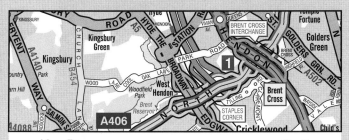

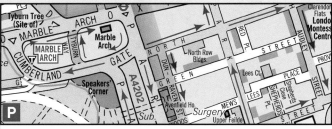

C000148137

London Main Routes at 1" to 1 mile

Motorway ——— **M3**	Tunnel ———
Motorway Junction Number Unlimited Interchange — **18** Limited Interchange — **19**	Major Road Under Construction –
	Major Road Proposed —
	Selected Other Road —
Motorway Service Area – **S** **HESTON**	Junction Name — ELEPHANT & CASTLE
Mileage between Motorway Junctions – 6	Toll ——— **TOLL**
Primary Route ——— **A2**	Railway & Croydon Tramlink ———
North & South Circular Roads and Inner Ring Road **R**	Level Crossing and Tunnel –
	Railway Station — KINGSTON
Primary Route Junction Number – **12**	Underground Station — BOND ST.
Primary Route Destination – **ROMFORD**	DLR Station & Tramlink Stop — SOUTH QUAY
A Road ——— **A320**	Airport ——— *LONDON CITY AIRPORT* ✈
B Road ——— B466	Airport Runway ———
Dual Carriageway ———	Built-up Area ———
Transport for London Road Network (Red Route) Primary Route North & South Circular Roads and Inner Ring Road **R** A Road	County Boundary ———
	Map Continuation **5**
	National Grid Reference — 490
One Way Road —➔— (Motorway, Primary Route & A Road only) - Traffic flow indicated by heavy line on driver's left)	River or Canal ———
	Wood, Park, Cemetery, Etc. ———

C CONGESTION CHARGING ZONE
The area contained within the Congestion Charging Zone is shown with reduced colours.

Scale: 1:63,360
1 inch (2.54cm) to 1 mile or 1.58 cm to 1 kilometre

0 ——— 1 ——— 2 Miles
0 — 1 — 2 — 3 Kilometres

Major Sporting Venues

Cricket	🏏	Rugby	🏉
Football	⚽	Tennis	🎾
Golf Course	**9** 9 Hole – **18** 18 Hole	Stadium	⬭
Horse Racing	🏇	Place of Interest — • *Windsor Castle*	
Motor Racing	🏁	Viewpoint — 180° 360°	

Central London at 9" to 1 mile

A Road ——— **A10**	**Buildings**	
B Road ——— **B326**	Educational Establishment	
Dual Carriageway ———	Hospital or Hospice	
One Way Street ——➔	Industrial	
	Leisure or Recreational Facility	
Inner Ring Road — **R**	Office	
Width Restriction — 7'0"	Place of Interest - Public Access	
	Place of Interest - No Public Access	
Restricted Access — Mon. - Sat. 7am - 7pm	Place of Worship	
Pedestrianized Road —	Public Building	
House Numbers — 34 62 (A & B Roads only)	Residential	
	Shopping Centre or Market	
On Street Parking (Restrictions may apply)	Other Selected Building	
Junction Name — MARBLE ARCH	Car Park — **P**	
Railway Station —	Cinema — 🎦	
Railway Station Entrance National Rail Network ≋ Underground ⊖ Docklands Light Railway **DLR**	Fast Ferry —	
	Fire Station —	
	Information Centre — 🛈	
	National Grid Reference — ¹78	
	Police Station — ▲	
Borough Boundary —	Post Office — ★	
Postal Boundary —	River Boat Trip —	
C Congestion Charging Zone Boundary	Theatre — 🎭	
	Toilet with facilities for the Disabled — ▽ without facilities for the Disabled — ▽ for exclusive use by the Disabled — ▽	
Map Continuation **75**		

Scale: 1:7,040
9 inches (22.86 cm) to 1 mile or 14.2 cm to 1 kilometre

0 — 100 — 200 — 300 Yards — ¼ Mile
0 — 100 — 200 — 300 — 400 Metres

Copyright of Geographers' A-Z Map Company Limited
Fairfield Road, Borough Green, Sevenoaks, Kent TN15 8PP
Telephone: 01732 781000 (Enquiries & Trade Sales) or 01732 783422 (Retail Sales)

 Ordnance Survey This product includes mapping data licensed from Ordnance Survey ® with the permission of the Controller of Her Majesty's Stationery Office. © Crown Copyright 2005. All rights reserved. Licence number 100017302

EDITION 4 2005
Copyright © Geographers' A-Z Map Company Limited 2005
www.a-zmaps.co.uk

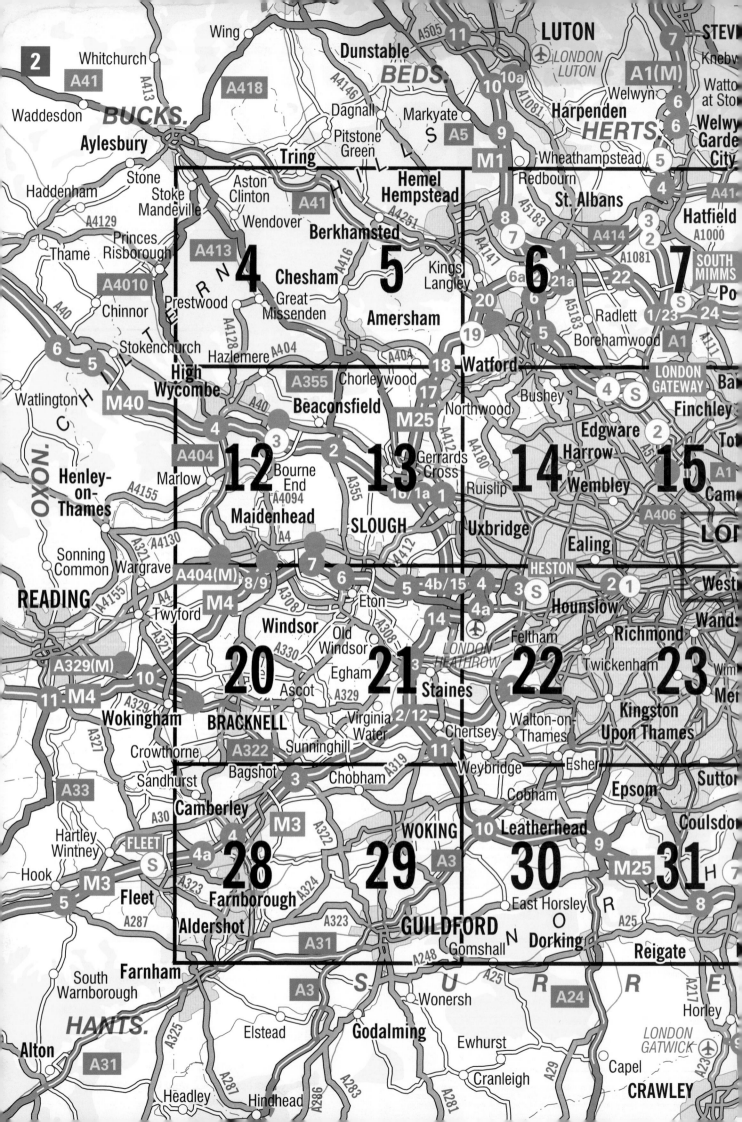

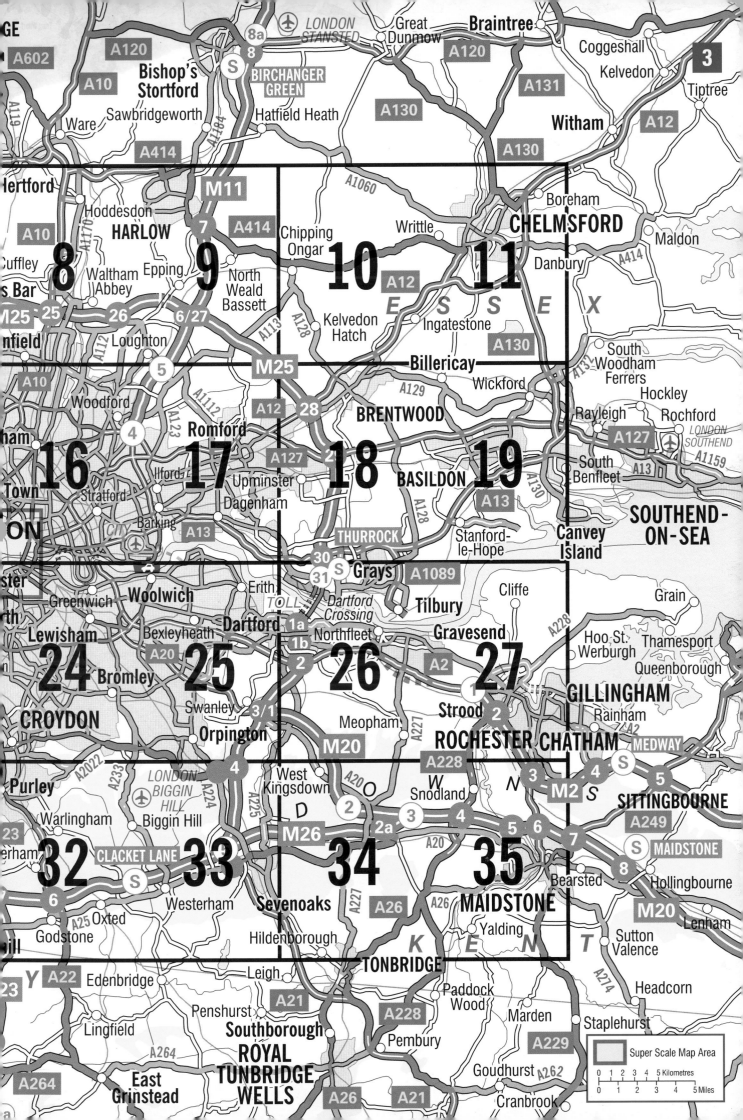

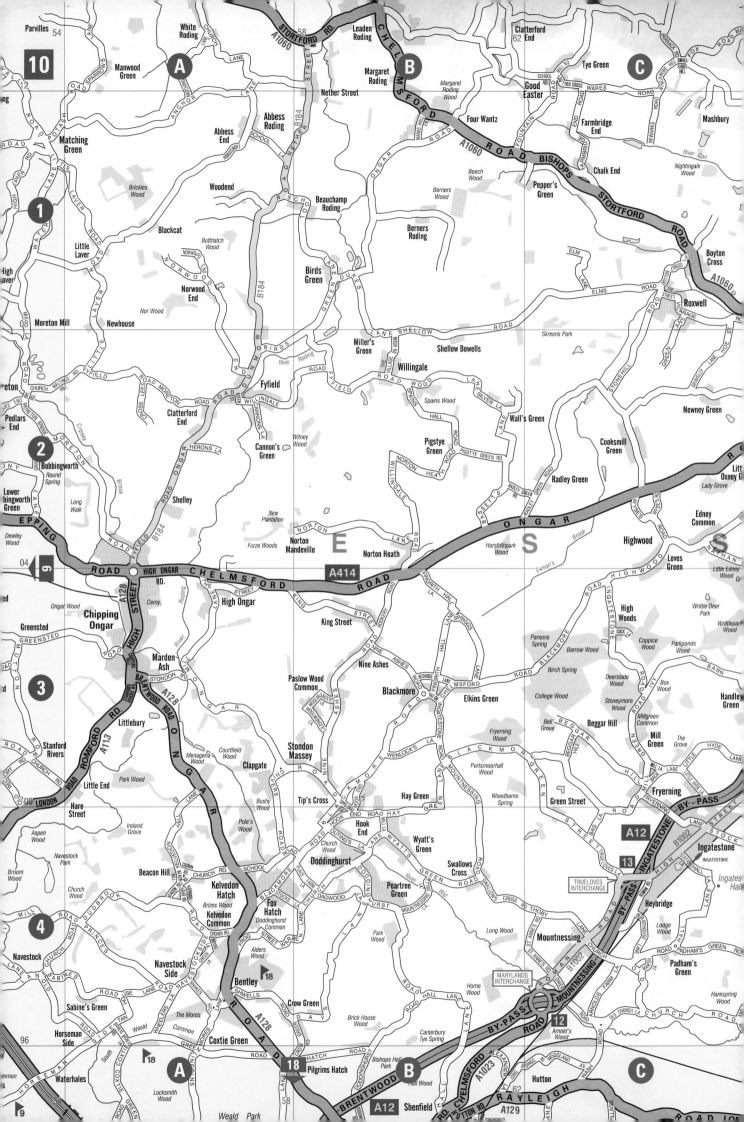

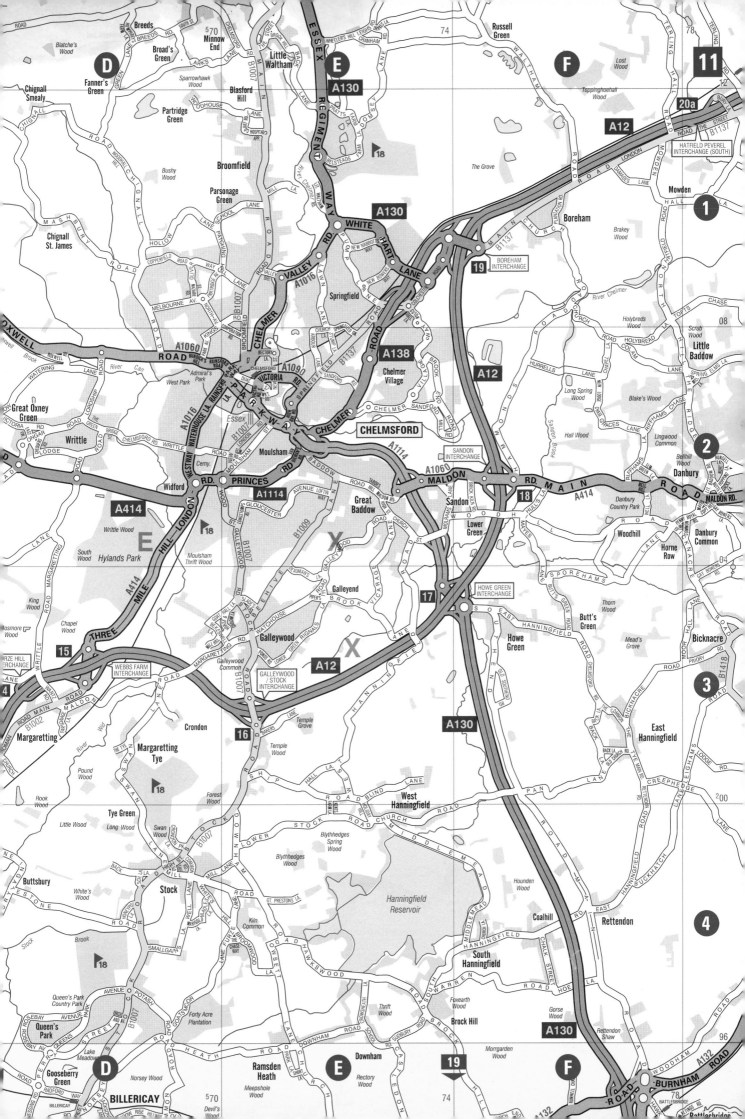

INDEX

Including Streets, Places & Areas, Junction Names and Selected Places of Interest.

HOW TO USE THIS INDEX

1. Each street name is followed by its Postal District (or, if outside the London Postal Districts, by its Posttown or Postal Locality), and then by its map reference; e.g. Abbey Barn La. *High W* . . . 2B **12** is in the High Wycombe Posttown and is to be found in square 2B on page **12**. The page number being shown in bold type.
A strict alphabetical order is followed in which Av., Rd., St. etc. (though abbreviated) are read in full and as part of the street name; e.g. Ash Chu. Rd. appears after Ashburton Rd. but before Ashcombe Rd.

2. Streets and a selection of Subsidiary names not shown on the Maps, appear in this index in *Italics* with the thoroughfare to which it is connected shown in brackets; e.g. *Parkside. Mat T . . . 1F **9** (off Rainbow Rd.)*

3. Places and areas are shown in the index in **blue type**, the map reference referring to the actual map square in which the town or area is located and not to the place name; e.g. **Abbess End. 1A 10**

4. An example of a selected place of interest is Arsenal F.C. 3A 16

5. Junction names are shown in the index in **bold type**; e.g. **Aldgate. (Junct.)** 4A 16

GENERAL ABBREVIATIONS

All : Alley
App : Approach
Arc : Arcade
Av : Avenue
Bk : Back
Boulevd : Boulevard
Bri : Bridge
B'way : Broadway
Bldgs : Buildings
Bus : Business
Cvn : Caravan
Cen : Centre
Chu : Church
Chyd : Churchyard
Circ : Circle
Cir : Circus
Clo : Close
Comn : Common
Cotts : Cottages
Ct : Court
Cres : Crescent
Cft : Croft
Dri : Drive
E : East
Embkmt : Embankment
Est : Estate
Fld : Field
Gdns : Gardens
Gth : Garth
Ga : Gate
Gt : Great
Grn : Green
Gro : Grove
Ho : House
Ind : Industrial
Info : Information
Junct : Junction
La : Lane
Lit : Little
Lwr : Lower
Mc : Mac
Mnr : Manor
Mans : Mansions
Mkt : Market
Mdw : Meadow
M : Mews
Mt : Mount
Mus : Museum
N : North
Pal : Palace
Pde : Parade
Pk : Park
Pas : Passage
Pl : Place
Quad : Quadrant
Res : Residential
Ri : Rise
Rd : Road
Shop : Shopping
S : South
Sq : Square
Sta : Station
St : Street
Ter : Terrace
Trad : Trading
Up : Upper
Va : Vale
Vw : View
Vs : Villas
Vis : Visitors
Wlk : Walk
W : West
Yd : Yard

POSTTOWN AND POSTAL LOCALITY ABBREVIATIONS

Ab R : Abbess Roding
Ab L : Abbots Langley
Ab C : Abinger Common
Ab H : Abinger Hammer
Abr : Abridge
Adtn : Addington
Add : Addlestone
Alb : Albury
Ald : Aldbury
Alder : Aldershot
Amer : Amersham
Art : Artington
Asc : Ascot
Ash : Ash (Aldershot)
As : Ash (Sevenoaks)
Ashf : Ashford
Ash G : Ashley Green
Asht : Ashtead
Ash V : Ash Vale
Ast C : Aston Clinton
Ave : Aveley
Ayl : Aylesbury
Ayle : Aylesford
Badg M : Badgers Mount
Bad L : Badshot Lea
Bag : Bagshot
Bans : Banstead
Bark : Barking
B'side : Barkingside
Barm : Barming
Barn : Barnet
Bas : Basildon
B Hth : Batchworth Heath
Bat : Battlesbridge
B'frd : Bayford
Beac : Beaconsfield
Bean : Bean
Beau R : Beauchamp Roding
Beck : Beckenham
Bedd : Beddington
Bedm : Bedmond
Bell : Bellingdon
Belv : Belvedere
Ben : Benfleet
Berk : Berkhamsted
Berr G : Berrys Green
Bet : Betchworth
Bex : Bexley
Bexh : Bexleyheath
Big H : Biggin Hill
Bill : Billericay
B'bear : Billingbear
Binf : Binfield
Birl : Birling
Bish : Bisham
Bisl : Bisley
B'more : Blackmore
B'water : Blackwater
Bled R : Bledloe Ridge
Blet : Bletchingley
Blue B : Blue Bell Hill
Bookh : Bookham
Bore : Boreham
Borwd : Borehamwood
Bor G : Borough Green
Bough B : Bough Beech
Bou M : Boughton Monchelsea
Bour E : Bourne End
Bov : Bovingdon
Boxl : Boxley
Brack : Bracknell
Brmly : Bramley
Bras : Brasted
Bray : Bray
Braz E : Braziers End
Bred : Bredhurst
Bren : Brentford
Brtwd : Brentwood
Brick : Brickendon
Brock : Brockham
Brom : Bromley
Brook P : Brooklands Ind. Pk.
Brk P : Brookmans Park
Brkwd : Brookwood
Broom : Broomfield
Brox : Broxbourne
Buck H : Buckhurst Hill
Bkld : Buckland (Aylesbury)
Buck : Buckland (Reigate)
Buck C : Buckland Common
Bulp : Bulphan
Bur G : Burchetts Green
Bur : Burcott
Burh : Burham
Burn : Burnham
Bush : Bushey
Bush H : Bushey Heath
But C : Butlers Cross
Byfl : Byfleet
Camb : Camberley
Can I : Canvey Island
Cars : Carshalton
Cat : Caterham
Chad H : Chadwell Heath
Chaf H : Chafford Hundred
Chal G : Chalfont St Giles
Chal P : Chalfont St Peter
Chalv : Chalvey
Chan X : Chandlers Cross
Chart : Chartridge
Cha S : Chart Sutton
Chat : Chatham
Chatt : Chattenden
Cheam : Cheam
Chelm : Chelmsford
Chels : Chelsfield
Cher : Chertsey
Che : Chesham
Ches B : Chesham Bois
Chesh : Cheshunt
Chess : Chessington
Chev : Chevening
Chid : Chiddingstone
Chid C : Chiddingstone Causeway
Chig S : Chignal Smealey
Chig : Chigwell
Chil : Chilworth
Chfd : Chipperfield
Chip : Chipstead
Chst : Chislehurst
Chob : Chobham
C'bry : Cholesbury
Chor : Chorleywood
C Crook : Church Crookham
Cipp : Cippenham
Clay : Claygate
Cli : Cliffe
Cobh : Cobham (Esher)
Cob : Cobham (Strood)
Cockf : Cockfosters
Col G : Cole Green
Coles : Coleshill
Coll S : Collier Street
Coln : Colnbrook
Col H : Colney Heath
Comp : Compton
Cook : Cookham
Cook D : Cookham Dean
Cook G : Cooksmill Green
C'ing : Cooling
Coop : Coopersale
Corr : Corringham
Coul : Coulsdon
Cow : Cowley
Cox : Coxheath
Cran : Cranford
Cray : Crayford
Cray H : Crays Hill
Cre P : Cressex Business Park
Crock : Crockenhill
Crock H : Crockham Hill
Crou : Crouch
Crow : Crowhurst
Crowt : Crowthorne
Crox G : Croxley Green
Croy : Croydon
Cud : Cudham
Cuff : Cuffley
Culv : Culverstone
Cux : Cuxton
Dag : Dagenham
Dan : Danbury
Dart : Dartford
Dat : Datchet
Deep : Deepcut
Den : Denham
Det : Detling
Dit : Ditton
Dodd : Doddinghurst
Dork : Dorking
Dor : Dorney
Dor R : Dorney Reach
Dow : Downe
D'ham : Downham
D'ley : Downley
D'side : Downside
Down : Downswood
Dud : Dudswell
D Grn : Dunks Green
Dun : Dunton
Dun G : Dunton Green
E Clan : East Clandon
E Far : East Farleigh
E Han : East Hanningfield
E Hor : East Horsley
E Mal : East Malling
E Mol : East Molesey
E Peck : East Peckham
E Til : East Tilbury
E'wck : Eastwick
Eccl : Eccles
Eden : Edenbridge
Edgw : Edgware
Ed C : Edney Common
Eff : Effingham
Eff J : Effingham Junction
Egh : Egham
Els : Elstree
Enf : Enfield
Epp : Epping
Epp G : Epping Green
Eps : Epsom
Eri : Erith
Esh : Esher
Ess : Essendon
Eton : Eton
Ewe : Ewell
Ews : Ewshot
Eyns : Eynsford
Fair : Fairseat
Farn : Farnborough
Farnh : Farnham
Farn C : Farnham Common
Farn R : Farnham Royal
F'ham : Farningham
Fawk : Fawkham
Fel : Felden
Felt : Feltham
Fet : Fetcham
Fif : Fifield
Finch : Finchampstead
Five G : Five Oak Green
F Hth : Flackwell Heath
Flau : Flaunden
Fleet : Fleet
Fob : Fobbing
Four E : Four Elms
Frim : Frimley
Frim G : Frimley Green
Frog : Frogmore
Fry : Fryerning
Ful : Fulmer
Fyf : Fyfield
Gad R : Gaddesden Row
Gall : Galleywood
G Grn : George Green
Ger X : Gerrards Cross
Gid P : Gidea Park
Gill : Gillingham
God : Godstone
G Oak : Goffs Oak
Gold G : Golden Green
Gom : Gomshall
Good E : Good Easter
Grav : Gravesend
Grays : Grays
Gt Amw : Great Amwell
Gt Bad : Great Baddow
Gt Gad : Great Gaddesden
Gt Kim : Great Kimble
Gt Kin : Great Kingshill
Gt Miss : Great Missenden
Gt Wal : Great Waldingfield
Gt Walt : Great Waltham
Gt War : Great Warley
Gnfd : Greenford
Grnh : Greenhithe
Grn St : Green Street Green
Guild : Guildford
Had : Hadleigh
Hdlw : Hadlow
Hail : Hailey
Hall : Halling
H'std : Halstead (Braintree)
Hals : Halstead (Otford)
Hal : Halton
Hamp : Hampton
Hamp H : Hampton Hill
Hamp W : Hampton Wick
Hand : Handcross
Hanw : Hanworth
Hare : Harefield
Hare H : Hare Hatch
Harl : Harlington
H'low : Harlow
Harm : Harmondsworth
Hpdn : Harpenden
H'shm : Harrietsham
Harr : Harrow
Hart : Hartley
Hasl : Haslemere
H'wd : Hastingwood
Hast : Hastoe
Hat : Hatfield
Hat H : Hatfield Heath
Hat P : Hatfield Peverel
Hav : Havering-atte-Bower
Hawr : Hawridge
Hay : Hayes
H'ley : Headley
H'row A : London Heathrow Airport
Hedg : Hedgerley
Hem H : Hemel Hempstead
Hem I : Hemel Hempstead Ind. Est.
Hem : Hempstead
Heron : Herongate
Hert : Hertford
Hert H : Hertford Heath
Hever : Hever
Hex : Hextable
High : Higham
High Bar : High Barnet
H Bee : High Beech
H Hals : High Halstow
H Lav : High Laver
H Ong : High Ongar
Hghwd : Highwood
High W : High Wycombe
Hild : Hildenborough
Hod : Hoddesdon
Hods : Hodsoll Street
Holl : Hollingbourne
Holm G : Holmer Green
Holyp : Holyport
Hoo : Hoo
Hook E : Hook End
Hool : Hooley
Horn : Hornchurch
Horn H : Horndon-on-the Hill
Hors : Horsell
Hort : Horton
Hort K : Horton Kirby
Houn : Hounslow
H Grn : Howe Green
Hugh : Hughenden
Hugh V : Hughenden Valley
Hun : Hunsdon
Hunt : Hunton
Hur : Hurley
Hut : Hutton
Hyde H : Hyde Heath
Ide H : Ide Hill
Igh : Ightham
Ilf : Ilford
Ing : Ingatestone
Ingve : Ingrave
Iswth : Isleworth
Iver : Iver
Ivy H : Ivy Hatch
Jor : Jordans
Kel C : Kelvedon Common
Kel H : Kelvedon Hatch
Kems : Kemsing
Kenl : Kenley
Kes : Keston
Kiln G : Kiln Green
King H : Kings Hill
K Lan : Kings Langley
King T : Kingston upon Thames
Kgswd : Kingswood
Knap : Knaphill
Knat : Knatts Valley
Knock : Knockholt
Knot : Knotty Green
Know H : Knowl Hill
Lac G : Lacey Green
Ladd : Laddingford
Lain : Laindon
Lale : Laleham
L End : Lane End
Lang H : Langdon Hills
Langl : Langley
Lark : Larkfield
Lea R : Leaden Roding
Lea : Leatherhead
Leav : Leavesden
Lee : Leedon
Leeds : Leeds
Lee G : Lee Gate
L'gh : Leigh (Reigate)
Leigh : Leigh (Tonbridge)
Lgh S : Leigh-on-Sea
Lem : Lemsford
Let H : Letchmore Heath
Let G : Letty Green
Leyb : Leybourne
Light : Lightwater
Limp : Limpsfield
Linf : Linford
Ling : Lingfield
Lin : Linton
L Bad : Little Baddow
L Berk : Little Berkhamsted
L Bur : Little Burstead
L Chal : Little Chalfont
L Gad : Little Gaddesden
Lit H : Little Heath (Berkhamsted)
L Hth : Little Heath (Romford)
L Kim : Little Kimble
L Kin : Little Kingshill
L Mar : Little Marlow
L Mis : Little Missenden
L Sand : Little Sandhurst
L Walt : Little Waltham
L War : Little Warley
L Grn : Littlewick Green
Lon C : London Colney
Longc : Longcross
Long : Longfield
Loose : Loose
L Row : Loosley Row
Loud : Loudwater
Lou : Loughton
Lwr K : Lower Kingswood
Lwr U : Lower Upnor
Ludd : Luddesdown
Lyne : Lyne
M'head : Maidenhead
Maid : Maidstone
Mard : Marden
Mar R : Margaret Roding
Marg : Margaretting
Mar : Marlow
Mash : Mashbury
Mat G : Matching Green
Mat T : Matching Tye
Mayf : Mayford
Medm : Medmenham
Meop : Meopham
Mere : Mereworth
Mers : Merstham
Mick : Mickleham
Mill G : Mill Green
Mitc : Mitcham
Mon R : Monks Risborough
Mord : Morden
More : Moreton
Mount : Mountnessing
Myt : Mytchett
Nap : Naphill
Nash : Nash
Nave : Navestock
N'side : Navestockside
Naze : Nazeing
Nett : Nettlestead
New Ad : New Addington
New Ash : New Ash Green
New H : New Haw
N Mald : New Malden
New S : Newgate Street
Noak H : Noak Hill
Norm : Normandy
N Asc : North Ascot
N'thaw : Northaw
N Ben : North Benfleet
N'chu : Northchurch
N Dean : North Dean
N'fleet : Northfleet
N Har : North Harrow
N Holm : North Holmwood
N'holt : Northolt
N Mym : North Mymms
N Ock : North Ockendon
N Stif : North Stifford
N Hth : Northumberland Heath
N Wea : North Weald
N'wd : Northwood
Nup : Nuptown
Nutf : Nutfield
Oak G : Oakley Green
Ock : Ockham
Off : Offham
Old Win : Old Windsor
Old Wok : Old Woking
Ong : Ongar
Orch : Orchard Leigh
Orp : Orpington
Ors : Orsett
Otf : Otford
Otham : Otham
Ott : Ottershaw
Out : Outwood
Oxs : Oxshott
Oxt : Oxted
Pad W : Paddock Wood
Park : Park Street
Par H : Parslows Hillock
Penn : Penn
Penn S : Penn Street
Pic E : Piccotts End
Pid : Piddington
Pil H : Pilgrims Hatch
Pim : Pimlico
Pinn : Pinner
Pirb : Pirbright
Pits : Pitsea
Platt : Platt
Plax : Plaxtol
Pott E : Potten End
Pot B : Potters Bar
Pot C : Potters Crouch
Prat B : Pratts Bottom
P'wd : Prestwood
P Ris : Princes Risborough
Purf : Purfleet
Purl : Purley
Putt : Puttenham
Pyr : Pyrford
Rad : Radlett
R'ge : Radnage
Rain : Rainham
Rams H : Ramsden Heath
Ran C : Ranmore Common
Raw : Rawreth
Ray : Rayleigh
Redb : Redbourn
Red : Redhill
Red A : Redhill Aerodrome
Reig : Reigate
Ret C : Rettendon Common
Rich : Richmond
Rick : Rickmansworth
Ridge : Ridge
Rip : Ripley
Roch : Rochester
Romf : Romford
Rough : Roughway
Rox : Roxwell
Roy : Roydon
Ruis : Ruislip
Runf : Runfold
Runw : Runwell
Rya : Ryarsh
St Alb : St Albans
St L : St Leonards
St M : St Mary Cray
St P : St Pauls Cray
Salf : Salfords
Sand : Sandhurst
S'lng : Sandling
S'don : Sandon
Sandr : Sandridge
Sarr : Sarratt
S'ton : Saunderton
Saw : Sawbridgeworth
Seal : Seal
Seale : Seale
Send : Send
Sev : Sevenoaks
Shalf : Shalford
Srng : Sheering
Shenf : Shenfield
Shenl : Shenley
Shep : Shepperton
Shere : Shere
S'brne : Shipbourne
Ship : Shipley
Shor : Shoreham
Shorne : Shorne
Short : Shortlands
Shur R : Shurlock Row
Sidc : Sidcup
Slou : Slough
Smal : Smallford
Snod : Snodland
Sole S : Sole Street
S'hall : Southall
S Croy : South Croydon
S Dar : South Darenth
S'fleet : Southfleet
S God : South Godstone
S Han : South Hanningfield
S Nut : South Nutfield
S Ock : South Ockendon
S Pk : South Park
S Wea : South Weald
Speen : Speen
Spri : Springfield
Stai : Staines
Stan H : Stanford-le-Hope
Stan : Stanmore
Stan A : Stanstead Abbotts

Stans : Stansted
Stanw : Stanwell
Stap A : Stapleford Abbotts
S'hrst : Staplehurst
Stock : Stock
Stoke D : Stoke D'Abernon
Stoke M : Stoke Mandeville
Stok : Stokenchurch
Stoke P : Stoke Poges
Ston M : Stondon Massey
Stone : Stone
Strood : Strood
Str G : Strood Green
Sun : Sunbury-on-Thames
Sund : Sundridge
S'dale : Sunningdale
S'hill : Sunninghill
Surb : Surbiton
Sur R : Surrey Research Park
Sutt : Sutton
S at H : Sutton at Hone
Sut G : Sutton Green
Swan : Swanley
Swans : Swanscombe

Tad : Tadworth
Tand : Tandridge
Tap : Taplow
Tats : Tatsfield
Tedd : Teddington
Terl : Terling
Ter : Terrick
Tstn : Teston
Th Dit : Thames Ditton
They B : Theydon Bois
They G : Theydon Garnon
They M : Theydon Mount
Thorn : Thornwood
Thr B : Threshers Bush
Til : Tilbury
T'sey : Titsey
Tonb : Tonbridge
Tong : Tongham
Ton : Tonwell
Toot : Toot Hill
Tovil : Tovil
Tring : Tring
T'frd : Tringford

Tros : Trottiscliffe
Twic : Twickenham
Tyngr : Tyttenhanger
Under : Underriver
Upm : Upminster
Upnor : Upnor
Up H'lng : Upper Halling
Uxb : Uxbridge
Van : Vange
Vir W : Virginia Water
Wain : Wainscott
Wald : Waldershare
W'slde : Walderslade
Wall : Wallington
Wal A : Waltham Abbey
Wal X : Waltham Cross
Wal L : Waltham St Lawrence
W on T : Walton-on-Thames
Wanb : Wanborough
Ware : Ware
Warf : Warfield
War : Warley
Warl : Warlingham
Wat E : Water End

W'bury : Wateringbury
Wat : Watford
Weald : Weald
W'stone : Wealdstone
Weav : Weavering
Well : Welling
Wel G : Welwyn Garden City
Wemb : Wembley
Wen : Wennington
W Byf : West Byfleet
W Cla : West Clandon
Westc : Westcott
W Dray : West Drayton
W End : West End
W'ham : Westerham
W Far : West Farleigh
W Horn : West Hornden
W H'dn : West Horndon
W Hor : West Horsley
Westh : Westhumble
W'ton T : Weston Turville
Wex : Wexham
W King : West Kingsdown

W Mal : West Malling
W Mol : West Molesey
W Peck : West Peckham
W Thur : West Thurrock
W Til : West Tilbury
W Wick : West Wickham
W Wyc : West Wycombe
Wey : Weybridge
Wheat : Wheathampstead
Wtf : Whiteleaf
Whit : Whitton
Whyt : Whyteleafe
W'fd : Wickford
Wid : Widford
Wig : Wigginton
Will : Willingale
Winch H : Winchmore Hill
W'sham : Windlesham
Wind : Windsor
Wink : Winkfield
Wink R : Winkfield Row
Wok : Woking
Wokgm : Wokingham
Wold : Woldingham

Won : Wonersh
Wbrn G : Wooburn Green
Wbrn M : Wooburn Moor
Wfd G : Woodford Green
Wdhm : Woodham
Wdrow : Woodrow
Wood S : Wood Street Village
Wor Pk : Worcester Park
Worm : Wormley
Worp : Worplesdon
Wott : Wotton
Woul : Wouldham
Wray : Wraysbury
Writ : Writtle
Wro : Wrotham
Wro H : Wrotham Heath
Wy G : Wyatts Green
Yald : Yalding
Yat : Yateley
Yiew : Yiewsley

INDEX

Bedford Park—Buckhold Rd.

Bedford Park. 1D 23
Bedford Rd. SW4 2A 24
Bedfords Hill. Good E 1C 10
Bedford Sq. W1 4F 15
Bedgrove. 1A 4
Bedgrove. Ayl 1A 4
Bedmond. 3A 6
Bedmond La. Ab L & St Alb 2B 6
Bedmond La. St Alb 2B 6
Bedmond Rd. Ab L 3A 6
Bedmond Rd. Hem H 2A 6
Bedrose La. Ing 3B 10
Beech Av. Eff 4B 30
Beechen Gro. Wat 4B 6
Beechenlea La. Swan 3F 25
Beeches Av. Cars 1F 31
Beeches Rd. Farn C 3D 13
Beeches Rd. Raw 1F 19
Beech Farm Rd. Warl 2C 32
Beechfield Rd. Hem H 2F 5
Beech Hill. Barn 4F 7
Beech Hyde La. Wheat 1D 7
Beechin Bank Rd. Chat 1F 35
Beechin Wood La. Platt 2C 34
Beechmont Rd. Sev 3F 33
Beech Rd. Mere 3C 34
Beech Rd. St Alb 1C 6
Beech Rd. Will 2B 10
Beech St. EC1 4A 16
Beech Tree Rd. Holm G 4B 4
Beechwood Av. St Alb 1C 6
Beehive La. Chelm 3E 11
Beehive La. Ilf 2D 17
Beehive La. Wel G 1E 7
Beenham's Heath. 2A 20
Beesfield La. F'ham 4A 26
Beggar Hill. 3C 10
Beggar Hill. Fry 3C 10
Beggar's Bush. 3D 21
Beggar's Hill. (Junct.) 1D 31
Beggars La. W'ham 3D 33
Bekeswell La. Chelm 3D 11
Beldam Bri. Rd. Wok 1D 29
Belgrave Pl. SW1 1F 23
Belgrave Rd. SW1 1F 23
Belgrave Sq. SW1 1F 23
Belgravia. 1F 23
Bell Bar. 2E 7
Bell Common. 3D 9
Bellegrove Rd. Well 1D 25
Bellevue Rd. SW17 2F 23
Bellew Rd. Deep 2B 28
Bellfield Rd. High W 1B 12
Bellfields. 3E 29
Bell Foundry La. Wokgm 3A 20
Bell Green. 3B 24
Bell Grn. SE26 3B 24
Bell Grn. La. SE26 3B 24
Bellingdon. 2D 5
Bellingdon Rd. Che 3D 5
Bellingham. 2B 24
Bellingham Rd. SE6 2C 24
Bell La. NW4 2E 15
Bell La. Amer 4E 5
Bell La. Boxl 1F 35
Bell La. Brk P 2E 7
Bell La. Brox 2B 8
Bell La. Burh 1E 35
Bell La. Enf 4B 8
Bell La. Fet 3C 30
Bell La. Lon C 3D 7
Bell La. N'chu & Berk 1D 5
Bellmead. Chelm 2E 11
Bells Farm Rd. Hdlw 4C 34
Bells Hill. Stoke P 4E 13
Bells Hill Rd. Van 3E 19
Bell's La. Hoo 2F 27
Bell St. Reig 4E 31
Bellswood La. Iver 4E 13
Bell, The. (Junct.) 2B 16
Belmont. 2C 14 (Harrow)
Belmont. 1E 31 (Sutton)
Belmont Hill. SE13 2C 24
Belmont Pk. Av. M'head 4B 12
Belmont Ri. Sutt 1E 31
Belmont Rd. N17 & N15 2A 16
Belmont Rd. Eri 1E 25
Belmont Rd. M'head 4B 12
Belmont Rd. Uxb 3F 13
Belsize. 3F 5
Belsize Av. NW3 3F 15
Belsize Pk. NW3 3F 15
Belsize Rd. NW6 4E 15
Belsteads Farm La. L Walt 1E 11
Belswains La. Hem H 2A 6
Beltring. 4D 35
Beltring Rd. Pad W 4D 35
Belvedere. 1E 25
Belvedere Rd. Bexh 2E 25
Benhill Av. Sutt 4F 23
Benhill Rd. Sutt 4F 23
Benhilton. 4F 23
Ben Jonson Rd. E1 4B 16
Benner La. W End 1D 29
Bennets End Rd. Hem H 2A 6
Bennetts Castle La. Dag 3E 17
Bennetts End. 2A 6
Benover. 4E 35
Benover Rd. Yald 4D 35
Bensham La. Croy & T Hth 4A 24
Bentham Rd. SE28 4E 17
Bentley. 4A 10
Bentley Heath. 4E 7
Benton Rd. Ilf 3D 17
Beresford Av. Wemb 4D 15
Beresford Hill. Bou M 4F 35
Beresford St. SE18 1D 25
Bericot Way. Wel G 1F 7
Berkeley St. W1 4F 15
Berkhamstead Rd. Che 3D 5
Berkhamsted. 1D 5
Berkhamsted By-Pass. Wig & Berk 1D 5
Berkhamsted La. Ess 2F 7
Berkhamsted Rd. Hem H 1F 5
Berkshire Way. Brack 3A 20
Bermondsey. 1B 24
Bermondsey St. SE1 4A 16
Bernard's Heath. 1C 6
Bernard St. WC1 4A 16
Berners Roding. 1B 10
Berrygrove. (Junct.) 4B 6
Berry Gro. La. Wat 4B 6
Berry Hill. Tap 4C 12
Berrylands. 4D 23
Berry La. Rick 1F 13
Berry La. Worp & Wok 3D 29
Berry's Green. 2D 33
Berry's Grn. Rd. Berr G 2D 33
Berry's Hill. Berr G 2D 33
Berwick La. Ong 3F 9
Berwick Pond Rd. Rain & Upm 4A 18
Berwick Rd. Mar 3A 12
Bessborough Rd. Harr 3C 14
Bessels Green. 3F 33
Bessels Grn. Rd. Sev 3F 33
Besson St. SE14 1B 24
Best St. Chat 4F 27
Betchworth. 4D 31
Bethnal Green. 4B 16
Bethnal Grn. Rd. E1 4A 16
Bethune Rd. N4 3A 16
Betsham. 3B 26
Betsham Rd. S'fleet 3B 26
Betts La. Naze 2C 8
Between Streets. Cobh 1B 30
Beulah Hill. SE19 3A 24
Beulah Rd. T Hth 3A 24
Beverley Dri. Edgw 2D 15
Beverley Gdns. Chesh 3B 8
Beverley Rd. Dag 3E 17
Beverley Rd. Whyt 2A 32
Beverley Way. SW20 & N Mald 3D 23
Bewley La. Plax 3B 34
Bexley. 2E 25
Bexleyheath. 2E 25
Bexley High St. Bex 2E 25
Bexley La. Sidc 2E 25
Bexley Rd. SE9 2D 25
Bexley Rd. Eri 1F 25 (in two parts)
Beynon Rd. Cars 4F 23
Bickley. 3D 25
Bickley Pk. Rd. Brom 3D 25
Bickley Rd. Brom 3C 24
Bicknacre. 3F 11
Bicknacre Rd. Dan 3F 11
Bicknacre Rd. E Han 3F 11
Big Comn. La. Blet 4A 32
Bigfrith La. Cook 3B 12
Biggin Hill. 2C 32
Biggin Hill Airport. 1C 32
Bignells Corner. 3E 7
Bignells Corner. (Junct.) 3E 7
Billericay. 1D 19
Billericay Rd. Heron & Bill 2C 18
Billet Hill. As 4B 26
Billet La. Berk 1E 5
Billet La. Horn 3F 17
Billet La. Slou & Iver 4E 13
Billet La. Stan H 4D 19
Billet Rd. E17 2B 16
Billet Rd. Romf 2E 17
Billingbear. 2A 20
Billingbear La. Binf 2A 20
Bill St. Rd. Roch 3E 27
Bilton Rd. Gnfd 4C 14
Bilton Way. Enf 4B 8
Bincote Rd. Enf 4A 8
Binfield. 3A 20
Binfield Rd. Brack 3A 20
Binfield Rd. Wokgm 3A 20
Bingham Rd. Croy 4B 24
Binton La. Seale 4B 28
Birchall La. Col G 1F 7
Birchanger Rd. SE25 4B 24
Birch Green. 1F 7
Birch Hill Rd. Brack 4B 20
Birchin Cross Rd. Knat 2A 34
Birch La. Flau 3E 5
Birchwood. 1E 7
Birchwood Av. Hat 1E 7
Birchwood Rd. Swan & Dart 3F 25
Bird La. Gt War 2B 18
Bird La. Upm 2A 18
Birds Green. 1B 10
Birds Grn. Will 2A 10
Birkbeck Rd. W3 4D 15
Birling. 1D 35
Birling Hill. Snod 1D 35
Birling Rd. Rya 2D 35
Birling Rd. Snod 1D 35
Birling Rd. W Mal 2D 35
Bisham. 3A 12
Bisham Abbey. 3A 12
Bishops Av., The. N2 3F 15
Bishop's Bri. W2 4E 15
Bishopsford Rd. Mord 4F 23
Bishopsgate. EC3 4A 16
Bishopsgate Rd. Egh 2E 21
Bishop's La. Hunt 4E 35
Bishop's La. Wink 2B 20
Bishops Ri. Hat 2D 7
Bishops Stortford Rd. Rox 1C 10
Bishopstone. Ayl 1A 4
Bishop's Way. E2 4B 16
Bisley. 2D 29
Bisley Camp. 2C 28
Bitchet Green. 3A 34
Bittacy Hill. NW7 2E 15
Blackamoor La. M'head 4B 12
Blackbird Hill. NW9 3D 15
Blackborough Rd. Reig 4F 31
Black Boy La. N15 2A 16
Blackbrook La. Brom 4D 25
Blackbrook Rd. Dork 4C 30
Black Bush La. Horn H 4C 18
Blackcat. 1A 10
Blackdown Rd. Deep 2C 28
Blacketts Wood Dri. Chor 1E 13
Black Fan Rd. Wel G 1E 7
Blackfen. 2E 25
Blackfen Rd. Sidc 2E 25
Blackfriars Bri. SE1 4A 16
Blackfriars Rd. SE1 4A 16
Blackhall La. Sev 3A 34
Blackheath. 2C 24
Blackheath Hill. SE10 1C 24
Blackheath La. Alb & Won 4F 29
Blackheath Park. 2C 24
Blackheath Rd. SE8 1B 24
Blackheath Village. SE3 1C 24
Blackhorse Lane. (Junct.) 2B 16
Blackhorse La. E17 2B 16
Blackhorse La. Croy 4B 24
Blackhorse La. Pot B 3E 7
Blackhorse La. Tad 3E 31
Blackhorse Rd. E17 2B 16
Blackhorse Rd. Wok 2D 29
Black Lion Hill. Shenl 3D 7
Blackmans La. Hdlw 4C 34
Blackmans La. Warl 1C 32
Blackmore. 3B 10
Blackmore Rd. B'more & Fry 3B 10
Blackmore Rd. Ing & Hghwd 3C 10
Blackmore Rd. Kel H & Ing 4A 10
Blackness La. Kes 1C 32
Blacknest. 3D 21
Blacknest Rd. Asc & Vir W 3D 21
Black Pk. Rd. Slou 4E 13
Blackpond La. Slou 3D 13
Black Prince Interchange. (Junct.) 2E 25
Blackshaw Rd. SW17 3F 23
Blackshots La. Grays 4C 18
Blacksmith La. Chil 4F 29
Blacksmiths La. Den 3F 13
Blacksmith's La. Orp 4E 25
Blackstock Rd. N5 & N4 3A 16
Blackstroud La. E. Light 1C 28
Blackwall La. SE10 1C 24 (in two parts)
Blackwall Tunnel Northern App. E14 & E3 4C 16
Blackwall Tunnel Southern App. SE10 1C 24
Blackwater. 2A 28
Blackwater La. Hem H 2A 6
Blackwater Valley Relief Rd. Camb 2A 28
Blackwater Valley Route. Farnh & Alder 4B 28
Blackwell Dri. Wat 1B 14
Blackwell Hall La. Che 3E 5
Blake Hall Rd. E11 3C 16
Blake Hall Rd. Ong 2F 9
Blakeney Rd. Beck 3B 24
Blanchards Hill. Guild 3E 29
Blanch La. Pot B 3D 7
Blandford Rd. S. Slou 1E 21
Blasford Hill. 1E 11
Blay's La. Egh 3E 21
Blendon Rd. Bex 2E 25
Bletchingley. 4A 32
Bletchingley Rd. God 4B 32
Bletchingley Rd. Mers 3F 31
Bletchingley Rd. Nutf 4A 32
Blighton La. Farnh 4B 28
Bligh Way. Roch 3E 27
Blind La. Bour E & F Hth 3B 12
Blind La. W Han 3E 11
Blindley Heath. 4B 32
Bloemfontein Rd. W12 4E 15
Bloomsbury St. WC1 4F 15
Blue Anchor La. W Til 1C 26
Blue Bell Hill. 1F 35
Blue Bell Hill By-Pass. W'slde 1F 35
Blueberry La. Knock 2E 33
Blue Bri. Rd. Brk P 2E 7
Bluehouse Hill. St Alb 2B 6
Bluehouse La. Oxt 3C 32
Bluewater. 2A 26
Bluewater Parkway. Grnh 2A 26
Blundel La. Stoke D 2B 30
Blunts La. Pot C 2B 6
Blyth Rd. Hay 1A 22
Boarley. 2F 35
Boarley La. S'lng 2F 35 (in two parts)
Bobbingworth. 2F 9
Bob Dunn Way. Dart 2F 25
Bobmore La. Mar 3A 12
Bockingford La. Maid 3F 35
Bockmer. Mar 3A 12
Bois La. Amer 4D 5
Bois Moor Rd. Che 3D 5
Boley Hill. Roch 3F 27
Boleyn Rd. N16 3A 16
Bolingbroke Gro. SW11 2F 23
Bollo La. W4 & W3 1D 23
Bolters La. Bans 1E 31
Bolton Av. Wind 2D 21
Bolton Rd. Wind 2D 21
Boltons La. Wok 2F 29
Bolton St. W1 4F 15
Bond St. W5 4C 14
Bond St. Egh 3E 21
Bond Way. SW8 1A 24
Bonner Rd. E2 4B 16
Bonsor Dri. Tad 2E 31
Booker. 2A 12
Bookham Rd. D'side 2B 30
Booth Rd. HA8 2D 15
Border's La. Lou 4D 9
Bordyke. Tonb 4B 34
Boreham. 1F 11
Borehamwood. 4D 7
Borough Green. 2B 34
Borough Grn. Rd. Igh 2B 34
Borough Grn. Rd. Wro 2B 34
Borough High St. SE1 1A 24
Borough Rd. SE1 1A 24
Borough Rd. Iswth 1C 22
Borough, The. 1A 24
Borstal. 4E 27
Borstal Rd. Roch 4E 27
Borstal St. Roch 4E 27
Boss La. Hugh V 4B 4
Bostall Hill. SE18 1E 25
Boston Manor. 1C 22
Boston Mnr. Rd. Bren 1C 22
Boston Rd. W7 1C 22
Botany Bay. 4F 7
Botley. 3E 5
Botley Rd. Che 3D 5
Botney Hill Rd. L Bur 2C 18
Botsom La. W King 1A 34
Bottle La. L Grn 1A 20
Bottle La. Warf 2A 20
Bottlescrew Hill. Bou M 4F 35
Bottom La. Holm G 4C 4
Bottom Ho. Farm La. Chal G 1D 13
Bottom Ho. La. New G 1D 5
Bottom La. Seer 2D 13
Bottom La. K Lan 4F 5
Bottom Rd. R'ge 1A 12
Bottom Rd. St L & Buck C 2C 4
Bottrells La. Coles & Chal G 1D 13
Botwell Comn. Rd. Hay 4A 14
Botwell La. Hay 4A 14
Bough Beech. 4E 33
Bough Beech Rd. Four E 4E 33
Boughton Green. 4F 35
Boughton La. Maid 3F 35
Boughton Monchelsea. 4F 35
Boughton Monchelsea Place. 4F 35
Bounces Rd. N9 1B 16
Boundary Rd. E13 4C 16
Boundary Rd. E17 3B 16
Boundary Rd. NW6 4E 15
Boundary Rd. Cars 1F 31
Boundary Rd. Farn 3B 28
Boundary Rd. Loud & Wbrn G 2C 12
Boundary Rd. Tap 4C 12
Boundary Way. Hem H 1A 6
Bounds Green. 2F 15
Bounds Grn. Rd. N22 & N11 2F 15
Bourley Rd. C Crook & Alder 4A 28
Bournebridge. 1E 17
Bournebridge La. Stap A 1E 17
Bourne End. 3C 12 (Cores End)
Bourne End. 2E 5 (Hemel Hempstead)
Bourne End Rd. Bour E 3C 12
Bourne Hill. N13 1A 16
Bourne La. Sev 3B 34
Bourne Rd. Bex & Dart 2E 25
Bourne, The. N14 1F 15
Bourne Way. Brom 4C 24
Boveney. 1C 20
Boveney Rd. Dor 1C 20
Boveney Wood La. Burn 3C 12
Bovingdon. 3E 5
Bovingdon Green. 3E 5 (Bovingdon)
Bovingdon Green. 3A 12 (Marlow)
Bovingdon Grn. La. Hem H 3E 5
Bovinger. 2F 9
Bow. 4B 16
Bow Common. 4B 16
Bow Comn. La. E3 4B 16
Boweashe La. Sev 2C 34
Bowerdean Rd. High W 1B 12
Bower Hill. Epp 3E 9
Bower Hill La. S Nut 4F 31
Bower La. Eyns & Sev 4A 26
Bower Mt. Rd. Maid 3F 35
Bowers Gifford. 2F 19
Bowes Park. 2A 16
Bowes Rd. N13 & N11 1F 15
Bow Interchange. (Junct.) 4C 16
Bowood La. Wen 2B 4
Bow Rd. E3 4B 16
Bow Rd. W'bury 3D 35
Bow St. WC2 4A 16
Bowstridge La. Chal G 1E 13
Bowyer's La. Warf 2B 20
Bowzell Rd. Weald 4F 33
Bowzell's La. Chid C 4F 33
Boxall's La. Alder 4B 28
Boxgrove Rd. Guild 4E 29
Box Hill. 4D 31
Boxhill Rd. Tad 4D 31
Box La. Hem H 2F 5
Boxley. 2F 35
Boxley Rd. Boxl 2F 35
Boxley Rd. Chat 1F 35
Boxley Rd. W'slde 1F 35
Boxmoor. 2F 5
Boxted. Hem H 1F 5
Boxtree Rd. Harr 2C 14
Boyn Hill. 4B 12
Boyn Hill Rd. M'head 4B 12
Boyn Valley Rd. M'head 4B 12
Boyton Cross. 1C 10
Boyton Cross La. Rox 1C 10
Bracknell. 3B 20
Bracknell Rd. Bag 4C 20
Bracknell Rd. Crowt 4A 20
Bracknell Rd. Warf 3B 20
Bradbourne Pk. Rd. Sev 3F 33
Bradbourne Rd. Sev 2F 33
Bradbourne Vale Rd. Sev 2F 33
Bradcutts La. Cook 3B 12
Bradden La. Gad R 1F 5
Bradenham. 4A 4
Bradenham La. Mar 3A 12
Bradenham Rd. W Wyc 4A 4
Bradenham Wood La. Walt A 4A 4
Bradley La. Brk P 2E 7
Bragmans La. Rick 3F 5
Braham St. E1 4A 16
Bramble La. Upm 4A 18
Bramley Hill. S Croy 4A 24
Bramley Rd. N14 1F 15
Brampton Rd. Bexh 1E 25
Bramshot La. Fleet 3A 28
Bramston Way. Lain 2D 19
Branbridges. 4D 35
Branbridges Rd. E Peck 4D 35 (in two parts)
Brancaster La. Purl 1A 32
Branch Hill. NW3 3F 15
Branch Rd. St Alb 2B 6
Brands Hatch Motor Racing Circuit. 4A 26
Brands Hatch Rd. Fawk 4B 26
Brands Hill. 1E 21
Branksome Av. Stan H 4D 19
Branksome Hill Rd. Camb 1A 28
Brasted. 3E 33
Brasted Chart. 3E 33
Brasted Hill. Knock & W'ham 2E 33
Brasted Hill Rd. Bras 2E 33
Brasted La. Knock 2E 33
Brasted Rd. W'ham 3D 33
Brawlings La. Ger X 1E 13
Bray. 1C 20
Bray Rd. M'head 4B 12
Bray Rd. Stoke D 2B 30
Brays Grn. La. Hyde H 4C 4
Brays Grove. 1E 9
Brays La. Hyde H 3C 4
Bray Wick. 1B 20
Braywick Rd. M'head 4B 12
Braywoodside. 2B 20
Braziers End. Braz E 2C 4
Braziers La. Wink R 3C 20
Bread and Cheese La. Chesh 2A 8
Breakspear Rd. Ruis 2A 14
Breakspear Rd. N. Hare 2F 13
Breakspear Rd. S. Uxb 3A 14
Breakspear Way. Hem H 2A 6
Brecknock Rd. N7 & N19 3F 15
Breeds Rd. Gt Walt 1D 11
Brenchley Gdns. SE23 2B 24
Brennan Rd. Til 1C 26
Brent Cross. 3E 15
Brent Cross Interchange. (Junct.) 2E 15
Brentfield. NW10 3D 15
Brentfield Rd. NW10 3D 15
Brentford End. 1C 22
Brentford F.C. 1C 22
Brentmoor Rd. W End 1D 29
Brent St. NW4 2E 15
Brent, The. Dart 2A 26
Brentwood. 1B 18
Brentwood By-Pass. Brtwd 1A 18
Brentwood Rd. Bulp & Grays 3C 18
Brentwood Rd. Grays 1C 26
Brentwood Rd. Heron 2C 18
Brentwood Rd. Ingve 1B 18
Brentwood Rd. Ong 3A 10
Brentwood Rd. Romf 2F 17
Brentwood Rd. W H'dn 3C 18
Brewers Rd. Shorne 3D 27
Brewer St. Blet 4A 32
Brewery La. Byfl 1A 30
Brewery Rd. N7 3A 16
Brewery Rd. SE18 1D 25
Brewery Rd. Wok 2E 29
Brickendon. 1A 8
Brickendon La. Brick 1A 8
Bricket Wood. 3B 6
Brick Hill. 4D 21
Brick Kiln La. Oxt 3C 32
Brick Kiln Rd. S'don 2F 11
Brick La. E1 & E2 4A 16
Bricklayer's Arms. (Junct.) 1A 24
Bridge End. 2A 30
Bridge Hill. Epp 3D 9
Bridge La. Vir W 4E 21
Bridgen Rd. Bex 2E 25
Bridge Rd. E15 4C 16
Bridge Rd. N22 2A 16
Bridge Rd. Bag 1C 28
Bridge Rd. Beck 3B 24
Bridge Rd. Cher 4F 21
Bridge Rd. Chess 4D 23
Bridge Rd. E Mol 3C 22
Bridge Rd. Eps 1D 31
Bridge Rd. Eri 1F 25
Bridge Rd. Farn 3A 28
Bridge Rd. Grays 1B 26
Bridge Rd. Houn 2C 22
Bridge Rd. K Lan 3A 6
Bridge Rd. M'head 4B 12
Bridge Rd. More 2F 9
Bridge Rd. Rain 4F 17
Bridge Rd. Wemb 3D 15
Bridge Rd. Wey 4A 22
Bridge Rd. E. Wel G 1E 7
Bridge St. Coln 1F 21
Bridge St. Gt Kim 2A 4
Bridge St. Guild 4E 29
Bridge St. Pinn 2B 14
Bridge St. W on T 4A 22
Bridge St. Writ 2D 11
Bridge, The. Harr 2C 14
Bridgewater Rd. Berk 1E 5
Bridgewater Rd. Wemb 3C 14
Bridle Rd. Croy 4B 24 (in two parts)
Bridle Rd. Pinn 2B 14
Bridle Rd., The. Purl 1A 32
Bridle Way N. Hod 1B 8
Bridle Way S. Hod 1B 8
Bridport Rd. N18 2A 16
Brighton Rd. Add 4F 21
Brighton Rd. Bans 2E 31
Brighton Rd. Hool & Coul 3F 31
Brighton Rd. Purl & S Croy 1A 32
Brighton Rd. Red 4F 31
Brighton Rd. Salf 4F 31
Brighton Rd. Surb 4C 22
Brighton Rd. Tad & Bans 2E 31
Brighton Rd. T Hth 4A 24
Brimmers Hill. Wid E 4B 4
Brimmers Rd. P Ris 3A 4
Brimsdown. 4B 8
Brimsdown Av. Enf 4B 8
Brimstone Hill. Meop 4C 26
Brimstone La. Meop 4C 26
Brishing La. Bou M 4F 35
Brishing Rd. Cha S 4F 35
Britannia Rd. H Hals 2F 27
Brittains La. Sev 3F 33
Brittania Junction. (Junct.) 3F 15
Britwell. 4D 13
Britwell Rd. Slou 4C 12
Brixton. 2A 24
Brixton Hill. SW2 2A 24
Brixton Rd. SW9 2A 24
Brixton Water La. SW2 2A 24
Broad Colney. 3C 6
Broad Ditch Rd. Meop 3C 26
Broadfields Av. Edgw 1D 15
Broad Grn. B'frd 1A 8
Broadgreen Wood. 1A 8
Broadham Green. 4C 32
Broadham Grn. Rd. Oxt 4C 32
Broadhurst Gdns. NW6 3E 15
Broad La. N15 2A 16
Broad La. Brack 3B 20
Broad La. Dart 3F 25
Broad La. Hamp 3B 22
Broad La. Wbrn G & Beac 2C 12
Broadley Common. 2D 9
Broadmayne. Bas 2E 19
Broadmead Rd. Hay & N'holt 4B 14
Broadmead Rd. Send 2E 29
Broadmead Rd. Wfd G 2C 16
Broadmoor La. Wal L & White 1A 20
Broad Sanctuary. SW1 1F 23
Broad's Green. 1D 11
Broad Street. 3F 27
Broad St. Che 3D 5
Broad St. Dag 3E 17
Broad St. Guild 4D 29
Broad St. Tedd 3C 22
Broad Wlk. SE3 1C 24
Broadwater Rd. Wel G 1E 7
Broadwater Rd. W Mal 2D 35
Broadway. E15 4C 16 (in two parts)
Broadway. Amer 4D 5
Broadway. Bexh 2E 25
Broadway. Knap 2D 29
Broadway. M'head 4B 12
Broadway. Maid 3F 35
Broadway. Rain 4F 17
Broadway. Surb 4D 23
Broadway. Swan 4F 25
Broadway. W'fd 1F 19
Broadway Mkt. E2 4B 16
Broadway Rd. Light & W'sham 1C 28
Broadway, The. N8 2A 16
Broadway, The. N9 1B 16
Broadway, The. NW7 1D 15
Broadway, The. NW9 2D 15
Broadway, The. SW19 3E 23
Broadway, The. W7 4C 14
Broadway, The. Cheam 1E 31
Broadway, The. Gnfd 4C 14
Broadway, The. Horn 3F 17
Broadway, The. Lou 4D 9
Broadway, The. S'hall 4B 14
Broadway, The. Stai 1F 21
Broadway, The. Stan 1C 14
Broadway, The. Wok 2E 29
Brockenhurst Rd. Asc 3C 20
Brocket Rd. Hod 1B 8
Brocket Rd. Lem & Wel G 1D 7
Brockham. 4D 31
Brockhamhurst Rd. Bet 4D 31
Brockham La. Brock 4D 31
Brock Hill. 4E 11
Brock Hill. Runw 4E 11
Brockley. 2B 24
Brockley Gro. SE4 2B 24
Brockley Hill. Stan 1C 14
Brockley Ri. SE23 2B 24
Brockley Rd. SE23 2B 24
Brockley Rd. Ilf 2D 17
Bromley. 4B 16 (Bow)
Bromley. 3C 24 (Chislehurst)
Bromley Common. 4D 25
Bromley Comn. Brom 3C 24
Bromley Hill. Brom 3C 24
Bromley La. Chst 3D 25
Bromley Rd. SE6 & Brom 2B 24
Bromley Rd. Beck & Brom 3B 24
Bromley Rd. Chst 3D 25
Brompton. 1F 23 (Belgravia)
Brompton. 3F 27 (Chatham)
Brompton Farm Rd. Roch 3E 27
Brompton Rd. SW7 1F 23
Brompton Rd. Gill 3F 27
Brondesbury. 3E 15
Brondesbury Park. 3E 15
Brondesbury Pk. NW6 & NW2 3E 15
Brondesbury Rd. NW6 4E 15
Bronze Age Way. Eri 1F 25
Brook Av. Wemb 3D 15
Brookbank. Wbrn G 3C 12
Brookdene Av. Wat 1B 14
Brook End. W'ton T 1A 4
Brook End Rd. Chelm 2E 11
Brookers Row. Crowt 4A 20
Brookfield La. W. Chesh 3B 8
Brook Green. 1E 23
Brook Hill. L Walt 1E 11
Brookhill Rd. Barn 1F 15
Brooklands. 1A 30
Brooklands Rd. Wey 1A 30
Brook La. Gall 3E 11
Brook La. Plax 3B 34
Brook La. Wal L 2B 20
Brookmans Park. 3E 7
Brookmill Rd. SE8 1B 24
Brook Pl. Ide H 3E 33
Brook Rd. Borwd 4D 7
Brook Rd. Buck H 1C 16
Brook Rd. Epp 3E 9
Brook Rd. Ilf 2D 17
Brookshill. Harr 1C 14
Brookside. 3C 20
Brookside S. EN4 1F 15
Brook Street. 1A 18
Brook St. Ast C 1B 4
Brook St. Belv & Eri 1E 25
Brook St. Brtwd 1A 18
Brook St. Snod 1E 35
Brook St. Tring 1C 4
Brook, The. Chat 3F 27
Brookwood. 2D 29
Brookwood Lye Rd. Wok 2D 29
Broombarn La. Gt Miss 3B 4
Broomfield. 1E 11
Broomfield Av. N13 1A 16
Broomfield La. N13 1A 16
Broomfield Rd. Chelm 2E 11
Broomhall. 4D 21
Broomhall La. Asc 4D 21
Broomhill Rd. Wfd G 1C 16 (in two parts)
Broomhills. 2D 19
Broom Rd. Tedd 3C 22
Broomstick Hall Rd. Wal A 3C 8
Broomwood La. Stock & Rams H 4E 11
Broomwood Rd. SW11 2F 23
Browells La. Felt 2B 22
Brownhill Rd. SE6 2C 24
Browning Rd. E12 3D 17
Browning Rd. Enf 4A 8
Brownlow Rd. N11 2A 16
Brownlow Rd. Berk 1E 5
Browns La. Eden 4D 33
Browns Rd. Hyde E 3C 4
Brown's Rd. Holm G 4C 4
Brownswood Rd. N4 3A 16
Brox. 1F 29
Broxbourne. 2B 8
Broxhill Rd. Hav 1F 17
Brox Rd. Ott 1F 29
Bruce Gro. N17 2A 16
Brunel Rd. SE16 1B 24
Brunswick Av. N11 1F 15
Brunswick Park. 1F 15
Brunswick Pk. Rd. N11 1F 15
Brunswick Rd. W5 4C 14
Bruton St. W1 4F 15
Bryant Av. Romf 2F 17
Bryant's Bottom. 4A 4
Bryant's Bottom Rd. Gt Miss 3A 4
Bucketsland La. Borwd 4D 7
Buckhatch La. Ret C 4F 11
Buckhold Rd. SW18 2E 23

Church La.—Darland Av.

Church La. Warf 2A 20
Church La. Warl 2B 32
Church La. Wen 2B 4
Church La. W'ham 2C 32
Church La. W'ton T 1A 4
Church La. Wex 4E 13
Church La. Wind 2C 20
Church La. E. Alder 4B 28
Church La. W. Alder 4A 28
Church Langley 1E 9
Church Langley Way. H'low 1E 9
Church Rd. E10 3B 16
Church Rd. E12 3D 17
Church Rd. NW4 2E 15
Church Rd. NW10 3D 15
Church Rd. SE19 3A 24
Church Rd. SW13 1E 23
Church Rd. SW19 3E 23
Church Rd. SW19 & Mitc 3F 23
Church Rd. W7 4C 14
Church Rd. Add 4F 21
Church Rd. Alder 4B 28
Church Rd. Asc 4D 21
Church Rd. As 4B 26
Church Rd. Ashf 2A 22
Church Rd. Bas 2E 19
Church Rd. Bexh 2E 25
Church Rd. Bookh 3B 30
Church Rd. Brack 3B 20
Church Rd. Bulp 3C 18
(in two parts)
Church Rd. Byfl 1A 30
Church Rd. Cat 3A 32
Church Rd. Chels 1E 33
Church Rd. Clay 1C 30
Church Rd. Cob 3C 26
Church Rd. Cook 3B 12
Church Rd. Corr 4E 19
Church Rd. Dun 2C 18
Church Rd. Egh 3E 21
Church Rd. Eps 1D 31
Church Rd. Farn 4D 25
Church Rd. Frim 2B 28
Church Rd. Had 2F 19
Church Rd. Hals 1E 33
Church Rd. Hart 4B 26
Church Rd. Hay 4A 14
Church Rd. H Bee 4C 8
Church Rd. Houn 1B 22
Church Rd. Igh 3A 34
Church Rd. Iver 4F 13
Church Rd. Kel H 4A 10
Church Rd. Kes 1C 32
Church Rd. Lea 2C 30
Church Rd. L Berk 2F 7
Church Rd. L Gad 1E 5
Church Rd. Mar 2B 12
Church Rd. More 2F 9
Church Rd. Mount & Ing 4C 10
Church Rd. Nave 4F 9
Church Rd. Noak H 1F 17
Church Rd. N'holt 4B 14
Church Rd. N'wd 2A 14
Church Rd. Ong 3F 9
Church Rd. Otham 3F 35
Church Rd. Penn 1C 12
Church Rd. Pits 2F 19
Church Rd. Pot B 3E 7
Church Rd. Rams H 1E 19
Church Rd. Raw 1F 19
Church Rd. Red 4F 31
Church Rd. Rich 2D 23
Church Rd. Sand 1A 28
Church Rd. Sev 4F 33
Church Rd. Shep 4A 22
Church Rd. Short 3C 24
Church Rd. Stan 1C 14
Church Rd. Sund 3E 33
Church Rd. Surb 4C 22
Church Rd. S at H 3A 26
Church Rd. Swan 4F 25
(Crockenhill)
Church Rd. Swan 3F 25
(Swanley Village)
Church Rd. Tedd 3C 22
Church Rd. Til 1D 27
Church Rd. Tovil 3F 35
Church Rd. Uxb 4F 13
Church Rd. W Dray 1A 22
Church Rd. W'ham 3E 33
Church Rd. W Han 4E 11
Church Rd. W Mal 2C 34
Church Rd. W Peck 3C 34
Church Rd. W'sham 1C 28
Church Rd. Wind 2E 21
Church Rd. Wold 2B 32
Church Rd. Wor Pk 4D 23
Church Street 2E 27
Church St. N9 1A 16
Church St. Amer 4D 5
Church St. Bill 1D 19
Church St. Bou M 4F 35
Church St. Bov 3E 5
Church St. Bur 1E 35
Church St. Che 3D 5
Church St. Cli 2E 27
Church St. Cobh 2B 30
Church St. Enf 4A 8
Church St. Eps 1D 31
Church St. Gill 3F 27
Church St. Gt Bad 2E 11
Church St. Hamp 3C 22
Church St. High 2E 27
Church St. High W 1B 12
Church St. Hoo 2F 27
Church St. Lea 2C 30
Church St. Loose 3F 35
Church St. Reig 4E 31
Church St. Rick 1A 14
Church St. Seal 2A 34
Church St. Shor 1F 33
Church St. Slou 1D 21
Church St. Stai 3F 21
Church St. W on T 4B 22
Church St. Wey 4A 22
Church St. W. Wok 2E 29
Church Town 4B 32
Church Wlk. Hay 4A 14
Church Way. S Croy 1A 32
Cippenham 4D 13
Cippenham La. Slou 4D 13
Circus Rd. NW8 4F 15
City 4A 16
City Rd. EC1 4A 16
City Way. Roch 4F 27
Clacket La. W'ham 3D 33
Clacton Rd. E13 4C 16
Clamp Hill. Stan 1C 14
Clandon Park 4F 29
Clandon Rd. Chat 1F 35
Clandon Rd. Send & Guild 3F 29
Clanking 2A 4
Clapgate 3A 10
Clapham 2F 23
Clapham Common. (Junct.) 2F 23
Clapham Comn. N. Side. SW11 2F 23
Clapham Comn. S. Side. SW4 2F 23
Clapham Comn. W. Side. SW11 2F 23
Clapham High St. SW4 2F 23
Clapham Junction 2F 23
Clapham Park 2F 23
Clapham Pk. Rd. SW4 2F 23
Clapham Rd. SW9 2A 24
Clappins La. N Dean & Nap 4A 4
Clapton Comn. N16 3A 16
Clapton Park 3B 16
Clare La. E Mal 2D 35
Claremont Av. N Mald 4E 23
Claremont Av. Wok 2E 29
Claremont La. Esh 4B 22
Claremont Park 1B 30
Claremont Rd. NW4 3E 15
Claremont Rd. Surb 4D 23
Claremont St. N18 2B 16
Clarence Av. N Mald 3D 23
Clarence La. SW15 2D 23
Clarence Rd. Grays 1B 26
Clarence Rd. Wind 1D 21
Clarence St. King T 3D 23
Clarence St. Stai 3F 21
Clarendon Rd. W11 4E 15
Clarendon Rd. P'wd 3B 4
Clarendon Rd. Wat 4B 6
Clare Rd. Stai 2F 21
Clarke's Grn. Rd. Sev 1A 34
Clarks La. Warl & W'ham 3C 32
Clatterford End 2A 10
(Fyfield)
Clatterford End 1C 10
(Good Easter)
Clatterford End 3A 10
(High Ongar)
Clatterford End 3F 9
(North Weald Bassett)
Claverhambury 3C 8
Claverhambury Rd. Wal A 3C 8
Claverton St. SW1 1F 23
Claycart Rd. Alder 4A 28
Claygate 1C 30
(Esher)
Claygate 4B 34
(Shipbourne)
Claygate Cross 3B 34
Claygate La. S'brne 3B 34
Claygate La. Th Dit 4C 22
Claygate Rd. Ladd 4D 35
Clayhall 2D 17
Clayhall Av. Ilf 2D 17
Clayhall La. Reig 4E 31
Clay Hill 4A 8
Clay Hill. Enf 4A 8
Clay Hill Rd. Bas 2E 19
Clay La. Guild 3E 29
Clay La. H'ley 3D 31
Clay La. High W 2A 12
Clay La. S Nut 4F 31
Claypit Hill. Wal A 4C 8
Clay's La. Lou 4D 9
Clay St. Knot 1C 12
Clayton Rd. Chess 4C 22
Clayton Rd. Hay 1A 22
Clay Tye Rd. Upm 3B 18
Clement St. Swan & Dart 3F 25
Clerkenwell 4A 16
Clerkenwell Rd. EC1 4A 16
Cleveland Rd. W13 4C 14
Cleveland St. W1 4F 15
Cleve Rd. NW6 3E 15
Clewer Green 1D 21
Clewer Hill Rd. Wind 1D 21
Clewer New Town 1D 21
Clewer Village 1D 21
Clew's La. Bisl 2D 29
Cliffe 1E 27
Cliffe Rd. Roch 3E 27
Cliffe Woods 2E 27
Cliff Hill. Bou M 4F 35
Cliff Hill Rd. Bou M 4F 35
Clifford Av. SW14 1D 23
(in two parts)
Clifford Rd. SE25 3B 24
Clifton Gdns. W9 4F 15
Clinch St. H Hals 1F 27
Clinton La. Bough B 4E 33
Cliveden 3C 12
Cliveden Pl. SW1 1F 23
Cliveden Rd. Tap 4C 12
Clive Rd. Gt War 2B 18
Clock House 1F 31
Clockhouse La. Ashf & Felt 3A 22
Clockhouse La. N Stif 1B 26
(in two parts)
Clockhouse La. Romf 2E 17
Clock Ho. Rd. Beck 3B 24
Clock Ho. Rd. L Bur 1D 19
Clockhouse Roundabout. (Junct.) 2A 22
Clubhouse Rd. Alder 3A 28
Coach Rd. Sev 3B 34
Coalhill 4F 11
Coalhouse Fort 1D 27
Coast Hill. Westc 4B 30
Coates La. D'ley 1A 12
Cobbett Hill. Norm 3D 29
Cobblershill 3B 4
Cobblershill La. Gt Miss 3B 4
Cobden Hill. Rad 4C 6
Cobham 1B 30
(Esher)
Cobham 3D 27
(Henley Street)
Cobham 3D 27
(Meopham)
Cobhambury Rd. Cob 3D 27
Cobham Pk. Rd. Cobh 2A 30
Cobham Rd. Stoke D & Lea 2B 30
Coborn Rd. E3 4B 16
Cockerhurst Rd. Shor 1F 33
Cockett Rd. Slou 1E 21
Cockfosters 4F 7
Cockfosters Rd. Pot B & Barn 4F 7
Cock La. Hghwd 3C 10
(in two parts)
Cock La. High W & Penn 1B 12
Cock La. Hod 2B 8
Cockmannings La. Orp 4E 25
Cockmannings Rd. Orp 4E 25
Cockpit Rd. Gt Kin 4B 4
Cockshot Hill. Reig 4E 31
Cock's La. Warf 2B 20
Cock Street 4F 35
Cocksure La. Sidc 2E 25
Codmore 3D 5
Codmore Wood Rd. Che 3E 5
Coke's La. Chal G 4E 5
Colam La. L Bad 2F 11
Colchester Rd. Romf 2F 17
Colchester Rd. Spri 1E 11
Cold Arbor Rd. Sev 3F 33
Coldblow 2F 25
Coldharbour 4B 34
Coldharbour La. SE5 & SW9 2A 24
Coldharbour La. Bush 1B 14
Coldharbour La. Dork 4C 30
Coldharbour La. Egh 3F 21
Coldharbour La. Hay 4B 14
Coldharbour La. Hild 4A 34
Coldharbour Rd. N'fleet 2C 26
Coldharbour Rd. W Byf & Wok 1F 29
Coldmoorholme La. Bour E 3B 12
Coleford Bri. Rd. Myt 3B 28
Cole Green 1E 7
Cole Grn. By-Pass. Col G & Hert 1F 7
Cole Grn. La. Wel G 1E 7
Coleman Green 1D 7
Coleman Grn. La. Wheat 1C 6
Cole Park 2C 22
Coleshill 1D 13
Coleshill La. Winch H 1C 12
Coles La. Bras 3E 33
Coles Meads 4F 31
Colham Green 4A 14
Colham Grn. Rd. Uxb 4A 14
Colindale 2D 15
Colindale Av. NW9 2D 15
Colindeep La. NW4 & NW9 2D 15
College Av. Harr 2C 14
College Cres. NW3 3F 15
College Hill Rd. Harr 2C 14
College La. Hat 2D 7
College Ride. Camb 1B 28
College Rd. SE19 & SE2 2A 24
College Rd. Ab L 3B 6
College Rd. Ast C 1B 4
College Rd. Brom 3C 24
College Rd. Chesh 3B 8
College Rd. Eps 1D 31
College Rd. Harr 2C 14
College Rd. Iswth 1C 22
College Rd. M'head 4B 12
College Rd. Maid 3F 35
College Rd. Swan 3F 25
College Rd. Wok 2E 29
College St. NW1 3F 15
College Town 1A 28
Collier Row 2E 17
Collier Row La. Romf 2E 17
Collier Row Rd. Romf 2E 17
Colliers Hatch 3F 9
Colliers Water La. T Hth 4A 24
Collier's Wood 3F 23
Colliers Wood. (Junct.) 3F 23
Collingwood Rd. Sutt 4E 23
Collinswood Rd. Farn C 3D 13
Collum Grn. Rd. Slou 3D 13
Colmore Rd. Enf 4B 8
Colnbrook 1F 21
Colnbrook By-Pass. Slou & W Dray 1F 21
Colne Way. Wat 4B 6
Colney Hatch 2F 15
Colney Hatch La. N10 & N11 2F 15
Colney Heath 2D 7
Colney Heath La. St Alb 2D 7
Colney Street 3C 6
Colonial Way. Wat 4B 6
Colston Av. Cars 4F 23
Columbia Rd. E2 4A 16
Colyers La. Eri 1F 25
Colyton Rd. SE22 2B 24
Combe La. Brmly 4A 30
Comet Way. Hat 2D 7
Commercial Rd. E14 & E1 4B 16
Commercial Rd. Roch 3E 27
(in two parts)
Commercial St. E1 4A 16
Commercial Way. SE5 1A 24
Common Ga. Rd. Rick 1F 13
Common La. Bough B 3C 12
Common La. Cli 1F 27
Common La. Dart 2F 25
Common La. K Lan 3A 6
Common La. Let H & Rad 4C 6
Common Rd. Chat 1E 35
Common Rd. Chor 4F 5
Common Rd. Clay 1C 30
Common Rd. Cli 2E 27
Common Rd. Hdlw 4C 34
Common Rd. Igh 3B 34
Common Rd. Stan 1C 14
Common Rd. Wal A 2D 9
Common Rd. Wind 1C 20
Common Side. D'ley 1A 12
Commonside. Kes 4C 24
Commonside E. Mitc 3F 23
Commonside Rd. H'low 2D 9
Commonside W. Mitc 3F 23
Common, The. W5 4D 15
Common, The. Dan 2F 11
Common, The. E Han 3F 11
Common, The. Gt Kin 4B 4
Common, The. Holm G 4C 4
Common, The. K Lan 3F 5
Common, The. Pott E 1E 5
Common, The. S'hall 1B 22
Common, The. Stan 1C 14
Commonwood 3F 5
Commority Rd. Meop 1C 34
Comp 2C 34
Compasses Rd. Leigh 4F 33
Comp La. Platt & W Mal 2C 34
Compton 4D 29
Compton Rd. N21 1A 16
Conduit La. N18 1B 16
Conduit La. Hod 1B 8
Conduit St. W1 4F 15
Coney Hall 4C 24
Coney Hill Rd. W Wick 4C 24
Congelow 4D 35
Coningsby La. Fif 1C 20
Coniston Way. Reig 4F 31
Connaught Bri. E16 4C 16
Connaught Gdns. N13 1A 16
Connaught Rd. Brkwd 2D 29
Connaught St. W2 4F 15
Constitution Hill. Snod 1D 35
Convent Rd. Ashf 3A 22
Conways Rd. Ors 4C 18
Cookham 3B 12
Cookham Dean 3B 12
Cookham Dean Bottom. Cook 3B 12
Cookham Rise 3B 12
Cookham Rd. M'head 4B 12
Cookham Rd. Swan 3E 25
Cooksmill Green 2C 10
Cooling 2F 27
Cooling Comn. Cli 2F 27
Cooling Rd. Cli 2E 27
(in two parts)
Cooling Rd. Roch 3E 27
Cooling Street 2F 27
Cooling St. Cli 2F 27
Cool Oak La. NW9 3D 15
Coombe 3D 23
(Kingston Upon Thames)
Coombe 2A 4
(Wendover)
Coombe Lane. (Junct.) 3D 23
Coombe La. SW20 3E 23
Coombe La. Croy 4B 24
Coombe La. Hugh & Nap 4A 4
Coombe La. Flyover. King T & SW20 3D 23
Coombe La. W. King T 3D 23
Coombe Rd. Croy 4A 24
Coombe Rd. King T 3D 23
Coombe Rd. N Mald 3D 23
Coombe St. Hem H 2F 5
Coomb Hill 4D 27
Coopersale Common 3E 9
Coopersale Comn. Coop 3E 9
Coopersale La. They B 4E 9
Coopersale Street 3E 9
Coopersale St. Coop 3E 9
Cooper's Corner 4E 33
Cooper's Green 1D 7
Coopers Grn. La. St Alb & Hat 1D 7
Cooper's Hill. Ong 3A 10
Coopers Hill Rd. S Nut 4A 32
Cooper's La. Pot B 3F 7
Cooper's La. W Til 1C 26
Cooper's La. Rd. Pot B 3F 7
Copenhagen St. N1 4A 16
Copes Rd. Gt Kin 4B 4
Copperfield Rd. Chelm 1D 11
Copperkins La. Amer 4D 5
Coppermill La. Rick & Uxb 2F 13
Coppermill Rd. Wray 2E 21
Coppetts Rd. N10 2F 15
Coppice Row. They B 4D 9
Copping's Rd. Leigh 4F 33
Copse Hill 3E 23
Copse Hill. SW20 3E 23
Copsem La. Esh & Lea 1B 30
Copthall Green 3C 8
Copthall La. Chal P 2E 13
Copt Hall La. Cob 3C 26
Copt Hall Rd. Igh 3B 34
Copt Hill. Dan 2F 11
Copthorne Rd. Lea 2C 30
Corbets Tey 3A 18
Corbets Tey Rd. Upm 3A 18
Cores End 3B 12
Cores End Rd. Bour E 3B 12
Corkscrew Hill. W Wick 4C 24
Cormongers La. Nutf 4F 31
Cornell Way. Romf 1E 17
Cornerfield. Hat 1E 7
Cornwall Cres. W11 4E 15
Cornwallis Av. Gill 4F 27
(in two parts)
Cornwallis Av. Tonb 4B 34
Cornwall Rd. Ruis 3B 14
Coronation Av. G Grn 4E 13
Coronation Dri. Horn 3F 17
Coronation Rd. NW10 4D 15
Coronation Rd. Asc 4C 20
Coronation Rd. Cre P 2A 12
Coronation Rd. L Grn 4A 12
Corporation Rd. Chelm 1E 11
Corporation St. Roch 3F 27
Corringham 4E 19
Corringham Rd. Stan H & Corr 4D 19
(in two parts)
Coryton 4E 19
Cotman's Ash 2A 34
Cotman's Ash La. Kems 1A 34
Coton St. E14 4C 16
Cotswold Rd. Sutt 1E 31
Cottenham Park 3E 23
Cottenham Pk. Rd. SW20 3E 23
Cotton La. Dart & Grnh 2A 26
Cottonmill La. St Alb 2C 6
Coulsdon 2F 31
Coulsdon La. Coul 2F 31
Coulsdon Rd. Coul & Cat 2A 32
Counters End 2F 5
Country Way. Hanw 3B 22
County La. Warf 3B 20
Coursers Rd. Col H 3D 7
Courtauld Rd. Bas 2E 19
Courtenay Av. Harr 2C 14
Courthill Rd. SE13 2C 24
Courthouse Rd. M'head 4B 12
Courtlands Dri. Wat 4A 6
Court La. SE21 2A 24
Court La. Burn 4C 12
Court La. Dor 1C 20
Court La. Hdlw 4C 34
Court Rd. SE9 2D 25
Court Rd. Broom 1E 11
Court Rd. Bur 1E 35
Court Rd. Orp 4E 25
Coval La. Chelm 2E 11
Cove 2A 28
Cove Rd. Farn 3A 28
Cove Rd. Fleet 3A 28
Cowbridge. Hert 1A 8
Cow La. Tring 1C 4
Cowley 4F 13
Cowley Hill. Borwd 4D 7
Cowley Mill Rd. Uxb 4F 13
Cowley Peachey 4F 13
Cowley Rd. Uxb 4F 13
Cow Watering La. Writ 2D 11
Coxes Farm Rd. Bill 1D 19
Cox Green 1B 20
Cox Grn. La. M'head 1B 20
Cox Grn. Rd. M'head 1B 20
Coxheath 4E 35
Cox La. Chess 4D 23
Coxtie Green 1A 18
Coxtie Grn. Rd. Brtwd 1A 18
Crabb's Hill. Hat P 1F 11
Crabhill La. S Nut 4A 32
Craddocks Av. Asht 2D 31
Crammavill St. Grays 4B 18
Cranbourne 2C 20
Cranbrook 3D 17
Cranbrook Rd. Ilf 2D 17
Cranbrook Rd. P Ris 2A 4
Cranes 2E 19
Cranes Farm Rd. Bas 2D 19
Cranes Way. Borwd 1D 15
Cranfield Pk. Rd. W'fd 2F 19
Cranford 1B 22
Cranford La. Hay 1A 22
Cranford La. Houn 1B 22
Cranham 3A 18
Cranham Rd. L Walt 1E 11
Cranley Gardens 2F 15
Cranley Gdns. N10 2F 15
Cranmer Rd. Mitc 3F 23
Cranmore La. Alder 4A 28
Cranston Rd. SE23 2B 24
Craufurd Ri. M'head 4B 12
Cravells Rd. Hpdn 1B 6
Craven Gdns. Ilf 2D 17
Craven Hill. W2 4F 15
Craven Pk. NW10 4D 15
Craven Pk. Rd. NW10 4D 15
Craven Rd. W2 4F 15
Crawley Hill 1B 28
Crawley Hill. Camb 1B 28
Crawley Ridge. Camb 1B 28
Crawley's La. Wig 1D 5
Cray Av. Orp 4E 25
Crayford 2F 25
Crayford Rd. Dart 2F 25
Crayford Way. Dart 2F 25
Craylands La. Swans 2B 26
Cray Rd. Sidc 3E 25
Cray Rd. Swan 4F 25
Crays Hill 2E 19
Crays Hill. Bill 2E 19
Creekmouth 4D 17
Creek Rd. SE10 & SE8 1B 24
Creek Rd. E Mol 3C 22
Creephedge La. E Han 3F 11
Creffield Rd. W3 & W5 4D 15
Creighton Av. N10 & N2 2F 15
Creighton Rd. N17 2A 16
Cremorne Rd. SW10 1F 23
Crescent E. Barn 4F 7
Crescent Rd. War 1B 18
Crescent, The. Lea 2C 30
Crescent W. Barn 4F 7
Cressex 2A 12
Cressex Rd. High W 2A 12
Crest Rd. Hand 2A 12
Crews Hill 4A 8
Cricketers La. Warf 3B 20
Cricketfield Rd. E5 3B 16
Cricket Grn. Mitc 3F 23
Cricket Hill 1A 28
Cricket Hill La. Yat 2A 28
Crickets Hill 3E 29
Cricklewood 3E 15
Cricklewood B'way. NW2 3E 15
Cricklewood La. NW2 3E 15
Crimp Hill. Wind & Egh 2D 21
Cripple St. Maid 3F 35
Crittall's Corner. (Junct.) 3E 25
Critten La. Dork 4B 30
Crockenhill 4F 25
Crockenhill La. Swan & Eyns 4F 25
Crockenhill Rd. Orp & W Wick 4E 25
Crockford Pk. Rd. Add 4F 21
Crockham Hill 4D 33
Crocknorth Rd. E Hor & Dork 4A 30
Crofton 4D 25
Crofton La. Orp 4D 25
Crofton Rd. Orp 4D 25
Croham Rd. S Croy 4A 24
Croham Valley Rd. S Croy 1B 32
Cromwell Av. Chesh 3B 8
Cromwell Rd. SW7 & SW5 1E 23
Cromwell Rd. Houn 2B 22
Cromwell Rd. King T 3D 23
Cromwell Rd. Red 4F 31
Crondall La. Farnh 4A 28
Crondon 3D 11
Crondon Pk. La. Stock 4D 11
Cronks Hill. Reig 4F 31
Crooked Billet. (Junct.) 2B 16
Crooked Billet Roundabout. (Junct.) 3F 21
Crooked Mile. Wal A 3C 8
Crook Log. Bexh 2E 25
Crooksbury Rd. Farnh 4B 28
Croom's Hill. SE10 1C 24
Crossbrook St. Chesh 3B 8
Cross Deep. Twic 2C 22
Cross Keys 3F 33
Cross Lances Rd. Houn 2B 22
Cross La. Beac 2D 13
Cross La. Hpdn 1B 6
Cross La. E. Grav 2C 26
Cross La. W. Grav 2C 26
Cross Lees. More 2A 10
Crossley's Hill. Chal G 1E 13
Cross Oak Rd. Berk 2E 5
Crossoaks La. Borwd & Pot B 3D 7
Cross Rd. Brom 4D 25
Cross Rd. Tad 2E 31
Cross Roads. Lou 4C 8
Cross St. N1 4A 16
Crossway. KT3 3E 23
Crossway. SE28 4E 17
Crossways Boulevd. Dart 2A 26
Crouch 3B 34
Crouch End 2F 15
Crouch End Hill. N8 3F 15
Crouch Hill. N4 & N8 2A 16
Crouch Ho. Rd. Eden 4D 33
Crouch La. Bor G 2B 34
Crouch La. Chesh 3A 8
Crouch La. Wink 2C 20
Crowbrook Rd. P Ris 2A 4
Crow Green 4B 10
Crow Grn. Rd. Pil H 1B 18
Crowhurst 4C 32
Crowhurst La. Crow 4C 32
Crowhurst La. Igh 3B 34
Crowhurst La. W King 1B 34
Crowhurst Lane End 4B 32
Crowhurst Village Rd. Crow 4C 32
Crowlands 3E 17
Crow La. Romf 3E 17
Crown Dale. SE19 3A 24
Crowndale Rd. NW1 4F 15
Crownfield Rd. E15 3C 16
Crown Hill. Wal A & Epp 3D 9
Crown La. SW16 3A 24
Crown La. Brom 4C 24
Crown La. Farn R 4D 13
Crown La. Mord 3E 23
Crown La. Penn 1C 12
Crown La. Shorne 3D 27
Crown Rd. Grays 1B 26
Crown Rd. Kel H 4A 10
Crown Rd. Mord 3E 23
Crown Rd. N'side 4A 10
Crown Rd. Sutt 4E 23
Crown Rd. Twic 2C 22
Crown Rd. Vir W 4E 21
Crown St. W3 4D 15
Crow Piece La. Farn R 3D 13
Crowsheath La. D'ham 4E 11
Crowthorne 1A 28
Crowthorne Rd. Brack 4B 20
Crowthorne Rd. Crowt & Brack 4A 20
Crowthorne Rd. Sand 1A 28
Croxley Green 1A 14
Croxted Rd. SE24 & SE2 2A 24
Croydon 4A 24
Croydon La. Bans 1F 31
Croydon Rd. SE20 3B 24
Croydon Rd. Beck 4B 24
Croydon Rd. Cat 3B 32
Croydon Rd. Kes 4C 24
Croydon Rd. Mitc & Croy 3F 23
Croydon Rd. Reig 4E 31
Croydon Rd. Wall & Croy 4F 23
Croydon Rd. W'ham 3D 33
Croydon Rd. W Wick & Brom 4C 24
Crutches La. Roch & Strd 3E 27
Cryers Hill 4B 4
Cryers Hill La. Cry H 4B 4
Cryers Hill Rd. Cry H 4B 4
Crystal Palace 3A 24
Crystal Palace F.C. 3A 24
Crystal Pal. Pde. SE19 3A 24
Crystal Pal. Pk. Rd. SE26 3A 24
Cubitt Town 1C 24
Cuckoo Hill. Pinn 2B 14
Cuckoo La. Tonb 4B 34
Cucumber La. Ess 2F 7
Cudham 2D 33
Cudham La. N. Cud & Orp 1D 33
Cudham La. S. Sev 2D 33
Cudham Rd. Orp 1D 33
Cuffley 3A 8
Cuffley Hill. Chesh 3A 8
Culver Gro. Stan 2C 14
Culverstone Green 1C 34
Cumberland Av. Guild 3E 29
Cumberland Av. Slou 4D 13
Cumberland Ga. W2 4F 15
Cumberland Rd. Camb 2C 28
Cumberland Rd. Stan 2D 15
Cupid Green 1A 6
Cupid Grn. La. Hem H 1A 6
Curriers La. Slou 3C 12
Curtain Rd. EC2 4A 16
Curtismill Green 4F 9
Curzon St. W1 4F 15
Custom House 4C 16
Cuton Hall La. Spri 1E 11
Cutter Ridge Rd. Ludd 4D 27
Cut, The. SE1 1A 24
Cutting, The. Red 4F 31
Cuxton 4E 27
Cuxton Rd. Roch 3E 27

Dagenham 3E 17
Dagenham Av. Dag 4E 17
(in two parts)
Dagenham Rd. Romf & Dag 3F 17
Dagger La. Borwd 1C 14
Dagnall Rd. Gt Gad 1E 5
Dagnam Pk. Dri. Romf 1A 18
Dagwood La. Dodd 4A 10
Daiglen Dri. S Ock 4B 18
Dairy La. Crock H 4D 33
Dairy La. Mard 4E 35
Dale Rd. S'fleet 3B 26
Dalling Rd. W6 1E 23
Dalston 3A 16
Dalston La. E8 3A 16
Daltons Rd. Orp & W Wick 4F 25
Damases La. Bore 1F 11
Dames Rd. E7 3C 16
Danbury 2F 11
Danbury Common 3F 11
Dancers End La. Tring 1B 4
Dancers Hill 4E 7
Dancers Hill Rd. Barn 4E 7
Danes Hill. Gill 3F 27
Daneshill. Red 4F 31
Danson Interchange. (Junct.) 2E 25
Danson La. Well 2E 25
Danson Rd. Bex & Bexh 2E 25
(in two parts)
Darby Green 1A 28
Darby Grn. La. B'water 1A 28
Darby Grn. Rd. B'water 1A 28
Darenth 3A 26
Darenth Hill. Dart 3A 26
Darenth Interchange. (Junct.) 2A 26
Darenth Rd. Dart 2A 26
Dargets Rd. Chat 1F 35
Darkes La. Pot B 3E 7
Dark La. Chesh 3B 8
Dark La. Gt War 1A 18
Darland 4F 27
Darland Av. Gill 4F 27

Darman La.—Fickleshole

Darman La. Pad W & Ladd 4D 35
Darnicle Hill. Chesh 2A 8
Darnley Rd. E8 3B 16
Darnley Rd. Grav 2C 26
(in two parts)
Darnley Rd. Roch 3E 27
Darr's La. N'chu 1D 5
Dartford. 2A 26
Dartford By-Pass. Bex & Dart 2F 25
Dartford Heath. (Junct.) 2F 25
Dartford Rd. Bex 2F 25
Dartford Rd. Dart 2F 25
Dartford Rd. F'ham 4A 26
(in two parts)
Dartford Rd. Sev 3F 33
Dartmouth Hill. SE13 1C 24
Dartmouth Park. 3F 15
Dartmouth Pk. Hill. N6 3F 15
Dartmouth Rd. SE23 & SE2 2B 24
Dartnell Park. 1F 29
Darvills La. Shur R 2A 20
Dashwood Av. High W 1A 12
Dashwood Rd. Grav 2C 26
Datchet. 1E 21
Datchet Common. 1E 21
Datchet Rd. Hort 2E 21
Datchet Rd. Old Win 2E 21
Datchet Rd. Slou 1D 21
Datchet Rd. Wind 1D 21
Daubeney Rd. E5 3B 16
Davenants. Bas 2E 19
Davidson Rd. Croy 4A 24
David Street. 4C 26
David St. Meop 4C 26
Dawesgreen. 4D 31
Dawes La. Sarr 4F 5
Dawes Rd. SW6 1E 23
Dawley Rd. Hay 4A 14
Dawney Hill. Pirb 2D 29
Daws Hill. E4 4C 8
Daws Hill La. High W 2B 12
Daws La. NW7 1D 15
Days La. Pil H 4B 10
Deacons Hill. Borwd 1D 15
Deacons Hill. Wat 1B 14
Deacons Hill Rd. Els 4D 7
Deadhearn La. Chal G 1E 13
Deadman's Ash La. Sarr 4F 5
Deadman's La. Chelm 3E 11
Dean La. Cook 3B 12
Dean La. Meop 1C 34
Dean La. Red 3F 31
Dean Rd. Meop 4C 26
Deansbrook Rd. Edgw 2D 15
Deans La. Edgw 2D 15
Deans La. Tad 3E 31
Dean Street. 4E 35
Dean St. W1 4F 15
Dean St. E Far 4E 35
Dean St. Mar 3A 12
Dean Way. Chal G 1E 13
Debden. 4D 9
Debden Green. 4D 9
Debden La. Lou 4D 9
De Beauvoir Rd. N1 4A 16
De Beauvoir Town. 4A 16
Decoy Hill Rd. H Hals 1F 27
Dedmere Rd. Mar 3A 12
Dedworth. 1D 21
Dedworth Rd. Wind 1C 20
Deepcut. 2C 28
Deepcut Bri. Rd. Deep 2C 28
Deepdene Av. Dork 4C 30
Deep Mill La. L Kin 4C 4
Deeves Hall La. Pot B 3D 7
Delancey St. NW1 4F 15
Delce Rd. Roch 4F 27
Dellsome La. N Mym 2E 7
Demesne Rd. Wall 4F 23
Dene Rd. Asht 2D 31
Dene Rd. N'wd 2A 14
Dene St. Dork 4C 30
Denham. 3F 13
Denham Aerodrome. 2F 13
Denham Av. Den 3F 13
Denham Garden Village. 2F 13
Denham Green. 2F 13
Denham Grn. La. Den 2F 13
Denham La. Chal P 2E 13
Denham Rd. Iver & Uxb 3F 13
Denham Roundabout. (Junct.)
3F 13
Denham Way. Den & Rick 2F 13
Denmark Hill. 2A 24
Denmark Hill. SE5 1A 24
Dennett Rd. Croy 4A 24
Dennettsland Rd. Crock H 4D 33
Denning Av. Croy 4A 24
Dennises La. Upm 4A 18
Dennis La. Stan 1C 14
Dennis Rd. S Ock 4B 18
Densham Rd. E15 4C 16
Denton. 2D 27
Denton Rd. Dart 2F 25
Denton Way. Wok 2D 29
Denzil Rd. NW10 3D 15
Deptford. 1B 24
Deptford Bri. SE8 1B 24
Deptford B'way. SE14 1B 24
Deptford Chu. St. SE8 1B 24
Deptford High St. SE8 1B 24
Derby Rd. Croy 4A 24
Derby Rd. Grays 1B 26
Deringwood Dri. Down 3F 35
Derry Downs. 4E 25
Desborough Av. High W 2A 12
Desborough Rd. High W 1A 12
Detillens La. Oxt 3C 32
Devas St. E3 4B 16
Devenish Rd. Asc 4C 20
Deville Way. Lain 2D 19
Devon Rd. S Dar 3A 26
Devonshire Rd. NW4 2E 15
Devonshire Rd. SE23 2B 24
Devonshire Rd. Chaf H 1B 26
Devons Rd. E3 4B 16
Dibden. 3F 33
Dibden La. Ide H & Sev 3F 33
Dickens Cen. 3F 27
Dickerage La. N Mald 3D 23
Dickerage Rd. King T 3D 23
Dillywood La. Roch & High 3E 27
Dimmocks La. Sarr 4F 5
Ditches La. Coul & Cat 2A 32
Ditton. 2E 35
Ditton Hill. Surb 4C 22
Ditton Hill Rd. Surb 4C 22
Ditton Pk. Rd. Slou 1E 21
Ditton Rd. Slou 1E 21
(Datchet)
Ditton Rd. Slou 1E 21
(Langley)
Ditton Rd. Surb 4C 22
Dixons Hill Rd. N Mym 2E 7
Dobb's Weir Rd. Hod 1C 8
Dockett Eddy La. Shep 4A 22
Docklands. 4D 17
Dock Rd. Chat 3F 27
Dock Rd. Grays & Til 1C 26
Dock St. E1 4B 16
Doctors La. Cat 3A 32
Doddinghurst. 4B 10
Doddinghurst Rd. Brtwd 4B 10
Dodds La. Chal G 1E 13
Dodds La. Pic E 1F 5
Doesgate La. Bulp 3C 18
Dogflud Way. Farnh 4A 28
Doghurst La. Coul 2F 31
Dogkennel Green. 4B 30
Dog Kennel Hill. SE22 2A 24
Dog Kennel La. Chor 4F 5
Dollis Hill. 3E 15
Dollis Rd. N3 & NW7 2E 15
Dollis Hill La. NW10 3D 15
Dome, The. (Junct.) 4B 6
Domsey La. L Walt 1E 11
Doncastle Rd. Brack 3A 20
Donkey La. F'ham 4A 26
Donkey Town. 1C 28
Donnington Rd. NW10 4E 15
Dora's Green. 4A 28
Dora's Grn. La. Farnh 4A 28
Dorchester Gro. W4 1D 23
Dorking Rd. Bookh 3B 30
Dorking Rd. Chil 4F 29
Dorking Rd. Eps 2D 31
Dorking Rd. Gom & Ab H 4A 30
Dorking Rd. Lea 2C 30
Dorking Rd. Tad 3D 31
Dormer's Wells. 4B 14
Dormer's Wells La. S'hall 4B 14
Dorney. 1C 20
Dorney Hill N. Beac 2D 13
Dorney Hill S. Slou 3D 13
Dorney Reach. 1C 20
Dorney Wood Rd. Burn 3C 12
Dorset Rd. SW19 3E 23
Douglas Rd. Maid 3F 35
Dover Ho. Rd. SW15 2E 23
Dover Rd. N'fleet 2C 26
Dover Rd. Slou 4D 13
Dover Rd. E. Grav 2C 26
Dovers Corner. (Junct.) 4F 17
Doversgreen. 4E 31
Dovers Grn. Rd. Reig 4E 31
Dowding Way. Wal A 4C 8
Dowlesgreen. 3A 20
Downe. 1D 33
Downe Rd. Cud 1D 33
Downe Rd. Kes 1D 33
Downfield Rd. Hert H 1B 8
Down Grn. La. Wheat 1C 6
Downhall Rd. Mat G 1F 9
Downham. 2C 24
(Bromley)
Downham. 1E 19
(Ramsden Heath)
Downham Rd. N1 4A 16
Downham Rd. Rams H 4E 11
Downham Rd. Stock 4E 11
Downham Way. Brom 3C 24
Downhills Pk. Rd. N17 2A 16
Down La. Comp 4D 29
Downley. 1A 12
Downley Rd. Nap 4A 4
Downs Ct. Rd. Purl 1A 32
Downs Hill Rd. Eps 2D 31
Downshills Way. N17 2A 16
Downshire Way. Brack 3B 20
Downside. 2B 30
Downside Bri. Rd. Cobh 2B 30
Downside Comn. Rd. D'side 2B 30
Downside Rd. D'side 2B 30
Downside Rd. Sutt 1F 31
Downs Rd. Enf 4A 8
Downs Rd. Eps 1D 31
Downs Rd. Grav 3C 26
Downs Rd. Sutt 1E 31
Downsview Rd. CR7 3A 24
Dowsett La. Rams H 4E 11
Dowsett Rd. N17 2B 16
Doyle Gdns. NW10 4E 15
Drake Rd. Chaf H 1B 26
Drake's Dri. St Alb 2C 6
Drakes La. L Walt 1E 11
Drapers Rd. Enf 4A 8
Draycott Av. Harr 2C 14
Drayton Beauchamp. 1C 4
Drayton Gdns. SW10 1F 23
Drayton Grn. Rd. W13 4C 14
Drayton Pk. N5 3A 16
Drewstead Rd. SW16 2F 23
Drift Bridge. (Junct.) 1E 31
Drift Rd. M'head 2A 20
Drive, The. Gt War 2B 18
Drive, The. Ilf 2D 17
Drive, The. Mord 4F 23
Drive, The. Rick 1F 13
Drive, The. Sidc 2E 25
Drop La. Brick 3B 6
Drummond Rd. Burn 4C 12
Druid St. SE1 1A 24
Drury La. WC2 4A 16
Drury Way. NW10 3D 15
Dry Arch Rd. Asc 4D 21
Drydell La. Che 3D 5
Dryhill. 3E 33
Dryhill La. Sund 3E 33
Dry Hill Pk. Rd. Tonb 4B 34
Dry Street. 3D 19
Dry St. Bas 3D 19
Du Cane Rd. W3 4D 15
Duck La. Thorn 2E 9
Duckmore La. Tring 1C 4
Duck's Hill Rd. N'wd 2A 14
Ducks Island. 1E 15
Dudbrook Rd. Kel C 4A 10
Dudden Hill. 3E 15
Dudden Hill La. NW10 3D 15
Dudswell. 1D 5
Dudswell La. Dud 1D 5
Duffield La. Stoke P 3D 13
Dugdale Hill La. Pot B 3E 7
Duke's Av. N10 2F 15
Dukes Av. Rich & King T 3C 22
Dukes La. Will 1B 10
Duke's Ride. Crowt 1A 28
Duke St. Chelm 2E 11
Duke St. Hod 1B 8
Dulwich. 2A 24
Dulwich Comn. SE21 2A 24
Dulwich Rd. SE24 2A 24
Dulwich Village. 2A 24
Dulwich Village. SE21 2A 24
Dulwich Wood Pk. SE19 3A 24
Dunbar Rd. N22 2A 16
Dunbridge St. E2 4B 16
Duncan Rd. Gill 3F 27
Dundale Rd. Tring 1C 4
Dungells La. Yat 2A 28
Dungrove Hill La. M'head 4A 12
Dunkery Rd. SE12 3C 24
Dunk's Green. 3B 34
Dunks Grn. Rd. S'brne 3B 34
Dunmow Rd. Fyf 2A 10
Dunnings La.
W H'dn & Upm 3B 18
Dunn St. Rd. Bred 1F 35
Dunny La. Chfd 3F 5
Dunsmore. 2B 4
Dunsmure Rd. N16 3A 16
Dunton Green. 2F 33
Dunton Rd. SE1 1A 24
Dunton Rd. Bill & Bas 2C 18
Dunton Rd. Dun 2C 18
Duppas Hill Rd. Croy 4A 24
Durants Rd. Enf 4B 8
Durham Rd. SW20 3E 23
Durham Rd. Lain & Bas 2D 19
Durnsford Rd. N22 2F 15
Durnsford Rd. SW18 2E 23
Durrants Hill Rd. Hem H 2F 5
Durrants La. Berk 2D 5
Durrants Rd. Berk 1D 5
Dury Rd. Barn 4E 7
Dutch Village. 4F 19
Dux Ct. Rd. Hoo 2F 27
Dux Hill. Plax 3B 34
Dux La. Plax 3B 34
Dwelly La. Eden 4C 32
Dyke La. Wheat 1C 6
Dytchleys La. N'side 4A 10
Dytchleys Rd. Brtwd 4A 10

Eagle Way. Gt War 2B 18
Eagle Wharf Rd. N1 4A 16
Ealing. 4C 14
Ealing Common. (Junct.) 4D 15
Ealing Grn. W5 4C 14
Ealing Rd. Bren 1C 22
Ealing Rd. Wemb 3D 15
Eardley Rd. SW16 3F 23
Earl Howe Rd. Holm G 4C 4
Earl Rd. N'fleet 2C 26
Earls Court. 1E 23
Earls Court Exhibition Cen. 1E 23
Earls Ct. Rd. SW5 & W8 1E 23
Earlsfield. 2F 23
Earlsfield Rd. SW18 2F 23
Earls La. Pot B 3D 7
Earl's Path. Lou 4C 8
Earl St. Maid 3F 35
Earlswood. 4F 31
East Acton. 4D 15
E. Acton La. W3 4D 15
East Av. E6 3D 17
East Barnet. 1F 15
E. Barnet Rd. Barn 4F 7
East Bedfont. 2A 22
Eastbourne Rd. God 4B 32
Eastbourne Rd. S God 4B 32
Eastbourne Ter. W2 4F 15
East Burnham. 3D 13
E. Burnham La. Farn R 4D 13
Eastbury. 1A 14
Eastbury Av. N'wd 1A 14
Eastbury Rd. N'wd 2A 14
Eastbury Rd. Wat 1B 14
E. Churchfield Rd. W3 4D 15
Eastchurch Rd. H'row A 1A 22
East Clandon. 4F 29
East Comn. Ger X 2E 13
Eastcote. 3B 14
Eastcote High Rd. Pinn 2B 14
Eastcote La. Harr 3B 14
Eastcote La. N'holt 3B 14
Eastcote La. N. N'holt 3B 14
Eastcote Rd. Pinn 2B 14
Eastcote Rd. Ruis 3A 14
Eastcote Village. 2B 14
East Dulwich. 2B 24
E. Dulwich Gro. SE21 2A 24
E. Dulwich Rd. SE15 & SE2 2A 24
Eastend. 1C 8
E. End Rd. N2 & N3 2E 15
Easter Av. Grays 1A 26
Easterfields. E Mal 2E 35
Eastern Av. E11 & Ilf 2C 16
Eastern Av. Pinn 3B 14
Eastern Av. E. Romf 2F 17
Eastern Av. W. Romf 2E 17
(in two parts)
Eastern Dene. Hasl 4B 4
Eastern Way. SE28 & Eri 1E 25
East Ewell. 1E 31
East Farleigh. 3E 35
Eastferry Rd. E14 1B 24
Eastfield Rd. Burn 4C 12
Eastfield Rd. Enf 4B 8
Eastfields Rd. Mitc 3F 23
East Finchley. 2F 15
E. Hall Hill. Bou M 4F 35
E. Hall La. Wen 4F 17
E. Hall Rd. Orp 4E 25
East Ham. 4D 17
Easthampstead. 4B 20
Easthampstead Rd. Brack 3B 20
Easthampstead Rd. Wokgm 3A 20
East Hanningfield. 3F 11
E. Hanningfield Rd.
H Grn & E Han 3F 11
E. Hanningfield Rd. Ret C 4F 11
E. Heath Rd. NW3 3F 15
East Hill. 1A 34
East Hill. SW18 2F 23
East Hill. Dart 2A 26
East Hill. Oxt 3C 32
East Hill. S Dar 3A 26
East Hill. Wok 2F 29
E. Hill Rd. Knat 1A 34
E. Hill Rd. Oxt 3C 32
East Horsley. 3A 30
E. India Dock Rd. E14 4B 16
East La. Wal L 1A 20
East La. Wemb 3C 14
East La. W Hor 3A 30
E. Lodge La. Enf 4F 7
Eastly End. 3F 21
East Malling. 2E 35
East Malling Heath. 3D 35
East Mayne. Bas 2E 19
E. Milton Rd. Grav 2C 26
East Molesey. 3C 22
Easton St. High W 1B 12
East Peckham. 4D 35
East Ramp. H'row A 1A 22
East Ridgeway. Cuff 3A 8
East Rd. EC1 4A 16
E. Rochester Way.
Sidc & Bex 2D 25
East Row. Roch 3F 27
East Sheen. 2D 23
East Smithfield. E1 4A 16
East St. Eps 1D 31
East St. Farnh 4A 28
East St. Hunt 4E 35
E. Thurrock Rd. Grays 1C 26
East Tilbury. 1D 27
E. Tilbury Rd. Linf 1D 27
East Vw. Writ 2D 11
East Way. E9 3B 16
Eastwick. 1D 9
Eastwick Hall La. E'wck 1D 9
East Wickham. 1E 25
Eastwick Rd. Bookh 3B 30
Eastwick Rd. H'low 1C 8
(in two parts)
Eastworth. 4F 21
Eastworth Rd. Cher 4F 21
Eaton Ri. W5 4C 14
Eaton Rd. Enf 4A 8
Eaton Sq. SW1 1F 23
Ebbisham Rd. Tad 3E 31
Ebury Bri. Rd. SW1 1F 23
Eccles. 1E 35
Eccleston St. SW1 1F 23
Echo Pit Rd. Guild 4E 29
Edenbridge. 4D 33
Eden Park. 4B 24
Eden Pk. Av. Beck 3B 24
(in two parts)
Edgehill Rd. Purl 1A 32
Edgemoor Rd. Frim 2C 28
Edgeworth Rd. Barn 4F 7
Edgington Way. Sidc 3E 25
Edgware. 2D 15
Edgware Bury. 1D 15
Edgwarebury La. Edgw 1D 15
Edgware Rd. NW2 3E 15
Edgware Rd. NW9 2D 15
Edgware Rd. W9 & W2 4F 15
Edgware Way. Edgw 1C 14
Edinburgh Av. Slou 4D 13
Edinburgh Way. H'low 1D 9
Edison Gro. SE18 1D 25
Edison Rd. SE18 & Well 1D 25
Edith Gro. SW10 1F 23
Edmonton. 1B 16
Edney Common. 2C 10
Edward St. SE8 & SE14 1B 24
Effingham. 3B 30
Effingham Comn. Rd. Eff 3B 30
Effingham Junction. 3B 30
Effingham Rd. Surb 4C 22
Effra Rd. SW2 2A 24
Egerton Dri. SE10 1B 24
Egerton Rd. Guild 4D 29
Eggar's Hill. Alder 4B 28
Eggpie La. Weald 4F 33
Egham. 3E 21
Egham By-Pass. Egh 3E 21
Egham Hill. Egh 3E 21
Egham Hythe. 3F 21
Egham Wick. 3E 21
Eglantine La. F'ham 4A 26
Egley Rd. Wok 2E 29
Egypt. 3D 13
Egypt La. Farn C 3D 13
Elder Rd. SE27 3A 24
Eleanor Cross Rd. Wal X 3B 8
Elephant & Castle. (Junct.)
1A 24
Elgin Av. W9 4E 15
Elgin Cres. W11 4E 15
Elizabeth Rd. Grays 1B 26
Elizabeth Way. H'low 1D 9
Elkins Green. 3B 10
Elkstone Rd. W10 4E 15
Ellenbrook. 1D 7
Ellenbrook La. Hat 1D 7
Ellen Rd. Ayl 1A 4
Ellesborough. 2A 4
Ellesborough Rd.
But C & Wen 2A 4
Ellesfield Av. Brack 3A 20
Ellesmere Rd. W4 1D 23
Elles Rd. Farn 3A 28
Elliman Av. Slou 4D 13
Elm Av. Ruis 3B 14
Elmbridge Av. Surb 4D 23
Elmbridge Rd. Ilf 2E 17
Elm Corner. 2A 30
Elmers End. 3B 24
Elmers End Rd.
SE20 & Beck 3B 24
Elm Grn. La. Dan 2F 11
Elm La. Bour E 2B 12
Elm La. Rox 1C 10
Elmore Rd. Coul 2F 31
Elm Park. 3F 17
Elm Pk. Av. Horn 3F 17
Elm Pk. Rd. Pinn 2B 14
Elm Rd. Chelm 2E 11
Elm Rd. Penn 1C 12
Elm Rd. Sidc 3E 25
Elmshott La. Slou 4D 13
Elms Perrin. Wemb 3C 14
Elms Rd. Alder 4B 28
Elms Rd. Harr 2C 14
Elmstead. 3D 25
Elmstead La. Chst 3D 25
Elmwood Av. Felt 2B 22
Elmwood Dri. Bex 2E 25
Elsdale St. E9 3B 16
Elspeth Rd. SW11 2F 23
Elstead Rd. Seale 4B 28
Elstree. 1C 14
Elstree Airport. 4C 6
Elstree Hill N. Els 1C 14
Elstree Hill S. Els 1C 14
Elstree Rd. Bush H & Borwd 1C 14
Elstree Way. Borwd 4D 7
Eltham. 2D 25
Eltham High St. SE9 2D 25
Eltham Hill. SE9 2C 24
Eltham Palace. 2D 25
Eltham Rd. SE9 & SE12 2C 24
Elthorne Heights. 4C 14
Elton Way. Wat 4B 6
Elvetham Rd. Fleet 3A 28
Embercourt Rd. Th Dit 4C 22
Ember La. Esh & E Mol 4C 22
Emerson Park. 2A 18
Emmanuel Rd. SW12 2F 23
Emmet Hill La. Ladd 4D 35
Emmetts La. W'ham 3E 33
Empire Way. Wemb 3D 15
Endell St. WC2 4A 16
Endlebury Rd. E4 1C 16
Endwell Rd. SE4 1B 24
Endymion Rd. N4 3A 16
Enfield. 4A 8
Enfield Highway. 4B 8
Enfield Lock. 4B 8
Enfield Rd. Enf 4A 8
Enfield Town. 4A 8
Enfield Wash. 4B 8
Engineers Way. Wemb 3D 15
Englands La. NW3 3F 15
Englands La. Lou 4D 9
Englefield Green. 3E 21
Englefield Rd. N1 3A 16
Engliff La. Wok 2F 29
Enterdent Rd. God 4B 32
Epping. 3E 9
Epping Green. 2D 9
(Epping Upland)
Epping Green. 2F 7
(Tylers Causeway)
Epping New Rd.
Buck H & Lou 1C 16
Epping Rd. Epp 3E 9
(Epping)
Epping Rd. Epp 4D 9
(Epping Forest)
Epping Rd. Ong 2F 9
Epping Rd. Roy & Epp G 1C 8
Epping Rd. Toot 3F 9
Epping Upland. 2D 9
Epsom. 1D 31
Epsom Downs. 2D 31
Epsom La. N. Eps & Tad 2E 31
Epsom Racecourse. 2D 31
Epsom Rd. Asht 2D 31
Epsom Rd. Croy 4A 24
Epsom Rd. Eps 1D 31
Epsom Rd. Guild & Eff 4E 29
Epsom Rd. Lea 2C 30
Epsom Rd. Sutt & Mord 4E 23
Erith. 1F 25
Erith High St. Eri 1F 25
Erith Rd. Belv & Eri 1E 25
Erith Rd. Bexh & N Hth 2E 25
Erriff Dri. S Ock 4B 18
Erskine Rd. Meop 1C 34
Esher. 4B 22
Esher By-Pass. Chess 4C 22
Esher By-Pass. Esh & Cob 1B 30
Esher By-Pass. Lea 1C 30
Esher Common. (Junct.) 1C 30
Esher Rd. E Mol 4C 22
Esher Rd. W on T 4B 22
Eskdale Av. Che 3D 5
Esplanade. Roch 4E 27
Essendon. 1E 7
Essendon Hill. Ess 1F 7
Essex Av. Slou 4D 13
Essex Regiment Way.
L Walt & Chelm 1E 11
Essex Rd. E11 & E10 2C 16
Essex Rd. N1 4A 16
Essex Rd. Hod 1B 8
(in two parts)
Essex Rd. S. E11 3C 16
Essex Way. Ben 3F 19
Eton. 1D 21
Eton Rd. Dat 1D 21
Eton St. Rich 2D 23
Eton Wick. 1D 21
Eton Wick Rd. Wind 1D 21
Euston Av. Wat 1A 14
Euston Rd. NW1 4F 15
Euston Underpass. (Junct.) 4F 15
Evelina Rd. SE15 2B 24
Evelyn St. SE8 1B 24
Evering Rd. E5 & N16 3A 16
Eve Rd. Wok 2E 29
Eversholt St. NW1 4F 15
Eversley. 2F 19
Eversley Pk. Rd. N21 1A 16
Ewell. 1D 31
Ewell By-Pass. Eps 1E 31
Ewell La. W Far 3E 35
Ewell Rd. Surb 4C 22
(Long Ditton)
Ewell Rd. Surb 4D 23
(Surbiton)
Ewell Rd. Sutt 1E 31
Ewshot. 4A 28
Ewshot La. Ews 4A 28
Exchange Rd. Wat 4B 6
Exedown Rd. Sev 1B 34
Exhibition Rd. SW7 1F 23
Eynsford. 4A 26
Eynsford Rd. F'ham 4A 26
Eynsford Rd. Sev 1F 33
Eynsford Rd. Swan 4F 25
Eynsham Dri. SE2 1E 25

Fackenden La. Shor 1F 33
Factory Rd. E16 1D 25
Faggoters La. Mat T 1F 9
Fagg's Rd. Felt 2A 22
Fagnall La. Winch H 1C 12
Fairchildes Rd. Warl 1C 32
Fair Cross. 3D 17
Fairfield Av. Stai 3F 21
Fairfield La. Farn R 4D 13
Fairfield N. King T 3D 23
Fairfield Rd. E3 4B 16
Fairfield Rd. Croy 4A 24
Fairfield S. King T 3D 23
Fairfield St. SW18 2E 23
Fairlands. 3D 29
Fair La. Coul 3F 31
Fairlie Rd. Slou 4D 13
Fairlop. 2D 17
Fairlop Rd. E11 3C 16
Fairmeadow. Maid 2F 35
Fairmead Rd. Lou 1C 16
Fairmile. 1B 30
Fairmile La. Cobh 1B 30
Fairoak La. Oxs & Chess 1C 30
Fairoaks Airport. 1E 29
Fairseat. 1C 34
Fairseat La. Fair 1B 34
Fairseat La. Wro 1B 34
Fairtrough Rd. Orp 1E 33
Fairway. Grays 4B 18
Fairway. Orp 4D 25
Fairway, The. Ruis 3B 14
Fakenham Way. Camb 1A 28
Falconer Rd. Bush 1B 14
Falcon Rd. SW11 1F 23
Falconwood. 2D 25
Falconwood. (Junct.) 2D 25
Falkland Rd. Dork 4C 30
Falling La. W Dray 4A 14
Falloden Way. NW11 2E 15
Falmouth Av. E4 1C 16
Fane Way. M'head 1B 20
Fanner's Green. 1D 11
Fanshawe Av. Bark 3D 17
Fant. 3F 35
Fantail, The. (Junct.) 4D 25
Fant La. Maid 3E 35
Faraday Av. Sidc 2E 25
Faringdon Av. Romf 2F 17
Farleigh. 2B 32
Farleigh Ct. Rd. Warl 1B 32
Farleigh Green. 3E 35
Farleigh Hill. Tovil 3F 35
Farleigh La. Maid 3E 35
Farleigh Rd. Warl 2B 32
Farley La. W'ham 3D 33
Farley Rd. S Croy 1B 32
Farmbridge End. 1C 10
Farm Hill Rd. Wal A 3C 8
Farm La. Asht & Eps 2D 31
Farm Rd. N21 1A 16
Farm Rd. Mord 4E 23
Farm Way. Buck H 1C 16
Farnaby Rd. Brom 3C 24
Farnborough. 3B 28
(Aldershot)
Farnborough. 4D 25
(Orpington)
Farnborough Airport. 3A 28
Farnborough Comn. Orp 4D 25
Farnborough Hill. Orp 4D 25
Farnborough Park. 3B 28
Farnborough Rd. Alder 4A 28
Farnborough Rd. Farn 3B 28
Farnborough Rd. Farnh 4A 28
Farnborough Street. 2B 28
Farnborough Way. Orp 4D 25
Farnham. 4A 28
Farnham By-Pass. Farnh 4A 28
Farnham Common. 3D 13
Farnham La. Slou 4D 13
Farnham Pk. La. Farn R 4D 13
Farnham Rd. Ews 4A 28
Farnham Rd. Guild 4D 29
Farnham Rd. Slou 4D 13
Farnham Royal. 4D 13
Farningham. 4A 26
Farningham. Brack 4B 20
Farquhar Rd. SE19 3A 24
Farringdon Rd. WC1 4A 16
Fartherwell Rd. W Mal 2D 35
Farthing Grn. La. Stoke P 4E 13
Farthing Street. 1D 33
Farthing St. Orp 1D 33
Farthing Way. Coul 2F 31
Fassett Rd. King T 3D 23
Faversham Rd. Mord 4E 23
Fawke Common. 3A 34
Fawke Comn. Under 3A 34
Fawke Wood Rd. Sev 3A 34
Fawkham. 4B 26
Fawkham Green. 4B 26
Fawkham Grn. Rd. Fawk 4B 26
Fawkham Rd.
Fawk & W King 4A 26
Fawkham Rd. Long 3B 26
Featherbed La. Croy & Warl 1B 32
Featherbed La. Hem H 2F 5
Feenan Highway. Til 1C 26
Felday Rd. Ab H 4A 30
Felden. 2F 5
Felden La. Fel 2F 5
Fellowes La. Col H 2D 7
Fellow Grn. W End 1D 29
Felmore. 2E 19
Felmores. Bas 2E 19
Feltham. 2B 22
Felthambrook Way. Felt 2B 22
Felthamhill. 3A 22
Feltham Hill Rd. Ashf 3A 22
Felthamhill Rd. Felt 3B 22
Feltham Rd. Ashf 3A 22
Fencepiece Rd. Chig & Ilf 1D 17
Fen La. Ors 4C 18
Fen La. Upm 3B 18
Fen La. W Horn 3B 18
Fenner Rd. Grays 1B 26
Fenns La. W End 1D 29
Fennycroft Rd. Hem H 1F 5
Fen Pond Rd. Igh 2B 34
Fentiman Rd. SW8 1A 24
Fenton Way. Bas 2D 19
Ferme Pk. Rd. N4 & N8 2A 16
Fern. 2B 12
Fernbank Rd. Asc 3C 20
Fernhall La. Wal A 3C 8
Fernhead Rd. W9 4E 15
Fernhill La. B'water 2A 28
Fernhill Rd. B'water & Farn 2A 28
Fernlea Rd. SW12 2F 23
Ferrers La. Hpdn & Wheat 1C 6
Ferry La. N17 2B 16
Ferry La. Bour E 3B 12
Ferry La. Lale 3F 21
Ferry La. Rain 4F 17
Ferry La. Shep 4A 22
Ferry Rd. Ben 3F 19
Ferry Rd. Til 2C 26
Fetcham. 3C 30
Fetter La. EC4 4A 16
Fickleshole. 1C 32

Fiddlers Hamlet—Grubwood La.

Fiddlers Hamlet. 3E 9
Fieldcommon. 4B 22
Field End Rd. Pinn & Ruis 2B 14
Field La. Frim 2B 28
Fields End. 2F 5
Fields End La. Hem H 1F 5
Field Way. New Ad 1B 32
Field Way. Rick 1F 13
Fife Rd. SW14 2D 23
Fifield. 1C 20
Fifield La. Wink 2C 20
Fifield Rd. Fif 1C 20
Fifth Av. H'low 1D 9
Fifth Cross Rd. Twic 2C 22
Fifth Way. Wemb 3D 15
Filston La. Sev 2F 33
Finchley. 2E 15
Finchley La. NW4 2E 15
Finchley Rd.
NW3, NW8 & NW11 2E 15
Fine Bush La. Hare 2A 14
Fingrith Hall La. Ing 3B 10
(in two parts)
Finsbury. 4A 16
Finsbury Park. 3A 16
Firbank Rd. Romf 1E 17
Firbank Rd. St Alb 1C 6
Firgrove Rd. Yat 1A 28
Firmingers Rd. Orp 4E 25
Firs La. N21 & N21 1A 16
First Av. Enf 1A 16
First Av. H'low 1D 9
First Av. Stan H 4D 19
First Way. Wemb 3D 15
Fir Tree Av. Stoke P 4D 13
Fir Tree Hill. Chan X 4A 6
Fir Tree Rd. Eps & Bans 2E 31
Fishers Green. 3B 8
Fishery. 4B 12
Fishery Rd. Hem H 2F 5
Fishponds Rd. Kes 4C 24
Fish St. Redb 1B 6
Fitzjohn's Av. NW3 3F 15
Five Elms Rd. Brom 4C 24
Five Fields La. Four E 4E 33
Fiveways. (Junct.) 2D 25
Fiveways Corner. (Junct.) 4A 24
(Croydon)
Fiveways Corner. (Junct.) 2E 15
(Hendon)
Flackwell Heath. 2B 12
Flamstead End. 3B 8
Flamstead End Rd. Chesh 3B 8
Flanchford Rd. L'gh 4E 31
Flanchford Rd. Reig 4E 31
Flaunden. 3E 5
Flaunden Bottom.
Che & Hem H 4E 5
Flaunden Hill. Flau 3E 5
Flaunden La. Hem H 3E 5
Flaunden La. Rick 3F 5
Fleece Rd. Surb 4C 22
Fleet. 3A 28
Fleet Downs. 2A 26
Fleet Rd. NW3 3F 15
Fleet Rd. Farn & Alder 3A 28
Fleet Rd. Fleet 3A 28
Fleet St. EC4 4A 16
Fleetville. 2C 6
Fleming Rd. Chaf H 1B 26
Fletcher's Green. 4F 33
Fletcher Way. Hem H 1F 5
Flexford. 4C 28
Flexford Rd. Norm 4C 28
Flint Hill. Dork 4C 30
Florence Rd. SE14 1B 24
Flower La. NW7 2D 15
Flower La. God 3B 32
Flowers Bottom La. Speen 4A 4
Floyd's La. Wok 2F 29
Fobbing. 4E 19
Fobbing Rd. Corr 4E 19
Folder's La. Brack 3B 20
Folly Hill. Farnh 4A 28
Folly La. St Alb 2C 6
Fonthill Rd. N4 3A 16
Foots Cray. 3E 25
Foots Cray La. Sidc 2E 25
Footscray Rd. SE9 2D 25
Force Green. 3D 33
Force Grn. La. W'ham 3D 33
Fordbridge Rd. Ashf 3A 22
Fordbridge Rd. Shep & Sun 4A 22
Fordbridge Roundabout. (Junct.) 3A 22
Ford La. Rain 3F 17
Ford La. Tros 2C 34
Ford Rd. Wok 2D 29
Fords Gro. N21 1A 16
Fordwater Rd. Cher 4F 21
Foreman Rd. Ash 4B 28
Foremans Barn Rd. Maid 4E 35
Forestdale. 1B 32
Forest Dri. E12 3C 16
Forest Edge. Buck H 1C 16
Foresters Dri. Wall 1F 31
Foresters Way. Crowt 4A 20
Forest Gate. 3C 16
Forest Grn. Rd. Fif 1B 20
Forest Hill. 2B 24
Forest Hill Rd. SE23 & SE22 2B 24
Forest La. E7 & E15 3C 16
Forest La. Chig 1D 17
Fore St. N9 & N18 2B 16
Fore St. Pinn 2A 14
Forest Rd. E17 2B 16
Forest Rd. Felt 2B 22
Forest Rd. Ilf 2D 17
Forest Rd. Lea 3A 30
Forest Rd. Lou 4C 8
Forest Rd. Sutt 4E 23
Forest Rd. Wink R & N Asc 3B 20
Forest Rd. Wokgm 3A 20
Forest Side. E4 1C 16
Forest Side. Wal A 4C 8
Forge La. Alder 3A 28
Forge La. E Far 3E 35
Forge La. High 3E 27
Forge La. Hort K 3A 26
Forge La. Leeds 4F 35
Forge La. Maid 3C 34
Forge La. Shorne 3D 27
Forge La. Yald 4E 35
Forlease Rd. M'head 4B 12
Formby Rd. Hall 4E 27
Forstal. 2E 35
Forstal La. Cox 4F 35
Forstal Rd. Ayle & Sandl 2E 35
Fort Amherst. 3F 27
Fortess Rd. NW5 3F 15
Fortis Green. 2F 15
Fortis Grn. N10 & N2 2F 15
Fortis Grn. Rd. N10 2F 15
Fort Pitt Hill. Chat 4F 27
Fort Rd. Til 2C 26
Fortune Green. 3E 15
Fortune Grn. NW6 3E 15
Forty Av. Wemb 3D 15
Forty Green. 2C 12
Forty Grn. Rd. Knot 2C 12
Forty Hill. 4A 8
Forty Hill. Enf 4A 8
Forty La. Wemb 3D 15
Foster Street. 1E 9
Foster St. H'low 1E 9
Fostington Way. W'slde 1F 35
Foundry La. L Row 3A 4
Fountain Dri. SE19 3A 24
Fountain La. Maid 3E 35
Fountain Rd. Red 4F 31
Four Ashes Rd. Cry H 4B 4
Four Elms. 4E 33
Four Elms Hill. Chatt 3F 27
Four Elms Rd. Eden 4D 33
Fourth Av. E12 3D 17
Fourth Av. H'low 1D 9
Fourth Way. Wemb 3D 15
Four Wantz. 1B 10
Fox Corner. 3D 29
Fox Corner. Worp 3D 29
Foxendown. 4C 26
Foxendown La. Meop 4C 26
Fox Hatch. 4A 10
Foxhills Rd. Ott 4E 21
Foxhounds La. S'fleet 2B 26
Fox Lane. 2A 28
Fox La. N13 1A 16
Fox La. Kes 4C 24
Foxley Hill Rd. Purl 1A 32
Foxley La. Binf 3A 20
Foxley La. Purl 1F 31
Foxley Rd. SW9 1A 24
Fox Rd. Mash 1C 10
Fox Rd. Wig 1C 4
Foyle Dri. S Ock 4B 18
Framewood Rd. Slou 3E 13
Frances Rd. Wind 1D 21
Frances St. SE18 1D 25
Francis Rd. E10 3C 16
Franks La. Hort K 4A 26
Franks Wood Av. Orp 4D 25
Frant Rd. T Hth 4A 24
Frascati Way. M'head 4B 12
Fraser Rd. Eri 1F 25
Freelands Rd. Brom 3C 24
Freemans La. Hay 4A 14
Freemasons Rd. E16 4C 16
Free Prae Rd. Cher 4F 21
Freezy Water. 4B 8
Fremantle Rd. Ilf 2D 17
Fremnells, The. Bas 2E 19
Frenches Rd. Red 4F 31
French Horn La. Hat 1E 7
French Street. 3D 33
French St. Sun 3B 22
Frendsbury Rd. SE4 2B 24
Friars Av. Shenf 1B 18
Friars Pl. La. W3 4D 15
Friars Stile Rd. Rich 2D 23
Friary Bri. Guild 4E 29
Friary Island. 2E 21
Friary Rd. N12 1F 15
Friary Rd. W3 4D 15
Friday Hill. 1C 16
Friday Hill. E4 1C 16
Friern Barnet. 1F 15
Friern Barnet La. N11 & N20 1F 15
Friern Barnet Rd. N11 1F 15
Frieth Rd. Medm 2A 12
Frimley. 2B 28
Frimley By-Pass. Frim 2B 28
Frimley Green. 2B 28
Frimley Grn. Rd. Frim G 2B 28
Frimley Gro. Gdns. Frim 2B 28
Frimley High St. Frim 2B 28
Frimley Ridge. 2B 28
Frimley Rd. Ash V 3B 28
Frimley Rd. Camb & Frim 1B 28
Frindsbury. 3F 27
Frindsbury Hill. Roch 3F 27
Frindsbury Rd. Strood 3E 27
Frithe, The. Slou 4E 13
Frith Hill. Gt Miss 3B 4
Frith La. NW7 1E 15
Frithsden. 1E 5
Frizlands La. Dag 3E 17
Frobisher Rd. St Alb 2C 6
Frog Gro. La. Wood S 3D 29
Froggy La. Uxb 3F 13
Froghole. 4D 33
Frogmoor. High W 1B 12
Frogmore. 1A 28
(Sandhurst)
Frogmore. 3C 6
(St Albans)
Frogmore. St Alb 3C 6
Frogmore Rd. B'water 1A 28
Frogmore St. Tring 1C 4
Frognal. NW3 3F 15
Frognal Av. Sidc 2E 25
Frognal Corner. (Junct.) 3D 25
Frognal La. NW3 3E 15
Frog St. Kel H 4A 10
Front La. Upm 3A 18
Front, The. Pott E 1E 5
Fryent Way. NW9 2D 15
Fryerning. 3C 10
Fryerning La. Ing 3C 10
Fryerns. 2E 19
Fulbourne Rd. E17 2C 16
Fulham. 1E 23
Fulham Broadway. (Junct.) 1E 23
Fulham F.C. 1E 23
Fulham High St. SW6 1E 23
Fulham Pal. Rd. SW6 & W6 1E 23
Fulham Rd.
SW3, SW6 & SW10 1E 23
Fuller's Hill. Che 3D 5
Fuller St. Sev 2A 34
Fullers Way N. Surb 4D 23
Fullers Way S. Chess 4D 23
Fullers Wood La. S Nut 4F 31
Fullwell Cross. 2D 17
Fullwell Cross. Ilf 2D 17
Fulmer. 3E 13
Fulmer Comn. Rd.
Ful & Iver 3E 13
Fulmer La. Ful & Ger X 3E 13
Fulmer Rd. Ful & Ger X 3E 13
Fulwell. 3C 22
Fulwell Rd. Tedd 3C 22
Furlong Rd. Bour E 3B 12
Furness Rd. Mord 4E 23
Furzebushes La. St Alb 2B 6
Furzedown. 3F 23
Furzehill Rd. Borwd 4D 7
Furze La. Stock 4E 11
Furze Platt. 4B 12
Furze Platt Rd. M'head 4B 12
Fyfield. 2A 10
Fyfield Rd. More 2A 10
Fyfield Rd. Ong 2A 10
Fyfield Rd. Will 2B 10

Gadbrook Rd. Bet 4D 31
Gaddesden La. Redb 1A 6
Gaddesden Row. 1F 5
Gaddesden Row. Gad R 1F 5
Gadebridge. 1F 5
Gadebridge La. Hem H 1F 5
Gadebridge Rd. Hem H 1F 5
Gadshill. 3E 27
Gads Hill. Gill 3F 27
Gainsborough Rd. E11 3C 16
Gainsborough Rd. N12 1E 15
Gainsthorpe Rd. Ong 2F 9
Gale St. Dag 3E 17
Gallants La. E Far 3E 35
Gallery Rd. SE21 2A 24
Galleyend. 3E 11
Galley Hill. Hem H 1F 5
Galley Hill Rd.
Swans & N'fleet 2B 26
Galleyhill Rd. Wal A 3C 8
Galley La. Barn 4E 7
Galleywood. 3E 11
Galleywood Rd. Chelm 2E 11
Galleywood Rd. Gt Bad 2E 11
Galliard Rd. N9 1B 16
Gallows Corner. (Junct.) 2F 17
Gallows Hill. K Lan 3A 6
Gallows Hill La. Ab L 3A 6
Gallows La. High W 1A 12
Gallwey Rd. Alder 4B 28
Gallys Rd. Wind 1C 20
Galpins Rd. T Hth 3A 24
Galsworthy Rd. King T 3D 23
Gambles La. Wok 3F 29
Gammons La. Wat 4A 6
Gander Grn. La. Sutt 4E 23
Gandy's La. Bou M 4F 35
Gangers Hill. God 3B 32
Gannondown Rd. Cook 3B 12
Gants Hill. 2D 17
Gants Hill. (Junct.) 2D 17
Gants Hill Cross. Ilf 2D 17
Ganwick Corner. 4E 7
Gapemouth Rd. Pirb 2C 28
Gap Rd. SW19 3E 23
Gardeners Green. 4A 20
Gardens, The. Harr 2C 14
Gardiners La. N. Cray H 1E 19
Gardiners La. S. Bas 2E 19
Gardner Rd. M'head 4B 12
Garfield Rd. Add 4F 21
Garlands Rd. Lea 2C 30
Garnet St. E1 4B 16
Garrad's Rd. SW16 2F 23
Garratt La. SW17 & SW1 2E 23
Garratts La. Bans 2E 31
Garrison La. Chess 1C 30
Garson's La. Warf 2B 20
Garston. 4B 6
Garston La. Wat 3B 6
Garth Rd. Mord 4E 23
Gascoigne Rd. Bark 4D 17
Gascoigne Rd. New Ad 1C 32
Gascoyne Rd. E9 3B 16
Gascoyne Way. Hert 1A 8
Gaston Bri. Rd. Shep 4A 22
Gates Grn. Rd.
W Wick & Brom 4C 24
Gateshead Rd. Borwd 4D 7
Gatland La. Maid 3E 35
Gatton. 3F 31
Gatton Bottom. Reig & Red 3F 31
Gatton Pk. Rd. Reig & Red 4F 31
Gay Bowers La. Dan 2F 11
Gay Bowers Rd. Dan 3F 11
Gellatly Rd. SE15 1B 24
General Wolfe Rd. SE10 1C 24
George V Av. Pinn 2B 14
George Green. 4E 13
George Grn. Slou 4E 13
George La. E18 2C 16
(in two parts)
George St. W2 4F 15
George St. Berk 2E 5
George St. Hunt 4E 35
George St. Rich 2C 22
George Wood Rd. Hem H 2A 6
Germain St. Che 3D 5
Gerpins La. Upm 4A 18
Gerrard's Cross. 2E 13
Gerrards Cross Rd. Stoke P 3E 13
Gervase Rd. Edgw 2D 15
Ghyllgrove. 2E 19
Ghyllgrove. Bas 2E 19
Gibbet La. Camb 1B 28
Gibbon Rd. SE15 1B 24
Gibbs Brook La. Oxt 4C 32
Gibbs Hill. Nett 3D 35
Gibraltar Hill. Chat 4F 27
Gibson Dri. King H 3D 35
Gidea Park. 2F 17
Giffard Dri. Farn 2A 28
Giffords Cross Rd. Corr 4E 19
Gighill Rd. Leyb 2D 35
Giggshill. 4C 22
Giggshill Rd. Th Dit 4C 22
Gilbert Rd. Belv 1F 25
Gilbert's Hill. St L 2C 4
Gildenhill Rd. Swan 3F 25
Gillan Way. H'low 1E 9
Gill Av. Guild 4D 29
Gillespie Rd. N5 3A 16
Gillette Corner. (Junct.) 1C 22
Gillingham. 3F 27
Gillingham F.C. 3F 27
Gillingham Rd. Gill 3F 27
Gills Rd. S Dar & Dart 3A 26
Gilston. 1D 9
Giltspur St. EC4 4A 16
Gipsy Hill. SE19 3A 24
Gipsy La. Wel G 1E 7
Gipsy Rd. SE27 3A 24
Givons Grove. 3C 30
Glade Rd. Mar 3A 12
Glade, The. Croy 4B 24
Glanty. 3F 21
Glanty, The. Egh 3F 21
Glasford St. SW17 3F 23
Glassmill La. Brom 3C 24
(in two parts)
Glaziers La. Norm 4C 28
Gleaming Wood Dri. Chat 1F 35
Glebe La. Maid 3E 35
Glebe Rd. Weald 4F 33
Glebe Way. W Wick 4C 24
Glencoe Rd. Hay 4B 14
Glenthorne Rd. W6 1E 23
Globe Rd. E1 & E2 4B 16
Globe Town. 4B 16
Gloucester Av. NW1 4F 15
Gloucester Av. Chelm 2E 11
Gloucester Pl. W1 & NW1 4F 15
Gloucester Rd. W8 1F 23
Gloucester Rd. Hamp 3B 22
Gloucester Rd. King T 3D 23
Gloucester Ter. W2 4E 15
Goat Hall La. Chelm 3D 11
Goathurst Common. 3E 33
Goat Rd. Mitc 4F 23
Goatsmoor La. Bill & Stock 4D 11
Goatswood La. Nave 1F 17
Goddard Rd. Beck 3B 24
Godden Green. 3A 34
Goddington. 4E 25
Goddington La. Orp 4E 25
Godstone. 4B 32
Godstone By-Pass. God 3B 32
Godstone Hill. Cat & God 3B 32
Godstone Interchange. (Junct.) 3B 32
Godstone Rd. Blet 4A 32
Godstone Rd. Cat 3B 32
Godstone Rd. Oxt 4B 32
Godstone Rd. Purl & Whyt 1A 32
Goffers Rd. SE3 1C 24
Goff's La. Chesh 3A 8
Goff's Oak. 3A 8
Goldcrest Way. New Ad 1C 32
Golden Ball La. M'head 4A 12
Golden Green. 4C 34
Golden La. EC1 4A 16
Golders Green. 2E 15
Golders Grn. Rd. NW11 2E 15
Goldhawk Rd. W12 & W6 1D 23
Gold Hill E. Chal P 2E 13
Gold Hill N. Chal P 2E 13
Gold Hill W. Chal P 2E 13
Goldings Hill. Lou 4D 9
Goldsel Rd. Swan 4F 25
Goldsmith Rd. W3 4D 15
Goldsmith's Row. E2 4B 16
Gold St. Sole S 4C 26
Goldsworth Park. 2D 29
Goldsworth Rd. Wok 2E 29
Gole Rd. Pirb 2C 28
Golf Ho. Rd. Oxt 3C 32
Gomshall. 4A 30
Gomshall La. Shere 4A 30
Gomshall Rd. Gom 4A 30
Good Easter. 1C 10
Goodge St. W1 4F 15
Goodley Stock. 3D 33
Goodley Stock Rd.
Crock H & W'ham 4D 33
Goodmayes. 3E 17
Goodmayes La. Ilf 3E 17
Goodmayes Rd. Ilf 3E 17
Goods Way. NW1 4A 16
Goodwyns Va. N10 2F 15
Gooseberry Green. 1D 19
Goose Green. 4C 34
(Hadlow)
Goose Green. 1B 8
(Hoddesdon)
Goose Grn. Gom & Brmly 4A 30
Goose La. Wok 2E 29
Goose Rye Rd. Worp 3D 29
Gooshays Dri. Romf 1A 18
Gordon Av. Stan 2C 14
Gordon Hill. Enf 4A 8
Gordon Ho. Rd. NW5 3F 15
Gordon Rd. Cars 1F 31
Gordon Rd. Corr 4D 19
Gordon Sq. WC1 4F 15
Gordons Way. Oxt 3C 32
Gore Ct. Rd. Otham 3F 35
Gore Grn. La. High 2E 27
Gore Hill. Amer 4D 5
Gorelands La.
Chal G & Ger X 1E 13
Gore Rd. Burn 4C 12
Gore Rd. Dart 2A 26
Goresbrook Rd. Dag 4E 17
Gorse Hill. F'ham 4A 26
Gorse Rd. Orp 4E 25
Goslar Way. Wind 1D 21
Gospel Oak. 3F 15
Gosport Rd. E17 2B 16
Gossamers, The. Wat 4B 6
Gosset St. E2 4B 16
Goss Hill. Swan 3F 25
Gossom's End. Berk 1E 5
Goswell Rd. EC1 4A 16
Goswell Rd. Wind 1D 21
Goulds Green. 4A 14
Gover Hill. 3C 34
Gover Hill. Rough 3C 34
Government Ho. Rd. Alder 3B 28
Government Rd. Alder 4B 28
Gower St. NW1 4F 15
Graces La. L Bad 2F 11
Gracious La. Sev 3F 33
Gracious Pond Rd. Chob 1D 29
Grafton Rd. Wor Pk 4D 23
Grahame Park. 2D 15
Grahame Pk. Way.
NW9 & NW7 2D 15
Graham Rd. E8 3B 16
Grand Depot Rd. SE18 1D 25
Grand Dri. SW20 3E 23
Grand Pde. N4 2A 16
Grandstand Rd. Eps 2E 31
Grange Hill. 2D 17
Grange Hill. Plax 3B 34
Grange La. Hart 4B 26
Grange La. Let H 4C 6
Grange La. S'Ing 2F 35
(in two parts)
Grange Park. 1A 16
Grange Rd. E16 4C 16
Grange Rd. SE1 1A 24
Grange Rd. Bill 1D 19
Grange Rd. Cook 3B 12
Grange Rd. Gill 3F 27
(in two parts)
Grange Rd. Guild 3E 29
Grange Rd. Lea 2C 30
Grange Rd. Pirb 2C 28
Grange Rd. Platt 3C 34
Grange Rd. T Hth & SE19 3A 24
Grants La. Oxt 4C 32
Granville Rd. N12 2F 15
Granville Rd. N'chu 1D 5
Grasmere Rd. Purl 1A 32
Gravel Hill. N3 2E 15
Gravel Hill. Bexh 2E 25
Gravel Hill. Chal P 2E 13
Gravel Hill. Croy 1B 32
Gravel Hill. Lou 4C 8
Gravel La. Chig 1E 17
Gravelly Hill. Cat 3A 32
Gravelly Ways. Ladd 4D 35
Gravel Path. Berk 2E 5
Gravel Rd. Brom 4D 25
Gravesend. 2C 26
Gravesend Rd. High 3E 27
Gravesend Rd. Roch 3E 27
Gravesend Rd. Shorne 3D 27
Gravesend Rd. Wro 2B 34
Gravetts La. Guild 3D 29
Grays. 1B 26
Gray's Inn Rd. WC1 4A 16
Grays Pk. Rd. Stoke P 4E 13
Grays Rd. W'ham & Sev 2D 33
Great Amwell. 1B 8
Great Baddow. 2E 11
Great Berry. 2D 19
Great Bookham. 3B 30
Gt. Braitch La. Hat 1D 7
Great Buckland. 1D 35
Great Burgh. 2E 31
Great Burstead. 1D 19
Great Cambridge Junction. (Junct.) 1A 16
Gt. Cambridge Rd. N9 1A 16
Gt. Cambridge Rd.
N18 & N17 2A 16
Gt. Cambridge Rd.
Enf & Wal X 1A 16
Gt. Central Way.
Wemb & NW10 3D 15
Gt. Chertsey Rd. W4 1D 23
Gt. Chertsey Rd. Felt & Twic 2B 22
Gt. Dover St. SE1 1A 24
Gt. Eastern Rd. E15 3C 16
Gt. Eastern St. EC2 4A 16
Great Gaddesden. 1F 5
Great Hampden. 3A 4
Greatham Rd. Bush 4B 6
Great Hivings. 3D 5
Great Hollands. 4A 20
Gt. Hollands Rd. Brack 4A 20
Great Kimble. 2A 4
Great Kingshill. 4B 4
Gt. Knightleys. Bas 2D 19
Gt. Marlborough St. W1 4F 15
Great Missenden. 3B 4
Greatness. 2F 33
Gt. Norman St. Sev 3E 33
Gt. North Rd. N6 & N2 2F 15
Gt. North Rd. Barn 1E 15
Gt. North Rd. Brk P 2E 7
Gt. North Rd. Hat & Pot B 2E 7
Gt. North Rd. High Bar 4E 7
Gt. North Rd. Wel G 1E 7
(in two parts)
Gt. North Way. NW4 2E 15
Great Oxney Green. 2D 11
Great Parndon. 1D 9
Gt. Portland St. W1 4F 15
Gt. Prestons La. Stock 4E 11
Gt. Queen St. WC2 4A 16
Great Rd. Hem H 2A 6
Gt. Ropers La. War 2B 18
Gt. South W. Rd.
Felt & Houn 2A 22
Gt. Tattenhams. Eps 2E 31
Great Waltham. 1D 11
Great Warley. 2B 18
Gt. Warley St. Gt War 2B 18
Gt. Western Rd. W11 & W9 4E 15
Gt. West Rd. W4 1D 23
Gt. West Rd. W6 & W4 1D 23
Gt. West Rd. Houn & Iswth 1B 22
Grn. Common La. Beac 3C 12
Green Comn. La. Wbrn G 3C 12
Green Ct. Rd. Swan 4F 25
Green Dene. E Hor 4A 30
Green Dragon La. N21 1A 16
Green Dragon La. F Hth 2B 12
Green End. 2F 5
Green End St. Ast C 1B 4
Green Farm La. Shorne 2D 27
Greenford. 4C 14
Greenford Av. W7 4C 14
Greenford Rd. S'hall & Harr 4C 14
Greenford Roundabout. (Junct.) 4C 14
Greengate St. E13 4C 16
Green Hailey. 3A 4
Greenhill. 2C 14
Green Hill. High W 1B 12
Greenhill Pk. NW10 4D 15
Greenhill Way. Harr 2C 14
Greenhithe. 2B 26
Greenhurst La. Oxt 4C 32
Greenlands La. P'wd 3B 4
Green La. NW4 2E 15
Green La. SE9 & Chst 2D 25
Green La. SE20 3B 24
Green La. SW16 & T Hth 3A 24
Green La. B'water 2A 28
Green La. Bou M 4F 35
Green La. Bov 3E 5
Green La. Burn 4C 12
Green La. Chelm 1D 11
Green La. Cher & Add 4F 21
Green La. Felt 3B 22
Green La. Four E 4E 33
Green La. Hem H 2A 6
Green La. Houn 2B 22
Green La. Ilf & Dag 3D 17
Green La. Kel H 4A 10
Green La. Meop 4C 26
Green La. Mord 4E 23
Green La. N'wd 2A 14
Green La. Ock 3A 30
Green La. P'wd 3B 4
Green La. Rox 2C 10
(in two parts)
Green La. Shep 4A 22
Green La. Stan 1C 14
Green La. Tad & Coul 3E 31
Green La. Thr B 1E 9
Green La. Uxb 4A 14
Green La. E. Norm 4C 28
Green Lanes. N8 2A 16
Green Lanes. N16 & N4 2A 16
Green Lanes. N21 & N13 2A 16
Green Lanes. Lem & Hat 1D 7
Green La. W. Ash 4C 28
Green Man Roundabout. (Junct.) 2C 24
Green Rd. Dart 3B 26
Green Rd. High W 1B 12
Green Rd. Vir W & Egh 4E 21
Greens Farm La. Bill 1D 19
Greensted. 3F 9
Greensted Green. 3F 9
Greensted Rd. Ong 3F 9
Green Street. 4C 10
Green St. E13 & E7 3C 16
Green St. Dart 2A 26
Green St. Enf 4B 8
Green St. High W 1A 12
Green St. Ing 3C 10
Green St. Rick 4F 5
Green St. Shenl 3D 7
Green St. Sun 3B 22
Green Street Green. 3B 26
(Dartford)
Green Street Green. 1D 33
(Orpington)
Green, The. E4 1C 16
Green, The. N9 1B 16
Green, The. N14 1F 15
Green, The. N21 1A 16
Green, The. B'more 3B 10
Green, The. Bou M 4F 35
Green, The. Clay 1C 30
Green, The. Crox G 1A 14
Green, The. Egh 3E 21
Green, The. Orp 4D 25
Green, The. Sarr 4F 5
Green, The. Sidc 3E 25
Green, The. S'hall 1B 22
Green, The. They B 4D 9
Green, The. Til 1C 26
Green, The. Twic 2C 22
Green, The. Warl 2B 32
Green, The. W Dray 1F 21
Green, The. Writ 2D 11
Green Wlk. Wfd G 2D 17
Greenway. Che 3D 5
Greenway, The. Uxb 4F 13
Greenwich. 1C 24
Greenwich High Rd. SE8 1B 24
Greenwich Millennium Village. 1C 24
Greenwich S. St. SE10 1C 24
Green Wrythe La. Cars 4F 23
Grenfell Pl. M'head 4B 12
Grenfell Rd. M'head 4B 12
Gresham Rd. Houn 1C 22
Gresham Rd. Stai 3F 21
Greville Pl. NW6 4E 15
Greyhound Hill. NW4 2E 15
Greyhound La. SW16 3F 23
Greyhound La. Pot B 3E 7
Greyhound Ter. SW16 3F 23
Griffin Rd. SE18 1D 25
Griggs App. Ilf 3D 17
Grimsdell's La. Amer 4D 5
Gringer Hill. M'head 4B 12
Grosvenor Av. N5 3A 16
Grosvenor Av. Cars 1F 31
Grosvenor Gdns. SW1 1F 23
Grosvenor Pl. SW1 1F 23
Grosvenor Rd. N10 2F 15
Grosvenor Rd. SW1 1F 23
Grosvenor Rd. Alder 4B 28
Grosvenor Rd. Wall 1F 31
Grosvenor Rd. Wat 4B 6
Grosvenor St. W1 4F 15
Ground La. Hat 1E 7
Grove Av. N10 2F 15
Grove Cres. King T 3D 23
Grove Cross Rd. Frim 2B 28
Grove End. Bag 1C 28
Grove End Rd. NW8 4F 15
Grove Green. 2F 35
Grove Grn. Rd. E11 & E10 3C 16
Grove Heath Rd. Rip 3F 29
Grovehill. 1A 6
Grove La. SE5 1A 24
Grove La. Chal P 2E 13
Grove La. Che 3E 5
Grove La. Gt Kim 2A 4
Grove La. King T 3D 23
Groveley Rd. Sun & Felt 3A 22
Grove Mill La. Rick & Wat 4A 6
Grove Park. 2C 24
(Bromley)
Grove Park. 1D 23
(Chiswick)
Grove Pk. Rd. SE12 2C 24
Grove Pk. Rd. W4 1D 23
Grove Rd. E9 4B 16
Grove Rd. E17 2B 16
Grove Rd. Burn 4C 12
Grove Rd. Hpdn 1C 6
Grove Rd. Houn 2B 22
Grove Rd. Mitc 3F 23
Grove Rd. Romf 3E 17
Grove Rd. Seal 2A 34
Grove Rd. Sutt 1E 31
Grove Rd. Tring 1C 4
Grove St. SE8 1B 24
Grove, The. (Junct.) 2B 24
Grove, The. E15 3C 16
Grove, The. Iswth 1C 22
Grove, The. Slou 1E 21
Grove Va. SE22 2A 24
Grovewood Dri. Maid 2F 35
Grubb St. 3B 26
Grubs La. Hat 2E 7
Grubwood La. Cook 3B 12

Gubbins La.—High St.

Gubbins La. Romf 2A 18
Guildables La. Eden 4D 33
Guildford. 4E 29
Guildford & Godalming By-Pass Rd. Comp & Guild 4D 29
Guildford La. Alb 4F 29
Guildford Park. 4E 29
Guildford Pk. Rd. Guild 4E 29
Guildford Rd. Ab C 4A 30
Guildford Rd. Ash & Norm 4C 28
Guildford Rd. Bag 1C 28
Guildford Rd. Farnh 4A 28
Guildford Rd. Fet 3C 30
Guildford Rd. Frim G 2B 28
Guildford Rd. Guild & Wok 3E 29
Guildford Rd. Lea 3A 30
Guildford Rd. Light & Wok 1C 28
Guildford Rd. Mayf 2E 29
Guildford Rd. Norm 4C 28
Guildford Rd. Pirb & Guild 3D 29
Guildford Rd. Runf 4B 28
Guildford Rd. Westc 4B 30
Guildford Rd. Wok & Cher 1E 29
Guildford St. Cher 4F 21
Guileshill La. Ock 2A 30
Guilford St. WC1 4A 16
Gun Hill. W Til 1C 26
Gun La. Strood 3E 27
Gunnersbury. 1D 23
Gunnersbury Av. W3 & W5 4D 15
Gunnersbury Dri. W5 1D 23
Gunnersbury La. W3 1D 23
Gunnersbury Park. (Junct.) 1D 23
Gunter Gro. SW10 1F 23
Gypsy Corner. (Junct.) 4D 15
Gypsy La. Gt Amw 1B 8
Gypsy La. Stoke P 3D 13
Gyratory Rd. Wat 1B 14

Hackbridge. 4F 23
Hackbridge Rd. Wall 4F 23
Hackney. 3B 16
Hackney Rd. E2 4A 16
Hackney Rd. Maid 3F 35
Hackney Wick. 3B 16
Hackney Wick. (Junct.) 3B 16
Hacton. 3A 18
Hacton La. Horn & Upm 3A 18
Haddon Rd. M'head 4B 12
Hadley. 4E 7
Hadley Comn. Barn 4E 7
Hadley Grn. Rd. Barn 4E 7
Hadley Highstone. Barn 4E 7
Hadley Rd. Barn 4E 7
Hadley Rd. Cockf & Enf 4F 7
Hadley Way. N21 1A 16
Hadley Wood. 4F 7
Hadlow. 4C 34
Hadlow Rd. Tonb 4B 34 (in two parts)
Hadlow Rd. E. Tonb 4B 34
Hadlow Stair. 4B 34
Hagden La. Wat 4A 6 (in two parts)
Haggerston. 4A 16
Hag Hill La. Tap 4C 12
Ha Ha Rd. SE18 1D 25
Hailey. 1B 8
Hailey La. Hail 1B 8
Hainault. 2E 17
Hainault Rd. E10 3C 16
Hainault Rd. Chig 1D 17
Hainault Rd. Romf 2E 17
Hale. 4A 28 (Farnham)
Hale. 4F 27 (Gillingham)
Halebourne La. Wok 1D 29
Hale End. 2C 16
Hale End Rd. E17 & E4 2C 16
Hale La. Edgw & NW7 1D 15
Hale La. Wen 2B 4
Hale Oak Rd. Chid & Weald 4F 33
Hale Oak Rd. Weald 4F 33
Hale Rd. N17 2B 16
Hale Rd. Farnh 4A 28
Hale Rd. Hert 1A 8
Hale Rd. Wen 2B 4
Hale Street. 4D 35
Hale St. E Peck 4D 35
Hale, The. 1D 15
Half Acre. Bren 1C 22
Halfhide La. Chesh 3B 8
Half Moon La. SE24 2A 24
Halfpence La. Cob 3D 27
Halfpenny La. Guild 4F 29
Halfway St. Sidc 2D 25
Haling Pk. Rd. S Croy 4A 24
Hall Grn. La. Hut 1C 18
Hall Gro. 1E 7
Hall Gro. Wel G 1E 7
Hall Hill. Oxt 4C 32
Hall Hill. Sev 3A 34
Halliford Rd. Shep & Sun 4A 22
Halliford St. N1 3A 16
Halling. 4E 27
Halling By-Pass. Hall 4E 27
Hall Lane. (Junct.) 1B 16
Hall La. E4 1B 16
Hall La. Ing 4C 10
Hall La. Shenf 4B 10
Hall La. Upm 3A 18
Hall La. Yat 1A 28
Hall Rd. E11 3C 16
Hall Rd. W9 4F 15
Hall Rd. Ayle 2E 35
Hall Rd. Iswth 2C 22
Hall Rd. N'fleet 2C 26
Hall Rd. Woul 1E 35
Halls Green. 1C 8 (Roydon)
Hall's Green. 4F 33 (Sevenoaks Weald)
Halls La. Wal L 1A 20
Halstead. 1E 33
Halstead Hill. Chesh 3A 8
Halstead La. Knock 2E 33
Halstead Rd. N21 1A 16
Halton. 1B 4
Halton Camp. 1B 4
Halton La. Wen 1B 4
Ham. 2C 22
Hamberlins La. N'chu 1D 5
Ham Comn. Rich 2C 22
Hamesmoor Rd. Myt 3B 28
Ham Ga. Av. Rich 2D 23
Hamilton Rd. High W 1B 12
Hamilton Rd. K Lan 3A 6
Ham Island. 2E 21
Ham La. Gill 1F 35
Ham La. Old Win 2E 21
Hamlet Hill. Roy 2C 8
Hamlet Rd. SE19 3A 24
Hammerfield. 2F 5
Hammers La. NW7 1E 15
Hammersley La. High W & Penn 2B 12
Hammersmith. 1E 23
Hammersmith Broadway. (Junct.) 1E 23
Hammersmith Flyover. (Junct.) 1E 23
Hammersmith Flyover. W6 1E 23
Hammersmith Rd. W14 & W6 1E 23
Hammond's La. Sandr 1C 6
Hammonds Rd. S'don & L Bad 2F 11
Hammond Street. 3A 8
Hammondstreet Rd. Chesh 2A 8
Ham Moor. 4F 21
Hampden Bottom. 3B 4
Hampden Rd. P'wd 3A 4
Hampden Rd. Speen 4A 4
Hampden Way. N14 1F 15
Hampermill La. Wat 1B 14
Hampstead. 3F 15
Hampstead Garden Suburb. 2F 15
Hampstead High St. NW3 3F 15
Hampstead La. N6 & NW3 3F 15
Hampstead La. Yald 4D 35
Hampstead Rd. NW1 4F 15
Hampstead Way. NW11 2E 15
Hampton. 3B 22
Hampton Court. 3C 22
Hampton Court. (Junct.) 3C 22
Hampton Ct. Bri. E Mol 3C 22
Hampton Court Palace. 3C 22
Hampton Ct. Rd. E Mol & King T 3C 22
Hampton Ct. Rd. Hamp & E Mol 3C 22
Hampton Ct. Way. Th Dit & E Mol 4C 22
Hampton Hill. 3C 22
Hampton La. Felt 3B 22
Hampton Rd. Tedd 3C 22
Hampton Rd. Twic 2C 22
Hampton Rd. E. Felt 3B 22
Hampton Rd. W. Felt 2B 22
Hamptons. 3C 34
Hamptons Rd. D Grn 3B 34
Hampton Wick. 3C 22
Hamsey Green. 2B 32
Ham St. Rich 2C 22
Handcroft Rd. Croy 4A 24
Handford La. Yat 1A 28
Handley Green. 3C 10
Handside. 1E 7
Handy Cross. 2A 12
Hanger Hill. 4D 15
Hanger Hill. Wey 1A 30
Hanger Lane. (Junct.) 4D 15
Hanger La. HA0 4D 15
Hanging Hill La. Hut 1B 18
Hangings La. P'wd 3B 4
Hangrove Hill. Orp 1D 33
Hanley Rd. N19 3A 16
Hanover Pk. SE15 1B 24
Hanwell. 4C 14
Hanworth. 4B 20 (Bracknell)
Hanworth. 3B 22 (Feltham)
Hanworth Rd. Brack 4B 20
Hanworth Rd. Felt 2B 22
Hanworth Rd. Hamp 3B 22
Hanworth Rd. Houn 2B 22
Hanworth Rd. Sun 3B 22 (in two parts)
Harberts Rd. H'low 1D 9
Harbet Rd. E4 & N18 2B 16
Harbourland. 2F 35
Hardings Dean. 3B 12
Hardings Elms Rd. Cray H 2E 19
Hardwick La. Lyne 4F 21
Hare & Billet Rd. SE10 & SE1 1C 24
Harebreaks, The. Wat 4B 6
Harefield. 2F 13
Harefield Rd. Rick 1F 13
Harefield Rd. Uxb 3F 13
Harehatch La. Slou 3D 13
Hare Hill. Add 1F 29
Hare La. Clay 4C 22
Hare La. L Kin 4B 4
Haresfoot Pk. Berk 2E 5
Harestone Valley Rd. Cat 3A 32
Hare Street. 1E 9 (Harlow)
Hare Street. 4A 10 (Little End)
Hareward Rd. Guild 4F 29
Harfield Rd. Sun 3B 22
Harlequins R.U.F.C. 2C 22
Harlesden. 4D 15
Harlesden Rd. NW10 4E 15
Harleyford Rd. SW8 1A 24
Harlington. 1A 22
Harlington Corner. (Junct.) 1A 22
Harlington Rd. Uxb 4A 14
Harlington Rd. E. Felt 2B 22
Harlington Rd. W. Felt 2B 22
Harlow. 1D 9
Harlow Comn. H'low 1E 9
Harlow Rd. Mat T 1F 9
Harlow Rd. More 1F 9
Harlow Rd. Roy 1C 8
Harlow Rd. Saw 1E 9
Harlow Rd. Srng 1E 9
Harmanswater. 3B 20
Harmans Water Rd. Brack 4B 20
Harmer St. Grav 2C 26
Harmondsworth. 1F 21
Harmondsworth La. W Dray 1A 22
Harmondsworth Rd. W Dray 1A 22
Harold Hill. 1A 18
Harold Park. 2A 18
Harold Rd. SE19 3A 24
Harold Wood. 2A 18
Harpenden. 1B 6
Harpenden La. Redb 1B 6
Harpenden Rd. St Alb 1B 6
Harper La. Rad 3C 6
Harper Rd. SE1 1A 24
Harper's Rd. Ash 4C 28
Harp Farm Rd. Boxl 1F 35
Harple La. Det 2F 35
Harps Oak La. Red 3F 31
Harringay. 2A 16
Harris La. Shenl 3D 7
Harrow. 2C 14
Harrow La. M'head 4B 12
Harrow Mnr. Way. SE28 1E 25
Harrow on the Hill. 3C 14
Harrow Road. (Junct.) 3D 15
Harrow Rd. E11 3C 16
Harrow Rd. W9, NW10 & W10 4E 15
Harrow Rd. Knock 2E 33
Harrow Rd. N Ben 2F 19
Harrow Rd. Warl 2B 32
Harrow Rd. Wemb 3C 14 (Sudbury)
Harrow Rd. Wemb 3D 15 (Wembley)
Harrow Vw. Harr 2C 14
Harrow Weald. 2C 14
Hartfield Rd. SW19 3E 23
Hartforde Rd. Borwd 4D 7
Harthall La. K Lan & Hem H 3A 6
Hartington Rd. W4 1D 23
Hartlake Rd. Gold G 4C 34
Hartland Way. Croy 4B 24
Hartley. 3B 26
Hartley Bottom Rd. Sev & Hart 1B 34
Hartley Down. Purl 2A 32
Hartley Green. 4B 26
Hartley Hill. 4B 26
Hartley Hill. Hart 4B 26
Hartley Rd. Long 3B 26
Hartmann Rd. E16 4D 17
Hart Rd. Ben 2F 19
Hart's La. S God 4B 32
Hartspring La. Bush & Wat 4B 6
Hartswood Rd. War & Brtwd 1B 18
Harvel. 1C 34
Harvel La. Meop 1C 34
Harvel Rd. Fair 1C 34
Harvel St. Meop 1C 34
Harvest Hill. Bour E 3C 12
Harvest Hill Rd. M'head 1B 20
Harvest Ride. Brack 3B 20
Harvest Rd. Egh 3E 21
Harvey Rd. Guild 4E 29
Harvil Rd. Hare & Uxb 2F 13
Harvist Rd. NW10 4E 15
Harwood Hall La. Upm 3A 18
Harwood Rd. SW6 1E 23
Harwoods Rd. Wat 4B 6
Haselbury Rd. N9 & N18 1A 16
Haste Hill Rd. Bou M 4F 35
Hastings Rd. Brom 4D 25
Hastings Rd. Maid 3F 35
Hastingwood. 2E 9
Hastingwood Rd. H'wd 2E 9
Hastoe. 1C 4
Hastoe Hill. Hast 1C 4
Hastoe La. Hast 1C 4
Hatch End. 2B 14
Hatches Farm Rd. L Bur 1C 18
Hatches La. E Peck 4C 34
Hatches La. Gt Kin 4B 4
Hatchet La. N Asc 3C 20
Hatchford. 2A 30
Hatching Green. 1B 6
Hatchlands Pk. 3A 30
Hatchlands Rd. Red 4F 31
Hatch La. E4 1C 16 (in two parts)
Hatch La. W Dray 1F 21
Hatch La. Wind 2D 21
Hatch Rd. Pil H 1B 18
Hatfield. 1E 7
Hatfield Airport. 1D 7
Hatfield Garden Village. 1D 7
Hatfield House. 1E 7
Hatfield Hyde. 1E 7
Hatfield Rd. L Bad 1F 11
Hatfield Rd. Pot B 3F 7
Hatfield Rd. St Alb & Smal 2C 6
Hatham Grn. La. Stans 1B 34
Hathaway Rd. Grays 1B 26
Hatherley Gdns. E6 4C 16
Hatterill. Lain 2D 19
Hatter's La. High W 1B 12
Hatton. 2B 22
Hatton Cross. (Junct.) 2A 22
Hatton Garden. EC1 4A 16
Hatton Hill. W'sham 4C 20
Hatton Rd. Felt 2A 22
Havelock Rd. N17 2B 16
Havelock Rd. S'hall 1B 22
Haven Grn. W5 4C 14
Haven Hill. Hods 1B 34
Haven Rd. Can I 4F 19
Haven St. Wain 2E 27
Havering-atte-Bower. 1F 17
Havering Rd. Romf 2F 17
Havering's Grove. 1C 18
Haverstock Hill. NW3 3F 15
Haviker St. Coll S 4E 35
Hawk Hill. Bat 1F 19
Hawkhurst Gdns. Chess 4D 23
Hawkshead La. N Mym 3E 7
Hawkshead Rd. Pot B 3E 7
Hawks Hill. Bour E 3C 12
Hawkshill Way. Esh 1B 30
Hawks Rd. King T 3D 23
Hawkstone Rd. SE16 1B 24
Hawkswood La. Slou & Ger X 3E 13
Hawkswood Rd. D'ham 4E 11
Hawley. 3A 26 (Dartford)
Hawley. 2A 28 (Farnborough)
Hawley Lane. 2B 28
Hawley La. Farn 2B 28
Hawley Rd. NW1 3F 15
Hawley Rd. B'water 2A 28
Hawley Rd. Dart 2A 26
Hawley's Corner. 2D 33
Hawstead La. Orp 4E 25
Hawthorn Hill. 2B 20
Hawthorn Hill Rd. Holyp 2B 20
Hawthorn La. Farn C 3D 13
Hawthorn Rd. NW10 3E 15
Haydens Rd. H'low 1D 9
Haydons Rd. SW19 3E 23
Hayes. 4C 24 (Bromley)
Hayes. 4A 14 (Uxbridge)
Hayes End. 4A 14
Hayes End Rd. Hay 4A 14
Hayes Hill Rd. Brom 4C 24
Hayes La. Beck 3C 24
Hayes La. Brom 4C 24
Hayes La. Kenl 2A 32 (in two parts)
Hayes Rd. Brom 3C 24
Hayes Rd. S'hall 1B 22
Hayes St. Brom 4C 24
Hayes Town. 1A 22
Hay Green. 3B 10
Hay Grn. La. Hook E & B'more 4B 10
Hay La. NW9 2D 15
Hayle Rd. Maid 3F 35
Hayley Grn. Warf 3B 20
Hayling Rd. Wat 1B 14
Haymarket. SW1 4F 15
Haymill Rd. Slou 4C 12
Hazel Av. Farn 3A 28
Hazelbank Rd. SE6 2C 24
Hazellville Rd. N19 3F 15
Hazelwood. 1D 33
Hazelwood La. N13 1A 16
Hazelwood La. Ab L 3A 6
Hazelwood La. Binf 3A 20
Hazelwood La. Coul 2F 31
Hazlemere. 1B 12
Hazlemere Rd. Penn 1C 12
Headley. 3D 31
Headley Comn. Rd. H'ley & Tad 3D 31
Headley Dri. New Ad 1B 32
Headley Rd. Dork 3C 30
Headley Rd. Eps 2D 31
Headley Rd. Lea & Eps 2C 30
Headstone. 2C 14
Headstone Dri. Harr 2C 14
Headstone Gdns. Harr 2C 14
Headstone La. Harr 2B 14
Headstone Rd. Harr 2C 14
Heathbourne Rd. Bush H & Stan 1C 14
Heathclose Rd. Dart 2F 25
Heathcote Rd. Camb 1B 28
Heath End. 4A 28 (Aldershot)
Heath End. 4B 4 (Great Kingshill)
Heath End. 2D 5 (Shootersway)
Heath End. Berk 2D 5
Heath End Rd. F Hth 2B 12
Heath End Rd. Gt Kin 4B 4
Heatherside. 2C 28
Heathfield La. Chst 3D 25
Heathfield Rd. Burn 3C 12
Heathfield Rd. Kes 4C 24
Heathfield Ter. W4 1D 23
Heath Ho. Rd. Wok 2D 29
Heathlands Rd. Wokgm 4A 20
Heath La. Dart 2F 25
Heath La. Ews 4A 28
Heath La. Hem H 2F 5
Heath Park. 2F 17
Heath Pk. Rd. Romf 2F 17
Heath Rd. Grays 4C 18
Heath Rd. Houn 2C 22
Heath Rd. Maid 3E 35
Heath Rd. Oxs 1C 30
Heath Rd. Rams H 1D 19
Heath Rd. Twic 2C 22
Heath Rd. W Far & Cox 4E 35
Heath Rd. Wey 4A 22
Heathrow Airport. 2A 22
Heathside Cres. Wok 2E 29
Heathside Rd. Wok 2E 29
Heath St. NW3 3F 15
Heath, The. E Mal 2D 35
Heathvale Bri. Rd. Ash V 3B 28
Heathway. (Junct.) 4E 17
Heathway. Dag 3E 17
Heavens Lea. Bour E 3C 12
Heaverham. 2A 34
Heaverham Rd. Kems 2A 34
Hedge La. N13 1A 16
Hedgemans Rd. Dag 3E 17
Hedge Pl. Rd. Grnh 2A 26
Hedgerley. 3D 13
Hedgerley Green. 3D 13
Hedgerley Hill. 3D 13
Hedgerley Hill. Hedg 3D 13
Hedgerley La. Beac & Ger X 2D 13
Hedsor Hill. Bour E 3C 12
Hedsor La. Wbrn G 3C 12
Hedsor Rd. Bour E 3B 12
Hemel Hempstead. 1A 6
Hemel Hempstead Rd. Hem H & St Alb 2A 6
Hemel Hempstead Rd. Redb 1A 6
Hemp La. Wig 1D 5
Hempstead. 4F 27
Hempstead La. L Hth & Pott 1E 5
Hempstead Rd. Bov 2E 5
Hempstead Rd. Hem 1F 35
Hempstead Rd. K Lan 2A 6
Hempstead Rd. Wat 4A 6
Henderson Dri. Dart 2A 26
Hendon. 2E 15
Hendon La. NW4 2E 15
Hendon Way. NW2 & NW4 2E 15
Hendon Wood La. EN5 1D 15
Henhurst. 3D 27
Henhurst Rd. Sole S 3C 26
Henley Rd. Hur & M'head 4A 12
Henley Rd. Medm 3A 12
Henley Street. 4D 27
Henley St. Ludd 4D 27
Henlys Corner. (Junct.) 2E 15
Henlys Roundabout. (Junct.) 1B 22
Henniker Gdns. E6 4C 16
Henrys Rd. Wfd G 2C 16
Hepworth Way. W on T 4A 22
Herbert Rd. SE18 1D 25
Herberts Hole. S Hth 3C 4
Hercies Rd. Uxb 3A 14
Heriot Rd. Cher 4F 21
Herkomer Rd. Bush 1B 14
Hermitage La. NW2 3E 15
Hermitage La. SW16 3A 24
Hermitage La. Ayle & Barm 2E 35
Hermitage La. Bou M 4F 35
Hermitage Rd. N15 & N4 3A 16
Hermitage Rd. SE19 3A 24
Hermitage Rd. High 3E 27
Hermitage Rd. Wok 2D 29
Hermit Rd. E16 4C 16
Hermon Hill. E18 & E11 2C 16
Herne Hill. 2A 24
Herne Hill. SE24 2A 24
Herne Hill Rd. SE24 2A 24
Herne Pound. 3C 34
Herns La. Wel G 1E 7
Herongate. 2C 18
Heron Hill. Belv 1E 25
Heronsgate. 1F 13
Heronsgate Rd. Chor 1E 13
Herons La. Fyf 2A 10 (in two parts)
Heronswood Rd. Wel G 1E 7
Heron Way. Grays 1B 26
Hersham. 4B 22
Hersham By-Pass. W on T 4B 22
Hersham Rd. W on T 4B 22
Hertford. 1A 8
Hertford Heath. 1B 8
Hertford Rd. N9 1B 16
Hertford Rd. Enf 4B 8
Hertford Rd. Hat 1E 7
Hertford Rd. Hod 1B 8
Hertingfordbury. 1A 8
Hertingfordbury Rd. Hert 1A 8 (in two parts)
Hesiers Hill. Warl 2C 32
Hesiers Rd. Warl 2C 32
Heston. 1B 22
Heston Rd. Houn 1B 22
Hever Ct. Rd. Grav 3C 26
Hewitts Rd. Orp 1E 33
Hewitts Roundabout. (Junct.) 1E 33
Hextable. 3F 25
Heybridge. 4C 10
Hibbert Rd. M'head 1B 20
Hibernia Rd. Houn 2B 22
Hicks Farm Ri. High W 1B 12
Hickstars La. Bill 1D 19
Higham. 2E 27
Higham Hill. 2B 16
Higham Hill Rd. E17 2B 16
Higham La. Tonb 4B 34
Higham Rd. Cli 2E 27
Higham Rd. Wain 3F 27
Highams La. Chob 1D 29
Highams Park. 1C 16
Higham Wood. 4B 34
High Banks. Loose 3F 35
High Barnet. 4E 7
High Barn Rd. Eff & Dork 3B 30
High Beech. 4C 8
High Bri. Rd. Chelm 2E 11
Highbridge St. Wal A 3B 8 (in two parts)
Highbury. 3A 16
Highbury Corner. (Junct.) 3A 16
Highbury Gro. N5 3A 16
Highbury Pk. N5 3A 16
High Canons. Borwd 4D 7
High Cross. 4C 6
High Cross. Ald 4C 6
High Cross Rd. Ivy H 3B 34
Highcross Rd. S'fleet 3B 26
High Curley. 1C 28
High Easter Rd. Lea R 1B 10
High Elms Rd. Dow 1D 33
Higher Denham. 3F 13
Higher Dri. Purl 1A 32
Highfield. 1A 6
Highfield Av. NW2 3E 15
Highfield La. M'head 1B 20
Highfield La. Putt 4C 28
Highfield La. Tyngr 2C 6
Highfield Pk. Dri. St Alb & Tyngr 2C 6
Highfield Rd. Dart 2F 25
Highfield Rd. Felt 2B 22
Highfield Rd. Purl 1A 32
Highgate. 3F 15
Highgate High St. N6 3F 15
Highgate Hill. N19 & N6 3F 15
Highgate La. Farn 2B 28
Highgate Rd. NW5 & N6 3F 15
Highgate W. Hill. N6 3F 15
High Halstow. 2F 27
High Holborn. WC2 4A 16
High Ho. La. Grays 1C 26
High Ho. La. Hdlw 4B 34
Highlands Hill. Swan 3F 25
Highlands Rd. Lea 2C 30
High La. Srng 1F 9
High Laver. 1F 9
High Laver Rd. Mat G 1F 9
High Ongar. 3A 10
High Ongar Rd. Ong 3A 10
High Rd. E18 2C 16
High Rd. N17 & N15 2A 16
High Rd. N22 2A 16
High Rd. NW10 3D 15
High Rd. Ben 2F 19
High Rd. Bush H 1C 14
High Rd. Byfl 1A 30
High Rd. Chesh 2B 8
High Rd. Chig 1D 17
High Rd. Cook 3B 34
High Rd. Cow 4F 13
High Rd. Dart 2F 25
High Rd. Epp 3D 9
High Rd. Ess 2F 7
High Rd. Harr 2C 14
High Rd. Horn H 3E 19
High Rd. Ilf & Romf 3D 17 (in five parts)
High Rd. Lang H & Lain 3D 19 (in two parts)
High Rd. Leav 3A 6
High Rd. N Stif 4B 18
High Rd. N Wea 3E 9
High Rd. Ors 4C 18
High Rd. Reig & Coul 3F 31
High Rd. Stan H 4D 19
High Rd. Thorn 2E 9
High Rd. Uxb 3A 14
High Rd. Van & Pits 3E 19
High Rd. Wemb 3D 15
High Rd. Wfd G & Lou 1C 16
High Rd. Worm & Brox 2B 8
High Rd. E. Finchley. N12 2F 15
High Rd. Leyton. E10 3C 16
High Rd. Leytonstone. E11 & E15 3C 16
High Rd. N. Lain 2D 19
High Rd. N. Finchley. N12 1F 15
High Rd. Turnford. Chesh 2B 8
High Rd. Whetstone. N20 1F 15
High Rd. Woodford Grn. Wfd G & E18 2C 16
High St. E11 2C 16
High St. E13 4C 16
High St. E15 4C 16
High St. N8 2A 16
High St. N14 1F 15
High St. SE18 1D 25
High St. SE20 3B 24
High St. SE25 3A 24
High St. SW19 3E 23
High St. W3 4D 15
High St. W5 4C 14
High St. Ab L 3A 6
High St. Add 4F 21
High St. Alder 4B 28
High St. Amer 4D 5
High St. Asc 3C 20
High St. Ave 4A 18
High St. Ayle 2E 35
High St. Bag 1C 28
High St. Bans 2E 31
High St. B'side 2D 17
High St. Barn 4E 7
High St. Bean 2B 26
High St. Beck 3B 24
High St. Bedm 3A 6
High St. Ben 3F 19
High St. Berk 1D 5
High St. Bill 1D 19
High St. Blet 4A 32
High St. Bookh 3B 30
High St. Bor G 2B 34
High St. Bov 3E 5
High St. Brack 3B 20
High St. Bras 3E 33
High St. Bray 1C 20
High St. Bren 1C 22
High St. Brtwd 1B 18
High St. Brom 3C 24
High St. Burn 4C 12
High St. Bush 1B 14
High St. Cars 4F 23
High St. Cat 3A 32
High St. Chal G 1E 13
High St. Chal P 2E 13
High St. Chalv 1D 21
High St. Chat 4F 27 (in two parts)
High St. Cheam 1E 31
High St. Che 3D 5
High St. Chesh 3B 8
High St. Chip 2F 33
High St. Chst 3D 25
High St. Chob 1D 29
High St. Cobh 1B 30
High St. Coln 1F 21
High St. Col H 2D 7
High St. Cook 3B 12
High St. Cow 4F 13
High St. Cran 1B 22
High St. Cray 2F 25
High St. Crowt 1A 28
High St. Croy 4A 24
High St. Dart 2A 26
High St. Dat 1E 21
High St. Dork 4C 30
High St. Dow 1D 33
High St. D'ley 1A 12
High St. E Mal 2E 35
High St. Edgw 2D 15
High St. Egh 3E 21 (in two parts)
High St. Els 1C 14
High St. Enf 1B 16
High St. Epp 3D 9
High St. Eps 1D 31
High St. Esh 4B 22
High St. Eton 1D 21
High St. Ewe 1D 31
High St. Eyns 4A 26
High St. Farn 4D 25
High St. F'ham 4A 26
High St. Felt 2B 22
High St. Gill 3F 27 (in four parts)
High St. God 4B 32
High St. Gt Bad 2E 11
High St. Gt Miss 3B 4
High St. Grnh 2B 26
High St. Grn St 1D 33
High St. Guild 4E 29 (in two parts)
High St. Hdlw 4C 34
High St. Hall 4E 27
High St. Hamp 3C 22
High St. Hamp H 3C 22
High St. Hamp W 3C 22
High St. Hare 2F 13
High St. Harl 1A 22
High St. H'low 1E 9 (in two parts)
High St. Harr 3C 14
High St. Hem H 1A 6
High St. High W 1B 12
High St. Hod 2B 8
High St. Horn 3F 17
High St. Hors 2E 29
High St. Ing 4C 10
High St. Iver 4F 13
High St. Kems 2A 34
High St. K Lan 3A 6
High St. King T 3C 22
High St. Knap 2D 29
High St. Langl 1E 21
High St. Limp 3C 32
High St. L Sand 1A 28
High St. Lon C 2C 6
High St. M'head 4B 12
High St. Maid 3F 35
High St. Mar 3A 12
High St. Mers 3F 31
High St. N Mald 3D 23
High St. N'fleet 2B 26
High St. N'wd 2A 14
High St. Nutf 4A 32
High St. Old Wok 2E 29

High St.—Knightsbridge

High St. Ong 3A 10
High St. Orp 4E 25
High St. Otf 2F 33
High St. Oxs 1C 30
High St. Oxt 3C 32
High St. Pinn 2B 14
High St. Pot B 3F 7
High St. P'wd 3B 4
High St. Redb 1B 6
High St. Red 4F 31
High St. Reig 4E 31
High St. Rick 1F 13
High St. Rip 2F 29
High St. Roch 3F 27
(in two parts)
High St. Roy 1C 8
High St. Ruis 3A 14
High St. Sand 1A 28
High St. Sandr 1C 6
High St. Seal 2A 34
High St. Sev 3F 33
High St. Shep 4A 22
High St. Shor 1F 33
High St. Sidc 3E 25
High St. Slou 1E 21
High St. Snod 1E 35
(in two parts)
High St. S'hall 4B 14
High St. Stai 3F 21
High St. Stan H 4D 19
High St. Stan A 1C 8
High St. Stanw 2F 21
High St. Stock 4D 11
High St. St M 4E 25
High St. Strood 3E 27
High St. S'dale 4D 21
High St. S'hill 4C 20
High St. Sutt 4E 23
High St. Swan 3F 25
High St. Swans 2B 26
High St. Tedd 3C 22
High St. Th Dit 4C 22
High St. T Hth 3A 24
High St. Tonb 4B 34
High St. Tring 1C 4
High St. Upnor 3F 27
High St. Uxb 3F 13
High St. Wal X 3B 8
High St. W'stone 2C 14
High St. Wen 2B 4
High St. W'ham 3D 33
High St. W Mal 2D 35
High St. W Mol 4B 22
High St. W Wick 4B 24
High St. W Wyc 1A 12
High St. Wey 4A 22
High St. Whit 2C 22
High St. W'fd 1F 19
High St. Wind 1D 21
High St. Wok 2E 29
High St. Woul 1E 35
High St. Wray 2E 21
High St. Wro 2B 34
High St. Yald 4D 35
High St. Yiew 4F 13
High St. Colliers Wood. SW19 3F 23
High St. Grn. Hem H 2F 5
High St. Harlesden. NW10 4D 15
High St. N. E6 & E12 3D 17
High St. S. E6 4D 17
High, The. 1D 9
High Vw. Gom 4A 30
Highway. 4B 12
Highway, The. E1 4B 16
Highway, The. Orp 4E 25
Highwood. 2C 10
Highwood Hill. 1E 15
Highwood Hill. NW7 1D 15
(in two parts)
Highwood Rd. Hghwd & Ed C 3C 10
(in two parts)
High Woods. 3C 10
High Wych Rd. Saw 1D 9
High Wycombe. 1B 12
Hildenborough. 4A 34
Hildenborough Rd. Leigh 4A 34
Hildenborough Rd. S'brne 4A 34
Hilfield La. Ald 4B 6
Hillbury Rd. Whyt 2B 32
Hillcroome Rd. Sutt 1F 31
Hillcross Av. Mord 4E 23
Hilldene Av. Romf 2F 17
Hill End. 2F 13
Hill End La. St Alb 2C 6
Hill End Rd. Hare 2F 13
Hill Farm Av. Wat 3B 6
Hill Farm Rd. Tap 4C 12
Hillgrove Rd. NW6 3F 15
Hilliers La. Croy 4A 24
Hillingdon. 4A 14
Hillingdon Heath. 4A 14
Hillingdon Hill. Uxb 4A 14
Hillingdon Rd. Uxb 4F 13
Hillmarton Rd. N7 3A 16
Hillreach. SE7 1D 25
Hill Rd. S Nut 4A 32
Hillside. NW10 4D 15
Hillside Av. Wfd G 2C 16
Hillside Rd. Bill 1D 19
Hillside Rd. Chat 3C 24
Hillside Rd. N'wd 2B 14
Hills La. Cook 3B 12
Hills La. Knat 1A 34
Hill, The. N'fleet 2C 26
Hill, The. Winch H 1C 12
Hilltop. 3D 5
Hill Top. Hunt 4E 35
Hilltop La. Cat & Red 3A 32
Hillway. Bill 1D 19
Hillyfields. Lou 4D 9
Hinchley Wood. 4C 22
Hindes Rd. Harr 2C 14
Hinton Rd. SW9 2A 24
Historic Dockyard, The. 3F 27
Hitcham La. Tap & Burn 4C 12
Hitcham Rd. Burn & Tap 4C 12
Hither Green. 2C 24
Hither Grn. La. SE13 2C 24
Hivings Hill. Che 3D 5
Hobbs Cross. 4E 9
(Epping)
Hobb's Cross. 1E 9
(Harlow)
Hobbs Cross Rd. H'low 1E 9
Hockenden. 3E 25
Hockenden La. Swan 3E 25
Hockering Rd. Wok 2E 29
Hockers La. Weav 2F 35
Hockett La. Cook 3B 12
Hoddesdon. 1B 8
Hoddesdon Rd. Stan A 1C 8
Hodford Rd. NW11 3E 15
Hodgson Way. W'fd 1F 19
Hodsoll Street. 1C 34
Hodsoll St. Sev 1C 34
Hoe La. Abr 4E 9
Hoe La. Enf 4B 8
Hoe La. Naze 2C 8
Hoe La. Ret C 4F 11
Hoe La. Ware 1B 8
Hoe St. E17 2B 16
Hoe St. Rox 2C 10
Hogarth La. W4 1D 23
Hogarth Roundabout. (Junct.) 1D 23
Hogden La. Ran C 4B 30
Hogfair La. Burn 4C 12
Hogg End La. Hem H & St Alb 1A 6
Hogg La. Grays 1B 26
Hog Hill Rd. Romf 2E 17
Hog La. Ash G 2D 5
Hogpits Bottom. 3E 5
Hog's Back. Runf & Seale 4B 28
(in two parts)
Hogscross La. Coul 3F 31
Hogtrough Hill. Bras & Sev 2D 33
Hogtrough La. S Nut 4F 31
Holbeck La. Chesh 2A 8
Holborn. 4A 16
Holborn. WC1 4A 16
Holborn Viaduct. EC4 & EC1 4A 16
Holborough. 1E 35
Holborough Rd. Snod 1E 35
Holbrook Way. Brom 4D 25
Holcome Hill. NW7 1E 15
Holdbrook. 3B 8
Holders Hill. 2E 15
Holders Hill Rd. NW7 & NW4 2E 15
Hole La. Eden 4D 33
Holiday Hill. W Han 4E 11
Holland. 4C 32
Holland Av. Sutt 1E 31
Holland La. Oxt 4C 32
Holland Pk. Av. W11 4E 15
Holland Park Roundabout. (Junct.) 1E 23
Holland Rd. W12 1E 23
Holland Rd. Maid 2F 35
Holland Rd. Oxt 4C 32
Hollis Rd. High W 1B 12
Holloway. 4A 12
(Maidenhead)
Holloway. 3F 15
(Tufnell Park)
Holloway Hill. Cher 4F 21
Holloway La. W Dray 1A 22
Holloway Rd. N7 & N19 3F 15
Holloways La. N Mym 2E 7
Holloway, The. Tring 1C 4
Holloway, The. Wtlf 2A 4
Hollow Hill La. Iver 4E 13
Hollow La. Broom 1D 11
Hollow La. Snod 1D 35
Hollow La. Wott 4B 30
Hollow Way. Che 3C 4
Hollow Way La. Amer 4D 5
Holly Bank Rd. Wok 2E 29
Hollybush Hill. E11 2C 16
Hollybush Hill. Stoke P 3E 13
Hollybush La. Den 3F 13
Hollybush La. Iver 4E 13
Hollybush La. Wel G 1E 7
Hollycross Rd. Stan A 1B 8
Hollydown Way. E11 3C 16
Hollyfield Rd. Surb 4D 23
Holly Hedges La. Bov 3F 5
Holly Hill. 1D 35
Holly Hill Rd. Meop 1D 35
Holly La. Bans 2E 31
Holly La. Worp 3D 29
Hollymeoak Rd. Coul 2F 31
Holly Spring La. Brack 3B 20
Hollywood La. Wain 3F 27
Holme Green. 4A 20
Holmer Green. 4C 4
Holmer Grn. Rd. Hasl 1B 12
Holmers Farm Way. High W 2A 12
Holmesdale Hill. S Dar 3A 26
Holmesdale Rd. S Dar 3A 26
Holmethorpe. 4F 31
Holmshill La. Borwd 4D 7
Holmstall Av. Edgw 2D 15
Holtsmere End. 1A 6
Holtspur. 2C 12
Holtspur Av. Wbrn G 2C 12
Holtspur La. Wbrn G 2C 12
Holtspur Top La. Beac 2C 12
Holtwhite's Hill. Enf 4A 8
Holybread La. L Bad 4F 11
Holy Cross Hill. Worm 2B 8
Holyfield. 3C 8
Holyfield Rd. Wal A 3C 8
Holyport. 1B 20
Holyport Rd. Holyp 1B 20
Holywell. 1A 14
Holywell Hill. St Alb 2C 6
Homedean Rd. Chip 3F 33
Home Farm Rd. L War 2B 18
Homefield Rd. Brom 3C 24
Home Gdns. Dart 2A 26
Home Hill. Hex 3F 25
Home Pk. Mill Link Rd. K Lan 3A 6
Home Pk. Rd. SW19 2E 23
Homerton. 3B 16
Homerton High St. E9 3B 16
Homerton Rd. E9 3B 16
Homesdale Rd. Brom 3C 24
Homestall Rd. SE22 2B 24
Homestead La. Wel G 1E 7
Homestead Rd. SW6 1E 23
Honeycroft Hill. Uxb 3A 14
Honey Hill. Uxb 3A 14
Honey Hill. Wokgm 4A 20
Honey La. Hur 4A 12
Honey La. Wal A 3C 8
Honeypot La. Brtwd 1B 18
Honeypot La. Eden 4C 32
Honeypot La. Kems 2A 34
Honeypot La. Stan & NW9 2C 14
Honeypot La. Stock 4D 11
Honor End La. P'wd 3B 4
Honor Oak. 2B 24
Honor Oak Park. 2B 24
Honor Oak Pk. SE23 2B 24
Honor Oak Rd. SE23 2B 24
Hook. 4C 22
Hook End. 4B 10
Hook End La. Hook E 3B 10
Hook End Rd. Hook E 4B 10
Hook Green. 3B 26
(Gravesend)
Hook Green. 4C 26
(Meopham)
Hook Grn. La. Dart 2F 25
Hook Grn. Rd. Meop 3B 26
Hook Heath. 2E 29
Hook Heath Av. Wok 2E 29
Hook Heath Rd. Wok 2D 29
Hook Hill La. Wok 2E 29
Hook Junction. (Junct.) 4C 22
Hook La. Putt 4C 28
Hook La. Romf 1E 17
Hook La. Shere 4A 30
Hook La. Well 2E 25
Hook Mill La. Light 1C 28
Hook Rise N. Surb 4D 23
Hook Rise S. Surb 4D 23
Hook Rd. Chess & Surb 4C 22
Hook Rd. Eps 1D 31
Hookstone La. W End 1D 29
Hookwood Rd. Orp 1E 33
Hooley. 2F 31
Hooley La. Red 4F 31
Hoop La. NW11 3E 15
Hoo Rd. Wain 3F 27
Hoo St Werburgh. 2F 27
Hope's Green. 3F 19
Hop Farm. 4D 35
Hoppers Rd. N13 1A 16
Hopping Jacks La. Dan 2F 11
Horley Rd. Red 4F 31
Hornchurch. 3F 17
Hornchurch Rd. Horn 3F 17
Horndon on the Hill. 4D 19
Horndon Rd. Horn H 4D 19
Hornfair Rd. SE7 1C 24
Hornhatch La. Guild 4E 29
Hornhill Rd. Ger X & Rick 1E 13
Horn La. W3 4D 15
Hornsby Way. Bas 2D 19
Horns Cross. 2A 26
Hornsey. 2A 16
Hornsey La. N19 3F 15
Hornsey Pk. Rd. N8 2A 16
Hornsey Ri. N19 3F 15
Hornsey Rd. N7 & N19 3A 16
Hornsey Vale. 2A 16
Horns Green. 2D 33
Horns Hill. 3D 33
Horns La. High W 2A 12
Horns La. Mere 3C 34
Horns Lodge Rd. Sev 1B 34
Horns Mill Rd. Hert 1A 8
Horn's Oak Rd. Meop 4C 26
Horns Rd. Ilf 2D 17
Horn Street. 1D 35
Horse Fair. King T 3C 22
Horseferry Rd. SW1 1F 23
Horse Hill. Che 3E 5
Horsell. 2E 29
Horsell Birch. Wok 2E 29
Horsell Comn. Rd. Wok 1E 29
Horseman Side. 4A 10
Horseman Side. N'side 1F 17
Horsemoor La. Winch H 1C 12
Horsenden La. N. Gnfd 3C 14
Horsenden La. S. Gnfd 4C 14
Horseshoe Hill. Burn 3C 12
Horseshoe Hill. Wal A 3C 8
Horseshoe La. Wat 3B 6
Horsham Rd. Dork 4C 30
Horsham Rd. N Holm 4C 30
Horsley Rd. Cobh 2B 30
Horsted Way. Roch 4F 27
Horton. 2E 21
Horton Kirby. 3A 26
Horton La. Eps 1D 31
Horton Rd. Dat 1E 21
Horton Rd. Hort 1E 21
Horton Rd. Hort K 3A 26
Horton Rd. Slou & Stai 2F 21
Horton Rd. W Dray 4A 14
Hosey Comn. La. W'ham 3D 33
Hosey Comn. Rd. Eden & W'ham 4D 33
Hosey Hill. 3D 33
Hosey Hill. W'ham 3D 33
Hospital App. Broom 1E 11
Hospital Bri. Rd. Twic 2B 22
Hospital Bridge Roundabout. (Junct.) 2B 22
Hospital Hill. Alder 4B 28
Hospital Rd. Alder 4B 28
Hotley Bottom. 3B 4
Hotley Bottom La. P'wd 3B 4
Houblons Hill. Coop 3E 9
Hound Ho. Rd. Shere 4A 30
Houndsden Rd. N21 1A 16
Hounslow. 2C 22
Hounslow Rd. Felt 2B 22
Hounslow Rd. Hanw 2B 22
Hounslow Rd. Twic 2B 22
Hounslow West. 2B 22
House La. Sandr 1C 6
Housham Tye. 1F 9
Howard Lodge Rd. Kel C 4A 10
Howard Rd. Eff J 3B 30
Howard Way. H'low 1D 9
Howbury La. Eri 1F 25
Howe Green. 3F 11
Howe La. Binf 2A 20
How Grn. La. Hever 4E 33
Howlands. Wel G 1E 7
How La. Coul 2F 31
Howletts La. Ruis 2A 14
How Wood. 3C 6
Hoxton. 4A 16
Hubbard's Hill. Weald & Sev 4F 33
Hubbard's La. Bou M 4F 35
Hudnall. 1E 5
Hudnall La. L Gad 1E 5
Hughenden Av. High W 1A 12
Hughenden Manor. 1B 12
Hughenden Rd. High W 1B 12
Hughenden Valley. 4B 4
Huguenot Pl. SW18 2F 23
Hull's La. S'don 2F 11
Hume Av. Til 2C 26
Humphrey's Farm La. Chelm 1D 11
Hungerford La. Shur R 2A 20
Hungry Hill La. Send 3F 29
Hunsdonbury. 1D 9
Hunsdon Rd. Stan A 1C 8
Huntercombe La. N. Burn 4C 12
Hunter's Rd. Chess 4D 23
Hunton. 4E 35
Hunton Bridge. 3A 6
Hunton Bridge. (Junct.) 4A 6
Hunton Bri. Hill. K Lan 3A 6
Hunton Hill. Hunt 4E 35
Hunton Rd. Mard 4E 35
Hunts Hill Rd. Nap 4A 4
Hunts Hill Rd. Norm 3C 28
Hunts Slip Rd. SE21 2A 24
Hunt St. W Far 3D 35
Huntswood La. Tap 3C 12
Hurley. 4A 12
Hurley Bottom. 4A 12
Hurley High St. Hur 3A 12
Hurley La. Hur 4A 12
Hurlingham. 2E 23
Hurrells La. L Bad 2F 11
Hurst Green. 4C 32
(Oxted)
Hurst Green. 4F 35
(Stilebridge)
Hurst Grn. Rd. Oxt 4C 32
Hurstlands. Oxt 4C 32
Hurst La. H'ley 3D 31
Hurst Park. 3B 22
Hurst Rd. H'ley & Tad 3D 31
Hurst Rd. Sidc & Bex 2E 25
Hurst Rd. W on T & W Mol 4B 22
Hurst, The. Sev & Ton 3C 34
Hutton. 1C 18
Hutton Mount. 1B 18
Hutton Rd. Ash V 3B 28
Hutton Rd. Shenf 1B 18
Hutton Village. Hut 1C 18
Hyde Heath. 3C 4
Hyde Heath Rd. Hyde H 3C 4
Hyde La. Hyde E 4C 4
Hyde La. Hem H 3A 6
Hyde Park Corner. (Junct.) 1F 23
Hyde Pk. St. W2 4F 15
Hyde, The. 2D 15
Hyde, The. NW9 2D 15
Hyde Va. SE10 1C 24
Hythe End. 2E 21

Ickenham. 3A 14
Ickenham Rd. Ruis 3A 14
Icknield Way. Tring 1C 4
Ide Hill. 3E 33
Ide Hill Rd. Four E 4E 33
Ide Hill Rd. Sev 4E 33
(in two parts)
Idleigh Ct. Rd. Meop 4B 26
Ightham. 2B 34
Ightham By-Pass. Sev 2B 34
Ightham Common. 3B 34
Ightham Mote. 3B 34
Ightham Rd. Sev 3B 34
Ilderton Rd. SE15 & SE1 1B 24
Ilford. 3D 17
Ilford Hill. Ilf 3D 17
Ilford La. Ilf 3D 17
Imperial Dri. Harr 3B 14
Imperial Rd. SW6 1E 23
Imperial Rd. Wind 2D 21
Ingatestone. 4C 10
Ingatestone By-Pass. Ing 4C 10
Ingatestone Rd. B'more 3B 10
Ingatestone Rd. Hghwd 3C 10
Ingatestone Rd. Ing 4D 11
Ingatestone Rd. Stock 4D 11
Inglis Rd. W5 4D 15
Ingram Rd. Gill 3F 27
Ingram Rd. T Hth 3A 24
Ingrave. 1C 18
Ingrave Rd. Brtwd 1B 18
Ingrebourne Rd. Rain 4F 17
Inholms La. N Holm 4C 30
Inner Pk. Rd. SW19 2E 23
Inner Ring E. H'row A 2A 22
Inner Ring W. H'row A 2A 22
Institute Rd. Tap 4C 12
Instone Rd. Dart 2A 26
Inverness Ter. W2 4F 15
Inwood Rd. Houn 2C 22
Iron Mill La. Dart 2F 25
Island Farm Rd. W Mol 4B 22
Isledon Rd. N7 3A 16
Isleworth. 1C 22
Islingham Farm Rd. Chatt 3F 27
Islington. 4A 16
Islington Pk. St. N1 3A 16
Ismays Rd. Sev 3B 34
Istead Rise. 3C 26
Itchingwood Common. 4C 32
Itchingwood Comn. Rd. Oxt 4C 32
Ively Rd. Farn 3A 28
Iver. 4F 13
Iver Heath. 4F 13
Iver La. Iver & Uxb 4F 13
Iverson Rd. NW6 3E 15
Ivy Barn La. Marg 3C 10
Ivy Chimneys. 3D 9
Ivy Chimneys Rd. Epp 3D 9
Ivydale Rd. SE15 2B 24
Ivy Hatch. 3B 34
Ivy Ho. La. Berk 2E 5
Ivy Ho. La. Sev 2F 33
Ivy Mill La. God 4B 32

Jackass La. Kes 4C 24
Jackass La. Tand 4B 32
Jacksons La. Bill 1D 19
Jacobswell. 3E 29
Jacob's Well Rd. Guild 3E 29
Jail La. Big H 2D 33
Jamaica Rd. SE16 & SE1 1A 24
James La. E11 2C 16
James St. W1 4F 15
James St. Gill 3F 27
Jasons Hill. Che 3E 5
Jealott's Hill. 2B 20
Jeffery St. Gill 3F 27
Jenkins La. St L 2C 4
Jermyn St. SW1 4F 15
Jersey Rd. Houn & Iswth 1C 22
Jeskyns Rd. Meop & Grav 3C 26
Jewels Hill. Warl 1C 32
Jig's La. N. Warf 3B 20
Jig's La. S. Warf 3B 20
Jock's La. Brack 3A 20
Jodrell Rd. E3 3B 16
Joel St. Pinn & N'wd 2B 14
John Hall Way. High W 2A 12
John Islip St. SW1 1F 23
John Nike Way. Brack 3A 20
Johns La. Ash G 2D 5
John Wilson St. SE18 1D 25
Joiners La. Chal P 2E 13
Jones Rd. Chesh 2A 8
Jordans. 2D 13
Jordans La. Jor 2D 13
Joyce Green. 2A 26
Joydens Wood. 3F 25
Jubilee Rd. L Grn 4A 12
Jubilee Rd. Orp 1E 33
Jubilee St. E1 4B 16
Jubilee Way. SW19 3E 23
Jubilee Way. Chess 4D 23
Judd St. WC1 4A 16
Judge Heath La. Hay 4A 14
Judge's Hill. N'thaw 3F 7
Junction Rd. NW5 3F 15
Jupiter Dri. Hem H 1A 6
Jutsums La. Romf 2E 17

Katherine Rd. E6 & E7 3C 16
Katherines. 1D 9
Katherine's Way. H'low 1D 9
Kavanaghs Rd. Brtwd 1B 18
Keats La. Wind 1D 21
Keel Dri. Slou 1D 21
Keens La. Guild 3D 29
Keepers La. Hyde H 4C 4
Keephatch Rd. Wokgm 3A 20
Kelvedon Common. 4A 10
Kelvedon Hall La. Kel H 4A 10
Kelvedon Hatch. 4A 10
Kelvedon Rd. SW6 1E 23
Kemprow. 4C 6
Kemprow. Ald 4C 6
Kempton Pk. Racecourse. 3B 22
Kemsing. 2A 34
Kemsing Rd. Sev 2B 34
Kendal Rd. NW10 3E 15
Kender St. SE14 1B 24
Kenley. 2A 32
Kenley Airfield. 2A 32
Kenley La. Kenl 2A 32
Kenley Rd. King T 3D 23
Kennel La. Bill 1D 19
Kennel La. Farn 3A 28
Kennel La. W'sham 4C 20
Kenneth Rd. Ben 2F 19
Kenninghall. (Junct.) 2B 16
Kenninghall Rd. E5 3B 16
Kennington. 1A 24
Kennington La. SE11 1A 24
Kennington Oval. (Junct.) 1A 24
Kennington Oval. SE11 1A 24
Kennington Pk. Rd. SW9 1A 24
Kennington Rd. SE11 & SE1 1A 24
Kensal Green. 4E 15
Kensal Rise. 4E 15
Kensal Rd. W10 4E 15
Kensal Town. 4E 15
Kensington. 1E 23
Kensington Av. T Hth 3A 24
Kensington Chu. St. W8 4E 15
Kensington Gore. SW7 1F 23
Kensington High St. W8 & W14 1E 23
Kensington Palace. 4E 15
Kensington Pk. Rd. W11 4E 15
Kensington Rd. W8 1E 23
Kensington Rd. N'holt 4B 14
Kent Gdns. W13 4C 14
Kent Ga. Way. Croy 1B 32
Kent Hatch. 4D 33
Kent Hatch Rd. Oxt & Eden 3C 32
Kent Ho. La. Beck 3B 24
Kent Ho. Rd. SE26 & SE2 3B 24
Kentish La. Brk P 2F 7
Kentish Town. 3F 15
Kentish Town Rd. NW5 & NW1 3F 15
Kentish Way. Brom 3C 24
Kenton. 2C 14
Kenton La. Harr 2C 14
Kenton Rd. E9 3B 16
Kenton Rd. Harr 3C 14
Kent Rd. Hall 4E 27
Kent Rd. Orp 4E 25
Kents Farm La. W Han 4E 11
Kents Hill Rd. Ben 3F 19
Kents La. N Wea 2F 9
Kent Street. 3D 35
Kent St. Mere 3C 34
Kenward. 4D 35
Kenward Rd. Yald 4D 35
Kenworthy Rd. E9 3B 16
Keston. 4C 24
Keston Mark. 4D 25
Keston Mark. (Junct.) 4C 24
Kettle La. E Far 3E 35
Kettlewell Hill. Wok 1E 29
Kevington. 4E 25
Kew. 1D 23
Kew Bridge. (Junct.) 1D 23
Kew Bri. Bren & Rich 1D 23
Kew Bri. Rd. Bren 1D 23
Kewferry Rd. N'wd 2A 14
Kew Gardens. 1D 23
Kew Gdns. Rd. Rich 1D 23
Kew Green. (Junct.) 1D 23
Kew Rd. Rich 2D 23
Keysers Estate. 2B 8
Kidbrooke. 1C 24
Kidbrooke Pk. Rd. SE3 1C 24
Kilburn. 4E 15
Kilburn High Rd. NW6 3E 15
Kilburn La. W9 & W10 4E 15
Kilburn Pk. Rd. W9 4E 15
Kilburn Priory. NW6 4E 15
Kiln Barn Rd. Dit & E Mal 2E 35
Kiln Green. 1A 20
Kiln La. Bour E 3C 12
Kiln La. Brock 4D 31
Kiln La. H'low 1C 8
Kiln La. Hedg 3D 13
Kiln La. P'wd 3B 4
Kiln Rd. Ben 3F 19
Kiln Rd. Hast 1C 4
Kimberley Av. SE15 2B 24
Kimblewick La. Ayl 1A 4
Kimblewick Rd. Ayl 1A 4
King Charles Rd. Surb 4D 23
King Edward VII Av. Wind 1D 21
King Edwards Rd. Bark 4D 17
Kingfield. 2E 29
Kingfield Rd. Wok 2E 29
Kingfisher Dri. Guild 4F 29
King George Rd. Chat 1F 35
King Harolds Way. Bexh 1E 25
King Harry La. St Alb 2B 6
King Henry's Dri. New Ad 1C 32
King Hill. W Mal 3D 35
Kingsash. 2B 4
King's Av. SW4 & SW12 2F 23
King's Av. Wfd G 2C 16
Kingsbury. 2D 15
Kingsbury Circ. NW9 2D 15
Kingsbury Green. 2D 15
Kingsbury Rd. NW9 2D 15
Kingscroft La. Warf 2B 20
Kings Cross. (Junct.) 4A 16
Kings Cross La. S Nut 4A 32
King's Cross Rd. WC1 4A 16
Kingsdowne Rd. Surb 4D 23
Kingsend. Ruis 3A 14
Kings Farm. 2C 26
Kingsgate Rd. King T 3D 23
Kings Gro. M'head 4B 12
Kings Hall Rd. Beck 3B 24
Kings Head Hill. E4 1B 16
Kings Highway. SE18 1D 25
Kings Hill. 3D 35
Kingshill Av. Hay & N'holt 4A 14
Kings Hill Av. King H 3D 35
Kingshill Rd. High W 1B 12
Kingshill Way. Berk 2E 5
Kingsland. 3A 16
Kingsland High St. E8 3A 16
Kingsland Rd. E8 & E2 4A 16
King's La. S Hth 3C 4
King's La. Chfd 3F 5
Kings La. Cook 3B 12
Kings La. Egh 3E 21
King's La. Gt Miss 3B 4
King's La. Lee G 2B 4
Kings Langley. 3A 6
Kings Langley By-Pass. Hem H & K Lan 2F 5
Kingsley Rd. Houn 1B 22
Kingsley Way. N2 2F 15
Kingsmead Rd. High W & Loud 2B 12
Kings Mill La. Red A & S Nut 4F 31
Kingsmoor. 2D 9
Kingsmoor Rd. H'low 1D 9
King's Ride. Asc 4C 20
Kings Ride. Camb 1B 28
Kings Rd. E4 1C 16
King's Rd. SW3, SW6 & SW10 1F 23
King's Rd. Asc 4C 20
Kings Rd. Berk 2E 5
Kings Rd. Brtwd 1B 18
Kings Rd. Chelm 2D 11
Kings Rd. Fleet 3A 28
King's Rd. King T 3D 23
King's Rd. Lon C 2C 6
Kings Rd. Rich 2D 23
Kings Rd. Shalf 4E 29
King's Rd. Wind 1D 21
Kings St. Stan H 4D 19
Kingston Bri. King T 3C 22
Kingston By-Pass. Surb 4C 22
Kingston By-Pass Rd. Esh 4C 22
Kingston Hall Rd. King T 3C 22
Kingston Hill. King T 3D 23
Kingston La. Tedd 3C 22
Kingston La. Uxb 4A 14
Kingston Rd. SW15 2E 23
Kingston Rd. SW19 & SW2 3E 23
Kingston Rd. Eps 1D 31
Kingston Rd. King T & N Mald 3D 23
Kingston Rd. Lea 2C 30
(in two parts)
Kingston Rd. Stai & Ashf 3F 21
Kingston Rd. Tedd 3C 22
Kingston Rd. Wor Pk & Eps 4D 23
Kingston upon Thames. 3D 23
Kingston Vale. 2D 23
Kingston Va. SW15 3D 23
King Street. 3B 10
King St. W6 1E 23
King St. M'head 4B 12
King St. Maid 3F 35
King St. Ong 3B 10
King St. S'hall 1B 22
King St. Twic 2C 22
Kingsway. WC2 4A 16
Kingsway. Chal P 2E 13
Kingsway. Farn C 3D 13
Kingsway. Hay 4A 14
Kingsway. W Wick 4C 24
Kingsway. Wok 2E 29
Kingsway N. Orbital Rd. Wat 4A 6
Kingswood. 3E 19
(Basildon)
Kingswood. 2E 31
(Tadworth)
Kingswood. 3B 6
(Watford)
Kingswood Dri. SE19 3A 24
Kingswood Rd. Tad 2E 31
Kippington. 3F 33
Kirkdale. SE26 2B 24
Kitchener Rd. Alder 3B 28
Kitchener Rd. Chatt 2F 27
Kit's Coty. 1F 35
Kitsmead La. Longc 4E 21
Kitto Rd. SE14 1B 24
Kitts End. 4E 7
Kitts End Rd. Barn 4E 7
Knaphill. 2D 29
Knares, The. Bas 3D 19
Knatts La. Knat 1A 34
Knatts Valley. 1A 34
Knatts Valley Rd. Knat 1A 34
Knaves Beech. Loud 2C 12
Knaves Beech Way. Loud 2C 12
Knee Hill. SE2 1E 25
Kneller Rd. Twic 2C 22
Knight Rd. Roch 3E 27
(in two parts)
Knightsbridge. 1F 23

Maidstone Rd.—Newtown

Maidstone Rd.
E Peck & Nett 4D 35
(in two parts)
Maidstone Rd. Hdlw 4C 34
Maidstone Rd. Mard 4F 35
Maidstone Rd. Roch 4E 27
Maidstone Rd. Seal 2A 34
Maidstone Rd.
Sidc & W Wick 3E 25
Maidstone Rd. S'hrst 4F 35
Maidstone Rd. W'slde 1F 35
Main Av. Enf 1B 16
Main Rd. Bore 1F 11
Main Rd. Buck & Reig 4E 31
Main Rd. Crock 4D 25
Main Rd. Crock H 4D 33
Main Rd. Dan 2F 11
Main Rd. Eden 4D 33
Main Rd. Hex 3F 25
Main Rd. Lac G 3A 4
Main Rd. L Walt & Broom 1E 11
Main Rd. Long 3B 26
Main Rd. Nap & Walt A 4A 4
Main Rd. Orp 3E 25
Main Rd. Ret C 4F 11
Main Rd. Romf 2F 17
Main Rd. Sev 3E 33
Main Rd. Sidc 2D 25
Main Rd. S at H 3A 26
Main Rd. W'ham & Brom 1C 32
Main St. Felt 3B 22
Main St. W'ton T 1A 4
Maize La. Warf 3B 20
Major Rd. E15 3C 16
Majors Farm Rd. Slou 1E 21
Malden Cres. NW1 3F 15
Malden Green. 4E 23
Malden Junction. (Junct.) 4D 23
Malden Rd. NW5 3F 15
Malden Rd.
N Mald & Wor Pk 4D 23
Malden Rd. Sutt 4E 23
Malden Rushett. 1C 30
Malden Way. N Mald 4D 23
Malders La. M'head 4B 12
Maldon Rd. Dan 2F 11
Maldon Rd. Gt Bad 2E 11
Maldon Rd. Marg 3D 11
Malling Rd. King H 1D 35
Malling Rd. Maid 3D 35
Malling Rd. Mere 3D 35
Malling Rd. Snod 1D 35
Malling Rd. Tstn 3D 35
Mall, The. W5 4D 15
Mall, The. Harr 3D 15
Malpas Rd. SE4 2B 24
Malt Hill. Warf 3B 20
Malthouse Rd. Stans 1B 34
Maltings Hill. More 2F 9
Maltings La. Epp 3E 9
Manchester Rd. E14 1C 24
Mandeville Rd. Ayl 1A 4
Mandeville Rd. N'holt 3B 14
Mandeville St. E5 3B 16
Mandeville Way. Lain 2D 19
Manford Way. Chig 1D 17
Mangrove La. Hert 1A 8
Mangrove Rd. Hert 1A 8
Manor Circus. (Junct.) 2D 23
Manorcrofts Rd. Egh 3E 21
Manor Dri. N20 1F 15
Manor Farm Rd. Wemb 4C 14
Manor House. (Junct.) 3A 16
Manorhouse La. Bookh 3B 30
Manor La. SE12 & SE1 2C 24
Manor La. Fawk & Sev 4B 26
Manor Park. 3C 16
(Ilford)
Manor Park. 4D 13
(Slough)
Manor Pk. Rd. NW10 4D 15
Manor Pk. Rd. Chst 3D 25
Manor Pk. Rd. W Wick 4B 24
Manor Rd. E15 & E16 4C 16
Manor Rd. N16 3A 16
Manor Rd. SE25 3B 24
Manor Rd. Abr 1E 17
Manor Rd. Beck 3B 24
Manor Rd. Bren 1C 22
Manor Rd. Dart 2F 25
Manor Rd. Eri 1F 25
Manor Rd. Guild 4E 29
Manor Rd. Hat 1D 7
Manor Rd. H Bee 4C 8
Manor Rd. Long 4C 26
Manor Rd. Lou 1C 10
Manor Rd. Mitc 3F 23
Manor Rd. Rich 2D 23
Manor Rd. Swans 2B 26
Manor Rd. Tedd 3C 22
Manor Rd. Tong & Alder 4B 28
Manor Rd. Wall 4F 23
Manor Rd. Wind 1D 21
Manor Rd. Wfd G & Chig 2D 17
Manor Rd. N. Esh & Th Dit 4C 22
Manor Rd. S. Esh 4C 22
Manor Vw. N3 2E 15
Manor Way. Borwd 4D 7
Manorway, The. Stan H 4D 19
Mansell St. EC3 4A 16
Mansfield Hill. E4 1B 16
Mansfield Rd. NW3 3F 15
Mansion La. Iver 4F 13
Mantle Rd. SE4 2B 24
Mantles Green. 4D 5
Manwood Green. 1A 10
Manwood Rd. SE4 2B 24
Mapesbury Rd. NW6 3E 15
Maple Cross. 1F 13
Maple Rd. SE20 3B 24
Maple Rd. Red 4F 31
Maple Rd. Surb 4C 22
Maplescombe. 4A 26
Maplescombe La.
F'ham & Sev 4A 26
Mapleton Rd.
W'ham & Eden 3D 33
Maple Way. Can I 4F 19
Marble Arch. (Junct.) 4F 15
Marcilly Rd. SW11 2F 23
Marden Ash. 3A 10
Mare St. E8 4B 16
Marford Rd. Wheat & Lem 1D 7
Margaret Rd. Barn 4F 7
Margaret Roding. 1B 10
Margaretting. 3D 11
Margaretting Rd. Gall 3D 11
Margaretting Rd. Writ 3D 11
Margaretting Tye. 3D 11
Margery. 3E 31
Margery La. Tad 3E 31
Margery St. WC1 4A 16
Margetts La. Bur 1E 35
Marigold La. Stock 4D 11
Markedge La. Coul & Reig 3C 32
Marketfield Way. Red 4F 31
Market La. Slou 1F 21
Market Pl. NW11 2E 15
Market Pl. Abr 4E 9
Market Pl. Chal P 2E 13
Market Pl. Wokgm 3A 20
Market Rd. N7 3A 16
Market Rd. Chelm 2E 11
Market Sq. Brom 3C 24
Market Sq. W'ham 3D 33
Market St. Brack 3B 20
Market St. Dart 2A 26
Mark Hall North. 1E 9
Mark Hall South. 1E 9
Markhams Chase. Bas 2D 19
Markhouse Rd. E17 2B 16
Marks Gate. 2E 17
Marks Hall La. Mar R 1B 10
Marlborough Av. Ruis 2A 14
Marlborough Rd. N19 3F 15
Marling Park. 3B 22
Marlin Hill. Wig 1C 4
Marlow. 3A 12
Marlow Bottom. 2A 12
Marlow Bottom. Mar 2A 12
Marlow Comn. Mar 3A 12
Marlowes. Hem H 2F 5
Marlow Hill. High W 2A 12
Marlow Rd. SE20 3B 24
Marlow Rd. Bish 3A 12
Marlow Rd. High W 2A 12
Marlow Rd. L End 2A 12
Marlow Rd. L Mar & Bour 3B 12
Marlow Rd. M'head 4B 12
Marlow Rd. Mar 3A 12
Marlpit Hill. 4D 33
Marlpit La. Coul 2A 32
Marrod's Bottom. Amer 1C 12
Marroway. W'ton T 1A 4
Marrowbrook La. Farn 3A 28
Marsh. 1A 4
Marshall Rd. Camb 1A 28
Marshalswick. 1C 6
Marshalswick La. St Alb 1C 6
Marsham St. SW1 1F 23
Marshcroft La. Tring 1C 4
Marshfoot Rd. Grays 1C 26
Marshgate La. E15 3B 16
Marsh Hill. E9 3B 16
Marsh Hill. Wal A 3C 8
Marsh La. NW7 1D 15
Marsh La. Dor R & Tap 4C 12
Marsh La. Stan 1C 14
Marsh La. Stoke M 1A 4
Marshmoor. 2E 7
Marsh Rd. Pinn 2B 14
Marsh Wall. E14 1B 24
Martindale Av. Camb 2C 28
Martindale Rd. Houn 2B 22
Martinsend La. Gt Miss 3B 4
Martin's Heron. 3B 20
Martins La. E Peck 4D 35
Martin Way. SW20 & Mord 3E 23
Martyr's Green. 2A 30
Martyr's La. Wok 1E 29
Marvels La. SE12 2C 24
Marylebone. 4F 15
Marylebone Flyover. (Junct.)
4F 15
Marylebone High St. W1 4F 15
Marylebone Rd. W2 4F 15
Mascalls La. Gt War 1A 18
Mashbury. 1C 10
Mashbury Rd. Gt Wal 1D 11
Mashbury Rd. Mash 1C 10
Masons Av. Harr 2C 14
Mason's Bri. Rd. Red 4F 31
Masons Hill. Brom 3C 24
Master Brewer. (Junct.) 3A 14
Maswell Park. 2C 22
Matching. 1F 9
Matching Green. 1A 10
Matching Rd. H'low 1E 9
Matching Tye. 1F 9
Matthews La. Hdlw 4C 34
Matthias Rd. N16 3A 16
Maultway, The. Camb 1B 28
Maury Rd. N16 3B 16
Mawney. 2E 17
Mawney Rd. Romf 2E 17
Maxted Rd. Hem I 1A 6
Maybank Av. Wemb 3C 14
Maybury. 2F 29
Maybury Hill. Wok 2E 29
Maybury Rd. Wok 2E 29
Mayes La. Dan 2F 11
Mayes La. S'don 2F 11
Mayes Rd. N22 2A 16
Mayfair. 4F 15
Mayfield Rd. W3 4D 15
Mayfield Rd. Farn 2A 28
Mayfield Rd. S Croy 1A 32
Mayfield Rd. W on T 4B 22
Mayford. 2E 29
Maygrove Rd. NW6 3E 15
Maylands Av. Hem H 1A 6
Mayow Rd. SE23 & SE2 3B 24
Mayplace Rd. E. Bexh 2E 25
Mayplace Rd. W. Bexh 2E 25
Maypole. 1E 33
Maypole Rd. Orp 4E 25
May's Green. 2A 30
Mays La. Barn 1E 15
Maze Hill. SE3 & SE10 1C 24
Mead La. Cher 4F 21
Meadow La. Eton 1D 21
Meadow Ri. Bill 1D 19
Mead Vale. 4F 31
Meadway. NW11 2E 15
Meadway. Barn 4E 7
Mead Way. Brom 4C 24
Mead Way. Coul 2A 32
Meadway. Twic 2C 22
Medfield St. SW15 2E 23
Medhurst Row. 4E 33
Median Rd. E5 3B 16
Medlar St. SE5 1A 24
Medway Rd. Gill 3F 27
(in two parts)
Medway St. Chat 3F 27
Melbourne Av. Chelm 1D 11
Melbourne Rd. Bush 1B 14
Melfort Rd. T Hth 3A 24
Melliker La. Meop 4C 26
Mellow La. E. Hay 4A 14
Mellow La. W. Uxb 4A 14
Melton St. NW1 4F 15
Melville Av. Gnfd 3C 14
Melville Gdns. N13 2A 16
Meopham. 4C 26
Meopham Green. 4C 26
Meopham Station. 4C 26
Merantun Way. SW19 3F 23
Mercian Way. Slou 4C 12
Mercury Gdns. Romf 2F 17
Mere Rd. Slou 1D 21
Mere Rd. Tad 3E 31
Mereworth. 3C 34
Mereworth Rd. Maid 3C 34
Meriden. 4B 6
Meriden Way. Wat 4B 6
Meridian Way. N18 & Enf 1B 16
Meridian Way. Wal A 3B 8
Merland Ri. Eps & Tad 2E 31
Merle Common. 4C 32
Merlin Cres. Edgw 2D 15
Merlin Way. N Wea 2E 9
Merrick Rd. S'hall 1B 22
Merrivale. N14 1F 15
Merrow. 4E 29
Merrow La. Guild 4F 29
Merrow Way. New Ad 1C 32
Merryboys Rd. Cli 2E 27
Merry Hill. 1B 14
Merry Hill Rd. Bush 1B 14
Merstham. 3F 31
Merstham Rd. Red 3A 32
Merton. 3F 23
Merton High St. SW19 3F 23
Merton Park. 3E 23
Merton Rd. SW18 2E 23
Merton Rd. SW19 3E 23
Merttins Rd. SE15 2B 24
Meudon Av. Farn 3B 28
Mewshurst. 4D 33
Michaels La. Fawk & Sev 4B 26
Micklefield. 1B 12
Micklefield Green. 4F 5
Micklefield Rd. High W 1B 12
Mickleham. 3C 30
Mickleham By-Pass. Mick 3C 30
Mickleham Downs. 3C 30
Middlefield Rd. Hod 1B 8
Middle Green. 4E 13
Middle Grn. Slou 4E 13
Middlegreen Rd. Slou 1E 21
Middle Hill. Egh 3E 21
Middle La. N8 2A 16
Middle La. Bov 3E 5
Middlemead. S Han 4E 11
Middle Pk. Av. SE9 2C 24
Middle St. Brock 4D 31
Middle St. Naze 2C 8
Middle St. Shere 4A 30
Middleton Hall La. Brtwd 1B 18
Middleton Rd. Mord & Cars 4E 23
Midfield Way. Orp 3E 25
Midland Rd. NW1 4F 15
Midland Rd. Hem H 2F 5
Midleton Rd. Guild 4E 29
Mid St. S Nut 4A 32
Milbourne La. Esh 1C 30
Mildmay Gro. N1 3A 16
Mildmay Pk. N1 3A 16
Mile End. 4B 16
Mile End Rd. E3 & E1 4B 16
Mile Ho. La. St Alb 2C 6
Miles Gray Rd. Bas 2D 19
Miles Green. 2D 29
Miles La. Cobh 1B 30
Miles La. S God 4B 32
Milespit Hill. NW7 1E 15
Milestone Green. (Junct.) 2D 23
Milkwood Rd. SE24 2A 24
Millbank. SW1 1A 24
Mill Bri. Hert 1A 8
Millbrook. Guild 4E 29
Millbrook Rd. St M 3E 25
Mill End. 1F 13
Mill End Rd. High W 1A 12
Millennium Dome. 4C 16
Millennium Way. SE10 1C 24
Miller's Green. 2B 10
Miller's La. Chig 1E 17
Milley Bridge. 1A 20
Milley La. Hare H 1A 20
Milley Rd. Wal L 1A 20
Millfields. Che 3D 5
Millfields Rd. E5 3B 16
Mill Green. 3C 10
(Ingatestone)
Mill Green. 1E 7
(Welwyn Garden City)
Mill Grn. Hat 1F 7
Mill Grn. La. Wel G & Mill G 1E 7
Mill Grn. Rd. Ing 3C 10
Mill Grn. Rd. Mitc 4F 23
Mill Hill. 1E 15
Mill Hill. W3 1D 23
Mill Hill. Chelm 3D 11
Mill Hill. Tovil 3F 35
Mill Hill Circus. (Junct.) 1D 15
Mill Hill La. Shorne 3D 27
Mill Hill Rd. SW13 1E 23
Mill Ho. La. Egh & Cher 3F 21
Mill La. NW2 3E 15
Mill La. Asc 3D 21
Mill La. Blue B 1F 35
Mill La. Brack 3A 20
Mill La. Brox 2B 8
Mill La. Chal G 1E 13
Mill La. Dan 2F 11
Mill La. Egh 3F 21
Mill La. Ger X 2E 13
Mill La. Hild 4A 34
Mill La. Hook E 4B 10
Mill La. Hur 4A 12
Mill La. Igh 2B 34
Mill La. Ing 3C 10
Mill La. K Lan 3A 6
Mill La. L Bad 2F 11
Mill La. Mon R 2A 4
Mill La. More 1F 9
Mill La. Nave 4F 9
Mill La. Ong 3A 10
Mill La. Orp 1D 33
Mill La. Oxt 4C 32
Mill La. Romf 2E 17
Mill La. Stock 4D 11
Mill La. Tap 4C 12
Mill La. Toot 3F 9
Mill La. Under 4A 34
Mill La. Yald 4E 35
Mill La. Yat 1A 28
Mill Meads. 4C 16
Mill Pond Rd. Dart 2A 26
Mill Rd. Ave 4A 18
Mill Rd. Bill 1D 19
Mill Rd. Cobh 2B 30
Mill Rd. Eps 1D 31
Mill Rd. Gill 3F 27
Mill Rd. Good E 1C 10
Mill Rd. Stock 4D 11
Mill Rd. Tad 3E 31
Mill Rd. W Dray 1F 21
Mill Street. 2D 35
Mill St. E Mal 2D 35
Mill St. H'low 1E 9
Mill St. Loose 3F 35
Mill St. Red 4F 31
Millwall. 1B 24
Millwall F.C. 1B 24
Mill Way. Dork 3D 31
Milman Rd. NW6 4E 15
Milton. 2C 26
Milton Rd. Cat 2A 32
Milton Rd. Grav 2C 26
(in two parts)
Milton Rd. Swans 2B 26
Milton St. Swans 2B 26
Mimbridge. 1E 29
Mimms Hall Rd. Pot B 3E 7
Mimms La. Shenl & Pot B 3D 7
Mincing La. Chob 1D 29
Minley. 2A 28
Minley La. B'water 2A 28
Minley Link Rd. Farn 3A 28
Minley Rd. B'water & Farn 2A 28
Minley Rd. Farn 2A 28
Minley Rd. Fleet 2A 28
Minnow End. 1D 11
Minories. EC3 4A 16
Missenden Rd. Che 3D 5
Missenden Rd. Gt Kin 4B 4
Miswell La. Tring 1C 4
Mitcham. 3F 23
Mitcham La. SW16 3F 23
Mitcham Rd. SW17 3F 23
Mitcham Rd. Croy 4A 24
Mitchley Av. Purl & S Croy 1A 32
Mitchley Hill. S Croy 1A 32
Moat La. P'wd 3B 4
Mobwell. 3B 4
Moby Dick. (Junct.) 2E 17
Mockbeggar. 4E 35
(Marden)
Mockbeggar. 2E 27
(Wainscott)
Mogador. 3E 31
Mogador Rd. Tad 3E 31
Mogden La. Iswth 2C 22
Molesey Rd.
W on T & W Mol 4B 22
Molesworth St. SE13 2C 24
Mollison Av. Enf 4B 8
Mollison Dri. Wall 1A 32
Mollison Way. Edgw 2D 15
Molrams La. Gt Bad 2E 11
Molsey Pk. Rd. W Mol 4B 22
Monarchs Way. Chesh 3B 8
Moneyhill. 1F 13
Moneyrow Green. 1B 20
Moneyrow Grn. Holyp 1B 20
Monkham's La. Wfd G 1C 16
(in two parts)
Monks La. Eden 4C 32
Monks Orchard. 4B 24
Monks Orchard Rd. Beck 4B 24
Monks Risborough. 2A 4
Monkswell La. Coul 3E 31
Monkton Hadley. 4E 7
Monkton La. Farnh 4A 28
Monmouth Rd. N9 1B 16
Monmouth St. WC2 4A 16
Montague Pl. WC1 4F 15
Montague Waye. S'hall 1B 22
Montagu Rd. N9 & N18 1B 16
Montem La. Slou 4D 13
Montpelier Row. SE3 1C 24
Montrose Av. Edgw 2D 15
Monument Hill. Wey 4A 22
Monument La. Chal P 2E 13
Monument Rd. Wok 1E 29
Monument Way. N15 2A 16
Moore's Rd. Dork 4C 30
Moorfield Rd. Den 3F 13
Moorgate. EC2 4A 16
Moor Hall La. E Han 3F 11
Moorhall Rd. Hare 2F 13
Moor Hall Rd. H'low 1E 9
Moorhouse. 3D 33
Moorhouse Bank. 3D 33
Moorhouse Rd.
Oxt & W'ham 4D 33
Moor Junction. (Junct.) 1F 21
Moor La. Chess 4D 23
Moor La. Rick 1A 14
Moor La. Sarr 4F 5
Moor La. Stai 2F 21
Moor Park. 1A 14
Moors Wlk. Wel G 1F 7
Morants Ct. Rd. Dun G 2F 33
Morden. 3E 23
Morden Hall Rd. Mord 3F 23
Morden Park. 4E 23
Morden Rd. SW19 3E 23
Morden Rd. Mitc 3F 23
Moreland St. EC1 4A 16
More La. Esh 4B 22
Mores La. Pil H 1A 18
Moreton. 2F 9
Moreton Bri. More 2F 9
Moreton Mill. 1F 9
Moreton Rd. Fyf 2A 10
Moreton Rd. More 2F 9
Moreton Rd. Ong 2A 10
Morgan's La. Hay 4A 14
Morland Rd. Croy 4A 24
Morley Hill. Stan H 3D 19
Morley's Rd. Weald 4F 33
Morning La. E9 3B 16
Mornington Rd. Gnfd 4B 14
Morris Rd. E3 4B 16
Mortimer Rd. NW10 4E 15
Mortimer St. W1 4F 15
Mortlake. 2D 23
Mortlake High St. SW14 2D 23
Mortlake Rd. Rich 1D 23
Morton Way. N14 1F 15
Morval Rd. SW2 2A 24
Moss End. 2B 20
Moss La. Pinn 2B 14
Mote Rd. Maid 3F 35
Mote Rd. S'brne & Ivy H 3A 34
Motherwell Way. Grays 1B 26
Motspur Park. 4E 23
Motspur Pk. N Mald 4D 23
Mottingham. 2C 24
Mottingham La. SE9 2C 24
Mottingham Rd. SE9 2D 25
Mott St. E4 & Lou 4C 8
Moulsham. 2E 11
Moulsham St. Chelm 2E 11
(in two parts)
Mount Av. W5 4C 14
Mount End. 3E 9
Mount End. They M 3E 9
Mountgrove Rd. N5 3A 16
Mt. Harry Rd. Sev 3F 33
Mount La. Den 3F 13
Mountnessing. 4C 10
Mountnessing By-Pass.
Mount & Ing 4C 10
Mountnessing La. Dodd 4B 10
Mountnessing Rd. Bill 1D 19
Mountnessing Rd.
B'more & Brtwd 3B 10
Mt. Nugent. Che 2D 5
Mount Pleasant. 2F 13
Mt. Pleasant. Barn 4F 7
Mt. Pleasant. Wemb 4D 15
Mt. Pleasant La. Brick 3B 6
Mt. Pleasant Rd. N17 2A 16
Mount Rd. They G 3E 9
Mounts Hill. Wink 2C 20
Mounts Rd. Grnh 2B 26
Movers Lane. (Junct.) 4D 17
Movers La. Bark 4D 17
Mowden. 1F 11
Mowden Hall La. Hat P 1F 11
Mucking. 4D 19
Muckingford. 1D 27
Muckingford Rd. W Til 1C 26
Mucking Wharf Rd. Stan H 4D 19
Mugswell. 3E 31
Mulberry Grn. H'low 1E 9
Mulberry Way. E18 2C 16
Mulgrave Rd. Sutt 1E 31
Mumfords La. Chal P 2E 13
Mundaydean La. Mar 2A 12
Mungo Pk. Rd. Rain 3F 17
Munster Rd. SW6 1E 23
Murchison Av. Bex 2E 25
Murdoch Rd. Wokgm 3A 20
Murray Rd. Ott 1F 29
Murrellhill La. Binf 3A 20
Murthering La. Romf 1F 17
Mussenden La.
Hort K & Dart 4A 26
Muswell Hill. 2F 15
Muswell Hill. N10 2F 15
Muswell Hill B'way. N10 2F 15
Muswell Hill Rd. N10 & N6 2F 15
Mutton La. Pot B 3E 7
Mutton Row. Ong 3F 9
Myddelton Av. Enf 4A 8
Myddelton Pk. N20 1F 15
Myddleton Rd. N22 2A 16
Myrke. 1D 21
Mytchett. 3B 28
Mytchett Pl. Rd. Myt 3B 28
Mytchett Rd. Myt 3B 28

Nag's Head. (Junct.) 3A 16
Nag's Head La. Gt Miss 4B 4
Nags Head La.
Upm & Brtwd 2A 18
Nags Head Rd. Enf 4B 8
Nairdwood La. P'wd 3B 4
Nallhead Rd. Felt 3B 22
Naphill. 4A 4
Napier Rd. Gill 4F 27
Napsbury. 2C 6
Napsbury La. St Alb 2C 6
Nap, The. K Lan 3A 6
Narcot La. Chal G 1E 13
Narrow La. Warl 2B 32
Nascott Wood Rd. Wat 4A 6
Nash. 4C 24
Nash Bank. Meop 3C 26
Nashdom La. Burn 3C 12
Nash La. Kes 1C 32
Nash Lee. 1A 4
Nash Lee Rd. Ter & Wen 1A 4
Nashleigh Hill. Che 3D 5
Nash Mills. 2A 6
Nash Mills La. Hem H 2A 6
Nash Street. 3C 26
Nast Hyde. 2D 7
Nathan's La. Hghwd 2C 10
Nathan Way. SE28 1D 25
National Sports Cen. 3B 24
(Crystal Palace)
Navestock Heath. 4F 9
Navestock Side. 4A 10
Navestockside. Brtwd 4A 10
Nazaire Rd. Chelm 1D 11
Nazeing. 2C 8
Nazeing Comn. Naze 2C 8
Nazeing New Rd. Brox 2B 8
Nazeing Rd. Naze 2C 8
Neasden. 3D 15
Neasden Junction. (Junct.)
3D 15
Neasden La. NW10 3D 15
Neasden La. N. NW10 3D 15
Nelson Rd. E4 2B 16
Nelson Rd. Gill 4F 27
Nelson Rd. Houn & Twic 2B 22
Nelson Rd. H'row A 1A 22
Nene Rd. H'row A 1A 22
Nepicar La. Wro 2C 34
Netherlands Rd. Barn & N20 1F 15
Nether Mayne. Bas 2E 19
Netherne Dri. Coul 2F 31
Netherne La. Coul 3F 31
Netherne-on-the-Hill. 2F 31
Nether Street. 1B 10
Nether St. N12 & N3 2E 15
Nether St. Ab R 1B 10
Nettleden. 1F 5
Nettleden Rd. L Gad & Wat E 1E 5
Nettleden Rd. Lit H 1E 5
Nettlestead. 3D 35
Nettlestead Green. 4D 35
Nettlestead La. Mere 3D 35
Nettleswell. 1D 9
Nevedon. 2E 19
Nevendon Rd. Bas & W'fd 2E 19
Nevendon Rd. By-Pass.
W'fd 1F 19
New Addington. 1C 32
Newark La. Wok 2F 29
Newarks Rd. Good E 1C 10
New Ash Green. 4B 26
New Barn. 3C 26
New Barnet. 4F 7
Newbarn La. Seer 1D 13
New Barn La. W'ham & Sev 2D 33
New Barn Rd. Long & Grav 3C 26
New Barn Rd. Swan 3F 25
New Barn St. E13 4C 16
New Beckenham. 3B 24
New Bond St. W1 4F 15
New Bowers Way. Chelm 1E 11
New Bri. St. EC4 4A 16
Newbury Av. Enf 4B 8
Newbury Park. 2D 17
Newbury Rd. H'row A 1A 22
New Cavendish St. W1 4F 15
New Charlton. 1C 24
New Chu. Rd. SE5 1A 24
New City Rd. E13 4C 16
New Cross. 1B 24
New Cross. (Junct.) 1B 24
New Cross Gate. 1B 24
New Cross Gate. (Junct.) 1B 24
New Cross Rd. SE14 1B 24
New Cut. E Far 3F 35
New Cut Rd. Weav 3F 35
New Denham. 3F 13
Newell Green. 3B 20
New Eltham. 2D 25
New Forest Ride. Brack 4B 20
Newgate Street. 2A 8
Newgate St. Hert 2F 7
Newgatestreet Rd. G Oak 2A 8
Newgate St. Village. Hert 2A 8
New Greens. 1C 6
New Ground. 1D 5
Newground Rd. New G 1D 5
Newham Way. E6 & E16 4C 16
New Haw. 1F 29
New Haw Rd. Add 4F 21
New Heston Rd. Houn 1B 22
Newhouse. 1A 10
(Moreton)
New House. 2C 26
(Northfleet)
New Ho. La. Grav 2C 26
New Hythe. 2E 35
New Hythe La. Lark 2E 35
Newington. 1A 24
Newington Butts. SE11 1A 24
Newington Causeway. SE1 1A 24
Newington Grn. N1 3A 16
Newington Grn. Rd. N1 3A 16
New Inn La. Guild 4E 29
New Kent Rd. SE17 1A 24
New King's Rd. SW6 1E 23
Newlands. 1C 14
Newlands La. Meop 1C 34
Newlands Pk. SE26 3B 24
New La. Wok & Guild 2E 29
New Lodge Chase. L Bad 2F 11
New London Rd. Chelm 2E 11
(in two parts)
New Malden. 3D 23
Newman's End. 1F 9
New Mile Rd. Asc 3C 20
New Mill. 1C 4
New Nabbotts Way. Chelm 1E 11
Newney Green. 2C 10
New N. Rd. N1 3A 16
New N. Rd. Ilf 2D 17
New Oxford St. W1 4F 15
New Pk. Rd. SW2 2A 24
New Plaistow Rd. E15 4C 16
New Pond Rd. Holm G 4C 4
Newport Rd. H'row A 1A 22
New Pound La. Mere 3C 34
New Rd. E1 4B 16
New Rd. E4 1B 16
New Rd. SE2 1E 25
New Rd. Abr 1E 17
New Rd. Alb 4F 29
New Rd. Asc 3C 20
New Rd. Bag & W'sham 1C 28
New Rd. Berk 1F 5
New Rd. Bur 4F 27
New Rd. Chat 4F 27
New Rd. Cher 4F 21
New Rd. Chil 4E 29
New Rd. Coles 4D 5
New Rd. Crox G 1A 14
New Rd. Dag & Rain 4E 17
New Rd. Dit 2E 35
New Rd. E Mal 2E 35
New Rd. Felt 2A 22
New Rd. Grays 1B 26
(in two parts)
New Rd. High W 1A 12
New Rd. Lac G & Walt H 4A 4
New Rd. Limp 3C 32
New Rd. N'chu 1D 5
New Rd. Penn 1C 12
New Rd. P Ris 3A 4
New Rd. Rad 4C 6
New Rd. Sarr 4F 5
New Rd. Shep 3A 22
New Rd. Sund 3E 33
New Rd. Tad 3E 31
New Rd. Tand 4B 32
New Rd. Uxb 4A 14
New Rd. W Mol 3B 22
New Rd. W'ton T 1A 4
New Rd. Av. Chat 4F 27
New Rd. Hill. Kes & Brom 1D 33
New Southgate. 2F 15
New Street. 4C 26
New St. Chelm 2E 11
New St. Rd. Meop & Sev 4C 26
New Tank Hill Rd. Purf 1A 26
New Thundersley. 2F 19
Newtown. 3D 5
(Chesham)

New Town—Phipps Hatch La.

New Town. 2A 26 (Dartford)
Newtown Rd. Mar 3A 12
New Wanstead. E11 2C 16
New Way La. Thr B 1F 9
New Wickham La. Egh 3E 21
New Windsor. 1D 21
New Windsor St. Uxb 4F 13
New Wokingham Rd. Crowt 4A 20
Newyears Green. 3A 14
Newyears Grn. La. Hare 2A 14
New Years La. Knock & Orp 2D 33
New Zealand Av. W on T 4A 22
Nightingale La. SW4 & SW12 2F 23
Nightingale La. Brom 3C 24
Nightingale La. Ide H 4E 33
Nightingale La. St Alb 2C 6
Nightingale Pl. SE18 1D 25
Nightingale Rd. N9 1B 16
Nightingale Rd. Cars 4F 23
Nightingale Rd. Rick 1F 13
Nightingales La. Chal G 4E 5
Nine Ashes. 3B 10
Nine Ashes Rd. B'more & Brtwd 3B 10
Nine Elms. 1F 23
Nine Elms La. SW8 1F 23
Ninehams Rd. Cat 2A 32
Nine Mile Ride. Brack 4A 20
Nine Mile Ride. Wokgm & Crowt 4A 20
Nizels. 4A 34
Nizels La. Hild 4A 34
Noah's Ark. 2A 34
Noah's Ark. Kems 2A 34
Noak Bridge. 2D 19
Noak Hill. 1A 18 (Harold Hill)
Noak Hill. 2D 19 (Steeple View)
Noak Hill Rd. Bill & Bas 1D 19
Noak Hill Rd. Romf 1F 17
Noble Tree Rd. Hild 4A 34
Noel Park. 2A 16
Noel Rd. W3 4D 15
Noke La. St Alb 2B 6
Norbiton. 3D 23
Norbury. 3A 24
Norbury Av. SW16 & T Hth 3A 24
Norbury Cres. SW16 3A 24
Norden Rd. M'head 4B 12
Norfolk Rd. M'head 4B 12
Norheads La. Warl & Big H 2C 32
Nork. 2E 31
Norlands La. Egh 3F 21
Normandy. 4C 28
Normandy Rd. St Alb 1C 6
Norman Rd. SE8 1B 24
Norman Rd. W Mal 2D 35
Normansland. 1C 6
Norreys Dri. M'head 1B 20
Norris Hill Rd. Fleet 3A 28
Norsey Rd. Bill 1D 19
Norsted La. Prat B 1E 33
North Acton. 4D 15
N. Acton Rd. NW10 4D 15
Northall Rd. Bexh 1F 25
North App. Wat 3B 6
North Ascot. 3C 20
N. Ash Rd. New Ash 4B 26
N. Audley St. W1 4F 15
North Av. Chelm 1D 11
Northaw. 3F 7
Northaw Rd. E. Cuff 3F 7
Northaw Rd. W. N'thaw 3F 7
North Benfleet. 2F 19
N. Birkbeck Rd. E11 3C 16
Northborough Rd. Slou 4D 13
Northbrook Rd. Ilf 3D 17
North Camp. 3B 28
North Cheam. 4E 23
Northchurch. 1D 5
N. Circular Rd. N12 & N2,N3 2E 15
N. Circular Rd. N13 1A 16
N. Circular Rd. NW2 & NW4 3E 15
N. Circular Rd. NW4 3E 15
N. Circular Rd. NW10 4D 15
N. Circular Rd. NW11 2E 15
Northcote Rd. SW11 2F 23
Northcote Rd. Croy 4A 24
Northcote Rd. Roch 3E 27
North Cray. 3E 25
N. Cray Rd. Sidc & Bex 3E 25
Northcroft Rd. Egh 3E 21
N. Dane Way. Chat 4F 27
Northdown Rd. Wold 3B 32
North End. 1F 25 (Erith)
North End. 3F 15 (Hampstead)
North End. W14 1E 23
Northend. Hem H 2A 6
N. End La. Orp 1D 33
N. End Rd. NW11 3E 15
Northend Rd. Eri 1F 25
N. End Way. NW3 3F 15
Northern Perimeter Rd. H'row A 1A 22
Northern Perimeter Rd. W. H'row A 1A 22
Northern Rd. Slou 4D 13
Northern Woods. F Hth 2C 12
Northey Av. Sutt 1E 31
North Farnborough. 3B 28
North Feltham. 2B 22
Northfield Av. W5 & W13 4C 14
Northfields. 1C 22
North Finchley. 1F 15
Northfleet. 2C 26
Northfleet Green. 3C 26
Northfleet Grn. Rd. S'fleet 3C 26
N. Folly Rd. E Far 4E 35
North Ga. Roch 3F 27
North Halling. 4E 27
North Harrow. 2B 14
North Hatton Rd. Harl 1A 22
North Hill. N6 2F 15
North Hill. Horn H 3D 19
North Hill. L Bad 1F 11
North Hill. Rick 4F 5
N. Hill Dri. Romf 1F 17
North Hillingdon. 3A 14
North Holmwood. 4C 30
N. Hyde La. S'hall & Houn 1B 22
N. Hyde Rd. Hay 1A 22
Northiam. N12 1E 15
North Kensington. 4E 15
North La. Alder 4B 28
North Lee. 1A 4
N. Lee La. Ter 1A 4
North Looe. 1E 31
North Mdw. Off 2C 34
North Mymms. 2D 7
North Ockendon. 3B 18
Northolt. 3B 14
Northolt Rd. Harr 3B 14
N. Orbital Rd. Wat & St Alb 3B 6
Northover. Brom 2C 24
N. Park Rd. Iver 1F 21
N. Pole La. Kes 1C 32
N. Pole Rd. W12 4E 15
N. Pole Rd. E Mal & Barm 3D 35
Northridge Way. Hem H 2F 5
North Rd. N6 3F 15
North Rd. N7 3A 16
North Rd. Wid E 1B 12
North Rd. Ches B 4D 5
North Rd. Hav 1F 17
North Rd. Hert 1A 8
North Rd. S'hall 4B 14
North Rd. S Ock & Upm 4B 18
North Sheen. 2D 23
North Stifford. 4B 18
North St. SW8 1F 23
North St. Barm 3E 35
North St. Cars 4F 23
North St. Guild 4E 29
North St. Horn 3F 17
North St. Naze 2C 8
North St. Romf 2F 17
North St. Strood 3E 27
North St. Wink 3C 20
North Town. 4B 28 (Aldershot)
North Town. 4B 12 (Maidenhead)
Northumberland Av. SW1 4A 16
Northumberland Heath. 1F 25
Northumberland Pk. N17 2B 16
Northumberland Rd. Maid 3F 35
North Vw. Pinn 3B 14
North Watford. 4B 6
North Weald Airfield. 2E 9
North Weald Bassett. 2F 9
North Wembley. 3C 14
N. Western Av. Wat 4A 6 (in two parts)
N. Western Way. Bush 4B 6
Northwick. 4F 19
Northwick Rd. Can I 4F 19
Northwold Rd. E5 & N16 3A 16
Northwood. 2A 14
Northwood Hills. 2A 14
Northwood Rd. Hare 2F 13
Northwood Rd. T Hth & SE19 3A 24
Northwood Way. N'wd 2B 14
North Woolwich. 4D 17
N. Woolwich Rd. E16 4C 16
Norton Heath. 2B 10
Norton Heath Rd. Will 2B 10
Norton La. H Ong 2B 10
Norton Mandeville. 2B 10
Norwich Rd. N'wd 2A 14
Norwood. 3A 24
Norwood End. 1A 10
Norwood End. Fyf 1A 10
Norwood Green. 1B 22
Norwood High St. SE27 3A 24
Norwood La. Iver 4F 13
Norwood La. Meop 4C 26
Norwood New Town. 3A 24
Norwood Rd. SE24 & SE2 2A 24
Norwood Rd. S'hall 1B 22
Notting Hill. 4E 15
Notting Hill Ga. W11 4E 15
Nower Hill. Pinn 2B 14
Nower, The. W'ham 2D 33
Nunhead. 2B 24
Nunhead La. SE15 2B 24
Nuper's Hatch. 1F 17
Nupton Dri. Barn 1E 15
Nuptown. 2B 20
Nuptown La. Nup 2B 20
Nursery Rd. Lou 4C 8
Nursery Rd. Sun 3A 22
Nurstead Chu. La. Meop 3C 26
Nurstead La. Long 3C 26
Nutfield. 4A 32
Nutfield Marsh Rd. Nutf 4F 31
Nutfield Rd. Mers 3F 31
Nutfield Rd. Red 4F 31
Nuxley Rd. Belv 1E 25

Oak Av. Hamp 3B 22
Oakcroft Rd. W Byf 1F 29
Oakdene Rd. Cobh 1B 30
Oakenden Rd. Ludd 4C 26
Oak End Way. Ger X 2E 13
Oaken La. Clay 4C 22
Oak Farm La. Fair 1C 34
Oakfield La. Dart 2F 25
Oakfield Rd. SE20 3B 24
Oakfield Rd. Croy 4A 24
Oak Hill. Wfd G 2C 16
Oak Hill. Wood S 4D 29
Oak Hill Rd. Stap A 1F 17
Oakhurst. 4A 34
Oakington Av. Wemb 3D 15
Oaklands La. Big H 1C 32
Oaklands La. Smal 1D 7
Oak La. Sev 3F 33
Oak La. St L 2C 4
Oaklawn Rd. Lea 2C 30
Oakleigh Park. 1F 15
Oakleigh Pk. N. N20 1F 15
Oakleigh Pk. S. N20 1F 15
Oakleigh Rd. N. N20 1F 15
Oakleigh Rd. S. N11 1F 15
Oakley Green. 1C 20
Oakley Grn. Rd. Oak G 1C 20
Oakley Rd. Brom 4D 25
Oakley Sq. NW1 4F 15
Oakley St. SW3 1F 23
Oakridge La. Ald 4C 6
Oak Rd. Cray H 2F 19
Oaks Rd. Croy 4B 24
Oaks Rd. Stai 2F 21
Oakthorpe Rd. N13 1A 16
Oakwood. 1A 16
Oakwood Av. Beck 3C 24
Oakwood Hill. Lou 1D 17
Oakwood Rd. Brick 3B 6
Oakwood Rd. Maid 3F 35
Oatlands Av. Wey 4A 22
Oatlands Chase. Wey 4A 22
Oatlands Dri. Slou 4D 13
Oatlands Dri. Wey 4A 22
Oatlands Park. 4A 22
Occam Rd. Guild 4D 29
Ockendon Rd. Upm & N Ock 3A 18
Ockham. 2A 30
Ockham La. Ock & Cob 2A 30
Ockham Rd. N. Ock & Lea 2A 30
Ockham Rd. S. E Hor 3A 30
Ockwells Rd. M'head 1B 20
Odiham Rd. Farnh 4A 28
Offham. 2C 34
Offham Rd. W Mal 2D 35
Offord Rd. N1 3A 16
Okehampton Cres. Well 1E 25
Old Bethnal Grn. Rd. E2 4B 16
Old Bexley. 2E 25
Old Bexley La. Bex & Dart 2F 25 (in two parts)
Old Bisley Rd. Frim 2B 28
Old Brentford. 1C 22
Old Brompton Rd. SW7 & SW5 1E 23
Oldbury. 2B 34
Oldbury La. Igh 2B 34
Old Chapel Rd. Swan 4F 25
Old Chatham Rd. Blue B 2F 35
Old Chatham Rd. S'lng 1F 35
Old Chertsey Rd. Chob 1E 29
Old Chu. Hill. Lang H 3D 19
Old Chu. La. NW9 3D 15
Old Chu. La. E Peck 3D 35
Old Chu. La. Mount 4C 10
Old Chu. La. Stan 1C 14
Old Chu. Rd. E4 1B 16
Old Chu. Rd. Burh 1E 35
Old Chu. Rd. E Han 3F 11
Old Chu. Rd. Mount 4C 10 (in three parts)
Oldchurch Rd. Romf 2F 17
Old Chu. Rd. Ton 3C 34
Old Coach Rd., The. Col G 1F 7
Old Coulsdon. 2A 32
Old Dover Rd. SE3 1C 24
Old Farley Rd. S Croy & Warl 1B 32
Oldfield La. N. Gnfd 4C 14
Oldfield La. S. Gnfd 4C 14
Oldfield Rd. M'head 4B 12
Oldfields Rd. Sutt 4E 23
Old Ford. 4B 16
Old Ford. (Junct.) 4B 16
Old Ford Rd. E3 & E2 4B 16
Old Gorhambury House. 2B 6
Old Harlow. 1E 9
Old Highway. Hod 1B 8
Old Hill. Chst 3D 25
Old Hill. Orp 1D 33
Oldhouse La. K Lan 4A 6
Old Isleworth. 1C 22
Old Kent Rd. SE15 & SE1 1A 24
Old La. Tats 2C 32
Old La. Wok & Cob 2A 30
Old Lodge La. Purl 1A 32
Old London Rd. Badg M 1E 33
Old London Rd. Eps 2E 31
Old London Rd. H'low 1E 9
Old London Rd. Knock 2E 33
Old London Rd. Mick 3C 30
Old London Rd. Raw 1F 19
Old London Rd. St Alb 2C 6
Old London Rd. Wro 2B 34
Old Loose Hill. Loose 4F 35
Old Maidstone Rd. Sidc 3E 25
Old Malden. 4D 23
Old Malden La. Wor Pk 4D 23
Old Marylebone Rd. W2 4F 15
Old Mill La. Uxb 4F 13
Old Mill Rd. Den 3F 13
Old Mill Rd. K Lan 3A 6
Old Nazeing Rd. Brox 2B 8
Old Oak Common. 4D 15
Old Oak Comn. La. W3 & NW10 4D 15
Old Oak La. NW10 4D 15
Old Oak Rd. W3 4D 15
Old Oxford Rd. Pid 1A 12
Old Oxted. 4C 32
Old Pk. Av. Enf 1A 16
Old Pk. Ridings. N21 1A 16
Old Portsmouth Rd. Art 4E 29
Old Rectory La. Den 3F 13
Old Rectory Rd. Ong 3F 9
Old Redding. Harr 1B 14
Old Reigate Rd. Bet 4D 31
Old Rd. Bkld 4D 31
Old Rd. Dart 2F 25
Old Rd. E Peck 4D 35
Old Rd. H'low 1E 9
Old Rd. Nave & Brtwd 4F 9
Old Rd. W'bury 3D 35
Old Rd. E. Grav 2C 26
Old Rd. W. Grav 2C 26
Old Roxwell Rd. Writ 2D 11
Old School La. Brock 4D 31
Old Soar Rd. Plax 3B 34
Old Southend Rd. H Grn 3F 11
Old Sta. Rd. Lou 1D 17
Old Street. (Junct.) 4A 16
Old St. EC1 4A 16
Old Terry's Lodge Rd. Sev 2A 34
Old Tilburstow Rd. S God 4B 32
Old Tovil Rd. Maid 3F 35
Old Town. SW4 2F 23
Old Town. Croy 4A 24
Old Tree La. Bou M 4F 35
Old Uxbridge Rd. Rick 1F 13
Old Watling St. Roch 3E 27
Old Windsor. 2E 21
Old Woking. 2E 29
Old Wokingham Rd. Wokgm & Crowt 4A 20
Old Woking Rd. Wok & W Byf 2F 29
Oliver Rd. E10 3B 16
Oliver Rd. Grays 1B 26
Oliver Way. Chelm 1D 11
Olleberrie La. Sarr 3F 5
Olympia. 1E 23
One Pin La. Farn C 3D 13
One Tree Hill. Stan H & Bas 3D 19
One Tree Hill Rd. Guild 4E 29
Ongar Hill. Add 1F 29
Ongar Rd. Abr 4E 9
Ongar Rd. Fyf 2A 10
Ongar Rd. Ing & Cook G 2C 10
Ongar Rd. Kel H & Brtwd 3A 10
Ongar Rd. Mar R 1B 10
Ongar Rd. Ston M 3A 10
Ongar Rd. Writ 2D 11
Onslow Sq. SW7 1F 23
Onslow St. Guild 4E 29
Onslow Village. 4D 29
Opladen Way. Brack 4A 20
Orange Hill Rd. Edgw 2D 15
Orange Tree Hill. Hav 1F 17
Orchard Av. Bill 4D 11
Orchard Av. Croy 4B 24
Orchard Gdns. Chess 4D 23
Orchard Leigh. 3E 5
Orchard Rd. Beac 1D 13
Orchard Rd. King T 3D 23
Orchard Way. Croy 4B 24
Ordnance Cres. SE10 1C 24
Ordnance Rd. Alder 4B 28
Ordnance Rd. Enf 4B 8
Organ Crossroads. (Junct.) 1E 31
Oriental Rd. Wok 2E 29
Orient Way. E10 3C 18
Orphanage Rd. Wat 4B 6
Orpington. 4E 25
Orpington By-Pass Rd. Orp & Bad M 1E 33
Orpington Rd. Chst 3D 25
Orsett. 4C 18
Orsett Heath. 4C 18
Orsett Rd. Grays 1B 26
Orsett Rd. Ors & Stan H 4C 18
Orwell Dri. Ayl 1A 4
Osborne La. Warf 3B 20
Osborne Rd. Wind 2D 21
Osidge. 1F 15
Osidge La. N20 1F 15
Ossulton Way. N2 2F 15
Osterley. 1C 22
Osterley Rd. Iswth 1C 22
Otford. 2F 33
Otford La. Hals 1E 33
Otford Rd. Sev 2F 33
Ottershaw. 1F 29
Otterspool Way. Wat 4B 6
Ottways La. Asht 2C 30
Outing's La. Dodd 4B 10
Outram Rd. Croy 4A 24
Outwood Comn. Rd. Bill 1D 19
Outwood Farm Rd. Bill 1D 19
Outwood La. Blet 4A 32
Outwood La. Red 4A 32
Outwood La. Tad & Coul 2E 31
Oval Cricket Ground, The. 1A 24
Oval Rd. N. Dag 4E 17
Ovenden Rd. Sund 2E 33
Overcliffe. Grav 2C 26
Overton Dri. E11 3C 16
Overy St. Dart 2A 26
Owletts. 3D 27
Owlsmoor. 1A 28
Owlsmoor Rd. Camb 1A 28
Oxenden Rd. Tong 4B 28
Oxenhoath Rd. Hdlw 4C 34
Oxestall's Rd. SE8 1B 24
Oxford Rd. Den & Uxb 3F 13
Oxford Rd. Ger X 2D 13
Oxford Rd. High W 1A 12
Oxford Rd. Mar 3A 12
Oxford Rd. Stok 1A 12
Oxford St. Lee C 2C 4
Oxford St. W1 4F 15
Oxford St. High W 1B 12
Oxgate La. NW2 3E 15
Oxhey. 1B 14
Oxhey Dri. N'wd & Wat 1B 14
Oxhey La. Wat & Pinn 1B 14
Oxhey Rd. Wat 1B 14
Oxlease. 1E 7
Oxlease Dri. Hat 2E 7
Oxlow La. Dag 3E 17
Oxshott. 1C 30
Oxshott Rd. Lea 2C 30
Oxted. 3C 32
Oxted Rd. God 4B 32
Oyster La. Byfl 1F 29

Pachesham Park. 2C 30
Packet Boat La. Uxb 4F 13
Packhorse La. Ridge 3D 7
Packhorse Rd. Ger X 2E 13
Paddenswick Rd. W12 1E 23
Paddington. 4F 15
Paddlesworth. 1D 35
Paddlesworth Rd. Snod 1D 35
Paddocks, The. Wemb 3D 15
Padham's Green. 4C 10
Padham's Grn. Rd. Ing 4C 10
Page Heath La. Brom 3C 24
Pages La. N10 2F 15
Page St. NW7 2E 15
Pagnell St. SE14 1B 24
Paines La. Pinn 2B 14
Pains Hill. 4C 32
Painshill. (Junct.) 1A 30
Pains Hill. Oxt 4C 32
Painters Rd. Ilf 2E 17
Palace Av. Maid 3F 35
Palace Gdns. Ter. W11 4E 15
Palace Ga. W8 1F 23
Palace Gates Rd. N22 2F 15
Palermo Rd. NW10 4E 15
Paley Street. 1B 20
Paley St. M'head 1B 20
Pall Mall. SW1 4F 15
Palmers Av. Grays 1C 26
Palmers Green. 1A 16
Palmers Hill. Epp 3E 9
Palmerston Rd. E17 2B 16
Palmerston Rd. N22 2A 16
Palmerston Rd. Buck H 1C 16
Pampisford Rd. Purl & S Croy 1A 32
Pancake La. Hem H 2A 6
Pancras Rd. NW1 4F 15
Pan La. E Han 3F 11
Panshanger Dri. Wel G 1E 7
Papercourt La. Rip 2F 29
Parade, The. Bour E 3B 12
Paradise Rd. Rich 2D 23
Parchmore Rd. T Hth 3A 24
Paringdon Rd. H'low 2D 9
Parish La. SE20 3B 24
Parish La. Farn C 3D 13
Park Av. N22 2A 16
Park Av. Bush 4B 6
Park Av. Chelm 2D 11
Park Av. Enf 1A 16
Park Av. S'hall 1B 22
Park Barn. 4D 29
Pk. Corner Rd. S'fleet 3B 26
Park Cres. W1 4F 15
Parker's Farm Rd. Ors 3C 18
Parker's Green. 4B 34
Parker's Hill. Asht 2D 31
Pk. Farm Rd. Upm 3A 18
Park Fields. Roch 3E 27
Parkfields. Wel G 1E 7
Parkgate Rd. SW11 1F 23
Parkgate Rd. Orp 4F 25
Parkgate Rd. Wall 4F 23
Pk. Hall Rd. SE21 2A 24
Park Hill. Cars 1F 31
Park Hill. Meop 3C 26
Pk. Hill Rd. NW3 3F 15
Parkhill Rd. Bex 2E 25
Pk. Hill Rd. Croy 4A 24
Parkhurst Rd. N7 3A 16
Parklands. Wal A 3C 8
Park La. W1 4F 15
Park La. Asht 2D 31
Park La. Beac 2D 13
Park La. Bou M 4F 35
Park La. Brox 2B 8
Park La. Cars 4F 23
Park La. Chesh 2A 8
Park La. Croy 4A 24
Park La. Guild 4F 29
Park La. Hare 2F 13
Park La. Hay 4A 14
Park La. Horn 2F 17
Park La. Houn 1B 22
Park La. L End 1A 12
Park La. Rams H 1E 19
Park La. Reig 4E 31
Park La. Sev 2A 34
Park La. Slou 3D 13
Park La. Wemb 3D 15
Park La. E. Reig 4E 31
Park La. Paradise. Chesh 2B 8
Park Langley. 3C 24
Parkpale La. Brock 4D 31
Park Pde. NW10 4D 15
Park Rd. N8 2F 15
Park Rd. N12 1F 15
Park Rd. N18 1B 16
Park Rd. NW8 4F 15
Park Rd. NW9 3E 15
Park Rd. SE25 3A 24
Park Rd. Alb 4A 30
Park Rd. Bans 2F 31
Park Rd. Brack 3B 20
Park Rd. Camb 2B 28
Park Rd. Che 3D 5
Park Rd. Chst 3D 25
Park Rd. Crow 4D 33
Park Rd. Dart 2A 26
Park Rd. E Peck 3D 35
Park Rd. Farn 3B 28
Park Rd. Hdlw 3C 34
Park Rd. Hamp H 3B 22
Park Rd. Hamp W 3C 22
Park Rd. Kenl 2A 32
Park Rd. King T 3D 23
Park Rd. Leyb 2D 35
Park Rd. Rad 4C 6
Park Rd. Rick 1A 14
Park Rd. Slou 4D 13
Park Rd. Stai 2F 21
Park Rd. Sun 3B 22
Park Rd. Tedd 3C 22
Park Rd. Tring 1C 4
Park Rd. Uxb 3A 14
Park Rd. Warl 1C 32
Park Rd. W Mal 2C 34
Park Royal. 4D 15
Park Royal Junction. (Junct.) 4D 15
Pk. Royal Rd. NW10 4D 15
Parkside. SW19 2E 23
Parkside. Mat T 1F 9 (off Rainbow Rd.)
Parkside Av. Bexh 1F 25
Parkside Av. Til 1C 26
Parkside Gdns. Barn 1F 15
Parkside Way. Harr 2B 14
Park Street. 2C 6
Park St. SW8 1A 24
Park St. W1 4F 15
Park St. Camb 1B 28
Park St. Coln 1F 21
Park St. St Alb 2C 6
Park St. La. Park 3B 6
Pk. View Rd. N17 2B 16
Pk. View Rd. Uxb 4A 14
Pk. View Rd. Well 2E 25
Parkway. NW1 4F 15
Parkway. Chelm 2E 11
Parkway. Guild 4E 29
Parkway. New Ad 1C 32
Park Way. Ruis 3B 14
Parkway. Wel G 1E 7
Parkway, The. Houn 1B 22
Parkway, The. S'hall & Hay 1B 22
Park Wood. 4F 35
Parlaunt Rd. Slou & Iver 1E 21
Parley Dri. Wok 2E 29
Parliament La. Burn 3C 12
Parnall Rd. H'low 1D 9
Parnell Rd. E3 4B 16 (in two parts)
Parrock Rd. Grav 2C 26
Parrock St. Grav 2C 26
Parrott's La. C'bry & Buck C 2C 4
Parsloe Rd. Epp G & H'low 2D 9
Parsloes Av. Dag 3E 17
Parslow's Hillock. 3A 4
Parsonage Green. 1E 11
Parsonage La. Enf 4A 8
Parsonage La. Marg 3D 11
Parsonage La. Sidc 3E 25
Parsonage La. Slou 3D 13
Parsonage La. Wind 1D 21
Parsonage Manorway. Belv 1E 25
Parsonage Rd. Egh 3E 21
Parsons Green. 1E 23
Parson's Grn. La. SW6 1E 23
Parsons La. Dart 2F 25
Parsons Mead. Croy 4A 24
Parson St. NW4 2E 15
Partridge Av. Chelm 1D 11
Partridge Green. 1D 11
Partridge Rd. H'low 1D 9
Parvilles. 1F 9
Parvis Rd. W Byf 1F 29
Paslow Wood Common. 3B 10
Passingford Bridge. 4F 9
Passmores. 1D 9
Pastures, The. High W 1A 12
Patchetts Green. 4C 6
Patching Hall La. Chelm 1D 11
Paternoster Hill. Wal A 3C 8
Patmos Rd. SW9 1A 24
Pattens La. Roch 4F 27
Pauls Hill. Penn 1C 12
Paul St. EC1 4A 16
Pawsons Rd. Croy 4A 24
Peach St. Wokgm 3A 20
Peacock La. Wokgm & Brack 4A 20
Peakes La. Chesh 3A 8
Peakes Way. Chesh 3A 8
Pea La. Upm 3B 18
Peartree. 1E 7
Peartree Green. 4B 10
Peartree La. Dan 3F 11
Pear Tree La. H'std 4F 27
Peartree La. Shorne & High 3D 27
Peartree La. Wel G 1E 7
Peasbody Rd. Farn 3B 28
Peascod St. Wind 1D 21
Peascroft Rd. Hem H 2A 6
Pease Hill. As 1B 34
Pebble Hill Rd. Bet 4D 31
Peckham. 1B 24
Peckham Bush. 4C 34
Peckham High St. SE15 1B 24
Peckham Hill St. SE15 1B 24
Peckham Hurst Rd. W Peck 3C 34
Peckham Pk. Rd. SE15 1B 24
Peckham Rd. SE15 & SE5 1A 24
Peckham Rye. SE22 & SE2 2B 24 (in two parts)
Peck's Hill. Naze 2C 8
Pedlars End. 2F 9
Pednor Bottom. Chart 3C 4
Pednormead End. 3D 5
Pednor Rd. Che 3C 4
Peeble Hill. Lea 4A 30
Peens La. Bou M 4F 35
Pegmire La. Ald 4C 6
Pegs La. Hert 1A 8
Pelham Rd. Grav 2C 26
Pelham Rd. S. Grav 2C 26
Pelham St. SW7 1F 23
Pells La. W King 1B 34
Pembridge La. Brox 2A 8
Pembridge Rd. W11 4E 15
Pembridge Vs. W2 & W11 4E 15
Pembroke B'way. Camb 1B 28
Pembroke Rd. W14 1E 23
Pembroke Rd. Chat 3F 27
Pembroke Rd. Eri 1F 25
Pembroke Rd. Ruis 3A 14
Pembroke Rd. Sev 3F 33
Pembroke Rd. Wemb 3C 14
Pembury Rd. E8 3B 16
Pendell Rd. Blet 4A 32
Pendleton Rd. Reig 4F 31
Penenden Heath. 2F 35
Penenden Heath Rd. Maid 2F 35
Penfold La. Holm G & L Mis 4C 4
Penge. 3B 24
Penge Rd. SE20 & SE2 3B 24
Penhill Rd. Bex 2E 25
Penn. 1C 12
Penn Bottom. Penn 1C 12
Penn Rd. Beac 1C 12
Penn Rd. Hasl 1B 12
Penn Rd. Knot 1C 12
Penn St. 4C 4
Penn St. Amer 1C 12
Penny Pot. 1D 29
Pennypot La. Chob 1D 29
Penny Royal Rd. Dan 2F 11
Penrhyn Rd. King T 3D 23
Penton St. N1 4A 16
Pentonville Rd. N1 4A 16
Penwith Rd. SW18 2E 23
Pepper Hill. Gt Amw 1B 8
Pepper's Green. 1C 10
Pepys Rd. SE14 1B 24
Percival St. EC1 4A 16
Percy Rd. N21 1A 16
Percy Rd. Hamp 3B 22
Percy Rd. Twic 2C 22
Perivale. 4C 14
Perks La. P'wd 4B 4
Perry Hall Rd. Orp 4D 25
Perry Hill. SE23 2B 24
Perry Hill. Cli 2F 27
Perry Hill. Worp 3D 29
Perry Ri. SE23 2B 24
Perrys La. Prat B 1E 33
Perry Street. 2C 26
Perry St. Bill 1D 19
Perry St. Chst 3D 25
Perry St. Dart 2F 25
Perry St. N'fleet 2C 26
Perry Va. SE23 2B 24
Perth Rd. N22 2A 16
Perth Rd. Ilf 2D 17
Pested Bars Rd. Bou M 3F 35
Peterborough Rd. Harr 3C 14
Peterley. Gt Miss 4B 4
Petersfield Av. Romf 2A 18
Petersham. 2D 23
Petersham Rd. Rich 2C 22
Peters La. Mon R 3A 4
Petherton Rd. N5 3A 16
Pettings. 1B 34
Pettits La. Dodd 4B 10
Pettits La. Romf 2F 17
Pettits La. N. Romf 2F 17
Pettman Cres. SE28 1D 25
Pett's Hill. N'holt 3B 14
Petts Wood. 4D 25
Petts Wood Rd. Orp 4D 25
Pheasant Hill. Chal G 1E 13
Pheasant La. Maid 3F 35
Philanthropic Rd. Red 4F 31
Philip La. N15 2A 16
Philpot La. Chob 1E 29
Philpots La. Leigh 4F 33
Phipps Hatch La. Enf 4A 8

Picardy Manorway—Roxeth Hill

Picardy Manorway. Belv 1E 25
Picardy Rd. Belv 1E 25
Picardy St. Belv 1E 25
Piccadilly. W1 4F 15
Piccotts End. 1F 5
Piccotts End. Hem H 1F 5
Piccotts End Rd. Hem H 1F 5
Pickford La. Bexh 1E 25
Pickhurst La. W Wick & Brom 4C 24
Pield Heath Rd. Uxb 4A 14
Pierce Mill Rd. Hdlw 4C 34
Piercing Hill. They B 4D 9
Pier Rd. E16 1D 25
Pier Rd. Gill 3F 27
Pigeonhouse La. Wink 2C 20
Piggott's Hill. N Dean 4A 4
Pigstye Green. 2B 10
Pigstye Grn. Rd. Will 2B 10
Pikefish La. Pad W & Ladd 4D 35
Pike La. Upm 3A 18
Pikey La. E Mal 2D 35
Pilgrims Hatch. 1B 18
Pilgrims La. N Stif 4B 18
Pilgrims La. T'sey & W'ham 3C 32
Pilgrims Way. Ayle 1E 35
Pilgrims Way. Boxl 2F 35
Pilgrims Way. Cux 1D 35
Pilgrims Way. Guild 4E 29
Pilgrims Way. Sev 2B 34
Pilgrims Way. Sund & Sev 2A 34
Pilgrims Way. Tros 1C 34
Pilgrims Way. W'ham & Sev 3D 33
Pilgrims Way E. Otf 2F 33
Pilgrims Way W. Sev & Otf 2F 33
Pillar Box Rd. Sev 2A 34
Pimlico. 2A 6 (Bedmond)
Pimlico. 1F 23 (Westminster)
Pimlico Rd. SW1 1F 23
Pinesfield La. Tros 1C 34
Pines Rd. Brom 3D 25
Pine Tree La. Ivy H 3B 34
Pinewood Rd. Iver 3E 13
Pinkham Way. N11 2F 15
Pink Hill. Par H 3A 4
Pink La. Burn 4C 12
Pinkneys Dri. M'head 4A 12
Pinkneys Green. 4A 12
Pinkneys Rd. M'head 4B 12
Pink Rd. Lac G 3A 4
Pinnacles. 1D 9
Pinner. 2B 14
Pinner Green. 2B 14
Pinner Grn. Pinn 2B 14
Pinner Hill Rd. Pinn 2B 14
Pinner Rd. Harr 2B 14
Pinner Rd. N'wd 2A 14
Pinner Rd. Pinn 2B 14
Pinner Rd. Wat 1B 14
Pinner Vw. Harr 2C 14
Pinnerwood Park. 2B 14
Piper's Hill. Gt Gad 1F 5
Pipers La. Gt Kin 4B 4
Pipers La. Hpdn 1C 6
Pipps Hill. 2D 19
Pipps Hill Rd. N. Cray H 2E 19
Pirbright. 2D 29
Pirbright Camp. 2C 28
Pirbright Grn. Wok 3D 29
Pirbright Rd. Norm 4C 28
Pitch Place. 3D 29
Pitfield St. EC1 4A 16
Pitsea. 3E 19
Pitsea Hall La. Pits 3E 19
Pitsea Rd. Pits 2E 19
Pitshanger La. W5 4C 14
Pittswood. 4B 34
Pix Farm La. Hem H 2E 5
Pixham. 4C 30
Pixham La. Dork 4C 30
Pizien Well. 3D 35
Pizien Well Rd. W'bury 3D 35
Place Farm La. Dodd 4B 10
Place Farm Rd. Blet 4A 32
Placehouse La. Coul 2A 32
Plain, The. Epp 3E 9
Plaistow. 3C 24 (Bromley)
Plaistow. 4C 16 (West Ham)
Plaistow La. Brom 3C 24 (in two parts)
Plaistow Rd. E15 4C 16
Plantagenet Rd. Barn 4F 7
Plantation Rd. Amer 4D 5
Plantation Rd. Bore 1F 11
Plashet. 3C 16
Plashet Gro. E13 4C 16
Plashet Rd. E13 4C 16
Platt Ho. La. Fair 1C 34
Platts La. NW3 3E 15
Plaxdale Grn. Rd. Stans 1B 34
Plaxtol. 3B 34
Plaxtol La. Plax 3B 34
Pleasure Pit Rd. Asht 2D 31
Plevna Rd. N9 1B 16
Plomer Grn. La. D'ley 1A 12
Plomer Hill. High W 1A 12
Plough Hill. Cuff 3A 8
Plough Hill. Igh 3B 34
Plough La. SW17 & SW1 3F 23
Plough La. D'side 2B 30
Plough La. Purl 1A 32
Plough La. Sarr 3F 5
Plough La. Stoke P 4A 12
Plough La. Wall 4A 24
Plough La. Wokgm 3A 20
Plough Rd. SW11 2F 23
Plough Way. SE16 1B 24
Ployters Rd. H'low 2D 9
Plug La. Meop 4C 26
Plumstead. 1D 25
Plumstead Common. 1D 25
Plumstead Comn. Rd. SE18 1D 25
Plumstead High St. SE18 1D 25
Plumstead Rd. SE18 1D 25
Pococks La. Eton 1D 21
Pointers Green. 2A 30
Polehanger La. Hem H 1F 5
Pole Hill Rd. Uxb 4A 14
Polesden Lacey. 3B 30
Polesden La. Wok 3F 29
Poles Hill. Sarr 3F 5
Polesteeple Hill. Big H 2C 32
Polhill. Hals 2F 33
Polish War Memorial. (Junct.) 3B 14
Pollard Rd. N20 1F 15
Pollards Wood Hill. Oxt 3C 32
Pollards Wood Rd. Oxt 4C 32
Polsted La. Comp 4D 29
Pomeroy St. SE15 1B 24
Pond App. Holm G 4C 4
Ponders End. 1B 16
Pondfield La. Brtwd 1B 18
Pond La. Ivy H 3A 34
Pond Park. 3D 5
Pond Pk. Rd. Che 3D 5
Ponds Rd. Chelm 3E 11
Pond St. NW3 3F 15
Pondtail. 3A 28
Pont St. SW3 1F 23
Poole St. N1 4A 16
Pooley Green. 3F 21
Pooley Grn. Rd. Egh 3E 21
Pool Rd. W Mol 4B 22
Pootings. 4D 33
Pootings Rd. Four E 4D 33
Popes La. W5 1C 22
Popes La. Cook 3B 12
Popes La. Oxt 4C 32
Popeswood. 3A 20
Popeswood Rd. Binf 3A 20
Poplar. 4B 16
Poplar High St. E14 4B 16
Poplar Way. Felt 2B 22
Porchester Rd. W2 4E 15
Porlock Av. Harr 3C 14
Porters Av. Dag 3E 17
Porters Way. W Dray 1A 22
Port Hill. Hert 1A 8
Port Hill. Prat B 1E 33
Portland Pl. W1 4F 15
Portland Rd. SE25 3B 24
Portman Sq. W1 4F 15
Portnalls Rd. Coul 2F 31
Portsmouth Rd. Esh 1B 30
Portsmouth Rd. Frim & Camb 2B 28
Portsmouth Rd. Guild 4E 29
Portsmouth Rd. King T 3C 22
Portsmouth Rd. Rip & Cobh 2F 29
Portsmouth Rd. Th Dit & Surb 4C 22
Portsmouth Rd. Wok 3F 29
Portway. E15 4C 16
Potash La. Platt 2C 34
Potash Rd. Bill 4D 11
Potash Rd. Mat G 1F 9
Potkiln La. Jor 2D 13
Potley Hill Rd. Yat 1A 28
Potten End. 1F 5
Potten End Hill. Wat E 1F 5
Potter Row. Gt Miss 3B 4
Potters Bar. 3E 7
Potters Crouch. 2B 6
Potterscrouch La. Pot C 2B 6
Potters La. Borwd 4D 7
Potters La. Send 3E 29
Potter's Rd. Barn 4E 7
Potter Street. 1E 9
Potter St. H'low 1E 9
Potter St. N'wd & Pinn 2B 14
Pouchen End. 2F 5
Pouchen End La. Hem H 2F 5
Pound Farm La. Ash 4C 28
Pound La. NW10 3E 15
Pound La. Eps 1D 31
Pound La. Knock 2E 33
Pound La. Pits & N Ben 2F 19
Pound La. W'sham 1C 28
Pound Rd. E Peck 4D 35
Pound St. Cars 4F 23
Pound St. Wen 2B 4
Pound, The. Cook 3B 12
Poverest. 4E 25
Poverest Rd. Orp 4D 25
Powder Mill La. Twic 2B 22
Powder Mills. 4A 34
Powerscroft Rd. E5 3B 16
Powys La. N14 & N13 1A 16
Poyle. 1F 21
Poyle La. Burn 4C 12
Poyle Rd. Coln 2F 21
Poyle Rd. Tong 4B 28
Poynders Rd. SW4 2F 23
Praed St. W2 4F 15
Pratling Street. 2E 35
Pratling St. Ayle 2E 35
Pratt's Bottom. 1E 33
Pratt's Bottom. (Junct.) 1E 33
Pratts Farm La. L Walt 1E 11 (in two parts)
Pratt St. NW1 4F 15
Prebendal Av. Ayl 1A 4
Prebend St. N1 4A 16
Preston. 3D 15
Preston Hill. Harr 3D 15
Preston La. Tad 2E 31
Preston Rd. Harr & Wemb 3D 15
Prestons Rd. Brom 4C 24
Prestwick Rd. Wat 1B 14
Prestwood. 3B 4
Pretoria Rd. N18 & N17 2A 16
Pretoria Rd. N. N18 2A 16
Prey Heath Rd. Wok 3E 29
Prices La. Reig 4E 31
Priestfield. Roch 4E 27
Priest Hill. Egh & Wind 2E 21
Priestley Rd. Sur R 4D 29
Priests Bri. SW15 & SW1 2D 23
Priests La. Brtwd 1B 18
Priestwood. 3B 20 (Bracknell)
Priestwood. 4C 26 (Meopham Green)
Priestwood Green. 4C 26
Priestwood Rd. Meop 1C 34
Primrose Hill. 4F 15
Primrose Hill. Wid E 4B 4
Primrose Hill. K Lan 3A 6
Primrose Hill Rd. NW3 3F 15
Prince Albert Rd. NW1 & NW8 4F 15
Prince Arthur Rd. Gill 3F 27
Prince Charles Av. Chat 1F 35
Prince Charles Av. Ors 4C 18
Prince Charles Rd. SE3 1C 24
Prince George Av. N14 1F 15
Prince Imperial Rd. Chst 3D 25
Prince of Wales Dri. SW11 1F 23
Prince of Wales Rd. NW3 3F 15
Prince of Wales Rd. SE3 1C 24
Prince of Wales Rd. Out 4A 32
Prince Regent La. E16 & E13 4C 16
Prince's Av. Alder 3B 28
Princes Av. Chat 1F 35
Princes Park. 1F 35
Princes Risborough. 3A 4
Prince's Rd. Brtwd 4A 10
Princes Rd. Chelm 2E 11
Princes Rd. Dart 2F 25
Princes Road Interchange. (Junct.) 2A 26
Princess Margaret Rd. Linf & E Til 1D 27
Princess Way. Red 4F 31
Printinghouse La. Hay 1A 22
Prior Rd. Camb 1B 28
Priorsfield Rd. Comp 4D 29
Priory La. SW15 2D 23
Priory La. Warf 3B 20
Priory Rd. N8 2F 15
Priory Rd. NW6 4E 15
Priory Rd. Burn 4C 12
Priory Rd. Roch 3E 27
Priory Rd. S'dale 3B 20
Priory Rd. Sutt 4E 23
Pritchard's Rd. E2 4B 16
Prospect Av. Farn 2B 28
Prospect Hill. E17 2B 16
Prospect Rd. Ash V 3B 28
Prospect Rd. Farn 3B 28
Prospect Rd. St Alb 2C 6
Prune Hill. Egh 3E 21
Pudding La. Chig 1D 17
Puddledock. 4E 33
Puddledock La. Dart 3F 25
Puddledock La. W'ham 4D 33
Pudds Cross. 3E 5
Pumpkin Hill. Slou 3D 13
Pump La. Hay 1B 22
Pump La. Spri 1E 11
Pump La. N. Mar 2A 12
Pump St. Horn H 4D 19
Punchbowl La. Dork 4C 30
Punch Bowl La. Hem H & St Alb 1A 6
Purfleet. 1A 26
Purfleet By-Pass. Purf 1A 26
Purfleet Rd. Ave 1A 26
Purley. 1A 32
Purley Cross. (Junct.) 1A 32
Purley Downs Rd. Purl & S Croy 1A 32
Purley Way. Croy & Kenl 4A 24
Pursley Rd. NW7 2E 15
Purton La. Farn R 3D 13
Putney. 2E 23
Putney Bri. SW6 & SW15 2E 23
Putney Bri. Rd. SW18 & SW1 2E 23
Putney Heath. 2E 23
Putney Heath. SW15 2E 23
Putney High St. SW15 2E 23
Putney Hill. SW15 2E 23
Puttenden Rd. S'brne 4B 34
Puttenham. 4C 28
Puttenham Heath Rd. Putt 4C 28
Puttenham Hill. Putt 4C 28
Puttenham Rd. Seale 4B 28
Pye Corner. 1D 9
Pyenest Rd. H'low 1D 9
Pyestock. 3A 28
Pyle Hill. 3E 29
Pynest Grn. La. Wal A 4C 8
Pyrcroft Rd. Cher 4F 21
Pyrford. 2F 29
Pyrford Comn. Rd. Wok 2F 29
Pyrford Green. 2F 29
Pyrford Rd. W Byf & Wok 1F 29
Pyrford Village. 2F 29
Pyrles La. Lou 4D 9

Quadrant, The. Rich 2D 23
Quaker La. Wal A 3C 8
Quakers Hall La. Sev 2F 33
Quarries, The. Bou M 4F 35
Quarry Hill Rd. Bor G 2B 34
Quarry St. Guild 4E 29
Quarry Wood Rd. Mar & Cook D 3A 12
Queen Alexandra Rd. High W 1B 12
Queen Anne Av. Brom 3C 24
Queen Elizabeth Rd. King T 3D 23
Queen's Av. N10 2F 15
Queen's Av. Alder 4B 28
Queen's Av. Wat 1A 14
Queensbridge Rd. E2 & E8 3A 16
Queensbury. 2D 15
Queen's Club. 1E 23 (Tennis)
Queens Dri. W5 4D 15
Queens Farm Rd. Shorne 2D 27
Queens Ga. SW7 1F 23
Queens Mead Rd. Brom 3C 24
Queens Pk. Av. Bill 4D 11
Queens Pk. Rangers F.C. 4E 15
Queen's Pk. 4D 11
Queens Ride. SW15 & SW1 2E 23
Queens Rd. E17 2B 16
Queens Rd. NW4 2E 15
Queens Rd. SE14 & SE1 1B 24
Queens Rd. SW19 3E 23
Queen's Rd. Alder 4A 28
Queens Rd. Bisl 2D 29
Queens Rd. Brtwd 1B 18
Queens Rd. Buck H 1C 16
Queens Rd. Croy 4A 24
Queen's Rd. Dat 1E 21
Queens Rd. Eri 1F 25
Queen's Rd. Farn 3B 28
Queen's Rd. King T 3D 23
Queen's Rd. Maid 3E 35
Queen's Rd. Rich 2D 23
Queen's Rd. Tedd 3C 22
Queen's Rd. Wat 4B 6
Queens Rd. Wey & W on T 4A 22
Queenstown Rd. SW8 1F 23
Queen St. Gom 4A 30
Queen St. M'head 4B 12
Queensway. W2 4E 15
Queensway. Hat 1E 7
Queensway. Hem H 2F 5
Queensway. Orp 4D 25
Queen Victoria. (Junct.) 4E 23
Queen Victoria St. EC4 4A 16
Quex Rd. NW6 4E 15
Quickley La. Rick 1F 13
Quickmoor La. K Lan 3F 5
Quinta Dri. Barn 1E 15

Rabbit's Cross. 4F 35
Rabbits Rd. S Dar 3A 26
Rabies Heath Rd. Blet 4A 32
Rabley. 3D 7
Rackstraw Rd. Camb 1A 28
Radford Way. Bill 1D 19
Radlett. 3C 6
Radlett La. Shenl 3C 6
Radlett Rd. Ald 4B 6
Radlett Rd. Frog 3C 6
Radlett Rd. Wat 4B 6
Radley Green. 2C 10
Radley Grn. Rd. Rox 2B 10
Radwater Av. W'fd 1F 19
Raeburn Av. Surb 4D 23
RAF Halton Airfield. 1B 4
RAF Northolt Airfield. 3A 14
Ragged Hall La. St Alb 2B 6
Rag Hill Rd. Tats 2C 32
Raglan Rd. Reig 4E 31
Ragmans La. Mar 2A 12
Rags La. Chesh 3A 8
Ragstone Rd. Slou 1D 21
Raikes La. Ab H 4B 30
Railton Rd. SW2 2A 24
Railway App. Cher 4F 21
Railway App. Harr 2C 14
Railway St. Chat 4F 27
Railway St. Gill 3F 27
Railway Ter. K Lan 3A 6
Rainbow La. Stan H 4D 19
Rainbow Rd. Chaf H 1B 26
Rainham. 4F 17
Rainham Rd. Gill 4F 27
Rainham Rd. Horn & Rain 3F 17
Rainham Rd. N. Dag 3F 17
Rainham Rd. S. Dag 3F 17
Rainsford La. Chelm 2D 11
Rainsford Rd. Chelm 2D 11
Ralph's Ride. Brack 3B 20
Ramsden. 4E 25
Ramsden Bellhouse. 1E 19
Ramsden Heath. 1E 19
Ramsden Pk. Rd. Bill 1E 19
Ram St. SW18 2E 23
Rances La. Wokgm 3A 20
Rancliffe Rd. E6 4D 17
Randalls Rd. Lea 2C 30
Randles La. Sev 2E 33
Ranger's Rd. E4 & Lou 1C 16
Ranmore Common. 4C 30
Ranmore Comn. Rd. Westh 4B 30
Ranmore Rd. Dork 4C 30
Ratcliffe Highway. Chatt 2F 27
Ravensbourne Pk. SE6 2B 24
Ravenscourt Gro. Horn 3A 18
Ravens La. Berk 2E 5
Ravensworth Rd. W Wick 4C 24
Rawlings La. Seer 1D 13
Rawreth. 1F 19
Rawreth La. Raw 1F 19
Rawreth Shot. 1F 19
Rayleigh Rd. Hut 1B 18
Rayley La. N Wea 2E 9
Ray Mead Rd. M'head 4C 12
Ray Mill Rd. E. M'head 4B 12
Ray Mill Rd. W. M'head 4B 12
Raymouth Rd. SE16 1B 24
Rayners Lane. 3B 14
Rayners La. Pinn 2B 14
Raynes Park. 3E 23
Ray Pk. Av. M'head 4B 12
Ray Pk. Rd. M'head 4B 12
Ray's Hill. Braz E 2C 4
Rays Hill. Hort K 3A 26
Ray St. M'head 4B 12
Reading Rd. Farn 3B 28
Reading Rd. Yat 1A 28
Reading Rd. S. Fleet 3A 28
Rectory Hill. Amer 4D 5
Rectory La. SW17 3F 23
Rectory La. Asht 2D 31
Rectory La. Bans 2F 31
Rectory La. Barm 3E 35
Rectory La. Bookh 3B 30
Rectory La. Brack 4B 20
Rectory La. Bras 3E 33
Rectory La. Byfl 1A 30
Rectory La. Chelm 2E 11
Rectory La. Igh 2B 34
Rectory La. K Lan 3A 6
Rectory La. Lou 4D 9
Rectory La. Shenl 3D 7
Rectory La. Sidc 3E 25
Rectory La. Surb 4C 22
Rectory La. W'ham 3D 33
Rectory Pk. S Croy 1A 32
Rectory Rd. N16 3A 16
Rectory Rd. As 4B 26
Rectory Rd. Beck 3B 24
Rectory Rd. Cli 2E 27
Rectory Rd. Coul 3F 31
Rectory Rd. Farn 3B 28
Rectory Rd. Grays 1C 26
Rectory Rd. L Bur 2D 19
Rectory Rd. Ors 4C 18
Rectory Rd. Pits 2F 19 (in three parts)
Rectory Rd. Rick 1F 13
Rectory Rd. Tap 4C 12
Rectory Rd. W Til 1C 26
Rectory Rd. Wokgm 3A 20
Redan Rd. Alder 4B 28
Redbourn. 1B 6
Redbourn La. Hpdn 1B 6
Redbourn Rd. Hem H 1A 6
Redbourn Rd. St Alb 1B 6
Redbridge. 2D 17
Redbridge La. E. Ilf 2D 17
Redbridge La. W. E11 2C 16
Redbridge Roundabout. (Junct.) 2C 16
Redcliffe Gdns. SW5 1E 23
Rede Ct. Rd. Strood 3E 27
Redhall La. Chan X 4A 6
Redhill. 4F 31 (Reigate)
Red Hill. 3D 35 (Wateringbury)
Red Hill. Chst 3D 25
Red Hill. W'bury 3D 35
Redhill Aerodrome. 4A 32
Redhill Rd. New Ash 4B 26
Redland End. 1C 4
Red La. Clay 1C 30
Red La. Oxt 4C 32
Red Lion La. SE18 1D 25
Red Lion La. Sarr 4F 5
Red Lion Rd. Chob 1D 29
Red Lion Rd. Surb 4D 23
Red Lion Sq. WC1 4A 16
Red Lion St. Che 3D 5
Red Lion St. Rich 2C 22
Red Lodge Rd. W Wick 4C 24
Redmans La. Sev 1F 33
Red Post Hill. SE24 2A 24
Redricks La. E'wck 1D 9
Redriff Rd. SE16 1B 24
Red Rd. Light 1C 28
Red Rover. (Junct.) 2D 23
Redstone Hill. Red 4F 31
Redstone Hollow. Red 4F 31
Red St. S'fleet 3B 26
Redvers. Alder 3B 28
Redwall La. Hunt & Lint 4E 35
Redwell La. Igh 3B 34
Reede Rd. Dag 3E 17
Reed's Hill. Brack 4B 20
Reeds La. S'brne 3B 34
Reed St. Cli 1E 27
Reeves La. Roy 2C 8
Regent's Park. 4F 15
Regent's Pk. Rd. NW3 4F 15
Regents Pk. Rd. NW11 2E 15
Regent St. SW1 & W1 4F 15
Regina Rd. S'hall 1B 22
Reigate. 4E 31
Reigate Av. Sutt 4E 23
Reigate Hill. Reig 4E 31
Reigate Hill Interchange. (Junct.) 3E 31
Reigate Rd. Dork & Bet 4C 30
Reigate Rd. Eps & Tad 1E 31
Reigate Rd. Lea 3C 30
Reigate Rd. Reig & Red 4F 31
Renfree Rd. Shep 4A 22
Renwick Rd. Bark 4E 17
Replingham Rd. SW18 2E 23
Repository Rd. SE18 1D 25
Reservoir Rd. Lou 4C 8
Rettendon. 4F 11
Rettendon Rd. E Han 3F 11
Rhodeswell Rd. E1 4B 16
Richings Park. 1F 21
Richings Way. Iver 1F 21
Richmond. 2C 22
Richmond Bri. Twic & Rich 2C 22
Richmond Circus. (Junct.) 2D 23
Richmond Hill. Rich 2D 23
Richmond Rd. E8 3A 16
Richmond Rd. Gill 3F 27
Richmond Rd. Iswth 2C 22
Richmond Rd. King T 3C 22
Richmond Rd. Twic 2C 22
Ricketts Hill Rd. Tats 2C 32
Rickford. Guild 3D 29
Rickmansworth. 1F 13
Rickmansworth La. Chal P 2E 13
Rickmansworth Rd. Amer 4D 5
Rickmansworth Rd. Chor 4F 5
Rickmansworth Rd. Hare 2F 13
Rickmansworth Rd. N'wd 1A 14
Rickmansworth Rd. Pinn 2B 14
Rickmansworth Rd. Wat 4A 6
Riddlesdown. 1A 32
Riddlesdown Rd. Purl 1A 32
Ridge. 3D 7
Ridge Av. N21 1A 16
Ridge La. Wat 4A 6
Ridgemead Rd. Egh 2E 21
Ridge Rd. N21 1A 16
Ridge Rd. Sutt 4E 23
Ridge, The. L Bad 2F 11
Ridge, The. Wold & Warl 3B 32
Ridgeway. High W 1B 12
Ridgeway. Wel G 1E 7
Ridgeway Rd. Iswth 1C 22
Ridgeway, The. E4 1B 16
Ridgeway, The. NW7 1E 15
Ridgeway, The. Chat 4F 27
Ridgeway, The. Cuff 3F 7
Ridgeway, The. Enf 4A 8
Ridgeway, The. Lea 3C 30
Ridgeway, The. N Har 2B 14
Ridgeway, The. Pot B & Enf 4F 7
Ridgeway, The. Shorne 3D 27
Ridgeway, The. St Alb 1C 6
Ridgeway, The. Tonb 4B 34
Ridgway. 2F 29
Ridgway. SW19 3E 23
Riding Ct. Rd. Dat 1E 21
Riding La. Hild 4A 34
Ridlands La. Oxt 3C 32
Ridley. 1B 34
Riefield Rd. SE9 2D 25
Riffhams Chase. L Bad 2F 11
Riffhams La. Dan 2F 11
Rignall Rd. Gt Miss 3B 4
Rignals La. Chelm 3E 11
Ringlestone. 2F 35
Ringmead. Brack 4A 20
Rings Hill. Hild 4A 34
Ring, The. Brack 3B 20
Ripley. 2F 29
Ripley By-Pass. Rip 3F 29
Ripley La. Wok & Lea 3A 30
Ripley Rd. Send & Guild 3F 29
Ripley Springs. 3E 21
Ripon Way. Borwd 1D 15
Ripple Rd. Bark & Dag 4D 17
Ripple Road Junction. (Junct.) 4E 17
Risborough Rd. Stoke M 1A 4
Rise Park. 2F 17
Rise Rd. Asc 4D 21
Rise, The. Gnfd & Wemb 3C 14
River Bank. E Mol 3C 22
Riverhead. 2F 33
River Hill. Sev 3A 34
River Rd. Bark 4D 17
Riverside. Eyns 4F 25
Riverside Dri. Rich 2C 22
Riverside Dri. Rick 1F 13
Riverside Rd. Stanw 2F 21
Riverside Wlk. Iswth 2C 22
Riverside Way. Camb 2B 28
River Vw. Grays 1C 26
Riverview Park. 3D 27
Roberts La. Chal P 1E 13
Robert St. NW1 4F 15
Robert Way. W'fd 1F 19
Robin Hood. (Junct.) 2D 23
Robin Hood La. Sut G 3E 29
Robin Hood La. W'slde 1F 35
Robin Hood Rd. Wok 2D 29
Robin Hood Way. SW20 & SW1 2D 23
Robins Nest Hill. L Berk 1F 7
Robinsway. W on T 4B 22
Robson Av. NW10 4E 15
Robson Rd. SE27 2A 24
Rocfort Rd. Snod 1E 35
Rochester. 3F 27
Rochester Airport. 4F 27
Rochester Av. Brom 3C 24
Rochester Castle. 3E 27
Rochester Rd. Ayle 2E 35
Rochester Rd. Burh 1E 35
Rochester Rd. Cux 4E 27 (in two parts)
Rochester Rd. Grav 2D 27
Rochester Rd. Roch & Chat 4F 27
Rochester Rd. Woul 4E 27
Rochester Row. SW1 1F 23
Rochester Way. SE9 & SE3 2C 24
Rochester Way. Dart 2F 25
Rochester Way Relief Rd. SE9 & SE3 1C 24
Rock Av. Gill 4F 27
Rockfield Rd. Oxt 3C 32
Rock Hill. Orp 1E 33
Rockingham Rd. Uxb 4F 13
Rock Rd. Bor G 2B 34
Rockshaw Rd. Red 3F 31
Rocks La. SW13 2E 23
Rocks Rd., The. E Mal 2E 35
Rocky La. Reig 3F 31
Rodborough Rd. NW11 3E 15
Roding La. Buck H & Chig 1D 17
Roding La. N. Wfd G 2D 17
Roding La. S. Ilf & Wfd G 2C 16
Roding Rd. Lou 1D 17
Rodney Rd. SE17 1A 24
Roe Green. 1E 7 (Hatfield)
Roe Green. 2D 15 (Hendon)
Roe Grn. NW9 2D 15
Roehampton. 2E 23
Roehampton High St. SW15 2E 23
Roehampton Lane. (Junct.) 2E 23
Roehampton La. SW15 2E 23
Roehampton Va. SW15 2D 23
Roehyde Way. Hat 2D 7
Roestock La. Col H 2D 7
Roffe's La. Cat 3A 32
Rogers La. Stoke P 3D 13
Rogers Wood La. Fawk 4B 26
Rokesly Av. N8 2A 16
Rolls Rd. SE1 1A 24
Roman Rd. E3 & E2 4B 16
Roman Rd. Mount 4C 10
Roman Villa Rd. Dart 3A 26
Roman Way. Croy 4A 24
Romford. 2F 17
Romford Rd. E12 & E15 3C 16
Romford Rd. Ave 4A 18
Romford Rd. Chig 1E 17
Romford Rd. Ong 3A 10
Romford Rd. Romf 2E 17
Romney Rd. SE10 1C 24
Romney Street. 1A 34
Romney St. Knat 1A 34
Rom Valley Way. Romf 3F 17
Ron Leighton Way. E6 4D 17
Roodlands La. Four E 4E 33
Rookery Hill. Corr 4E 19
Rookery Rd. B'more 3B 10
Rookery Rd. Orp 1D 33
Rookery, The. 1B 14
Rook La. Cat 3A 32
Roothill Rd. Bet 4D 31
Roper's La. H Hals 2F 27
Rosebay Av. Bill 4D 11
Rosebery Av. EC1 4A 16
Rosedale. 3B 8
Rosedale Way. Chesh 3B 8
Rosehill. 4F 23
Rose Hill. Burn 4C 12
Rose Hill. Sutt 4E 23
Rose Hill Roundabout. (Junct.) 4F 23
Rose La. Rip 2F 29
Rose La. Romf 2E 17
Rosemary La. B'water 1A 28
Rosemary La. Hods 1C 34
Rosendale Rd. SE24 2A 24
Rose St. Wokgm 3A 20
Rosherville. 2C 26
Rosslyn Hill. NW3 3F 15
Rossmore Rd. NW1 4F 15
Rossway. Berk 2D 5
Rossway La. Wig 1D 5
Rothbury Rd. E9 3B 16
Rotherhithe. 1B 24
Rotherhithe New Rd. SE1 1B 24
Roughetts Rd. Rya 2D 35
Roughway. 3B 34
Roughway La. D Grn & Rough 3B 34
Roughwood La. Chal G 1E 13
Round Acre. Bas 2D 19
Round Bush. 4C 6
Round Clo. Yat 1A 28
Roundshaw. 1A 32
Round Street. 3C 26
Round St. Sole S 3C 26
Roundway, The. N17 2A 16
Roundwood Rd. NW10 3D 15
Rowan Rd. SW16 3F 23
Rowdow. Otf 2A 34
Rowdow La. Sev 1F 33
Rowhill. 1F 29
Rowley Green. 4D 7
Rowley Grn. Rd. Barn 1E 15
Rowley La. Borwd & Barn 4D 7
Rowley La. Wex 4E 13
Rowley Rd. Ors 4C 18
Row Town. 1F 29
Rowtown. Add 1F 29
Roxeth. 3C 14
Roxeth Grn. Av. Harr 3B 14
Roxeth Hill. Harr 3C 14

S. Park Dri.—Tibbet's Ride

S. Park Dri. Ilf & Bark 3D 17
S. Park Hill Rd. S Croy 4A 24
S. Park La. Blet 4B 32
South Rd. S'hall 1B 22
South Rd. S Ock 4B 18
South Rd. Twic 2C 22
South Rd. Wok 2E 29
South Ruislip. 3B 14
Southside Comn. SW19 . . . . . . 3E 23
South Stifford. 1B 26
South Street. 1C 34
(Meopham)
South Street. 2D 33
(Westerham Hill)
South St. Barm 3E 35
South St. Dork 4C 30
South St. Enf 1B 15
South St. Eps 1D 31
South St. Farnh 4B 28
South St. Gt Walt 1D 11
South St. Iswth 2C 22
South St. Meop 1C 34
South St. Romf 2F 17
South St. Stai 3F 21
South St. Wen 2B 4
South Tottenham. 2A 16
Southwark. 4A 16
Southwark Bri. SE1 . . . . 4A 16
Southwark Bri. Rd. SE1 . . . . . . 1A 24
Southwark Pk. Rd. SE16 . . . . . 1B 24
Southwark St. SE1 . . . . 4A 16
South Way. Ab L 3A 6
Southway. Guild 4D 29
South Way. Hat 2E 7
South Way. Wemb 3D 15
South Weald. 1A 18
Southwell Pk. Rd. Camb 1B 28
South Wimbledon. 3E 23
Southwood. 3A 28
South Woodford. 2C 16
S. Woodford to Barking Relief Rd.
E18 & Bark 2C 16
Southwood La. N6 . . . . 3F 15
Southwood Rd. SE9 . . . . 2D 25
Southwood Rd. Farn 3A 28
Spa Hill. SE19 . . . . 3A 24
Spains Hall Rd. Will 2B 10
Spaniards Rd. NW3 . . . . 3F 15
Sparepenny La. Eyns 4F 25
Sparrow Row. 1D 29
Sparrow Row. Wok 1D 29
Sparrow's Herne. Bas 3E 19
Sparrows Herne. Bush 1B 14
Sparrows La. Hat H 1A 10
Speedgate Hill. Fawk 4B 26
Speen. 4A 4
Speen Rd. N Dean 4A 4
Speer Rd. Th Dit 4C 22
Spelthorne La. Ashf 3A 22
Spencer Pk. SW18 . . . . 2F 23
Spencer Rd. E Mol 3C 22
Spencers Rd. M'head 4B 12
Spencer St. EC1 . . . . 4A 16
Spendiff. 2F 27
Spinfield La. Mar 3A 12
Spinney Hill. Add 4F 21
Spital. 2D 21
Spitalbrook. 1B 8
Spitalfields. 4B 16
Spitals Cross. 4D 33
Spital St. Mar 3A 12
Spook Hill. N Holm 4C 30
Sporehams La. Dan 3F 11
Spout Hill. Croy 4B 24
Spout La. Crock H 4D 33
Spriggs La. B'more 3B 10
Spring Bottom La. Blet 3A 32
Springbridge Rd. W5 . . . . 4C 14
Spring Coppice La. Speen 4A 4
Spring Elms La. L Bad 2F 11
Springfield. 1E 11
Springfield Grn. Chelm 1E 11
Springfield Rd. Chelm 2E 11
(in two parts)
Spring Grove. 1C 22
Spring Gro. Rd.
Houn & Iswth 1B 22
Springhead Rd. N'fleet 2C 26
Springhouse La. Corr 4E 19
Springhouse Rd. Corr 4D 19
Spring La. SE25 . . . . 4B 24
Spring La. Farn R 3D 13
Spring La. F Hth 2B 12
Spring La. Igh 2B 34
Spring La. M'head 3B 12
Spring La. Oxt 4C 32
Spring Park. 4B 24
Spring St. W2 . . . . 4F 15
Spring St. Eps 1D 31
Spring Wlk. Worm 2B 8
Springwell La. Rick & Uxb 1F 13
Spurlands End Rd. Gt Kin 4B 4
Spur Rd. Edgw 1D 15
Spur Rd. Iswth 1C 22
Spur Rd. Orp 4E 25
Square Hill Rd. Maid 3F 35
Squire's Bri. Rd. Shep 3A 22
Squires La. N3 . . . . 2E 15
Squirrel's Heath. 2F 17
Squirrels Heath La.
Romf & Horn 2F 17
Squirrels Heath Rd. Romf 2A 18
Stablebridge Rd. Ast C 1B 4
Stack La. Hart K 3A 26
Staffhurst Wood La. Eden 4C 32
Staffordlake. 2D 29
Stafford Rd. Cat 3A 32
Stafford Rd. Wall & Croy 1F 31
Stagg Hill. Barn 4F 7
Stag Lane. (Junct.) 2D 23
Stag La. Chor 1F 13
Stag La. Edgw & NW9 . . . . 2D 15
Stag La. Gt Kin 4B 4
Staines. 3F 21
Staines By-Pass. Stai 2F 21
Staines Green. 1A 8
Staines Rd. Cher 4F 21
Staines Rd. Felt & Houn 2A 22
Staines Rd. Hamp & Twic 2B 22
Staines Rd. Stai 3F 21
Staines Rd. Wray 2E 21
Staines Rd. E. Sun 3B 22
Staines Rd. W. Ashf & Sun 3A 22
Stallion's Green. 4B 34
Stamford Brook Rd. W4 . . . . . . 1D 23
Stamford Hill. 2A 16
Stamford Hill. N16 . . . . 3A 16
Stamford Rd. N1 . . . . 3A 16
Stamford St. SE1 . . . . 4A 16
Stanborough. 1E 7
Stanborough Rd. Wel G 1E 7
Staneway. Bas 3D 19
Stanford La. Hdlw 4C 34
Stanford-le-Hope. 4D 19
Stanford Rivers. 3F 9
Stanford Rivers Rd. Ong 3A 10
Stanford Rd. Grays 1C 26
Stangate Rd. Birl 1D 35
Stanhope Gdns. SW7 . . . . 1F 23
Stanhope Rd. St Alb 2C 6
Stanhope Rd. Swans 2B 26
Stan La. W Peck 3C 34
Stanley Hill. Amer 4D 5
Stanley Hill. Pirb 2D 29
Stanley Pk. Rd. Cars & Wall . . . 1F 31
Stanley Rd. Grays 1B 26
Stanley Rd. Twic & Tedd 3C 22
Stanmore. 2C 14
Stanmore Hill. Stan 1C 14
Stanners Hill. 1E 29
Stansfeld Rd. E16 . . . . 4C 16
Stanstead Abbots. 1C 8
Stanstead Rd. SE6 & SE23 . . . . 2B 24
Stanstead Rd. Cat 3A 32
Stanstead Rd. Hert & Gt A 1B 8
Stanstead Rd. Hod 1B 8
Stansted. 1B 34
Stansted Hill. Sev 1B 34
Stansted La. Sev 1B 34
Stanwell. 2F 21
Stanwell Moor. 2F 21
Stanwell Moor Rd.
Stai & W Dray 2F 21
Stanwell Rd. Ashf 2A 22
Stanwell Rd. Felt 2A 22
Stanwell Rd. Hort 2E 21
Stapleford Abbotts. 1F 17
Stapleford Rd. Romf 1F 17
Stapleford Tawney. 4F 9
Stapleford Tawney Airfield. . . . 4E 9
Staple Hill Rd. Wok 1D 29
Staplehurst Rd. Cars 1F 31
Staplehurst Rd. S'hrst 4F 35
Staple La. Guild 4F 29
Staples Corner. (Junct.) 3E 15
Stapleton Hall Rd. N4 . . . . 3A 16
Stapleton Rd. Borwd 4D 7
Star & Garter Hill. Rich 2D 23
Star Hill. Roch 3F 27
Star Hill. Wok 2E 29
Star Hill Rd. Dun G 2E 33
Star La. Coul 2F 31
Star La. Orp 3E 25
Startins La. Cook 3B 12
Starts Hill Rd. Orp 4D 25
Station App. Gt Miss 3B 4
Station App. Hay 4C 24
Station App. Oxt 3C 32
Station App. Rick 4F 5
Station App. Ruis 3B 14
Station App. Wok 2E 29
Station App. Rd. Tad 2E 31
Station Av. Cat 3B 32
Station Av. W on T 4B 22
Station Hall La. Ing 4C 10
Station Hill. Asc 3C 20
Station Hill. Brom 4C 24
Station Hill. Cook 3B 12
Station Hill. E Far 3E 35
Station La. Horn 3A 18
Station Rd. E4 . . . . 1C 16
Station Rd. N11 . . . . 1F 15
Station Rd. N21 . . . . 1A 16
Station Rd. N22 . . . . 2A 16
Station Rd. NW9 . . . . 2E 15
Station Rd. NW10 . . . . 4D 15
Station Rd. SW13 . . . . 1D 23
Station Rd. Add 4F 21
Station Rd. Amer 4D 5
Station Rd. Asc 4D 21
Station Rd. Barn 1E 15
Station Rd. Beac 2C 12
Station Rd. Bet 4D 31
Station Rd. Bor G 2B 34
Station Rd. Bour E 3B 12
Station Rd. Bras 3E 33
Station Rd. Brick 3B 6
Station Rd. Brk P 2C 7
Station Rd. Brox 2B 8
Station Rd. Cat 2B 32
Station Rd. Chob 1D 29
Station Rd. Cipp 4D 13
Station Rd. Cli 2E 27
Station Rd. Cray 2F 25
Station Rd. Cux 4E 27
Station Rd. Dag & Romf 3E 17
Station Rd. Dit 2E 35
Station Rd. Dork 4C 30
Station Rd. Dun G 2F 33
Station Rd. E Til 1D 27
Station Rd. Eden 4D 33
Station Rd. Edgw 2D 15
Station Rd. Epp 3E 9
Station Rd. Esh 4C 22
Station Rd. Eyns 4F 25
Station Rd. Gid P 2F 17
Station Rd. Gom 4A 30
Station Rd. Grnh 2B 26
(in two parts)
Station Rd. Hals 1E 33
Station Rd. H'low 3A 26
Station Rd. Harr 2C 14
Station Rd. Hat P 1E 31
Station Rd. Hay 1A 22
Station Rd. Hem H 2F 5
Station Rd. K Lan 3A 6
Station Rd. Langl 1E 21
Station Rd. Lea 2C 30
Station Rd. Let G 1F 7
Station Rd. Loud 2C 12
Station Rd. Lou 1D 17
Station Rd. Mar 3A 12
Station Rd. Meop 3B 26
Station Rd. Nett 4D 35
Station Rd. N Har 2B 14
Station Rd. Orp 4D 25
Station Rd. Otf 2F 33
Station Rd. Pot B 3A 8
Station Rd. Red 4F 31
Station Rd. Shor 1F 33
Station Rd. Short 3C 24
Station Rd. Sidc 2E 25
Station Rd. Smal 2D 7
Station Rd. Stan A 1C 8
Station Rd. Stoke D 2B 30
Station Rd. Stoke M 1A 4
Station Rd. St P 3E 25
Station Rd. Strood 3E 27
Station Rd. Sutt 1E 31
Station Rd. S at H 3A 26
Station Rd. Tap 4C 12
Station Rd. Th Dit 4C 22
Station Rd. Tring & A'bry 1C 4
Station Rd. Upm 3A 18
Station Rd. Uxb 4F 13
Station Rd. Wal X 3B 8
Station Rd. Wat 4B 6
Station Rd. W Dray 1A 22
Station Rd. W H'dn 2C 18
Station Rd. W Wick 4C 24
Station Rd. Wray 2E 21
Station Rd. E. Oxt 3C 32
Station Rd. W. Oxt 3C 32
Station Way. Buck H 1C 16
Station Way. Sutt 1E 31
Staveley Rd. W4 . . . . 1D 23
Staverton Rd. NW10 . . . . 3E 15
Steel's La. Oxs 1B 30
Steep Hill. Chob 1D 29
Steeple View. 2D 19
Stembridge Rd. SE20 . . . . 3B 24
Stephenson St. E16 . . . . 4C 16
Stephenson Way. Wat 4B 6
Stepney. 4B 16
Stepney Grn. E1 . . . . 4B 16
Stepney Way. E1 . . . . 4B 16
Sterling Way. N18 . . . . 1A 16
Sternhold Av. SW2 . . . . 2A 24
Stevens Hill. Yat 1A 28
Stevens La. Clay 1C 30
Stewards. 2D 9
Stewards Green. 3E 9
Stewards Grn. Rd. Epp 3E 9
Stewart's Dri. Farn C 3D 13
Steyne Rd. W3 . . . . 4D 15
Stickens La. E Mal 2D 35
Stifford Clays Rd. N Stif 4B 18
(in three parts)
Stifford Hill. S Ock & Grays . . . 4B 18
Stifford Rd. S Ock 4A 18
Stilebridge. 4F 35
Stilebridge La. Mard 4F 35
(in two parts)
Stirling Corner. (Junct.) 1D 15
Stites Hill Rd. Cat 2A 32
Stoats Nest Rd. Coul 1A 32
Stock. 4D 11
Stockett La. Cox & L'se 4F 35
Stockett La. E Far 3F 35
Stock Hill. Big H 2C 32
Stocking La. Nap 4A 4
Stock La. Ing 4C 10
Stockley Park. 4A 14
Stockley Rd. W Dray 4A 14
Stock Rd. Bill 1D 19
Stock Rd. Gall 3E 11
Stock Rd. Stock 4D 11
Stocks Green. 4A 34
Stocks Grn. Rd. Hild 4A 34
Stocks La. Kel H 4A 10
Stocks Rd. Ald 1D 5
Stockton Rd. N18 . . . . 2B 16
Stockwell. 1A 24
Stockwell Rd. SW9 . . . . 1A 24
Stoke Common. 3E 13
Stoke Comn. Rd. Ful 3E 13
Stoke D'Abernon. 2B 30
Stoke Green. 4E 13
Stoke Grn. Stoke P 4E 13
Stoke Mandeville. 1A 4
Stoke Newington. 3A 16
Stoke Newington Chu. St.
N16 . . . . 3A 16
Stoke Newington High St.
N16 . . . . 3A 16
Stoke Newington Rd. N16 . . . . . 3A 16
Stoke Poges. 4D 13
Stoke Poges La. Slou 4D 13
Stoke Rd. Ayl 1A 4
Stoke Rd. Cobh 2B 30
Stoke Rd. Guild 4E 29
Stoke Rd. Hoo 2F 27
Stoke Rd. Slou 4D 13
Stompond La. W on T 4B 22
Stomp Rd. Burn 4C 12
Stonard Rd. N13 . . . . 1A 16
Stonards Hill. Epp 3E 9
Stondon Massey. 3B 10
Stondon Pk. SE23 . . . . 2B 24
Stondon Rd. Ong 3A 10
Stone. 2A 26
Stonebridge. 4D 15
Stonebridge Rd. N'fleet 2B 26
Stonecot Hill. Sutt 4E 23
Stonecross. St Alb 2C 6
Stonegrove. 1D 15
Stonegrove. Edgw 1D 15
Stonehill. 1E 29
Stonehill Rd. Chob & Cher 1E 29
Stonehill Rd. Rox 2C 10
Stonehouse La. Hals 1E 33
Stonehouse La. Purf 1A 26
Stoneings La. Knock 2D 33
Stoneleigh. 4E 23
Stoneness Rd. Grays 1B 26
Stone Pk. Av. Beck 3B 24
Stone Pl. Rd. Grnh 2A 26
Stones Cross Rd. Swan 4F 25
Stone Street. 3A 34
Stone St. Rd. Ivy H 3A 34
Stoney Rd. Brack 3B 20
Stony Corner. Meop 3C 26
Stony Green. 4B 4
Stony Hill. Esh 1B 30
Stony La. Amer 4E 5
Stony La. Ong 2F 9
Stopford Rd. E13 . . . . 4C 16
Stortford Rd. Hat H 1A 10
Stoughton. 4E 29
Stoughton Rd. Guild 4E 29
Straight Bit. F Hth 2B 12
Straight Mile, The. Shur R 2A 20
Straight Rd. Old Win 2E 21
Straight Rd. Romf 1F 17
Strait Rd. E6 . . . . 4D 17
Strand. WC2 . . . . 4A 16
Stratford. 3C 16
Stratford Marsh. 4B 16
Stratford New Town. 3C 16
Stratford Rd. Ash V 3B 28
Stratford Rd. Wat 4B 6
Strathearn Rd. SW19 . . . . 3E 23
Stratheden Rd. SE3 . . . . 1C 24
Strath Ter. SW11 . . . . 2F 23
Strathyre Av. CR7 . . . . 3A 24
Stratton. 4B 32
Strawberry Hill. 2C 22
Strawberry Hill. Warf 3B 20
Strawberry Va. Twic 2C 22
Straw Mill Hill. Maid 3F 35
Streatfield Rd. Harr 2C 14
Streatham. 3A 24
Streatham Common. 3A 24
Streatham Comn. N. SW16 . . . . 3A 24
Streatham High Rd. SW16 . . . . 2A 24
Streatham Hill. 2F 23
Streatham Hill. SW2 . . . . 2A 24
Streatham Park. 3F 23
Streatham Pl. SW2 . . . . 2A 24
Streatham Rd.
Mitc & SW16 . . . . 3F 23
Streatham Vale. 3F 23
Streatham Va. SW16 . . . . 3F 23
Street End Rd. Chat 4F 27
Streets Heath. W End 1D 29
Street, The. Alb 4F 29
Street, The. As 4B 26
Street, The. Asht 2D 31
Street, The. Bet 4D 31
Street, The. Bore 1F 11
Street, The. Boxl 2F 35
Street, The. Chfd 3F 5
Street, The. Cob 3D 27
Street, The. Comp 4D 29
Street, The. Eff 3B 30
Street, The. Fet 2C 30
Street, The. Grav 3D 27
Street, The. Guild 3F 29
Street, The. H Hals 2F 27
Street, The. H Ong 3A 10
Street, The. Hort K 3A 26
Street, The. Igh 2B 34
Street, The. L Walt 1E 11
Street, The. Maid 3C 34
Street, The. Meop 4C 26
Street, The. Plax 3B 34
Street, The. Putt 4C 28
Street, The. Rox 1C 10
Street, The. Rya 2D 35
Street, The. Shalf 4E 29
Street, The. Shorne 3D 27
Street, The. Shur R 2A 20
Street, The. Tstn 3E 35
Street, The. Tong 4B 28
Street, The. Up H'ing 1D 35
Street, The. Wal L 1A 20
Street, The. W Hor 3A 30
Strood. 3E 27
Strood Green. 4D 31
Stroude. 3E 21
Stroude Rd. Egh 3E 21
Stroude Rd. Vir W & Egh 3E 21
Stroud Green. 3A 16
Stroud Grn. Rd. N4 . . . . 3A 16
Stuart Rd. Grav 2C 26
Stubbers La. Upm 3A 18
Stubbles La. Cook 3B 12
Stubbs Hill. Brack 3A 20
Stubbs Hill. Orp 1E 33
Stubbs La. Lwr K 3E 31
Stud Green. 1B 20
Studio Way. Borwd 4D 7
Studland St. W6 . . . . 1E 23
Studridge La. Speen 4A 4
Stumble Hill. S'brne 4B 34
Stump La. Chelm 2E 11
Sturt Grn. Holyp 1B 20
Sturt Rd. Frim G 2B 28
Styants Bottom. 2A 34
Styants Bottom Rd. Sev 2A 34
Succombs Hill. Warl 2B 32
Sudbury. 3C 14
Sudbury Ct. Dri. Harr 3C 14
Sudbury Hill. Harr 3C 14
Sudbury Rd. D'ham 4E 11
Suffield La. Putt 4C 28
Suffield Rd. High W 1A 12
Suffolk Rd. Harr 2B 14
Sugden Rd. Th Dit 4C 22
Summer Hill. Chst 3D 25
Summerhouse Dri.
Bex & Dart 2F 25
Summerhouse La. Ald 4C 6
Summerleaze Rd. M'head 4B 12
Summer Rd. Th Dit 4C 22
Summers La. N12 . . . . 2F 15
Summerstown. 2F 23
Summerstown. SW17 . . . . 2F 23
Summerswood La. Borwd 3D 7
Summit Av. Farn 3A 28
Sumner Rd. Croy 4A 24
Sumners. 2D 9
Sunbury. 3B 22
Sunbury Common. 3A 22
Sunbury Cross. (Junct.) 3B 22
Sunbury Rd. Felt 2A 22
Sunbury Way. Felt 3B 22
Sunderland Rd. SE23 . . . . 2B 24
Sundridge. 3C 24
(Bromley)
Sundridge. 3E 33
(Sevenoaks)
Sundridge Av. Brom & Chst 3C 24
Sundridge Hill. Cux 4E 27
Sundridge Hill. Sev 2E 33
Sundridge La. Sev 2E 33
Sundridge Rd. Ide H 2E 33
Sun Hill. Fawk 4B 26
Sun-in-the-Sands. (Junct.) . . . 1C 24
Sunningdale. 4D 21
Sunningdale Golf Course. 4D 21
Sunninghill. 4C 20
Sunninghill Rd. Asc 4C 20
Sunninghill Rd. W'sham 4C 20
Sunninghill Rd. Wind & Asc . . . 3C 20
Sunnings La. Upm 3A 18
Sunningvale Av. Big H 2C 32
Sunnybank. Warl 2B 32
Sunnymeads. 2E 21
Sunnymede. 1D 19
Sunnyside Rd. Che 3D 5
Sunray Av. SE24 . . . . 2A 24
Sun St. EC2 . . . . 4A 16
Surbiton. 4C 22
Surbiton Cres. King T 3C 22
Surbiton Hill Pk. Surb 4D 23
Surbiton Hill Rd. Surb 4D 23
Surbiton Rd. King T 3C 22
Surrey Canal Rd.
SE14 & SE1 . . . . 1B 24
Surrey Quays Rd. SE16 . . . . . . 1B 24
Sussex Gdns. W2 . . . . 4F 15
Sussex Pl. W2 . . . . 4F 15
Sussex Pl. Slou 1E 21
Sussex Ring. N12 . . . . 1E 15
Sutherland Av. W9 . . . . 4E 15
Sutton. 4E 23
(Ewell)
Sutton. 1F 21
(Slough)
Sutton at Hone. 3A 26
Sutton Comn. Rd. Sutt 4E 23
Sutton Ct. Rd. W4 . . . . 1D 23
Sutton Green. 3E 29
Sutton Grn. Rd. Guild 3E 29
Sutton La. Houn 1B 22
Sutton La. Slou 1E 21
Sutton La. Sutt & Bans 1E 31
Sutton Pk. Rd. Sutt 1E 31
Sutton Rd. Cook 3B 12
Sutton Rd. Houn 1B 22
Sutton Rd. Maid 3F 35
Suttons Av. Horn 3F 17
Suttons La. Horn 3F 17
Swains La. F Hth 2B 12
Swakeleys Rd. Uxb 3A 14
Swakeleys Roundabout. (Junct.)
. . . . 3A 14
Swallowdale La. Hem I 1A 6
Swallows Cross. 4B 10
Swallows Cross Rd. Mount 4B 10
Swallow St. Iver 4F 13
Swan Bottom. Lee 2C 4
Swandon Way. SW18 . . . . 2E 23
Swanland Rd. Pot B & Hat 3E 7
Swan La. B'water 1A 28
Swan La. Dart 2F 25
Swan La. Eden 4D 33
Swan La. Lee 2C 4
Swan La. Runw 1F 19
Swan La. Stock 3D 11
Swanley. 3F 25
Swanley Bar. 3E 7
Swanley Bar La. Pot B 3E 7
Swanley By-Pass.
Sidc & Swan 3E 25
Swanley Interchange. (Junct.)
. . . . 4F 25
Swanley La. Swan 3F 25
Swanley Village. 3F 25
Swanley Village Rd. Swan 3F 25
Swan Rd. Felt 3B 22
Swan Rd. W Dray 1F 21
Swanscombe. 2B 26
Swanscombe St. Swans 2B 26
Swansea Rd. Felt 2A 22
Swan St. W Mal 2D 35
Swan, The. (Junct.) 4C 24
Swanton. 3C 34
Swanton Rd. W Peck 3C 34
Swanton Valley La. W Peck 3C 34
Swaynesland Rd. Eden 4D 33
Sweeps La. Orp 4E 25
Sweetcroft La. Uxb 3A 14
Sweets La. E Mal 3E 35
Swift Cres. Chat 4F 27
Swillet, The. 1E 13
Swingate La. SE18 . . . . 1D 25
Swinley Rd. Asc 4C 20
Swiss Cottage. (Junct.) 3F 15
Switchback Rd. N. M'head 4B 12
Switchback Rd. S. M'head 4B 12
Swyncombe Av. TW8 . . . . 1C 22
Sycamore Rd. Amer 4D 5
Sycamore Rd. Farn 3B 28
Sydenham. 3B 24
Sydenham Hill. SE23 & SE2 . . . 3B 24
Sydenham Rd. SE26 . . . . 3B 24
Sydenham Rd. Croy 4A 24
Sydenham Rd. Guild 4E 29
Sydney Rd. Enf 4A 8
Sydney Rd. Guild 4E 29
Sydney St. SW3 . . . . 1F 23
Sylvan Hill. SE19 . . . . 3A 24
Sylvan Way. Wel G 1F 7
Symonds La. Yald 4D 35
Syon House. 1C 22
Syon La. Iswth 1C 22
Sythwood. Wok 2E 29

Taddington. W'slde 1F 35
Tadpole La. Ews 4A 28
Tadworth. 2E 31
Tadworth St. Tad 3E 31
Talgarth Rd. W. W6 . . . . 1E 23
Tally Rd. Oxt 4D 33
Tamworth La. Mitc 3F 23
Tandridge. 4B 32
Tandridge Hill La. God 3B 32
Tandridge La. Ling 4B 32
Tandridge La. Oxt 4B 32
Tanfield Av. NW2 . . . . 3D 15
Tangley La. Guild 3D 29
Tan Ho. La. N'side 4A 10
Tanhouse Rd. Oxt 4C 32
Tank Hill Rd. Purf 1A 26
Tank Rd. Camb 1A 28
Tanner's Hill. Brock 4D 31
Tanners La. Ilf 2D 17
Tanner St. SE1 . . . . 1A 24
Tannery La. Send 3F 29
Tanyard Hill. Shorne 3D 27
Taplow. 4C 12
Taplow Comn. Rd. Burn 3C 12
Taplow Rd. Tap 4C 12
Tapner's Rd. Bet 4D 31
Target Roundabout. (Junct.)
. . . . 4B 14
Tarpots. 2F 19
Tate Rd. Sutt 4E 23
Tatling End. 3E 13
Tatsfield. 2C 32
Tatsfield Green. 2D 33
Tatsfield La. W'ham 2D 33
Tattenham Corner. 2E 31
Tattenham Corner Rd. Eps 2D 31
Tattenham Cres. Eps 2E 31
Tattenham Way. Tad 2E 31
Taunton Way. Stan & Edg 2D 15
Taverners Way. Hod 1B 8
Tavistock Pl. WC1 . . . . 4A 16
Tavistock Sq. NW1 . . . . 4F 15
Tawney Common. 3E 9
Tawney Comn. They M 3E 9
Tawneys Rd. H'low 1D 9
Taylor's La. High 3E 27
Taylor's La. Tros 1C 34
Teasaucer. Tovil 3F 35
Teddington. 3C 22
Tees Dri. Romf 1F 17
Teignmouth Gdns. Gnfd 4C 14
Telegraph Hill. High 3E 27
Telford Dri. Slou 1D 21
Telford Rd. N11 . . . . 1F 15
Temple. 3A 12
Temple End. High W 1B 12
Temple Fields. 1E 9
Temple Fortune. 2E 15
Temple Fortune La. NW11 . . . . 2E 15
Temple Hill. 2A 26
Temple Hill. Dart 2A 26
Temple Hill Sq. Dart 2A 26
Temple La. Bish 3A 12
Temple Mill La. E15 & E10 . . . . 3C 16
Temple Mills. 3B 16
Temple Rd. Eps 1D 31
Temple St. High W 1B 12
Temple Way. Binf 3A 20
Templewood La. Slou 3D 13
Ten Acre La. Egh 3F 21
Tendring Rd. H'low 1D 9
(in two parts)
Tennison Rd. SE25 . . . . 4A 24
Tentelow La. S'hall 1B 22
Terling Hall Rd. Terl 1F 11
Terling Rd. Hat P 1F 11
Terrace Rd. W on T 4B 22
Terrace Rd. N. Binf 3A 20
Terrace Rd. S. Binf 3A 20
Terrace, The. SW13 . . . . 1D 23
Terrace, The. Grav 2C 26
(in three parts)
Terrace, The. Wfd G 2C 16
Terrick. 1A 4
Terriers. 1B 12
Terry's La. Cook 3B 12
Terry's Lodge Rd. Wro 1B 34
Teston. 3E 35
Teston La. Tstn 3E 35
Teston Rd. Off 2C 34
Teston Rd. W Mal 2C 34
Tetherdown. N10 . . . . 2F 15
Thames Ditton. 4C 22
Thames Haven. 4E 19
Thamesmead. 4E 17
Thamesmead Central. 4D 17
Thamesmead E. 1E 25
Thamesmead N. 4E 17
Thamesmead S. 1E 25
Thamesmead W. 1D 25
Thames Rd. Bark 4D 17
Thames Rd. Dart 1F 25
Thames Side. Stai & Cher 3F 21
Thames St. Hamp 3B 22
Thames St. Stai 3F 21
Thames St. Sun 3B 22
Thames St. Wey 4A 22
Thames St. Wind 1D 21
Thames Way. Grav 2C 26
(in two parts)
Theberton St. N1 . . . . 4A 16
Theobalds La. Chesh 3B 8
Theobalds Pk. Rd. Enf 4A 8
Theobalds Rd. WC1 . . . . 4A 16
Theobald St. Rad & Borwd 4C 6
Thesiger Rd. SE20 . . . . 3B 24
Theydon Bois. 4D 9
Theydon Garnon. 4E 9
Theydon Mount. 4E 9
Theydon Mt. They M 3E 9
Theydon Rd. Epp 4D 9
Thicket Rd. SE20 . . . . 3B 24
Thieves La. Hert 1A 8
Third Av. H'low 1D 9
Thoby La. Mount 4C 10
Thomas More St. E1 . . . . 4B 16
Thompkins La. Farn R 3D 13
Thong. 3D 27
Thong La. Grav 3D 27
Thong La. Sev 2B 34
Thorkhill Rd. Th Dit 4C 22
Thornbury Rd. Iswth 1C 22
Thorncliffe Rd. S'hall 1B 22
Thorndon Av. W H'dn 2C 18
Thorndown La. W'sham 1C 28
Thorney. 1F 21
Thorney Bay Rd. Can I 4F 19
Thorney La. N. Iver 4F 13
Thorney La. S. Iver 1F 21
Thorney Mill Rd.
Iver & W Dray 1F 21
Thornhill Av. SE18 . . . . 1D 25
Thornhill Rd. N1 . . . . 3A 16
Thornhill Rd. Alder 4B 28
Thornhill Rd. Surb 4D 23
Thornton Av. SW2 . . . . 2F 23
Thornton Heath. 3A 24
Thornton Heath Pond. (Junct.)
. . . . 4A 24
Thornton Rd. SW12 . . . . 2F 23
Thornton Rd. Croy & T Hth 4A 24
Thornwood Common. 2E 9
Thornwood Rd. Epp 3E 9
Thorpe. 3F 21
Thorpe By-Pass. Egh 3E 21
Thorpe Green. 3E 21
Thorpe Lea. 3E 21
Thorpe Lea Rd. Egh 3E 21
Thorpe Pk. 3F 21
Thorpe Rd. Cher 4F 21
Thorpe Rd. Stai 3F 21
Thrale Rd. SW16 . . . . 3F 23
Three Arch Rd. Red 4F 31
Three Cherry Trees La.
Hem H 1A 6
Three Colts La. E2 . . . . 4B 16
Three Elm La. Gold G 4B 34
Three Gates Rd. Fawk 4A 26
Three Households. Chal G 1D 13
Three Mile Hill. Ing 3D 11
Threshers Bush. 1F 9
Threshers Bush. H'low 1E 9
Throwley Way. Sutt 4E 23
Thundersley. 2F 19
Thurloe Gdns. Romf 2F 17
Thurlow Pk. Rd. SE27 . . . . 2A 24
Thurlow St. SE17 . . . . 1A 24
Thurrock Lakeside. 1B 26
Thurston Rd. SE13 . . . . 1B 24
Tibbet's Corner. (Junct.) 2E 23
Tibbet's Ride. SW15 . . . . 2E 23

W. Barnes La.—Zig Zag Rd.

W. Barnes La. *N Mald* 3E 23
West Bedfont. 2A 22
Westbere Rd. *NW2* 3E 15
Westbourne Green. 4E 15
Westbourne Gro. *W2* 4E 15
Westbourne Gro. *W11* 4E 15
Westbourne Pk. *W10* 4E 15
Westbourne Rd. *N7* 3A 16
Westbourne Ter. *W2* 4F 15
Westbridge Rd. *SW11* 1F 23
Westbrook Rd. *Houn* 1B 22
Westbury Av. *N22* 2A 16
W. Bury St. *N9* 1A 16
West Byfleet. 1F 29
Westcar La. *W on T* 1B 30
West Clandon. 3F 29
Westcombe Hill. *SE3* 1C 24
West Comn. *Ger X* 2E 13
W. Common Rd. *Brom* 4C 24
Westcote Rd. *SW16* 3F 23
Westcott. 4C 30
Westcott Rd. *Dork* 4C 30
Westcott St. *Westc* 4B 30
Westcourt. 2D 27
West Drayton. 1A 22
W. Drayton Rd. *Uxb* 4A 14
West Dri. *SW16* 3F 23
West Dulwich. 2A 24
West Ealing. 4C 14
Wested La. *Swan* 4F 25
West End. ....1D 29 **(Bisley)**
West End. ....4B 22 **(Esher)**
West End. ....3B 20 **(Newell Green)**
West End. ....4B 14 **(Northolt)**
West End. ....2A 20 **(Waltham St Lawrence)**
West End. ....1E 7 **(Welwyn Garden City)**
West End. ....4F 15 **(Westminster)**
West End. *Ess* 2F 7
West End. *Kems* 2A 34
W. End La. *NW6* 3E 15
W. End La. *Esh* 1B 30
W. End La. *Pinn* 2B 14
W. End La. *Stoke P* 4D 13
W. End Rd. *N'holt* 3B 14
W. End Rd. *Ruis* 3A 14
W. End Rd. *Worm* 2A 8
Westerham. 3D 33
Westerham Hill. 2D 33
Westerham Hill. *W'ham* 2D 33
Westerham Rd. *Kes* 4D 25
Westerham Rd. *Oxt & W'ham* 3C 32
Westerham Rd. *Sev* 3E 33
Westerham Rd. *W'ham* 3E 33
Westerhill Rd. *Cox* 4F 35
Western Av. *W3 & UB6,W5* 4C 14
Western Av. *Brtwd* 1B 18
Western Av. *Den & Uxb* 3F 13
Western Av. *Gnfd* 4B 14
Western Av. *Ruis & N'holt* 3A 14
Western Circus. (Junct.) 4D 15
Western Dene. *Hasl* 4B 4
Western Perimeter Rd. *W Dray & H'row A* 1F 21
Western Rd. *SW19 & Mitc* 3F 23
Western Rd. *Bill* 1D 19
Western Rd. *Bor G* 2B 34
Western Rd. *Brack* 3A 20
Western Rd. *Brtwd* 1B 18
Western Rd. *Romf* 2F 17
Western Rd. *S'hall* 1B 22
Western Rd. *Tring* 1C 4
Western Way. *SE28* 1D 25
West Ewell. 1D 31
West Farleigh. 3E 35
Westferry Rd. *E14* 4B 16
Westfield. 2E 29
Westfield Av. *Wok* 2E 29
Westfield Rd. *Berk* 1D 5
Westfield Rd. *Wok* 2E 29
Westfield Sole. 1F 35
Westfield Sole Rd. *Boxl* 1F 35
Westgate Rd. *Dart* ....2F 25 (in two parts)
West Green. 2A 16
W. Green Rd. *N15* 2A 16
West Gro. *W on T* 4B 22
Westhall Rd. *Warl* 2B 32
West Ham. 4C 16
W. Ham La. *E15* 3C 16
West Hampstead. 3E 15
West Ham United F.C. 4C 16
West Hanningfield. 3E 11
W. Hanningfield Rd. *W Han* 3E 11
West Harrow. 3C 14
Westhatch La. *Warf* 3B 20
West Heath. ....1E 25 **(Abbey Wood)**
West Heath. ....2A 28 **(Farnborough)**
W. Heath Rd. *DA7* 1E 25
W. Heath Rd. *NW3* 3E 15
W. Heath Rd. *Farn* 2A 28
West Hendon. 3E 15
West Hill. 2E 23
West Hill. *SW18 & SW1* 2E 23
West Hill. *Dart* 2F 25
West Hill. *Eps* 1D 31
West Hill. *Oxt* 3C 32
West Horndon. 2C 18
Westhorne Av. *SE9 & SE12* 2C 24
West Horsley. 3A 30
Westhumble. 4C 30
Westhumble St. *Westh* 4C 30
West Hyde. 2F 13
W. Hyde La. *Chal P* 2E 13
W. India Dock Rd. *E14* 4B 16
West Kensington. 1E 23
West Kilburn. 4E 15
West Kingsdown. 1A 34
West Leith. 1C 4
West Malling. 2D 35
West Mayne. *Bas* 2C 18
Westmead Rd. *Sutt* 4F 23
Westminster. 1F 23
Westminster Bri. *SE1 & SW1* 1A 24
Westminster Bri. Rd. *SE1* 1A 24
West Molesey. 4B 22
Westmoreland Rd. *Brom* 4C 24
Westmorland Dri. *Warf* 3B 20
Westmount Rd. *SE9* 1D 25
West Norwood. 3A 24
Weston Av. *Grays* 1A 26
Weston Dri. *Stan* 2C 14
Weston Green. 4C 22
Weston Grn. Rd. *Th Dit* 4C 22
Weston Rd. *Ast C* 1B 4
Weston Turville. 1A 4
Westow Hill. *SE19* 3A 24
Westow St. *SE19* 3A 24
West Pk. *SE9* 2D 25
West Peckham. 3C 34
Westpole Av. *Barn* 4F 7
West Ramp. *H'row A* 1A 22
West Riding. *Brick* 3B 6
West Rd. *Reig* 4E 31
West Rd. *S Ock* 4B 18
West Ruislip. 3A 14
W. Side Comn. *SW19* 3E 23
W. Smithfield. *EC4* 4A 16
West Street. 1E 27
West St. *Cars* 4F 23
West St. *Dork* 4C 30
West St. *Eri* 1F 25
West St. *Grav* 2C 26
West St. *Grays* 1B 26
West St. *Harr* 3C 14
West St. *Hunt* 4E 35
West St. *Mar* 3A 12
West St. *Reig* 4E 31
West St. *Sutt* 4E 23
West St. *W Mal* 2D 35
West Thurrock. 1B 26
W. Thurrock Way. *W Thur* 1B 26
West Tilbury. 1D 27
West Watford. 1B 14
Westway. *SW20* 3E 23
Westway. *W12* 4E 15
Westway. *Cat* 3A 32
Westway. *Chelm* 2D 11
West Wickham. 4C 24
Westwick Row. 2A 6
Westwick Row. *Hem H* 2A 6
Westwood Hill. *SE26* 3B 24
Westwood La. *Norm & Wanb* 4C 28
Westwood La. *Well* 2D 25
Westwood Rd. *S'fleet* 3B 26
Westwood Rd. *W'sham* 4C 20
West Wycombe. 1A 12
West Wycombe Pk. 1A 12
West Wycombe Rd. *W Wyc & High W* 1A 12
West Yoke. 4B 26
West Yoke. *As* 4B 26
W. Yoke Rd. *New Ash* 4B 26
Wexham. 4E 13
Wexham Court. 4E 13
Wexham Pk. La. *Wex* 4E 13
Wexham Rd. *Slou* 1E 21
Wexham Street. 4E 13
Wexham St. *Slou* 4E 13
Weybourne. 4A 28
Weybourne Rd. *Farnh & Alder* 4A 28
Weybridge. 4A 22
Weybridge Rd. *Add & Wey* 4A 22
Wey La. *Che* 3D 5
Weymouth St. *W1* 4F 15
Whalebone La. N. *Romf* 2E 17
Whalebone La. S. *Romf & Dag* 3E 17
Wharfdale Rd. *N1* 4A 16
Wharf La. *Dud* 1D 5
Wharf Rd. *Ash V* 4B 28
Wharf Rd. *Fob* 4D 19
Wharf Rd. *Frim G* 2B 28
Wharncliffe Rd. *SE25* 3A 24
Wheatfield Way. *King T* 3D 23
Wheeler's Hill. *L Walt* 1E 11
Wheelers La. *Brock* 4D 31
Wheelers La. *Lin* 4F 35
Wheelers La. *Pil H* 4A 10
Whelpley Hill. 2E 5
Whelpley Hill. *Che* 2E 5
Whetsted Rd. *Five G* ....4D 35 (in two parts)
Whetstone. 1F 15
Whielden La. *Winch H* 1C 12
Whielden St. *Amer* 4D 5
Whippendell Rd. *Wat* 1A 14
Whipps Cross Rd. *E11* 2C 16
Whiston Rd. *E2* 4B 16
Whitchurch La. *Edgw* 2C 14
Whitchurch Rd. *Romf* 1F 17
Whitechapel. 4B 16
Whitechapel Rd. *E1* 4B 16
White City. 4E 15
White City. (Junct.) 4E 15
Whitefoot La. *Brom* 3C 24
Whitehall. *SW1* 4A 16
Whitehall La. *Egh* 3E 21
Whitehall La. *Eri* 1F 25
Whitehall La. *S Pk* 4E 31
Whitehall Rd. *E4 & Wfd G* 1C 16
White Hart La. *N17 & N22* 2A 16
White Hart La. *SW13* 1D 23
White Hart La. *Chelm* 1E 11
White Hart La. *Romf* 2E 17
White Hart Rd. *Hem H* 2A 6
White Hill. *Ash G* 2E 5
White Hill. *B Hth* 2A 14
Whitehill. *Berk* 1E 5
White Hill. *Che* 3D 5
White Hill. *Chip* 3F 31
White Hill. *High W* 1B 12
White Hill. *Wbrn M* 2C 12
Whitehill La. *Blet* 3A 32
Whitehill La. *Grav* 2C 26
Whitehill Rd. *Grav* 2C 26
Whitehill Rd. *Long & Grav* 3B 26
Whitehill Rd. *Meop* 4C 26
White Horse Hill. *Chst* 3D 25
Whitehorse La. *CR7* 3A 24
White Horse La. *E1* 4B 16
White Horse La. *Lon C* 2C 6
Whitehorse Rd. *Croy & T Hth* 4A 24
White Horse Rd. *Meop* 1C 34
Whitehouse La. *Bedm* 2B 6
Whitehouse La. *Wbrn G* 2C 12
White Ho. Rd. *Sev* 3F 33
Whitelands Way. *Romf* 2A 18
White La. *Alb* 4F 29
White La. *Ash* 4C 28
White La. *Guild* 4F 29
White La. *Oxt & W'ham* 3C 32
Whiteleaf. 2A 4
Whiteley Village. 1A 30
White Lion Rd. *Amer* 4D 5
Whitepit La. *Wbrn G & F Hth* 2C 12
White Post. 4A 32
Whitepost Hill. *Red* 4F 31
Whitepost La. *Culv* 1C 34
White Post La. *Meop* 3C 26
White Roding. 1A 10
White Rose La. *Wok* 2E 29
White's Hill. *Stock* 4D 11
White Stubbs La. *B'frd & EN10* 2A 8
White Waltham. 1A 20
White Waltham Airfield. 1A 20
Whitewebbs La. *Enf* 4A 8
Whitewebbs Rd. *Enf* 4A 8
Whitley Row. 3E 33
Whitmoor La. *Guild* 3E 29
Whitmore La. *Asc* 4D 21
Whitmore Rd. *Harr* 3C 14
Whitmore Way. *Bas* 2E 19
Whittington Rd. *N22* 2A 16
Whittington Way. *Pinn* 2B 14
Whitton. 2C 22
Whitton Av. E. *Gnfd* 3C 14
Whitton Av. W. *N'holt & Gnfd* 3C 14
Whitton Dene. *Houn & Iswth* 2C 22
Whitton Rd. *Houn* 2B 22
Whitton Rd. *Twic* 2C 22
Whitton Road Roundabout. (Junct.) 2C 22
Whitworth Rd. *SE25* 3A 24
Whyteladyes La. *Cook* 3B 12
Whyteleafe. 2A 32
Whyteleafe Hill. *Whyt* 2A 32
Whyteleafe Rd. *Cat* 3A 32
Wickford. 1F 19
Wickford Av. *Bas* 2E 19
Wickham Ct. Rd. *W Wick* 4C 24
Wickham La. *SE2* 1E 25
Wickham Rd. *SE4* 2B 24
Wickham Rd. *Beck* 3B 24
Wickham Rd. *Croy* 4B 24
Wickham St. *Well* 1E 25
Wickham Way. *Beck* 3C 24
Wickhurst. 4F 33
Wick La. *E3* ....4B 16 (in two parts)
Wick La. *Egh* 3D 21
Wick Rd. *E9* 3B 16
Wick Rd. *Egh* 3E 21
Wick's Grn. *Binf* 3A 20
Wide Way. *Mitc* 3F 23
Widford. 2D 11
Widmere La. *Mar* 2A 12
Widmer End. 4B 4
Widmore. 3C 24
Widmore Rd. *Brom* 3C 24
Wierton. 4F 35
Wierton Hill. *Bou M* 4F 35
Wierton Rd. *Bou M* 4F 35
Wiggenhall Rd. *Wat* 1B 14
Wigginton. 1C 4
Wigginton Bottom. 1D 5
Wightman Rd. *N4 & N8* 2A 16
Wigley Bush La. *S Wea* 1A 18
Wigmore St. *W1* 4F 15
Wilbury Way. *N18* 1A 16
Wildernesse. 2A 34
Wildhill. 1E 7
Wild Hill. *Hat* 2F 7
Wildridings. 4B 20
Wildridings Rd. *Brack* 4B 20
Wildwood Rd. *NW11* 2E 15
Wilkin's Grn. La. *Smal & Hat* 2D 7
Willesden. 3E 15
Willesden Green. 3E 15
Willesden La. *NW6 & NW2* 3E 15
Willey Green. 4C 28
William Barefoot Dri. *SE9* 3D 25
William St. *Slou* 4D 13
Willingale. 2B 10
Willingale Rd. *Fyf* 2A 10
Willingale Rd. *Lou* 4D 9
Willingale Rd. *Ong* 2B 10
Willingale Rd. *Will* 2B 10
Willington. 3F 35
Willington St. *Maid* 3F 35
Willoughby La. *N17* 2B 16
Willowbank. 3F 13
Willow Brook Rd. *SE15* 1A 24
Willowfield. *Lain* 2D 19
Willow Rd. *Enf* 4A 8
Willow Tree La. *Hay* 4B 14
Willow Wents. *Mere* 3C 34
Wilmerhatch La. *Eps* 2D 31
Wilmer Way. *N11* 1F 15
Wilmington. 3F 25
Wilson La. *S Dar* 3A 26
Wilsons La. *E Far* 3E 35
Wilson St. *EC2* 4A 16
Wiltshire Rd. *Mar* 2A 12
Wiltshire Rd. *Wokgm* 3A 20
Wimbledon. 3E 23
Wimbledon Hill Rd. *SW19* 3E 23
Wimbledon Park. 2E 23
Wimbledon Pk. Rd. *SW18 & SW1* 2E 23
Wimbledon Pk. Side. *SW19* 2E 23
Wimbledon Rd. *SW17* 3F 23
Wimbledon. (Tennis Courts) 3E 23
Winchbottom La. *High W* 2A 12
Winchbottom La. *Mar* 2B 12
Winchelsea Rd. *NW10* 4D 15
Winchester Rd. *E17* 2C 16
Winchester Rd. *N9* 1A 16
Winchester St. *W3* 1D 23
Winchmore Hill. ....1C 12 **(Amersham)**
Winchmore Hill. ....1A 16 **(Enfield)**
Winchmore Hill. *Good E* 1C 10
Winchmore Hill Rd. *N21 & N14* 1F 15
Windermere Av. *Wemb* 3C 14
Wind Hill. *H Lav* 2F 9
Windlesham. 4C 20
Windlesham Rd. *Chob* 1D 29
Windlesham Rd. *W End* 1D 29
Windmill Hill. *Coles* 1D 13
Windmill Hill. *Enf* 4A 8
Windmill Hill. *K Lan* 3F 5
Windmill Hill. *Ruis* 3A 14
Windmill Hill. *Sev* 2C 34
Windmill La. *E15* 3C 16
Windmill La. *Wid E* 4B 4
Windmill La. *Chesh* 3B 8
Windmill La. *Eps* 1D 31
Windmill La. *S'hall & Iswth* 1C 22
Windmill Rd. *SW18* 2F 23
Windmill Rd. *W5 & Bren* 1C 22
Windmill Rd. *Croy* 4A 24
Windmill Rd. *Ful* 3E 13
Windmill Rd. *Mitc* 3F 23
Windmill Rd. *Sev* 3F 33
Windmill Rd. *Sun* 3A 22
Windmill Rd. *Weald* 4F 33
Windmill St. *Grav* ....2C 26 (in two parts)
Windsor. 1D 21
Windsor & Eton Relief Rd. *Wind* 1D 21
Windsor Av. *SW19* 3F 23
Windsor Castle. 1D 21
Windsor Dri. *Hert* 1A 8
Windsor End. *Beac* 2D 13
Windsor Hill. *Wbrn G* 2C 12
Windsor La. *Burn* 4C 12
Windsor La. *L Kin* 4B 4
Windsor Rd. *Asc* 3C 20
Windsor Rd. *Chob* 4D 21
Windsor Rd. *Dat* 1E 21
Windsor Rd. *Egh* 2E 21
Windsor Rd. *M'head & Oak G* 1B 20
Windsor Rd. *Slou* 1D 21
Windsor Rd. *Stoke P & Ger X* 3E 13
Windsor Rd. *Wind* ....1C 20 (Windsor)
Windsor Rd. *Wind* ....3C 20 (Windsor Great Park)
Windsor Rd. *Wray* 2E 21
Windsor St. *Cher* 4F 21
Windsor Way. *Alder* 4B 28
Winfield La. *Bor G* 3B 34
Wingletye La. *Horn* 3A 18
Wingrave Rd. *Tring* 1C 4
Winkfield. 2C 20
Winkfield La. *Wink* 2C 20
Winkfield Rd. *Asc* 3C 20
Winkfield Rd. *Wink* 2C 20
Winkfield Row. 3B 20
Winkfield Row. *Brack* 3B 20
Winkfield Street. 2C 20
Winkfield St. *Wink* 2C 20
Winkhurst Green. 4E 33
Winkhurst Grn. Rd. *Bough B* 4E 33
Winkworth Rd. *Bans* 1E 31
Winn Rd. *SE12* 2C 24
Winston Way. *Ilf* 3D 17
Winterfield La. *W Mal* 2D 35
Winter Gardens. 3F 19
Winter Hill. *Cook* 3B 12
Winter Hill Rd. *Cook* 3B 12
Wise La. *NW7* 1E 15
Wisley. 2A 30
Wisley Interchange. (Junct.) 2A 30
Wisley La. *Wok* 2F 29
Witches La. *Sev* 2F 33
Witheridge La. *Penn & Knot* 1C 12
Withies La. *Comp* 4D 29
Witney Green. 2B 10
Woburn Grn. La. *Wbrn G* 2C 12
Woburn Hill. *Add* 4F 21
Woburn Pl. *WC1* 4A 16
Woking. 2E 29
Wokingham. 3A 20
Wokingham Rd. *Brack* 3A 20
Wokingham Rd. *Crowt & Sand* 1A 28
Wokingham Without. 4A 20
Woking Rd. *Guild* 3E 29
Woldingham. 3B 32
Woldingham Garden Village. 2B 32
Woldingham Rd. *Wold* 2B 32
Wolf La. *Wind* 2C 20
Wolf's Hill. *Oxt* 4C 32
Wolf's Rd. *Oxt* 3C 32
Wolf's Row. *Oxt* 3C 32
Wolseley Rd. *N8* 2F 15
Wolves La. *N13 & N22* 2A 16
Wonham La. *Bet* 4D 31
Wooburn. 3C 12
Wooburn Common. 3C 12
Wooburn Comn. Rd. *Wbrn G* 3C 12
Wooburn Green. 2C 12
Wooburn Moor. 2C 12
Woodberry Gro. *N4* 3A 16
Woodbridge Hill. 4E 29
Woodbridge Meadows. *Guild* 4E 29
Woodbridge Rd. *Guild* 4E 29
Woodcock Hill. *Borwd* 1D 15
Woodcock Hill. *Harr* 2C 14
Woodcockhill. *Sandr* 1C 6
Woodcock La. *Chob* 1D 29
Woodcote. ....2D 31 **(Epsom)**
Woodcote. ....1F 31 **(Purley)**
Woodcote Green. 1F 31
Woodcote Grn. *Wall* 1F 31
Woodcote Grn. Rd. *Eps* 2D 31
Woodcote Gro. Rd. *Coul* 2F 31
Woodcote Rd. *Eps* 1D 31
Woodcote Rd. *Wall & Kenl* 1F 31
Woodcote Side. *Eps* 2D 31
Woodcote Valley Rd. *Purl* 1F 31
Woodcroft Av. *NW7* 2D 15
Woodend. ....1A 10 **(Abbess Roding)**
Wood End. ....3C 20 **(Ascot)**
Wood End. ....4A 14 **(Hayes)**
Wood End. *Hay* 4A 14
Wood End. *Medm* 2A 12
Wood End Green. 4A 14
Wood End Grn. Rd. *Hay* 4A 14
Wood End La. *N'holt* 3B 14
Woodfield Av. *SW16* 2F 23
Woodfield La. *Asht* 2D 31
Woodfield La. *Hat* 2F 7
Woodfield Rd. *W5* 4C 14
Woodford. 2C 16
Woodford Av. *Ilf* 2D 17
Woodford Bridge. 2D 17
Woodford Bri. Rd. *Ilf* 2D 17
Woodford Green. 1C 16
Woodford New Rd. *E18 & E17* 2C 16
Woodford Rd. *E7* 3C 16
Woodford Rd. *E11* 2C 16
Woodford Rd. *Wat* 4B 6
Woodford Side. 1C 16
Woodford Wells. 1C 16
Woodgate Rd. *W Mal* 2C 34
Woodgrange Rd. *E7* 3C 16
Wood Green. ....2A 16 **(Hornsey)**
Wood Green. ....3C 8 **(Waltham Abbey)**
Woodgreen Rd. *Wal A* 3C 8
Woodhall La. *Wel G* 1E 7
Woodham. 1F 29
Woodham La. *Wok & Add* 1E 29
Woodham Pk. Rd. *Wdhm* 1F 29
Woodham Rd. *Bat* 1F 19
Woodham Rd. *Wok* 2E 29
Woodhatch. ....3F 9 **(Epping)**
Woodhatch. ....4F 31 **(Reigate)**
Woodhatch Rd. *Reig* 4F 31
Woodhayes Rd. *SW19* 3E 23
Woodhill. 2F 11
Wood Hill. *Meop* 4C 26
Woodhill. *Send* 3F 29
Woodhill Rd. *S'don & Dan* 2F 11
Woodhouse La. *Broom & L Walt* 1D 11
Woodhouse Rd. *N12* 2F 15
Woodhurst La. *Oxt* 4C 32
Woodland Av. *Hut* 1C 18
Woodland Rd. *Rick* 1F 13
Woodlands. ....1C 22 **(Hounslow)**
Woodlands. ....1A 34 **(Kemsing)**
Woodlands Hill. *Beac* 2D 13
Woodlands La. *Shorne* 3D 27
Woodlands La. *W'sham* 1C 28
Woodlands Park. 1B 20
Woodlands Pk. Rd. *M'head* 1B 20
Woodlands Rd. *Cobh & Lea* 2B 30
Woodlands Rd. *Gill* 4F 27
Woodlands Rd. *Iswth* 2C 22
Woodlands Rd. *Lea* 2C 30
Wood La. *NW9* 3D 15
Wood La. *W12* 4E 15
Wood La. *Dag* 3E 17
Wood La. *Horn* 3F 17
Wood La. *Iswth* 1C 22
Wood La. *Iver* 4F 13
Wood La. *Ruis* 3A 14
Wood La. *Stan* 1C 14
Wood La. *W'slde* 1F 35
Wood La. *Will* 2B 10
Wood La. End. *Hem H* 2A 6
Woodman Rd. *War* 1B 18
Woodmansterne. 2F 31
Woodmansterne La. *Bans* ....2F 31 (Park Rd.)
Woodmansterne La. *Bans & Cars* ....1F 31 (Croydon La.)
Woodmansterne Rd. *Cars* 1F 31
Woodmansterne St. *Bans* 2F 31
Woodmere Av. *Wat* 4B 6
Woodplace La. *Coul* 2F 31
Woodridden Hill. *Wal A* 4C 8
Woodrow. 4C 4
Woods Av. *Hat* 1E 7
Woodside. ....3B 6 **(Abbots Langley)**
Woodside. ....3C 20 **(Ascot)**
Woodside. ....4B 24 **(Croydon)**
Woodside. ....2E 7 **(Welham Green)**
Woodside. *SW19* 3E 23
Woodside. *Hat* 2E 7
Woodside. *Thorn* 2E 9
Woodside Av. *N10 & N6* 2F 15
Woodside Grn. *CR0* 4B 24
Woodside Park. 1E 15
Woodside Rd. *Amer* 4D 5
Woods, The. *N'wd* 1B 14
Woodstock La. N. *Surb* 4C 22
Woodstock La. S. *Clay & Chess* 1C 30
Woodstock, The. (Junct.) 4E 23
Wood Street. 4D 29
Wood Street. (Junct.) 2C 16
Wood St. *E17* 2C 16
Wood St. *Barn* 4E 7
Wood St. *Chelm* 2E 11
Wood St. *Gill* 3F 27
Wood St. *King T* 3D 23
Wood St. *Swan* 3F 25
Wood St. Grn. *Wood S* 4D 29
Woodthorpe Rd. *Ashf* 3F 21
Wood Va. *SE22* 2B 24
Wood Vw. *Grays* 1C 26
Woodward Rd. *Dag* 3E 17
Woodway. *P Ris* ....3A 4 (in two parts)
Woollensbrook. 1B 8
Woolley Green. 1A 20
Woolmead Rd. *Farnh* 4A 28
Woolmers La. *Let G* 1F 7
Woolmonger's La. *Ing* 3B 10
Woolstone Rd. *SE23* 2B 24
Woolwich. 1D 25
Woolwich Chu. St. *SE18* 1D 25
Woolwich Comn. *SE18* 1D 25
Woolwich Mnr. Way. *E16 & E6* 4D 17
Woolwich New Rd. *SE18* 1D 25
Woolwich Rd. *SE2 & Belv* 1E 25
Woolwich Rd. *SE10* 1C 24
Woolwich Rd. *Bexh* 2E 25
Wootton Way. *M'head* 4B 12
Worcester Park. 4E 23
Worcester Pk. Rd. *Wor Pk* 4D 23
Workhouse La. *E Far* 3F 35
Workhouse Rd. *W Mal* 2D 35
World's End. ....4A 8 **(Enfield)**
World's End. ....1A 4 **(Wendover)**
World's End La. *N21 & Enf* 1A 16
Worlds End La. *Orp* 1D 33
World's End La. *W'ton T* 1A 4
Wormley. 2B 8
Wormley West End. 2A 8
Worple Rd. *SW19 & SW2* 3E 23
Worple Rd. *Stai* 3F 21
Worplesdon. 3D 29
Worplesdon Hill. *Wok* 2D 29
Worplesdon Rd. *Guild* 3D 29
Worships Hill. *Sev* 3F 33
Worship St. *EC2* 4A 16
Worton Rd. *Iswth* 2C 22
Wotton. 4B 30
Wouldham. 1E 35
Wouldham Rd. *Woul* 4E 27
Wrangling La. *Ludd* ....1D 35 (in two parts)
Wray La. *Reig* 3F 31
Wraysbury. 2E 21
Wraysbury Rd. *Stai* 2E 21
Wrentham Av. *NW10* 4E 15
Wren Way. *Farn* 2A 28
Wrights Bri. Rd. *S Wea* 1A 18
Writtle. 2D 11
Writtle Rd. *Chelm* 2D 11
Writtle Rd. *Marg* 3D 11
Wrotham. 2B 34
Wrotham By-Pass. *Wro* 2B 34
Wrotham Heath. 2C 34
Wrotham Hill Rd. *Wro* 1B 34
Wrotham Rd. *Bor G* 2B 34
Wrotham Rd. *Meop & Grav* 4C 26
Wrotham Water La. *Tros* 2C 34
Wrotham Water Rd. *Wro H* 1C 34
Wrottesley Rd. *NW10* 4E 15
Wrythe Grn. Rd. *Cars* 4F 23
Wrythe La. *Cars* 4F 23
Wrythe, The. 4F 23
Wyatt's Green. 4B 10
Wyatt's Grn. Rd. *Wy G* 4B 10
Wych Hill. *Wok* 2E 29
Wych Hill La. *Wok* 2E 29
Wycombe Air Pk. 2A 12
Wycombe End. *Beac* 2D 13
Wycombe La. *Wbrn G* 2C 12
Wycombe Marsh. 2B 12
Wycombe Rd. *Holm G* 4B 4
Wycombe Rd. *Mar* 3A 12
Wycombe Rd. *P'wd* 3B 4
Wycombe Rd. *W Wyc* 4A 4
Wycombe Wanderers F.C. 1A 12
Wyke. 4C 28
Wyke La. *Ash* 4C 28
Wymer's Wood Rd. *Burn* 4C 12
Wyndham Rd. *SE5* 1A 24
Wyse's Rd. *Hghwd* 2C 10

Yalding. 4D 35
Yalding Hill. *Yald* 4D 35
Yardley Pk. Rd. *Tonb* 4B 34
Yarnton Way. *SE2 & Eri* 1E 25
Yateley. 1A 28
Yateley Rd. *Sand* 1A 28
Yeading. 4B 14
Yeading La. *Hay & N'holt* 4B 14
Yelsted La. *Boxl* 1F 35
Yeovil Rd. *Camb* 1A 28
Yester Rd. *Chst* 3D 25
Yew Tree Bottom Rd. *Eps* 2E 31
Yew Tree Rd. *Slou* 1E 21
Yiewsley. 4F 13
Yopps Green. 3B 34
Yopps Grn. *Plax* 3B 34
York Cres. *Borwd* 4D 7
York Rd. *E10* 3C 16
York Rd. *SE1* 1A 24
York Rd. *SW11* 2F 23
York Rd. *Alder* 4A 28
York Rd. *Barn* 1F 15
York Rd. *Guild* 4E 29
York Rd. *M'head* 4B 12
York Rd. *Sutt* 1E 31
York Rd. *Uxb* 3F 13
York Rd. *Wok* 2E 29
Yorks Hill Rd. *Ide H* 4E 33
Yorkshire Grey (Eltham Hill). (Junct.) 2C 24
York St. *W1* 4F 15
York St. *Twic* 2C 22
York Town. 1B 28
Yorktown Rd. *B'water* 1A 28
Yorktown Rd. *Camb* 1A 28
York Way. *N1 & N7* 3A 16
Young St. *Fet* 3C 30

Zig Zag Rd. *Dork & Tad* 3C 30

CENTRAL LONDON

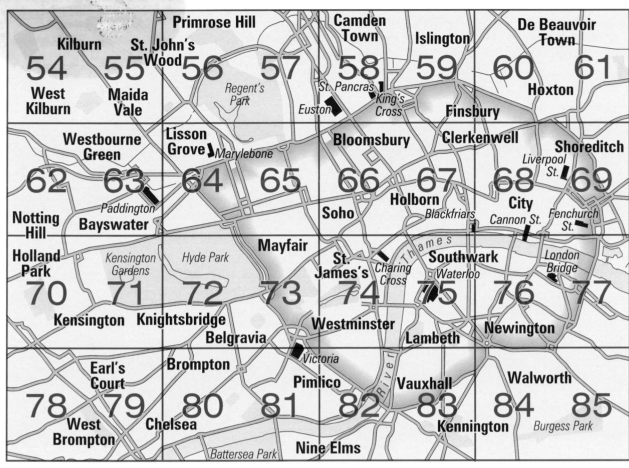

Kilburn	St. John's Wood			Camden Town	Islington	De Beauvoir Town
54	**55**	**56**	**57**	**58**	**59**	**60** **61**
West Kilburn	Maida Vale	Regent's Park		St. Pancras Euston King's Cross	Finsbury	Hoxton
Westbourne Green	Lisson Grove Marylebone			Bloomsbury	Clerkenwell	Shoreditch Liverpool St.
62	**63**	**64**	**65**	**66**	**67**	**68** **69**
Notting Hill	Paddington Bayswater		Soho	Holborn Blackfriars	City Cannon St.	Fenchurch St.
Holland Park	Kensington Gardens	Hyde Park	Mayfair	St. James's Charing Cross	Southwark Waterloo	London Bridge
70	**71**	**72**	**73**	**74**	**75**	**76** **77**
Kensington	Knightsbridge		Belgravia	Westminster	Lambeth	Newington
Earl's Court	Brompton		Victoria			Walworth
78	**79**	**80**	**81** Pimlico	**82** Vauxhall	**83**	**84** **85**
West Brompton	Chelsea Battersea Park		Nine Elms		Kennington	Burgess Park

REFERENCE

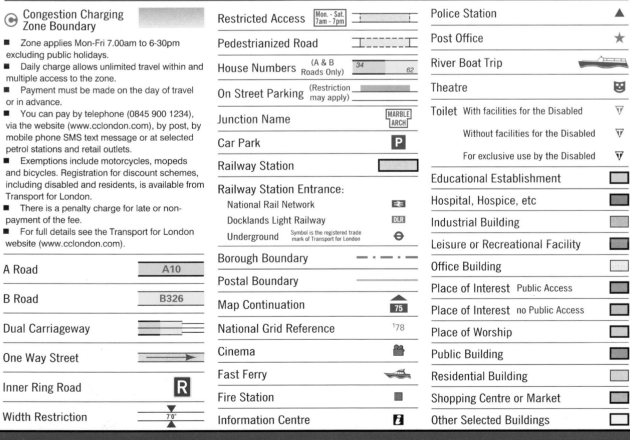

Congestion Charging Zone Boundary (C)

- Zone applies Mon-Fri 7.00am to 6-30pm excluding public holidays.
- Daily charge allows unlimited travel within and multiple access to the zone.
- Payment must be made on the day of travel or in advance.
- You can pay by telephone (0845 900 1234), via the website (www.cclondon.com), by post, by mobile phone SMS text message or at selected petrol stations and retail outlets.
- Exemptions include motorcycles, mopeds and bicycles. Registration for discount schemes, including disabled and residents, is available from Transport for London.
- There is a penalty charge for late or non-payment of the fee.
- For full details see the Transport for London website (www.cclondon.com).

A Road	A10
B Road	B326
Dual Carriageway	
One Way Street	
Inner Ring Road	R
Width Restriction	7'0"

Restricted Access	Mon. - Sat. 7am - 7pm
Pedestrianized Road	
House Numbers (A & B Roads Only)	34 62
On Street Parking (Restriction may apply)	
Junction Name	MARBLE ARCH
Car Park	P
Railway Station	

Railway Station Entrance:
National Rail Network	⊟
Docklands Light Railway	DLR
Underground (Symbol is the registered trade mark of Transport for London)	⊖
Borough Boundary	
Postal Boundary	
Map Continuation	75
National Grid Reference	78
Cinema	🎬
Fast Ferry	
Fire Station	■
Information Centre	𝒊

Police Station	▲
Post Office	★
River Boat Trip	
Theatre	😈
Toilet With facilities for the Disabled	▽
Without facilities for the Disabled	▽
For exclusive use by the Disabled	▽
Educational Establishment	□
Hospital, Hospice, etc	□
Industrial Building	□
Leisure or Recreational Facility	□
Office Building	□
Place of Interest Public Access	□
Place of Interest no Public Access	□
Place of Worship	□
Public Building	□
Residential Building	□
Shopping Centre or Market	□
Other Selected Buildings	□

SCALE

0 50 100 200 300 Yards ¼ ½ Mile
0 50 100 200 300 400 500 750 Metres

1:7,040 9 inches (22.7cm) to 1 mile 14.2cm to 1km

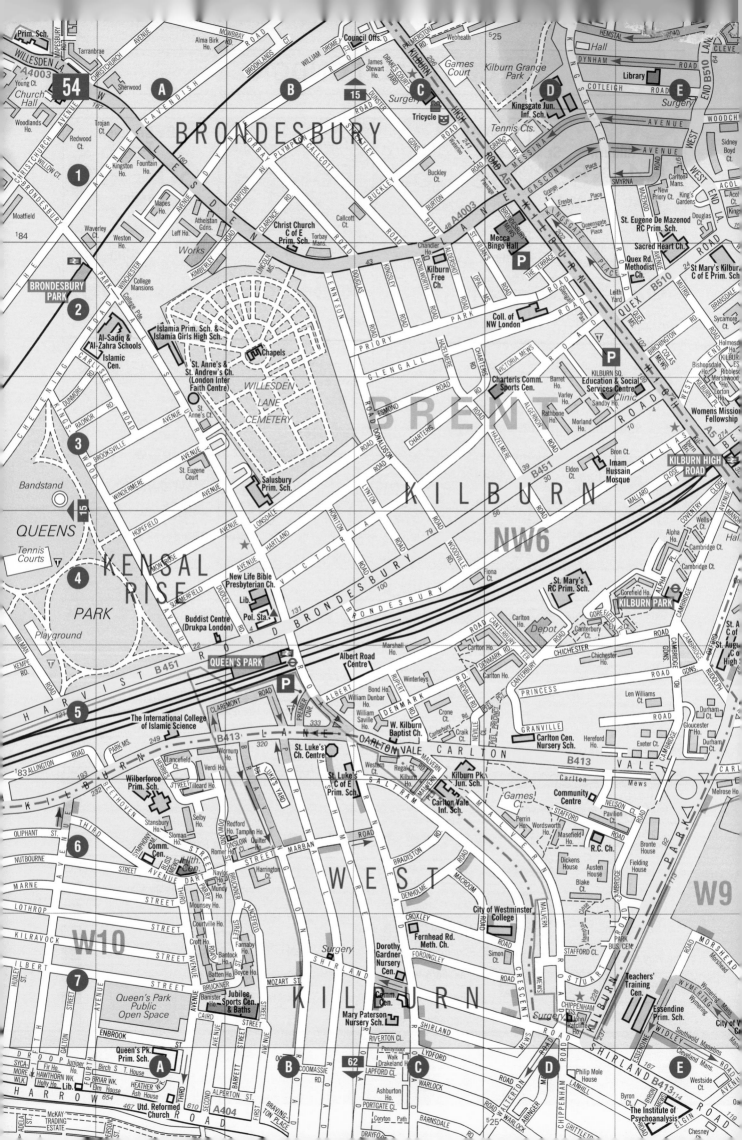

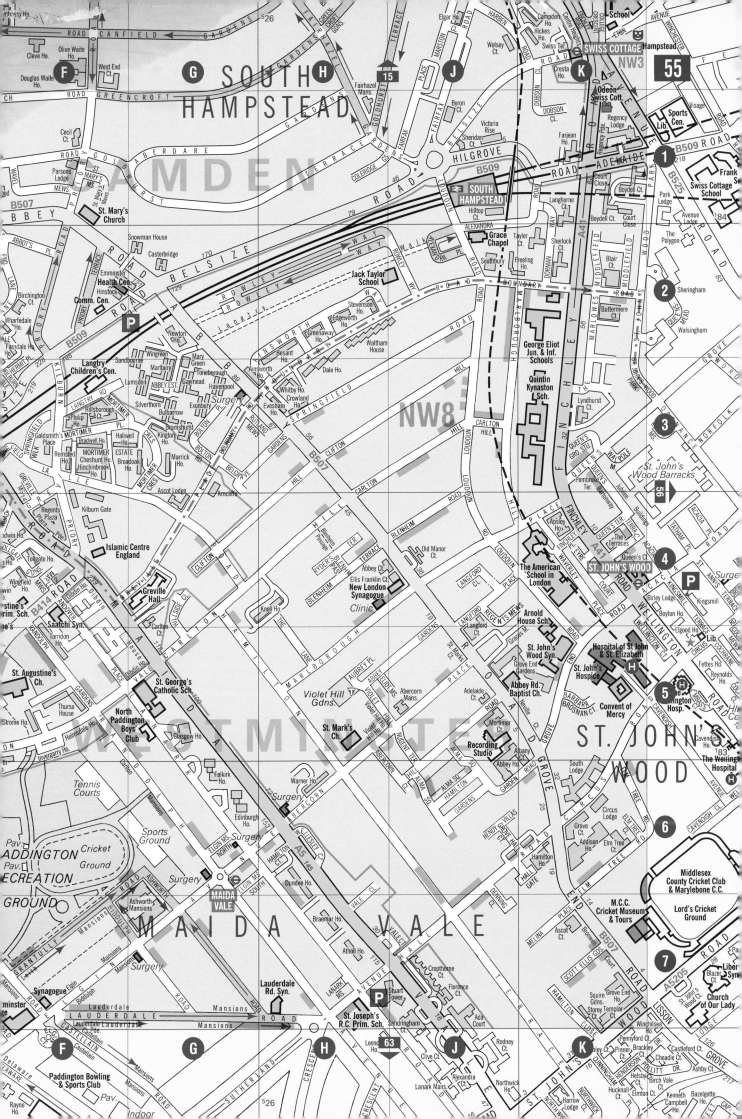

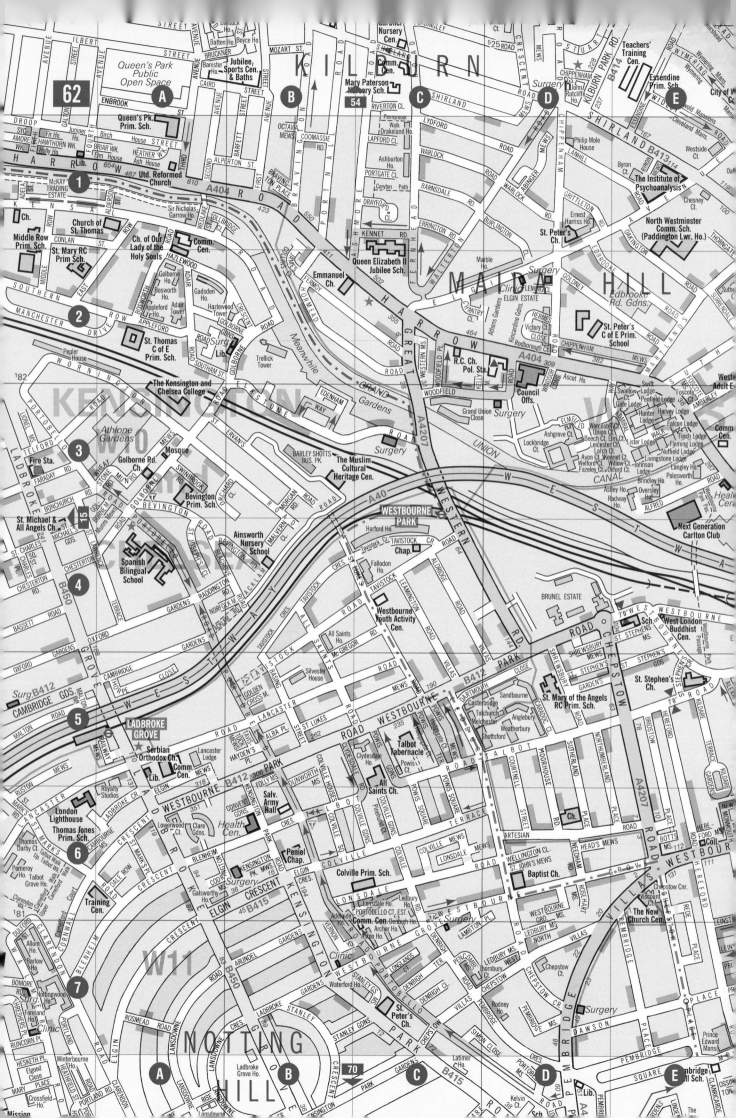

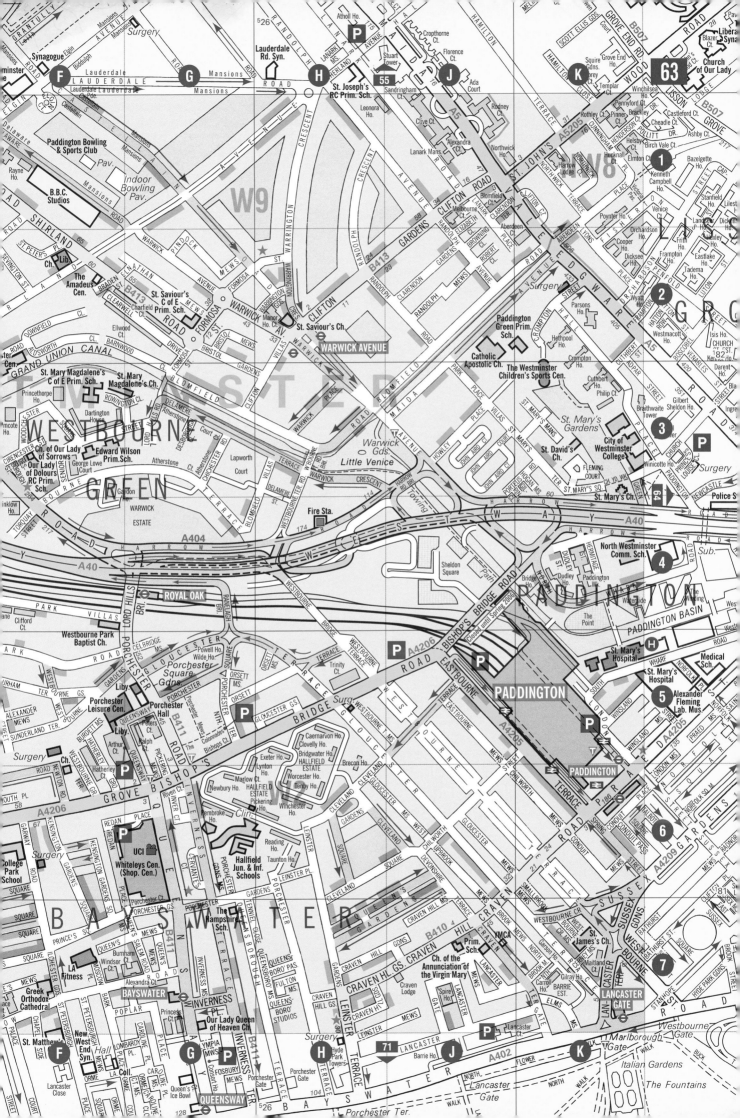

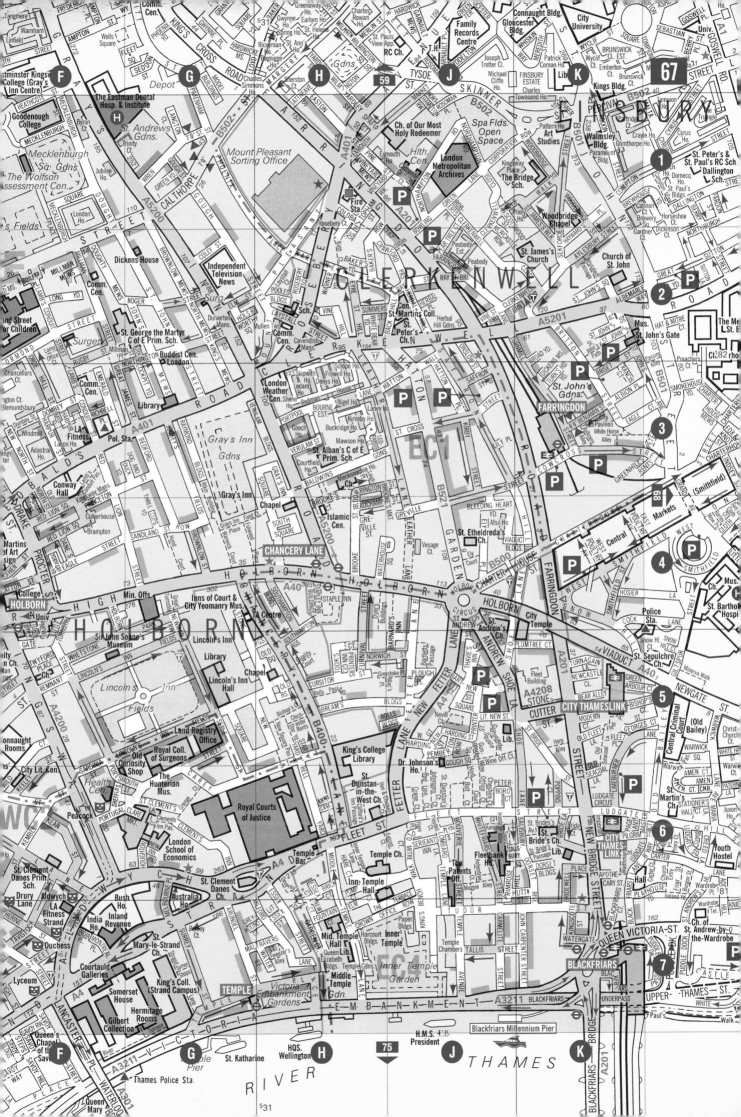

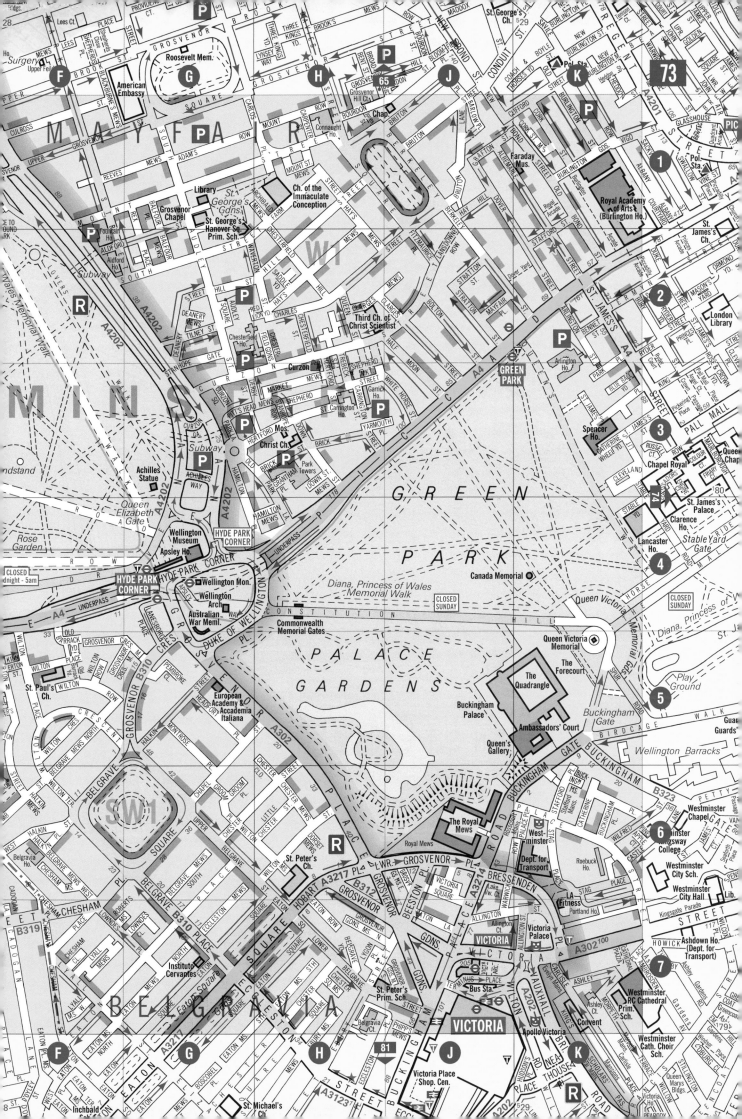

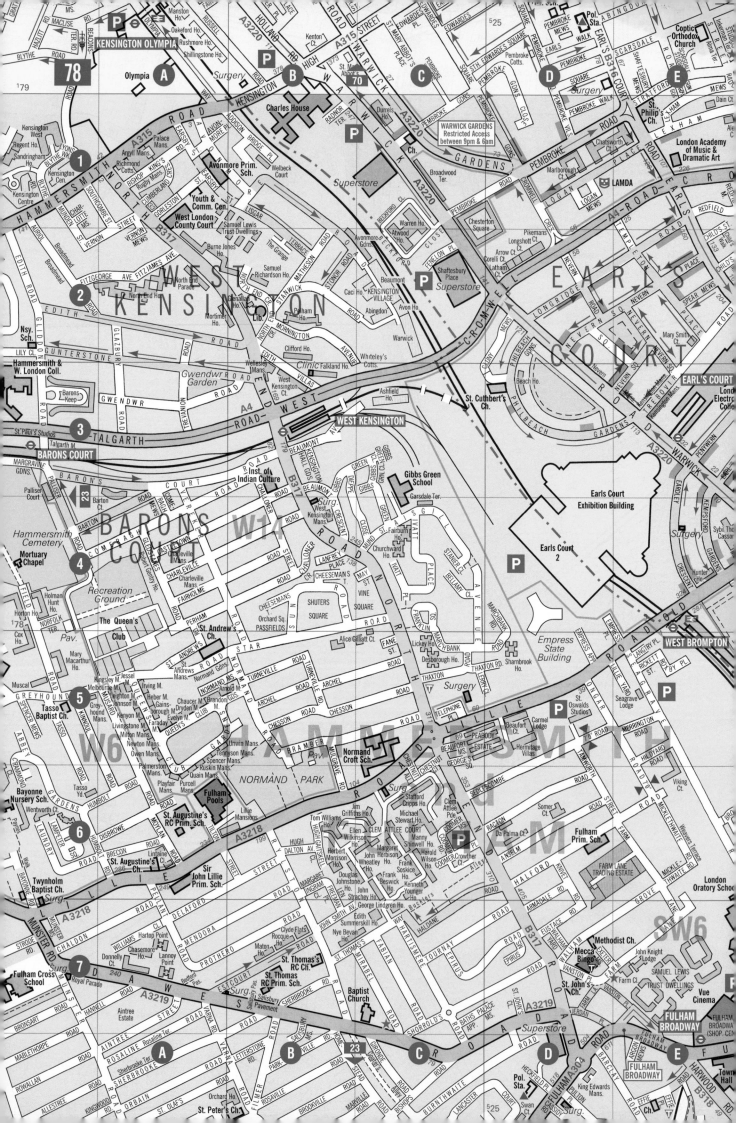

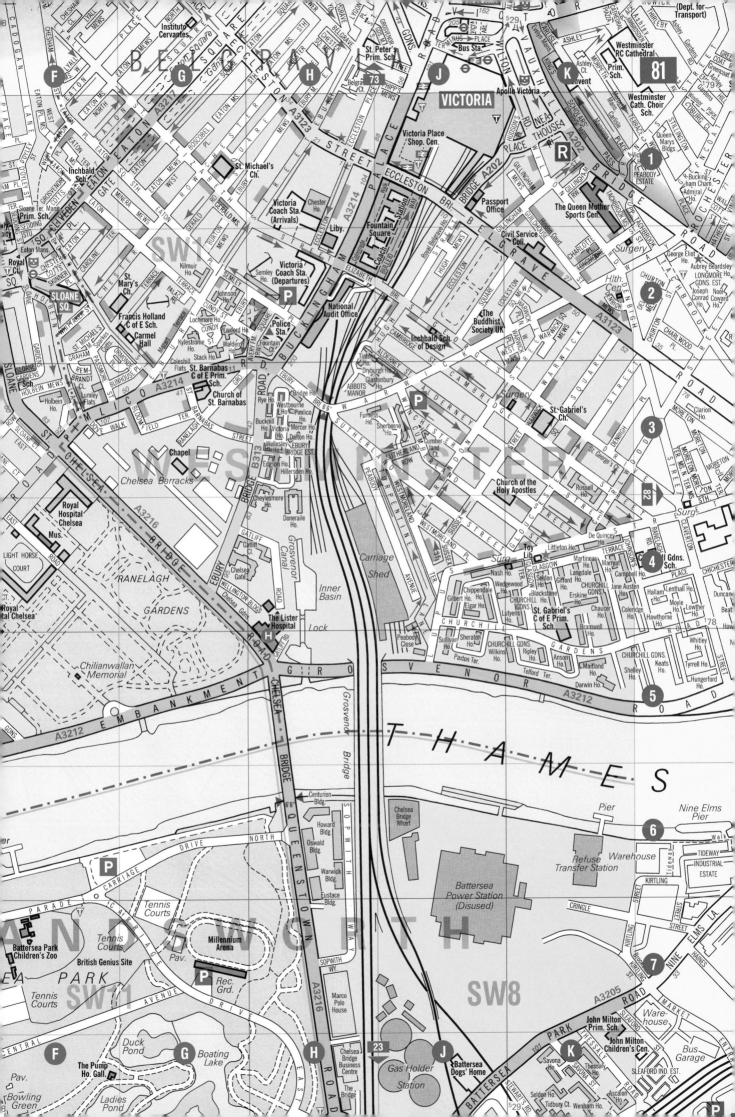

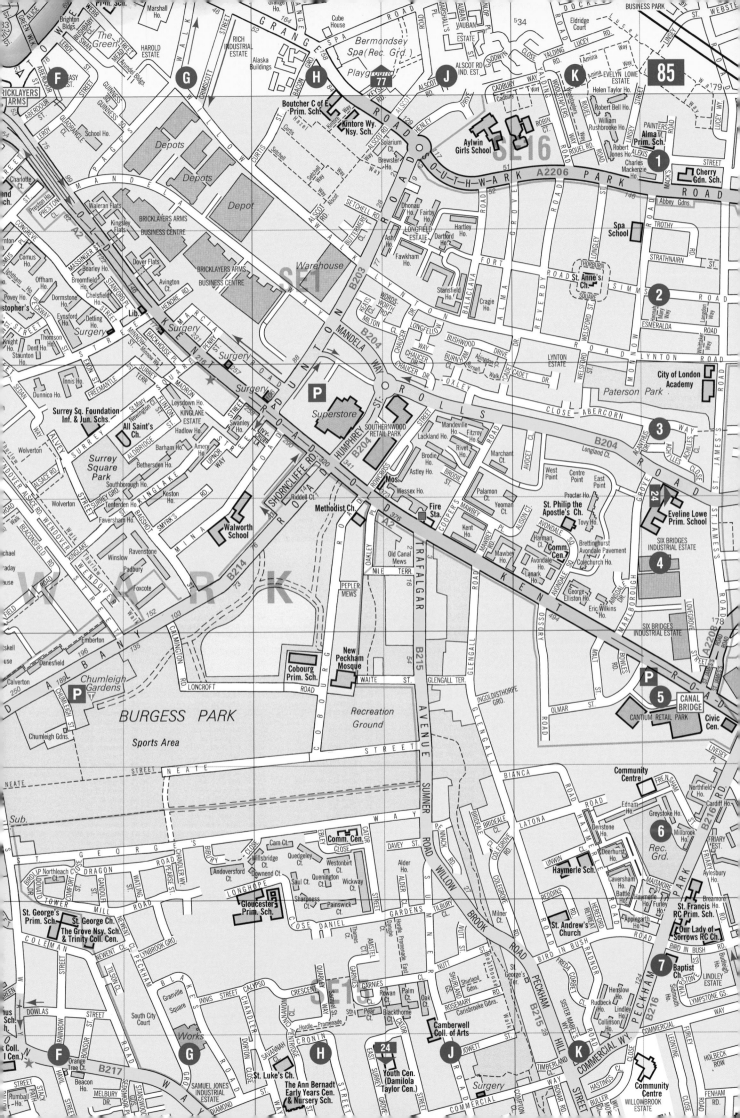

INDEX

Including Streets, Places & Areas, Junction Names and Selected Places of Interest.

HOW TO USE THIS INDEX

1. Each street name is followed by its Postal District and then by its map reference; e.g. **Abbey Gdns.** NW8 . . . .5H **55** is in the North West 8 Postal District and is to be found in square 5H on page **55**. The page number being shown in bold type. A strict alphabetical order is followed in which Av., Rd., St. etc. (though abbreviated) are read in full and as part of the street name; e.g. **Ash Ho.** appears after **Ashgrove Ho.** but before **Ashland Pl.**

2. Streets and a selection of Subsidiary names not shown on the Maps, appear in this index in *Italics* with the thoroughfare to which it is connected shown in brackets; e.g. **Aldgate.** E1 . . . .*5H 69 (off Whitechapel High St.)*

3. Places and areas are shown in the index in **blue type**, the map reference referring to the actual map square in which the town or area is located and not to the place name; e.g. **BAYSWATER. 7H 63**

4. An example of a selected place of interest is **Alexander Fleming Mus. 5A 64**

5. Junction names are shown in the index in **bold type**; e.g. **Aldgate. 6J 69**

GENERAL ABBREVIATIONS

All. : Alley
App. : Approach
Arc. : Arcade
Av. : Avenue
Bk. : Back
Bri. : Bridge
B'way. : Broadway
Bldg. : Building
Bldgs. : Buildings
Bus. : Business
C'way. : Causeway
Cen. : Centre
Chu. : Church
Chyd. : Churchyard
Circ. : Circle
Cir. : Circus
Cl. : Close
Coll. : College
Cnr. : Corner
Cotts. : Cottages
Ct. : Court
Cres. : Crescent
Cft. : Croft
Dr. : Drive
E. : East
Emb. : Embankment
Est. : Estate
Flds. : Fields
Gdn. : Garden
Gdns. : Gardens
Ga. : Gate
Gt. : Great
Grn. : Green
Gro. : Grove
Hgts. : Heights
Ho. : House
Ho's. : Houses
Ind. : Industrial
Info. : Information
Junc. : Junction
La. : Lane
Lit. : Little
Lwr. : Lower
Mnr. : Manor
Mans. : Mansions
Mkt. : Market
M. : Mews
Mt. : Mount
Mus. : Museum
Nth. : North
Pal. : Palace
Pde. : Parade
Pk. : Park
Pas. : Passage
Pav. : Pavilion
Pl. : Place
Pct. : Precinct
Prom. : Promenade
Ri. : Rise
Rd. : Road
Shop. : Shopping
Sth. : South
Sq. : Square
Sta. : Station
St. : Street
Ter. : Terrace
Twr. : Tower
Trad. : Trading
Up. : Upper
Va. : Vale
Vw. : View
Vs. : Villas
Vis. : Visitors
Wlk. : Walk
W. : West
Yd. : Yard

INDEX

Abady Ho. SW1 . . . .1C **82**
Abbey Ct. NW8 . . . .4H **55**
SE17 . . . .4C **84**
Abbey Est. NW8 . . . .3G **55**
Abbey Gdns. NW8 . . . .5H **55**
SE16 . . . .1K **85**
W6 . . . .5A **78**
Abbey Ho. NW8 . . . .6J **55**
Abbey Lodge NW8 . . . .7C **56**
Abbey Orchard St. SW1 . . . .6B **74**
Abbey Orchard St. Est.
SW1 . . . .6C **74**
(not continuous)
Abbey Rd. NW6 . . . .1F **55**
NW8 . . . .2G **55**
Abbey St. SE1 . . . .6G **77**
Abbotsbury Cl. W14 . . . .5A **70**
Abbotsbury Rd. W14 . . . .4A **70**
Abbot's Ho. W14 . . . .7B **70**
Abbots La. SE1 . . . .3G **77**
Abbots Mnr. SW1 . . . .3H **81**
Abbot's Pl. NW6 . . . .2F **55**
Abbots Wlk. W8 . . . .7F **71**
Abbotts Ho. SW1 . . . .4B **82**
Abchurch La. EC4 . . . .7E **68**
(not continuous)
Abchurch Yd. EC4 . . . .7D **68**
Abel Ho. SE11 . . . .5J **83**
Abercorn Cl. NW8 . . . .5H **55**
Abercorn Mans. NW8 . . . .5J **55**
Abercorn Pl. NW8 . . . .6H **55**
Abercorn Way SE1 . . . .3K **85**
Aberdare Gdns. NW6 . . . .1G **55**
Aberdeen Ct. W9 . . . .2J **63**
Aberdeen Mans. WC1 . . . .1D **66**
Aberdeen Pl. NW8 . . . .2K **63**
Aberdour St. SE1 . . . .7F **77**
Aberfeldy Ho. SE5 . . . .7K **83**
(not continuous)
Abingdon W14 . . . .2C **78**
Abingdon Cl. SE1 . . . .2J **85**
Abingdon Ct. W8 . . . .7E **70**
Abingdon Gdns. W8 . . . .7E **70**
Abingdon Ho. E2 . . . .1H **69**
Abingdon Lodge W8 . . . .7F **71**
Abingdon Rd. W8 . . . .6D **70**
Abingdon St. SW1 . . . .6E **75**
Abingdon Vs. W8 . . . .7D **70**
Abinger Ho. SE1 . . . .5D **76**
Abinger M. W9 . . . .1D **62**
Acacia Gdns. NW8 . . . .4A **56**
Acacia Pl. NW8 . . . .4A **56**
Acacia Rd. NW8 . . . .4A **56**
Academy Bldgs. N1 . . . .6F **61**
Academy Gdns. W8 . . . .4D **70**
Acanthus Dr. SE1 . . . .3K **85**
Achilles Cl. SE1 . . . .3K **85**
Achilles Statue 3G **73**
Achilles Way W1 . . . .3G **73**
Acklam Rd. W10 . . . .4A **62**
(not continuous)
Acol Ct. NW6 . . . .1E **54**
Acol Rd. NW6 . . . .1E **54**
Acorn Production Cen.
N7 . . . .1D **58**
Acton Ho. E8 . . . .2H **61**
Acton M. E8 . . . .2H **61**
Acton St. WC1 . . . .7F **59**
Ada Ct. N1 . . . .3B **60**
W9 . . . .7J **55**
Adair Rd. W10 . . . .2A **62**
Adair Twr. W10 . . . .2A **62**
Adam & Eve Ct. W1 . . . .5A **66**
Adam & Eve M. W8 . . . .6E **70**
Adam Ct. SE11 . . . .2K **83**
SW7 . . . .1J **79**
Adams Ct. EC2 . . . .5E **68**
Adam's Row W1 . . . .1G **73**
Adam St. WC2 . . . .1E **74**
Adastral Ho. WC1 . . . .3F **67**
Addington Sq. SE5 . . . .7C **84**
(not continuous)
Addington St. SE1 . . . .5G **75**
Addisland Ct. W14 . . . .4A **70**
Addison Av. W11 . . . .2A **70**
Addison Bri. Pl. W14 . . . .1B **78**
Addison Cres. W14 . . . .6A **70**
(not continuous)
Addison Ho. NW8 . . . .6K **55**
Addison Pl. W11 . . . .3A **70**
Addison Rd. W14 . . . .4A **70**
Addle Hill EC4 . . . .6A **68**
Addle St. EC2 . . . .5C **68**
Adelaide Ct. NW8 . . . .5J **55**
Adelaide Ho. W11 . . . .6B **62**
Adelaide Rd. NW3 . . . .1K **55**
Adelaide St. WC2 . . . .1D **74**
Adela St. W10 . . . .1A **62**
Adeline Pl. WC1 . . . .4C **66**
Adelphi Ct. E8 . . . .1J **61**
Adelphi Ter. WC2 . . . .1E **74**
Adelphi Theatre 1E **74**
Adeyfield Ho. EC1 . . . .7E **60**
Adler St. E1 . . . .5K **69**
Admiral Ct. W1 . . . .4F **65**
Admiral Ho. SW1 . . . .1A **82**
Admirals Ct. SE1 . . . .3H **77**
Admiralty Arch 2C **74**
Admiral Wlk. W9 . . . .3E **62**
Adpar St. W2 . . . .3K **63**
Adrian Ho. N1 . . . .3G **59**
SW8 . . . .7D **82**
Adrian M. SW10 . . . .5G **79**
Adstock Ho. N1 . . . .1K **59**
Affleck St. N1 . . . .5G **59**
Afsil Ho. EC1 . . . .4J **67**
Agar Gro. NW1 . . . .1A **58**
Agar Gro. Est. NW1 . . . .1B **58**
Agar Pl. NW1 . . . .1A **58**
Agar St. WC2 . . . .1D **74**
Agdon St. EC1 . . . .1K **67**
Aigburth Mans. SW9 . . . .7H **83**
Ainger M. NW3 . . . .1E **56**
(not continuous)
Ainger Rd. NW3 . . . .1D **56**
Ainsdale NW1 . . . .5K **57**
Ainsdale Dr. SE1 . . . .4K **85**
Ainsworth Ho. NW8 . . . .3G **55**
Ainsworth Way NW8 . . . .2H **55**
Aintree Est. SW6 . . . .7A **78**
Aintree St. SW6 . . . .7A **78**
Aird Ho. SE1 . . . .7B **76**
Airdrie Cl. N1 . . . .1F **59**
Airlie Gdns. W8 . . . .3D **70**
Air St. W1 . . . .1A **74**
Aisgill Av. W14 . . . .4C **78**
(not continuous)
Aitken Cl. E8 . . . .2K **61**
Alaska Bldgs. SE1 . . . .7H **77**
Alaska St. SE1 . . . .3H **75**
Alban Highwalk EC2 . . . .4C **68**
(not continuous)
Albany W1 . . . .1K **73**
Albany Ct. NW8 . . . .5K **55**
Albany Courtyard W1 . . . .1A **74**
Albany Mans. SW11 . . . .7C **80**
Albany M. SE5 . . . .6C **84**
Albany Rd. SE5 . . . .6C **84**
Albany St. NW1 . . . .4H **57**
Albany Ter. NW1 . . . .2J **65**
Alba Pl. W11 . . . .5B **62**
Albemarle St. W1 . . . .1J **73**
Albemarle Way EC1 . . . .2K **67**
Alberta Est. SE17 . . . .3A **84**
Alberta St. SE17 . . . .3K **83**
Albert Barnes Ho. SE1 . . . .7B **76**
Albert Bri. SW8 . . . .6C **80**
Albert Bri. Rd. SW11 . . . .7C **80**
Albert Cotts. E1 . . . .3K **69**
Albert Ct. SW7 . . . .5K **71**
Albert Ct. Ga. SW7 . . . .5D **72**
Albert Emb. SE1 . . . .7F **75**
(Lambeth Pal. Rd.)
SE1 . . . .4E **82**
(Vauxhall Bri.)
Albert Ga. SW1 . . . .4E **72**
Albert Gray Ho. SW10 . . . .7K **79**
Albert Hall Mans. SW7 . . . .5K **71**
(not continuous)
Albert Memorial 5K **71**
Albert M. W8 . . . .6H **71**
Albert Pl. W8 . . . .5G **71**
Albert Rd. NW6 . . . .5B **54**
Albert St. NW1 . . . .3J **57**
Albert Ter. NW1 . . . .2F **57**
Albert Ter. M. NW1 . . . .2F **57**
Albert Westcott Ho.
SE17 . . . .3A **84**
Albery Ct. E8 . . . .1H **61**
Albery Theatre 7D **66**
Albion Bldgs. N1 . . . .5E **58**
Albion Cl. W2 . . . .7C **64**
Albion Dr. E8 . . . .1H **61**
Albion Ga. W2 . . . .7C **64**
(not continuous)
Albion M. N1 . . . .1H **59**
W2 . . . .7C **64**
Albion Pl. EC1 . . . .3K **67**
EC2 . . . .4E **68**
Albion Sq. E8 . . . .1H **61**
(not continuous)
Albion St. W2 . . . .6C **64**
Albion Ter. E8 . . . .1H **61**
Albion Wlk. N1 . . . .5E **58**
Albion Way EC1 . . . .4B **68**
Albion Wharf SW11 . . . .7B **80**
Albion Yd. N1 . . . .5E **58**
Albury Ho. SE1 . . . .5A **76**
Aldbridge St. SE17 . . . .3G **85**
Aldburgh M. W1 . . . .5G **65**
(not continuous)
Aldbury Ho. SW3 . . . .2B **80**
Aldenham Ho. NW1 . . . .5A **58**
Aldenham St. NW1 . . . .5A **58**
Alder Cl. SE15 . . . .6J **85**
Alder Ho. SE15 . . . .6J **85**
Aldermanbury EC2 . . . .5C **68**
Aldermanbury Sq. EC2 . . . .4C **68**
Aldermans Wlk. EC2 . . . .4F **69**
Alderney St. SW1 . . . .2J **81**
Aldersgate St. EC1 . . . .3B **68**
Aldershot Rd. NW6 . . . .2C **54**
Alderson St. W10 . . . .1A **62**
Aldford Ho. W1 . . . .2F **73**
Aldford St. W1 . . . .2F **73**
ALDGATE 6J **69**
Aldgate *E1 . . . .5H 69*
(off Whitechapel High St.)
EC3 . . . .6H **69**
Aldgate Av. E1 . . . .5H **69**
Aldgate Barrs E1 . . . .5J **69**
Aldgate High St. EC3 . . . .6H **69**
Aldgate Triangle E1 . . . .5K **69**
Aldrick Ho. N1 . . . .3G **59**
Aldridge Rd. Vs. W11 . . . .4C **62**
Aldsworth Cl. W9 . . . .2F **63**
Aldwych WC2 . . . .7F **67**
Aldwych Ct. E8 . . . .1J **61**
Aldwych Theatre 6F **67**
Aldwyn Ho. SW8 . . . .7D **82**
Alexa Ct. W8 . . . .1E **78**
Alexander Fleming Mus.
. . . .5A **64**
Alexander M. W2 . . . .5F **63**
Alexander Pl. SW7 . . . .1B **80**
Alexander Sq. SW3 . . . .7B **72**
Alexander St. W2 . . . .5E **62**
Alexandra Ct. SW7 . . . .6J **71**
W2 . . . .7G **63**
W9 . . . .1J **63**
Alexandra Mans. SW3 . . . .6K **79**
Alexandra Pl. NW8 . . . .2J **55**
Alexandra Rd. NW8 . . . .2J **55**
Alexis St. SE16 . . . .1K **85**
Alford Ct. N1 . . . .5C **60**
(not continuous)
Alford Pl. N1 . . . .5C **60**
Alfred M. W1 . . . .3B **66**
Alfred Pl. WC1 . . . .3B **66**
Alfred Rd. W2 . . . .3E **62**
Algar Ho. SE1 . . . .5K **75**
Algernon Rd. NW6 . . . .3D **54**
Alice Gilliatt Ct. W14 . . . .5B **78**
Alice Owen Technology Cen.
EC1 . . . .6K **59**
Alice St. SE1 . . . .7F **77**
(not continuous)
Alie St. E1 . . . .6J **69**
Alison Ct. SE1 . . . .4K **85**
Allensbury Pl. NW1 . . . .1C **58**
Allen St. W8 . . . .6E **70**
Allerton Ho. N1 . . . .6D **60**
Allerton St. N1 . . . .6D **60**
Allestree Rd. SW6 . . . .7A **78**
Alleyn Ho. SE1 . . . .7E **76**
Allgood St. E2 . . . .5J **61**
Allhallows La. EC4 . . . .1D **76**
Allingham M. N1 . . . .4B **60**
Allingham St. N1 . . . .4B **60**
Allington Ct. SW1 . . . .7J **73**
Allington Rd. W10 . . . .5A **54**
Allington St. SW1 . . . .7J **73**
Alliston Ho. E2 . . . .7J **61**
Allitsen Rd. NW8 . . . .5B **56**
(not continuous)
Allom Ho. W11 . . . .7A **62**
All Saints Ho. W11 . . . .4B **62**
All Saints Rd. W11 . . . .4B **62**
All Saints St. N1 . . . .4F **59**
Allsop Pl. NW1 . . . .2E **64**
All Souls' Pl. W1 . . . .4J **65**
Alma Birk Ho. NW6 . . . .1A **54**
Alma Gro. SE1 . . . .2J **85**
Alma Sq. NW8 . . . .5J **55**
Alma Ter. W8 . . . .7E **70**
Almeida St. N1 . . . .2K **59**
Almeida Theatre 2K **59**
Almorah Rd. N1 . . . .1D **60**
Alperton St. W10 . . . .1A **62**
Alpha Cl. NW1 . . . .7C **56**
Alpha Ho. NW6 . . . .4E **54**
NW8 . . . .2B **64**
Alpha Pl. NW6 . . . .4E **54**
SW3 . . . .5C **80**
Alsace Rd. SE17 . . . .3F **85**
Alscot Rd. SE1 . . . .1H **85**
(not continuous)
Alscot Rd. Ind. Est. SE1 . . . .7J **77**
Alscot Way SE1 . . . .1H **85**
Alverstone Ho. SE11 . . . .6H **83**
Alvey St. SE17 . . . .3F **85**
Alwyne La. N1 . . . .1A **60**
Alwyne Rd. N1 . . . .1B **60**
Ambassadors Ct. E8 . . . .1J **61**
SW1 . . . .3A **74**
Ambassadors Theatre 6C **66**
Ambergate St. SE17 . . . .3K **83**
Amberley Rd. W9 . . . .3E **62**
Amber Wharf E2 . . . .3H **61**
Ambleside NW1 . . . .5J **57**
Ambrosden Av. SW1 . . . .7K **73**
Amelia St. SE17 . . . .3A **84**
Amen Cnr. EC4 . . . .6A **68**
Amen Ct. EC4 . . . .6A **68**
America Sq. EC3 . . . .7H **69**
America St. SE1 . . . .3B **76**
Amery Ho. SE17 . . . .3G **85**
Amias Ho. EC1 . . . .1B **68**
Amigo Ho. SE1 . . . .6J **75**
Amina Way SE16 . . . .7K **77**
Amory Ho. N1 . . . .3G **59**
Ampthill Est. NW1 . . . .5A **58**
Ampthill Sq. NW1 . . . .5A **58**
Ampton Pl. WC1 . . . .7F **59**
Ampton St. WC1 . . . .7F **59**
Amstel Ct. SE15 . . . .7H **85**
Amwell St. EC1 . . . .6H **59**
Anchor Brewhouse SE1 . . . .3H **77**
Anchor Ct. SW1 . . . .2B **82**
Anchor Ho. EC1 . . . .1B **68**
Anchor Yd. EC1 . . . .1C **68**
Anderson Sq. N1 . . . .3K **59**
Anderson St. SW3 . . . .3D **80**
Andover Pl. NW6 . . . .4F **55**
Andoversford Ct. SE15 . . . .6G **85**
Andrew Borde St. WC2 . . . .5C **66**
Andrewes Highwalk EC2 . . . .4C **68**
Andrewes Ho. EC2 . . . .4C **68**
Andrews Crosse WC2 . . . .6H **67**
Andrews Wlk. SE17 . . . .6A **84**
ANGEL 5J **59**
Angel All. E1 . . . .5J **69**
Angel Cen., The N1 . . . .5J **59**
Angel Ct. EC2 . . . .5E **68**
SW1 . . . .3A **74**
Angel Ga. EC1 . . . .6A **60**
(not continuous)
Angelis Apartments N1 . . . .5A **60**
Angel M. N1 . . . .5J **59**
Angel Pas. EC4 . . . .1D **76**
Angel Pl. SE1 . . . .4D **76**
Angel Sq. EC1 . . . .5K **59**
Angel St. EC1 . . . .5B **68**
Anglebury W2 . . . .5D **62**
Angrave Ct. E8 . . . .2J **61**
Angrave Pas. E8 . . . .2J **61**
Anhalt Rd. SW11 . . . .7C **80**
Anna Cl. E8 . . . .2J **61**
Annette Cres. N1 . . . .1C **60**
Anning St. EC2 . . . .1G **69**
Ann La. SW10 . . . .7K **79**
Ann's Cl. SW1 . . . .5E **72**
Ann's Pl. E1 . . . .4H **69**
Ansdell St. W8 . . . .6G **71**
Ansdell Ter. W8 . . . .6G **71**
Anselm Rd. SW6 . . . .6D **78**
Anson Ho. SW1 . . . .5K **81**
Anthony Cope Ct. N1 . . . .6E **60**
Anthony Ho. NW8 . . . .2B **64**
Antonine Hgts. SE1 . . . .5F **77**
Apollo Ct. E1 . . . .1K **77**
Apollo Ho. SW10 . . . .7K **79**
Apollo Pl. SW10 . . . .7K **79**
Apollo Theatre
Soho 7B **66**
Victoria 7K **73**
Apollo West End Cinema
. . . .1B **74**
Apothecary St. EC4 . . . .6K **67**
Apple Blossom Ct. SW8 . . . .7C **82**
Appleby St. E2 . . . .4H **61**
Appleford Ho. W10 . . . .2A **62**
Appleford Rd. W10 . . . .2A **62**
Applegarth Ho. SE1 . . . .4A **76**
SE15 . . . .7K **85**
Apple Tree Yd. SW1 . . . .2A **74**
Appold St. EC2 . . . .3F **69**
Apsley House 4G **73**
Apsley Ho. NW8 . . . .4K **55**
Apsley Way W1 . . . .4G **73**
(not continuous)
Aquila St. NW8 . . . .4A **56**
Aquinas St. SE1 . . . .3J **75**
Arbon Ct. N1 . . . .3C **60**
Arbutus St. E8 . . . .2H **61**
Arcade, The EC2 . . . .4F **69**
Arcadia Ct. E1 . . . .5H **69**
Archdale Ho. SE1 . . . .6F **77**
Archel Rd. W14 . . . .5B **78**
Archer Ho. W11 . . . .7C **62**
Archer St. W1 . . . .7B **66**
Archery Cl. W2 . . . .6C **64**
Archery Steps W2 . . . .7C **64**
Arches, The NW1 . . . .1H **57**
SW8 . . . .7B **82**
WC2 . . . .2E **74**
Archibald M. W1 . . . .1H **73**
Archie St. SE1 . . . .5G **77**
Arch St. SE1 . . . .7B **76**
Arden Est. N1 . . . .5F **61**
Arden Ho. N1 . . . .5F **61**
SE11 . . . .2F **83**
Argon M. SW6 . . . .7E **78**
Argyle Sq. WC1 . . . .6E **58**
Argyle St. WC1 . . . .6D **58**
Argyle Wlk. WC1 . . . .7D **58**
Argyll Mans. SW3 . . . .6A **80**
W14 . . . .1A **78**
Argyll Rd. W8 . . . .5D **70**
Argyll St. W1 . . . .6K **65**
Ariel Ct. SE11 . . . .2K **83**
Arklow Ho. SE17 . . . .6D **84**
Arlington Av. N1 . . . .4C **60**
(not continuous)
Arlington Ho. EC1 . . . .6J **59**
SW1 . . . .2K **73**
Arlington Rd. NW1 . . . .2H **57**
Arlington Sq. N1 . . . .3C **60**
Arlington St. SW1 . . . .2K **73**
Arlington Way EC1 . . . .6J **59**
Armadale Rd. SW6 . . . .7D **78**
Armstrong Rd. SW7 . . . .7K **71**
Arncliffe NW6 . . . .4G **55**
Arne Ho. SE11 . . . .3F **83**
Arne St. WC2 . . . .6E **66**
Arneway St. SW1 . . . .7C **74**
Arnold Cir. E2 . . . .7H **61**
Arnold Est. SE1 . . . .5J **77**
(not continuous)
Arnold Ho. SE17 . . . .4A **84**
Arnold Mans. W14 . . . .5A **78**
Arnside St. SE17 . . . .5C **84**
Arrol Ho. SE1 . . . .7C **76**
Arrow Ct. SW5 . . . .2D **78**
Arrowsmith Ho. SE11 . . . .3F **83**
Artesian Rd. W2 . . . .6D **62**
Arthur Ct. W2 . . . .5F **63**
Arthur Deakin Ho. E1 . . . .3K **69**
Arthur St. EC4 . . . .1E **76**
Artillery La. E1 . . . .4G **69**
Artillery Pas. E1 . . . .4G **69**
Artillery Pl. SW1 . . . .7B **74**
Artillery Row SW1 . . . .7B **74**
Artizan St. E1 . . . .5G **69**
Arts Theatre 7D **66**
Arundel Bldgs. SE1 . . . .7G **77**
Arundel Ct. SW3 . . . .3C **80**
Arundel Gdns. W11 . . . .7B **62**
Arundel Gt. Ct. WC2 . . . .7G **67**
Arundel St. WC2 . . . .7G **67**
Ascalon Ho. SW8 . . . .7K **81**
Ascot Ct. NW8 . . . .7K **55**
Ascot Ho. NW1 . . . .6J **57**
W9 . . . .2D **62**
Ascot Lodge NW6 . . . .3G **55**
Ashbridge St. NW8 . . . .2B **64**
Ashburn Gdns. SW7 . . . .1H **79**
Ashburnham Mans.
SW10 . . . .7J **79**
Ashburnham Rd. SW10 . . . .7J **79**
Ashburnham Twr. SW10 . . . .7K **79**
Ashburn Pl. SW7 . . . .1H **79**
Ashburton Ho. W9 . . . .1C **62**
Ashby Ct. NW8 . . . .1A **64**

Ashby Ho.—Boswell Ho.

Ashby Ho. N1 1C 60
Ashby St. EC1 7A 60
Ashdown Ho. *SW1* *7A 74*
(off Victoria St.)
Ashenden SE17 1B 84
Ashentree Ct. EC4 6J 67
Asher Way E1 1K 77
Ashfield Ho. W14 3C 78
Ashford St. N1 6F 61
Ashgrove Ct. W9 3D 62
Ashgrove Ho. SW1 3C 82
Ash Ho. SE1 2J 85
W10 1A 62
Ashland Pl. W1 3F 65
Ashley Ct. SW1 7K 73
Ashley Gdns. SW1 7A 74
(not continuous)
Ashley Pl. SW1 7K 73
(not continuous)
Ashmill St. NW1 3B 64
Ashmole Pl. SW8 6H 83
(not continuous)
Ashmole St. SW8 6G 83
Ashmore NW1 1B 58
Ashmore Ho. W14 7A 70
Ashmore Rd. W9 6B 54
Ashton Ho. SW9 7J 83
Ash Tree Ho. SE5 7B 84
Ashworth Mans. W9 7G 55
Ashworth Rd. W9 6G 55
Aske Ho. N1 6F 61
(not continuous)
Aske St. N1 6F 61
Asolando Dr. SE17 3C 84
Aspen Lodge W8 7F 71
Assam St. E1 5K 69
Association Gallery, The 1F 69
Astbury Ho. SE11 7H 75
Astell St. SW3 3C 80
Astey's Row N1 2A 60
Astley Ho. SE1 3J 85
W2 3E 62
Aston Ho. W11 7C 62
Astor Ct. SW6 7H 79
Astoria, The 5C 66
Astoria Ct. E8 1J 61
Astwood M. SW7 1G 79
Athelstan Gdns. NW6 1A 54
Athene Pl. *EC4* *5J 67*
(off St Andrew St.)
Athens Gdns. W9 2D 62
Atherstone Ct. W2 3G 63
Atherstone M. SW7 1J 79
Atholl Ho. W9 7H 55
Atkin Bldg. WC1 3G 67
Atkinson Ho. SE17 2E 84
Atrium Apartments N1 3E 60
Atterbury St. SW1 2D 82
Attilburgh Ho. SE1 6H 77
Attneave St. WC1 1H 67
Atwood Ho. W14 2C 78
Aubrey Beardsley Ho.
SW1 2A 82
Aubrey Mans. NW1 3B 64
Aubrey Pl. NW8 5H 55
Aubrey Rd. W8 2C 70
Aubrey Wlk. W8 3C 70
Auckland St. SE11 4F 83
Auden Pl. NW1 2F 57
(not continuous)
Audley Sq. W1 2G 73
Audrey St. E2 4K 61
Augustus Ho. NW1 5K 57
Augustus St. NW1 5J 57
Aulton Pl. SE11 4J 83
Auriol Rd. W14 2A 78
Austen Ho. NW6 6D 54
Austin Friars EC2 5E 68
(not continuous)
Austin Friars Pas. EC2 5E 68
Austin Friars Sq. EC2 5E 68
Austin St. E2 7H 61
Austin Ter. SE1 6J 75
Australian War Memorial
4G 73
Austral St. SE11 1K 83
Avebury Ct. N1 3D 60
Avebury St. N1 3D 60
Aveline St. SE11 4H 83
Ave Maria La. EC4 6A 68
Avenfield Ho. W1 7E 64
Avenue Cl. NW8 3C 56
Avenue Ct. SW3 2D 80
Avenue Ho. NW8 5B 56
Avenue Lodge NW8 1A 56
Avenue Rd. NW3 1K 55
Avery Farm Row SW1 2H 81
Avery Row W1 7H 65
Avington Ct. SE1 2G 85
Avocet Cl. SE1 3K 85
Avon Ct. W9 3D 62
Avondale Ho. SE1 4K 85
Avondale Pavement SE1 4K 85
Avondale Sq. SE1 4K 85
Avon Ho. W8 6E 70
W14 2C 78
Avonmore Gdns. W14 2C 78
Avonmore Pl. W14 1A 78
Avonmore Rd. W14 1A 78
Avonmouth St. SE1 6B 76
Avon Pl. SE1 5C 76
Aybrook St. W1 4F 65
Aylesbury Ho. SE15 6K 85
Aylesbury Rd. SE17 4E 84
Aylesbury St. EC1 2K 67
Aylesford Ho. SE1 5E 76
Aylesford St. SW1 3B 82
Aylwin Est. SE1 6G 77
Ayres St. SE1 4C 76
Ayrton Rd. SW7 6K 71
Ayton Ho. SE5 7E 84
Azure Ho. *E2* *7K 61*
(off Buckfast St.)

Babington Ct. WC1 3F 67
Babington Ho. SE1 4C 76
Babmaes St. SW1 1B 74
Bacchus Wlk. N1 5F 61
Bache's St. N1 7E 60
Back All. EC3 6G 69
Bk. Church La. E1 6K 69
Back Hill EC1 2J 67
Backhouse Pl. SE17 2G 85
Back Passage EC1 3A 68
Bacon Gro. SE1 7H 77
Bacon St. E1 1J 69
E2 1J 69
Baddesley Ho. SE11 3G 83
Baddow Wlk. N1 2B 60
Baden Pl. SE1 4D 76
Baden Powell Ho. SW7 7J 71
Bagnigge Ho. WC1 7H 59
Bagshot Ho. NW1 6J 57
Bagshot St. SE17 4G 85
Bailey Ho. SW10 7G 79
Bainbridge St. WC1 5C 66
Baird St. EC1 1C 68
Baker Ho. WC1 2E 66
Bakers Hall Ct. EC3 1F 77
Baker's M. W1 5F 65
Baker's Rents E2 7H 61
Baker's Row EC1 2H 67
BAKER STREET 3E 64
Baker St. NW1 2E 64
W1 2E 64
Baker's Yd. EC1 2H 67
Balaclava Rd. SE1 2J 85
Balcombe Ho. NW1 1C 64
Balcombe St. NW1 1D 64
Balderton Flats W1 6G 65
Balderton St. W1 6G 65
Baldwins Gdns. EC1 3H 67
Baldwin St. EC1 7D 60
Baldwin Ter. N1 4B 60
Balfe St. N1 4E 58
Balfour M. W1 2G 73
Balfour Pl. W1 1G 73
Balfour St. SE17 1D 84
Balin Ho. SE1 4D 76
Ball Ct. EC3 6E 68
Ballow Cl. SE5 7F 85
Balmes Rd. N1 2E 60
Balmoral Apartments
W2 4B 64
Balmoral Ct. SE17 4D 84
Balniel Ga. SW1 3C 82
Baltic Pl. N1 3G 61
Baltic St. E. EC1 2B 68
Baltic St. W. EC1 2B 68
Baltimore Ho. SE11 2H 83
Balvaird Pl. SW1 4C 82
Banbury Ct. WC2 7D 66
Banister Ho. W10 7A 54
Bank End SE1 2C 76
Bank of England 6D 68
Bank of England Mus. 6E 68
Bank of England Offices
EC4 6B 68
Banks Ho. SE1 7B 76
Bankside SE1 1B 76
(not continuous)
Bankside Art Gallery 1A 76
Bannerman Ho. SW8 6F 83
Banner St. EC1 2C 68
Banqueting House 3D 74
Bantock Ho. W10 7A 54
Bantry St. SE5 7E 84
Barbara Brosnan Ct.
NW8 5K 55
Barbican Arts Cen. 3C 68
Barbican Cinema 3C 68
Barbican Theatre 3C 68
Barbican Trade Cen. EC1 3C 68
Barbon All. EC2 5G 69
Barbon Cl. WC1 3E 66
Barclay Rd. SW6 7D 78
Bardell Ho. SE1 5K 77
Barfett St. W10 1B 62
Barford St. N1 3J 59
Barge Ho. St. SE1 2J 75
Barham Ho. SE17 3G 85
Baring St. N1 3D 60
Barker Dr. NW1 1A 58
Barkers Arc. W8 5F 71
Barker St. SW10 5H 79
Barkham Ter. SE1 6J 75
Bark Pl. W2 7F 63
Barkston Gdns. SW5 2F 79
Barley Mow Pas. EC1 4A 68
Barley Shotts Bus. Pk.
W10 3B 62
Barlow Ho. N1 6D 60
W11 7A 62
Barlow Pl. W1 1J 73
Barlow St. SE17 2E 84
Barnaby Ct. SE16 5K 77
Barnaby Pl. SW7 2K 79
Barnard Lodge *W9* *3E 62*
(off Admiral Wlk.)
Barnard's Inn EC1 5J 67
Barnbrough NW1 3K 57
Barnby St. NW1 5A 58
Barnes Ct. N1 1H 59
Barnet Gro. E2 6K 61
Barnham St. SE1 4G 77
BARNSBURY 1F 59
Barnsbury Est. N1 3G 59
(not continuous)
Barnsbury Pk. N1 1H 59
Barnsbury Rd. N1 4H 59
Barnsbury Sq. N1 1H 59
Barnsbury St. N1 1H 59
Barnsbury Ter. N1 1G 59
Barnsdale Rd. W9 1C 62
Barnston Wlk. N1 2B 60
Barnwood Cl. W9 2F 63
Baroness Rd. E2 6J 61
BARONS COURT 4A 78
Baron's Ct. Rd. W14 3A 78
Barons Court Theatre *3A 78*
(off Comeragh Rd.)
Barons Keep W14 3A 78
Baron's Pl. SE1 5J 75
Baron St. N1 4H 59
Barratt Ho. N1 1A 60
Barret Ho. NW6 3D 54
Barrett Ho. SE17 3C 84
Barrett St. W1 6G 65
Barrie Est. W2 7K 63
Barrie Ho. W2 1J 71
Barrow Hill Est. NW8 5B 56
Barrow Hill Rd. NW8 5B 56
Barter St. WC1 4E 66
Bartholomew Cl. EC1 4A 68
(not continuous)
Bartholomew Ct. EC1 1C 68
Bartholomew La. EC2 6E 68
Bartholomew Pl. EC1 4B 68
Bartholomew Sq. EC1 7C 60
Bartholomew St. SE1 7E 76
Bartlett Ct. EC4 5J 67
Bartletts Pas. EC4 5J 67
Barton Ct. W14 4A 78
Barton Ho. N1 1A 60
Barton Rd. W14 4A 78
Barton St. SW1 6D 74
Bartonway NW8 3K 55
Basildon Ct. W1 3G 65
Basil Ho. SW8 7D 82
Basil St. SW3 6D 72
Basinghall Av. EC2 5D 68
Basinghall St. EC2 5C 68
Basing Ho. Yd. E2 6G 61
Basing Pl. E2 6G 61
Basing St. W11 5B 62
Basire St. N1 2B 60
Bassett Rd. W10 4A 62
Bassingbourn Ho. N1 1J 59
Bassishaw Highwalk
EC2 4D 68
Basterfield Ho. EC1 2B 68
Bastion Highwalk EC2 4C 68
Bastion Ho. EC2 4B 68
Bastwick St. EC1 1B 68
Batchelor St. N1 4J 59
Bateman Ho. SE17 6K 83
Bateman's Bldgs. W1 6B 66
Bateman's Row EC2 1G 69
Bateman St. W1 6B 66
Bath Ct. EC1 2H 67
Bath Gro. E2 5K 61
Bath Ho. E2 1K 69
SE1 6B 76
Bath Pl. EC2 7F 61
Baths App. SW6 7C 78
Bath St. EC1 7C 60
Bath Ter. SE1 7B 76
Bathurst M. W2 7A 64
Bathurst St. W2 7A 64
Batson Ho. E1 6K 69
Batten Ho. W10 7A 54
Battersea Bri. SW11 7B 80
Battersea Bri. Rd. SW11 7B 80
Battersea Chu. Rd.
SW11 7B 80
Battersea Pk. 7E 80
Battersea Pk. Children's Zoo
7F 81
Battersea Pk. Rd. SW11 7J 81
Battishill St. N1 1K 59
Battlebridge Ct. N1 4E 58
Battle Bri. La. SE1 3F 77
Battle Bri. Rd. NW1 5D 58
Battle Ho. SE15 6K 85
Batty St. E1 5K 69
Baxendale St. E2 6K 61
Bayer Ho. EC1 2B 68
Bayham Pl. NW1 3K 57
Bayham St. NW1 2J 57
Bayley St. WC1 4B 66
Baylis Rd. SE1 5H 75
Baynes St. NW1 1A 58
Bayonne Rd. W6 6A 78
BAYSWATER 7H 63
Bayswater Rd. W2 1F 71
Bazalgette Ho. NW8 1A 64
Bazeley Ho. SE1 5K 75
BBC Broadcasting House 4J 65
Beach Ho. SW5 3D 78
Beacon Ho. SE5 7F 85
Beaconsfield Rd. SE17 5E 84
Beaconsfield Ter. Rd.
W14 7A 70
Beak St. W1 7K 65
Beaminster Ho. SW8 7F 83
Bear All. EC4 5K 67
Bear Gdns. SE1 2B 76
Bear La. SE1 2A 76
Bear St. WC2 7C 66
Beatrice Pl. W8 7F 71
Beatrix Ho. SW5 3G 79
Beatty Ho. NW1 1K 65
SW1 4A 82
Beatty St. NW1 4K 57
Beauchamp Pl. SW3 6C 72
Beauchamp St. EC1 4H 67
Beaufort Ct. SW6 5D 78
Beaufort Gdns. SW3 6C 72
Beaufort Ho. SW1 4B 82
Beaufort M. SW6 5C 78
Beaufort St. SW3 4K 79
Beaufoy Ho. SW8 7F 83
Beaufoy Wlk. SE11 2G 83
Beaumont W14 2C 78
Beaumont Av. W14 3B 78
Beaumont Bldgs. WC2 6E 66
Beaumont Ct. W1 3G 65
Beaumont Cres. W14 3B 78
Beaumont M. W1 3G 65
Beaumont Pl. W1 1A 66
Beaumont St. W1 3G 65
Beaumont Wlk. NW3 1E 56
Becket Ho. SE1 5D 76
Becket St. SE1 6D 76
Beckfoot NW1 5A 58
Beckford Cl. W14 1C 78
Beckford Pl. SE17 4C 84
Beckham Ho. SE11 2G 83
Beckway St. SE17 2E 84
(not continuous)
Bedale St. SE1 3D 76
Bedefield WC1 7E 58
Bedford Av. WC1 4C 66
Bedfordbury WC2 1D 74
Bedford Ct. WC2 1D 74
(not continuous)
Bedford Ct. Mans. WC1 4C 66
Bedford Gdns. W8 3D 70
Bedford Pas. SW6 7A 78
W1 3A 66
Bedford Pl. WC1 3D 66
Bedford Row WC1 3G 67
Bedford Sq. WC1 4C 66
Bedford St. WC2 7D 66
Bedford Way WC1 2C 66
Bedlam M. SE11 1H 83
Bedmond Ho. SW3 3B 80
Bedser Cl. SE11 5G 83
Beech Ct. W9 3D 62
Beech Gdns. EC2 3B 68
Beech St. EC2 3B 68
Beech Tree Cl. N1 1H 59
Beechwood Ho. E2 4K 61
Beehive Cl. E8 1H 61
Bee Pas. EC3 6F 69
Beeston Ho. SE1 7D 76
Beeston Pl. SW1 7J 73
Beethoven St. W10 6A 54
Belford Ho. E8 2J 61
Belgrave Gdns. NW8 3G 55
Belgrave Ho. SW9 7H 83
Belgrave M. Nth. SW1 6F 73
Belgrave M. Sth. SW1 6G 73
Belgrave M. W. SW1 6F 73
Belgrave Pl. SW1 6G 73
Belgrave Rd. SW1 2J 81
Belgrave Sq. SW1 6F 73
Belgrave Yd. SW1 7H 73
BELGRAVIA 7G 73
Belgravia Ct. SW1 7H 73
Belgravia Ho. SW1 6F 73
Belgrove St. WC1 6E 58
Belitha Vs. N1 1G 59
Bella Best Ho. *W1* *3J 81*
(off Westmoreland Ter.)
Bellamy Cl. W14 4C 78
Bell Inn Yd. EC3 6E 68
Bell La. E1 4H 69
Bell St. NW1 3B 64
Bell Wharf La. EC4 1C 76
Bell Yd. WC2 6H 67
Bell Yd. M. SE1 5G 77
Belmont St. NW1 1G 57
Belsize Rd. NW6 3E 54
Belvedere Bldgs. SE1 5A 76
Belvedere Ct. N1 2F 61
Belvedere Pl. SE1 5A 76
Belvedere Rd. SE1 4G 75
Bemerton Est. N1 1F 59
Bemerton St. N1 2F 59
Bendall M. NW1 3C 64
Ben Ezra Ct. SE17 2C 84
Benfleet Ct. E8 2J 61
Bengal Ct. EC3 6E 68
Benham Ho. SW10 7G 79
Benhill Rd. SE5 7E 84
Benjamin Franklin House
2D 74
(off Craven St.)
Benjamin St. EC1 3K 67
Ben Jonson Ct. N1 4G 61
Ben Jonson Ho. EC2 3C 68
Ben Jonson Pl. EC2 3C 68
Bennet's Hill EC4 7A 68
Bennet St. SW1 2K 73
Bennett Ho. SW1 1C 82
Bennett's Yd. SW1 7C 74
Ben Smith Way SE16 6K 77
Benson Ho. E2 1H 69
SE1 3J 75
Bentham Ct. N1 1B 60
Bentham Ho. SE1 6D 76
Bentinck Cl. NW8 5C 56
Bentinck M. W1 5G 65
Bentinck St. W1 5G 65
Bentworth Ct. E2 1K 69
Benville Ho. SW8 7G 83
Benyon Ct. N1 2F 61
Benyon Ho. EC1 6J 59
Benyon Rd. N1 2E 60
Berenger Twr. SW10 7K 79
Berenger Wlk. SW10 7K 79
Bergholt M. NW1 1A 58
Berkeley Ct. NW1 2E 64
Berkeley Gdns. W8 3E 70
Berkeley M. W1 6E 64
Berkeley Sq. W1 1J 73
Berkeley St. W1 1J 73
Berkley Gro. NW1 1E 56
Berkley Rd. NW1 1E 56
BERMONDSEY 5K 77
Bermondsey Sq. SE1 6G 77
Bermondsey St. SE1 3F 77
Bermondsey Wall E.
SE16 5K 77
Bermondsey Wall W.
SE16 4K 77
Bernard Mans. WC1 2D 66
Bernard Shaw Ct. NW1 1K 57
Bernard St. WC1 2D 66
Bernard Sunley Ho. SW9 7H 83
Berners Ho. N1 4H 59
Berners M. W1 4A 66
Berners Pl. W1 5A 66
Berners Rd. N1 3K 59
Berners St. W1 4A 66
Berner Ter. E1 6K 69
Bernhardt Cres. NW8 1B 64
Berryfield Rd. SE17 3A 84
Berry Pl. EC1 7A 60
Berry St. EC1 1A 68
Berwick Ct. SE1 5C 76
Berwick St. W1 5A 66
Besant Ho. NW8 2H 55
Bessborough Gdns. SW1 3C 82
Bessborough Pl. SW1 3B 82
Bessborough St. SW1 3B 82
Bessemer Ct. NW1 1A 58
Bethal Est. SE1 3G 77
Bethersden Ho. SE17 3G 85
Bethnal Green Cen. for Sports &
Performing Arts 7J 61
Bethnal Grn. Rd. E1 1H 69
E2 1H 69
Bethwin Rd. SE5 7A 84
Betsham Ho. SE1 4D 76
Betterton Ho. WC2 6E 66
Betterton St. WC2 6E 66
Bevan Ho. WC1 3E 66
Bevan St. N1 3C 60
Bevenden St. N1 6E 60
Beverston M. W1 4D 64
Bevin Ct. WC1 6G 59
Bevington Path *SE1* *5H 77*
(off Tanner St.)
Bevington Rd. W10 3A 62
Bevington St. SE16 5K 77
Bevin Way WC1 6H 59
Bevis Marks EC3 5G 69
Bewdley St. N1 1H 59
Bianca Rd. SE15 6J 85
Bibury Cl. SE15 6G 85
(not continuous)
Bickenhall Mans. W1 3E 64
(not continuous)
Bickenhall St. W1 3E 64
Bicknell Ho. E1 6K 69
Bidborough St. WC1 7D 58
Biddesden Ho. SW3 2D 80
Biddulph Mans. W9 7F 55
Biddulph Rd. W9 7F 55
Big Ben 5E 74
Billingley NW1 3K 57
Billing Pl. SW10 7G 79
Billing Rd. SW10 7G 79
Billing St. SW10 7G 79
Billiter Sq. EC3 6G 69
Billiter St. EC3 6G 69
Bilton Towers W1 6E 64
Bina Gdns. SW5 2H 79
Bingfield St. N1 2E 58
(not continuous)
Bingham Ct. N1 1A 60
Bingham Pl. W1 3F 65
Binney St. W1 6G 65
Binnie Ho. SE1 7B 76
Birch Ho. W10 1A 62
Birchington Ct. NW6 2F 55
Birchington Rd. NW6 2E 54
Birchin La. EC3 6E 68
Birch Va. Ct. NW8 1A 64
Birdbrook Ho. N1 1B 60
Birdcage Wlk. SW1 5K 73
Bird in Bush Rd. SE15 7K 85
Birdlip Cl. SE15 6F 85
Bird St. W1 6G 65
Birkbeck College 3C 66
Birkenhead St. WC1 6E 58
Birley Lodge NW8 4A 56
Bishopgate Chu. Yd. EC2 5F 69
Bishop King's Rd. W14 1A 78
Bishop's Bri. Rd. W2 6G 63
Bishops Ct. EC4 5K 67
W2 5G 63
WC2 5H 67
Bishopsdale Ho. NW6 2E 54
Bishopsgate EC2 5F 69
Bishopsgate Arc. EC2 4G 69
Bishopsgate Institute & Libraries
4G 69
Bishops Ho. SW8 7E 82
Bishops Mead SE5 7C 84
Bishops Rd. SW6 7C 78
SW11 7C 80
Bishop's Ter. SE11 1J 83
Bishop St. N1 2B 60
Bittern Ho. SE1 5B 76
Bittern St. SE1 5B 76
Blackall St. EC2 1F 69
Blackbird Yd. E2 6J 61
Blackburne's M. W1 7F 65
Blackfriars Bri. SE1 1K 75
Blackfriars Ct. EC4 7K 67
Black Friars La. EC4 7K 67
(not continuous)
Blackfriars Pas. EC4 7K 67
Blackfriars Rd. SE1 5K 75
Blackfriars Underpass
EC4 7K 67
Black Horse Ct. SE1 6E 76
Blacklands Ter. SW3 2D 80
Blackmans Yd. E2 1K 69
Blackmore Ho. N1 3G 59
Black Prince Rd. SE1 2F 83
SE11 2F 83
Blackstone Ho. SW1 4K 81
Black Swan Yd. SE1 4F 77
Blackthorne Ct. SE15 7J 85
Blackwater Ho. NW8 3A 64
Blackwood St. SE17 3D 84
Blades Ho. SE11 6H 83
Blagrove Rd. W10 4A 62
Blair Ct. NW8 2K 55
Blake Ct. NW6 6D 54
Blake Ho. SE1 6H 75
Blakeney Cl. NW1 1B 58
Blake's Rd. SE15 7G 85
Blandford Ct. N1 1G 61
Blandford Ho. SW8 7F 83
Blandford Sq. NW1 2C 64
Blandford St. W1 5E 64
Bland Ho. SE11 3G 83
Blantyre St. SW10 7K 79
Blantyre Twr. SW10 7K 79
Blantyre Wlk. SW10 7K 79
Blashford NW3 1D 56
Blazer Ct. NW8 7A 56
Bledlow Ho. NW8 2A 64
Bleeding Heart Yd. EC1 4J 67
Blemundsbury WC1 3F 67
Blendon Row SE17 2D 84
Blenheim Cres. W11 7A 62
Blenheim Pas. NW8 4H 55
(not continuous)
Blenheim Rd. NW8 4J 55
Blenheim St. W1 6H 65
Blenheim Ter. NW8 4H 55
Bletchley Ct. N1 5D 60
(not continuous)
Bletchley St. N1 5C 60
Bletsoe Wlk. N1 4C 60
Bliss M. W10 6A 54
Blisworth Ho. E2 3K 61
Blithfield St. W8 7F 71
Blomfield Ct. W9 1G 63
Blomfield Rd. W9 3G 63
Blomfield St. EC2 4E 68
Blomfield Vs. W2 4G 63
Bloomburg St. SW1 2A 82
Bloomfield Ho. E1 4K 69
Bloomfield Pl. W1 7J 65
Bloomfield Ter. SW1 3G 81
BLOOMSBURY 3D 66
Bloomsbury Ct. WC1 4E 66
Bloomsbury Pl. WC1 4E 66
Bloomsbury Sq. WC1 4E 66
Bloomsbury St. WC1 4C 66
Bloomsbury Theatre 1B 66
Bloomsbury Way WC1 4D 66
Blore Ct. W1 7B 66
Blore Ho. SW10 7H 79
Blossom St. E1 2G 69
Blue Anchor Yd. E1 7K 69
Blue Ball Yd. SW1 3K 73
Blue Elephant Theatre 7B 84
Blue Lion Pl. SE1 6F 77
Blythe Ho. SE11 5J 83
Blythe Rd. W14 7A 70
(not continuous)
Boadicea St. N1 3F 59
Boarley Ho. SE17 2F 85
Boathouse Wlk. SE15 7J 85
(not continuous)
Boden Ho. E1 3K 69
Boldero Pl. NW8 2B 64
Bolney Ga. SW7 5B 72
Bolney St. SW8 7F 83
Bolsover St. W1 2J 65
Bolt Ct. *EC4* *6J 67*
(off Fleet St.)
Bolton Cres. SE5 7K 83
Bolton Gdns. SW5 3F 79
Bolton Gdns. M. SW10 3G 79
Bolton Pl. NW8 3G 55
Bolton Rd. NW8 3G 55
Boltons, The SW10 3H 79
Boltons Ct. SW5 3G 79
Boltons Pl. SW5 3H 79
Bolton St. W1 2J 73
Bolton Studios SW10 4J 79
Bomore Rd. W11 7A 62
Bonar Rd. SE15 7K 85
Bonchurch Rd. W10 3A 62
Bond Ct. EC4 6D 68
Bond Ho. NW6 5C 54
Bondway SW8 6E 82
Bonhill St. EC2 2E 68
Bonnington Ho. N1 5F 59
Bonnington Sq. SW8 5F 83
Bonny St. NW1 1K 57
Bonsor St. SE5 7F 85
Booth La. EC4 7B 68
Booth's Pl. W1 4A 66
Boot St. N1 7F 61
Boreas Wlk. N1 5A 60
BOROUGH, THE 5C 76
Borough High St. SE1 5C 76
Borough Mkt. SE1 3D 76
Borough Rd. SE1 6K 75
Borough Sq. SE1 5B 76
Borrett Cl. SE17 4B 84
Borrowdale NW1 7K 57
Boscobel Pl. SW1 1G 81
Boscobel St. NW8 2A 64
Boss Ho. SE1 4H 77
Boss St. SE1 4H 77
Boston Pl. NW1 1D 64
Boswell Ct. WC1 3E 66
Boswell Ho. WC1 3E 66

Boswell St.—Carrington St.

Boswell St. WC1 3E 66
Bosworth Ho. W10 2A 62
Bosworth Rd. W10 2A 62
Botolph All. EC3 7F 69
Botolph La. EC3 1F 77
Botts M. W2 6E 62
Boughton Ho. SE1 4D 76
Boulogne Ho. SE1 6H 77
Boundary Ho. SE5 7B 84
Boundary La. SE17 6C 84
Boundary Pas. E1 1H 69
Boundary Rd. NW8 3G 55
Boundary Row SE1 4K 75
Boundary St. E2 7H 61
Bourchier St. W1 7B 66
(not continuous)
Bourdon Pl. W1 7J 65
Bourdon St. W1 7J 65
Bourlet Cl. W1 4K 65
Bourne Est. EC1 3H 67
Bourne M. W1 5G 65
Bourne St. SW1 2F 81
Bourne Ter. W2 4F 63
Bouverie Pl. W2 5A 64
Bouverie St. EC4 6J 67
Bowater Ho. EC1 2B 68
SW1 5D 72
Bow Chyd. EC4 6C 68
Bowden St. SE11 3J 83
Bowhill Cl. SW9 7J 83
Bowland Yd. SW1 5E 72
Bow La. EC4 6C 68
Bowl Ct. EC2 2G 69
Bowles Rd. SE1 5K 85
Bowley Ho. SE16 6K 77
Bowling Grn. La. EC1 2J 67
Bowling Grn. Pl. SE1 4D 76
Bowling Grn. St. SE11 5H 83
Bowling Grn. Wlk. N1 6F 61
Bowman's Bldgs. NW1 3B 64
Bowman's M. E1 7K 69
Bowmore Wlk. NW1 1C 58
Bow St. WC2 6E 66
Bowyer Ho. N1 3G 61
Bowyer Pl. SE5 7C 84
Bowyer St. SE5 7C 84
Boxworth Gro. N1 2G 59
Boyce Ho. W10 7B 54
Boydell Ct. NW8 1K 55
(not continuous)
Boyd St. E1 6K 69
Boyfield St. SE1 5A 76
Boyle St. W1 7K 65
Boyne Ter. M. W11 2B 70
Boyson Rd. SE17 5C 84
(not continuous)
Boyson Wlk. SE17 5C 84
Boyton Ho. NW8 4A 56
Brabant Ct. EC3 7F 69
Brabner Ho. E2 6K 61
Bracer Ho. N1 3G 61
Brackley Ct. NW8 1K 63
Brackley St. EC1 3C 68
Bracklyn Ct. N1 4D 60
(not continuous)
Bracklyn St. N1 4D 60
Bradenham SE17 5D 84
Bradenham Cl. SE17 5D 84
Braden St. W9 2F 63
Bradfield Ct. NW1 1J 57
Bradiston Rd. W9 6C 54
Bradley's Cl. N1 4J 59
Brad St. SE1 3J 75
Bradwell Ho. NW6 3F 55
Braemar Ho. W9 7H 55
Braes St. N1 1A 60
Braganza St. SE17 3K 83
Braham Ho. SE11 4G 83
Braham St. E1 6J 69
Braidwood Pas. EC1 3B 68
Braidwood St. SE1 3F 77
Braithwaite Ho. EC1 1D 68
Braithwaite Twr. W2 3K 63
Bramah Tea & Coffee Mus. 3C 76
Bramber WC1 7D 58
Bramber Rd. W14 5B 78
Bramerton St. SW3 5B 80
Bramham Gdns. SW5 3F 79
Bramley Cres. SW8 7C 82
Brampton WC1 4F 67
Bramshurst NW8 3G 55
Bramwell Ho. SE1 7C 76
SW1 4K 81
Bramwell M. N1 2G 59
Branch Pl. N1 3E 60
Brandon Est. SE17 6K 83
Brandon Mans. W14 5A 78
Brandon M. EC2 4D 68
Brandon Rd. N7 1D 58
Brandon St. SE17 2C 84
(not continuous)
Brangton Rd. SE11 4G 83
Branksome Ho. SW8 7F 83
Branscombe NW1 3A 58
Bransdale Cl. NW6 2E 54
Brantwood Ho. SE5 7B 84
Brathay NW1 5A 58
Bratley St. E1 2K 69
Bravington Pl. W9 1B 62
Bravington Rd. W9 5B 54
Bravingtons Wlk. *N1* *5E 58*
(off York Way)
Brawne Ho. SE17 6A 84
Bray NW3 1B 56
Brayfield Ter. N1 1H 59
Bray Pl. SW3 3D 80
Bread St. EC4 7C 68
(not continuous)
Bream's Bldgs. EC4 5H 67
Brechin Pl. SW7 3J 79
Brecon Ho. W2 5H 63
Brecon Rd. W6 6A 78
Bredin Ho. SW10 7G 79
Breezer's Hill E1 1K 77
Bremner Rd. SW7 6J 71
Brendon St. W1 5C 64
Brenley Ho. SE1 4D 76
Bressenden Pl. SW1 6J 73
Breton Highwalk EC1 3C 68
Breton Ho. EC2 3C 68
SE1 6H 77
W1 1E 72
Brettell St. SE17 4E 84
Brettinghurst SE1 4K 85
Brewer's Grn. SW1 6B 74
Brewer's Hall Gdn. EC2 4C 68
Brewer St. W1 1A 74
Brewery, The EC2 3D 68
Brewery Ind. Est., The
N1 5C 60
Brewery Sq. EC1 1K 67
SE1 3H 77
Brewhouse Yd. EC1 1K 67
Brewster Ho. SE1 1J 85
Briant Ho. SE1 7H 75
Briar Wlk. W10 1A 62
Briary Cl. NW3 1B 56
Brickbarn Cl. SW10 7J 79
Brick Ct. EC4 6H 67
Brick La. E1 3J 69
BRICKLAYER'S ARMS 7E 76
Bricklayers Arms Bus. Cen.
SE1 1G 85
Brick St. W1 3H 73
Brideale Cl. SE15 6J 85
Bride Ct. EC4 6K 67
Bride La. EC4 6K 67
Bridel M. N1 3K 59
Brides Pl. N1 1F 61
Bridewain St. SE1 6H 77
(not continuous)
Bridewell Pl. EC4 6K 67
Bridford M. W1 3J 65
Bridge, The SW8 7H 81
Bridge App. NW1 1F 57
Bridgefoot SE1 4E 82
Bridge Ho. NW3 1F 57
SW1 3H 81
W2 4K 63
Bridgehouse Ct. SE1 4K 75
Bridgeman Rd. N1 1F 59
Bridgeman St. NW8 5B 56
Bridge Pl. SW1 1J 81
Bridgeport Pl. E1 2K 77
Bridges Ho. SE5 7D 84
Bridgeside Ho. N1 5B 60
Bridge St. SW1 5D 74
Bridgewalk Hgts. SE1 4E 76
Bridgewater Highwalk
EC2 3C 68
Bridgewater Sq. EC2 3B 68
Bridgewater St. EC2 3B 68
Bridgeway St. NW1 5A 58
Bridge Yd. SE1 2E 76
Bridgnorth Ho. SE15 6K 85
Bridgwater Ho. W2 5H 63
Bridle La. W1 7A 66
Bridport SE17 4D 84
Bridport Ho. N1 3E 60
Bridport Pl. N1 2E 60
(not continuous)
Bridstow Pl. W2 5E 62
Brierfield NW1 3K 57
Briggs Ho. E2 6J 61
Brighton Bldgs. SE1 7F 77
Brill Pl. NW1 5C 58
Brindley Ho. W2 3E 62
Brinklow Ho. W2 4F 63
Brinton Wlk. SE1 3K 75
Brisbane St. SE5 7D 84
Briset St. EC1 3K 67
Bristol Gdns. W9 2G 63
Bristol Ho. SE11 7H 75
Bristol M. W9 2G 63
Britain & London Vis. Cen. 2B 74
Britain at War Experience 3F 77
BRITANNIA JUNC. 2J 57
Britannia Leisure Cen. 3E 60
Britannia Rd. SW6 7F 79
(not continuous)
Britannia Row N1 2A 60
Britannia St. WC1 6F 59
Britannia Wlk. N1 5D 60
(not continuous)
Britannic Highwalk EC2 4D 68
Britannic Twr. EC2 3D 68
British Cartoon Cen., The *2E 66*
(off Bernard St.)
British Genius Site 7F 81
British Library 6C 58
British Mus. 4D 66
British Telecom Cen.
EC1 5B 68
Brittany Point SE11 2H 83
Britten St. SW3 4B 80
Britton St. EC1 2K 67
Brixton Rd. SE11 6H 83
SW9 7H 83
Broadbent St. W1 7H 65
Broad Ct. WC2 6E 66
Broadfield La. NW1 1D 58
Broadgate EC2 4F 69
Broadgate Circ. EC2 4F 69
Broadgate Ice Rink 4F 69
Broadgates Ct. SE11 4J 83
Broad La. EC2 3F 69
Broadley St. NW8 3A 64
Broadley Ter. NW1 2C 64
Broadmayne SE17 3D 84
Broadmead W14 2A 78
Broadoak Ho. NW6 3G 55
Broad Sanctuary SW1 5C 74
Broadstone Ho. SW8 7F 83
Broadstone Pl. W1 4F 65
Broad St. Av. EC2 4F 69
Broad St. Pl. EC2 4E 68
Broad Wlk. NW1 4G 57
W1 1E 72
Broad Wlk., The W8 1G 71
Broadwalk Ct. W8 2E 70
Broadwalk Ho. EC2 2F 69
SW7 5H 71
Broadwall SE1 2J 75
Broadway SW1 6B 74
Broadway Shop. Mall
SW1 6B 74
Broadwick St. W1 7A 66
Broadwood Ter. W8 1C 78
Broad Yd. EC1 2K 67
Brocas Cl. NW3 1C 56
Brockham Ho. NW1 3A 58
Brockham St. SE1 6C 76
Brockwell Ho. SE11 5G 83
Brodie Ho. SE1 3J 85
Brodie St. SE1 3J 85
Broken Wharf EC4 7B 68
Broke Wlk. E8 2J 61
Bromfield St. N1 4J 59
Bromleigh Ho. SE1 6H 77
Bromley Pl. W1 3K 65
BROMPTON 7C 72
Brompton Arc. SW3 5E 72
Brompton Cotts. SW10 5H 79
Brompton Oratory 7B 72
Brompton Pk. Cres. SW6 6E 78
Brompton Pl. SW3 6C 72
Brompton Rd. SW1 1B 80
SW3 1B 80
Brompton Sq. SW3 6B 72
Bron Ct. NW6 3D 54
BRONDESBURY 1C 54
Brondesbury M. NW6 1D 54
BRONDESBURY PARK 2A 54
Brondesbury Pk. NW6 1A 54
Brondesbury Rd. NW6 4B 54
Brondesbury Vs. NW6 4C 54
Bronsart Rd. SW6 7A 78
Bronte Ho. NW6 6E 54
Bronti Cl. SE17 4C 84
Bronwen Ct. NW8 7K 55
Brook Dr. SE11 7J 75
Brooke's Ct. EC1 4H 67
Brooke's Mkt. EC1 3H 67
Brooke St. EC1 4H 67
Brook Ga. W1 1E 72
Brook Ho's. NW1 5A 58
Brooklands Ct. NW6 1B 54
Brook M. WC2 6C 66
Brook M. Nth. W2 7J 63
Brooksby M. N1 1J 59
Brooksby St. N1 1H 59
Brooks Ct. SW8 7A 82
Brooks Lodge N1 4G 61
Brooks M. W1 7H 65
Brook St. W1 7G 65
W2 7A 64
Brooksville Av. NW6 3A 54
Brookville Rd. SW6 7B 78
Brookwood Ho. SE1 5A 76
Broome Way SE5 7D 84
Broomfield Ct. SE16 6K 77
Broomfield Ho. SE17 2F 85
Brougham Rd. E8 2K 61
Brough Cl. SW8 7E 82
Brown Hart Gdns. W1 7G 65
Browning Cl. W9 2J 63
Browning M. W1 4G 65
Browning St. SE17 3C 84
Brownlow Ho. SE16 5K 77
Brownlow M. WC1 2G 67
Brownlow Rd. E8 2J 61
Brownlow St. WC1 4G 67
Browns Arc. W1 1A 74
Brown's Bldgs. EC3 6G 69
Brown St. W1 5D 64
Broxwood Way NW8 3C 56
Bruckner St. W10 6B 54
Bruges Pl. NW1 1A 58
Brune Ho. E1 4H 69
Brunei Gallery 3C 66
Brunel Est. W2 4D 62
Brune St. E1 4H 69
Brunlees Ho. SE1 7B 76
Brunswick Cen. WC1 1D 66
Brunswick Cl. Est. EC1 7K 59
Brunswick Ct. EC1 7K 59
SE1 5G 77
SW1 2C 82
Brunswick Gdns. W8 3E 70
Brunswick Ho. E2 4J 61
Brunswick Mans. WC1 1E 66
Brunswick M. W1 5E 64
Brunswick Pl. N1 7E 60
NW1 2G 65
(not continuous)
Brunswick Sq. WC1 1E 66
Brushfield St. E1 4G 69
Bruton La. W1 1J 73
Bruton Pl. W1 1J 73
Bruton St. W1 1J 73
Brutus Ct. SE11 2K 83
Bryanston Ct. W1 5D 64
(not continuous)
Bryanston Mans. W1 3D 64
Bryanston M. E. W1 4D 64
Bryanston M. W. W1 4D 64
Bryanston Pl. W1 4D 64
Bryanston Sq. W1 4D 64
Bryanston St. W1 6D 64
Bryant Ct. E2 4H 61
(not continuous)
Brydges Pl. WC2 1D 74
Brydon Wlk. N1 2E 58
Bryer Ct. EC2 3B 68
Bryher Ct. SE11 3H 83
Buckfast St. E2 7K 61
Buck Hill Wlk. W2 1A 72
Buckingham Arc. WC2 1E 74
Buckingham Chambers
SW1 1A 82
Buckingham Ga. SW1 6K 73
Buckingham M. SW1 6K 73
Buckingham Palace 5J 73
Buckingham Pal. Rd.
SW1 2H 81
Buckingham Pl. SW1 6K 73
Buckingham St. WC2 1E 74
Buckland Ct. N1 4F 61
Buckland St. N1 5E 60
Bucklebury NW1 1K 65
Bucklers All. SW6 7C 78
(not continuous)
Bucklersbury EC4 6D 68
Bucklersbury Pas. EC4 6D 68
Buckle St. E1 6J 69
Buckley Ct. NW6 1C 54
Buckley Rd. NW6 1C 54
Bucknall St. WC2 5C 66
Bucknill Ho. SW1 3H 81
Buckridge Ho. EC1 3H 67
Buck St. NW1 1J 57
Budge Row EC4 6D 68
Budge's Wlk. W2 3H 71
Budleigh Ho. SE15 7K 85
Bulbarrow NW8 3G 55
Bulinga St. SW1 2D 82
Bulleid Way SW1 2J 81
Buller Cl. SE15 7K 85
Bullingham Mans. W8 4E 70
Bull Inn Ct. WC2 1E 74
Bulls Gdns. SW3 1C 80
(not continuous)
Bulls Head Pas. EC3 6F 69
Bull Wharf La. EC4 7C 68
Bull Wharf Wlk. *EC4* *1C 76*
(off Bull Wharf La.)
Bulmer M. W11 2D 70
Bulmer Pl. W11 2C 70
Bulstrode Pl. W1 4G 65
Bulstrode St. W1 5G 65
Bunhill Row EC1 1D 68
Bunhouse Pl. SW1 3F 81
Bunyan Ct. EC2 3B 68
Buonaparte M. SW1 3B 82
Burbage Cl. SE1 7D 76
Burbage Ho. N1 3E 60
Burchell Ho. SE11 3G 83
Burden Ho. SW8 7D 82
Burdett M. W2 5F 63
Burgess Bus. Pk. SE5 7E 84
Burgess Pk. Kart Track 6E 84
Burge St. SE1 7E 76
Burgh St. N1 4A 60
Burgon St. EC4 6A 68
Burleigh Ho. SW3 6A 80
Burleigh St. WC2 7F 67
Burlington Arc. W1 1K 73
Burlington Cl. W9 1D 62
Burlington Gdns. W1 1K 73
Burnaby St. SW10 7J 79
Burne Jones Ho. W14 2A 78
Burnell Wlk. SE1 3J 85
Burne St. NW1 3B 64
Burnham NW3 1B 56
Burnham Cl. SE1 2J 85
Burnham Ct. W2 7F 63
Burnsall St. SW3 3C 80
Burns Ho. SE17 4A 84
Burnthwaite Rd. SW6 7C 78
Burr Cl. E1 2K 77
Burrell St. SE1 2A 76
Burrows M. SE1 4K 75
Bursar St. SE1 3F 77
Burton Bank N1 1D 60
Burton Ct. SW3 3E 80
(not continuous)
Burton Gro. SE17 4D 84
Burton M. SW1 2G 81
Burton Pl. WC1 7C 58
Burton Rd. NW6 1C 54
Burton St. WC1 7C 58
Burtt Ho. N1 6F 61
Burwash Ho. SE1 5E 76
Burwood Pl. W2 5C 64
Bury Ct. EC3 5G 69
Bury Pl. WC1 4D 66
Bury St. EC3 6G 69
SW1 2K 73
Bury Wlk. SW3 2B 80
Bushbaby Cl. SE1 7F 77
Bushell St. E1 2K 77
Bush La. EC4 7D 68
Bushwood Dr. SE1 2J 85
Business Design Cen. 3J 59
Bute St. SW7 1K 79
Butler Pl. SW1 6B 74
Butlers & Colonial Wharf
SE1 4J 77
Butlers Wharf SE1 4H 77
Buttermere NW1 6J 57
Buttermere Cl. SE1 2H 85
Buttermere Ct. NW8 2K 55
Butterworth Ter. SE17 4C 84
Buttesland St. N1 6E 60
Buxted Rd. E8 1H 61
Buxton Ct. N1 6C 60
Buxton St. E1 2J 69
Byng Pl. WC1 2C 66
Byron Cl. E8 2K 61
Byron Ct. NW6 1J 55
W9 1E 62
WC1 1F 67
Byron M. W9 1E 62
Byward St. EC3 1G 77
Bywater St. SW3 3D 80
Bywell Pl. W1 4K 65

Cabbell St. NW1 4B 64
Cable Ho. WC1 6H 59
Cable St. E1 7K 69
Caci Ho. W14 2B 78
Cadbury Way SE16 7J 77
Cadell Cl. E2 5J 61
Cadet Dr. SE1 3J 85
Cadiz St. SE17 4C 84
Cadman Cl. SW9 7K 83
Cadmore Ho. N1 1K 59
Cadogan Ct. SW3 2D 80
Cadogan Gdns. SW3 1E 80
Cadogan Ga. SW1 1E 80
Cadogan Ho. SW3 6A 80
Cadogan La. SW1 7F 73
Cadogan Mans. SW3 2E 80
Cadogan Pl. SW1 6E 72
Cadogan Sq. SW1 7D 72
Cadogan St. SW3 2D 80
Caernarvon Ho. W2 5H 63
Cahill St. EC1 2C 68
Caird St. W10 7A 54
Caithness Ho. N1 2F 59
Calderon Ho. NW8 4B 56
Caldew St. SE5 7D 84
Caleb St. SE1 4C 76
Caledonian Rd. N1 5E 58
N7 1F 59
Caledonia St. N1 5E 58
Cale St. SW3 3B 80
Calgarth NW1 5A 58
Caliban Twr. N1 5F 61
Calico Ho. EC4 6C 68
Callcott Ct. NW6 1B 54
Callcott Rd. NW6 1B 54
Callcott St. W8 2D 70
Callendar Rd. SW7 6K 71
Callow St. SW3 5J 79
Cally Swimming Pool 2F 59
Calmington Rd. SE5 5G 85
Calshot Ho. N1 4F 59
Calshot St. N1 4F 59
Calstock NW1 3B 58
Calstock Ho. SE11 3J 83
Calthorpe St. WC1 1G 67
Calvert Av. E2 7G 61
Calverton SE5 5F 85
Calvert's Bldgs. SE1 3D 76
Calvert St. NW1 2F 57
Calvin St. E1 2H 69
Calypso Cres. SE15 7G 85
Camberley Ho. NW1 5J 57
Camberwell New Rd.
SE5 6H 83
Camberwell Rd. SE5 5C 84
Cambourne M. W11 6A 62
Cambridge Av. NW6 4E 54
Cambridge Cir. WC2 6C 66
Cambridge Ct. NW6 4E 54
W2 4B 64
Cambridge Gdns. NW6 4E 54
W10 5A 62
Cambridge Ga. NW1 1H 65
Cambridge Ga. M. NW1 1J 65
Cambridge Pl. W8 5G 71
Cambridge Rd. NW6 6E 54
(not continuous)
Cambridge Sq. W2 5B 64
Cambridge St. SW1 2J 81
Cambridge Ter. NW1 7H 57
Cambridge Ter. M. NW1 7J 57
Cambridge Theatre 6D 66
Cam Ct. SE15 6H 85
Camden Ct. NW1 1A 58
Camden Gdns. NW1 1J 57
Camden High St. NW1 1J 57
Camden Lock Market 1H 57
Camden Lock Pl. NW1 1H 57
Camden Market 2J 57
Camden Pas. N1 4K 59
(not continuous)
Camden Peoples Theatre 1K 65
Camden Rd. NW1 1K 57
Camden St. NW1 1J 57
Camden Studios NW1 3A 58
CAMDEN TOWN 2J 57
Camden Wlk. N1 3K 59
(not continuous)
Camelford NW1 3A 58
Camelford Ct. W11 7A 62
Camelford Ho. SE1 4E 82
Camelford Wlk. W11 6A 62
Camera Pl. SW10 6K 79
Cameron Ho. NW8 4B 56
SE5 7B 84
Camlet St. E2 1H 69
Camley St. NW1 1B 58
Camomile St. EC3 5F 69
Campbell Ct. SW7 7H 71
Campbell Ho. SW1 4K 81
Campbell Wlk. N1 2E 58
Campden Gro. W8 4E 70
Campden Hill W8 4C 70
Campden Hill Ct. W8 4E 70
Campden Hill Gdns. W8 2D 70
Campden Hill Ga. W8 4D 70
Campden Hill Mans. W8 2E 70
Campden Hill Pl. W11 2C 70
Campden Hill Rd. W8 2D 70
Campden Hill Sq. W8 2C 70
Campden Ho. NW6 1K 55
W8 3E 70
Campden Ho. Cl. W8 4E 70
Campden Ho's. W8 3D 70
Campden Ho. Ter. W8 3E 70
Campden St. W8 3D 70
Camperdown St. E1 6J 69
Canada Memorial 4J 73
CANAL BRIDGE 5K 85
Canal Bldg. N1 4B 60
Canal Mkt. NW1 1H 57
Canal Path E2 3H 61
Canal St. SE5 6D 84
Canal Wlk. N1 2E 60
Candover St. W1 4K 65
Canfield Gdns. NW6 1F 55
Cann Ho. W14 7A 70
Canning Pas. W8 6H 71
(not continuous)
Canning Pl. W8 6H 71
Canning Pl. M. W8 5H 71
Cannon Ct. EC1 1K 67
Cannon Ho. SE11 2G 83
Cannons Health Club
Cannon Street 1D 76
Cannon St. EC4 6B 68
Canon All. *EC4* *6B 68*
(off Queen's Head Pas.)
Canonbury Bus. Cen. N1 2C 60
Canonbury Ct. N1 1A 60
Canonbury Cres. N1 1C 60
Canonbury Gro. N1 1B 60
Canonbury Rd. N1 1A 60
Canonbury St. N1 1B 60
Canonbury Vs. N1 1A 60
Canon Row SW1 5D 74
(not continuous)
Canon St. N1 3B 60
Canterbury Ct. NW6 4D 54
SW9 7J 83
Canterbury Ho. SE1 6G 75
Canterbury Pl. SE17 2A 84
Canterbury Rd. NW6 5C 54
(not continuous)
Canterbury Ter. NW6 4D 54
Cantium Retail Pk. SE1 5K 85
Canvey St. SE1 2B 76
Capel Ct. EC2 6E 68
Capener's Cl. SW1 5E 72
Cape Yd. E1 2K 77
Capland Ho. NW8 1A 64
Capland St. NW8 1A 64
Caple Ho. SW10 7J 79
Capper St. WC1 2A 66
Caradoc Cl. W2 5D 62
Carburton St. W1 3J 65
Cardiff Ho. SE15 6K 85
Cardigan St. SE11 3H 83
Cardinal Bourne St. SE1 7E 76
Cardinal Cap All. SE1 2B 76
Cardinal Ct. E1 1K 77
Cardington St. NW1 6A 58
Carey Ct. SE5 7B 84
Carey La. EC2 5B 68
Carey Mans. SW1 1B 82
Carey Pl. SW1 2B 82
Carey St. WC2 6G 67
Carfree Cl. N1 1J 59
Carisbrooke Gdns. SE15 7J 85
Carlisle Av. EC3 6H 69
Carlisle La. SE1 7G 75
Carlisle Mans. SW1 1K 81
Carlisle Pl. SW1 7K 73
Carlisle Rd. NW6 2A 54
Carlisle St. W1 6B 66
Carlos Pl. W1 1G 73
Carlow St. NW1 4K 57
Carlton Ct. W9 4G 55
Carlton Gdns. SW1 2B 74
Carlton Hill NW8 5G 55
Carlton Ho. NW6 5C 54
(not continuous)
Carlton Ho. Ter. SW1 3B 74
Carlton Mans. NW6 1E 54
W9 6G 55
Carlton M. NW6 5D 54
Carlton St. SW1 1B 74
Carlton Twr. Pl. SW1 6E 72
Carlton Va. NW6 5C 54
Carlyle's House 6B 80
Carlyle Sq. SW3 4A 80
Carmarthen Pl. SE1 4F 77
Carmel Ct. W8 4F 71
Carmelite St. EC4 7J 67
Carmel Lodge SW6 5D 78
Carnaby St. W1 6K 65
Carnegie St. N1 3F 59
Carnival Ho. SE1 4J 77
Carnoustie Dr. N1 1F 59
(not continuous)
Caroline Cl. W2 1G 71
Caroline Gdns. E2 6G 61
Caroline Pl. W2 7G 63
Caroline Pl. M. W2 1G 71
Caroline Ter. SW1 2F 81
Carol St. NW1 2K 57
Carpenters Ct. NW1 2K 57
Carpenter St. W1 1H 73
Carriage Dr. E. SW11 7G 81
Carriage Dr. Nth. SW11 6F 81
(Carriage Dr. E.)
SW11 7D 80
(Parade, The)
Carriage Dr. W. SW11 7D 80
Carrick Ho. SE11 3K 83
Carrington Ho. W1 3H 73
Carrington St. W1 3H 73

Carroll Ho.—Colyer Cl.

Carroll Ho. W2 7K 63
Carroun Rd. SW8 7F 83
Carter Ct. EC4 6A 68
Carteret St. SW1 5B 74
Carter Ho. E1 4H 69
Carter La. EC4 6A 68
Carter Pl. SE17 4C 84
Carter St. SE17 5B 84
Carthusian St. EC1 3B 68
Carting La. WC2 1E 74
Cartmel NW1 6K 57
Carton Ho. SE16 6K 77
Cartwright Gdns. WC1 7D 58
Cartwright Ho. SE1 7C 76
Cartwright St. E1 7J 69
Casby Ho. SE16 6K 77
Casey Cl. NW8 7B 56
Caspian St. SE5 7D 84
Cassidy Rd. SW6 7D 78
(not continuous)
Casson Ho. E1 3K 69
Castellain Mans. W9 1F 63
(not continuous)
Castellain Rd. W9 1F 63
Casterbridge NW6 2G 55
W11 5C 62
Castleacre W2 6B 64
Castle Baynard St. EC4 7A 68
Castlebrook Ct. SE11 1K 83
Castle Ct. EC3 6E 68
Castleford Ct. NW8 1A 64
Castlehaven Rd. NW1 1H 57
Castle Ho. SE1 1B 84
SW8 7E 82
Castle Ind. Est. SE17 1B 84
Castle La. SW1 6K 73
Castle Mead SE5 7C 84
Castlereagh St. W1 5D 64
Castletown Rd. W14 4A 78
Castle Yd. SE1 2A 76
Catesby St. SE17 2E 84
Cathcart Rd. SW10 5G 79
Cathedral Lodge EC1 3B 68
Cathedral Mans. SW1 1K 81
Cathedral Piazza SW1 7K 73
Cathedral St. SE1 2D 76
Catherine Griffiths Ct.
EC1 1J 67
Catherine Ho. N1 3F 61
Catherine Pl. SW1 6K 73
Catherine St. WC2 7F 67
Catherine Wheel All. E1 4G 69
(not continuous)
Catherine Wheel Yd.
SW1 3K 73
Catherwood Ct. N1 6D 60
(not continuous)
Cator St. SE15 7J 85
(Commercial Way)
SE15 6H 85
(Ebley Cl.)
Cato St. W1 4C 64
Catton St. WC1 4F 67
Caughley Ho. SE11 7H 75
Causton Ho. SE5 7C 84
Causton St. SW1 2C 82
Cavaye Pl. SW10 4J 79
Cavell Ho. N1 3F 61
Cavendish Av. NW8 5A 56
Cavendish Cl. NW8 6A 56
Cavendish Ct. EC3 5G 69
Cavendish Ho. NW8 5A 56
Cavendish Mans. EC1 2H 67
Cavendish M. Nth. W1 3J 65
Cavendish M. Sth. W1 4J 65
Cavendish Pl. W1 5J 65
Cavendish Rd. NW6 1A 54
Cavendish Sq. W1 5J 65
Cavendish St. N1 5D 60
Caversham Ho. SE15 6K 85
Caversham St. SW3 5D 80
Cavour Ho. SE17 3A 84
Caxton St. SW1 6A 74
Caxton Wlk. WC2 6C 66
Cayenne Ct. SE1 4H 77
Cayton Pl. EC1 7D 60
Cayton St. EC1 7D 60
Cecil Ct. NW6 1F 55
SW10 5H 79
WC2 1D 74
Cecil Rhodes Ho. NW1 4B 58
Cecil Sharp House 2G 57
Cedar Ct. N1 1C 60
SE1 5F 77
Cedar Ho. W8 6F 71
Cedarne Rd. SW6 7F 79
Cedar Way NW1 1B 58
Cedar Way Ind. Est.
NW1 1B 58
Celandine Dr. E8 1J 61
Celbridge M. W2 5G 63
Celia Ho. N1 5F 61
Cenotaph 4D 74
Centaur St. SE1 6G 75
Central Av. SW11 7D 80
Central Markets (Smithfield)
4K 67
Central St Martins College of
Art & Design 4F 67
Central St. EC1 6B 60
Cen. for the Magic Arts, The
1A 66
Centre Hgts. NW3 1K 55
Centre Point SE1 3K 85
Centrepoint WC2 5C 66
Centre Point Ho. WC2 5C 66
Centric Cl. NW1 2H 57
Centurion Bldg. SW8 6H 81
Cerney M. W2 7K 63
Cervantes Ct. W2 6G 63
Cester St. E2 3K 61
Chadston Ho. N1 1A 60
Chadswell WC1 7E 58
Chadwick St. SW1 7C 74
Chadworth Ho. EC1 7B 60
Chagford St. NW1 2D 64
Chalbury Wlk. N1 4G 59
Chalcot Cres. NW1 1E 56
Chalcot Rd. NW1 1F 57
Chalcot Sq. NW1 1E 56
(not continuous)
Chaldon Rd. SW6 7A 78
Chalfont Ct. NW1 2E 64
CHALK FARM 1G 57
Chalk Farm Rd. NW1 1F 57
Challoner Cres. W14 4B 78
Challoner St. W14 3B 78
Chalmers Wlk. SE17 6A 84
Chalton Ho. NW1 6B 58
Chalton St. NW1 4A 58
(not continuous)
Chamberlain Ho. NW1 5B 58
SE1 5H 75
Chamberlain St. NW1 1E 56
Chambers St. SE16 4K 77
Chamber St. E1 7J 69
Chambers Wharf SE16 4K 77
Chambord St. E2 6J 61
Chancellors Ct. WC1 3F 67
Chancel St. SE1 3K 75
Chancery La. WC2 4G 67
Chance St. E1 1H 69
E2 1H 69
Chandler Ho. NW6 2C 54
WC1 2E 66
Chandler Way SE15 7G 85
(Calypso Cres.)
SE15 6G 85
(St George's Way)
Chandlery, The SE1 6J 75
Chandlery Ho. E1 6K 69
Chandos Pl. WC2 1D 74
Chandos St. W1 4J 65
Change All. EC3 6E 68
Chantry Cl. W9 2C 62
Chantry Sq. W8 7F 71
Chantry St. N1 3A 60
Chapel Ct. SE1 4D 76
Chapel Mkt. N1 4H 59
Chapel of St John the Evangelist
1H 77
(in Tower of London, The)
Chapel Pl. EC2 7F 61
N1 4J 59
W1 6H 65
Chapel Side W2 7F 63
Chapel St. NW1 4B 64
SW1 6G 73
Chaplin Cl. SE1 4J 75
Chapone Pl. W1 6B 66
Chapter Chambers SW1 2B 82
Chapter House 6A 68
Chapter Rd. SE17 4A 84
Chapter St. SW1 2B 82
Charfield Ct. W9 2G 63
Charing Cross SW1 2D 74
Charing Cross Rd. WC2 5C 66
Charing Cross Underground
Shop. Cen. WC2 1D 74
Charing Ho. SE1 4J 75
Charlbert Ct. NW8 4B 56
Charlbert St. NW8 4B 56
Charles II Pl. SW3 4C 80
Charles II St. SW1 2B 74
Charles Gardner Ct. N1 6E 60
Charles Ho. W14 1B 78
Charles La. NW8 5A 56
Charles Mackenzie Ho.
SE16 1K 85
Charles Pl. NW1 7A 58
Charles Rowan Ho. WC1 7H 59
Charles Simmons Ho.
WC1 7G 59
Charles Sq. N1 7E 60
Charles Sq. Est. N1 7E 60
Charles St. W1 2H 73
Charleston St. SE17 2C 84
Charles Townsend Ho.
EC1 7K 59
Charleville Mans. W14 4A 78
Charleville Rd. W14 4A 78
Charlie Chaplin Wlk.
SE1 3G 75
Charlotte Ct. SE1 1F 85
Charlotte M. W1 3A 66
W14 1A 78
Charlotte Pl. SW1 2K 81
W1 4A 66
Charlotte Rd. EC2 7F 61
Charlotte St. W1 3A 66
Charlotte Ter. N1 3G 59
Charlton Ct. E2 4J 61
Charlton Pl. N1 4K 59
Charlwood Ho. SW1 2B 82
Charlwood Ho's. WC1 7E 58
(off Midhope St.)
Charlwood Pl. SW1 2A 82
Charlwood St. SW1 4K 81
(not continuous)
Charmans Ho. SW8 7D 82
Charmouth Ho. SW8 7F 83
Charrington St. NW1 4B 58
Charterhouse 2A 68
Charter Ho. WC2 6E 66
Charterhouse Bldgs. EC1 2B 68
Charterhouse M. EC1 3A 68
Charterhouse Sq. EC1 3A 68
Charterhouse St. EC1 4J 67
Charteris Rd. NW6 2C 54
Chartes Ho. SE1 6G 77
Chartham Ho. SE1 6E 76
Chartridge SE17 5D 84
Chart St. N1 6E 60
Chasemore Ho. SW6 7A 78
Chateris Community Sports Cen.
3D 54
Chatham St. SE17 1D 84
Chatsworth Ct. W8 1D 78
Chaucer Dr. SE1 2J 85
Chaucer Ho. SW1 4K 81
Chaucer Mans. W14 5A 78
Chaucer Theatre 5J 69
(off Braham St.)
Chaulden Ho. EC1 7E 60
Cheadle Ct. NW8 1A 64
Cheapside EC2 6B 68
Chearsley SE17 1C 84
Cheddington Ho. E2 3K 61
Cheesemans Ter. W14 4B 78
(not continuous)
CHELSEA 4B 80
Chelsea Barracks 3G 81
Chelsea Bri. SW1 5H 81
Chelsea Bri. Bus. Cen.
SW8 7H 81
Chelsea Bri. Rd. SW1 3F 81
Chelsea Bri. Wharf SW8 6J 81
Chelsea Cinema 4C 80
Chelsea Cloisters SW3 2C 80
Chelsea College of Art &
Design 4B 80
Chelsea Emb. SW3 6B 80
Chelsea Farm Ho. Studios
SW10 6A 80
Chelsea FC 7F 79
Chelsea Gdns. SW1 4G 81
Chelsea Ga. SW1 4G 81
Chelsea Lodge SW3 5E 80
Chelsea Mnr. Ct. SW3 5C 80
Chelsea Mnr. Gdns.
SW3 5C 80
Chelsea Mnr. St. SW3 4B 80
Chelsea Pk. Gdns. SW3 5K 79
Chelsea Physic Garden 5D 80
Chelsea Reach Twr.
SW10 7K 79
Chelsea Sports Cen. 4C 80
Chelsea Sq. SW3 3A 80
Chelsea Studios SW6 7G 79
Chelsea Towers SW3 4C 80
Chelsea Village SW6 7G 79
Chelsea Wharf SW10 7K 79
Chelsfield Ho. SE17 2F 85
Cheltenham Ter. SW3 3E 80
Chelwood Ho. W2 6A 64
Chenies, The NW1 4C 58
Chenies M. WC1 2B 66
Chenies Pl. NW1 4C 58
Chenies St. WC1 3B 66
Cheniston Gdns. W8 6F 71
Chepstow Cnr. W2 6E 62
Chepstow Ct. W11 7D 62
Chepstow Cres. W11 7D 62
Chepstow Pl. W2 6E 62
Chepstow Rd. W2 4D 62
Chepstow Vs. W11 7C 62
Chequers Ct. EC1 2D 68
Chequers Ho. NW8 1B 64
Chequer St. EC1 2C 68
(not continuous)
Cherbury Ct. N1 5E 60
Cherbury St. N1 5E 60
Cherry Tree Ter. SE1 5G 77
Cherry Tree Wlk. EC1 2C 68
Cherwell Ho. NW8 2A 64
Chesham Cl. SW1 7F 73
Chesham Flats W1 7G 65
Chesham M. SW1 6F 73
Chesham Pl. SW1 7F 73
(not continuous)
Chesham St. SW1 7F 73
Cheshire Ct. EC4 6J 67
Cheshire St. E2 1J 69
Cheshunt Ho. NW6 3F 55
Chesil Ct. SW3 5C 80
Chesney Ct. W9 1E 62
Chesson Rd. W14 5B 78
Chester Cl. SW1 5H 73
Chester Cl. Nth. NW1 6J 57
Chester Cl. Sth. NW1 7J 57
Chester Cotts. SW1 2F 81
Chester Ct. NW1 6J 57
SE5 7D 84
Chesterfield Gdns. W1 2H 73
Chesterfield Hill W1 2H 73
Chesterfield Ho. W1 2G 73
Chesterfield St. W1 2H 73
Chester Ga. NW1 7H 57
Chester Ho. SW1 1H 81
SW9 7J 83
Chester M. SW1 6H 73
Chester Pl. NW1 6H 57
Chester Rd. NW1 7G 57
Chester Row SW1 2F 81
Chester Sq. SW1 1G 81
Chester Sq. M. SW1 7H 73
Chester St. SW1 6G 73
Chester Ter. NW1 6H 57
(not continuous)
Chesterton Rd. W10 4A 62
Chesterton Sq. W8 1C 78
Chester Way SE11 2J 83
Chestnut All. SW6 5C 78
Chestnut Ct. SW6 6C 78
W8 7F 71
Chettle Cl. SE1 6D 76
Chetwode Ho. NW8 1B 64
Cheval Pl. SW7 6C 72
Chevening Rd. NW6 3A 54
Cheylesmore Ho. SW1 4H 81
Cheyne Ct. SW3 5D 80
Cheyne Gdns. SW3 5C 80
Cheyne M. SW3 6C 80
Cheyne Pl. SW3 5D 80
Cheyne Row SW3 6B 80
Cheyne Wlk. SW3 6B 80
(not continuous)
SW10 7K 79
Chicheley St. SE1 4G 75
Chichester Ho. NW6 5D 54
SW9 7H 83
Chichester Rents WC2 5H 67
Chichester Rd. NW6 5D 54
W2 3G 63
Chichester St. SW1 4A 82
Chicksand Ho. E1 3K 69
Chicksand St. E1 4J 69
(not continuous)
Child's M. SW5 2E 78
Child's Pl. SW5 2E 78
Child's St. SW5 2E 78
Child's Wlk. SW5 2E 78
Chilham Ho. SE1 6E 76
Chilianwallan Memorial 5F 81
Chiltern Ct. NW1 2E 64
Chiltern St. W1 3F 65
Chilton St. E2 1J 69
Chilworth M. W2 6K 63
Chilworth St. W2 6J 63
China Wlk. SE11 7G 75
China Wharf SE1 4K 77
Ching Ct. WC2 6D 66
Chippendale Ho. SW1 4J 81
Chippenham Gdns. NW6 7D 54
Chippenham M. W9 2D 62
Chippenham Rd. W9 1D 62
Chipperfield Ho. SW3 3B 80
Chiswell St. EC1 3C 68
SE5 7E 84
Chitty St. W1 3A 66
Chocolate Studios N1 6D 60
Christchurch Av. NW6 1A 54
Christchurch Ct. EC4 5A 68
Christchurch St. SW3 5D 80
Christchurch Ter. SW3 5D 80
Christina St. EC2 1F 69
Christopher Pl. NW1 6C 58
Christophers M. W11 2A 70
Christopher St. EC2 2E 68
Chryssell Rd. SW9 7J 83
Chumleigh Gdns. SE5 5F 85
Chumleigh St. SE5 5F 85
Church Cloisters EC3 1F 77
Church Cl. W8 4F 71
Church Entry EC4 6A 68
Church Ho. EC1 1A 68
(off Compton St.)
SW1 6C 74
Churchill Gdns. SW1 4K 81
Churchill Gdns. Rd. SW1 4J 81
Churchill Mus. (Cabinet War
Rooms) 4C 74
Church Mead SE5 7C 84
Church Pas. EC2 5C 68
(off Guildhall Yd.)
Church Pl. SW1 1A 74
Church Row SW6 7F 79
Church St. NW8 3A 64
W2 3A 64
Church St. Est. NW8 2A 64
(not continuous)
Churchward Ho. W14 4C 78
Churchway NW1 6C 58
(not continuous)
Churchyard Row SE11 1A 84
Church Yd. Wlk. W2 3K 63
Churton Pl. SW1 2A 82
Churton St. SW1 2A 82
Cicely Ho. NW8 5A 56
Cine Lumiere 1K 79
Cinnabar Wharf Central
E1 3K 77
Cinnabar Wharf E. E1 3K 77
Cinnabar Wharf W. E1 3K 77
Cinnamon Cl. SE15 7H 85
Cinnamon Wharf SE1 4J 77
Circa Apartments NW1 1F 57
Circle, The SE1 4J 77
Circus Lodge NW8 6K 55
Circus M. W1 3D 64
Circus Pl. EC2 4E 68
Circus Rd. NW8 6K 55
Cirencester St. W2 3F 63
Citadel Pl. SE11 3F 83
City Apartments E1 5K 69
(off White Chu. La.)
City Central Est. EC1 7B 60
City Gdn. Row N1 5A 60
City Hgts. SE1 3G 77
CITY OF LONDON 5E 68
City of Westminster College
7A 66
City Pav. EC1 3K 67
City Rd. EC1 5K 59
City Twr. EC2 4D 68
City University 7K 59
City University Saddlers
Sports Cen. 1A 68
City Wlk. Apartments
EC1 7A 60
(off Seward St.)
Clabon M. SW1 7D 72
Clandon Ho. SE1 5A 76
Clanricarde Gdns. W2 1E 70
Clapham Rd. SW9 7G 83
Clare Ct. WC1 7E 58
Clare Gdns. W11 6A 62
Clare La. N1 1C 60
Clare Mkt. WC2 6G 67
Claremont Cl. N1 5H 59
Claremont Rd. W9 5A 54
Claremont Sq. N1 5H 59
Claremont Vs. SE5 7E 84
Clarence Gdns. NW1 7J 57
Clarence Ga. Gdns. NW1 2E 64
Clarence House 4A 74
Clarence Rd. NW6 1B 54
Clarence Ter. NW1 1E 64
Clarendon Cl. W2 7B 64
Clarendon Cross W11 1A 70
Clarendon Flats W1 6G 65
Clarendon Gdns. W9 2J 63
Clarendon Gro. NW1 6B 58
Clarendon Ho. NW1 5A 58
Clarendon M. W2 7B 64
Clarendon Pl. W2 7B 64
Clarendon Rd. W11 7A 62
Clarendon St. SW1 4J 81
Clarendon Ter. W9 1J 63
Clarendon Wlk. W11 6A 62
Clareville Gro. SW7 2J 79
Clareville Gro. M. SW7 2J 79
Clareville St. SW7 2J 79
Clarewood Ct. W1 4D 64
Clarges M. W1 2H 73
Clarges St. W1 2J 73
Clarion Ho. SW1 3A 82
W1 6B 66
Clarissa St. E8 2H 61
Clarke's M. W1 3G 65
Clark Ho. SW10 7H 79
Clarkson Row NW1 5K 57
Clark's Pl. EC2 5F 69
Claverton St. SW1 4A 82
Claydon SE17 1B 84
Claylands Pl. SW8 7H 83
Claylands Rd. SW8 6G 83
Clay St. W1 4E 64
Clayton Cres. N1 3E 58
Clayton St. SE11 5H 83
Clearwell Dr. W9 2F 63
Cleaver Ho. NW3 1D 56
Cleaver Sq. SE11 4J 83
Cleaver St. SE11 3J 83
Cleeve Workshops E2 7G 61
Clem Attlee Ct. SW6 6C 78
Clem Attlee Pde. SW6 6C 78
Clement's Inn WC2 6G 67
Clement's Inn Pas. WC2 6G 67
Clements La. EC4 7E 68
Clemson Ho. E8 3J 61
Clennam St. SE1 4C 76
Clenston M. W1 5D 64
Cleopatra's Needle 2F 75
Clere Pl. EC2 1E 68
Clere St. EC2 1E 68
CLERKENWELL 2J 67
Clerkenwell Cl. EC1 1J 67
(not continuous)
Clerkenwell Grn. EC1 2J 67
Clerkenwell Rd. EC1 2H 67
Cleve Ho. NW6 1F 55
Cleveland Gdns. W2 6H 63
Cleveland Mans. W9 1E 62
Cleveland M. W1 3K 65
Cleveland Pl. SW1 2A 74
Cleveland Rd. N1 1E 60
Cleveland Row SW1 3K 73
Cleveland Sq. W2 6H 63
Cleveland St. W1 2J 65
Cleveland Ter. W2 6H 63
Cleve Rd. NW6 1E 54
Clifford Ct. W2 4F 63
Clifford Ho. W14 2B 78
Clifford Rd. N1 2F 61
Clifford's Inn Pas. EC4 6H 67
Clifford St. W1 1K 73
Clifton Ct. NW8 1K 63
Clifton Gdns. W9 2H 63
Clifton Ga. SW10 5H 79
Clifton Hill NW6 4G 55
NW8 4G 55
Clifton Ho. E2 1H 69
Clifton Pl. W2 6A 64
Clifton Rd. W9 1J 63
Clifton St. EC2 2F 69
Clifton Vs. W9 3G 63
Climsland Ho. SE1 2J 75
Clinger Ct. N1 3F 61
Clink Exhibition, The 2C 76
Clink St. SE1 2C 76
Clink Wharf SE1 2D 76
Clipstone M. W1 3K 65
Clipstone St. W1 3J 65
Clive Ct. W9 1J 63
Cliveden Pl. SW1 1F 81
Cloak La. EC4 7C 68
Clock Mus., The 5C 68
Clock Pl. SE1 1A 84
Clock Twr. M. N1 3C 60
Cloisters, The 6D 74
Cloisters, The E1 3H 69
Cloth Ct. EC1 4A 68
Cloth Fair EC1 4A 68
Clothier St. E1 5G 69
Cloth St. EC1 3B 68
Cloudesley Pl. N1 3H 59
Cloudesley Rd. N1 2H 59
(not continuous)
Cloudesley Sq. N1 2H 59
Cloudesley St. N1 3J 59
Clovelly Ho. W2 5H 63
Clover M. SW3 5E 80
Cloysters Grn. E1 2K 77
Club Row E1 1H 69
E2 1H 69
Clunbury St. N1 5E 60
Cluny Est. SE1 6F 77
Cluny M. SW5 2D 78
Cluny Pl. SE1 6F 77
Cluse Ct. N1 4B 60
(not continuous)
Clyde Ct. NW1 4C 58
Clyde Flats SW6 7B 78
Clydesdale Ho. W11 5C 62
Clydesdale Rd. W11 5B 62
Coach & Horses Yd. W1 7J 65
Coalport Ho. SE11 1H 83
Coate St. E2 5K 61
Cobalt Sq. SW8 5F 83
Cobbett St. SW8 7G 83
Cobbold Ct. SW1 1B 82
Cobb's Ct. EC4 6A 68
Cobb St. E1 4H 69
Cobden Ho. NW1 4K 57
Cobham M. NW1 1B 58
Cobourg Rd. SE5 5H 85
Cobourg St. NW1 7A 58
Coburg Cl. SW1 1A 82
Cochrane Cl. NW8 5A 56
Cochrane M. NW8 5A 56
Cochrane St. NW8 5A 56
Cochrane Theatre 4E 66
Cockburn Ho. SW1 4C 82
Cock Hill E1 4G 69
Cock La. EC1 4K 67
Cockpit Steps SW1 5C 74
Cockpit Theatre 2B 64
Cockpit Yd. WC1 3G 67
Cockspur Ct. SW1 2C 74
Cockspur St. SW1 2C 74
Code St. E1 2J 69
Codrington M. W11 6A 62
Coin St. SE1 2H 75
(not continuous)
Coke St. E1 5K 69
Colas M. NW6 2E 54
Colbeck M. SW7 2G 79
Colchester St. E1 5J 69
Coldbath Sq. EC1 1H 67
Colebrook Ct. SW3 2C 80
Colebrooke Pl. N1 3A 60
Colebrooke Row N1 5K 59
Coleby Path SE5 7E 84
Colechurch Ho. SE1 4K 85
Colegrove Rd. SE15 6J 85
Coleherne Ct. SW5 4G 79
Coleherne Mans. SW5 3G 79
Coleherne M. SW10 4F 79
Coleherne Rd. SW10 4F 79
Cole Ho. SE1 5J 75
Coleman Flds. N1 2C 60
Coleman Rd. SE5 7F 85
Coleman St. EC2 5D 68
Coleman St. Bldgs. EC2 5D 68
Coleridge Gdns. NW6 1H 55
SW10 7G 79
Coleridge Ho. SE17 3C 84
SW1 4A 82
Coleridge Sq. SW10 7H 79
Coleshill Flats SW1 2G 81
Cole St. SE1 5C 76
Colet Ho. SE17 4A 84
Coley St. WC1 2G 67
Coliseum Theatre 1D 74
Collard Pl. NW1 1H 57
College Ct. SW3 4E 80
College Cres. NW3 1K 55
College Cross N1 1J 59
College E. E1 4J 69
College Gro. NW1 2B 58
College Hill EC4 7C 68
College Mans. NW6 2A 54
College M. N1 1J 59
(not continuous)
SW1 6D 74
College of Arms 7B 68
College Pde. NW6 2A 54
College Pl. NW1 2A 58
SW10 7H 79
College St. EC4 7C 68
Collett Rd. SE16 7K 77
Collier St. N1 5F 59
Collingham Gdns. SW5 2G 79
Collingham Pl. SW5 2F 79
Collingham Rd. SW5 1G 79
Collingwood Ho. SW1 4B 82
W1 3K 65
Collinson Ct. SE1 5B 76
Collinson Ho. SE15 7K 85
Collinson St. SE1 5B 76
Collinson Wlk. SE1 5B 76
Collin's Yd. N1 3K 59
Colnbrook St. SE1 7K 75
Colombo St. SE1 3K 75
Colombo Street Sports Cen. &
Community Cen. 3K 75
Colonnade WC1 2D 66
Colonnades, The W2 5G 63
Colonnade Wlk. SW1 2H 81
Colosseum Ter. NW1 7J 57
Colour Ct. SW1 3A 74
Columbia Rd. E2 6H 61
Columbia Road Flower Market
6J 61
(off Columbia Rd.)
Colville Est. N1 3E 60
Colville Est. W. E2 7J 61
Colville Gdns. W11 6C 62
(not continuous)
Colville Ho's. W11 5B 62
Colville M. W11 6C 62
Colville Pl. W1 4A 66
Colville Rd. W11 6C 62
Colville Sq. W11 6B 62
Colville Ter. W11 6B 62
Colworth Gro. SE17 2C 84
Colwyn Ho. SE1 7H 75
Colyer Cl. N1 4G 59

Combe, The—Doulton Ho.

Combe, The NW1 7J 57
Comber Gro. SE5 7C 84
Comber Ho. SE5 7C 84
Comedy Store 1B 74
Comedy Theatre 1B 74
Comeragh M. W14 4A 78
Comeragh Rd. W14 4A 78
Comfort St. SE15 6F 85
Commercial Rd. E1 5K 69
Commercial St. E1 2H 69
Commodity Quay E1 1J 77
Commonwealth Conference Cen. 3A 74
Commonwealth Institute 6C 70
Compass Ct. SE1 3H 77
Compton Cl. NW1 7J 57
SE15 7K 85
Compton Pas. EC1 1A 68
Compton Pl. WC1 1D 66
Compton St. EC1 1K 67
Comus Ho. SE17 2F 85
Comus Pl. SE17 2F 85
Conant Ho. SE11 5K 83
Conant M. E1 7K 69
Concert Hall App. SE1 3G 75
Conduit Ct. WC2 7D 66
Conduit M. W2 6K 63
Conduit Pas. W2 6K 63
Conduit Pl. W2 6K 63
Conduit St. W1 7J 65
Coney Way SW8 6G 83
Congreve St. SE17 1F 85
Coningham Ct. SW10 7J 79
Conisbrough NW1 3K 57
Coniston NW1 6K 57
Coniston Ct. W2 6C 64
Conistone Way N7 1E 58
Coniston Ho. SE5 7B 84
Conlan St. W10 1A 62
Connaught Cl. W2 6C 64
Connaught Ho. W1 1H 73
Connaught M. SE11 1J 83
Connaught Pl. W2 7D 64
Connaught Sq. W2 6D 64
Connaught St. W2 6B 64
Conrad Ho. SW8 7D 82
Consort Ho. W2 1G 71
Consort Lodge NW8 3D 56
Cons St. SE1 4J 75
Constable Ho. NW3 1E 56
Constitution Hill SW1 4H 73
Content St. SE17 2D 84
Convent Gdns. W11 6B 62
Conway M. W1 2K 65
Conway St. W1 2K 65
(not continuous)
Conybeare NW3 1C 56
Cookham Ho. E2 1H 69
Cook's Rd. SE17 5K 83
Coomassie Rd. W9 1B 62
Coombs St. N1 5A 60
Coomer M. SW6 6C 78
Coomer Pl. SW6 6C 78
Coomer Rd. SW6 6C 78
Cooper Cl. SE1 5J 75
Cooper Ho. NW8 2K 63
Coopers La. NW1 4C 58
(not continuous)
Coopers Lodge SE1 4H 77
Cooper's Rd. SE1 4J 85
Coopers Row EC3 7H 69
Cope Ho. EC1 7C 60
Copeland Ho. SE11 7G 75
Copenhagen Ho. N1 3G 59
Copenhagen St. N1 3E 58
Cope Pl. W8 7D 70
Copford Wlk. N1 2B 60
Copley Cl. SE17 6A 84
Copperfield Ho. SE1 5K 77
W1 3G 65
Copperfield St. SE1 4A 76
Copper Row SE1 3H 77
Copperworks, The N1 5E 58
Copthall Av. EC2 5E 68
(not continuous)
Copthall Bldgs. EC2 5D 68
Copthall Cl. EC2 5D 68
Coptic St. WC1 4D 66
Coral St. SE1 5J 75
Coram Ho. WC1 1D 66
Coram St. WC1 2D 66
Corbet Ct. EC3 6E 68
Corbet Ho. N1 4H 59
Corbet Pl. E1 3H 69
Corbett Ho. SW10 5H 79
Corbiere Ho. N1 2E 60
Cordelia Ho. N1 4G 61
Corelli Ct. SW5 2D 78
Corfe Ho. SW8 7F 83
Cork St. W1 1K 73
Cork St. M. W1 1K 73
Corlett St. NW1 3B 64
Cormorant Lodge E1 2K 77
Cornell Bldg. E1 5K 69
Corner Ho. St. WC2 2D 74
Cornhill EC3 6E 68
Cornish Ho. SE17 6K 83
Cornwall Cres. W11 7A 62
Cornwall Gdns. SW7 7G 71
Cornwall Gdns. Wlk.
SW7 7G 71
Cornwall Mans. SW10 7J 79
Cornwall M. Sth. SW7 7H 71
Cornwall M. W. SW7 7G 71
Cornwall Rd. SE1 2H 75
Cornwall Sq. SE11 3K 83
Cornwall Ter. NW1 2E 64
Cornwall Ter. M. NW1 2E 64
Coroners Ct. NW1 3B 58
Coronet Cinema 2D 70
Coronet St. N1 7F 61
Corporation Row EC1 1J 67
Corsham St. N1 7E 60
Coryton Path W9 1C 62
Cosgrove Ho. E2 3K 61
Cosmo Pl. WC1 3E 66
Cosser St. SE1 6H 75
Cosway Mans. NW1 3C 64
Cosway St. NW1 3C 64
Cotes Ho. NW8 2B 64
Cotham St. SE17 2C 84
Cotleigh Rd. NW6 1D 54
Cotman Ho. NW8 4B 56
Cotswold Ct. EC1 1B 68
Cottage Grn. SE5 7E 84
Cottage Pl. SW3 6B 72
Cottesloe Ho. NW8 1B 64
Cottesloe M. SE1 6J 75
Cottesloe Theatre *2G 75*
(in Royal National Theatre)
Cottesmore Ct. W8 6G 71
Cottesmore Gdns. W8 6G 71
Cottingham Rd. SW8 7G 83
Cottington St. SE11 3J 83
Cottons Cen. SE1 2F 77
Cotton's Gdns. E2 6G 61
Cottons La. SE1 2E 76
Coulson St. SW3 3D 80
Councillor St. SE5 7B 84
Counter Ct. SE1 3D 76
Counter St. SE1 3F 77
County Hall Apartments
SE1 5F 75
County Hall (Former) 4F 75
County St. SE1 7C 76
Courtauld Institute Galleries
7F 67
Court Cl. NW8 1K 55
(not continuous)
Courtenay Sq. SE11 4H 83
Courtenay St. SE11 3H 83
Courtfield Gdns. SW5 2F 79
Courtfield Ho. EC1 3H 67
Courtfield M. SW5 2G 79
Courtfield Rd. SW7 2H 79
Courthope Ho. SW8 7D 82
Courtnell St. W2 5D 62
Courtney Ho. W14 6A 70
Courtville Ho. W10 7A 54
Courtyard, The *EC3 6E 68*
(in Royal Exchange)
N1 1G 59
NW1 1G 57
Courtyard Theatre, The
King's Cross 5E 58
Cousin La. EC4 1D 76
COVENT GARDEN 7E 66
Covent Garden 7E 66
Covent Gdn. WC2 7E 66
Coventry Cl. NW6 4E 54
Coventry St. W1 1B 74
Coverley Cl. E1 3K 69
Coverley Point SE11 2F 83
Cowcross St. EC1 3K 67
Cowdenbeath Path N1 2F 59
Cowley St. SW1 7D 74
Cowling Cl. W11 2A 70
Cowper Ho. SE17 3C 84
SW1 4B 82
Cowper's Ct. EC3 6E 68
Cowper St. EC2 1E 68
Cox Ho. W6 5A 78
Cox's Ct. E1 4H 69
Coxson Way SE1 5H 77
Crabtree Cl. E2 5H 61
Crace St. NW1 6B 58
Crafts Council & Gallery 5J 59
Cragie Ho. SE1 2J 85
Craig's Ct. SW1 2D 74
Craik Ct. NW6 5C 54
Crail Row SE17 2E 84
Cramer St. W1 4G 65
Crammond Cl. W6 6A 78
Crampton St. SE17 2B 84
Cranbourn All. WC2 7C 66
Cranbourn St. WC2 7C 66
Cranbrook NW1 3A 58
Crane Ct. EC4 6J 67
Cranfield Ct. W1 4C 64
Cranfield Ho. WC1 3D 66
Cranfield Row SE1 6J 75
Cranleigh Ho's. NW1 5A 58
Cranleigh St. NW1 5A 58
Cranley Gdns. SW7 3J 79
Cranley M. SW7 3J 79
Cranley Pl. SW7 2K 79
Cranmer Ct. SW3 2C 80
Cranmer Ho. SW9 7H 83
Cranmer Rd. SW9 7J 83
Cranston Est. N1 4E 60
Cranwood Ct. EC1 7E 60
Cranwood St. EC1 7E 60
Craven Hill W2 7J 63
Craven Hill Gdns. W2 7H 63
(not continuous)
Craven Hill M. W2 7J 63
Craven Lodge W2 7J 63
Craven Pas. WC2 2D 74
Craven Rd. W2 7J 63
Craven St. WC2 2D 74
Craven Ter. W2 7J 63
Crawford Bldgs. W1 4C 64
Crawford Mans. W1 4C 64
Crawford M. W1 4D 64
Crawford Pas. EC1 2H 67
Crawford Pl. W1 5C 64
Crawford St. W1 4C 64
Crayford Ho. SE1 5E 76
Crayle Ho. EC1 1K 67
Creasy Est. SE1 7F 77
Creechurch La. EC3 6G 69
(not continuous)
Creechurch Pl. EC3 6G 69
Creed Ct. EC4 6A 68
Creed La. EC4 6A 68
Creek Ho. W14 6A 70
Cremer Bus. Cen. E2 5H 61
Cremer St. E2 5H 61
Cremorne Est. SW10 6A 80
Cremorne Rd. SW10 7J 79
Crescent EC3 7H 69
Crescent Ho. EC1 2B 68
Crescent Pl. SW3 1B 80
Crescent Row EC1 2B 68
Crescent St. N1 1G 59
Cresswell Gdns. SW5 3H 79
Cresswell Pl. SW10 3H 79
Cresta Ho. NW3 1K 55
Crestfield St. WC1 6E 58
Crewdson Rd. SW9 7H 83
Cricketers Ct. SE11 2K 83
Crimscott St. SE1 7G 77
Crimsworth Rd. SW8 7C 82
Crinan St. N1 4E 58
Cringle St. SW8 7K 81
Cripplegate St. EC2 3B 68
Crispe Ho. N1 3G 59
Crispin St. E1 4H 69
Criterion Ct. E8 1J 61
Criterion Theatre 1B 74
Crofters Way NW1 2B 58
Croft Ho. W10 7A 54
Crofts Ho. E2 4K 61
Crofts St. E1 1K 77
Cromer St. WC1 7D 58
Crompton Ct. SW3 1B 80
Crompton Ho. SE1 7C 76
W2 2K 63
Crompton St. W2 2K 63
Cromwell Cl. E1 2K 77
Cromwell Cres. SW5 1D 78
Cromwell Gdns. SW7 1A 80
Cromwell Highwalk EC2 3C 68
Cromwell M. SW7 1A 80
Cromwell Pl. EC2 3C 68
SW7 1A 80
Cromwell Rd. SW5 1E 78
SW7 1H 79
Cromwell Twr. EC2 3C 68
Crondall Ct. N1 5F 61
Crondall St. N1 5E 60
Crone Ct. NW6 5C 54
Cronin St. SE15 7H 85
Crooked Billet Yd. E2 6G 61
Cropley Ct. N1 4D 60
(not continuous)
Cropley St. N1 4D 60
Cropthorne Ct. W9 7J 55
Crosby Ct. SE1 4D 76
Crosby Row SE1 5D 76
Crosby Sq. EC3 6F 69
Crossfield Ho. W11 1A 70
Cross Keys Cl. W1 4G 65
Cross Keys Sq. EC1 4B 68
Cross La. EC3 1F 77
(not continuous)
Crosslet St. SE17 1E 84
Crossmount Ho. SE5 7C 84
Cross St. N1 2K 59
Crosswall EC3 7H 69
Crowland Ho. NW8 3H 55
Crown Ct. EC2 6C 68
WC2 6E 66
Crowndale Ct. NW1 4B 58
Crowndale Rd. NW1 4A 58
Crown Lodge SW3 2C 80
Crown Office Row EC4 7H 67
Crown Pas. SW1 3A 74
Crown Pl. EC2 3F 69
(not continuous)
Crown Reach SW1 4C 82
Crown St. SE5 7C 84
Crowther Cl. SW6 6C 78
Croxley Rd. W9 7C 54
Croydon Ho. SE1 4J 75
Crozier Ho. SW8 7F 83
Crucifix La. SE1 4F 77
Cruden Ho. SE17 6A 84
Cruden St. N1 3A 60
Cruikshank Ho. NW8 4C 56
Cruikshank St. WC1 6H 59
Crutched Friars EC3 7G 69
Crystal Wharf N1 5A 60
Cube Ho. SE16 7H 77
Cubitt St. WC1 7G 59
Cubitt's Yd. WC2 7E 66
Cuddington SE17 1B 84
Cuff Point E2 6H 61
Culford Gdns. SW3 2E 80
Culford Mans. SW3 2E 80
Culford Rd. N1 1F 61
Culham Ho. E2 7H 61
Cullum St. EC3 7F 69
Cullum Welch Ct. N1 6E 60
Cullum Welch Ho. EC1 2B 68
Culpepper Ct. SE11 1H 83
Culross Bldgs. NW1 5D 58
Culross St. W1 1F 73
Culverhouse WC1 4F 67
Culworth Ho. NW8 4B 56
Culworth St. NW8 5B 56
Cumberland Ct. SW1 3J 81
Cumberland Cres. W14 1A 78
(not continuous)
Cumberland Gdns. WC1 6H 59
Cumberland Ga. W1 7D 64
Cumberland Mans. W1 5D 64
Cumberland Mkt. NW1 6J 57
Cumberland Pl. NW1 6H 57
Cumberland St. SW1 3J 81
Cumberland Ter. NW1 5H 57
Cumberland Ter. M.
NW1 5H 57
(not continuous)
Cuming Mus. 2B 84
Cumming St. N1 5G 59
Cunard Pl. EC3 6G 69
Cundy St. SW1 2G 81
Cunningham Ho. SE5 7D 84
Cunningham Pl. NW8 1K 63
Cureton St. SW1 2C 82
Curlew St. SE1 4H 77
Curran Ho. SW3 2B 80
Cursitor St. EC4 5H 67
Curtain Pl. EC2 1G 69
Curtain Rd. EC2 7G 61
Curtis Ho. SE17 3D 84
Curtis St. SE1 1H 85
Curtis Way SE1 1H 85
Curzon Cinema
Mayfair 3H 73
Soho 7C 66
Curzon Ga. W1 3G 73
Curzon Sq. W1 3G 73
Curzon St. W1 3G 73
Custance Ho. N1 5D 60
Custance St. N1 6D 60
Custom House 1F 77
Custom Ho. Wlk. EC3 1F 77
Cut, The SE1 4J 75
Cuthbert Harrowing Ho.
EC1 2B 68
Cuthbert Ho. W2 3K 63
Cuthbert St. W2 2K 63
Cutlers Gdns. EC2 4G 69
Cutler St. E1 5G 69
Cygnet St. E1 1J 69
Cynthia St. N1 5G 59
Cypress Pl. W1 2A 66
Cyrus Ho. EC1 1A 68
Cyrus St. EC1 1A 68

Dabbs La. EC1 2J 67
Dacre Ho. SW3 6A 80
Dacre St. SW1 6B 74
Dagmar Pas. N1 2A 60
Dagmar Ter. N1 2A 60
Dain Ct. W8 1E 78
Dalehead NW1 5K 57
Dale Ho. NW8 3H 55
Dale Rd. SE17 6A 84
Dale Row W11 6A 62
Dali Universe 4F 75
Dalkeith Ct. SW1 2C 82
Dallington Sq. *EC1 1A 68*
(off Berry St.)
Dallington St. EC1 1A 68
DALSTON 1H 61
Dalton Ho. SW1 3H 81
Damer Ter. SW10 7J 79
Dame St. N1 4B 60
Danbury St. N1 4A 60
Dandridge Ho. E1 3H 69
Danes Ct. NW8 3D 56
Danesfield SE5 5F 85
Dane St. WC1 4F 67
Daniel Gdns. SE15 7H 85
Daniell Ho. N1 4E 60
Dan Leno Wlk. SW6 7F 79
Dansey Pl. W1 7B 66
Danson Rd. SE17 4A 84
Dante Pl. SE11 2A 84
Dante Rd. SE11 1K 83
Danube Ct. SE15 7J 85
Danube St. SW3 3C 80
Danvers Ho. E1 6K 69
Danvers St. SW3 6A 80
Da Palma Ct. SW6 6D 78
Daplyn St. E1 3K 69
D'Arblay St. W1 6A 66
Darent Ho. NW8 3A 64
Darfield NW1 3K 57
Dark Ho. Wlk. EC3 1E 76
Darley Ho. SE11 4F 83
Darlington Ho. SW8 7C 82
Darnay Ho. SE16 6K 77
Dartford Ho. SE1 2J 85
Dartford St. SE17 5C 84
Dartington NW1 3A 58
Dartington Ho. W2 3F 63
Dartle Ct. SE16 5K 77
Dartmouth Cl. W11 5C 62
Dartmouth St. SW1 5B 74
Dartrey Twr. SW10 7J 79
Dartrey Wlk. SW10 7J 79
Dart St. W10 6A 54
Darwin Ct. NW1 2G 57
SE17 2E 84
(off Barlow St.)
Darwin Ho. SW1 5K 81
Darwin St. SE17 2E 84
(not continuous)
Daryngton Ho. SW8 7D 82
Datchet Ho. NW1 6J 57
Datchworth Ho. N1 1K 59
Date St. SE17 4C 84
Dauncey Ho. SE1 5K 75
Davenant St. E1 4K 69
Davenport Ho. SE11 7H 75
Daventry St. NW1 3B 64
Daver Ct. SW3 4C 80
Davey's Ct. WC2 7D 66
Davey St. SE15 6J 85
Davidge Ho. SE1 5J 75
Davidge St. SE1 5K 75
David Ho. SW8 7D 82
David Lloyd Leisure
South Kensington 1G 79
David M. W1 3E 64
Davidson Gdns. SW8 7D 82
Davies M. W1 7H 65
Davies St. W1 6H 65
Dawes Ho. SE17 2D 84
Dawes Rd. SW6 7A 78
Dawes St. SE17 3E 84
Dawson Pl. W2 7D 62
Dawson St. E2 5J 61
Day Ho. SE5 7B 84
Deacon Ho. SE11 2G 83
Deacon M. N1 1E 60
Deacon Way SE17 1B 84
Deal St. E1 3K 69
Deal Wlk. SW9 7H 83
Dean Abbott Ho. SW1 1B 82
Dean Bradley St. SW1 7D 74
Dean Ct. SW8 7D 82
Deanery M. W1 2G 73
Deanery St. W1 2G 73
Dean Farrar St. SW1 6C 74
Dean Ryle St. SW1 1D 82
Dean's Bldgs. SE17 2D 84
Dean's Ct. EC4 6A 68
Dean's M. W1 5J 65
Dean Stanley St. SW1 7D 74
Dean St. W1 5B 66
Dean's Yd. SW1 6C 74
Dean Trench St. SW1 7D 74
Debdale Ho. E2 3K 61
De Beauvoir Ct. N1 1E 60
De Beauvoir Cres. N1 2F 61
De Beauvoir Est. N1 2F 61
De Beauvoir Rd. N1 2F 61
De Beauvoir Sq. N1 1G 61
DE BEAUVOIR TOWN 2F 61
Debenham Ct. E8 3K 61
Decima St. SE1 6F 77
Deerhurst Ho. SE15 6K 85
Defoe Ho. EC2 3B 68
Defoe Pl. EC2 3B 68
Delaford St. SW6 7A 78
Delamere St. W2 3H 63
Delamere Ter. W2 3G 63
Delancey Pas. NW1 3J 57
Delancey St. NW1 3H 57
Delancey Studios NW1 3J 57
Delarch Ho. SE1 5K 75
De Laune St. SE17 4K 83
Delaware Mans. W9 1F 63
Delaware Rd. W9 1F 63
Delfina Studio Trust 4F 77
Delhi St. N1 3E 58
(not continuous)
Dell's M. SW1 2A 82
Delmerend Ho. SW3 3B 80
Delta Point E2 6K 61
Delta St. E2 6K 61
Delverton Ho. SE17 3A 84
Delverton Rd. SE17 4A 84
Denbigh Cl. W11 7C 62
Denbigh Ho. SW1 6E 72
W11 6C 62
Denbigh M. SW1 2K 81
Denbigh Pl. SW1 3K 81
Denbigh Rd. W11 7C 62
Denbigh St. SW1 2K 81
(not continuous)
Denbigh Ter. W11 7C 62
Denby Ct. SE11 1G 83
Dence Ho. E2 7K 61
Dengie Wlk. N1 2B 60
Denholme Rd. W9 6C 54
Denland Ho. SW8 7G 83
Denman Pl. W1 7B 66
Denman St. W1 1B 74
Denmark Gro. N1 4H 59
Denmark Pl. WC2 5C 66
Denmark Rd. NW6 5C 54
(not continuous)
Denmark St. WC2 6C 66
Denne Ter. E8 3J 61
Denning Cl. NW8 6J 55
Denning Point E1 5J 69
Denny Cres. SE11 3J 83
Denny St. SE11 3J 83
Densham Ho. NW8 5A 56
Denstone Ho. SE15 6K 85
Dent Ho. SE17 2F 85
Denton Ho. N1 1A 60
Denyer St. SW3 2C 80
Denys Ho. EC1 3H 67
Depot St. SE5 6D 84
De Quincey Ho. SW1 4K 81
Derby Ga. SW1 4D 74
(not continuous)
Derby Ho. SE11 1H 83
Derby Lodge WC1 6F 59
Derbyshire St. E2 7K 61
(not continuous)
Derby St. W1 3G 73
Dereham Pl. EC2 7G 61
Dering St. W1 6H 65
Dering Yd. W1 6J 65
Derry St. W8 5F 71
Derwent NW1 7K 57
Derwent Ho. SW7 1J 79
Desborough Cl. W2 3G 63
Desborough Ho. W14 5C 78
Desborough St. W2 3F 63
Design Mus. 4J 77
Detling Ho. SE17 2F 85
De Vere Gdns. W8 5H 71
Deverell St. SE1 7D 76
De Vere M. W8 6H 71
Devereux Ct. WC2 6H 67
Devizes St. N1 3E 60
Devonia Rd. N1 4A 60
Devon Mans. *SE1 4H 77*
(off Tooley St.)
Devonport W2 5B 64
Devonshire Cl. W1 3H 65
Devonshire Ct. WC1 3E 66
Devonshire Ho. SE1 6B 76
SW1 3C 82
Devonshire M. SW10 6K 79
Devonshire M. Nth. W1 3H 65
Devonshire M. Sth. W1 3H 65
Devonshire M. W. W1 2G 65
Devonshire Pl. W1 2G 65
W8 7F 71
Devonshire Pl. M. W1 3G 65
Devonshire Row EC2 4G 69
Devonshire Row M. W1 2J 65
Devonshire Sq. EC2 5G 69
Devonshire St. W1 3G 65
Devonshire Ter. W2 6J 63
De Walden Ho. NW8 4B 56
De Walden St. W1 4G 65
Dewey Rd. N1 4H 59
Dewsbury Ter. NW1 2J 57
Dhonau Ho. SE1 1J 85
Diadem Ct. W1 6B 66
Dial Wlk., The W8 4G 71
Diamond St. SE15 7G 85
Diana, Princess of Wales
Memorial Walk 2G 71
Dibden St. N1 2A 60
Dibdin Ho. W9 4F 55
Dickens Est. SE1 5K 77
SE16 6K 77
Dickens House 2G 67
Dickens Ho. NW6 6D 54
NW8 1A 64
SE17 4A 84
WC1 1D 66
Dickens M. EC1 3K 67
Dickens Sq. SE1 6C 76
Dickinson Ct. EC1 2A 68
Dicksee Ho. NW8 2K 63
Dieppe Cl. W14 3B 78
Dighton Ct. SE5 6B 84
Dignum St. N1 4H 59
Dilke St. SW3 5E 80
Dingley Pl. EC1 7C 60
Dingley Rd. EC1 7B 60
Dinton Ho. NW8 1B 64
Disbrowe Rd. W6 6A 78
Discovery Bus. Pk. SE16 7K 77
Disney Pl. SE1 4C 76
Disney St. SE1 4C 76
Diss St. E2 6H 61
Distaff La. EC4 7B 68
Distin St. SE11 2H 83
Dobson Cl. NW6 1K 55
Dobson Ho. SE5 7E 84
Doby Ct. EC4 7C 68
Dockhead SE1 5J 77
Dockhead Wharf SE1 4J 77
Dockley Rd. SE16 7K 77
Dockley Rd. Ind. Est.
SE16 7K 77
Dock St. E1 7K 69
Doddington Gro. SE17 5K 83
Doddington Pl. SE17 5K 83
Dodson St. SE1 5J 75
Dog & Duck Yd. WC1 3G 67
Dolben St. SE1 3K 75
(not continuous)
Dolland Ho. SE11 4G 83
Dolland St. SE11 4G 83
Dolphin Sq. SW1 4A 82
Dombey Ho. SE1 5K 77
Dombey St. WC1 3F 67
(not continuous)
Domecq Ho. *EC1 1A 68*
(off Dallington St.)
Domingo St. EC1 2B 68
Dominion Ct. E8 1J 61
Dominion St. EC2 3E 68
Dominion Theatre 5C 66
Donaldson Rd. NW6 3C 54
Donato Dr. SE15 6F 85
Donegal St. N1 5G 59
Doneraile Ho. SW1 4H 81
Donmar Warehouse Theatre
6D 66
Donnelly Ct. SW6 7A 78
Donne Pl. SW3 1C 80
Donnington Ct. NW1 1J 57
Donovan Ct. SW10 4K 79
Doon St. SE1 3H 75
Dorchester Ct. N1 1G 61
Doric Way NW1 6B 58
Dorking Ho. SE1 6E 76
Dorman Way NW8 2K 55
Dormstone Ho. SE17 2F 85
Dorney NW3 1C 56
Dorrington St. EC1 3H 67
Dorrit St. SE1 4C 76
Dorset Bldgs. EC4 6K 67
Dorset Cl. NW1 3D 64
Dorset Ct. N1 1G 61
Dorset Ho. NW1 2E 64
Dorset M. SW1 6H 73
Dorset Ri. EC4 6K 67
Dorset Rd. SW8 7E 82
Dorset Sq. NW1 2D 64
Dorset St. W1 4E 64
Dorton Cl. SE15 7G 85
Doughty Ho. SW10 6J 79
Doughty M. WC1 2F 67
Doughty St. WC1 1F 67
Douglas Johnstone Ho.
SW6 6B 78
Douglas Pl. SW1 2B 82
Douglas Rd. NW6 2C 54
Douglas St. SW1 2B 82
Douglas Waite Ho. NW6 1F 55
Doulton Ho. SE11 7G 75

Douro Pl.—Fitzroy Ho.

Douro Pl. W8 6G 71
Dove Ct. EC2 6D 68
Dovehouse St. SW3 3A 80
Dove M. SW5 2H 79
Dover Flats SE1 2G 85
Dove Row E2 3K 61
Dover St. W1 1J 73
Dover Yd. W1 2K 73
Doves Yd. N1 3J 59
Dove Wlk. SW1 3F 81
Dovey Lodge N1 1J 59
Dowgate Hill EC4 7D 68
Dowland St. W10 6A 54
Dowlas St. SE5 7F 85
Downend Ct. SE15 6H 85
Downfield Cl. W9 2F 63
Downham Ct. N1 1E 60
Downham Rd. N1 1D 60
Downing St. SW1 4D 74
Down St. W1 3H 73
Down St. M. W1 3H 73
Dowrey St. N1 2H 59
Doyce St. SE1 4B 76
D'Oyley St. SW1 1F 81
Draco St. SE17 5B 84
Dragon Rd. SE15 6F 85
Dragon Yd. WC1 5E 66
Drake Ct. SE1 5C 76
Drake Ho. SW1 5B 82
Drakeland Ho. W9 1C 62
Drakes Courtyard NW6 1C 54
Drake St. WC1 4F 67
Draper Ho. SE1 1A 84
Draper Pl. N1 2A 60
Drapers Gdns. EC2 5E 68
Draycott Av. SW3 1B 80
Draycott Cl. SE5 7D 84
(not continuous)
Draycott Pl. SW3 2D 80
Draycott Ter. SW3 2E 80
Drayford Cl. W9 1C 62
Drayson M. W8 5E 70
Drayton Gdns. SW10 3J 79
Dresden Ho. SE11 1G 83
Drill Hall Arts Cen. 3B 66
Drinkwater Ho. SE5 7D 84
Dr Johnson's House 5J 67
Droop St. W10 1A 62
Druid St. SE1 4G 77
Drummond Cres. NW1 6B 58
Drummond Ga. SW1 3C 82
Drummond Ho. E2 4K 61
Drummond St. NW1 1K 65
Drum St. E1 5J 69
Drury La. WC2 5E 66
Drury Lane Theatre 6F 67
Dryburgh Ho. SW1 3H 81
Dryden Ct. SE11 2J 83
Dryden Mans. W14 5A 78
Dryden St. WC2 6E 66
Drysdale Ho. N1 6G 61
Drysdale Pl. N1 6G 61
Drysdale St. N1 7G 61
Dublin Av. E8 2K 61
Ducal St. E2 7J 61
Duchess M. W1 4J 65
Duchess of Bedford Ho.
W8 4D 70
Duchess of Bedford's Wlk.
W8 5C 70
Duchess St. W1 4J 65
Duchess Theatre 7F 67
Duchy St. SE1 2J 75
(not continuous)
Duck La. W1 6B 66
Dudley Ct. W1 6D 64
WC2 5D 66
Dudley Ho. W2 4K 63
Dudley Rd. NW6 4A 54
Dudley St. W2 4K 63
Dudmaston M. SW3 3A 80
Duffell Ho. SE11 4G 83
Dufferin Av. EC1 2D 68
Dufferin Ct. EC1 2D 68
Dufferin St. EC1 2C 68
Dufour's Pl. W1 6A 66
Dugard Way SE11 1K 83
Duke of Wellington Pl.
SW1 5G 73
Duke of York Column
(Memorial) 3B 74
Duke of York Sq. SW3 2E 80
Duke of York's Theatre 1D 74
Duke of York St. SW1 2A 74
Duke's Ho. SW1 1C 82
Dukes La. W8 4E 70
Duke's La. Chambers *W8* 4F 71
(off Dukes La.)
Duke's La. Mans. *W8* 4F 71
(off Dukes La.)
Duke's M. W1 5G 65
Duke's Pl. EC3 6G 69
Duke's Rd. WC1 7C 58
Duke St. SW1 2A 74
W1 5G 65
Duke St. Hill SE1 2E 76
Duke St. Mans. W1 6G 65
Duke's Yd. W1 7G 65
Dulford St. W11 7A 62
Dulverton NW1 3A 58
Dulverton Mans. WC1 2G 67
Dumain Ct. SE11 2K 83
Dumpton Pl. NW1 1F 57
Dunbridge St. E2 1K 69
Duncan Ho. SW1 4A 82
Duncannon Ho. SW1 4C 82
Duncannon St. WC2 1D 74
Duncan St. N1 4K 59
Duncan Ter. N1 5K 59
(not continuous)
Dundee Ho. W9 6H 55
Dunloe Ct. E2 5J 61
Dunloe St. E2 5H 61
Dunlop Pl. SE16 7J 77
Dunmore Point E2 7H 61
Dunmore Rd. NW6 3A 54
Dunmow Ho. SE11 3G 83
Dunmow Wlk. N1 2B 60
Dunnico Ho. SE17 3F 85
Dunn's Pas. WC1 5E 66
Dunoon Ho. N1 3F 59
Dunraven St. W1 7E 64
Dunstable M. W1 3G 65
Dunster Ct. EC3 7G 69
Dunster Gdns. NW6 1C 54
Dunsterville Way SE1 5E 76
Dunston Rd. E8 3H 61
Dunston St. E8 2H 61
Dunton Rd. SE1 3H 85
Dunworth M. W11 5B 62
Duplex Ride SW1 5E 72
Durant St. E2 6K 61
Durham Ct. NW6 5E 54
(not continuous)
Durham Ho. St. WC2 1E 74
Durham Pl. SW3 4D 80
Durham St. SE11 4F 83
Durham Ter. W2 5F 63
Durrels Ho. W14 1C 78
Durweston M. W1 3E 64
Durweston St. W1 3E 64
Dyer's Bldgs. EC1 4H 67
Dyne Rd. NW6 1A 54
Dynham Rd. NW6 1D 54
Dyott St. WC1 5C 66
Dysart St. EC2 2F 69

Eagle Ct. EC1 3K 67
Eagle Ho. N1 4D 60
Eagle Pl. SW1 1A 74
SW7 3J 79
Eagle St. WC1 4F 67
Eagle Wharf Ct. SE1 3H 77
Eagle Wharf Rd. N1 4C 60
Eagle Works E. E1 2J 69
Eagle Works W. E1 2H 69
Eamont Ct. NW8 4C 56
Eamont St. NW8 4B 56
Eardley Cres. SW5 3E 78
Earlham St. WC2 6C 66
Earl Ho. NW1 2C 64
Earlom Ho. WC1 7H 59
EARL'S COURT 3E 78
Earls Court Exhibition Building
4D 78
Earl's Ct. Gdns. SW5 2F 79
Earl's Ct. Rd. W8 6D 70
Earl's Ct. Sq. SW5 3E 78
Earlsferry Way N1 1E 58
(not continuous)
Earls Ter. W8 7C 70
Earlstoke St. EC1 6K 59
Earl St. EC2 3E 68
(not continuous)
Earls Wlk. W8 7D 70
Early M. NW1 2J 57
Earnshaw St. WC2 5C 66
Earsby St. W14 1A 78
(not continuous)
Easleys M. W1 5G 65
East Block SE1 4G 75
Eastbourne M. W2 5J 63
Eastbourne Ter. W2 5J 63
Eastcastle St. W1 5K 65
Eastcheap EC3 7F 69
E. Harding St. EC4 5J 67
Eastlake Ho. NW8 2A 64
East La. SE16 5K 77
(not continuous)
Easton St. WC1 1H 67
East Pas. EC1 3A 68
East Point SE1 3K 85
E. Poultry Av. EC1 4K 67
East Rd. N1 7D 60
SW3 4F 81
East Row W10 2A 62
Eastry Ho. SW8 7D 82
East Smithfield E1 1J 77
East St. SE17 3C 84
E. Surrey Gro. SE15 7H 85
E. Tenter St. E1 6J 69
Eastwell Ho. SE1 6E 76
Eaton Cl. SW1 2F 81
Eaton Ga. SW1 1F 81
Eaton La. SW1 7J 73
Eaton Mans. SW1 2F 81
Eaton M. Nth. SW1 1F 81
Eaton M. Sth. SW1 1G 81
Eaton M. W. SW1 1G 81
Eaton Pl. SW1 7F 73
Eaton Row SW1 7H 73
Eaton Sq. SW1 1F 81
Eaton Ter. SW1 1F 81
Eaton Ter. M. SW1 1F 81
Ebbisham Dr. SW8 5F 83
Ebenezer Ho. SE11 2J 83
Ebenezer St. N1 6D 60
Ebley Cl. SE15 6H 85
Ebony Ho. *E2* 7K 61
(off Buckfast St.)
Ebor St. E1 1H 69
Ebury Bri. SW1 3H 81
Ebury Bri. Est. SW1 3H 81
Ebury Bri. Rd. SW1 4G 81
Ebury M. SW1 1G 81
Ebury M. E. SW1 1H 81
Ebury Sq. SW1 2G 81
Ebury St. SW1 2G 81
Ecclesbourne Rd. N1 1C 60
Eccleston Bri. SW1 1J 81
Eccleston M. SW1 7G 73
Eccleston Pl. SW1 2H 81
Eccleston Sq. SW1 2J 81
Eccleston Sq. M. SW1 2K 81
Eccleston St. SW1 7G 73
Eckford St. N1 4H 59
Edbrooke Rd. W9 2D 62
Eden Cl. W8 6E 70
Edenham Way W10 3B 62
Eden Ho. NW8 2B 64
Edgar Ho. SW8 7D 82
Edge St. W8 2E 70
Edgeworth Ho. NW8 2H 55
Edgson Ho. SW1 3H 81
Edgware Rd. W2 2K 63
Edinburgh Ga. SW1 4D 72
Edinburgh Ho. W9 6G 55
Edis St. NW1 2F 57
Edith Gro. SW10 6H 79
Edith Neville Cotts. NW1 6B 58
Edith Rd. W14 2A 78
Edith St. E2 4J 61
Edith Summerskill Ho.
SW6 7C 78
Edith Ter. SW10 7H 79
Edith Vs. W14 2B 78
Edith Yd. SW10 7J 79
Edmund Ho. SE17 4A 84
Edmund St. SE5 7D 84
Ednam Ho. SE15 6K 85
Edric Ho. SW1 1C 82
Edward Bond Ho. *WC1* 7E 58
(off Cromer St.)
Edward Dodd Ct. N1 6E 60
Edward Edward's Ho.
SE1 3K 75
Edwardes Pl. W8 7C 70
Edwardes Sq. W8 7C 70
Edward Ho. SE11 3G 83
Edward M. NW1 6J 57
Edwards M. W1 6F 65
Edward Sq. N1 3F 59
Effie Pl. SW6 7E 78
Effie Rd. SW6 7E 78
Egbert St. NW1 2F 57
Egerton Cres. SW3 1C 80
Egerton Gdns. SW3 7B 72
Egerton Gdns. M. SW3 7C 72
Egerton Pl. SW3 7C 72
Egerton Ter. SW3 7C 72
Eglington Ct. SE17 5B 84
Eglon M. NW1 1E 56
Eland Ho. *SW1* 6K 73
(off Bressenden Pl.)
Elba Pl. SE17 1C 84
Elbourn Ho. SW3 3B 80
Elcho St. SW11 7B 80
Elder St. E1 3H 69
(not continuous)
Elder Wlk. N1 2A 60
Eldon Ct. NW6 3D 54
Eldon Rd. W8 7G 71
Eldon St. EC2 4E 68
Eldridge Ct. SE16 7K 77
ELEPHANT & CASTLE 7A 76
Elephant & Castle SE1 1A 84
Elephant & Castle Superbowl
1B 84
Elephant Rd. SE17 1B 84
Elgar Ho. NW6 1J 55
SW1 4J 81
Elgin Av. W9 2C 62
Elgin Ct. W9 1F 63
Elgin Cres. W11 1A 70
Elgin Est. W9 2D 62
Elgin Mans. W9 7F 55
Elgin M. W11 6A 62
Elgin M. Nth. W9 6G 55
Elgin M. Sth. W9 6G 55
Elgood Cl. W11 1A 70
Elgood Ho. NW8 5A 56
Elias Pl. SW8 6H 83
Elia St. N1 5K 59
Elim Est. SE1 6F 77
Elim St. SE1 6E 76
(not continuous)
Eliot M. NW8 5H 55
Elizabeth Av. N1 2C 60
Elizabeth Bri. SW1 2H 81
Elizabeth Cl. W9 2J 63
Elizabeth Ct. SW1 7C 74
SW10 6A 80
Elizabeth Ho. SE11 2J 83
Elizabeth Newcomen Ho.
SE1 4D 76
Elizabeth St. SW1 1G 81
Elkington Point SE11 2H 83
Elkstone Rd. W10 3B 62
Ella M. N1 5K 59
Ellen St. E1 6K 69
Ellen Wilkinson Ho.
SW6 6B 78
Ellery Ho. SE17 2E 84
Ellington Ho. SE1 7C 76
Elliot Ho. W1 4C 64
Elliott's Pl. N1 3A 60
Elliott Sq. NW3 1C 56
Elliotts Row SE11 1K 83
Ellis Franklin Ct. NW8 4H 55
Ellis Ho. SE17 3D 84
Ellis St. SW1 1E 80
Ellwood Ct. W9 2F 63
Elm Ct. EC4 7H 67
W9 3E 62
Elmer Ho. *NW1* 3B 64
(off Penfold St.)
Elmfield Way W9 3D 62
Elm Friars Wlk. NW1 1C 58
Elm Ho. W10 1A 62
Elmington Est. SE5 7E 84
Elmore St. N1 1C 60
Elm Pk. Chambers SW10 4K 79
Elm Pk. Gdns. SW10 4K 79
Elm Pk. Ho. SW10 4K 79
Elm Pk. La. SW3 4K 79
Elm Pk. Mans. SW10 5J 79
Elm Pk. Rd. SW3 5K 79
Elm Pl. SW7 3K 79
Elm Quay Ct. SW8 6B 82
Elms M. W2 7K 63
Elm St. WC1 2G 67
Elmton Ct. NW8 1K 63
Elm Tree Cl. NW8 6K 55
Elm Tree Ct. NW8 6K 55
Elm Tree Rd. NW8 6K 55
Elnathan M. W9 2G 63
Elsham Rd. W14 5A 70
Elsham Ter. W14 6A 70
Elsie La. Ct. W2 4E 62
Elsinore Ho. N1 3H 59
Elsted St. SE17 2E 84
Elsworthy Ri. NW3 1C 56
Elsworthy Rd. NW3 2B 56
Elsworthy Ter. NW3 1C 56
Elvaston M. SW7 6J 71
Elvaston Pl. SW7 7H 71
Elverton St. SW1 1B 82
Elwin St. E2 6K 61
Elworth Ho. SW8 7G 83
Ely Cotts. SW8 7F 83
Ely Ct. EC1 4J 67
NW6 4D 54
Ely Pl. EC1 4J 67
Elystan Pl. SW3 3C 80
Elystan St. SW3 2B 80
Elystan Wlk. N1 3H 59
Embankment Gdns. SW3 5E 80
Embankment Pl. WC2 2E 74
Embassy Ct. NW8 5A 56
Embassy Ho. NW6 1F 55
Embassy Theatre 1K 55
(off College Cres.)
Emberton SE5 5F 85
Emberton Ct. EC1 7K 59
Emerald St. WC1 3F 67
Emerson St. SE1 2B 76
Emery Hill St. SW1 7A 74
Emery St. SE1 6J 75
Emmanuel Ho. SE11 2H 83
Emminster NW6 2F 55
Emperor's Ga. SW7 7G 71
Empire Cinema 7C 66
Empress App. SW6 5D 78
Empress Pl. SW6 4D 78
Empress State Bldg.
SW6 5D 78
Empress St. SE17 5C 84
Enbrook St. W10 7A 54
Endell St. WC2 5D 66
Endsleigh Gdns. WC1 1B 66
Endsleigh Pl. WC1 1C 66
Endsleigh St. WC1 1B 66
Enfield Cloisters N1 6F 61
Enfield Rd. N1 1G 61
Enford St. W1 3D 64
Engine Ct. SW1 3A 74
Englefield NW1 7K 57
Englefield Rd. N1 1G 61
English Grounds SE1 3F 77
Enid St. SE16 6J 77
Ennerdale NW1 6K 57
Ennismore Gdns. SW7 5B 72
Ennismore Gdns. M.
SW7 6B 72
Ennismore M. SW7 6B 72
Ennismore St. SW7 6B 72
Ensbury Ho. SW8 7F 83
Ensign Ind. Cen. E1 1K 77
Ensign St. E1 7K 69
Ensor M. SW7 3K 79
Epirus M. SW6 7D 78
Epirus Rd. SW6 7C 78
Epworth St. EC2 2E 68
Equity Sq. E2 7J 61
Erasmus St. SW1 2C 82
Eresby Ho. SW7 5C 72
Eresby Pl. NW6 1D 54
Eric Fletcher Ct. N1 1C 60
Eric Wilkins Ho. SE1 4K 85
Ernest Harriss Ho. W9 1D 62
Eros 1B 74
Errington Rd. W9 1C 62
Errol St. EC1 2C 68
Erskine Ho. SW1 4K 81
Erskine M. NW3 1E 56
Erskine Rd. NW3 1E 56
Eskdale NW1 5K 57
Esmeralda Rd. SE1 2K 85
Esmond Ct. W8 6G 71
Esmond Rd. NW6 3C 54
Esporta Health & Fitness
Islington 3K 59
Esprit Ct. E1 4H 69
Essendine Rd. W9 1E 62
Essex Ct. EC4 6H 67
Essex Rd. N1 3A 60
Essex St. WC2 6H 67
Essex Vs. W8 5D 70
Estcourt Rd. SW6 7A 78
Esterbrooke St. SW1 2B 82
Etal Ho. N1 1K 59
Etcetera Theatre 1J 57
Ethel St. SE17 2C 84
Eton Av. NW3 1K 55
Eugene Cotter Ho. SE17 2E 84
Europa Pl. EC1 7B 60
Eustace Bldg. SW8 6H 81
Eustace Ho. SE11 1F 83
Eustace Rd. SW6 7D 78
Euston Cen. NW1 1K 65
(not continuous)
Euston Gro. NW1 7B 58
Euston Rd. NW1 2J 65
Euston Sq. NW1 7B 58
(not continuous)
Euston Sta. Colonnade
NW1 7B 58
Euston St. NW1 1A 66
Euston Twr. NW1 1K 65
EUSTON UNDERPASS 1A 66
Evangelist Ho. *EC4* 6K 67
(off Black Friars La.)
Evans Ho. SW8 7C 82
Evelina Mans. SE5 7D 84
Evelyn Ct. N1 5D 60
(not continuous)
Evelyn Denington Ct. N1 1K 59
Evelyn Gdns. SW7 4J 79
Evelyn Lowe Est. SE16 7K 77
Evelyn Mans. SW1 7K 73
W14 5A 78
Evelyn Wlk. N1 5D 60
Evelyn Yd. W1 5B 66
Everard Ho. E1 6K 69
Everett Ho. SE17 3E 84
Evergreen Sq. E8 1H 61
Everilda St. N1 3G 59
Eversholt St. NW1 4A 58
Eversley Ho. E2 7K 61
Everton Bldgs. NW1 7K 57
Evesham Ho. NW8 3H 55
Ewen Ho. N1 3F 59
Ewer St. SE1 3B 76
Exbury Ho. SW1 3B 82
Excel Ct. WC2 1C 74
Exchange Arc. EC2 3G 69
Exchange Bldg. E1 2H 69
Exchange Ct. WC2 1E 74
Exchange Ho. EC2 3G 69
SW1 2B 82
Exchange Pl. EC2 3F 69
Exchange Sq. EC2 3F 69
Exchange St. EC1 7B 60
Exeter Ct. NW6 5E 54
Exeter Ho. W2 5H 63
Exeter M. SW6 7D 78
Exeter St. WC2 7E 66
Exhibition Rd. SW7 5A 72
Exmouth Ho. EC1 1H 67
Exmouth Mkt. EC1 1H 67
Exmouth M. NW1 7A 58
Exonbury NW8 3G 55
Exon St. SE17 2F 85
Export Ho. SE1 5G 77
Express Newspapers SE1 2K 75
Exton St. SE1 3H 75
Eynsford Ho. SE1 5D 76
SE17 2F 85
Eyre Ct. NW8 4K 55
Eyre St. Hill EC1 2H 67
Ezra St. E2 6J 61

Fabian Rd. SW6 7C 78
Fairbank Est. N1 5E 60
Fairburn Ho. W14 4C 78
Fairby Ho. SE1 1J 85
Fairchild Ho. N1 6F 61
Fairchild Pl. EC2 2G 69
Fairchild St. EC2 2G 69
Fairclough St. E1 6K 69
Fairfax Pl. NW6 1J 55
W14 7A 70
Fairfax Rd. NW6 1J 55
Fairfield NW1 3K 57
Fairford Ho. SE11 2J 83
Fairhazel Gdns. NW6 1H 55
Fairhazel Mans. NW6 1H 55
Fairholme Rd. W14 4A 78
Fairholt St. SW7 6C 72
Fairstead Wlk. N1 2B 60
Fair St. SE1 4G 77
Fakruddin St. E1 2K 69
Falcon WC1 3E 66
Falconberg Ct. W1 5C 66
Falconberg M. W1 5B 66
Falcon Cl. SE1 2A 76
Falcon Ct. EC4 6J 67
N1 5A 60
Falcon Highwalk EC2 4B 68
Falcon Lodge W9 3E 62
Falcon Point SE1 1A 76
Falkirk Ho. W9 6G 55
Falkirk St. N1 5G 61
Falkland Ho. W8 7F 71
W14 3B 78
Fallodon Ho. W11 4C 62
Falmouth Ho. SE11 3J 83
W2 7B 64
Falmouth Rd. SE1 7C 76
Falstaff Ct. SE11 2K 83
Falstaff Ho. N1 5F 61
Fane St. W14 5C 78
Fann St. EC1 2B 68
EC2 2B 68
(not continuous)
Fanshaw St. N1 6F 61
Faraday Ho. SE1 5D 76
Faraday Mans. W14 5A 78
Faraday Mus. 1K 73
Faraday Rd. W10 3A 62
Fareham St. W1 5B 66
Farjeon Ho. NW6 1K 55
Farley Ct. NW1 2E 64
Farm Cl. SW6 7E 78
Farmer's Rd. SE5 7A 84
Farmer St. W8 2D 70
Farm La. SW6 6E 78
(not continuous)
Farm La. Trad. Est. SW6 6D 78
Farm Pl. W8 2D 70
Farm St. W1 1H 73
Farnaby Ho. W10 7B 54
Farndale Ho. NW6 2F 55
Farnell M. SW5 3F 79
Farnham Ho. NW1 2C 64
Farnham Pl. SE1 3A 76
Farnham Royal SE11 4G 83
Farriers Ho. EC1 2C 68
Farrier St. NW1 1J 57
Farrier Wlk. SW10 5H 79
Farringdon La. EC1 2J 67
Farringdon Rd. EC1 1H 67
Farringdon St. EC4 4K 67
Farthing All. SE1 5K 77
Fashion & Textile Mus. 4G 77
Fashion St. E1 4H 69
Faulkners All. EC1 3K 67
Faunce Ho. SE17 5K 83
Faunce St. SE17 5K 83
Faversham Ho. NW1 3A 58
SE17 4F 85
Fawcett St. SW10 6G 79
Fawkham Ho. SE1 2J 85
Fazeley Ct. W9 3D 62
Featherstone St. EC1 1D 68
Fellmongers Path SE1 5H 77
Fellows Ct. E2 4H 61
(not continuous)
Fellows Rd. NW3 1A 56
Felton Ho. N1 3E 60
Felton St. N1 3E 60
Fenchurch Av. EC3 6F 69
Fenchurch Bldgs. EC3 6G 69
Fenchurch Pl. EC3 7G 69
Fenchurch St. EC3 7F 69
Fen Ct. EC3 6F 69
Fendall St. SE1 7G 77
(not continuous)
Fenelon Pl. W14 2C 78
Fenham Rd. SE15 7K 85
Fenning St. SE1 4F 77
Fentiman Rd. SW8 6E 82
Ferdinand Pl. NW1 1G 57
Ferdinand St. NW1 1G 57
Fermain Ct. E. N1 2G 61
Fermain Ct. Nth. N1 2G 61
Fermain Ct. W. N1 2F 61
Fermoy Rd. W9 2B 62
Fern Cl. N1 4F 61
Fernhead Rd. W9 5B 54
Fernsbury St. WC1 7H 59
Fernshaw Cl. SW10 6H 79
Fernshaw Rd. SW10 6H 79
Ferriby Cl. N1 1H 59
Ferrybridge Ho. SE11 7G 75
Festival Ct. E8 1J 61
Fetter La. EC4 6J 67
(not continuous)
Fettes Ho. NW8 5A 56
Field Ct. WC1 4G 67
Fieldgate St. E1 4K 69
Fielding Ho. NW6 6E 54
Fielding St. SE17 5B 84
Field Rd. W6 4A 78
Fields Est. E8 1K 61
Field St. WC1 6F 59
Fife Ter. N1 4G 59
Fifth Av. W10 1A 62
Figure Ct. SW3 4E 80
Filmer Rd. SW6 7B 78
Finborough Ho. SW10 5H 79
Finborough Rd. SW10 4F 79
Finborough Theatre, The
5G 79
Finch La. EC3 6E 68
Finchley Pl. NW8 4K 55
Finchley Rd. NW3 1K 55
NW8 3K 55
Finch Lodge W9 3E 62
Fingest Ho. NW8 1B 64
Finnemore Ho. N1 2B 60
Finn Ho. N1 6E 60
FINSBURY 7J 59
Finsbury Av. EC2 4E 68
(not continuous)
Finsbury Av. Sq. EC2 3F 69
Finsbury Cir. EC2 4E 68
Finsbury Est. EC1 7K 59
Finsbury Leisure Cen. 1B 68
Finsbury Mkt. EC2 2F 69
(not continuous)
Finsbury Pavement EC2 3E 68
Finsbury Sq. EC2 2E 68
Finsbury St. EC2 3D 68
Fiona Ct. NW6 4D 54
Fir Ho. W10 1A 62
First Av. W10 1B 62
First St. SW3 1C 80
Firth Ho. E2 7K 61
Fisher Ho. N1 3H 59
Fisher St. WC1 4F 67
Fisherton St. NW8 2K 63
Fishmongers Hall Wharf
EC4 1E 76
Fish St. Hill EC3 1E 76
Fish Wharf EC3 1E 76
Fitness First Health Club
Islington 5K 59
Fitrooms 6C 78
Fitzalan St. SE11 1G 83
Fitzgeorge Av. W14 2A 78
Fitzhardinge Ho. W1 5F 65
Fitzhardinge St. W1 5F 65
Fitzjames Av. W14 2A 78
Fitzmaurice Pl. W1 2J 73
FITZROVIA 3J 65
Fitzroy Ct. W1 2A 66
Fitzroy Ho. SE1 3J 85

Fitzroy M.—Grosvenor Gdns.

Fitzroy M. W1 2K 65
Fitzroy Rd. NW1 2F 57
Fitzroy Sq. W1 2K 65
Fitzroy St. W1 2K 65
(not continuous)
Fitzroy Yd. NW1 2F 57
Fives Ct. SE11 7K 75
Flamstead Ho. *SW3* *3B 80*
(off Cale St.)
Flank St. E1 7K 69
Flatiron Yd. SE1 3C 76
Flaxman Ct. W1 6B 66
WC1 7C 58
Flaxman Ter. WC1 7C 58
Flecker Ho. SE5 7D 84
Fleetbank Ho. EC4 6J 67
Fleet Bldg. EC4 5K 67
Fleetfield WC1 6E 58
Fleet Pl. EC4 5K 67
(not continuous)
Fleet Sq. WC1 7G 59
Fleet St. EC4 6H 67
Fleet St. Hill E1 2K 69
Fleetway WC1 6E 58
Fleming Cl. W9 2D 62
Fleming Ct. W2 3K 63
Fleming Ho. SE16 5K 77
Fleming Lodge W9 3E 62
Fleming Rd. SE17 5A 84
Flemming Cl. SW10 5J 79
Fletcher Bldgs. WC2 6E 66
Fletcher St. E1 7K 69
Fleur-de-Lis St. E1 2G 69
Flinton St. SE17 3G 85
Flint St. SE17 2E 84
Flitcroft St. WC2 6C 66
Flitton Ho. N1 1K 59
Flockton St. SE16 5K 77
Flood St. SW3 4C 80
Flood Wlk. SW3 5C 80
Floral St. WC2 7D 66
Florence Ct. N1 1K 59
W9 7J 55
Florence Nightingale Mus. 5F 75
Florence St. N1 1K 59
Florey Lodge *W9* *3E 62*
(off Admiral Wlk.)
Florida St. E2 7K 61
Florin Ct. SE1 5H 77
Flower & Dean Wlk. E1 4J 69
Flower Wlk., The SW7 5H 71
Foley St. W1 4K 65
Folgate St. E1 3G 69
(not continuous)
Foliot Ho. N1 4F 59
Follett Ho. SW10 7K 79
Follingham Ct. N1 6G 61
Folly M. W11 5B 62
Fontenoy Ho. SE11 2K 83
Forbes St. E1 6K 69
Fordingley Rd. W9 7C 54
Foreland Ho. W11 7A 62
Fore St. EC2 4C 68
Fore St. Av. EC2 4D 68
Formosa St. W9 3G 63
Forset Ct. W2 5C 64
Forset St. W1 5C 64
Forston St. N1 4C 60
Forsyth Gdns. SE17 5A 84
Forsyth Ho. SW1 3A 82
Fort Rd. SE1 2J 85
Fort St. E1 4G 69
Fortune Ct. E8 1J 61
Fortune Ho. EC1 2C 68
SE11 2H 83
Fortune St. EC1 2C 68
Fortune Theatre 6E 66
Forum Magnum Sq. SE1 4F 75
Fosbrooke Ho. SW8 7D 82
Fosbury M. W2 1G 71
Foscote Ct. W9 3E 62
Foscote M. W9 2E 62
Foster Ct. NW1 1K 57
Foster La. EC2 5B 68
Foubert's Pl. W1 6K 65
Foulis Ter. SW7 3A 80
Founders Ct. EC2 5D 68
Founders Ho. SW1 4B 82
Foundling Ct. WC1 1D 66
Foundling Mus., The 1E 66
Foundry M. NW1 1A 66
Fountain Ct. EC4 7H 67
SW1 2H 81
Fountain Ho. NW6 1A 54
W1 2F 73
Fountain Sq. SW1 2H 81
Fount St. SW8 7C 82
Fournier St. E1 3H 69
Fourscore Mans. E8 1K 61
Fourth Av. W10 1A 62
Fowey Ho. SE11 3J 83
Fowler Rd. N1 2A 60
Fox & Knot St. EC1 3A 68
Foxcote SE5 4G 85
Foxcroft WC1 5G 59
Foxfield NW1 3J 57
Foxley Rd. SW9 7J 83
Frampton NW1 1B 58
Frampton Ho. NW8 2A 64
Frampton St. NW8 2K 63
Francis Ct. EC1 3K 67
Francis Ho. N1 3F 61
SW10 7G 79
Francis St. SW1 1K 81
Francis Wlk. N1 2F 59
Frank Beswick Ho. SW6 6C 78
Frank Ho. SW8 7D 82
Frankland Rd. SW7 7K 71
Franklin Sq. W14 4C 78
Franklin's Row SW3 3E 80
Frank Soskice Ho. SW6 6C 78
Frazier St. SE1 5H 75
Frean St. SE16 6K 77
Frearson Ho. WC1 6G 59
Freda Corbet Cl. SE15 7K 85
Frederick Cl. W2 7C 64
Frederick Ct. *SW3* *2E 80*
(off Duke of York Sq.)
Frederick Rd. SE17 5A 84
Frederick's Pl. EC2 6D 68
Frederick's Row EC1 6K 59
Frederick St. WC1 7F 59
Frederick Ter. E8 1H 61
Frederic M. SW1 5E 72
Freeling Ho. NW8 2K 55
Freeling St. N1 1F 59
(Carnoustie Dr.)
N1 1E 58
(Pembroke St.)
Freemantle St. SE17 3F 85
French Ordinary Ct. EC3 7G 69
French Pl. E1 1G 69
Frensham St. SE15 6K 85
Freshfield Av. E8 1H 61
Freshwater Ct. *W1* *4C 64*
(off Crawford St.)
Frewell Ho. EC1 3H 67
Friars Cl. SE1 2A 76
Friar St. EC4 6A 68
Friary Ct. SW1 3A 74
Friary Est. SE15 6K 85
(not continuous)
Friary Rd. SE15 6K 85
Friday St. EC4 7B 68
Friendship Ho. SE1 5A 76
Friends House 1B 66
Friend St. EC1 6K 59
Frith Ho. NW8 2A 64
Frith St. W1 6B 66
Frobisher Cres. EC2 3C 68
Frobisher Ho. SW1 5B 82
Frome St. N1 4B 60
Frostic Wlk. E1 4J 69
Fruiterers Pas. EC4 1C 76
Frying Pan All. E1 4H 69
Fulcher Ho. N1 3F 61
FULHAM BROADWAY 7E 78
Fulham B'way. SW6 7E 78
Fulham B'way. Shop. Cen.
SW6 7E 78
Fulham Pools 6A 78
Fulham Rd. SW3 6H 79
SW6 7D 78
(Fulham High St.)
SW6 7F 79
(King's Rd.)
SW10 6H 79
Fuller Cl. E2 1K 69
Fullwood's M. N1 6E 60
Fulmer Ho. NW8 2C 64
Fulton M. W2 7H 63
Fulwood Pl. WC1 4G 67
Funland *1B 74*
(in Trocadero Cen.)
Furley Ho. SE15 7K 85
Furley Rd. SE15 7K 85
Furness Ho. SW1 3H 81
Furnival Mans. W1 4K 65
Furnival St. EC4 5H 67
Fursecroft W1 5D 64
Fusion Health & Leisure Cen.
1A 84
Fye Foot La. EC4 7B 68
(not continuous)
Fynes St. SW1 1B 82

Gabriel Ho. SE11 1F 83
Gabriels Wharf SE1 2J 75
Gaddesden Ho. EC1 7E 60
Gadebridge Ho. *SW3* *3B 80*
(off Cale St.)
Gadsden Ho. W10 2A 62
Gage St. WC1 3E 66
Gainford St. N1 2H 59
Gainsborough Ho. SW1 2C 82
Gainsborough Mans.
W14 5A 78
Gainsborough Studios E.
N1 3D 60
Gainsborough Studios Nth.
N1 3D 60
Gainsborough Studios Sth.
N1 3D 60
Gainsborough Studios W.
N1 3D 60
Gainsford St. SE1 4H 77
Gairloch Ho. NW1 1B 58
Gaitskell Ho. SE17 5F 85
Galaxy Ho. *EC2* *1E 68*
(off Leonard St.)
Galen Pl. WC1 4E 66
Gallery Ct. SE1 5D 76
SW10 *6H 79*
(off Gunter Gro.)
Galsworthy Ho. W11 6A 62
Galton St. W10 7A 54
Galway Ho. EC1 7C 60
Galway St. EC1 7C 60
Gambia St. SE1 3A 76
Gambier Ho. EC1 7C 60
Gandolfi St. SE15 6F 85
Ganton St. W1 7K 65
Garbett Ho. SE17 5K 83
Garbutt Pl. W1 4G 65
Garden Ct. EC4 7H 67
Garden M. W2 1E 70
Garden Pl. E8 3J 61
Garden Rd. NW8 6J 55
Garden Row SE1 7K 75
Garden Ter. SW1 3B 82
SW7 5C 72
Garden Wlk. EC2 1F 69
Gardner Ct. EC1 2K 67
Gardners La. EC4 7B 68
Gard St. EC1 6A 60
Garlick Hill EC4 7C 68
Garnault M. EC1 7J 59
Garnault Pl. EC1 7J 59
Garner St. E2 5K 61
Garnies Cl. SE15 7H 85
Garrett Ho. SE1 4K 75
Garrett St. EC1 1C 68
Garrick Ct. *E8* *1J 61*
(off Jacaranda Gro.)
Garrick Ho. W1 3H 73
Garrick St. WC2 7D 66
Garrick Theatre 1D 74
Garrick Yd. WC2 7D 66
Garsdale Ter. W14 3C 78
Garson Ho. W2 7K 63
Garston Ho. N1 1K 59
Garway Rd. W2 6F 63
Gascoigne Pl. E2 7H 61
(not continuous)
Gascony Av. NW6 1D 54
Gaskin St. N1 2K 59
Gaspar Cl. SW5 1G 79
Gaspar M. SW5 1G 79
Gastigny Ho. EC1 7C 60
Gate Cinema 2D 70
Gateforth St. NW8 2B 64
Gate Hill Ct. W11 2C 70
Gatehouse Sq. SE1 2C 76
Gate Lodge W9 3E 62
Gate M. SW7 5C 72
Gatesborough St. EC2 1F 69
Gates Ct. SE17 4B 84
Gatesden WC1 7E 58
Gate St. WC2 5F 67
Gate Theatre, The 2D 70
Gateway SE17 5C 84
Gateway Arc. N1 4K 59
Gateways, The SW3 2C 80
Gatliff Cl. SW1 4H 81
Gatliff Rd. SW1 4H 81
(not continuous)
Gattis Wharf N1 4E 58
Gaunt St. SE1 6B 76
Gavel St. SE17 1E 84
Gaydon Ho. W2 3F 63
Gayfere St. SW1 7D 74
Gayhurst SE17 5E 84
Gayhurst Ho. NW8 1B 64
Gayhurst Rd. E8 1K 61
Gaymead NW8 3G 55
Gaysley Ho. SE11 2H 83
Gaywood St. SE1 7A 76
Gaza St. SE17 4K 83
Gedling Pl. SE1 6J 77
Gees Ct. W1 6G 65
Gee St. EC1 1B 68
Geffrye Ct. N1 5G 61
Geffrye Est. N1 5G 61
Geffrye Mus. 5G 61
Geffrye St. E2 4H 61
Gemini Ct. E1 1K 77
Geoffrey Ho. SE1 6E 76
George Ct. WC2 1E 74
George Eliot Ho. SW1 2A 82
George Elliston Ho. SE1 4K 85
George Eyre Ho. NW8 5A 56
George Gillett Ct. EC1 1C 68
George Inn Yd. SE1 3D 76
George Lindgren Ho.
SW6 7C 78
George Loveless Ho. E2 6J 61
George Lowe Ct. W2 3F 63
George Mathers Rd.
SE11 1K 83
George M. NW1 7A 58
George Peabody Ct.
NW1 3B 64
George Row SE16 5K 77
George's Sq. SW6 5C 78
George St. W1 5D 64
George Tingle Ho. SE1 6J 77
George Yd. EC3 6E 68
W1 7G 65
Georgiana St. NW1 2K 57
Georgina Gdns. E2 6J 61
Geraldine St. SE11 7K 75
Gerald M. SW1 1G 81
Gerald Rd. SW1 1G 81
Gerrard Pl. W1 7C 66
Gerrard Rd. N1 4K 59
Gerrard St. W1 7B 66
Gerridge Ct. *SE1* *6J 75*
(off Gerridge St.)
Gerridge St. SE1 6J 75
Gertrude St. SW10 6J 79
Gibbings Ho. SE1 5A 76
Gibbon Ho. NW8 2A 64
Gibbon's Rents SE1 3F 77
Gibbs Grn. W14 3B 78
(not continuous)
Gibbs Grn. Cl. W14 3C 78
Gibraltar Wlk. E2 7J 61
Gibson Rd. SE11 2G 83
Gibson Sq. N1 2J 59
Gielgud Theatre 7B 66
Gifford Ho. SW1 4K 81
Gifford St. N1 1E 58
Gilbert Bri. *EC2* *4C 68*
(off Gilbert Ho.)
Gilbert Collection 7F 67
Gilbert Ho. EC2 4C 68
SW1 4J 81
SW8 7D 82
Gilbert Pl. WC1 4D 66
Gilbert Rd. SE11 2J 83
Gilbert Sheldon Ho. W2 3A 64
Gilbert St. W1 6G 65
Gilbeys Yd. NW1 1G 57
Gildea St. W1 4J 65
Giles High St. WC2 5C 66
Giles Ho. SE16 6K 77
Gillfoot NW1 5K 57
Gillingham M. SW1 1K 81
Gillingham Row SW1 1K 81
Gillingham St. SW1 2J 81
Gilpin Cl. W2 3K 63
Gilray Ho. W2 7K 63
Gilston Rd. SW10 4J 79
Giltspur St. EC1 5A 68
Girling Ho. N1 3F 61
Gironde Rd. SW6 7C 78
Gissing Wlk. N1 1J 59
Gladstone Ct. SW1 2C 82
Gladstone St. SE1 7K 75
Gladwin Ho. NW1 5A 58
Glasgow Ho. W9 5G 55
Glasgow Ter. SW1 4K 81
Glass Art Gallery, The 5F 77
Glasshill St. SE1 4A 76
Glass Ho. SE1 5F 77
Glasshouse St. W1 1A 74
Glasshouse Wlk. SE11 3E 82
Glasshouse Yd. EC1 2B 68
Glassworks Studios E2 6G 61
Glastonbury Ho. SW1 3H 81
Glazbury Rd. W14 2A 78
Glebe Pl. SW3 5B 80
Glebe Rd. E8 1H 61
Gledhow Gdns. SW5 2H 79
Gledstanes Rd. W14 4A 78
Glenallan Ho. W14 2B 78
Glencoe Mans. SW9 7H 83
Glendower Pl. SW7 1K 79
Glenfinlas Way SE5 7A 84
Glengall Pas. NW6 2D 54
(not continuous)
Glengall Rd. NW6 2C 54
SE15 5J 85
Glengall Ter. SE15 5J 85
Glenridding NW1 5A 58
Glenshaw Mans. SW9 7H 83
Glentworth St. NW1 2E 64
Gliddon Rd. W14 2A 78
Globe, The SE1 5D 76
Globe St. SE1 6D 76
Globe Yd. W1 6H 65
Gloucester Arc. SW7 1H 79
Gloucester Av. NW1 1F 57
Gloucester Ct. EC3 1G 77
Gloucester Cres. NW1 2H 57
Gloucester Gdns. W2 5H 63
Gloucester Ga. NW1 4H 57
(not continuous)
Gloucester Ga. M. NW1 4H 57
Gloucester Ho. NW6 5E 54
SW9 7J 83
Gloucester M. W2 6J 63
Gloucester M. W. W2 6H 63
Gloucester Pl. NW1 1D 64
W1 3E 64
Gloucester Pl. M. W1 4E 64
Gloucester Rd. SW7 6H 71
Gloucester Sq. E2 3K 61
W2 6A 64
Gloucester St. SW1 4K 81
Gloucester Ter. W2 5G 63
Gloucester Wlk. W8 4E 70
Gloucester Way EC1 7J 59
Glynde M. SW3 7C 72
Glynde Reach WC1 7E 58
Glyn St. SE11 4F 83
Goater's All. SW6 7C 78
Godfree Ct. *SE1* *4D 76*
(off Long La.)
Godfrey Ho. EC1 7D 60
Godfrey St. SW3 3D 80
Goding St. SE11 3E 82
Godliman St. EC4 6B 68
Godstone Ho. SE1 6E 76
Godwin Cl. N1 4C 60
Godwin Ct. NW1 4A 58
Godwin Ho. NW6 4F 55
(not continuous)
Golborne Gdns. W10 2B 62
Golborne Ho. W10 2A 62
Golborne M. W10 3A 62
Golborne Rd. W10 3A 62
Golden Cross M. W11 5B 62
Golden Hinde 2D 76
Golden La. EC1 1B 68
Golden La. Est. EC1 2B 68
Golden Lane Leisure Cen.
2B 68
Golden Sq. W1 7A 66
Goldhurst Ter. NW6 1F 55
Goldington Bldgs. NW1 3B 58
Goldington Cres. NW1 4B 58
Goldington St. NW1 4B 58
Goldman Cl. E2 1K 69
Goldney Rd. W9 2D 62
Goldsmith Ct. WC2 5E 66
Goldsmith's Pl. NW6 3F 55
Goldsmith's Row E2 5K 61
Goldsmith's Sq. E2 4K 61
Goldsmith St. EC2 5C 68
Goldthorpe NW1 3K 57
Gooch Ho. EC1 3H 67
Goodge Pl. W1 4A 66
Goodge St. W1 4A 66
Goodman's Ct. E1 7H 69
Goodman's Stile E1 5K 69
Goodmans Yd. E1 7H 69
Goodson St. N1 4H 59
Goods Way NW1 4D 58
Goodwin Cl. SE16 7J 77
Goodwins Ct. WC2 7D 66
Goodwood Ct. W1 3J 65
Goodyear Pl. SE5 6C 84
Goodyer Ho. SW1 3B 82
Gophir La. EC4 7D 68
Gopsall St. N1 3E 60
Gordon Ho. SW1 7A 74
Gordon Mans. WC1 2B 66
Gordon Pl. W8 4E 70
Gordon Sq. WC1 1B 66
Gordon St. WC1 1B 66
Gorefield Ho. NW6 4E 54
Gorefield Pl. NW6 4D 54
Gore St. SW7 6J 71
Goring St. EC3 5G 69
Gorleston St. W14 1A 78
(not continuous)
Gorsuch Pl. E2 6H 61
Gorsuch St. E2 6H 61
Gosfield St. W1 3K 65
Goslett Yd. WC2 6C 66
Gosset St. E2 6J 61
Goswell Pl. EC1 7A 60
Goswell Rd. EC1 5K 59
Gothic Ct. SE5 7B 84
Gough Ho. N1 2A 60
Gough Sq. EC4 5J 67
Gough St. WC1 1G 67
Goulston St. E1 5H 69
Govan St. E2 3K 61
Gowan Ho. E2 7J 61
Gower Ct. WC1 1B 66
Gower Ho. SE17 3C 84
Gower M. WC1 4C 66
Gower M. Mans. WC1 3C 66
Gower Pl. WC1 1A 66
Gower St. WC1 1A 66
Gower's Wlk. E1 5K 69
Gracechurch St. EC3 7E 68
Grace Ho. SE11 5G 83
Graces All. E1 7K 69
Graces M. NW8 5J 55
Graduate Pl. SE1 6F 77
Grafton M. W1 2K 65
Grafton Pl. NW1 7C 58
Grafton St. W1 1J 73
Grafton Way W1 2K 65
WC1 2K 65
Graham St. N1 5A 60
Graham Ter. SW1 2F 81
Granary St. NW1 3B 58
Granby Pl. SE1 5H 75
Granby St. E2 1J 69
(not continuous)
Granby Ter. NW1 5K 57
Grand Av. EC1 3A 68
Grand Central Hgts. *EC1* *6B 60*
(off Central St.)
Grand Junc. Wharf N1 5B 60
Grand Union W2 4A 64
Grand Union Cl. W9 3C 62
Grand Union Cres. E8 2K 61
Grand Union Wlk. NW1 1J 57
Grand Vitesse Ind. Cen.
SE1 3A 76
Grange, The SE1 6H 77
W14 2B 78
Grange Ct. WC2 6G 67
Grange Ho. SE1 7H 77
Grange Pl. NW6 1D 54
Grange Rd. SE1 7G 77
Grange St. N1 3E 60
Grange Wlk. SE1 6G 77
Grange Wlk. M. SE1 7G 77
Grange Way NW6 1D 54
Grange Yd. SE1 7H 77
Grantbridge St. N1 4A 60
Grantham Pl. W1 3H 73
Grant Mus. of Zoology &
Comparative Anatomy
2B 66
(off Gower St.)
Grants Quay Wharf EC3 1E 76
Grant St. N1 4H 59
Grantully Rd. W9 7F 55
Granville Ct. N1 2E 60
Granville Pl. W1 6F 65
Granville Rd. NW6 5D 54
(not continuous)
Granville Sq. SE15 7G 85
WC1 7G 59
Granville St. WC1 7G 59
Grape St. WC2 5D 66
Graphite Sq. SE11 3F 83
Grasmere NW1 7J 57
Gratton Rd. W14 7A 70
Gravel La. E1 5H 69
Gray Ho. SE17 3C 84
Grayling Sq. E2 6K 61
Gray's Inn 3G 67
Gray's Inn Bldgs. *EC1* *2H 67*
(off Rosebery Av.)
Gray's Inn Pl. WC1 4G 67
Gray's Inn Rd. WC1 6E 58
Gray's Inn Sq. WC1 3H 67
Grayson Ho. EC1 7C 60
Gray St. SE1 5J 75
Gray's Yd. W1 5G 65
Gt. Arthur Ho. EC1 2B 68
Gt. Bell All. EC2 5D 68
Gt. Castle St. W1 5J 65
Gt. Central St. NW1 3D 64
Gt. Chapel St. W1 5B 66
Great Coll. St. SW1 7E 74
Great Cft. WC1 7E 58
Gt. Cumberland M. W1 6D 64
Gt. Cumberland Pl. W1 5D 64
Gt. Dover St. SE1 5C 76
Gt. Eastern St. EC2 7F 61
Gt. Eastern Wlk. EC2 4G 69
Gt. Eastern Wharf SW11 7C 80
Gt. George St. SW1 5C 74
Gt. Guildford Bus. Sq.
SE1 3B 76
Gt. Guildford St. SE1 2B 76
Great Hall 4E 80
Gt. James St. WC1 3F 67
Gt. Marlborough St. W1 6K 65
Gt. Maze Pond SE1 4E 76
(not continuous)
Gt. Newport St. WC2 7C 66
Gt. New St. EC4 5J 67
Greatorex Ho. E1 3K 69
Greatorex St. E1 3K 69
Gt. Ormond St. WC1 3E 66
Gt. Percy St. WC1 6G 59
Gt. Peter St. SW1 7B 74
Gt. Portland St. W1 2J 65
Gt. Pulteney St. W1 7A 66
Gt. Queen St. WC2 6E 66
Gt. Russell St. WC1 5C 66
Gt. St Helen's EC3 5F 69
Gt. St Thomas Apostle
EC4 7C 68
Gt. Scotland Yd. SW1 3D 74
Gt. Smith St. SW1 6C 74
Gt. Suffolk St. SE1 3A 76
Gt. Sutton St. EC1 2A 68
Gt. Swan All. EC2 5D 68
(not continuous)
Gt. Titchfield St. W1 2J 65
Gt. Tower St. EC3 7F 69
Gt. Trinity La. EC4 7C 68
Great Turnstile WC1 4G 67
Gt. Western Rd. W9 2C 62
Gt. Winchester St. EC2 5E 68
Gt. Windmill St. W1 7B 66
Great Yd. SE1 4G 77
Greaves Twr. SW10 7J 79
Greek Ct. W1 6C 66
Greek St. W1 6C 66
Grn. Arbour Ct. EC1 5K 67
Greenaway Ho. NW8 2H 55
WC1 7H 59
Greenberry St. NW8 5B 56
Greencoat Mans. SW1 7A 74
Greencoat Pl. SW1 1A 82
Greencoat Row SW1 7A 74
Greencroft Gdns. NW6 1F 55
Grn. Dragon Ct. SE1 3D 76
Grn. Dragon Yd. E1 4K 69
Greene Ho. SE1 7D 76
Greenfield Rd. E1 4K 69
Greenham Cl. SE1 5H 75
Greenhill's Rents EC1 3K 67
Greenland Pl. NW1 2J 57
Greenland Rd. NW1 2J 57
Greenland St. NW1 2J 57
Greenman St. N1 1B 60
Green Pk. 3J 73
Green's Ct. W1 7B 66
W11 3B 70
Green St. W1 7E 64
Green Ter. EC1 7J 59
Green Wlk. SE1 7F 77
Greenwell St. W1 2J 65
Green Yd. WC1 1G 67
Green Yd., The EC3 6F 69
Greet Ho. SE1 5J 75
Greet St. SE1 3J 75
Gregory Pl. W8 4F 71
Greig Ter. SE17 5A 84
Grendon Ho. N1 5F 59
Grendon St. NW8 1B 64
Grenfell Ho. SE5 7B 84
Grenville Ho. SW1 5B 82
Grenville M. SW7 1H 79
Grenville Pl. SW7 7H 71
Grenville St. WC1 2E 66
Gresham St. EC2 5B 68
Gresse St. W1 4B 66
Greville Hall NW6 4G 55
Greville M. NW6 3F 55
Greville Pl. NW6 4G 55
Greville Rd. NW6 4F 55
Greville St. EC1 4H 67
(not continuous)
Greycoat Gdns. SW1 7B 74
Greycoat Pl. SW1 7B 74
Greycoat St. SW1 7B 74
Grey Eagle St. E1 3H 69
Greyfriars Pas. EC1 5A 68
Greyhound Ct. WC2 7G 67
Greyhound Mans. W6 5A 78
Greyhound Rd. W6 5A 78
W14 5A 78
Greystoke Ho. SE15 6K 85
Greystoke Pl. EC4 5H 67
Grigg's Pl. SE1 7G 77
Grimaldi Ho. N1 4F 59
Grimsby St. E2 2J 69
Grimsel Path SE5 7A 84
Grimthorpe Ho. EC1 1K 67
Grindal St. SE1 5H 75
Grisedale NW1 6K 57
Grittleton Rd. W9 1D 62
Grocer's Hall Ct. EC2 6D 68
Grocer's Hall Gdns. EC2 6D 68
Groome Ho. SE11 2G 83
Groom Pl. SW1 6G 73
Grosvenor Cotts. SW1 1F 81
Grosvenor Ct. SE5 6C 84
Grosvenor Ct. Mans. W2 6D 64
Grosvenor Cres. SW1 5G 73
Grosvenor Cres. M. SW1 5F 73
Grosvenor Est. SW1 1C 82
Grosvenor Gdns. SW1 6H 73

Grosvenor Gdns. M. E.—Hyde Pk. Ga. M.

Grosvenor Gdns. M. E.
SW1 ....6J 73
Grosvenor Gdns. M. Nth.
SW1 ....7H 73
Grosvenor Gdns. M. Sth.
SW1 ....7J 73
Grosvenor Ga. W1 ....1F 73
Grosvenor Hill W1 ....7H 65
Grosvenor Hill Ct. W1 ....7H 65
Grosvenor Pk. SE5 ....6B 84
Grosvenor Pl. SW1 ....4G 73
Grosvenor Rd. SW1 ....5H 81
Grosvenor Sq. W1 ....7G 65
Grosvenor St. W1 ....7H 65
Grosvenor Ter. SE5 ....7A 84
Grotto Ct. SE1 ....4B 76
Grotto Pas. W1 ....3G 65
Grove Cotts. SW3 ....5C 80
Grove Ct. NW8 ....6K 55
SW10 ....4J 79
Grove End Gdns. NW8 ....5K 55
Grove End Ho. NW8 ....7K 55
Grove End Rd. NW8 ....5K 55
Grove Gdns. NW8 ....7C 56
Grove Hall Ct. NW8 ....6J 55
Grove Ho. SW3 ....5C 80
Groveland Ct. EC4 ....6C 68
Grover Ho. SE11 ....4G 83
Guards Memorial 3C 74
Guards' Mus. 5A 74
Guildhall
City 5C 68
Westminster 5D 74
Guildhall Art Gallery 5D 68
Guildhall Bldgs. EC2 ....5D 68
Guildhall Library 5C 68
Guildhall Offices EC2 ....5C 68
Guildhall Yd. EC2 ....5C 68
Guildhouse St. SW1 ....1K 81
Guilford Pl. WC1 ....2F 67
Guilford St. WC1 ....2D 66
Guinea Ct. E1 ....7K 69
Guinness Ct. E1 ....6H 69
EC1 ....7C 60
NW8 ....3C 56
SE1 ....4F 77
SW3 ....2D 80
Guinness Sq. SE1 ....7F 77
Guinness Trust SW3 ....2D 80
Guinness Trust Bldgs.
SE11 ....3K 83
Gulliver's Ho. EC1 ....2B 68
Gulston Wlk. SW3 ....2E 80
Gunpowder Sq. EC4 ....5J 67
(not continuous)
Gun St. E1 ....4H 69
Gunter Gro. SW10 ....6H 79
Gunterstone Rd. W14 ....2A 78
Gunthorpe St. E1 ....4J 69
Gurney Ho. E2 ....4K 61
Guthrie Ct. SE1 ....5J 75
Guthrie St. SW3 ....3B 80
Gutter La. EC2 ....5B 68
Guy St. SE1 ....4E 76
Gwendwr Rd. W14 ....3A 78
Gwynne Ho. WC1 ....7H 59
Gwynne Pl. WC1 ....7G 59

Haberdasher Est. N1 ....6E 60
Haberdasher Pl. N1 ....6E 60
Haberdasher St. N1 ....6E 60
Habington Ho. SE5 ....7D 84
Hackford Rd. SW9 ....7H 83
Hackney City Farm 4K 61
Hackney Rd. E2 ....7H 61
Haddon Hall St. SE1 ....7E 76
Hadfield Ho. E1 ....6K 69
Hadlow Ho. SE17 ....3G 85
Hadrian Est. E2 ....5K 61
Hadstock Ho. NW1 ....6C 58
HAGGERSTON 5H 61
Haggerston Rd. E8 ....1H 61
Haig Ho. E2 ....5K 61
Haines St. SW8 ....7A 82
Halcomb St. N1 ....3F 61
Halcyon Wharf E1 ....3K 77
Haldane Rd. SW6 ....7C 78
Hale Ho. SW1 ....3C 82
Hales Prior N1 ....5F 59
Half Moon Ct. EC1 ....4B 68
Half Moon Cres. N1 ....4G 59
(not continuous)
Half Moon Pas. E1 ....6J 69
(not continuous)
Half Moon St. W1 ....2J 73
Halford Rd. SW6 ....6D 78
Haliwell Ho. NW6 ....3F 55
Halkin Arc. SW1 ....6E 72
Halkin M. SW1 ....6F 73
Halkin Pl. SW1 ....6F 73
Halkin St. SW1 ....5G 73
Hallam Ct. W1 ....3J 65
Hallam Ho. SW1 ....4A 82
Hallam M. W1 ....3J 65
Hallam St. W1 ....2J 65
Hallfield Est. W2 ....6G 63
(not continuous)
Hall Ga. NW8 ....6K 55
Halliford St. N1 ....1C 60
Hall Pl. W2 ....2K 63
(not continuous)
Hall Rd. NW8 ....7J 55
Hall St. EC1 ....6A 60
Hall Twr. W2 ....3A 64
Halpin Pl. SE17 ....2E 84
Halsey M. SW3 ....1D 80
Halsey St. SW3 ....1D 80
Halstead Ct. N1 ....5E 60
Halton Cross St. N1 ....2A 60
Halton Mans. N1 ....1A 60
Halton Pl. N1 ....2B 60
Halton Rd. N1 ....1A 60
Hambledon SE17 ....5E 84
Hamilton Bldgs. EC2 ....2G 69
Hamilton Cl. NW8 ....7K 55
Hamilton Ct. W9 ....6H 55
Hamilton Gdns. NW8 ....6J 55
Hamilton Ho. NW8 ....6K 55
Hamilton M. W1 ....4H 73
Hamilton Pl. W1 ....3G 73
Hamilton Sq. SE1 ....4E 76
Hamilton Ter. NW8 ....4G 55
Hamlet Ct. SE11 ....3K 83
Hamlet Way SE1 ....5E 76
Hammerfield Ho. SW3 ....3C 80
Hammersmith Rd. W14 ....1A 78
Hammett St. EC3 ....7H 69
Hammond Lodge *W9 ....3E 62*
(off Admiral Wlk.)
Hamond Sq. N1 ....4F 61
Hampden Cl. NW1 ....5C 58
Hampden Gurney St. W1 ....6D 64
Hampstead Rd. NW1 ....4K 57
Hampstead Theatre 1K 55
Hampton Cl. NW6 ....7D 54
Hampton St. SE17 ....2A 84
Ham Yd. W1 ....7B 66
Hanbury Ho. E1 ....3K 69
SW8 ....6E 82
Hanbury M. N1 ....3C 60
Hanbury St. E1 ....3H 69
Hand Ct. WC1 ....4G 67
Handel House Mus. *7H 65*
(off Brook St.)
Handel Mans. WC1 ....1E 66
Handels Bus. Cen. SW8 ....5E 82
Handel St. WC1 ....1D 66
Handforth Rd. SW9 ....7H 83
Hanging Sword All. EC4 ....6J 67
Hankey Pl. SE1 ....5E 76
Hannah Mary Way SE1 ....2K 85
Hannell Rd. SW6 ....7A 78
Hanover Flats W1 ....7G 65
(not continuous)
Hanover Gdns. SE11 ....6H 83
Hanover Ga. NW1 ....7C 56
Hanover Ga. Mans. NW1 ....1C 64
Hanover Ho. NW8 ....5B 56
Hanover Pl. WC2 ....6E 66
Hanover Sq. W1 ....6J 65
Hanover Steps W2 ....6C 64
Hanover St. W1 ....6J 65
Hanover Ter. NW1 ....7C 56
Hanover Ter. M. NW1 ....7C 56
Hanover Yd. N1 ....4A 60
Hans Cres. SW1 ....6D 72
Hanson St. W1 ....3K 65
Hans Pl. SW1 ....6E 72
Hans Rd. SW3 ....6D 72
Hans St. SW1 ....7E 72
Hanway Pl. W1 ....5B 66
Hanway St. W1 ....5B 66
Hanworth Ho. SE5 ....7K 83
(not continuous)
Harad's Pl. E1 ....1K 77
Harben Rd. NW6 ....1J 55
Harbet Rd. W2 ....4A 64
Harbledown Ho. SE1 ....5D 76
Harcourt Bldgs. EC4 ....7H 67
Harcourt St. W1 ....4C 64
Harcourt Ter. SW10 ....4G 79
Harding Cl. SE17 ....5B 84
Hardwicke M. WC1 ....7G 59
Hardwick Ho. NW8 ....1C 64
Hardwick St. EC1 ....7J 59
Hardwidge St. SE1 ....4F 77
Hare Ct. EC4 ....6H 67
Hare Marsh E2 ....1K 69
Hare Pl. EC4 ....6J 67
Hare Wlk. N1 ....5G 61
(not continuous)
Harewood Av. NW1 ....2C 64
Harewood Pl. W1 ....6J 65
Harewood Row NW1 ....3C 64
Harfleur Ct. SE11 ....2K 83
Harford Ho. SE5 ....6C 84
W11 ....4C 62
Harkness Ho. E1 ....6K 69
Harlequin Ct. E1 ....1K 77
Harleyford Ct. SE11 ....5F 83
Harleyford Rd. SE11 ....5F 83
Harleyford St. SE11 ....6H 83
Harley Gdns. SW10 ....4J 79
Harley Ho. NW1 ....2G 65
Harley Pl. W1 ....4H 65
Harley Rd. NW3 ....1A 56
Harley St. W1 ....2H 65
Harlowe Cl. E8 ....2K 61
Harlowe Ho. E8 ....2H 61
Harlynwood SE5 ....7B 84
Harman Cl. SE1 ....4K 85
Harmont Ho. W1 ....4H 65
Harmood Gro. NW1 ....1H 57
Harmood St. NW1 ....1H 57
Harmsworth M. SE11 ....7K 75
Harmsworth St. SE17 ....4K 83
Harold Est. SE1 ....7G 77
Harold Laski Ho. EC1 ....7A 60
Harold Maddison Ho.
SE17 ....3A 84
Harold Pl. SE11 ....4H 83
Harold Wilson Ho. SW6 ....6C 78
Harp All. EC4 ....5K 67
Harper Rd. SE1 ....6B 76
Harp La. EC3 ....1F 77
Harpur M. WC1 ....3F 67
Harpur St. WC1 ....3F 67
Harriet Cl. E8 ....2K 61
Harriet Ho. SW6 ....7G 79
Harriet St. SW1 ....5E 72
Harriet Wlk. SW1 ....5E 72
Harrington Ct. W10 ....6B 54
Harrington Gdns. SW7 ....2G 79
Harrington Ho. NW1 ....6K 57
Harrington Rd. SW7 ....1K 79
Harrington Sq. NW1 ....4K 57
Harrington St. NW1 ....5K 57
(not continuous)
Harrison Ho. SE17 ....3D 84
Harrison St. WC1 ....7E 58
Harris St. SE5 ....7E 84
Harrods 6D 72
Harrowby St. W1 ....5C 64
Harrow Lodge NW8 ....1K 63
Harrow Pl. E1 ....5G 69
Harrow Rd. W2 ....4G 63
(not continuous)
W9 ....2C 62
W10 ....1A 62
Harrow Rd. Bri. W2 ....3J 63
Harrow St. NW1 ....3C 64
Harry Hinkins Ho. SE17 ....4C 84
Hartington Ho. SW1 ....3C 82
Hartington Rd. SW8 ....7D 82
Hartismere Rd. SW6 ....7C 78
Hartland NW1 ....3A 58
Hartland Rd. NW1 ....1H 57
NW6 ....4B 54
Hartley Ho. SE1 ....1J 85
Hartop Point SW6 ....7A 78
Hartshorn All. EC3 ....6G 69
Hart St. EC3 ....7G 69
Harvard Ho. SE17 ....5K 83
Harvey Ho. N1 ....3E 60
SW1 ....4C 82
Harvey Lodge W9 ....3E 62
Harvey's Bldgs. WC2 ....1E 74
Harvey St. N1 ....3E 60
Harvist Rd. NW6 ....5A 54
Harwood Ct. N1 ....3E 60
Harwood Rd. SW6 ....7E 78
Hasker St. SW3 ....1C 80
Haslam Cl. N1 ....1J 59
Hassard St. E2 ....5J 61
Hastings Cl. SE15 ....7K 85
Hastings Ho. WC1 ....7D 58
Hastings St. WC1 ....7D 58
Hat & Mitre Ct. EC1 ....2A 68
Hatchers M. SE1 ....5G 77
Hatfield Ho. EC1 ....2B 68
Hatfields SE1 ....2J 75
Hathaway Ho. N1 ....6F 61
Hatherley Ct. W2 ....5F 63
Hatherley Gro. W2 ....5F 63
Hatherley St. SW1 ....2A 82
Hatton Gdn. EC1 ....3J 67
Hatton Pl. EC1 ....3J 67
Hatton Row NW8 ....2A 64
Hatton St. NW8 ....2A 64
Hatton Wall EC1 ....3J 67
Haunch of Venison Yd.
W1 ....6H 65
Havelock St. N1 ....2E 58
Haven M. N1 ....1J 59
Havenpool NW8 ....3G 55
Haven St. NW1 ....1J 57
Haverstock Pl. N1 ....6A 60
Haverstock St. N1 ....5A 60
Havil St. SE5 ....7F 85
Havisham Ho. SE16 ....5K 77
Hawes St. N1 ....1A 60
Hawkins Ho. SW1 ....5A 82
Hawkshead NW1 ....6K 57
Hawksmoor Pl. E2 ....1K 69
Hawkwell Wlk. N1 ....2C 60
Hawley Cres. NW1 ....1J 57
Hawley M. NW1 ....1H 57
Hawley Rd. NW1 ....1H 57
(not continuous)
Hawley St. NW1 ....1H 57
Hawthorne Ho. SW1 ....4A 82
Hawthorn Wlk. W10 ....1A 62
Hawtrey Rd. NW3 ....1B 56
Hayden's Pl. W11 ....5B 62
Haydon St. EC3 ....7H 69
Haydon Wlk. E1 ....7J 69
Hayes Pl. NW1 ....2C 64
Hay Hill W1 ....1J 73
Hayles Bldgs. SE11 ....1A 84
Hayles St. SE11 ....1K 83
Haymans Point SE11 ....3F 83
Hayman St. N1 ....1A 60
Haymarket SW1 ....1B 74
Haymarket Arc. SW1 ....1B 74
Haymarket Ct. *E8 ....1J 61*
(off Jacaranda Gro.)
Haymarket Theatre Royal
....2C 74
Haymerle Ho. SE15 ....6K 85
Haymerle Rd. SE15 ....6K 85
Hayne Ho. W11 ....2A 70
Hayne St. EC1 ....3A 68
Hay's Galleria SE1 ....2F 77
Hays La. SE1 ....3F 77
Hay's M. W1 ....1H 73
Hay St. E2 ....3K 61
Hayward Gallery 3G 75
Hayward's Pl. EC1 ....2K 67
Hazelmere Rd. NW6 ....2C 54
Hazel Way SE1 ....1H 85
Hazlewood Cres. W10 ....2A 62
Hazlewood Twr. W10 ....2A 62
Hazlitt M. W14 ....7A 70
Hazlitt Rd. W14 ....7A 70
Headbourne Ho. SE1 ....6E 76
Headfort Pl. SW1 ....5G 73
Head's M. W11 ....6D 62
Healey Ho. SW9 ....7J 83
Hearn's Bldgs. SE17 ....2E 84
Hearn St. EC2 ....2G 69
Heathcock Ct. *WC2 ....1E 74*
(off Exchange Ct.)
Heathcote St. WC1 ....1F 67
Heather Wlk. W10 ....1A 62
Heathfield St. W11 ....1A 70
Hebden Ct. E2 ....3H 61
Heber Mans. W14 ....5A 78
Heckfield Pl. SW6 ....7D 78
Heddon St. W1 ....7K 65
(not continuous)
Hedgegate Ct. W11 ....5C 62
Hedger St. SE11 ....1K 83
Hedingham Cl. N1 ....1B 60
Hedsor Ho. E2 ....1H 69
Heiron St. SE17 ....6A 84
Heldar Ct. SE1 ....5E 76
Helen Gladstone Ho. SE1 ....4K 75
Helen Taylor Ho. SE16 ....7K 77
Hellings St. E1 ....3K 77
Helmet Row EC1 ....7C 60
Helmsdale Ho. NW6 ....5F 55
Helsby Ct. NW8 ....1K 63
Helston NW1 ....4A 58
Helston Ho. SE11 ....3J 83
Hemans St. SW8 ....7C 82
Hemingford Rd. N1 ....3G 59
Hemp Wlk. SE17 ....1E 84
Hemstal Rd. NW6 ....1D 54
Hemsworth Ct. N1 ....4F 61
Hemsworth St. N1 ....4F 61
Hemus Pl. SW3 ....4C 80
Hen & Chicken Ct. EC4 ....6H 67
Henderson Dr. NW8 ....1G 63
Hendre Rd. SE1 ....2G 85
Heneage La. EC3 ....6G 69
Heneage Pl. EC3 ....6G 69
Heneage St. E1 ....3J 69
Henley Dr. SE1 ....1J 85
Henley Ho. E2 ....1J 69
Henley Prior N1 ....5F 59
Henniker M. SW3 ....5K 79
Henrietta M. WC1 ....1E 66
Henrietta Pl. W1 ....6H 65
Henrietta St. WC2 ....7E 66
Henriques St. E1 ....5K 69
Henry Ho. SE1 ....3J 75
SW8 ....7E 82
Henry Wise Ho. SW1 ....2A 82
Henshaw St. SE17 ....1D 84
Henslow Ho. SE15 ....7K 85
Henstridge Pl. NW8 ....4B 56
Hepworth Ct. N1 ....2K 59
Herald's Pl. SE11 ....1K 83
Herbal Hill EC1 ....2J 67
Herbal Hill Gdns. EC1 ....2J 67
Herbal Pl. EC1 ....2J 67
Herbert Cres. SW1 ....6E 72
Herbert Ho. E1 ....5H 69
Herbert Morrison Ho.
SW6 ....6B 78
Herbrand Est. WC1 ....1D 66
Herbrand St. WC1 ....1D 66
Hercules Rd. SE1 ....7G 75
Hereford Bldgs. SW3 ....5A 80
Hereford Ho. NW6 ....5D 54
SW3 ....6C 72
SW10 ....7G 79
Hereford M. W2 ....6E 62
Hereford Retreat SE15 ....7K 85
Hereford Rd. W2 ....5E 62
Hereford Sq. SW7 ....2J 79
Hereford St. E2 ....1K 69
Her Majesty's Theatre 2B 74
Hermes Cl. W9 ....2D 62
Hermes St. N1 ....5H 59
Hermitage Rooms 7G 67
Hermitage St. W2 ....4K 63
Hermitage Vs. SW6 ....5D 78
Hermitage Wall E1 ....3K 77
Hermitage Waterside E1 ....2K 77
Hermit Pl. NW6 ....3F 55
Hermit St. EC1 ....6K 59
Heron Ho. NW8 ....5B 56
Heron Pl. W1 ....5G 65
Herrick St. SW1 ....2C 82
Herries St. W10 ....5A 54
Hertford Pl. W1 ....2K 65
Hertford Rd. N1 ....2G 61
(not continuous)
Hertford St. W1 ....2H 73
Hesketh Pl. W11 ....1A 70
Hesper M. SW5 ....3F 79
Hester Rd. SW11 ....7B 80
Hestia Ho. SE1 ....5F 77
Hethpool Ho. W2 ....2K 63
Hewett St. EC2 ....2G 69
Heyford Av. SW8 ....7E 82
Heyford Ter. SW8 ....7E 82
Heygate St. SE17 ....2B 84
Hickes Ho. NW6 ....1K 55
Hickleton NW1 ....3K 57
Hide Pl. SW1 ....2B 82
Hide Twr. SW1 ....2B 82
Higgins Ho. N1 ....3F 61
High Holborn WC1 ....5D 66
Highstone Mans. NW1 ....1K 57
High Timber St. EC4 ....7B 68
Highway, The E1 ....1K 77
Highworth St. NW1 ....3C 64
Hilary Cl. SW6 ....7F 79
Hilborough Ct. E8 ....1J 61
Hildyard Rd. SW6 ....5E 78
Hilgrove Rd. NW6 ....1J 55
Hillersden Ho. SW1 ....3H 81
Hillery Cl. SE17 ....2E 84
Hillgate Pl. W8 ....2D 70
Hillgate St. W8 ....2D 70
Hillingdon St. SE17 ....6K 83
Hill Rd. NW8 ....6J 55
Hillsborough Ct. NW6 ....3F 55
Hillside Cl. NW8 ....4G 55
Hillsleigh Rd. W8 ....2C 70
Hills Pl. W1 ....6K 65
Hill St. W1 ....2G 73
Hilltop Ct. NW8 ....1J 55
Hill-Wood Ho. NW1 ....5A 58
Hinchinbrook Ho. NW6 ....3F 55
Hind Ct. EC4 ....6J 67
Hinde Ho. W1 ....5G 65
Hinde M. W1 ....5G 65
Hinde St. W1 ....5G 65
Hindmarsh Cl. E1 ....7K 69
Hindon Ct. SW1 ....1K 81
Hinstock NW6 ....2F 55
Hippodrome M. W11 ....1A 70
Hippodrome Pl. W11 ....1A 70
HMS Belfast 2G 77
Hobart Pl. SW1 ....7H 73
Hobbs Ct. SE1 ....4J 77
Hobbs Pl. N1 ....3F 61
Hobbs Pl. Est. N1 ....4F 61
Hobson's Pl. E1 ....3K 69
Hobury St. SW10 ....6J 79
Hocker St. E2 ....7H 61
Hoffman Sq. N1 ....6E 60
Hofland Rd. W14 ....6A 70
Hogan M. W2 ....3K 63
Hogarth Ct. E1 ....5K 69
EC3 ....7G 69
NW1 ....1A 58
Hogarth Ho. SW1 ....2C 82
Hogarth Pl. SW5 ....2F 79
Hogarth Rd. SW5 ....2F 79
Holbeck Row SE15 ....7K 85
Holbein Ho. SW1 ....3F 81
Holbein M. SW1 ....3F 81
Holbein Pl. SW1 ....2F 81
HOLBORN 4H 67
Holborn EC1 ....4H 67
Holborn Cir. EC1 ....4J 67
Holborn Pl. WC1 ....4F 67
Holborn Viaduct EC1 ....4J 67
Holcroft Ct. W1 ....3K 65
Holden Ho. N1 ....3B 60
Holford M. WC1 ....5H 59
Holford Pl. WC1 ....6G 59
Holford St. WC1 ....6H 59
Holford Yd. WC1 ....5H 59
Holland Gdns. W14 ....6A 70
Holland Gro. SW9 ....7J 83
HOLLAND PARK 3B 70
Holland Pk. 4B 70
Holland Pk. W11 ....3A 70
Holland Pk. Av. W11 ....3A 70
Holland Pk. Gdns. W14 ....3A 70
Holland Pk. M. W11 ....3A 70
Holland Pk. Rd. W14 ....7B 70
Holland Pk. Ter. W11 ....3A 70
Holland Pk. Theatre (Open Air)
....*5C 70*
(in Holland Pk.)
Holland Pas. N1 ....2B 60
Holland Pl. W8 ....4F 71
Holland Pl. Chambers
W8 ....4F 71
Holland Ri. Ho. SW9 ....7G 83
Holland Rd. W14 ....5A 70
Holland St. SE1 ....2A 76
W8 ....5E 70
Holland Vs. Rd. W14 ....4A 70
Holland Wlk. W8 ....3C 70
Hollen St. W1 ....5B 66
Holles St. W1 ....5J 65
Hollisfield WC1 ....7E 58
Holly Ho. W10 ....1A 62
Holly M. SW10 ....4J 79
Holly St. E8 ....1J 61
Hollywood M. SW10 ....5H 79
Hollywood Rd. SW10 ....5H 79
Holman Hunt Ho. W6 ....4A 78
Holmbrook NW1 ....5A 58
Holmead Rd. SW6 ....7G 79
Holmesdale Ho. NW6 ....2E 54
Holmes Pl. SW10 ....5J 79
Holmes Place Health Club
Barbican 3B 68
(off Aldersgate St.)
St Luke's 2D 68
Holmes Ter. SE1 ....4H 75
Holocaust Memorial Garden
....4E 72
Holst Ct. SE1 ....6H 75
Holsworthy Sq. WC1 ....2G 67
Holyoak Rd. SE11 ....2K 83
Holyrood St. SE1 ....3F 77
Holywell Cen. 1F 69
Holywell La. EC2 ....1G 69
Holywell Row EC2 ....2F 69
Homefield St. N1 ....5F 61
Homer Row W1 ....4C 64
Homer St. W1 ....4C 64
Homestead Rd. SW6 ....7B 78
Honduras St. EC1 ....1B 68
Honey La. EC2 ....6C 68
Honiton Rd. NW6 ....4B 54
Hood Ct. EC4 ....6J 67
Hood Ho. SW1 ....4B 82
Hooper's Ct. SW3 ....5D 72
Hooper Sq. E1 ....6K 69
Hooper St. E1 ....6K 69
Hopefield Av. NW6 ....4A 54
Hopetown St. E1 ....4J 69
Hopewell St. SE5 ....7E 84
Hopewell Yd. SE5 ....7E 84
Hop Gdns. WC2 ....1D 74
Hopkinsons Pl. NW1 ....2F 57
Hopkins St. W1 ....6A 66
Hopton's Gdns. SE1 ....2A 76
Hopton St. SE1 ....1K 75
Hopwood Rd. SE17 ....5E 84
Horatio Ho. E2 ....5J 61
Horatio St. E2 ....5J 61
Horbury Cres. W11 ....1D 70
Horbury M. W11 ....1C 70
Hordle Prom. E. SE15 ....7J 85
Hordle Prom. Sth. SE15 ....7H 85
Hormead Rd. W9 ....2B 62
Hornbeam Cl. SE11 ....1H 83
Hornby Cl. NW3 ....1A 56
Hornby Ho. SE11 ....5H 83
Horner Ho. N1 ....3G 61
Hornton Ct. W8 ....5E 70
Hornton Pl. W8 ....5E 70
Hornton St. W8 ....4E 70
Horse & Dolphin Yd. W1 ....7C 66
Horseferry Rd. SW1 ....7B 74
Horseferry Rd. Est. SW1 ....7B 74
Horseguards Av. SW1 ....3D 74
Horse Guards Parade 3D 74
Horse Guards Rd. SW1 ....3C 74
Horselydown La. SE1 ....4H 77
Horselydown Mans. SE1 ....4H 77
Horsemongers M. SE1 ....5C 76
Horse Ride SW1 ....4K 73
Horseshoe Ct. EC1 ....1A 68
Horseshoe Wharf SE1 ....2D 76
Horse Yd. N1 ....2A 60
Horsfield Ho. N1 ....1B 60
Horsley St. SE17 ....5D 84
Horsman Ho. SE5 ....6B 84
Horsman St. SE5 ....6C 84
Hortensia Ho. SW10 ....7H 79
Hortensia Rd. SW10 ....6H 79
Horton Ho. SW8 ....7F 83
W6 ....4A 78
Horwood Ho. NW8 ....1C 64
Hosier La. EC1 ....4K 67
Hotspur St. SE11 ....3H 83
Houghton St. WC2 ....6G 67
(not continuous)
Houndsditch EC3 ....5G 69
Houseman Way SE5 ....7E 84
Houses of Parliament 6E 74
Howard Bldg. SW8 ....6H 81
Howard Ho. SW1 ....4A 82
W1 ....2J 65
Howell Wlk. SE1 ....2A 84
Howick Pl. SW1 ....7A 74
Howie St. SW11 ....7B 80
Howland M. E. W1 ....3A 66
Howland St. W1 ....3K 65
Howley Pl. W2 ....3J 63
How's St. E2 ....4H 61
HOXTON 5F 61
Hoxton Hall Theatre 5G 61
Hoxton Mkt. N1 ....7F 61
Hoxton Sq. N1 ....7F 61
Hoxton St. N1 ....3F 61
HQS Wellington 1H 75
Huberd Ho. SE1 ....6E 76
Hubert Ho. NW8 ....2B 64
Hucknall Ct. NW8 ....1K 63
Hudson's Pl. SW1 ....1K 81
Huggin Ct. EC4 ....7C 68
Huggin Hill EC4 ....7C 68
Hugh Astor Ct. SE1 ....6A 76
Hugh Cubitt Ho. N1 ....5G 59
Hugh Dalton Av. SW6 ....6B 78
Hughenden Ho. NW8 ....1B 64
Hughes Ho. SE17 ....2A 84
Hugh Gaitskell Cl. SW6 ....6B 78
Hugh M. SW1 ....2J 81
Hugh St. SW1 ....2J 81
Huguenot Pl. E1 ....3J 69
Hullbridge M. N1 ....2D 60
Hull St. EC1 ....7B 60
Hulme Pl. SE1 ....5C 76
Humbolt Rd. W6 ....6A 78
Hume Ct. N1 ....1A 60
Humphrey St. SE1 ....3H 85
Hungerford Ho. SW1 ....5A 82
Hungerford La. WC2 ....2D 74
(not continuous)
Hunstanton Ho. NW1 ....3C 64
Hunter Cl. SE1 ....7E 76
Hunter Ho. SE1 ....5A 76
SW5 ....4E 78
SW8 ....7C 82
WC1 ....1D 66
Hunterian Mus., The 6G 67
Hunter Lodge W9 ....3E 62
Hunter St. WC1 ....1E 66
Huntingdon St. N1 ....1F 59
Huntley St. WC1 ....2A 66
Hunton St. E1 ....2K 69
Hunt's Ct. WC2 ....1C 74
Huntsman St. SE17 ....2E 84
Huntsworth M. NW1 ....1D 64
Hurdwick Pl. *NW1 ....4K 57*
(off Hampstead Rd.)
Hurley Ho. SE11 ....2K 83
Huron University 6A 72
Hurst Ho. WC1 ....5G 59
Huson Cl. NW3 ....1B 56
Hutchinson Ho. NW3 ....1D 56
Hutton St. EC4 ....6K 67
Huxley Ho. NW8 ....2A 64
Huxley St. W10 ....7A 54
Hyde Pk. 1C 72
Hyde Pk. Barracks 5C 72
HYDE PARK CORNER 4G 73
Hyde Pk. Cnr. W1 ....4G 73
Hyde Pk. Cres. W2 ....6B 64
Hyde Pk. Gdns. W2 ....7A 64
Hyde Pk. Gdns. M. W2 ....7A 64
(not continuous)
Hyde Pk. Ga. SW7 ....5H 71
(not continuous)
Hyde Pk. Ga. M. SW7 ....5J 71

Hyde Pk. Mans—Larissa St.

Hyde Pk. Mans. NW1 4B 64
(not continuous)
Hyde Pk. Pl. W2 7C 64
Hyde Pk. Sq. W2 6B 64
Hyde Pk. Sq. M. W2 6B 64
Hyde Pk. St. W2 6B 64
Hyde Pk. Towers W2 1H 71
Hyde Rd. N1 3F 61
Hydra Bldg., The EC1 7J 59

Ian Bowater Ct. N1 6E 60
Ibberton Ho. SW8 7F 83
W14 7A 70
ICA Cinema 3C 74
ICA Theatre 3C 74
Ice Wharf Marina N1 4E 58
Icknield Ho. SW3 3C 80
Icon Apartments SE1 6F 77
Idol La. EC3 1F 77
Ifield Rd. SW10 5G 79
Ightham Ho. SE17 2F 85
Ilbert St. W10 7A 54
Ilchester Gdns. W2 7F 63
Ilchester Pl. W14 6B 70
Ilfracombe Flats *SE1* *4C 76*
(off Marshalsea Rd.)
Iliffe St. SE17 3A 84
Iliffe Yd. SE17 3A 84
IMAX Cinema 3H 75
Imber St. N1 3D 60
Imperial College of Science, Technology & Medicine
Imperial Coll. Rd. 6K 71
Wilson House 5B 64
Imperial Coll. Rd. SW7 7J 71
Imperial Ct. NW8 4C 56
SE11 4H 83
Imperial Pde. EC4 6K 67
Imperial War Mus. 7J 75
India Pl. WC2 7F 67
India St. EC3 6H 69
Infirmary Ct. SW3 5E 80
Ingelow Ho. W8 4F 71
Ingestre Pl. W1 6A 66
Inglebert St. EC1 6H 59
Ingoldisthorpe Gro. SE15 5J 85
Ingram Cl. SE11 1G 83
Ingrebourne Ho. NW8 3A 64
Inigo Pl. WC2 7D 66
Inkerman Ter. W8 7E 70
Inner Circ. NW1 7F 57
Inner Temple 7J 67
Inner Temple Hall 6H 67
Inner Temple La. EC4 6H 67
Innis Ho. SE17 3F 85
Innis St. SE15 7G 85
Inns of Court & City Yeomanry Mus. 4G 67
Institute of Archaeology 1B 66
Institute of Classical Studies 1B 66
Institute of Contemporary Arts 3C 74
International Ho. E1 1J 77
Inver Ct. W2 6G 63
Invergarry Ho. NW6 5F 55
Inverness Gdns. W8 3F 71
Inverness M. W2 7G 63
Inverness Pl. W2 7G 63
Inverness St. NW1 2H 57
Inverness Ter. W2 6G 63
Invicta Plaza SE1 2K 75
Inville Rd. SE17 4E 84
Inville Wlk. SE17 4E 84
Inwood Ct. NW1 1A 58
Inworth Wlk. N1 2B 60
Ion Ct. E2 5K 61
Ion Sq. E2 5K 61
Ipsden Bldgs. SE1 4J 75
Ireland Yd. EC4 6A 68
Iron Bri. Ho. NW1 1E 56
Ironmonger La. EC2 6C 68
Ironmonger Pas. EC1 7C 60
Ironmonger Row EC1 7C 60
Ironmonger Row Baths 7B 60
Irving Ho. SE17 4K 83
Irving Mans. W14 5A 78
Irving St. WC2 1C 74
Isaac Way SE1 4C 76
Isabella Ho. SE11 3K 83
Isabella St. SE1 3K 75
Isis Ho. NW8 2A 64
Isleden Ho. N1 2B 60
ISLINGTON 3K 59
Islington Grn. N1 3K 59
Islington High St. N1 5J 59
(not continuous)
Islington Mus. 1K 59
Islington Pk. St. N1 1J 59
Ivatt Pl. W14 4C 78
Iveagh Ct. E1 6H 69
Iveagh Ho. SW10 7J 79
Iverna Ct. W8 6E 70
Iverna Gdns. W8 6E 70
Ives St. SW3 1C 80
Ivimey St. E2 6K 61
Ivor Ct. NW1 1D 64
Ivories, The N1 1B 60
Ivor Pl. NW1 2D 64
Ivor St. NW1 1K 57
Ivory Ho. E1 2J 77
Ivybridge La. WC2 1E 74
Ivychurch La. SE17 3H 85
Ivy St. N1 4F 61
Ixworth Pl. SW3 3B 80

Jacana Ct. E1 1J 77
Jacaranda Gro. E8 1J 61
Jacks Pl. E1 3H 69
Jacob St. SE1 4J 77
Jacob's Well M. W1 5G 65
Jago Wlk. SE5 7D 84
Jamaica Rd. SE1 5J 77
SE16 5J 77
James Anderson Ct. E2 4G 61
James Brine Ho. E2 6J 61
James Collins Cl. W9 2B 62
James Ct. N1 2C 60
James Hammett Ho. E2 6J 61
Jameson Ho. SE11 3F 83
Jameson St. W8 2E 70
James Stewart Ho.
NW6 1C 54
James St. W1 5G 65
WC2 6E 66
James Stroud Ho. SE17 4C 84
Jamestown Rd. NW1 2H 57
Jane Austen Ho. SW1 4K 81
Jason Ct. W1 5G 65
Jasper Wlk. N1 6D 60
Java Wharf SE1 4J 77
Jay M. SW7 5J 71
Jean Darling Ho. SW10 6K 79
Jeffrey's Pl. NW1 1K 57
Jeffrey's St. NW1 1J 57
Jeger Av. E2 3H 61
Jellicoe Ho. E2 5K 61
NW1 2J 65
Jenner Ho. WC1 1E 66
Jennifer Ho. SE11 2J 83
Jenningsbury Ho. *SW3* *3C 80*
(off Cale St.)
Jephson Ho. SE17 5K 83
Jerdan Pl. SW6 7D 78
Jermyn St. SW1 2K 73
Jermyn Street Theatre 1B 74
Jerome Cres. NW8 1B 64
Jerome Ho. NW1 3C 64
SW7 1K 79
Jerome St. E1 3H 69
Jerrold St. N1 5G 61
Jerusalem Pas. EC1 2K 67
Jervis Ct. W1 6K 65
Jerwood Space Art Gallery 4B 76
Jessel Ho. SW1 1C 82
WC1 7D 58
Jessel Mans. W14 5A 78
Jessie Duffett Ho. SE5 7B 84
Jesson Ho. SE17 2D 84
Jessop Ct. N1 5A 60
Jewel House *1H 77*
(in Tower of London, The)
Jewel Tower 6D 74
Jewish Mus.
Camden Town 3J 57
Jewry St. EC3 6H 69
Jim Griffiths Ho. SW6 6B 78
Joan St. SE1 3K 75
Jocelin Ho. N1 3G 59
Jockey's Flds. WC1 3G 67
Johanna St. SE1 5H 75
John Adam St. WC2 1E 74
John Aird Ct. W2 3J 63
(not continuous)
John Carpenter St. EC4 7K 67
John Fearon Wlk. *W10* *6A 54*
(off Dart St.)
John Felton Rd. SE16 5K 77
John Fisher St. E1 7K 69
John Horner M. N1 4B 60
John Islip St. SW1 3C 82
John Knight Lodge SW6 7E 78
John Maurice Cl. SE17 1D 84
John Parry Ct. N1 4G 61
John Prince's St. W1 5J 65
John Pritchard Ho. E1 2K 69
John Ratcliffe Ho. NW6 7D 54
John Roll Way SE16 6K 77
John Ruskin St. SE5 7K 83
John's M. WC1 2G 67
John Smith Av. SW6 7B 78
Johnson Cl. E8 2K 61
Johnson Ho. E2 7K 61
NW1 5A 58
NW3 1D 56
SW1 2G 81
Johnson Lodge W9 3E 62
Johnson Mans. W14 5A 78
Johnson's Ct. EC4 6J 67
Johnson's Pl. SW1 4K 81
John Strachey Ho. SW6 6C 78
John St. WC1 2G 67
John Trundle Ct. EC2 3B 68
John Trundle Highwalk
EC2 3B 68
John Wesley Highwalk
EC2 4B 68
John Wheatley Ho. SW6 6C 78
Joiner St. SE1 3E 76
Joiners Yd. N1 5E 58
Jonathan St. SE11 3F 83
Jones St. W1 1H 73
Jonson Ho. SE1 7E 76
Jordan Ho. N1 2E 60
Jordans Ho. NW8 1A 64
Joseph Conrad Ho. SW1 2A 82
Joseph Trotter Cl. EC1 7J 59
Jowett St. SE15 7J 85
Jubilee Bldgs. NW8 3K 55
Jubilee Hall Sports Cen. 7E 66
Jubilee Ho. SE11 2J 83
WC1 1F 67
Jubilee Mkt. WC2 7E 66
Jubilee Pl. SW3 3C 80
Jubilee Sports Cen. & Baths 7B 54
Jubilee Walkway SE1 1A 76
Jubilee Yd. SE1 4H 77
Judd St. WC1 6D 58
Juer St. SW11 7C 80
Juliet Ho. N1 5F 61
Julius Nyerere Cl. N1 3F 59
Junction M. W2 5B 64
Junction Pl. W2 5B 64
Juniper Ct. W8 7F 71
Juniper Cres. NW1 1G 57
Juniper Ho. W10 1A 62
Jurston Ct. SE1 5J 75
Justice Wlk. SW3 6B 80
Juxon Ho. EC4 6A 68
Juxon St. SE11 1G 83

Kay St. E2 4K 61
Kean Ho. SE17 5K 83
Kean St. WC2 6F 67
Keats Cl. SE1 2H 85
Keats Ho. SE5 7C 84
SW1 5A 82
Keats Pl. EC2 4D 68
Keeley St. WC2 6F 67
Keith Ho. NW6 6F 55
Kellet Ho's. *WC1* *7E 58*
(off Tankerton St.)
Kellett Ho. N1 3F 61
Kellow Ho. SE1 4D 76
Kell St. SE1 6A 76
Kelly M. W9 2C 62
Kelso Pl. W8 6G 71
Kelvin Ct. W11 1D 70
Kember St. N1 1F 59
Kemble St. WC2 6F 67
Kempe Ho. SE1 7E 76
Kempe Rd. NW6 5A 54
Kemp Ho. W1 7B 66
Kemps Ct. W1 6B 66
Kempsford Gdns. SW5 4E 78
Kempsford Rd. SE11 2J 83
(not continuous)
Kemsing Ho. SE1 5E 76
Kenbrook Ho. W14 6C 70
Kenchester Cl. SW8 7E 82
Kendal NW1 6J 57
Kendal Cl. SW9 7K 83
Kendal Ho. N1 4G 59
Kendall Pl. W1 4F 65
Kendal Steps W2 6C 64
Kendal St. W2 6C 64
Kendrick M. SW7 1K 79
Kendrick Pl. SW7 2K 79
Kenilworth Rd. NW6 2C 54
Kennedy Ho. SE11 3F 83
Kennedy Wlk. SE17 2E 84
Kennet Ct. W9 3E 62
Kenneth Campbell Ho.
NW8 1A 64
Kenneth Ct. SE11 1J 83
Kennet Ho. NW8 2A 64
Kenneth Younger Ho.
SW6 6C 78
Kennet Rd. W9 1C 62
Kennet St. E1 2K 77
Kennett Wharf La. EC4 1C 76
Kenning Ho. N1 2F 61
Kennings Way SE11 3J 83
KENNINGTON 5J 83
Kennington Grn. SE11 4H 83
Kennington Gro. SE11 5G 83
Kennington La. SE11 4F 83
KENNINGTON OVAL 6H 83
Kennington Oval SE11 5G 83
Kennington Pal. Ct.
SE11 3H 83
Kennington Pk. Gdns.
SE11 5K 83
Kennington Pk. Ho. SE11 4J 83
Kennington Pk. Pl. SE11 5J 83
Kennington Pk. Rd.
SE11 6H 83
Kennington Rd. SE1 6H 75
SE11 7H 75
Kenrick Pl. W1 3F 65
Kensal Rd. W10 1A 62
KENSAL TOWN 2A 62
KENSINGTON 5F 71
Kensington Arc. W8 5F 71
Kensington Cen. W14 1A 78
(not continuous)
Kensington Chu. Ct. W8 5F 71
Kensington Chu. St. W8 2E 70
Kensington Chu. Wlk.
W8 4F 71
(not continuous)
Kensington Ct. W8 5G 71
Kensington Ct. Gdns.
W8 6G 71
Kensington Ct. M. W8 6G 71
Kensington Ct. Pl. W8 6G 71
Kensington Gardens 2H 71
Kensington Gdns. Sq.
W2 6F 63
(not continuous)
Kensington Ga. W8 6H 71
Kensington Gore SW7 5J 71
Kensington Hall Gdns.
W14 3B 78
Kensington Hgts. W8 3D 70
Kensington High St. W8 7C 70
W14 1B 78
Kensington Mall W8 2E 70
Kensington Mans. SW5 3E 78
(not continuous)
Kensington Palace 3G 71
Kensington Pal. Gdns.
W8 2F 71
Kensington Pk. Gdns.
W11 1B 70
Kensington Pk. M. W11 6B 62
Kensington Pk. Rd. W11 6B 62
Kensington Pl. W8 3D 70
Kensington Rd. SW7 5G 71
W8 5G 71
Kensington Sq. W8 5F 71
Kensington Village W14 2C 78
Kensington W. W14 1A 78
Kensworth Ho. EC1 7E 60
Kent Ct. E2 4J 61
Kent Ho. SE1 4J 85
SW1 4B 82
Kentish Bldgs. SE1 3D 76
Kentish Town Rd. NW1 2J 57
Kenton Ct. W14 7B 70
Kenton St. WC1 1D 66
Kent Pas. NW1 1D 64
Kent St. E2 4J 61
Kent Ter. NW1 7C 56
Kent Yd. SW7 5C 72
Kenway Rd. SW5 2F 79
Kenwrick Ho. N1 3G 59
Kenyon Mans. W14 5A 78
Keppel Row SE1 3B 76
Keppel St. WC1 3C 66
Kerbela St. E2 1K 69
Kerrin Ho. SE17 3G 85
Kestrel Ho. EC1 6B 60
Kevan Ho. SE5 7B 84
Keybridge Ho. SW8 6E 82
Keyes Ho. SW1 4B 82
Key Ho. SE11 5H 83
Keyse Rd. SE1 7H 77
Keystone Cres. N1 5E 58
Keyworth Pl. SE1 6A 76
Keyworth St. SE1 6A 76
Kibworth St. SW8 7F 83
Kiffen St. EC2 1E 68
KILBURN 4B 54
Kilburn Bri. NW6 3E 54
Kilburn Ga. NW6 4F 55
Kilburn High Rd. NW6 1C 54
Kilburn Ho. NW6 5C 54
Kilburn La. W9 6A 54
W10 6A 54
Kilburn Pk. Rd. NW6 7D 54
Kilburn Pl. NW6 3E 54
Kilburn Priory NW6 3F 55
Kilburn Sq. NW6 2D 54
Kilburn Va. NW6 3F 55
Kilburn Va. Est. NW6 2E 54
Kildare Gdns. W2 5E 62
Kildare Ter. W2 5E 62
Killick St. N1 4F 59
Kilmuir Ho. SW1 2G 81
Kilner Ho. SE11 5H 83
Kilravock St. W10 7A 54
Kimberley Rd. NW6 2A 54
Kimble Ho. NW8 1C 64
Kimbolton Ct. SW3 2B 80
Kimbolton Row SW3 2B 80
Kincardine Gdns. W9 2D 62
Kinder Ho. N1 4E 60
Kindersley Ho. E1 6K 69
King & Queen St. SE17 3C 84
King Charles I Island
WC2 *2D 74*
(off Trafalgar Sq.)
King Charles Ct. SE17 5K 83
King Charles Ho. SW6 7G 79
King Charles St. SW1 4C 74
King Edward Bldg. EC1 5A 68
King Edwards Mans.
SW6 7D 78
King Edward St. EC1 5B 68
King Edward Wlk. SE1 6J 75
Kingfisher Ct. SE1 5C 76
King George IV Ct. *SE17* *3D 84*
(off Dawes St.)
King George VI Memorial 3B 74
King Henry's Rd. NW3 1A 56
Kinghorn St. EC1 3A 68
King James Ct. SE1 5A 76
King James St. SE1 5A 76
King John Ct. EC2 1G 69
Kinglake Est. SE17 3G 85
Kinglake St. SE17 4F 85
(not continuous)
Kingly Ct. W1 7K 65
Kingly St. W1 6K 65
Kings Arms Ct. E1 4K 69
Kings Arms Yd. EC2 5D 68
King's Bench St. SE1 4A 76
King's Bench Wlk. EC4 7J 67
Kings Coll. Ct. NW3 1C 56
King's College London
Strand Campus 7G 67
Waterloo Campus 3H 75
King's Coll. Rd. NW3 1B 56
Kingscote St. EC4 7K 67
Kings Ct. N7 1F 59
NW8 3D 56
SE1 4A 76
Kings Ct. Nth. SW3 4B 80
Kings Ct. Sth. SW3 5B 80
KING'S CROSS 6D 58
King's Cross Bri. N1 6E 58
King's Cross Rd. WC1 6F 59
King's Gdns. NW6 1E 54
Kingsgate Mans. WC1 4F 67
Kingsgate Pde. SW1 7A 74
Kingsgate Pl. NW6 1D 54
Kingsgate Rd. NW6 1D 54
Kings Head Theatre 2K 59
King's Head Yd. SE1 3D 76
Kingshill SE17 2C 84
Kings Ho. SW8 7E 82
Kingsland NW8 3C 56
Kingsland Rd. E2 6G 61
Kingsley Flats SE1 1F 85
Kingsley Ho. SW3 6A 80
Kingsley Mans. W14 5A 78
Kingsley M. W8 7G 71
Kingsley Rd. NW6 2C 54
King's M. WC1 2G 67
Kingsmill NW8 4A 56
Kingsmill Ho. *SW3* *3C 80*
(off Cale St.)
Kingsmill Ter. NW8 4A 56
King's Pl. SE1 5B 76
King Sq. EC1 7B 60
Kings Reach Twr. SE1 2J 75
King's Rd. SW3 6K 79
SW6 7G 79
SW10 7J 79
King's Scholars' Pas.
SW1 7K 73
King's Ter. NW1 3K 57
Kingston Ho. NW6 1A 54
Kingston Ho. E. SW7 5B 72
Kingston Ho. Nth. SW7 5B 72
Kingston Ho. Sth. SW7 5B 72
Kingstown St. NW1 2F 57
(not continuous)
King St. EC2 6C 68
SW1 3A 74
WC2 7D 66
Kings Wlk. Shop. Cen.
SW3 3D 80
Kingsway WC2 5F 67
Kingsway Mans. WC1 4F 67
Kingsway Pl. EC1 1J 67
Kings Wharf E8 2G 61
Kingswood Av. NW6 3A 54
Kingswood Cl. SW8 7E 82
Kingswood Ct. NW6 1E 54
Kington Ho. NW6 3G 55
Kingward Ho. E1 3K 69
King William St. EC4 6E 68
Kingwood Rd. SW6 7A 78
Kinnerton Pl. Nth. SW1 5E 72
Kinnerton Pl. Sth. SW1 5E 72
Kinnerton St. SW1 5F 73
Kinnerton Yd. SW1 5E 72
Kinnoul Rd. W6 5A 78
Kinsham Ho. E2 1K 69
Kintore Way SE1 1H 85
Kipling Est. SE1 5E 76
Kipling Ho. SE5 7C 84
Kipling St. SE1 5E 76
Kirby Gro. SE1 4F 77
Kirby St. EC1 3J 67
Kirkeby Ho. EC1 3H 67
Kirkman Pl. W1 4B 66
Kirkstone NW1 6K 57
Kirk St. WC1 2G 67
Kirtling St. SW8 6A 82
Kirton Gdns. E2 7J 61
Kirwyn Way SE5 7A 84
Kite Pl. E2 6K 61
Kitson Rd. SE5 7C 84
Kittiwake Ct. *SE1* *5C 76*
(off Swan St.)
Knaresborough Pl. SW5 1F 79
Knight Ho. SE17 2F 85
Knightrider Ct. EC4 7B 68
Knightrider St. EC4 7A 68
Knights Arc. SW1 5D 72
KNIGHTSBRIDGE 5D 72
Knightsbridge SW1 5C 72
SW7 5C 72
Knightsbridge Ct. SW1 5E 72
Knightsbridge Grn. SW1 5D 72
(not continuous)
Knight's Wlk. SE11 2K 83
(not continuous)
Knivet Rd. SW6 6D 78
Knoll Ho. NW8 4H 55
Knolly's Ho. WC1 1D 66
Knox St. NW1 3D 64
Kramer M. SW5 4E 78
Krupnik Pl. EC2 1G 69
Kylestrome Ho. SW1 2G 81
Kynance M. SW7 7G 71
Kynance Pl. SW7 7H 71

Laburnum Ct. E2 3H 61
Laburnum St. E2 3H 61
Lackington St. EC2 3E 68
Lackland Ho. SE1 3J 85
Lacland Ho. SW10 7K 79
Lacon Ho. WC1 3F 67
Ladbroke Cres. W11 6A 62
Ladbroke Gdns. W11 7B 62
Ladbroke Gro. W10 3A 62
Ladbroke Gro. Ho. W11 1B 70
Ladbroke M. W11 3A 70
Ladbroke Rd. W11 2A 70
Ladbroke Sq. W11 1B 70
Ladbroke Ter. W11 1C 70
Ladbroke Wlk. W11 2C 70
LA Fitness
Aldgate 7J 69
Bayswater 7F 63
Bloomsbury 3F 67
Covent Garden 7F 67
Leadenhall 6G 69
Marylebone 3D 64
Piccadilly 2B 74
St Pauls 4B 68
South Kensington 1B 80
Victoria 7K 73
Lafone St. SE1 4H 77
Laird Ho. SE5 7B 84
Lake Ho. SE1 5B 76
Lakeside Ter. EC2 3C 68
Lake Vw. Ct. SW1 6J 73
Laleham Ho. E2 1H 69
Lambert Jones M. EC2 3B 68
Lambert St. N1 1H 59
LAMBETH 7F 75
Lambeth Bri. SE1 1E 82
Lambeth High St. SE1 2F 83
Lambeth Hill EC4 7B 68
Lambeth Palace 7F 75
Lambeth Pal. Rd. SE1 7F 75
Lambeth Rd. SE1 1F 83
Lambeth Towers SE11 7H 75
Lambeth Wlk. SE11 7H 75
(not continuous)
Lambourne Ho. NW8 3A 64
Lamb's Bldgs. EC1 2D 68
Lamb's Conduit Pas.
WC1 3F 67
Lamb's Conduit St. WC1 2F 67
(not continuous)
Lambs Health & Fitness 2C 68
Lamb's M. N1 3K 59
Lamb's Pas. EC1 3D 68
Lamb St. E1 3H 69
Lambton Pl. W11 7C 62
Lamb Wlk. SE1 5F 77
LAMDA Theatre 1D 78
Lamlash St. SE11 1K 83
Lamont Rd. SW10 6J 79
Lamont Rd. Pas. SW10 6K 79
Lampern Sq. E2 6K 61
Lampeter Sq. W6 6A 78
Lamp Office Ct. WC1 2F 67
Lamps Ct. SE5 7B 84
Lanark Ho. SE1 4K 85
Lanark Mans. W9 1J 63
Lanark M. W9 7H 55
Lanark Pl. W9 1J 63
Lanark Rd. W9 5G 55
Lancashire Ct. W1 7H 65
Lancaster Cl. N1 1G 61
W2 1F 71
Lancaster Ct. SW6 7C 78
W2 7J 63
Lancaster Ga. W2 1H 71
Lancaster House 4A 74
Lancaster Lodge W11 5A 62
Lancaster M. W2 7J 63
Lancaster Pl. WC2 7F 67
Lancaster Rd. W11 6A 62
Lancaster St. SE1 5K 75
Lancaster Ter. W2 7K 63
Lancaster Wlk. W2 1J 71
Lancefield Ct. W10 5A 54
Lancefield St. W10 6B 54
Lancelot Pl. SW7 5D 72
Lancer Sq. W8 4F 71
Lanchester Ct. W2 6D 64
Lancing St. NW1 7B 58
Lancresse Ct. N1 2F 61
Landon Pl. SW1 6D 72
Landrake NW1 3A 58
Landseer Ho. NW8 1A 64
SW1 2C 82
Landulph Ho. SE11 3J 83
Landward Ct. W1 5C 64
Lane, The NW8 4H 55
Lanesborough Ct. *N1* *6F 61*
(off Fanshaw St.)
Lanesborough Pl. SW1 4G 73
Laney Ho. EC1 3H 67
Lanfrey Pl. W14 4B 78
Langdale NW1 6K 57
Langdale Cl. SE17 5B 84
Langdale Ho. SW1 4K 81
Langdon Ct. EC1 5A 60
Langdon Way SE1 2K 85
Langford Cl. NW8 4J 55
Langford Ct. NW8 4J 55
Langford Pl. NW8 4J 55
Langham Mans. SW5 4F 79
Langham Pl. W1 4J 65
Langham St. W1 4J 65
Langhorne Ct. NW8 1K 55
Lang Ho. SW8 7D 82
Langland Ho. SE5 7E 84
Langley Ct. WC2 7D 66
Langley Ho. W2 3E 62
Langley La. SW8 5E 82
Langley Mans. SW8 5F 83
Langley St. WC2 6D 66
Langmore Ho. E1 6K 69
Langthorn Ct. EC2 5E 68
Langton Cl. WC1 1G 67
Langton Ho. SE11 1G 83
Langton Rd. SW9 7A 84
Langton St. SW10 6J 79
Langtry Pl. SW6 5E 78
Langtry Rd. NW8 3F 55
Langtry Wlk. NW8 2G 55
Lanhill Rd. W9 1D 62
Lannoy Point SW6 7A 78
Lansdowne Ct. W11 1A 70
Lansdowne Cres. W11 1A 70
Lansdowne Dr. E8 1K 61
Lansdowne M. W11 3B 70
Lansdowne Pl. SE1 6E 76
Lansdowne Ri. W11 1A 70
Lansdowne Rd. W11 1A 70
Lansdowne Row W1 2J 73
Lansdowne Ter. WC1 2E 66
Lansdowne Wlk. W11 2A 70
Lant Ho. SE1 5B 76
Lant St. SE1 4B 76
Lapford Cl. W9 1C 62
Lapwing Ct. *SE1* *5C 76*
(off Swan St.)
Lapworth Ct. W2 3G 63
Larch Ct. SE1 5F 77
W9 3D 62
Larcom St. SE17 2B 84
Larissa St. SE17 3E 84

Lascelles Ho.—Marville Rd.

Lascelles Ho. NW1 . . . . . . .2C **64**
Latham Ct. SW5 . . . . .2D **78**
Latimer Ho. W11 . . . . .1C **70**
Latona Rd. SE15 . . . . .6K **85**
Lauderdale Mans. W9 . . . . .7F **55**
(not continuous)
Lauderdale Pde. W9 . . . . . .7F **55**
Lauderdale Pl. EC2 . . . . . . .3B **68**
Lauderdale Rd. W9 . . . . . . .7F **55**
Lauderdale Twr. EC2 . . . . . .3B **68**
Laud St. SE11 . . . . .3F **83**
Launcelot St. SE1 . . . . .5H **75**
Launceston Pl. W8 . . . . . . .6H **71**
Laundry La. N1 . . . . .1B **60**
Laundry Rd. W6 . . . . .6A **78**
Laurence Pountney Hill
EC4 . . . . .7D **68**
Laurence Pountney La.
EC4 . . . . .1D **76**
Laurie Ho. SE1 . . . . .7A **76**
Lavender Cl. SW3 . . . . .6A **80**
Lavender Gro. E8 . . . . .1J **61**
Lavendon Ho. NW8 . . . . . . .1C **64**
Laverton M. SW5 . . . . .2G **79**
Laverton Pl. SW5 . . . . .2G **79**
Lavina Gro. N1 . . . . .4F **59**
Lavington St. SE1 . . . . .3A **76**
Lawford Rd. N1 . . . . .1F **61**
Lawn La. SW8 . . . . .5E **82**
Lawrence Ho. SW1 . . . . . . .2C **82**
Lawrence La. EC2 . . . . .6C **68**
Lawrence Pl. N1 . . . . .2E **58**
Lawrence St. SW3 . . . . .6B **80**
Law St. SE1 . . . . .6E **76**
Laxfield Ct. E8 . . . . .3K **61**
Laxford Ho. SW1 . . . . .2G **81**
Laxley Cl. SE5 . . . . .7A **84**
Laxton Pl. NW1 . . . . .1J **65**
Laystall Ct. WC1 . . . . .2H **67**
Laystall St. EC1 . . . . .2H **67**
Layton's Bldgs. SE1 . . . . . . .4D **76**
Lazenby Ct. WC2 . . . . .7D **66**
Leadenhall Mkt. EC3 . . . . . .6F **69**
Leadenhall Pl. EC3 . . . . .6F **69**
Leadenhall St. EC3 . . . . .6F **69**
Lea Ho. NW8 . . . . .2B **64**
Leake Ct. SE1 . . . . .5G **75**
Leake St. SE1 . . . . .4G **75**
(not continuous)
Leamington Rd. Vs.
W11 . . . . .4C **62**
Leary Ho. SE11 . . . . .4G **83**
Leather La. EC1 . . . . .3H **67**
(not continuous)
Leathermarket, The SE1 . . .5F **77**
Leathermarket Ct. SE1 . . . . .5F **77**
Leathermarket St. SE1 . . . . .5F **77**
Lebus Ho. NW8 . . . . .5B **56**
Lecky St. SW7 . . . . .3K **79**
Le Cordon Bleu London Culinary
Arts Institute *4G 65*
(off Marylebone La.)
Ledam Ho. EC1 . . . . .3H **67**
Ledbury Ho. W11 . . . . .6C **62**
Ledbury M. Nth. W11 . . . . .7D **62**
Ledbury M. W. W11 . . . . . . .7D **62**
Ledbury Rd. W11 . . . . .5C **62**
Lee Ho. EC2 . . . . .4C **68**
Leeke St. WC1 . . . . .6F **59**
Lees Ct. W1 . . . . .7F **65**
Lees Pl. W1 . . . . .7F **65**
Lee St. E8 . . . . .2H **61**
Leff Ho. NW6 . . . . .1A **54**
Lefroy Ho. SE1 . . . . .5B **76**
Leicester Ct. W9 . . . . .3D **62**
WC2 . . . . .7C **66**
Leicester Flds. WC2 . . . . . . .1C **74**
Leicester Pl. WC2 . . . . .7C **66**
Leicester Sq. WC2 . . . . .1C **74**
Leicester St. WC2 . . . . .7C **66**
Leigh Pl. EC1 . . . . .3H **67**
Leigh St. WC1 . . . . .1D **66**
Leighton Ho. SW1 . . . . .2C **82**
Leighton House Art Gallery &
Mus. 6C **70**
Leighton Mans. W14 . . . . . .5A **78**
Leinster Gdns. W2 . . . . .6H **63**
Leinster M. W2 . . . . .1H **71**
Leinster Pl. W2 . . . . .6H **63**
Leinster Sq. W2 . . . . .6E **62**
(not continuous)
Leinster Ter. W2 . . . . .7H **63**
Leith Mans. W9 . . . . .7F **55**
Leith Yd. NW6 . . . . .2D **54**
Lelitia Cl. E8 . . . . .3K **61**
Leman Pas. E1 . . . . .6K **69**
Leman St. E1 . . . . .6J **69**
Len Freeman Pl. SW6 . . . . .6B **78**
Lenham Ho. SE1 . . . . .6E **76**
Lennox Gdns. SW1 . . . . . . .7D **72**
Lennox Gdns. M. SW1 . . . . .7D **72**
Lenthall Ho. SW1 . . . . .4A **82**
Lenthall Rd. E8 . . . . .1J **61**
Len Williams Ct. NW6 . . . . .5E **54**
Leonard Ct. WC1 . . . . .1C **66**
Leonard St. EC2 . . . . .1E **68**
Leonora Ho. W9 . . . . .1H **63**
Leontine Cl. SE15 . . . . .7K **85**
Leopards Ct. EC1 . . . . .3H **67**
Leopold Bldgs. E2 . . . . .6H **61**
Leo Yd. EC1 . . . . .2A **68**
Leroy St. SE1 . . . . .7F **77**
Lerry Cl. W14 . . . . .5C **78**
Leslie Prince Ct. SE5 . . . . . .7D **84**
Letterstone Rd. SW6 . . . . . .7B **78**
Leverett St. SW3 . . . . .1C **80**
Leverington Pl. N1 . . . . .7F **61**
Leverstock Ho. SW3 . . . . . .3C **80**
Lever St. EC1 . . . . .7A **60**
Levita Ho. NW1 . . . . .6C **58**
(not continuous)
Lewes Ho. SE1 . . . . .4G **77**
Lewisham St. SW1 . . . . . . .5C **74**
Lexham Gdns. W8 . . . . .1E **78**
Lexham Gdns. M. W8 . . . . .7G **71**
Lexham M. W8 . . . . .1E **78**
Lexham Wlk. W8 . . . . .7G **71**
Lexington Apartments
EC1 . . . . .1D **68**
Lexington St. W1 . . . . .6A **66**
Leybourne Rd. NW1 . . . . . . .1J **57**
Leybourne St. NW1 . . . . . . .1H **57**
Leyden St. E1 . . . . .4H **69**
Leysdown Ho. SE17 . . . . . . .3G **85**
Liberty Ho. E1 . . . . .1K **77**
Library St. SE1 . . . . .5K **75**
Lickey Ho. W14 . . . . .5C **78**
Lidlington Pl. NW1 . . . . . . .5A **58**
Light Horse Ct. SW3 . . . . . .4F **81**
Ligonier St. E2 . . . . .1H **69**
Lilac Pl. SE11 . . . . .2F **83**
Lilestone Ho. NW8 . . . . . . .1A **64**
Lilestone St. NW8 . . . . .1B **64**
Lilley Cl. E1 . . . . .3K **77**
Lillie Mans. SW6 . . . . .6B **78**
Lillie Rd. SW6 . . . . .7A **78**
Lillie Yd. SW6 . . . . .5E **78**
Lillington Gdns. Est.
SW1 . . . . .2A **82**
Lily Cl. W14 . . . . .2A **78**
(not continuous)
Lily Pl. EC1 . . . . .3J **67**
Limeburner La. EC4 . . . . . . .6K **67**
Lime Cl. E1 . . . . .2K **77**
Limerston St. SW10 . . . . . . .5J **79**
Limes, The W2 . . . . .1E **70**
Lime St. EC3 . . . . .7F **69**
Lime St. Pas. EC3 . . . . .7F **69**
Linale Ho. N1 . . . . .5D **60**
Lincoln Ho. SE5 . . . . .7J **83**
SW3 . . . . .5D **72**
Lincoln M. NW6 . . . . .2B **54**
Lincolns Inn Flds. WC2 . . . .5F **67**
Lincoln's Inn Hall **5G 67**
Lincoln St. SW3 . . . . .2D **80**
Linden Gdns. W2 . . . . .1E **70**
Linden M. W2 . . . . .1E **70**
Lindley Est. SE15 . . . . .7K **85**
Lindley Ho. SE15 . . . . .7K **85**
Lindsay Sq. SW1 . . . . .3C **82**
Lindsey M. N1 . . . . .1C **60**
Lindsey St. EC1 . . . . .3A **68**
Linfield WC1 . . . . .7F **59**
Lingfield Ho. SE1 . . . . .5A **76**
Linhope St. NW1 . . . . .1D **64**
Link Rd. E1 . . . . .7K **69**
Links Yd. E1 . . . . .3J **69**
Linkwood Wlk. NW1 . . . . . .1C **58**
Linley Sambourne House
. . . .**5D 70**
Linnell Ho. E1 . . . . .3H **69**
Linsey St. SE16 . . . . .1K **85**
(not continuous)
Linslade Ho. E2 . . . . .3K **61**
NW8 . . . . .1C **64**
Linstead Hall SW7 . . . . .6A **72**
Lintaine Cl. W6 . . . . .6A **78**
Linton St. N1 . . . . .3C **60**
(not continuous)
Lion Ct. N1 . . . . .3F **59**
SE1 . . . . .3G **77**
Lionel M. W10 . . . . .3A **62**
Lisgar Ter. W14 . . . . .1B **78**
Liskeard Ho. SE11 . . . . .3J **83**
Lisle St. WC2 . . . . .7C **66**
Lisson Grn. Est. NW8 . . . . . .1B **64**
LISSON GROVE **3C 64**
Lisson Gro. NW1 . . . . .1B **64**
NW8 . . . . .7A **56**
Lisson Ho. NW1 . . . . .3B **64**
Lisson St. NW1 . . . . .3B **64**
Lister Lodge W9 . . . . .3E **62**
Listowel Cl. SW9 . . . . .7J **83**
Litchfield St. WC2 . . . . .7C **66**
Lit. Albany St. NW1 . . . . . . .7J **57**
(Albany St.)
NW1 . . . . .1J **65**
(Longford St.)
Little Angel Theatre **2A 60**
Lit. Argyll St. W1 . . . . .6K **65**
Lit. Boltons, The SW5 . . . . .3G **79**
SW10 . . . . .4G **79**
Little Britain EC1 . . . . .4A **68**
Lit. Chester St. SW1 . . . . . .6H **73**
Little Cloisters SW1 . . . . . . .6D **74**
Little Coll. La. EC4 . . . . .7D **68**
Little Coll. St. SW1 . . . . . . .6D **74**
Lit. Dean's Yd. SW1 . . . . . . .6D **74**
Lit. Dorrit Ct. SE1 . . . . .4C **76**
Lit. Edward St. NW1 . . . . . . .6J **57**
Lit. Essex St. WC2 . . . . .7H **67**
Lit. George St. SW1 . . . . . . .5D **74**
Lit. London Ct. SE1 . . . . . . .5J **77**
Lit. Marlborough St.
W1 . . . . .6K **65**
Lit. Newport St. WC2 . . . . . .7C **66**
Lit. New St. EC4 . . . . .5J **67**
Lit. Portland St. W1 . . . . . . .5J **65**
Lit. Russell St. WC1 . . . . . . .4D **66**
Lit. St James's St. SW1 . . . .3K **73**
Little Sanctuary SW1 . . . . . .5D **74**
Lit. Smith St. SW1 . . . . .6C **74**
Lit. Somerset St. E1 . . . . . . .6K **69**
Lit. Titchfield St. W1 . . . . . .4K **65**
Littleton Ho. SW1 . . . . .4K **81**
Lit. Trinity La. EC4 . . . . . . .7C **68**
Little Turnstile WC1 . . . . . . .4F **67**
Livermere Ct. E8 . . . . .2J **61**
Livermere Rd. E8 . . . . .2H **61**
Liverpool Gro. SE17 . . . . . . .4C **84**
Liverpool Rd. N1 . . . . .1J **59**
Liverpool St. EC2 . . . . .4F **69**
Livesey Pl. SE15 . . . . .5K **85**
Livingstone Ho. SE5 . . . . . . .7C **84**
Livingstone Lodge W9 . . . . .3E **62**
Livingstone Mans. W14 . . . .5A **78**
Livingwell Health Club
Greville Rd. *4F 55*
(within Regents Plaza)
Livonia St. W1 . . . . .6A **66**
Lizard St. EC1 . . . . .7C **60**
Llewellyn St. SE16 . . . . .5K **77**
Lloyd Baker St. WC1 . . . . . .7G **59**
(not continuous)
Lloyd's Av. EC3 . . . . .6G **69**
Lloyds' Building **6F 69**
Lloyd Sq. WC1 . . . . .6H **59**
Lloyd's Row EC1 . . . . .7J **59**
Lloyd St. WC1 . . . . .6H **59**
Lloyds Wharf SE1 . . . . .4J **77**
Loanda Cl. E8 . . . . .2H **61**
Lochmore Ho. SW1 . . . . . . .2G **81**
Lockbridge Ct. W9 . . . . .3D **62**
Locksfields SE17 . . . . .2E **84**
Lockwood Ho. SE11 . . . . . . .6H **83**
Lockyer Est. SE1 . . . . .4E **76**
(not continuous)
Lockyer Ho. SW8 . . . . .7C **82**
Lockyer St. SE1 . . . . .5E **76**
Lodge Rd. NW8 . . . . .1A **64**
Loftie St. SE16 . . . . .5K **77**
Lofting Rd. N1 . . . . .1G **59**
Logan M. W8 . . . . .1D **78**
Logan Pl. W8 . . . . .1D **78**
Lohmann Ho. SE11 . . . . . . .5H **83**
Lolesworth Cl. E1 . . . . .4J **69**
Lollard St. SE11 . . . . .1G **83**
(not continuous)
Loman St. SE1 . . . . .4A **76**
Lombard Ct. EC3 . . . . .7E **68**
Lombard La. EC4 . . . . .6J **67**
Lombard St. EC3 . . . . .6E **68**
Lombardy Pl. W2 . . . . .1F **71**
Lomond Gro. SE5 . . . . .7D **84**
Loncroft Rd. SE5 . . . . .5G **85**
Londinium Twr. E1 . . . . .7J **69**
London Academy of Music &
Dramatic Art **1E 78**
London Aquarium **4F 75**
London Bri. EC4 . . . . .1E **76**
SE1 . . . . .2E **76**
London Bri. St. SE1 . . . . . . .3E **76**
London Bri. Wlk. SE1 . . . . . .2E **76**
London Business School
. . . .**1D 64**
London Canal Mus. **4E 58**
London City College **3H 75**
London Coliseum **1D 74**
London College of Fashion, The
St Luke's **2B 68**
London Dungeon **3E 76**
London Eye **4F 75**
London Fruit Exchange
E1 . . . . .4H **69**
London Guildhall University
Coke St. **5K 69**
London Ho. NW8 . . . . .4C **56**
WC1 . . . . .1F **67**
London Metropolitan University
City of London **6H 69**
Manningtree St. **5K 69**
London M. W2 . . . . .6A **64**
London Palladium **6K 65**
London Planetarium **2F 65**
London Rd. SE1 . . . . .6K **75**
London School of Economics &
Politics, The **6G 67**
London South Bank University
. . . .**6A 76**
London South Bank University
Sports Cen. **6A 76**
London Stock Exchange . . .**5A 68**
London St. EC3 . . . . .7G **69**
W2 . . . . .5K **63**
London Telecom Tower, The
. . . .**3K 65**
London Television Cen., The
. . . .**2H 75**
London Ter. E2 . . . . .5K **61**
London Transport Mus. **7E 66**
London Wall EC2 . . . . .4C **68**
London Wall Bldgs. EC2 . . .4E **68**
London Wildlife Trust **3C 58**
London Zoo **4F 57**
Long Acre WC2 . . . . .7D **66**
Longfellow Way SE1 . . . . . . .2J **85**
Longfield Est. SE1 . . . . .1J **85**
Longford St. NW1 . . . . .1J **65**
Longhope Cl. SE15 . . . . . . .6G **85**
Longland Ct. SE1 . . . . .3K **85**
Longlands Ct. W11 . . . . .7C **62**
Long La. EC1 . . . . .4A **68**
SE1 . . . . .5D **76**
Longleat Ho. SW1 . . . . .3B **82**
Longley St. SE1 . . . . .2K **85**
Longman Ho. E8 . . . . .3J **61**
Longmoore St. SW1 . . . . . . .2K **81**
Longmore Gdns. Est.
SW1 . . . . .2A **82**
Longridge Ho. SE1 . . . . .7C **76**
Longridge Rd. SW5 . . . . . . .2D **78**
Long's Ct. WC2 . . . . .1C **74**
Longshott Ct. SW5 . . . . .2D **78**
Longstone Ct. *SE1* *5C 76*
(off Gt. Dover St.)
Long St. E2 . . . . .6H **61**
Longville Rd. SE11 . . . . . . .1K **83**
Long Wlk. SE1 . . . . .6G **77**
Long Yd. WC1 . . . . .2F **67**
Lonsdale Ho. W11 . . . . .6C **62**
Lonsdale M. W11 . . . . .6C **62**
Lonsdale Pl. N1 . . . . .1J **59**
Lonsdale Rd. NW6 . . . . .4B **54**
W11 . . . . .6B **62**
Lonsdale Sq. N1 . . . . .1J **59**
Lonsdale Yd. W11 . . . . .1D **70**
Lorden Wlk. E2 . . . . .7K **61**
Lord Hills Bri. W2 . . . . .4G **63**
Lord Hills Rd. W2 . . . . .3G **63**
Lord North St. SW1 . . . . . . .7D **74**
Lord Roberts M. SW6 . . . . . .7F **79**
Lord's Cricket Ground
Marylebone & Middlesex
County Cricket Clubs **7A 56**
Lordship Pl. SW3 . . . . .6B **80**
Lords Vw. NW8 . . . . .7A **56**
Lorenzo St. WC1 . . . . .6F **59**
Lorne Cl. NW8 . . . . .7C **56**
Lorrimore Rd. SE17 . . . . . . .6A **84**
Lorrimore Sq. SE17 . . . . . . .5A **84**
Lorton Ho. NW6 . . . . .3E **54**
Lothbury EC2 . . . . .5D **68**
Lothrop St. W10 . . . . .6A **54**
Lots Rd. SW10 . . . . .7H **79**
Loudoun Rd. NW8 . . . . .1J **55**
Loughborough St. SE11 . . . .3G **83**
Lovat La. EC3 . . . . .7F **69**
(not continuous)
Lovegrove St. SE1 . . . . .4K **85**
Lovelace Ho. E8 . . . . .2J **61**
Love La. EC2 . . . . .5C **68**
Lovell Ho. E8 . . . . .2K **61**
Lovers' Wlk. W1 . . . . .2F **73**
Lowell Ho. SE5 . . . . .7C **84**
Lwr. Addison Gdns.
W14 . . . . .4A **70**
Lwr. Belgrave St. SW1 . . . .7H **73**
Lwr. Grosvenor Pl.
SW1 . . . . .6H **73**
Lwr. James St. W1 . . . . .7A **66**
Lwr. John St. W1 . . . . .7A **66**
Lower Marsh SE1 . . . . .5H **75**
Lwr. Merton Ri. NW3 . . . . . .1B **56**
Lower Rd. SE1 . . . . .4H **75**
Lwr. Robert St. WC2 . . . . . .1E **74**
Lwr. Sloane St. SW1 . . . . . .2F **81**
Lwr. Thames St. EC3 . . . . . .1E **76**
Lowerwood Ct. W11 . . . . . . .6A **62**
Lowndes Cl. SW1 . . . . .7G **73**
Lowndes Ct. SW1 . . . . .6E **72**
W1 . . . . .6K **65**
Lowndes Pl. SW1 . . . . .7F **73**
Lowndes Sq. SW1 . . . . .5E **72**
Lowndes St. SW1 . . . . .6E **72**
Lowther Gdns. SW7 . . . . . . .6A **72**
Lowther Ho. E8 . . . . .2H **61**
SW1 . . . . .4A **82**
Loxham St. WC1 . . . . .7E **58**
LSO St Lukes **1C 68**
Lucan Ho. N1 . . . . .3E **60**
Lucan Pl. SW3 . . . . .2B **80**
Lucas Ho. SW10 . . . . .7G **79**
Lucerne M. W8 . . . . .2E **70**
Lucey Rd. SE16 . . . . .7K **77**
Lucey Way SE16 . . . . .7K **77**
Lucy Brown Ho. SE1 . . . . . .3C **76**
Ludgate B'way. EC4 . . . . . . .6K **67**
Ludgate Cir. EC4 . . . . .6K **67**
Ludgate Hill EC4 . . . . .6K **67**
Ludgate Sq. EC4 . . . . .6A **68**
Ludlow St. EC1 . . . . .1B **68**
Luke St. EC2 . . . . .1F **69**
Lulworth NW1 . . . . .1B **58**
SE17 . . . . .3D **84**
Lulworth Ct. N1 . . . . .1G **61**
Lulworth Ho. SW8 . . . . .7F **83**
Lumley Ct. WC2 . . . . .7E **66**
Lumley Flats SW1 . . . . .3F **81**
Lumley St. W1 . . . . .6G **65**
Lumsdon NW8 . . . . .3G **55**
Luntley Pl. E1 . . . . .4K **69**
Lupino Ct. SE11 . . . . .1G **83**
Lupin Point SE1 . . . . .5J **77**
Lupus St. SW1 . . . . .5J **81**
Luscombe Way SW8 . . . . . .7D **82**
Luton St. NW8 . . . . .2A **64**
Lutyens Ho. SW1 . . . . .4K **81**
Luxborough Ho. W1 . . . . . . .3F **65**
Luxborough St. W1 . . . . .2F **65**
Luxborough Twr. W1 . . . . . .3F **65**
Lux Cinema **7F 61**
Lyall M. SW1 . . . . .7F **73**
Lyall M. W. SW1 . . . . .7F **73**
Lyall St. SW1 . . . . .7F **73**
Lyceum Theatre **7F 67**
Lydford NW1 . . . . .3A **58**
Lydford Rd. W9 . . . . .1C **62**
Lygon Ho. E2 . . . . .6J **61**
Lygon Pl. SW1 . . . . .7H **73**
Lyly Ho. SE1 . . . . .7E **76**
Lyme St. NW1 . . . . .1K **57**
Lyme Ter. NW1 . . . . .1K **57**
Lympstone Gdns. SE15 . . . .7K **85**
Lynbrook Gro. SE15 . . . . . . .7G **85**
Lyndhurst Ct. NW8 . . . . . . .3K **55**
Lynton Est. SE1 . . . . .2K **85**
Lynton Ho. W2 . . . . .6H **63**
Lynton Mans. SE1 . . . . .6H **75**
Lynton Rd. NW6 . . . . .3C **54**
SE1 . . . . .2J **85**
Lyon Ho. NW8 . . . . .2B **64**
Lyons Pl. NW8 . . . . .2K **63**
Lyon St. N1 . . . . .1F **59**
Lyons Wlk. W14 . . . . .1A **78**
Lyric Ct. *E8* *1J 61*
(off Holly St.)
Lyric Theatre
Westminster **7B 66**
Lytham St. SE17 . . . . .4D **84**
Lyttelton Cl. NW3 . . . . .1B **56**
Lyttelton Theatre *2G 75*
(in Royal National Theatre)

M

Mabledon Ct. WC1 . . . . .7C **58**
Mabledon Pl. WC1 . . . . .7C **58**
Mablethorpe Rd. SW6 . . . . .7A **78**
McAuley Cl. SE1 . . . . .6H **75**
Macbeth Ho. N1 . . . . .4F **61**
MCC Cricket Mus. and
Tours **7K 55**
Macclesfield Ho. EC1 . . . . .7B **60**
Macclesfield Rd. EC1 . . . . .6B **60**
Macclesfield St. W1 . . . . . . .7C **66**
McCoid Way SE1 . . . . .5B **76**
Macfarren Pl. NW1 . . . . . . .2G **65**
McGlashon Ho. E1 . . . . .2K **69**
McGregor Ct. N1 . . . . .6G **61**
McGregor Rd. W11 . . . . . . .4B **62**
McIndoe Ct. N1 . . . . .2D **60**
Macintosh Ho. W1 . . . . .3G **65**
McKay Trad. Est. W10 . . . . .1A **62**
Mackennal St. NW8 . . . . . . .5C **56**
Macklin St. WC2 . . . . .5E **66**
Mackonochie Ho. EC1 . . . . .3H **67**
Mack's Rd. SE16 . . . . .1K **85**
Mackworth Ho. NW1 . . . . . .6K **57**
Mackworth St. NW1 . . . . . . .6K **57**
McLaren House SE1 . . . . . . .5K **75**
McLeod's M. SW7 . . . . .7G **71**
Macleod St. SE17 . . . . .4C **84**
Maclise Ho. SW1 . . . . .2D **82**
Maclise Rd. W14 . . . . .7A **70**
Macnamara Ho. SW10 . . . . .7K **79**
Macready Ho. W1 . . . . .4C **64**
Macroom Rd. W9 . . . . .6C **54**
Mac's Pl. EC4 . . . . .5J **67**
Madame Tussaud's **2F 65**
Maddock Way SE17 . . . . . . .6A **84**
Maddox St. W1 . . . . .7J **65**
Madison, The SE1 . . . . .4D **76**
Madrigal La. SE5 . . . . .7A **84**
Madron St. SE17 . . . . .3G **85**
Magazine Ga. W2 . . . . .2C **72**
Magdalen Pas. E1 . . . . .7J **69**
Magdalen St. SE1 . . . . .3F **77**
Magee St. SE11 . . . . .5H **83**
Magnin Cl. E8 . . . . .2K **61**
Magnolia Lodge W8 . . . . . . .7F **71**
Magpie All. EC4 . . . . .6J **67**
Maguire St. SE1 . . . . .4J **77**
Maida Av. W2 . . . . .3J **63**
MAIDA HILL **2C 62**
MAIDA VALE **7F 55**
Maida Va. W9 . . . . .4F **55**
Maiden La. NW1 . . . . .1C **58**
SE1 . . . . .3C **76**
WC2 . . . . .1E **74**
Maidstone Bldgs. M.
SE1 . . . . .3C **76**
Mail Coach Yd. E2 . . . . .6G **61**
Maismore St. SE15 . . . . .6K **85**
Maitland Ct. W2 . . . . .7K **63**
Maitland Ho. SW1 . . . . .5K **81**
Makins St. SW3 . . . . .2C **80**
Malam Ct. SE11 . . . . .2H **83**
Malcolm Ho. N1 . . . . .5F **61**
Malcolmson Ho. SW1 . . . . . .4B **82**
Maldon Cl. N1 . . . . .2B **60**
Malet Pl. WC1 . . . . .2B **66**
Malet St. WC1 . . . . .2B **66**
Mall, The SW1 . . . . .4K **73**
Mallard Cl. NW6 . . . . .3E **54**
Mallard Ho. NW8 . . . . .5B **56**
Mall Chambers W8 . . . . . . .2E **70**
Mall Galleries **2C 74**
Mall Gallery *WC2* *6D* ***66***
(in Thomas Neals Shop. Mall)
Mallon Gdns. E1 . . . . .5J **69**
Mallord St. SW3 . . . . .5A **80**
Mallory St. NW8 . . . . .1C **64**
Mallow St. EC1 . . . . .1D **68**
Malmsey Ho. SE11 . . . . .3G **83**
Malta St. EC1 . . . . .1A **68**
Maltby St. SE1 . . . . .5H **77**
Maltings Pl. SE1 . . . . .5G **77**
Malton M. W10 . . . . .5A **62**
Malton Rd. W10 . . . . .5A **62**
Maltravers St. WC2 . . . . . . .7G **67**
Malt St. SE1 . . . . .5K **85**
Malvern Cl. W10 . . . . .4B **62**
Malvern Ct. SW7 . . . . .1A **80**
Malvern M. NW6 . . . . .6D **54**
Malvern Pl. NW6 . . . . .6C **54**
Malvern Rd. E8 . . . . .1K **61**
NW6 . . . . .5C **54**
(not continuous)
Malvern Ter. N1 . . . . .2H **59**
Manchester Dr. W10 . . . . . . .2A **62**
Manchester Ho. SE17 . . . . . .3C **84**
Manchester M. W1 . . . . .4F **65**
Manchester Sq. W1 . . . . . . .5G **65**
Manchester St. W1 . . . . .4F **65**
Manciple St. SE1 . . . . .5D **76**
Mandela Ho. E2 . . . . .7H **61**
Mandela St. NW1 . . . . .2A **58**
SW9 . . . . .7H **83**
(not continuous)
Mandela Way SE1 . . . . .1F **85**
Mandeville Ho. SE1 . . . . . . .3J **85**
Mandeville Pl. W1 . . . . .5G **65**
Manette St. W1 . . . . .6C **66**
Manley Ho. SE11 . . . . .3H **83**
Manley St. NW1 . . . . .2F **57**
Manneby Prior N1 . . . . .5G **59**
Manningford Cl. EC1 . . . . . .6K **59**
Manningtree St. E1 . . . . . . .5K **69**
Manny Shinwell Ho.
SW6 . . . . .6C **78**
Manor Ho. NW1 . . . . .3C **64**
Manor Ho. Ct. W9 . . . . .2H **63**
Manor M. NW6 . . . . .4E **54**
Manor Pl. SE17 . . . . .4A **84**
Manresa Rd. SW3 . . . . .4B **80**
Mansell St. E1 . . . . .6J **69**
Mansfield Ct. E2 . . . . .3J **61**
Mansfield M. W1 . . . . .4H **65**
Mansfield St. W1 . . . . .4H **65**
Mansion House **6D 68**
Mansion Ho. Pl. EC4 . . . . . .6D **68**
Mansion Ho. St. EC4 . . . . . .6D **68**
Mansions, The SW5 . . . . . . .3F **79**
Manson M. SW7 . . . . .2J **79**
Manson Pl. SW7 . . . . .2K **79**
Manston NW1 . . . . .1A **58**
Manston Ho. W14 . . . . .7A **70**
Mapesbury Rd. NW2 . . . . . .1A **54**
Mapes Ho. NW6 . . . . .1A **54**
Mapledene Est. E8 . . . . .1K **61**
Mapledene Rd. E8 . . . . .1J **61**
Maple Lodge W8 . . . . .7F **71**
Maple M. NW6 . . . . .4F **55**
Maple Pl. W1 . . . . .2A **66**
Maple St. W1 . . . . .3K **65**
Marathon Ho. NW1 . . . . . . .3D **64**
Marban Rd. W9 . . . . .6B **54**
Marble Arch **7E 64**
MARBLE ARCH **7D 64**
Marble Arch W1 . . . . .7D **64**
Marble Arch Apartments
W1 . . . . .5D **64**
Marble Ho. W9 . . . . .2C **62**
Marble Quay E1 . . . . .2K **77**
Marbles Ho. SE5 . . . . .5C **84**
Marchant Ct. SE1 . . . . .3J **85**
Marchbank Rd. W14 . . . . . .5C **78**
Marchmont St. WC1 . . . . . .1D **66**
Marcia Rd. SE1 . . . . .2G **85**
Marco Polo Ho. SW8 . . . . . .7H **81**
Mardyke Ho. SE17 . . . . .1E **84**
Margaret Ct. W1 . . . . .5K **65**
Margaret Herbison Ho.
SW6 . . . . .6C **78**
Margaret Ingram Cl.
SW6 . . . . .6B **78**
Margaret St. W1 . . . . .5J **65**
Margaretta Ter. SW3 . . . . . .5B **80**
Margaret White Ho.
NW1 . . . . .6B **58**
Margery St. WC1 . . . . .7H **59**
Margravine Gdns. W6 . . . . .3A **78**
Marie Lloyd Ho. N1 . . . . . . .5D **60**
Marigold All. SE1 . . . . .1K **75**
Marine St. SE16 . . . . .6K **77**
Market Ct. W1 . . . . .5K **65**
Market Entrance SW8 . . . . .7A **82**
Market M. W1 . . . . .3H **73**
Market Pl. W1 . . . . .5K **65**
Market Yd. M. SE1 . . . . . . .6G **77**
Markham Pl. SW3 . . . . .3D **80**
Markham Sq. SW3 . . . . .3D **80**
Markham St. SW3 . . . . .3C **80**
Mark La. EC3 . . . . .7G **69**
Mark Sq. EC2 . . . . .1F **69**
Markstone Ho. SE1 . . . . . . .5K **75**
Mark St. EC2 . . . . .1F **69**
Marlborough Av. E8 . . . . . . .3K **61**
(not continuous)
Marlborough Cl. SE17 . . . . .2A **84**
Marlborough Ct. W1 . . . . . .6K **65**
W8 . . . . .1D **78**
Marlborough Flats SW3 . . . .1C **80**
Marlborough Gro. SE1 . . . . .4K **85**
Marlborough Hill NW8 . . . . .2K **55**
Marlborough House **3A 74**
Marlborough Ho. NW1 . . . . .1J **65**
Marlborough Pl. NW8 . . . . .5H **55**
Marlborough Rd. SW1 . . . . .3A **74**
Marlborough St. SW3 . . . . .2B **80**
Marlbury NW8 . . . . .3G **55**
Marloes Rd. W8 . . . . .7F **71**
Marlowe Ct. SW3 . . . . .2C **80**
Marlowes, The NW8 . . . . . . .3K **55**
Marlow Ho. E2 . . . . .7H **61**
SE1 . . . . .6H **77**
W2 . . . .*6G* ***63***
(off Hallfield Est.)
Marlow Workshops E2 . . . . .7H **61**
Marne St. W10 . . . . .6A **54**
Marnock Ho. SE17 . . . . .3D **84**
Marrick Ho. NW6 . . . . .3G **55**
Marryat Ho. SW1 . . . . .4K **81**
Marshall Ho. N1 . . . . .4E **60**
NW6 . . . . .4C **54**
SE1 . . . . .7G **77**
SE17 . . . . .3D **84**
Marshall's Pl. SE16 . . . . . . .7J **77**
Marshall St. W1 . . . . .6A **66**
Marshall Street Leisure Cen.
. . . .**6A 66**
Marshalsea Rd. SE1 . . . . . . .4C **76**
Marsham Ct. SW1 . . . . .1C **82**
Marsham St. SW1 . . . . .7C **74**
Marsh Cen., The E1 . . . . . . .5J **69**
Marsh Ho. SW1 . . . . .4C **82**
Marshwood Ho. NW6 . . . . . .3E **54**
Marsland Cl. SE17 . . . . .4A **84**
Marsom Ho. N1 . . . . .5D **60**
Marston Cl. NW6 . . . . .1J **55**
Marsworth Ho. E2 . . . . .3K **61**
Martara M. SE17 . . . . .4B **84**
Martha's Bldgs. EC1 . . . . . .1D **68**
Martineau Ho. SW1 . . . . . . .4K **81**
Martin Ho. SE1 . . . . .7C **76**
SW8 . . . . .7D **82**
Martin La. EC4 . . . . .7E **68**
(not continuous)
Martlett Ct. WC2 . . . . .6E **66**
Marvell Ho. SE5 . . . . .7D **84**
Marville Rd. SW6 . . . . .7C **78**

A-Z London Motorists Atlas 95

Mary Flux Ct.—Nth. End Pde.

Mary Flux Ct. SW5 3F 79
Mary Grn. NW8 2G 55
Marylands Rd. W9 2E 62
Maryland Wlk. N1 2B 60
MARYLEBONE 3G 65
Marylebone Cricket Club
Lord's Cricket Ground 6A 56
MARYLEBONE FLYOVER 4B 64
Marylebone Fly-Over W2 4A 64
Marylebone High St. W1 3G 65
Marylebone La. W1 4G 65
Marylebone M. W1 4H 65
Marylebone Pas. W1 5A 66
Marylebone Rd. NW1 3C 64
Marylebone St. W1 4G 65
Marylee Way SE11 2G 83
Mary Macarthur Ho. W6 5A 78
Mary Pl. W11 1A 70
Mary Seacole Cl. E8 3H 61
Mary Smith Ct. SW5 2E 78
Marysmith Ho. SW1 3C 82
Mary St. N1 3C 60
Mary Ter. NW1 3J 57
Masefield Ho. NW6 6D 54
Mason's Arms M. W1 6J 65
Mason's Av. EC2 5D 68
Masons Pl. EC1 6A 60
Mason St. SE17 2E 84
Masons Yd. EC1 6A 60
SW1 2A 74
Massinger St. SE17 2F 85
Masterman Ho. SE5 7D 84
Matheson Lang Ho. SE1 5H 75
Matheson Rd. W14 2B 78
Mathews Yd. WC2 6D 66
Mathieson Ct. SE1 5A 76
Mathison Ho. SW10 7H 79
Matilda Ho. E1 2K 77
Matilda St. N1 3G 59
Matisse Ct. EC1 1D 68
Maton Ho. SW6 7B 78
Matthew Parker St. SW1 5C 74
Maude Ho. E2 5K 61
Maudlins Grn. E1 2K 77
Maunsel St. SW1 1B 82
Mavor Ho. N1 3G 59
Mawbey Ho. SE1 4J 85
Mawbey Pl. SE1 4J 85
Mawbey Rd. SE1 4J 85
Mawbey St. SW8 7D 82
Mawdley Ho. SE1 5J 75
Mawson Ct. N1 3E 60
Mawson Ho. EC1 3H 67
Maxwell Rd. SW6 7F 79
Maybury Ct. W1 4G 65
MAYFAIR 1H 73
Mayfair M. NW1 1E 56
Mayfair Pl. W1 2J 73
Mayfield Rd. E8 1H 61
Mayford NW1 4A 58
(not continuous)
Maygood St. N1 4H 59
Maylands Ho. SW3 2C 80
Maynard Cl. SW6 7G 79
Mays Ct. WC2 1D 74
May St. W14 4C 78
Mazenod Av. NW6 1E 54
Meadcroft Rd. SE11 6K 83
(not continuous)
Mead Ho. W11 2B 70
Meadowbank NW3 1D 56
Meadow Ct. N1 4F 61
Meadow M. SW8 6F 83
Meadow Pl. SW8 7E 82
Meadow Rd. SW8 7F 83
Meadow Row SE1 7B 76
Mead Row SE1 6H 75
Meakin Est. SE1 6F 77
Meard St. W1 6B 66
(not continuous)
Mecca Bingo
Camden 2J 57
Fulham Broadway 7D 78
Haggerston 5J 61
Islington 1B 60
Kilburn 1D 54
Mecklenburgh Pl. WC1 1F 67
Mecklenburgh Sq. WC1 1F 67
Mecklenburgh St. WC1 1F 67
Medburn St. NW1 4B 58
Medway Ct. WC1 7D 58
Medway Ho. NW8 2B 64
SE1 5E 76
Medway St. SW1 7B 74
Melbourne Ct. W9 1J 63
Melbourne Ho. W8 3D 70
Melbourne Mans. W14 5A 78
Melbourne Pl. WC2 7G 67
Melbourne Ter. SW6 7F 79
Melbury Ct. W8 6C 70
Melbury Dr. SE5 7F 85
Melbury Ho. SW8 7F 83
Melbury Rd. W14 6B 70
Melbury Ter. NW1 2C 64
Melchester W11 5C 62
Melcombe Ct. NW1 3D 64
Melcombe Ho. SW8 7F 83
Melcombe Pl. NW1 3D 64
Melcombe Regis Ct. *W1* *4G 65*
(off Weymouth St.)
Melcombe St. NW1 2E 64
Melford Ct. SE1 6G 77
Melina Pl. NW8 7K 55
Melior Pl. SE1 4F 77
Melior St. SE1 4F 77
Melon Pl. W8 4E 70
Melrose Ho. NW6 6E 54
Melton Ct. SW7 2A 80
(not continuous)
Melton St. NW1 7A 58
Melville Pl. N1 1B 60
Memel Ct. EC1 2B 68
Memel St. EC1 2B 68
Mendham Ho. SE1 6F 77
Mendora Rd. SW6 7A 78
Mepham St. SE1 3H 75
Mercer Ho. SW1 3H 81
Mercer St. WC2 6D 66
Meredith St. EC1 7K 59
Meriden Ct. SW3 4C 80
Merlins Ct. WC1 7H 59
Merlin St. WC1 7H 59
Mermaid Ct. E8 1H 61
SE1 4D 76
Merrick Sq. SE1 6D 76
Merrington Rd. SW6 5E 78
Merritt's Bldgs. EC2 2F 69
Merrivale NW1 3A 58
Merrow St. SE17 5C 84
Merrow Wlk. SE17 3E 84
Mertoun Ter. W1 4D 64
Messina Av. NW6 1D 54
Messiter Ho. N1 3G 59
Methley St. SE11 4J 83
Metro Central Hgts. SE1 7B 76
Metropolis SE11 7A 76
Metropolitan Bus. Cen.
N1 1G 61
Mews, The N1 2C 60
Mews St. E1 2K 77
Mexborough NW1 3K 57
Meymott St. SE1 3K 75
Miah Ter. E1 3K 77
Micawber Ct. N1 6C 60
Micawber Ho. SE16 5K 77
Micawber St. N1 6C 60
Michael Cliffe Ho. EC1 7J 59
Michael Faraday Ho.
SE17 4F 85
Michael Stewart Ho.
SW6 6C 78
Michelson Ho. SE11 2G 83
Mickledore NW1 5A 58
Micklethwaite Rd. SW6 6E 78
Middle Dartrey Wlk.
SW10 *7J 79*
(off Dartrey Wlk.)
Middlefield NW8 2K 55
Middle Row W10 2A 62
Middlesex County Cricket Club
Lord's Cricket Ground 6A 56
Middlesex Pas. EC1 4A 68
Middlesex St. E1 4G 69
Middle St. EC1 3B 68
Middle Temple 7H 67
Middle Temple Hall 7H 67
Middle Temple La. EC4 6H 67
Middleton Ho. E8 1J 61
SE1 7D 76
SW1 2C 82
Middleton Pl. W1 4K 65
Middleton Rd. E8 1H 61
Middle Yd. SE1 2F 77
Midford Pl. W1 2A 66
Midhope Ho. WC1 7E 58
Midhope St. WC1 7E 58
Midland Rd. NW1 5C 58
Midway Ho. EC1 6A 60
Milborne Gro. SW10 4J 79
Milcote St. SE1 5K 75
Miles Bldgs. NW1 3B 64
Miles Pl. *NW1* *3A 64*
(off Broadley St.)
Miles St. SW8 6D 82
(not continuous)
Miles St. Bus. Est. SW8 6D 82
Milford La. WC2 7G 67
Milk St. EC2 6C 68
Millais Ho. SW1 2D 82
Millbank SW1 7D 74
Millbank Ct. SW1 1D 82
Millbank Twr. SW1 2D 82
Millbrook Ho. SE15 6K 85
Millbrook Pl. *NW1* *4K 57*
(off Hampstead Rd.)
Millennium Bridge 1A 76
Millennium Sq. SE1 4J 77
Miller St. NW1 4K 57
(not continuous)
Millers Wharf Ho. E1 3K 77
Miller Wlk. SE1 3J 75
Millman M. WC1 2F 67
Millman Pl. WC1 2F 67
Millman St. WC1 2F 67
Mill Pond Cl. SW8 7C 82
Mill Row N1 3G 61
Mills Ct. EC2 1F 69
Millstream Rd. SE1 5H 77
Mill St. SE1 5J 77
W1 7K 65
Mill Yd. E1 7K 69
Milman Rd. NW6 4A 54
Milman's St. SW10 6K 79
Milner Ct. SE15 7J 85
Milner Pl. N1 2J 59
Milner Sq. N1 1J 59
Milner St. SW3 1D 80
Milroy Wlk. SE1 2K 75
Milson Rd. W14 7A 70
Milton Cl. SE1 2H 85
Milton Ct. EC2 3D 68
Milton Ct. Wlk. EC2 3D 68
Milton Ho. SE5 7D 84
Milton Mans. W14 5A 78
Milton St. EC2 3D 68
Milverton St. SE11 4J 83
Mina Rd. SE17 4G 85
Mincing La. EC3 7F 69
Minera M. SW1 1G 81
Minerva Cl. SW9 7J 83
(not continuous)
Minerva Wlk. EC1 5A 68
Miniver Pl. EC4 7C 68
Minnow St. SE17 2G 85
Minnow Wlk. SE17 2G 85
Minories EC3 6H 69
Minster Ct. EC3 7G 69
Minster Pavement EC3 7G 69
Mintern St. N1 4E 60
Minton Ho. SE11 1H 83
Mint St. SE1 4B 76
Mirabel Rd. SW6 7C 78
Missenden SE17 4E 84
Missenden Ho. NW8 1B 64
Mitali Pas. E1 6K 69
(not continuous)
Mitchell St. EC1 1B 68
(not continuous)
Mitre Ct. EC2 6C 68
Mitre Rd. SE1 4J 75
Mitre Sq. EC3 6G 69
Mitre St. EC3 6G 69
Mitre Yd. SW3 1C 80
Moatlands Ho. WC1 7E 58
Mobil Ct. WC2 6G 67
Model Bldgs. WC1 7G 59
Modern Ct. EC4 5K 67
Molesworth Ho. SE17 6K 83
Molton Ho. N1 3G 59
Molyneux St. W1 4C 64
Monck St. SW1 7C 74
Moncorvo Cl. SW7 5B 72
Moneyer Ho. N1 6D 60
Monica Shaw Ct. NW1 5C 58
(not continuous)
Monkton St. SE11 1J 83
Monkwell Sq. EC2 4C 68
Monmouth Pl. W2 6F 63
Monmouth Rd. W2 6E 62
Monmouth St. WC2 6D 66
Monnow Rd. SE1 3K 85
Montague Cl. SE1 2D 76
Montague Pl. WC1 3C 66
Montague St. EC1 4B 68
WC1 3D 66
Montagu Mans. W1 3E 64
Montagu M. Nth. W1 4E 64
Montagu M. Sth. W1 5E 64
Montagu M. W. W1 5E 64
Montagu Pl. W1 4D 64
Montagu Row W1 4E 64
Montagu Sq. W1 4E 64
Montagu St. W1 5E 64
Montaigne Cl. SW1 2C 82
Montclare St. E2 1H 69
Monteagle Ct. N1 4G 61
Montford Pl. SE11 4H 83
Monthope Rd. E1 4J 69
Montpelier M. SW7 6C 72
Montpelier Pl. SW7 6C 72
Montpelier Sq. SW7 5C 72
Montpelier St. SW7 6C 72
Montpelier Ter. SW7 5C 72
Montpelier Wlk. SW7 6C 72
Montreal Pl. WC2 7F 67
Montrose Av. NW6 4A 54
Montrose Ct. SW7 5A 72
Montrose Pl. SW1 5G 73
Monument, The 7E 68
Monument St. EC3 7E 68
Moon St. N1 2K 59
Moore Ct. N1 3K 59
Moore Pk. Ct. SW6 7G 79
Moore Pk. Rd. SW6 7F 79
Moore St. SW3 1D 80
Moorfields EC2 4D 68
Moorfields Highwalk
EC2 4D 68
(not continuous)
Moorgate EC2 5D 68
Moorgate Pl. EC2 5D 68
Moorgreen Ho. EC1 6K 59
Moorhouse Rd. W2 5D 62
Moor La. EC2 4D 68
(not continuous)
Moor Pl. EC2 4D 68
Moor St. W1 6C 66
Mora St. EC1 7C 60
Moravian Cl. SW10 6K 79
Moravian Pl. SW10 6A 80
Mordern Ho. NW1 2C 64
Morecambe St. SE17 2C 84
Moreland St. EC1 6A 60
More London Pl. SE1 3F 77
More's Gdn. SW3 6A 80
Moreton Cl. SW1 3A 82
Moreton Pl. SW1 3A 82
Moreton St. SW1 3A 82
Moreton Ter. SW1 3A 82
Moreton Ter. M. Nth.
SW1 3A 82
Moreton Ter. M. Sth.
SW1 3A 82
Morgan Ho. SW1 2A 82
Morgan Rd. W10 3B 62
Morland Ho. NW1 5A 58
NW6 3D 54
SW1 1D 82
Morland M. N1 1J 59
Morley St. SE1 6J 75
Mornington Av. W14 2B 78
Mornington Ct. NW1 4K 57
Mornington Cres. NW1 4K 57
Mornington Pl. NW1 4K 57
Mornington Sports &
Leisure Cen. *2J 57*
(off Stanmore Pl.)
Mornington St. NW1 4J 57
Mornington Ter. NW1 3J 57
Morocco St. SE1 5F 77
Morpeth Mans. SW1 1K 81
Morpeth Ter. SW1 7K 73
Morrel Ct. E2 4K 61
Morris Ho. NW8 2B 64
Morrison Bldgs. Nth. E1 5K 69
Morshead Mans. W9 7E 54
Morshead Rd. W9 7E 54
Mortimer Ct. NW8 5J 55
Mortimer Cres. NW6 3F 55
Mortimer Est. NW6 3F 55
Mortimer Ho. W14 2A 78
Mortimer Mkt. WC1 2A 66
Mortimer Pl. NW6 3F 55
Mortimer Rd. N1 1G 61
(not continuous)
Mortimer St. W1 5J 65
Morton M. SW5 2F 79
Morton Pl. SE1 7H 75
Morton Rd. N1 1C 60
Morwell St. WC1 4B 66
Moscow Pl. W2 7F 63
Moscow Rd. W2 7E 62
Mosedale NW1 7K 57
Mosque Ter. *E1* *4K 69*
(off Fieldgate St.)
Mosque Twr. *E1* *4K 69*
(off Fieldgate St.)
Moss Cl. E1 4K 69
Mossop St. SW3 1C 80
Motcomb St. SW1 6F 73
Motley Av. EC2 1F 69
Moules Ct. SE5 7B 84
Mounsey Ho. W10 6A 54
Mountain Ho. SE11 2G 83
Mt. Carmel Chambers
W8 4E 70
Mountfort Cres. N1 1H 59
Mountfort Ter. N1 1H 59
Mountjoy Cl. *EC2* *4C 68*
(off Thomas More Highwalk)
Mountjoy Ho. EC2 4C 68
Mount Mills EC1 7A 60
Mt. Pleasant WC1 2H 67
Mount Row W1 1H 73
Mount St. W1 1F 73
Mount St. M. W1 1H 73
Mowbray Rd. NW6 1B 54
Mowll St. SW9 7H 83
Moxon St. W1 4F 65
Moye Cl. E2 4K 61
Moylan Rd. W6 6A 78
Moyle Ho. SW1 4A 82
Mozart St. W10 7B 54
Mozart Ter. SW1 2G 81
Mulberry Cl. SW3 6A 80
Mulberry Ct. EC1 7A 60
Mulberry Housing Co-operative
SE1 2J 75
Mulberry Rd. E8 1H 61
Mulberry St. E1 5K 69
Mulberry Wlk. SW3 5A 80
Mulgrave Rd. SW6 5B 78
Mullen Twr. WC1 2H 67
Mullet Gdns. E2 6K 61
Mulletsfield WC1 7E 58
Mulready Ho. SW1 2D 82
Mulready St. NW8 2B 64
Mulvaney Way SE1 5E 76
(not continuous)
Mumford Ct. EC2 5C 68
Munday Ho. SE1 7D 76
Munden St. W14 1A 78
Mund St. W14 4C 78
Mundy Ho. W10 6A 54
Mundy St. N1 6F 61
Munro Ho. SE1 5H 75
Munro M. W10 4A 62
(not continuous)
Munro Ter. SW10 7K 79
Munster M. SW6 7A 78
Munster Rd. SW6 7A 78
Munster Sq. NW1 7J 57
Munton Rd. SE17 1C 84
Muriel St. N1 4G 59
(not continuous)
Murphy Ho. SE1 6A 76
Murphy St. SE1 5H 75
Murray Gro. N1 5C 60
Murray St. NW1 1B 58
Musard Rd. W6 5A 78
W14 6A 78
Muscal W6 5A 78
Muscovy St. EC3 1G 77
Museum Chambers WC1 4D 66
Museum La. SW7 7A 72
Mus. of Classical Archaeology
1B 66
(off Gower Pl.)
Mus. of Garden History 7F 75
Mus. of London 4B 68
Mus. of the Order of St John
2K 67
Museum St. WC1 4D 66
Mutrix Rd. NW6 2E 54
Myddelton Pas. EC1 6J 59
Myddelton Sq. EC1 6J 59
Myddelton St. EC1 7J 59
Myddleton Ho. N1 5H 59
Mylne St. EC1 6H 59
Myrtle Wlk. N1 5F 61
Mytton Ho. SW8 7F 83

N1 Shop. Cen. N1 4J 59
Nags Head Ct. EC1 2C 68
Nainby Ho. SE11 2H 83
Naish Ct. N1 2E 58
(not continuous)
Nantes Pas. E1 3H 69
Naoroji St. WC1 7H 59
Napier Cl. W14 6B 70
Napier Ct. N1 4D 60
Napier Gro. N1 4C 60
Napier Pl. W14 7B 70
Napier Rd. W14 7B 70
Napier Ter. N1 1K 59
Nashe Ho. SE1 7D 76
Nash Ho. SW1 4J 81
Nash St. NW1 6J 57
Nassau St. W1 4K 65
Nathan Ho. SE11 2J 83
Nathaniel Cl. E1 4J 69
National Army Mus. 5E 80
National Film Theatre, The
2G 75
National Gallery 1C 74
National Gallery
(Sainsbury Wing) 1C 74
National Portrait Gallery
1C 74
Natural History Mus. 7K 71
Nautilus Bldg., The EC1 6J 59
Navarre St. E2 1H 69
Naylor Ho. W10 6A 54
Nazrul St. E2 6H 61
Neal St. WC2 6D 66
Neal's Yd. WC2 6D 66
Neate St. SE5 6F 85
(not continuous)
Neathouse Pl. SW1 1K 81
Nebraska St. SE1 5D 76
Neckinger SE16 6J 77
Neckinger Est. SE16 6J 77
Neckinger St. SE1 5J 77
Needham Ho. SE11 2H 83
Needham Rd. W11 6D 62
Nelson Cl. NW6 6D 54
Nelson Ct. SE1 4A 76
Nelson Gdns. E2 6K 61
Nelson Ho. SW1 5A 82
Nelson Pas. EC1 6C 60
Nelson Pl. N1 5A 60
Nelson's Column 2C 74
Nelson Sq. SE1 4K 75
Nelsons Yd. NW1 4K 57
Nelson Ter. N1 5A 60
Nesham St. E1 2K 77
Ness St. SE16 6K 77
Netherton Gro. SW10 6J 79
Netley St. NW1 7K 57
Nettlecombe NW1 1B 58
Nettleden Ho. SW3 2C 80
Nettleton Ct. EC2 4B 68
Nevern Pl. SW5 2E 78
Nevern Rd. SW5 2D 78
Nevern Sq. SW5 2D 78
Nevill Ct. EC4 5J 67
Neville Cl. NW1 5C 58
NW6 5C 54
Neville Ct. NW8 5K 55
Neville Rd. NW6 5C 54
Neville St. SW7 3K 79
Neville Ter. SW7 3K 79
Nevitt Ho. N1 5E 60
Newall Ho. SE1 6C 76
New Bentham Ct. N1 1C 60
Newbery Ho. N1 1B 60
Newbolt Ho. SE17 3D 84
New Bond St. W1 6H 65
New Bri. St. EC4 6K 67
New Broad St. EC2 4E 68
Newburgh St. W1 6K 65
New Burlington M. W1 7K 65
New Burlington Pl. W1 7K 65
New Burlington St. W1 7K 65
Newburn Ho. SE11 3G 83
Newburn St. SE11 4G 83
Newbury Ho. W2 6G 63
Newbury St. EC1 3B 68
Newby NW1 7K 57
New Caledonian Mkt.
SE1 6G 77
Newcastle Cl. EC4 5K 67
Newcastle Ct. EC4 7C 68
Newcastle Ho. W1 3F 65
Newcastle Pl. W2 3A 64
Newcastle Row EC1 2J 67
New Cavendish St. W1 4G 65
New Change EC4 6B 68
New Charles St. EC1 6A 60
New Church Rd. SE5 7C 84
(not continuous)
New College M. N1 1J 59
Newcombe St. W8 2E 70
Newcomen St. SE1 4D 76
New Compton St. WC2 6C 66
New Concordia Wharf
SE1 4J 77
New Ct. EC4 7H 67
Newcourt St. NW8 5B 56
New Covent Garden Market
7B 82
New Coventry St. W1 1C 74
Newent Cl. SE15 7F 85
New Era Est. N1 3F 61
New Fetter La. EC4 5J 67
Newgate St. EC1 5A 68
New Globe Wlk. SE1 2B 76
New Goulston St. E1 5H 69
Newham's Row SE1 5G 77
NEWINGTON 7B 76
Newington Butts SE1 2A 84
SE11 2A 84
Newington C'way. SE1 7A 76
Newington Ct. Bus. Cen.
SE1 6B 76
Newington Ind. Est.
SE17 2B 84
New Inn B'way. EC2 1G 69
New Inn Pas. WC2 6G 67
New Inn Sq. EC2 1G 69
New Inn St. EC2 1G 69
New Inn Yd. EC2 1G 69
New Kent Rd. SE1 7B 76
Newland Ct. EC1 1D 68
Newlands NW1 6K 57
New London St. EC3 7G 69
New London Theatre 5E 66
Newlyn NW1 3A 58
Newman Pas. W1 4A 66
Newman's Ct. EC3 6E 68
Newman's Row WC2 4G 67
Newman St. W1 4A 66
Newman Yd. W1 5B 66
Newnham Ter. SE1 6H 75
New Nth. Pl. EC2 1F 69
New Nth. Rd. N1 1B 60
New Nth. St. WC1 3F 67
New Oxford St. WC1 5C 66
Newport Ct. WC2 7C 66
Newport Pl. WC2 7C 66
Newport St. SE11 2F 83
New Priory Ct. NW6 1E 54
Newquay Ho. SE11 3H 83
New Quebec St. W1 6E 64
New Ride SW1 4C 72
SW7 5A 72
New River Head EC1 6J 59
New River Wlk. N1 1B 60
New Row WC2 7D 66
New Spring Gdns. Wlk.
SE11 4E 82
New Sq. WC2 5H 67
New Sq. Pas. WC2 5H 67
New St. EC2 4G 69
New St. Sq. EC4 5J 67
Newton Ho. NW8 2G 55
Newton Mans. W14 5A 78
Newton Rd. W2 6E 62
Newton St. WC2 5E 66
New Turnstile WC1 4F 67
New Union St. EC2 4D 68
New Wharf Rd. N1 4E 58
Next Generation Carlton Club
Carlton 3E 62
Niagra Cl. N1 4C 60
Nicholas La. EC4 7E 68
(not continuous)
Nicholas Pas. EC4 7E 68
Nicholl St. E2 3K 61
Nichols Ct. E2 5H 61
Nicholson Ho. SE17 3D 84
Nicholson St. SE1 3K 75
Nickleby Ho. SE16 5K 77
Nigel Ho. EC1 3H 67
Nightingale Ho. E1 2K 77
E2 3G 61
Nightingale Lodge *W9* *3E 62*
(off Admiral Wlk.)
Nightingale M. SE11 1K 83
Nightingale Pl. SW10 6J 79
(not continuous)
Nile St. N1 6D 60
Nile Ter. SE15 4H 85
NINE ELMS 7A 82
Nine Elms La. SW8 7A 82
Nipponzan Myohoji Peace
Pagoda 7E 80
Nirvana Apartments *N1* *3K 59*
(off Islington Grn.)
Noble Ct. E1 7K 69
Noble St. EC2 5B 68
Noel Coward Ho. SW1 2A 82
Noel Rd. N1 4K 59
Noel St. W1 6A 66
Norfolk Cres. W2 5B 64
Norfolk Ho. SW1 1C 82
Norfolk M. W10 4A 62
Norfolk Pl. W2 5A 64
(not continuous)
Norfolk Rd. NW8 3A 56
Norfolk Row SE1 1F 83
(not continuous)
Norfolk Sq. W2 6A 64
Norfolk Sq. M. W2 6A 64
Norfolk Ter. W6 4A 78
Norland Pl. W11 3A 70
Norland Sq. W11 3A 70
Norland Sq. Mans.
W11 3A 70
Normand Gdns. W14 5A 78
Normand M. W14 5A 78
Normand Rd. W14 5B 78
Norman Ho. SW8 7D 82
Norman St. EC1 7B 60
Norris Ho. N1 3F 61
Norris St. SW1 1B 74
Northampton Rd. EC1 1J 67
Northampton Row EC1 1J 67
Northampton Sq. EC1 7K 59
Northampton St. N1 1B 60
Nth. Audley St. W1 6F 65
North Bank NW8 7B 56
North Block SE1 4G 75
Northburgh St. EC1 2A 68
Nth. Carriage Dr. W2 7B 64
Northchurch SE17 3E 84
(not continuous)
Northchurch Rd. N1 1D 60
(not continuous)
Northchurch Ter. N1 1F 61
North Ct. SW1 7D 74
W1 3A 66
North Cres. WC1 3B 66
Northdown St. N1 4E 58
Nth. End Cres. W14 2B 78
Nth. End Ho. W14 2A 78
Nth. End Pde. W14 2A 78

North End Rd.—Pinchin St.

North End Rd. SW6 ... 4C 78
W14 ... 1A 78
Northfield Ho. SE15 ... 6K 85
Northfleet Ho. SE1 ... 4D 76
Nth. Flock St. SE16 ... 4K 77
Nth. Flower Wlk. W2 ... 1J 71
North Ga. NW8 ... 5B 56
Nth. Gower St. NW1 ... 7A 58
Northiam WC1 ... 7E 58
Northington St. WC1 ... 2G 67
Northleach Ct. SE15 ... 6F 85
North M. WC1 ... 2G 67
Northport St. N1 ... 3E 60
North Ride W2 ... 1B 72
North Ri. W2 ... 6C 64
North Row W1 ... 7E 64
Nth. Row Bldgs. W1 ... 7F 65
Nth. Tenter St. E1 ... 6J 69
North Ter. SW3 ... 7B 72
Northumberland All. EC3 ... 6G 69
(not continuous)
Northumberland Av.
WC2 ... 2D 74
Northumberland Ho.
SW1 ... 2D 74
Northumberland Pl. W2 ... 5D 62
Northumberland St.
WC2 ... 2D 74
North Wlk. W8 ... 1G 71
Nth. Western Commercial Cen.
NW1 ... 1D 58
Northwest Pl. N1 ... 4J 59
Nth. Wharf Rd. W2 ... 4K 63
Northwick Cl. NW8 ... 1K 63
Northwick Ho. NW8 ... 1J 63
Northwick Ter. NW8 ... 1K 63
Norton Folgate E1 ... 3G 69
Norton Folgate Ho. E1 ... 3H 69
Norton Ho. SW1 ... 7C 74
Norwich St. EC4 ... 5H 67
Notley St. SE5 ... 7D 84
Nottingdale Sq. W11 ... 1A 70
Nottingham Ct. WC2 ... 6E 66
Nottingham Ho. WC2 ... 6D 66
Nottingham Pl. W1 ... 3F 65
Nottingham St. W1 ... 3F 65
Nottingham Ter. NW1 ... 2F 65
NOTTING HILL ... 7B 62
Notting Hill Ga. W11 ... 2C 70
Nottingwood Ho. W11 ... 7A 62
Nuffield Lodge W9 ... 3E 62
Nugent Ter. NW8 ... 5J 55
Nun Ct. EC2 ... 5D 68
Nursery La. E2 ... 3H 61
Nutbourne St. W10 ... 6A 54
Nutford Pl. W1 ... 5C 64
Nuttall St. N1 ... 4G 61
Nutt St. SE15 ... 7J 85
Nye Bevan Ho. SW6 ... 7B 78

Oak Ct. SE15 ... 7J 85
Oakden St. SE11 ... 1J 83
Oakeford Ho. W14 ... 7A 70
Oakey La. SE1 ... 6H 75
Oakfield St. SW10 ... 5H 79
Oakington Rd. W9 ... 1E 62
Oakley Cres. EC1 ... 5A 60
Oakley Gdns. SW3 ... 5C 80
Oakley Ho. SW1 ... 1E 80
Oakley Pl. SE1 ... 4H 85
Oakley Rd. N1 ... 1E 60
Oakley Sq. NW1 ... 4A 58
Oakley St. SW3 ... 5B 80
Oakley Yd. E2 ... 1J 69
Oak Lodge W8 ... 7F 71
Oakshott Ct. NW1 ... 5B 58
(not continuous)
Oak Tree Ho. W9 ... 1E 62
Oak Tree Rd. NW8 ... 7A 56
Oakwood Ct. W14 ... 6B 70
Oakwood La. W14 ... 6B 70
Oasis Sports Cen. ... 5D 66
Oat La. EC2 ... 5C 68
Oatwell Ho. SW3 ... 3C 80
Oberon Ho. N1 ... 4F 61
Observatory Gdns. W8 ... 4D 70
Occupation Rd. SE17 ... 3B 84
Octagon, The SW10 ... 7H 79
Octagon Arc. EC2 ... 4F 69
Octavia Ho. SW1 ... 7B 74
Octavia M. W10 ... 1B 62
Odeon Cinema
Camden Town ... 2J 57
Charing Cross ... 1C 74
Covent Garden ... 6C 66
Kensington ... 6D 70
Leicester Sq. ... 1C 74
Marble March ... 6E 64
Mezzanine ... 1C 74
Swiss Cen. ... 7B 66
Swiss Cottage ... 1K 55
Tottenham Ct. Rd. ... 4B 66
West End ... 1C 74
Odhams Wlk. WC2 ... 6D 66
O'Donnell Ct. WC1 ... 1E 66
Odontological Mus., The
... 5G 67
(in Royal College of Surgeons, The)
Offham Ho. SE17 ... 2F 85
Offley Rd. SW9 ... 7H 83
Offord Rd. N1 ... 1F 59
Offord St. N1 ... 1G 59
Ogle St. W1 ... 3K 65
O'Gorman Ho. SW10 ... 7J 79
Old Bailey EC4 ... 6A 68
Old Bailey (Central Criminal
Court) ... 5A 68
Old Barge Ho. All. SE1 ... 1J 75
Old Barracks W8 ... 4G 71
Old Barrack Yd. SW1 ... 5F 73
(not continuous)
Old Billingsgate Mkt.
EC3 ... 1F 77
Old Billingsgate Wlk.
EC3 ... 1F 77
Old Bond St. W1 ... 1K 73
Old Brewer's Yd. WC2 ... 6D 66
Old Broad St. EC2 ... 6E 68
Old Brompton Rd. SW5 ... 4E 78
SW7 ... 2K 79
Old Bldgs. WC2 ... 5K 67
Old Burlington St. W1 ... 7K 65
Oldbury Pl. W1 ... 2G 65
Old Canal M. SE15 ... 4J 85
Old Castle St. E1 ... 5H 69
Old Cavendish St. W1 ... 5H 65
Old Change Ct. EC4 ... 6B 68
Old Chelsea M. SW3 ... 6B 80
Old Church St. SW3 ... 3A 80
Old Compton St. W1 ... 7B 66
Old Ct. Ho. W8 ... 5F 71
Old Ct. Pl. W8 ... 4F 71
Old Curiosity Shop ... 6G 67
Old Fish St. Hill EC4 ... 7B 68
Old Fleet La. EC4 ... 5K 67
Old Gloucester St. WC1 ... 3E 66
Old Jamaica Rd. SE16 ... 6K 77
Old Jewry EC2 ... 6D 68
Old Kent Rd. SE1 ... 1F 85
Old Mnr. Ct. NW8 ... 4J 55
Old Mnr. Yd. SW5 ... 3F 79
Old Mkt. Sq. E2 ... 6H 61
Old Marylebone Rd.
NW1 ... 4C 64
Old Mitre Ct. EC4 ... 6J 67
Old Montague St. E1 ... 4K 69
Old Nichol St. E2 ... 1H 69
Old Nth. St. WC1 ... 3F 67
Old Pal. Yd. SW1 ... 6D 74
Old Paradise St. SE11 ... 1F 83
Old Pk. La. W1 ... 3G 73
Old Pye St. SW1 ... 6B 74
Old Pye St. Est. SW1 ... 7B 74
Old Quebec St. W1 ... 6E 64
Old Queen St. SW1 ... 5C 74
Old Red Lion Theatre ... 5J 59
Old Royal Free Pl. N1 ... 3J 59
Old Royal Free Sq. N1 ... 3J 59
Old Seacoal La. EC4 ... 6K 67
Old Sth. Lambeth Rd.
SW8 ... 7E 82
Old Spitalfields Market ... 3H 69
Old Sq. WC2 ... 5H 67
OLD STREET ... 7D 60
Old St. EC1 ... 2B 68
Old Theatre Ct. SE1 ... 2C 76
Old Vic Theatre, The ... 4J 75
Oliphant St. W10 ... 6A 54
Oliver Ho. SE16 ... 5K 77
SW8 ... 7D 82
Olivers Yd. EC1 ... 1E 68
Olive Waite Ho. NW6 ... 1F 55
Olivier Theatre ... 2G 75
(in Royal National Theatre)
Olmar St. SE1 ... 5K 85
Olney Ho. NW8 ... 1C 64
Olney Rd. SE17 ... 6A 84
(not continuous)
Olympia ... 7A 70
Olympia M. W2 ... 1G 71
Olympia Way W14 ... 7A 70
O'Meara St. SE1 ... 3C 76
Omega Pl. N1 ... 5E 58
O'Neill Ho. NW8 ... 5B 56
One Owen St. EC1 ... 5K 59
Ongar Rd. SW6 ... 5D 78
Onslow Cl. W10 ... 6B 54
Onslow Gdns. SW7 ... 2K 79
Onslow M. E. SW7 ... 2K 79
Onslow M. W. SW7 ... 2K 79
Onslow Sq. SW7 ... 1A 80
Onslow St. EC1 ... 2J 67
Ontario St. SE1 ... 6A 76
Opal M. NW6 ... 2C 54
Opal St. SE11 ... 2K 83
Operating Theatre Mus. ... 3E 76
Opie Ho. NW8 ... 4B 56
Oppidans Rd. NW3 ... 1D 56
Orangery Gallery, The ... 5B 70
Orange St. WC2 ... 1C 74
Orange Tree Ct. SE5 ... 7F 85
Orange Yd. W1 ... 6C 66
Oratory La. SW3 ... 3A 80
Orbain Rd. SW6 ... 7A 78
Orb St. SE17 ... 2D 84
Orchard Cl. N1 ... 1C 60
W10 ... 3A 62
Orchard Ho. SW6 ... 7A 78
W1 ... 5F 65
Orchard M. N1 ... 1E 60
Orchardson Ho. NW8 ... 1K 63
Orchardson St. NW8 ... 2K 63
Orchard Sq. W14 ... 4B 78
Orchard St. W1 ... 6F 65
Orde Hall St. WC1 ... 2F 67
Ordnance Hill NW8 ... 3A 56
Ordnance M. NW8 ... 4A 56
Orient St. SE11 ... 1K 83
Orkney Ho. N1 ... 3F 59
Orme Ct. W2 ... 1G 71
Orme Ct. M. W2 ... 1G 71
Orme Ho. E8 ... 2J 61
Orme La. W2 ... 1F 71
Orme Sq. W2 ... 1F 71
Ormond Cl. WC1 ... 3E 66
Ormonde Ct. NW8 ... 3D 56
Ormonde Ga. SW3 ... 4E 80
Ormonde Pl. SW1 ... 2G 81
Ormonde Ter. NW8 ... 3D 56
Ormond M. WC1 ... 2E 66
Ormond Yd. SW1 ... 2A 74
Ormsby St. E2 ... 4H 61
Orsett M. W2 ... 5G 63
(not continuous)
Orsett St. SE11 ... 3G 83
Orsett Ter. W2 ... 5G 63
Orsman Rd. N1 ... 3F 61
Orton St. E1 ... 3K 77
Orwell Ct. E8 ... 3K 61
Osbert St. SW1 ... 2B 82
Osborn Cl. E8 ... 2K 61
Osborn St. E1 ... 4J 69
Oscar Faber Pl. N1 ... 1G 61
Oslo Ct. NW8 ... 5B 56
Osmani School Sports Cen.
... 2K 69
Osnaburgh St. NW1 ... 2J 65
(Euston Rd.)
NW1 ... 7J 57
(Robert St.)
Osnaburgh Ter. NW1 ... 1J 65
Osprey Ct. E1 ... 1K 77
Ospringe Ho. SE1 ... 4J 75
Osric Path N1 ... 5F 61
Ossington Bldgs. W1 ... 3F 65
Ossington Cl. W2 ... 1E 70
Ossington St. W2 ... 1F 71
Ossory Rd. SE1 ... 4K 85
Ossulston St. NW1 ... 5B 58
Ostend Pl. SE1 ... 1B 84
Osten M. SW7 ... 7G 71
Oswald Bldg. SW8 ... 6H 81
Oswin St. SE11 ... 1A 84
Otford Ho. SE1 ... 5E 76
Othello Cl. SE11 ... 3K 83
Other Cinema, The ... 7B 66
Otterburn Ho. SE5 ... 7B 84
Otto St. SE17 ... 6K 83
Outer Circ. NW1 ... 4D 56
Outram Pl. N1 ... 2E 58
Outwich St. EC3 ... 5G 69
Oval Cricket Ground, The
... 5G 83
Oval House Theatre ... 6H 83
Oval Mans. SE11 ... 5G 83
Oval Pl. SW8 ... 7F 83
Oval Rd. NW1 ... 1H 57
Oval Way SE11 ... 4G 83
Oversley Ho. W2 ... 3E 62
Overy Ho. SE1 ... 5K 75
Ovington Gdns. SW3 ... 7C 72
Ovington M. SW3 ... 7C 72
Ovington Sq. SW3 ... 7C 72
Ovington St. SW3 ... 7C 72
Owen Mans. W14 ... 5A 78
Owen's Row EC1 ... 6K 59
Owen St. EC1 ... 5K 59
(not continuous)
Owgan Cl. SE5 ... 7E 84
Oxendon St. SW1 ... 1B 74
Oxenholme NW1 ... 5A 58
Oxford & Cambridge Mans.
NW1 ... 4C 64
Oxford Cir. W1 ... 6K 65
Oxford Cir. Av. W1 ... 6K 65
Oxford Ct. EC4 ... 7D 68
W9 ... 3D 62
Oxford Dr. SE1 ... 3F 77
Oxford Gdns. W10 ... 5A 62
Oxford Rd. NW6 ... 5E 54
Oxford Sq. W2 ... 6C 64
Oxford St. W1 ... 6E 64
Oxley Cl. SE1 ... 3J 85
Oxo Tower Wharf SE1 ... 1J 75
Oystergate Wlk. EC4 ... 1D 76

Packenham Ho. E2 ... 6J 61
Packington Sq. N1 ... 3B 60
(not continuous)
Packington St. N1 ... 2A 60
Padbury SE17 ... 4G 85
Padbury Ct. E2 ... 7J 61
Padbury Ho. NW8 ... 1C 64
PADDINGTON ... 6K 63
Paddington Bowling &
Sports Club ... 1F 63
Paddington Grn. W2 ... 3A 64
Paddington St. W1 ... 3F 65
Paddington Wlk. W2 ... 4K 63
Pageantmaster Ct. EC4 ... 6K 67
Page St. SW1 ... 1C 82
Page's Wlk. SE1 ... 1E 86
Paget St. EC1 ... 6K 59
Painswick Ct. SE15 ... 7H 85
Painters M. SE16 ... 1K 85
Pakeman Ho. SE1 ... 4A 76
Pakenham St. WC1 ... 7G 59
Palace Av. W8 ... 4G 71
Palace Bingo ... 1B 84
Palace Ct. W2 ... 7F 63
(not continuous)
Palace Gdns. M. W8 ... 2E 70
Palace Gdns. Ter. W8 ... 2E 70
Palace Ga. W8 ... 5H 71
Palace Grn. W8 ... 3F 71
Palace Mans. W14 ... 1A 78
Palace M. SW1 ... 2G 81
SW6 ... 7C 78
Palace Pl. SW1 ... 6K 73
Palace Pl. Mans. W8 ... 5G 71
Palace St. SW1 ... 6K 73
Palace Theatre
Soho ... 6C 66
Palamon Ct. SE1 ... 3J 85
Palfrey Pl. SW8 ... 7G 83
Palgrave Gdns. NW1 ... 1C 64
Palgrave Ho. SE5 ... 7B 84
Palissy St. E2 ... 7H 61
(not continuous)
Palladium Ct. E8 ... 1J 61
Pallant Ho. SE1 ... 7E 76
Palliser Ct. W14 ... 3A 78
Palliser Rd. W14 ... 3A 78
Pall Mall SW1 ... 3A 74
Pall Mall E. SW1 ... 2C 74
Pall Mall Pl. SW1 ... 3A 74
Palm Ct. SE15 ... 7J 85
Palmerston Ho. SE1 ... 5H 75
W8 ... 3D 70
Palmerston Mans. W14 ... 6A 78
Palmerston Rd. NW6 ... 1C 54
(not continuous)
Palmer St. SW1 ... 6B 74
(not continuous)
Pamela Ho. E8 ... 2J 61
Pancras La. EC4 ... 6C 68
Pancras Rd. NW1 ... 4B 58
Pangbourne NW1 ... 7K 57
Panton St. SW1 ... 1B 74
Paper Bldgs. EC4 ... 7J 67
Parade, The SW11 ... 7E 80
Paradise Wlk. SW3 ... 5D 80
Paragon M. SE1 ... 1E 84
Paramount Bldg. EC1 ... 1K 67
Paramount Ct. WC1 ... 2A 66
Pardoner Ho. SE1 ... 6E 76
Pardoner St. SE1 ... 6E 76
(not continuous)
Pardon St. EC1 ... 1A 68
Paris Gdn. SE1 ... 2K 75
Park Bus. Cen. NW6 ... 7E 54
Park Cl. SW1 ... 5D 72
W14 ... 6C 70
Park Cres. W1 ... 2H 65
Park Cres. M. E. W1 ... 2J 65
Park Cres. M. W. W1 ... 2H 65
Parker M. WC2 ... 5E 66
Parkers Row SE1 ... 5J 77
Parker St. WC2 ... 5E 66
Parkfield St. N1 ... 4J 59
Parkgate Rd. SW11 ... 7C 80
Parkhouse St. SE5 ... 7E 84
Parkinson Ho. SW1 ... 2A 82
Park La. W1 ... 7E 64
Park Lodge NW8 ... 1A 56
Park Lorne NW8 ... 7C 56
Park Mans. NW8 ... 5B 56
SW1 ... 5D 72
SW8 ... 5E 82
Park M. W10 ... 5A 54
Park Pl. N1 ... 2E 60
SW1 ... 3K 73
Park Pl. Vs. W2 ... 3J 63
Park Rd. NW1 ... 6B 56
NW8 ... 6B 56
Parkside SW1 ... 4E 72
Park Sq. E. NW1 ... 1H 65
Park Sq. M. NW1 ... 2H 65
Park Sq. W. NW1 ... 1H 65
Park Steps W2 ... 7C 64
Park St. SE1 ... 2B 76
W1 ... 7F 65
Park Towers W1 ... 3H 73
Pk. Village E. NW1 ... 3H 57
Pk. Village W. NW1 ... 4H 57
Parkville Rd. SW6 ... 7B 78
Park Wlk. SW10 ... 5J 79
Parkway NW1 ... 3H 57
Park W. W2 ... 5C 64
Park W. Pl. W2 ... 5C 64
Parkwood NW8 ... 3D 56
Parliament Ct. E1 ... 4G 69
Parliament Sq. SW1 ... 5D 74
Parliament St. SW1 ... 4D 74
Parliament Vw. SE1 ... 1F 83
Parmoor Ct. EC1 ... 1B 68
Parnell Ho. WC1 ... 4C 66
Parr Ct. N1 ... 4D 60
Parr St. N1 ... 4D 60
Parry Rd. W10 ... 6A 54
(not continuous)
Parry St. SW8 ... 5E 82
Parsons Ho. W2 ... 2K 63
Parsons Lodge NW6 ... 1F 55
Partridge Ct. EC1 ... 1K 67
Pascall Ho. SE17 ... 5B 84
Pascal St. SW8 ... 7C 82
Pasley Cl. SE17 ... 4B 84
Passfields W14 ... 4B 78
Passing All. EC1 ... 2A 68
Passmore House E2 ... 3H 61
Passmore St. SW1 ... 2F 81
Pastor St. SE11 ... 1A 84
(not continuous)
Patent Office, The EC4 ... 6J 67
Paternoster La. EC4 ... 6A 68
Paternoster Row EC4 ... 6B 68
Paternoster Sq. EC4 ... 6A 68
Paterson Ct. EC1 ... 7D 60
Pater St. W8 ... 7D 70
Paton St. EC1 ... 7B 60
Patrick Coman Ho. EC1 ... 7K 59
Patterdale NW1 ... 7J 57
Pattern Ho. EC1 ... 1K 67
Pattison Ho. SE1 ... 4C 76
Pauline Ho. E1 ... 3K 69
Paul St. EC2 ... 2E 68
Paul's Wlk. EC4 ... 7A 68
Paultons Sq. SW3 ... 5A 80
Paultons St. SW3 ... 6A 80
Paveley Dr. SW11 ... 7B 80
Paveley Ho. N1 ... 5F 59
Paveley St. NW8 ... 7B 56
Pavilion NW8 ... 7A 56
Pavilion, The SW8 ... 7C 82
Pavilion Ct. NW6 ... 6D 54
Pavilion Rd. SW1 ... 5E 72
Pavilion St. SW1 ... 7E 72
Paxton Ter. SW1 ... 5J 81
Payne Ho. N1 ... 3G 59
Paynes Wlk. W6 ... 6A 78
Peabody Av. SW1 ... 3H 81
Peabody Bldgs. E1 ... 7K 69
EC1 ... 2C 68
SW3 ... 6B 80
Peabody Cl. SW1 ... 5J 81
Peabody Ct. EC1 ... 2C 68
Peabody Est. EC1 ... 2C 68
(Dufferin St., not continuous)
EC1 ... 2J 67
(Farringdon La.)
N1 ... 2B 60
SE1 ... 3J 75
(Duchy St.)
SE1 ... 4C 76
(Marshalsea Rd.)
SE1 ... 3B 76
(Southwark St.)
SW1 ... 1A 82
SW3 ... 5C 80
SW6 ... 5C 78
Peabody Sq. SE1 ... 5K 75
(not continuous)
Peabody Ter. EC1 ... 2J 67
Peabody Twr. EC1 ... 2C 68
Peabody Trust SE17 ... 2D 84
Peabody Yd. N1 ... 2B 60
Peacock St. SE17 ... 2A 84
Peacock Theatre ... 6F 67
Peacock Yd. SE17 ... 2A 84
Pear Ct. SE15 ... 7H 85
Pearman St. SE1 ... 6J 75
Pear Pl. SE1 ... 4H 75
Pearse St. SE15 ... 6G 85
Pearson St. E2 ... 4G 61
Pear Tree Cl. E2 ... 3H 61
Pear Tree Ct. EC1 ... 2J 67
Pear Tree St. EC1 ... 1A 68
Peckham Gro. SE15 ... 7G 85
Peckham Hill St. SE15 ... 7K 85
Peckham Pk. Rd. SE15 ... 7K 85
Pecks Yd. E1 ... 3H 69
Pedley St. E1 ... 2J 69
Peel Pas. W8 ... 3D 70
Peel Prct. NW6 ... 5D 54
Peel St. W8 ... 3D 70
Peerless St. EC1 ... 7D 60
Pegasus Pl. SE11 ... 5H 83
Peldon Wlk. N1 ... 2A 60
Pelham Ct. SW3 ... 2B 80
Pelham Cres. SW7 ... 2B 80
Pelham Ho. W14 ... 2B 78
Pelham Pl. SW7 ... 1B 80
Pelham St. SW7 ... 1A 80
Pelier St. SE17 ... 5C 84
Pella Ho. SE11 ... 3G 83
Pellant Rd. SW6 ... 6A 78
Pelter St. E2 ... 6H 61
(not continuous)
Pemberton Row EC4 ... 5J 67
Pembridge Cres. W11 ... 7D 62
Pembridge Gdns. W2 ... 1D 70
Pembridge M. W11 ... 7D 62
Pembridge Pl. W2 ... 7E 62
Pembridge Rd. W11 ... 1D 70
Pembridge Sq. W2 ... 1E 70
Pembridge Vs. W2 ... 6E 62
W11 ... 1D 70
Pembroke Av. N1 ... 2E 58
Pembroke Cl. SW1 ... 5G 73
Pembroke Cotts. W8 ... 7D 70
Pembroke Gdns. W8 ... 1C 78
Pembroke Gdns. Cl. W8 ... 7C 70
Pembroke Ho. W2 ... 6G 63
Pembroke M. W8 ... 7D 70
Pembroke Pl. W8 ... 7D 70
Pembroke Rd. W8 ... 1C 78
Pembroke Sq. W8 ... 7D 70
Pembroke St. N1 ... 1E 58
(not continuous)
Pembroke Studios W8 ... 7C 70
Pembroke Ter. NW8 ... 3K 55
Pembroke Vs. W8 ... 1D 78
Pembroke Wlk. W8 ... 1D 78
Penally Pl. N1 ... 2E 60
Pencombe M. W11 ... 7C 62
Pendrell Ho. WC2 ... 6C 66
Penfield Lodge W9 ... 3E 62
Penfold Pl. NW1 ... 3B 64
Penfold St. NW1 ... 2A 64
NW8 ... 2A 64
Penhurst Pl. SE1 ... 7G 75
Peninsula Apartments
W2 ... 4B 64
Peninsula Hgts. SE1 ... 3E 82
Penley Ct. WC2 ... 7G 67
Penmayne Ho. SE11 ... 3J 83
Pennack Rd. SE15 ... 6J 85
Pennant M. W8 ... 1F 79
Penn Ho. NW8 ... 2B 64
Pennington St. E1 ... 1K 77
Penn St. N1 ... 3E 60
Pennyford Ct. NW8 ... 1K 63
Pennymoor Wlk. W9 ... 1C 62
Penrose Gro. SE17 ... 4B 84
Penrose Ho. SE17 ... 4B 84
(not continuous)
Penrose St. SE17 ... 4B 84
Penryn Ho. SE11 ... 3K 83
Penryn St. NW1 ... 4B 58
Penry St. SE1 ... 2G 85
Penton Gro. N1 ... 5H 59
Penton Ho. N1 ... 5H 59
Penton Pl. SE17 ... 2A 84
Penton Ri. WC1 ... 6G 59
Penton St. N1 ... 4H 59
PENTONVILLE ... 5F 59
Pentonville Rd. N1 ... 6E 58
Pentridge St. SE15 ... 7H 85
Penywern Rd. SW5 ... 3E 78
Penzance Ho. SE11 ... 3J 83
Penzance Pl. W11 ... 2A 70
Penzance St. W11 ... 2A 70
Peperfield WC1 ... 7F 59
Pepler Ho. W10 ... 2A 62
Pepler M. SE5 ... 4H 85
Pepper St. SE1 ... 4B 76
Pepys St. EC3 ... 7G 69
Percival David Foundation of
Chinese Art ... 2C 66
Percival St. EC1 ... 1K 67
Percy Cir. WC1 ... 6G 59
Percy M. W1 ... 4B 66
Percy Pas. W1 ... 4B 66
Percy St. W1 ... 4B 66
Percy Yd. WC1 ... 6G 59
Peregrine Ho. EC1 ... 6A 60
Perham Rd. W14 ... 4A 78
Perkin's Rents SW1 ... 7B 74
Perkins Sq. SE1 ... 2C 76
Perrin Ho. NW6 ... 6D 54
Perronet Ho. SE1 ... 7A 76
Perry's Pl. W1 ... 5B 66
Perseverance Pl. SW9 ... 7J 83
Perseverance Works E2 ... 6G 61
Perth Ho. N1 ... 1F 59
Peterborough Ct. EC4 ... 6J 67
Peter Butler Ho. SE1 ... 4K 77
Peter Ho. SW8 ... 7D 82
Peter Pan Statue ... 2K 71
Peters Ct. W2 ... 5G 63
Petersham Ho. SW7 ... 1K 79
Petersham La. SW7 ... 6H 71
Petersham M. SW7 ... 7H 71
Petersham Pl. SW7 ... 7H 71
Peter's Hill EC4 ... 7B 68
Peter's La. EC1 ... 3A 68
(not continuous)
Peter St. W1 ... 7B 66
Peto Pl. NW1 ... 1J 65
Petrie Mus. of Egyptian
Archaeology ... 2B 66
Petticoat La. E1 ... 4G 69
Petticoat Lane Market ... *4G 69*
(off Middlesex St.)
Petticoat Sq. E1 ... 5H 69
Petticoat Twr. E1 ... 5H 69
Petty France SW1 ... 6A 74
Petyt Pl. SW3 ... 6B 80
Petyward SW3 ... 2C 80
Peveril Ho. SE1 ... 7E 76
Phelp St. SE17 ... 5D 84
Phene St. SW3 ... 5C 80
Philadelphia Ct. SW10 ... 7J 79
Philbeach Gdns. SW5 ... 3D 78
Philchurch Pl. E1 ... 6K 69
Philip Ct. W2 ... 3K 63
Philip Ho. NW6 ... 3F 55
Philip Mole Ho. W9 ... 1D 62
Phillimore Gdns. W8 ... 5D 70
Phillimore Gdns. Cl. W8 ... 6D 70
Phillimore Pl. W8 ... 5D 70
Phillimore Ter. W8 ... 6E 70
Phillimore Wlk. W8 ... 6D 70
Phillipp St. N1 ... 3F 61
Philpot La. EC3 ... 7F 69
Phipp St. EC2 ... 1F 69
Phoenix Cl. E8 ... 2H 61
Phoenix Ct. NW1 ... 5C 58
Phoenix Pl. WC1 ... 1G 67
Phoenix Rd. NW1 ... 6B 58
Phoenix St. WC2 ... 6C 66
Phoenix Theatre ... 6C 66
Phoenix Wharf Rd. SE1 ... 5J 77
Phoenix Yd. WC1 ... 7G 59
Photographers' Gallery ... *7D 66*
(off Gt. Newport St.)
Physic Pl. SW3 ... 5D 80
Piazza, The WC2 ... 7E 66
(not continuous)
Piccadilly W1 ... 3H 73
Piccadilly Arc. SW1 ... 2K 73
Piccadilly Circus ... 1B 74
Piccadilly Cir. W1 ... 1B 74
Piccadilly Pl. W1 ... 1A 74
Piccadilly Theatre ... 7A 66
Pickard St. EC1 ... 6A 60
Pickering Ho. W2 ... 6H 63
Pickering M. W2 ... 5G 63
Pickering Pl. SW1 ... 3A 74
Pickering St. N1 ... 2A 60
Pickfords Wharf N1 ... 5B 60
SE1 ... 2D 76
Pickwick Ho. SE16 ... 5K 77
Pickwick St. SE1 ... 5B 76
Picton Pl. W1 ... 6G 65
Picton St. SE5 ... 7D 84
Pied Bull Yard *N1* ... *3K 59*
(off Theberton St.)
WC1 ... 4D 66
Pier Ho. SW3 ... 6C 80
Pierrepont Arc. N1 ... 4K 59
Pierrepont Row N1 ... 4K 59
Pietra Lara Bldg. EC1 ... 1B 68
Pikemans Ct. SW5 ... 2D 78
Pilgrimage St. SE1 ... 5D 76
Pilgrim Ho. SE1 ... 7E 76
Pilgrim St. EC4 ... 6K 67
Pilton Pl. SE17 ... 3C 84
Pilton Pl. Est. SE17 ... 3C 84
PIMLICO ... 4K 81
Pimlico Ho. SW1 ... 3H 81
Pimlico Rd. SW1 ... 3F 81
Pimlico Wlk. N1 ... 6F 61
Pinchin & Johnsons Yd.
E1 ... 7K 69
Pinchin St. E1 ... 7K 69

Pincombe Ho.—Robin Hood Ct.

Pincombe Ho. SE17 . . . 3D 84
Pindar St. EC2 . . . 3F 69
Pindock M. W9 . . . 2G 63
Pineapple Ct. SW1 . . . 6K 73
Pinehurst Ct. W11 . . . 6C 62
Pine St. EC1 . . . 1H 67
Pinner Ct. NW8 . . . 1K 63
Pinners Pas. *EC2* . . . *5F 69*
(off Austin Friars)
Pitfield Est. N1 . . . 6F 61
Pitfield St. N1 . . . 3F 61
Pitman St. SE5 . . . 7B 84
(not continuous)
Pitt's Head M. W1 . . . 3G 73
Pitt St. W8 . . . 4E 70
Place, The . . . 7C 58
Plaisterers Highwalk
EC2 . . . 4B 68
Plantain Pl. SE1 . . . 4D 76
Plantation Pl. EC3 . . . 7F 69
Platina St. EC2 . . . 1E 68
Platt St. NW1 . . . 4B 58
Playfair Mans. W14 . . . 6A 78
Playhouse Ct. SE1 . . . 4B 76
Playhouse Theatre . . . 2E 74
Playhouse Yd. EC4 . . . 6K 67
Plaza Cinema . . . 1B 74
Plaza Pde. NW6 . . . 4F 55
Plaza Shop. Cen., The
W1 . . . 5A 66
Pleasant Pl. N1 . . . 1A 60
Pleasant Row NW1 . . . 3J 57
Plender Pl. NW1 . . . 3A 58
Plender St. NW1 . . . 3K 57
Pleydell Ct. EC4 . . . 6J 67
Pleydell Est. EC1 . . . 7C 60
Pleydell St. EC4 . . . 6J 67
Plough Ct. EC3 . . . 7E 68
Ploughmans Cl. NW1 . . . 2B 58
Plough Pl. EC4 . . . 5J 67
Plough St. E1 . . . 5J 69
Plough Yd. EC2 . . . 2G 69
Plover Ho. SW9 . . . 7H 83
Plowden Bldgs. *EC4* . . . *7H 67*
(off Middle Temple La.)
Plumber's Row E1 . . . 4K 69
Plumtree Ct. EC4 . . . 5K 67
Plympton Av. NW6 . . . 1B 54
Plympton Pl. NW8 . . . 2B 64
Plympton Rd. NW6 . . . 1B 54
Plympton St. NW8 . . . 2B 64
Pocock St. SE1 . . . 4K 75
Point, The W2 . . . 4K 63
Point West SW7 . . . 1G 79
Poland St. W1 . . . 5A 66
Polesworth Ho. W2 . . . 3E 62
Pollard Ho. N1 . . . 5F 59
Pollard Row E2 . . . 6K 61
Pollen St. W1 . . . 6K 65
Pollitt Dr. NW8 . . . 1K 63
Pollock's Toy Mus. . . . 3A 66
Polperro M. SE11 . . . 1K 83
Polygon, The NW8 . . . 2A 56
Polygon Rd. NW1 . . . 5B 58
Pomell Way E1 . . . 5J 69
Pomeroy Ho. W11 . . . 6A 62
Pond Ho. SW3 . . . 2B 80
Pond Pl. SW3 . . . 2B 80
Ponsonby Pl. SW1 . . . 3C 82
Ponsonby Ter. SW1 . . . 3C 82
Ponton Rd. SW8 . . . 6C 82
Pont St. SW1 . . . 7D 72
Pont St. M. SW1 . . . 7D 72
Pontypool Pl. SE1 . . . 4K 75
Poole Ct. N1 . . . 1G 61
Poole Ho. SE11 . . . 1G 83
Pooles Bldgs. WC1 . . . 2H 67
Pooles La. SW10 . . . 7H 79
Poole St. N1 . . . 3D 60
Pool Ho. NW8 . . . 3A 64
Pope Ho. SE5 . . . 7D 84
Pope's Head All. EC3 . . . 6E 68
Pope St. SE1 . . . 5G 77
Popham Rd. N1 . . . 2B 60
Popham St. N1 . . . 2A 60
(not continuous)
Poplar Pl. W2 . . . 7F 63
Poppins Ct. EC4 . . . 6K 67
Porchester Ct. W2 . . . 7G 63
Porchester Gdns. W2 . . . 7G 63
Porchester Gdns. M. W2 . . . 6G 63
Porchester Ga. W2 . . . 1G 71
(not continuous)
Porchester Leisure Cen. . . . 5F 63
Porchester M. W2 . . . 5G 63
Porchester Pl. W2 . . . 6C 64
Porchester Rd. W2 . . . 5G 63
Porchester Sq. W2 . . . 5G 63
Porchester Ter. W2 . . . 6H 63
Porchester Ter. Nth. W2 . . . 5G 63
Porlock St. SE1 . . . 4E 76
Portcullis Ho. SW1 . . . 5D 74
Portelet Ct. N1 . . . 2F 61
Porters Lodge, The *SW10* . . . *7H 79*
(off Coleridge Gdns.)
Porter St. SE1 . . . 2C 76
W1 . . . 3E 64
Porteus Rd. W2 . . . 3J 63
Portgate Cl. W9 . . . 1C 62
Portia Ct. SE11 . . . 3K 83
Porticos, The SW3 . . . 6K 79
Portland Ct. N1 . . . 1G 61
SE1 . . . 6D 76
Portland Ho. SW1 . . . 7K 73
Portland M. W1 . . . 6A 66
Portland Pl. W1 . . . 2H 65
Portland Rd. W11 . . . 7A 62
Portland St. SE17 . . . 3D 84
Portland Wlk. SE17 . . . 5E 84
Portman Cl. W1 . . . 5E 64
Portman Ga. NW1 . . . 2C 64
Portman Mans. W1 . . . 3E 64
Portman M. Sth. W1 . . . 6F 65
Portman Sq. W1 . . . 5F 65
Portman St. W1 . . . 6F 65
Portman Towers W1 . . . 5E 64
Portnall Rd. W9 . . . 5B 54
Portobello Ct. Est. W11 . . . 6C 62
Portobello M. W11 . . . 1D 70
Portobello Rd. W10 . . . 3A 62
W11 . . . 5B 62
Portobello Road Market . . . 3A 62
Portpool La. EC1 . . . 3H 67
Portsea Hall W2 . . . 6D 64
Portsea M. W2 . . . 6C 64
Portsea Pl. W2 . . . 6C 64
Portsmouth St. WC2 . . . 6F 67
Portsoken St. E1 . . . 7H 69
Portugal St. WC2 . . . 6F 67
Pory Ho. SE11 . . . 2G 83
Postern, The EC2 . . . 4C 68
Post Office Ct. EC3 . . . 6E 68
Post Office Way SW8 . . . 7B 82
Potier St. SE1 . . . 7E 76
Potters Flds. SE1 . . . 3G 77
Pottery La. W11 . . . 2A 70
Poultry EC2 . . . 6D 68
Povey Ho. SE17 . . . 2F 85
Powell Ho. W2 . . . 5G 63
Powis Ct. W11 . . . 5C 62
Powis Gdns. W11 . . . 5C 62
Powis M. W11 . . . 5C 62
Powis Pl. WC1 . . . 2E 66
Powis Sq. W11 . . . 5C 62
(not continuous)
Powis Ter. W11 . . . 5C 62
Pownall Rd. E8 . . . 3J 61
Poynter Ho. NW8 . . . 1K 63
Praed M. W2 . . . 5A 64
Praed St. W2 . . . 6K 63
Pratt M. NW1 . . . 3K 57
Pratt St. NW1 . . . 3K 57
Pratt Wlk. SE11 . . . 1G 83
Preachers Ct. EC1 . . . 2A 68
Prebend St. N1 . . . 3B 60
Precinct, The N1 . . . 3B 60
Premier Cnr. W9 . . . 5B 54
Premier Ho. N1 . . . 1K 59
Prescot St. E1 . . . 7J 69
Prescott Ho. SE17 . . . 6A 84
President Ho. EC1 . . . 7A 60
President Quay E1 . . . 2J 77
President St. EC1 . . . 6B 60
Preston Cl. SE1 . . . 1F 85
Preston Ho. SE1 . . . 1F 85
(Preston Cl.)
SE1 . . . 6H 77
(Stanworth St.)
Prestwood St. N1 . . . 5C 60
Price Ho. N1 . . . 3B 60
Price's St. SE1 . . . 3A 76
Price's Yd. N1 . . . 3G 59
Prideaux Pl. WC1 . . . 6G 59
Priestley Ho. EC1 . . . 1B 68
Priest's Ct. EC2 . . . 5B 68
Prima Rd. SW9 . . . 7H 83
PRIMROSE HILL . . . 1E 56
Primrose Hill EC4 . . . 6J 67
Primrose Hill Ct. NW3 . . . 1D 56
Primrose Hill Rd. NW3 . . . 1D 56
Primrose Hill Studios
NW1 . . . 2F 57
Primrose M. NW1 . . . 1E 56
Primrose St. EC2 . . . 3F 69
Prince Albert Ct. NW8 . . . 3D 56
Prince Albert Rd. NW1 . . . 6B 56
NW8 . . . 6B 56
Prince Charles Cinema . . . 7C 66
Prince Consort Rd. SW7 . . . 6J 71
Princedale Rd. W11 . . . 2A 70
Prince Edward Mans.
W2 . . . 7E 62
Prince Edward Theatre . . . 6C 66
Princelet St. E1 . . . 3J 69
Prince of Wales Pas.
NW1 . . . 7K 57
Prince of Wales Ter.
W8 . . . 5G 71
Prince of Wales Theatre . . . 1B 74
Prince Regent Ct. NW8 . . . 4C 56
Prince Regent M. NW1 . . . 7K 57
Prince Regents Ga. NW8 . . . 1C 64
Princes Arc. SW1 . . . 2A 74
Princes Cir. WC2 . . . 5D 66
Prince's Ct. SW3 . . . 6D 72
Prince's Gdns. SW7 . . . 6A 72
Prince's Ga. SW7 . . . 5A 72
(not continuous)
Prince's Ga. Ct. SW7 . . . 5A 72
Prince's Ga. M. SW7 . . . 6A 72
Prince's M. W2 . . . 7E 62
Princes Pl. SW1 . . . 2A 74
W11 . . . 2A 70
Princess Ct. W1 . . . 4D 64
W2 . . . 7G 63
Princess Louise Cl. W2 . . . 3A 64
Princess Mary Ho. SW1 . . . 2C 82
Princes Sq. W2 . . . 7E 62
(not continuous)
Princess Rd. NW1 . . . 2F 57
NW6 . . . 5D 54
Princess St. SE1 . . . 7A 76
Princes St. EC2 . . . 6D 68
W1 . . . 6J 65
Prince's Yd. W11 . . . 3A 70
Princethorpe Ho. W2 . . . 3F 63
Princeton St. WC1 . . . 4F 67
Printers Inn Ct. EC4 . . . 5H 67
Printer St. EC4 . . . 5J 67
Printing Ho. Yd. E2 . . . 7G 61
Printwork Apartments
SE1 . . . *6F 77*
(off Long La.)
Prioress St. SE1 . . . 7E 76
Priory Ct. EC4 . . . 6A 68
Priory Grn. Est. N1 . . . 4G 59
Priory Ho. E1 . . . 3H 69
EC1 . . . 1K 67
SW1 . . . 3B 82
Priory Pk. Rd. NW6 . . . 2C 54
(not continuous)
Priory Rd. NW6 . . . 2F 55
Priory Ter. NW6 . . . 2F 55
Priory Wlk. SW10 . . . 4J 79
Priter Rd. SE16 . . . 7K 77
Priter Way SE16 . . . 7K 77
Probyn Ho. SW1 . . . 1C 82
Procter Ho. SE1 . . . 3K 85
SE5 . . . 7E 84
Procter St. WC1 . . . 4F 67
Prospect Ho. N1 . . . 5H 59
SE1 . . . 7K 75
Prothero Rd. SW6 . . . 7A 78
Provence St. N1 . . . 4B 60
Providence Ct. W1 . . . 7G 65
Providence Pl. N1 . . . 3K 59
Providence Row N1 . . . 5F 59
Providence Sq. SE1 . . . 4K 77
Providence Twr. SE16 . . . 4K 77
Providence Yd. E2 . . . 6K 61
Provost Est. N1 . . . 6D 60
Provost St. N1 . . . 5D 60
Prowse Pl. NW1 . . . 1K 57
Prudent Pas. EC2 . . . 6C 68
Pudding La. EC3 . . . 1E 76
Puddle Dock EC4 . . . 7A 68
(not continuous)
Pugin Ct. N1 . . . 1J 59
Pulham Ho. SW8 . . . 7F 83
Pullen's Bldgs. SE17 . . . 3A 84
Pulteney Ter. N1 . . . 3G 59
(not continuous)
Pulton Pl. SW6 . . . 7D 78
Puma Ct. E1 . . . 3H 69
Pump Ct. EC4 . . . 6H 67
Pump House Gallery, The
. . . 7F 81
Pump Ho. M. E1 . . . 7K 69
Purbeck Ho. SW8 . . . 7F 83
Purbrook Est. SE1 . . . 5G 77
Purbrook St. SE1 . . . 6G 77
Purcell Ho. SW10 . . . 6K 79
Purcell Mans. W14 . . . 6A 78
Purcell Room . . . 2G 75
Purcell St. N1 . . . 4F 61
Purchese St. NW1 . . . 4B 58
Purley Pl. N1 . . . 1K 59

Quadrangle, The W2 . . . 5B 64
Quadrangle Cl. SE1 . . . 1F 85
Quadrant Arc. W1 . . . 1A 74
Quadrant Ho. SE1 . . . 3K 75
Quain Mans. W14 . . . 6A 78
Quaker Ct. E1 . . . 2H 69
EC1 . . . 1C 68
Quaker St. E1 . . . 2H 69
Quality Ct. WC2 . . . 5H 67
Quarley Way SE15 . . . 7H 85
Quastel Ho. SE1 . . . 5D 76
Quayside Cotts. E1 . . . 2K 77
Quebec M. W1 . . . 6E 64
Quebec Wharf E8 . . . 2G 61
Quedgeley Ct. SE15 . . . 6H 85
Queen Alexandra Mans.
WC1 . . . 6D 58
Queen Anne M. W1 . . . 4J 65
Queen Anne's Ga. SW1 . . . 5B 74
Queen Anne St. W1 . . . 5H 65
Queen Anne's Wlk. WC1 . . . 2E 66
Queenbridge Sports &
Community Cen. . . . 1J 61
Queen Catherine Ho.
SW6 . . . 7G 79
Queen Elizabeth Bldgs.
EC4 . . . 7H 67
Queen Elizabeth Hall . . . 2F 75
Queen Elizabeth II Conference
Cen. . . . 5C 74
Queen Elizabeth St. SE1 . . . 4G 77
Queenhithe EC4 . . . 7C 68
Queen Isabella Way EC1 . . . 5A 68
Queen Marys Bldgs.
SW1 . . . 1A 82
Queen Mother Sports
Cen., The . . . 1K 81
Queensberry M. W. SW7 . . . 1K 79
Queensberry Pl. SW7 . . . 1K 79
Queensberry Way SW7 . . . 1K 79
Queensborough M. W2 . . . 7H 63
Queensborough Pas. W2 . . . 7H 63
Queensborough Studios
W2 . . . 7H 63
Queensborough Ter. W2 . . . 7G 63
Queensbridge Ct. E2 . . . 4J 61
Queensbridge Rd. E2 . . . 3J 61
E8 . . . 2J 61
Queensbury St. N1 . . . 1C 60
Queen's Chapel of the
Savoy, The . . . 7F 67
Queen's Club Gdns. W14 . . . 5A 78
Queen's Club, The (Tennis)
. . . 4A 78
Queens Ct. NW8 . . . 4K 55
W2 . . . 1G 71
Queensdale Rd. W11 . . . 3A 70
Queensdale Wlk. W11 . . . 3A 70
Queen's Elm Pde. *SW3* . . . *3A 80*
(off Old Chu. St.)
Queen's Elm Sq. SW3 . . . 4A 80
Queen's Gallery . . . 5J 73
Queen's Gdns. W2 . . . 7H 63
Queen's Ga. SW7 . . . 5J 71
Queen's Ga. Gdns. SW7 . . . 7H 71
Queen's Ga. M. SW7 . . . 5J 71
Queen's Ga. Pl. SW7 . . . 7J 71
Queen's Ga. Pl. M. SW7 . . . 7J 71
Queen's Ga. Ter. SW7 . . . 6H 71
Queen's Gro. NW8 . . . 3K 55
Queen's Gro. Studios
NW8 . . . 3K 55
Queen's Head Pas. EC4 . . . 5B 68
Queen's Head St. N1 . . . 3A 60
Queen's Head Yd. SE1 . . . 3D 76
Queens Ho. SW8 . . . 7E 82
Queen's Ice Bowl . . . *1G 71*
(off Queensway)
Queensmead NW8 . . . 2A 56
Queen's M. W2 . . . 7F 63
(not continuous)
Queen Sq. WC1 . . . 2E 66
Queen Sq. Pl. WC1 . . . 2E 66
Queen's Quay EC4 . . . 7C 68
Queen's Row SE17 . . . 5D 84
Queen's Ter. NW8 . . . 3K 55
Queen's Theatre
Westminster . . . 7B 66
Queen St. EC4 . . . 7C 68
(not continuous)
W1 . . . 2H 73
Queen St. Pl. EC4 . . . 1C 76
Queen's Wlk. SW1 . . . 2K 73
Queen's Wlk., The SE1 . . . 1J 75
(Oxo Tower Wharf)
SE1 . . . 2E 76
(Tooley St.)
SE1 . . . 2G 75
(Waterloo Rd.)
Queensway W2 . . . 5G 63
Queen's Yd. WC1 . . . 2A 66
Queen Victoria Memorial
. . . 5K 73
Queen Victoria St. EC4 . . . 7K 67
Quenington Ct. SE15 . . . 6H 85
Quentin Ho. SE1 . . . 5J 75
(not continuous)
Quex M. NW6 . . . 2E 54
Quex Rd. NW6 . . . 2E 54
Quick St. N1 . . . 5A 60
Quick St. M. N1 . . . 5K 59
Quickswood NW3 . . . 1C 56
Quilp St. SE1 . . . 4B 76
(not continuous)
Quilter Ho. W10 . . . 6B 54
Quilter St. E2 . . . 6K 61
Quinton Ho. SW8 . . . 7D 82

Rabbit Row W8 . . . 2E 70
Raceway, The (Go-Kart Track)
. . . 3D 58
Rackstraw Ho. NW3 . . . 1D 56
Racton Rd. SW6 . . . 6D 78
RADA . . . 3B 66
Radcliffe Rd. SE1 . . . 6G 77
Radcot St. SE11 . . . 4J 83
Raddington Rd. W10 . . . 4A 62
Radlett Pl. NW8 . . . 3B 56
Radley Ho. NW1 . . . 1D 64
Radley M. W8 . . . 7E 70
Radnor M. W2 . . . 6A 64
Radnor Pl. W2 . . . 6B 64
Radnor Rd. NW6 . . . 3A 54
SE15 . . . 7K 85
Radnor St. EC1 . . . 7C 60
Radnor Ter. W14 . . . 1B 78
Radnor Wlk. SW3 . . . 4C 80
Radstock St. SW11 . . . 7B 80
(not continuous)
Radway Ho. W2 . . . 3D 62
Railway App. SE1 . . . 3E 76
Railway Arches E2 . . . 4H 61
(Geffrye St.)
E2 . . . 4H 61
(Laburnam St.)
Railway M. W11 . . . 5A 62
Railway St. N1 . . . 5E 58
Rainbow St. SE5 . . . 7F 85
Rainham Ho. NW1 . . . 3A 58
Rainsford St. W2 . . . 5B 64
Raleigh Ho. SW1 . . . 5B 82
Raleigh M. N1 . . . 3A 60
Raleigh St. N1 . . . 3A 60
Ralph Brook Ct. N1 . . . 6E 60
Ralph Ct. W2 . . . 5G 63
Ralston St. SW3 . . . 4D 80
Ramar Ho. E1 . . . 3K 69
Ramillies Pl. W1 . . . 6K 65
Ramillies St. W1 . . . 6K 65
Rampayne St. SW1 . . . 3B 82
Ramsay Ho. NW8 . . . 4B 56
Ramsay M. SW3 . . . 5B 80
Ramsey St. E2 . . . 1K 69
Randall Rd. SE11 . . . 3F 83
Randall Row SE11 . . . 2F 83
Randell's Rd. N1 . . . 2D 58
(not continuous)
Randolph Av. W9 . . . 5F 55
Randolph Cres. W9 . . . 2H 63
Randolph Gdns. NW6 . . . 5F 55
Randolph M. W9 . . . 2J 63
Randolph Rd. W9 . . . 2H 63
Randolph St. NW1 . . . 1A 58
Ranelagh Bri. W2 . . . 4G 63
Ranelagh Gro. SW1 . . . 3G 81
Ranelagh Ho. SW3 . . . 3D 80
Ranelagh Rd. SW1 . . . 4A 82
Rangoon St. EC3 . . . 6H 69
Rankine Ho. SE1 . . . 7B 76
Ransome's Dock Bus. Cen.
SW11 . . . 7C 80
Ranston St. NW1 . . . 3B 64
Raphael St. SW7 . . . 5D 72
Rapley Ho. E2 . . . 7K 61
Raquel Ct. SE1 . . . 4F 77
Rashleigh Ho. WC1 . . . 7D 58
Ratcliffe Ct. *SE1* . . . *5C 76*
(off Gt. Dover St.)
Rathbone Ho. NW6 . . . 3D 54
Rathbone Pl. W1 . . . 4B 66
Rathbone St. W1 . . . 4A 66
Ravensbourne Ho.
NW8 . . . 3B 64
Ravenscar NW1 . . . 3K 57
Ravenscroft St. E2 . . . 5J 61
Ravensdon St. SE11 . . . 4J 83
Ravenstone SE17 . . . 4G 85
Ravent Rd. SE11 . . . 2G 83
Raven Wharf SE1 . . . 4H 77
Ravey St. EC2 . . . 1F 69
Rawlings St. SW3 . . . 1D 80
Rawreth Wlk. N1 . . . 2C 60
Rawstorne Pl. EC1 . . . 6K 59
Rawstorne St. EC1 . . . 6K 59
(not continuous)
Rayburne Ct. W14 . . . 6A 70
Ray Gunter Ho. SE17 . . . 4A 84
Ray Ho. N1 . . . 3E 60
Raymond Bldgs. WC1 . . . 3G 67
Raymond Revuebar . . . 7B 66
Rayne Ho. W9 . . . 1F 63
Raynham W2 . . . 5B 64
Raynor Pl. N1 . . . 2C 60
Ray St. EC1 . . . 2J 67
Ray St. Bri. EC1 . . . 2J 67
Reachview Cl. NW1 . . . 1A 58
Read Ho. SE11 . . . 5H 83
Reading Ho. W2 . . . 6H 63
Reapers Cl. NW1 . . . 2B 58
Rector St. N1 . . . 3B 60
Red Anchor Cl. SW3 . . . 6A 80
Redan Pl. W2 . . . 6F 63
Redburn St. SW3 . . . 5D 80
Redcar St. SE5 . . . 7B 84
Redchurch St. E2 . . . 1H 69
Redcliffe Cl. SW5 . . . 4F 79
Redcliffe Gdns. SW10 . . . 4G 79
Redcliffe M. SW10 . . . 4G 79
Redcliffe Pl. SW10 . . . 6H 79
Redcliffe Rd. SW10 . . . 4H 79
Redcliffe Sq. SW10 . . . 4G 79
Redcliffe St. SW10 . . . 5G 79
Red Cow La. EC1 . . . 1B 68
Redcross Way SE1 . . . 4C 76
Reddins Rd. SE15 . . . 6K 85
Rede Pl. W2 . . . 6E 62
Redesdale St. SW3 . . . 5C 80
Redfield La. SW5 . . . 1E 78
Redfield M. SW5 . . . 1E 78
Redford Ho. W10 . . . 6B 54
Redford Wlk. N1 . . . 2A 60
Redgrave Ter. E2 . . . 7K 61
Redhill St. NW1 . . . 5J 57
Redington Ho. N1 . . . 4G 59
Red Lion Cl. SE17 . . . 5D 84
Red Lion Ct. EC4 . . . 6J 67
SE1 . . . 2C 76
Red Lion Row SE17 . . . 5C 84
Red Lion Sq. WC1 . . . 4F 67
Red Lion St. WC1 . . . 3F 67
Red Lion Yd. W1 . . . 2H 73
Redman Ho. EC1 . . . 3H 67
SE1 . . . 5C 76
Redmead La. E1 . . . 3K 77
Redmond Ho. N1 . . . 3G 59
Red Pl. W1 . . . 7F 65
Redvers St. N1 . . . 6G 61
Redwing Ct. SE1 . . . 5C 76
Redwood Ct. NW6 . . . 1A 54
Redwood Mans. W8 . . . 7F 71
Reece M. SW7 . . . 1K 79
Reedworth St. SE11 . . . 2J 83
Rees St. N1 . . . 3C 60
Reeves Ho. SE1 . . . 5H 75
Reeves M. W1 . . . 1F 73
Reflection Ho. E2 . . . 1K 69
Regal Ct. NW6 . . . 5C 54
Regal La. NW1 . . . 3G 57
Regan Way N1 . . . 4F 61
Regency Ho. NW1 . . . 1J 65
Regency Lodge NW3 . . . 1K 55
Regency Pde. NW3 . . . 1K 55
Regency Pl. SW1 . . . 1C 82
Regency St. SW1 . . . 1C 82
Regency Ter. SW7 . . . 3K 79
Regent Ct. NW8 . . . 7B 56
Regent Ho. W14 . . . 1A 78
Regent Pl. W1 . . . 7A 66
Regent's Bri. Gdns. SW8 . . . 7E 82
Regents College . . . 1E 64
Regents Ct. E8 . . . 3J 61
Regents M. NW8 . . . 4J 55
REGENT'S PARK . . . 7J 57
Regent's Pk. . . . 5E 56
Regent's Pk. Barracks . . . 5H 57
Regents Pk. Est. NW1 . . . 6K 57
Regent's Pk. Gdns. M.
NW1 . . . 2E 56
Regents Pk. Golf &
Tennis School . . . 4D 56
Regent's Pk. Ho. NW8 . . . 7C 56
Regent's Pk. Open Air Theatre
. . . 7F 57
Regent's Pk. Rd. NW1 . . . 1E 56
(not continuous)
Regent's Pk. Ter. NW1 . . . 2H 57
Regents Plaza NW6 . . . 5J 55
Regent Sq. WC1 . . . 7E 58
Regent's Row E8 . . . 3K 61
Regent St. SW1 . . . 1B 74
W1 . . . 5J 65
Regents Wharf N1 . . . 4F 59
Regis Ct. NW1 . . . 3D 64
Regis Ho. W1 . . . 3G 65
Regnart Bldgs. NW1 . . . 1A 66
Reliance Sq. EC2 . . . 1G 69
Relton M. SW7 . . . 6C 72
Rembrandt Cl. SW1 . . . 3F 81
Remington St. N1 . . . 5A 60
Remnant St. WC2 . . . 5F 67
Remsted Ho. NW6 . . . 3F 55
Remus Bldg., The EC1 . . . 7J 59
Renfrew Rd. SE11 . . . 1K 83
Rennie Ct. SE1 . . . 2K 75
Rennie Ho. SE1 . . . 7B 76
Rennie St. SE1 . . . 2K 75
(not continuous)
Renoir Cinema . . . 2E 66
Rephidim St. SE1 . . . 7F 77
Repton Ho. SW1 . . . 2A 82
Reston Pl. SW7 . . . 5H 71
Restormel Ho. SE11 . . . 2J 83
Retford St. N1 . . . 5G 61
Reverdy Rd. SE1 . . . 2K 85
Rewell St. SW6 . . . 7H 79
Rex Pl. W1 . . . 1G 73
Reynolds Ho. NW8 . . . 5A 56
SW1 . . . 2C 82
Rheidol M. N1 . . . 4B 60
Rheidol Ter. N1 . . . 4A 60
Rhoda St. E2 . . . 1J 69
Rhodes Ho. N1 . . . 6D 60
Ribblesdale Ho. NW6 . . . 2E 54
Riceyman Ho. WC1 . . . 7H 59
Richardson Cl. E8 . . . 2H 61
Richardson's M. W1 . . . 2K 65
Richard's Pl. SW3 . . . 1C 80
Richbell Pl. WC1 . . . 3F 67
Richborne Ter. SW8 . . . 7F 83
Richbourne Ct. W1 . . . 5C 64
Rich Ind. Est. SE1 . . . 7G 77
Rich La. SW5 . . . 4F 79
Richmond American University
in London, The . . . 6G 71
Richmond Av. N1 . . . 2G 59
Richmond Bldgs. W1 . . . 6B 66
Richmond College
American Institute University
in London, The . . . 5G 71
Richmond Cotts. W14 . . . 1A 78
Richmond Ct. SW1 . . . 5E 72
Richmond Cres. N1 . . . 2G 59
Richmond Gro. N1 . . . 1K 59
(not continuous)
Richmond Ho. NW1 . . . 5J 57
SE17 . . . 3D 84
Richmond M. W1 . . . 6B 66
Richmond Rd. E8 . . . 1H 61
Richmond Ter. SW1 . . . 4D 74
Rickett St. SW6 . . . 5E 78
Riddell Ct. SE5 . . . 3H 85
Ridgewell Cl. N1 . . . 2C 60
Ridgmount Gdns. WC1 . . . 2B 66
Ridgmount Pl. WC1 . . . 3B 66
Ridgmount St. WC1 . . . 3B 66
Riding Ho. St. W1 . . . 4J 65
Rifle Ct. SE11 . . . 5J 83
Riley Ho. SW10 . . . 7K 79
Riley Rd. SE1 . . . 6G 77
Riley St. SW10 . . . 6K 79
Rill Ho. SE5 . . . 7E 84
Ring, The W2 . . . 1A 72
(not continuous)
Ringsfield Ho. SE17 . . . 4C 84
Ripley Ho. SW1 . . . 5K 81
Ripplevale Gro. N1 . . . 1G 59
Risborough SE17 . . . 1B 84
Risborough Ho. NW8 . . . 1C 64
Risborough St. SE1 . . . 4A 76
Risinghill St. N1 . . . 4H 59
Rising Sun Ct. EC1 . . . 4A 68
Rita Rd. SW8 . . . 6E 82
Ritchie St. N1 . . . 4J 59
Ritson Ho. N1 . . . 3F 59
Riven Ct. W2 . . . 6G 63
River Ct. SE1 . . . 1K 75
Riverfleet WC1 . . . 6E 58
River Pl. N1 . . . 1B 60
Riverside WC1 . . . 6E 58
Riverside Apartments
SE1 . . . 3H 77
Riverside Ct. SW8 . . . 5C 82
Riverside Ho. N1 . . . 1B 60
Riverside Workshops
SE1 . . . 2C 76
River St. EC1 . . . 6H 59
River Ter. WC2 . . . 1F 75
Riverton Cl. W9 . . . 7C 54
River Vw. Hgts. SE16 . . . 4K 77
Rivington Ho. SE1 . . . 3J 85
Rivington Pl. EC2 . . . 7G 61
Rivington St. EC2 . . . 7F 61
Rivington Wlk. E8 . . . 2K 61
Robert Adam St. W1 . . . 5F 65
Roberta St. E2 . . . 6K 61
Robert Bell Ho. SE16 . . . 1K 85
Robert Cl. W9 . . . 2J 63
Robert Dashwood Way
SE17 . . . 2B 84
Robert Gentry Ho. W14 . . . 4A 78
Robert Jones Ho. SE16 . . . 1K 85
Roberts Ct. N1 . . . 3A 60
Roberts M. SW1 . . . 7F 73
Roberts Pl. EC1 . . . 1J 67
Robert St. NW1 . . . 7J 57
WC2 . . . 1E 74
Robin Ct. SE16 . . . 1K 85
Robin Hood Ct. *EC4* . . . *5J 67*
(off Shoe La.)

Robin Ho.—Sebright Ho.

Robin Ho. NW8 5B 56
Robin Howard Dance Theatre 7C 58
Robinson Ct. N1 2A 60
Robinson St. SW3 5D 80
Roby Ho. EC1 1B 68
Rochelle St. E2 7H 61
(not continuous)
Rochemont Wlk. E8 3K 61
Rochester Ct. NW1 1A 58
Rochester Ho. SE1 5D 76
Rochester Pl. NW1 1K 57
Rochester Row SW1 1A 82
Rochester Sq. NW1 1A 58
Rochester St. SW1 7B 74
Rochester Wlk. SE1 3D 76
Rockingham St. SE1 7B 76
Rocliffe St. N1 5A 60
Rocque Ho. SW6 7B 78
Rodborough Ct. W9 2D 62
Rodin Ct. N1 3K 59
Roding Ho. N1 3H 59
Roding M. E1 2K 77
Rodmarton St. W1 4E 64
Rodmell WC1 7E 58
Rodney Ct. W9 1J 63
Rodney Ho. N1 5G 59
SW1 4A 82
W11 7D 62
Rodney Pl. SE17 1C 84
Rodney Rd. SE17 1C 84
(not continuous)
Rodney St. N1 4G 59
Roebuck Ho. SW1 6K 73
Rogers Ho. SW1 1C 82
Roger St. WC1 2G 67
Rohere Ho. EC1 6B 60
Roland Gdns. SW7 3J 79
Roland Ho. SW7 3J 79
Roland Way SE17 4E 84
SW7 3J 79
Rolls Bldgs. EC4 5H 67
Rolls Pas. EC4 5H 67
Rolls Rd. SE1 3J 85
Roman Ho. EC2 4C 68
Romer Ho. W10 6A 54
Romilly St. W1 7C 66
Romney M. W1 3F 65
Romney St. SW1 7C 74
Rood La. EC3 7F 69
Roof Ter. Apartments, The
EC1 *2A 68*
(off Gt. Sutton St.)
Roosevelt Memorial 7G 65
Ropemaker St. EC2 3D 68
Roper La. SE1 5G 77
Ropers Orchard SW3 6B 80
Ropewalk M. E8 1K 61
Ropley St. E2 5K 61
Rosalind Ho. N1 5G 61
Rosaline Rd. SW6 7A 78
Rosaline Ter. SW6 7A 78
Rosary Gdns. SW7 2H 79
Rosaville Rd. SW6 7B 78
Roscoe St. EC1 2C 68
(not continuous)
Roscoe St. Est. EC1 2C 68
Rose All. EC2 4G 69
SE1 2C 76
Rose & Crown Ct. EC2 5B 68
Rose & Crown Yd. SW1 3A 74
Rosebank Wlk. NW1 1C 58
Rosebery Av. EC1 2H 67
Rosebery Ct. EC1 1H 67
Rosebery Sq. EC1 2H 67
Rose Ct. E1 4H 69
N1 3K 59
Rosehart M. W11 6D 62
Rosemary Branch Theatre 2D 60
Rosemary Ho. N1 3E 60
Rosemary Rd. SE15 7J 85
Rosemary St. N1 2D 60
Rosemoor St. SW3 2D 80
Rose Sq. SW7 2A 80
Rose St. EC4 5A 68
WC2 7D 66
(not continuous)
Rosetta Cl. SW8 7E 82
Rosewood Ho. SW8 5F 83
Rosmead Rd. W11 7A 62
Rosoman Pl. EC1 1J 67
Rosoman St. EC1 7J 59
Rosscourt Mans. SW1 6J 73
Rossendale Way NW1 1A 58
Rossetti Ct. WC1 3B 66
Rossetti Ho. SW1 2C 82
Rossetti M. NW8 3A 56
Rossmore Cl. NW1 2C 64
Rossmore Ct. NW1 1D 64
Rossmore Rd. NW1 2C 64
Rotary St. SE1 6K 75
Rothay NW1 6J 57
Rotherfield Ct. *N1* *1D 60*
(off Rotherfield St., not continuous)
Rotherfield St. N1 1B 60
Rotherham Wlk. SE1 3K 75
Rotherwick Ho. E1 1K 77
Rothery St. N1 2A 60
Rothesay Ct. SE11 6H 83
Rothley Ct. NW8 1K 63
Rothsay St. SE1 6F 77
Rothwell St. NW1 2E 56
Rotten Row SW1 4D 72
SW7 4A 72
Rouel Rd. SE16 6K 77
(Dockley Rd.)
SE16 1K 85
(Southwark Pk. Rd.)
Roundhouse, The
Chalk Farm 1G 57
Roupell St. SE1 3J 75
Rousden St. NW1 1K 57
Rover Ho. N1 3G 61
Rowallan Rd. SW6 7A 78
Rowan Ct. SE15 7H 85
Rowan Lodge W8 7F 71
Rowcross St. SE1 3H 85
Rowington Cl. W2 3F 63
Rowland Hill Ho. SE1 4K 75
Rowley Way NW8 2G 55
Roxby Pl. SW6 5E 78
Royal Academy of Arts
(Burlington House) 1K 73
Royal Academy of Music Mus.
2G 65
Royal Air Force Memorial
3E 74
Royal Albert Hall 5K 71
Royal Arc. W1 1K 73
Royal Av. SW3 3D 80
Royal Av. Ho. SW3 3D 80
Royal Belgrave Ho. SW1 2J 81
Royal Ceremonial Dress
Collection, The 3F 71
Royal College of Art 5J 71
Royal College of Music 6K 71
Royal College of Obstetricians &
Gynaecologists 1D 64
Royal College of Physicians
1J 65
Royal College of Surgeons
5G 67
Royal Coll. St. NW1 1K 57
Royal Ct. EC3 6E 68
Royal Courts of Justice 6G 67
Royal Court Theatre 2F 81
Royal Cres. W11 3A 70
Royal Exchange 6E 68
Royal Exchange Av. EC3 6E 68
Royal Exchange Bldgs.
EC3 6E 68
Royal Festival Hall 3G 75
Royal Fusiliers Mus. *1H 77*
(in Tower of London, The)
Royal Geographical Society
5K 71
(off Kensington Gore)
Royal Hospital Chelsea Mus.
4F 81
Royal Hospital Rd. SW3 6D 80
Royal Mews, The 6J 73
Royal M. SW1 6J 73
Royal Mint Ct. EC3 1J 77
Royal Mint Pl. E1 7J 69
Royal Mint St. E1 7J 69
Royal National Theatre 2G 75
Royal Oak Ct. N1 6F 61
Royal Oak Yd. SE1 5F 77
Royal Opera Arc. SW1 2B 74
Royal Opera House 6E 66
Royal Pde. SW6 7A 78
Royal Rd. SE17 5K 83
Royal St. SE1 6G 75
Royal Twr. Lodge E1 1K 77
Royalty M. W1 6B 66
Royalty Studios W11 6A 62
Royal Westminster Lodge
SW1 1B 82
Royle Bldg. N1 4B 60
Rozel Ct. N1 2F 61
Rudbeck Ho. SE15 7K 85
Rudge Ho. SE16 6K 77
Rudgwick Ter. NW8 3C 56
Rudolf Pl. SW8 6E 82
Rudolph Rd. NW6 5E 54
Rufford St. N1 2E 58
Rufus Ho. SE1 6H 77
Rufus St. N1 7F 61
Rugby Mans. W14 1A 78
Rugby St. WC1 2F 67
Rumball Ho. SE5 7F 85
Rumbold Rd. SW6 7G 79
Rumford Ho. SE1 7B 76
Runacres Ct. SE17 4B 84
Runcorn Pl. W11 7A 62
Rupert Ct. W1 7B 66
Rupert Ho. SE11 2J 83
Rupert Rd. NW6 5C 54
Rupert St. W1 7B 66
Rushmore Ho. W14 7A 70
Rushton St. N1 4E 60
Rushworth St. SE1 4A 76
Ruskin Ho. SW1 2C 82
Ruskin Mans. W14 6A 78
Russell Ct. SW1 3A 74
WC1 2D 66
Russell Gdns. W14 6A 70
Russell Gdns. M. W14 5A 70
Russell Ho. SW1 3K 81
Russell Lodge SE1 6D 76
Russell Rd. W14 6A 70
Russell Sq. WC1 2D 66
Russell St. WC2 7E 66
Russia Ct. EC2 6C 68
Russia Row EC2 6C 68
Ruston M. W11 6A 62
Rust Sq. SE5 7D 84
Rutherford St. SW1 1B 82
Rutland Ct. SW7 5C 72
Rutland Gdns. SW7 5C 72
Rutland Gdns. M. SW7 5C 72
Rutland Ga. SW7 5C 72
Rutland Ga. M. SW7 5B 72
Rutland Ho. W8 7F 71
Rutland M. NW8 3G 55
Rutland M. E. SW7 6C 72
Rutland M. Sth. SW7 6B 72
Rutland M. W. SW7 6B 72
Rutland Pl. EC1 3A 68
Rutland St. SW7 6C 72
Rutley Cl. SE17 5K 83
Rydal Water NW1 7K 57
Ryder Ct. SW1 2A 74
Ryder's Ter. NW8 4H 55
Ryder St. SW1 2A 74
Ryder Yd. SW1 2A 74
Rydon St. N1 2C 60
Rye Ho. SW1 3H 81
Rylston Rd. SW6 6B 78
Rysbrack St. SW3 6D 72

Saatchi Collection 4F 75
Sable St. N1 1A 60
Sackville St. W1 1A 74
Saddle Yd. W1 2H 73
Sadler Ho. EC1 6K 59
Sadler's Wells Theatre 6J 59
Saffron Hill EC1 3J 67
Saffron St. EC1 3J 67
Saffron Wharf SE1 4J 77
Sage Way WC1 7F 59
Sail St. SE11 1G 83
St Agnes Pl. SE11 6J 83
St Agnes Well EC1 1E 68
St Albans Ct. EC2 5C 68
St Alban's Gro. W8 6G 71
St Albans Mans. W8 6G 71
St Alban's Pl. N1 3K 59
St Alban's St. SW1 1B 74
(not continuous)
St Albans Studios W8 6G 71
St Alphage Gdn. EC2 4C 68
St Alphage Highwalk
EC2 4C 68
St Alphage Ho. EC2 4D 68
St Andrews Chambers
W1 4A 66
St Andrew's Hill EC4 7A 68
(not continuous)
St Andrews Mans. W1 4F 65
W14 5A 78
St Andrew's Pl. NW1 1J 65
St Andrew's Rd. W14 5A 78
St Andrew St. EC4 4J 67
St Andrew's Wharf SE1 4J 77
St Anne's Ct. NW6 3A 54
W1 6B 66
St Anne's Flats NW1 6B 58
St Ann's Ho. WC1 7H 59
St Ann's La. SW1 7C 74
St Ann's St. SW1 6C 74
St Ann's Ter. NW8 4A 56
St Anselm's Pl. W1 7H 65
St Anthony's Cl. E1 2K 77
St Anthony's Flats NW1 5B 58
St Aubins Ct. N1 2E 60
St Augustine's Ho. NW1 6B 58
St Augustine's Mans.
SW1 2A 82
St Augustine's Rd. NW1 1B 58
St Barnabas St. SW1 3G 81
St Bartholomew's Hospital Mus.
4A 68
St Benet's Pl. EC3 7E 68
St Botolph Row EC3 6H 69
St Botolph St. EC3 6H 69
St Brelades Ct. N1 2E 60
St Bride's Av. EC4 6K 67
St Bride's Crypt Mus. 6K 67
St Bride's Pas. EC4 6K 67
St Bride St. EC4 5K 67
St Catherines M. SW3 1D 80
St Chad's Pl. WC1 6E 58
St Chad's St. WC1 6E 58
(not continuous)
St Charles Pl. W10 4A 62
St Charles Sq. W10 4A 62
St Christopher's Ho.
NW1 5A 58
St Christopher's Pl. W1 5G 65
St Clare St. EC3 6H 69
St Clement's Ct. EC4 7E 68
St Clements Ho. *E1* *4H 69*
(off Leyden St.)
St Clement's La. WC2 6G 67
St Cross St. EC1 3J 67
St Dunstan's All. EC3 1F 77
St Dunstan's Ct. EC4 6J 67
St Dunstans Hill EC3 1F 77
St Dunstan's La. EC3 1F 77
St Edmund's Cl. NW8 3D 56
St Edmund's Ct. NW8 3D 56
St Edmund's Ter. NW8 3C 56
St Ermin's Hill SW1 6B 74
St Ervan's Rd. W10 3A 62
St Eugene Ct. NW6 3A 54
St Francis' Ho. NW1 5B 58
St George's Bldgs. SE1 7K 75
St George's Cathedral 6J 57
St George's Cir. SE1 6K 75
St Georges Ct. EC4 5K 67
SW1 3K 81
St George's Dr. SW1 2J 81
St George's Flds. W2 6C 64
St George's Ho. NW1 5B 58
St George's La. EC3 7E 68
St George's Mans. SW1 3C 82
St George's M. NW1 1E 56
SE1 6J 75
St George's RC Cathedral
6J 75
St George's Rd. SE1 6J 75
St George's Sq. SW1 3B 82
St George's Sq. M. SW1 4B 82
St George's Ter. NW1 2E 56
SE15 7J 85
St George St. W1 6J 65
St George's Way SE15 6F 85
St George's Wharf SE1 4J 77
St George Wharf SW8 5D 82
St Giles Cir. W1 5C 66
St Giles Ct. WC2 5D 66
St Giles High St. WC2 5C 66
St Giles Pas. WC2 6C 66
St Giles Ter. EC2 4C 68
St Helena Ho. WC1 7H 59
St Helena St. WC1 7H 59
St Helen's Pl. EC3 5F 69
St Helier Ct. N1 2F 61
St James App. EC2 2F 69
St James' Ct. SW1 6A 74
St James Residences
W1 7B 66
ST JAMES'S 3A 74
St James's SW1 2A 74
St James's Chambers
SW1 2A 74
St James's Cl. NW8 3D 56
St James's Gdns. W11 2A 70
(not continuous)
St James's Mkt. SW1 1B 74
St James's Palace 4A 74
St James's Pk. 4B 74
St James's Pas. EC3 6G 69
St James's Pl. SW1 3K 73
St James's Rd. SE1 5K 85
SE16 6K 77
St James's Sq. SW1 2A 74
St James's St. SW1 2K 73
St James's Ter. NW8 4D 56
St James's Ter. M. NW8 3D 56
St James's Wlk. EC1 1K 67
St John's Cl. SW6 7D 78
St John's Est. N1 5E 60
SE1 4H 77
St John's Gdns. W11 1A 70
St John's Gate 2K 67
St Johns Ho. SE17 5D 84
St John's La. EC1 2K 67
St John's M. W11 6D 62
St John's Path EC1 2K 67
St John's Pl. EC1 2K 67
St John's Sq. EC1 2K 67
St John St. EC1 5J 59
St John's Vs. W8 7G 71
ST JOHN'S WOOD 5A 56
St John's Wood Ct. NW8 7A 56
St John's Wood High St.
NW8 4A 56
St John's Wood Pk. NW8 3K 55
St John's Wood Rd. NW8 1K 63
St John's Wood Ter. NW8 4A 56
St Joseph's Cl. W10 4A 62
St Joseph's Cotts. SW3 2D 80
St Joseph's Flats NW1 6B 58
St Julian's Rd. NW6 1C 54
St Katharine Docks 1J 77
St Katharine's Pct. NW1 4H 57
St Katharine's Way E1 2J 77
(not continuous)
St Katherine's Row EC3 7G 69
St Lawrence Ct. N1 2E 60
St Lawrence Ho. SE1 6G 77
St Lawrence Ter. W10 3A 62
St Leonard M. N1 4F 61
St Leonard's Ct. N1 6E 60
St Leonard's Ter. SW3 4D 80
St Loo Av. SW3 5C 80
ST LUKE'S 1C 68
St Luke's Cl. EC1 1C 68
St Luke's Est. EC1 7D 60
St Luke's M. W11 5B 62
St Luke's Rd. W11 4C 62
St Luke's St. SW3 3B 80
St Luke's Yd. W9 5B 54
(not continuous)
St Margarets Cl. EC2 5D 68
St Margarets Ct. SE1 3D 76
St Margaret's La. W8 7F 71
St Margaret St. SW1 5D 74
St Marks Ct. NW8 5J 55
St Mark's Cres. NW1 2G 57
St Mark's Gro. SW10 7G 79
St Marks Ho. SE17 5D 84
St Mark's Pl. W11 6A 62
St Mark's Rd. W10 6A 62
St Mark's Sq. NW1 3F 57
St Mark St. E1 6J 69
St Martin-in-the-Fields Church
1D 74
St Martin's Almshouses
NW1 2K 57
St Martin's Cl. NW1 2K 57
St Martins Ct. EC4 5B 68
N1 2G 61
WC2 7D 66
St Martin's La. WC2 7D 66
St Martin's le-Grand EC1 5B 68
St Martin's Pl. WC2 1D 74
St Martin's St. WC2 1C 74
(not continuous)
St Martin's Theatre 7D 66
St Mary Abbot's Ct. W14 7B 70
St Mary Abbot's Pl. W8 7C 70
St Mary Abbot's Ter.
W14 7B 70
St Mary at Hill EC3 1F 77
St Mary Axe EC3 6F 69
St Mary Graces Ct. E1 7J 69
St Mary le-Park Ct.
SW11 7C 80
St Mary Newington Cl.
SE17 3G 85
St Mary's Flats NW1 6B 58
St Mary's Gdns. SE11 1J 83
St Mary's Ga. W8 7F 71
St Mary's Ho. N1 2A 60
St Mary's Mans. W2 3K 63
St Mary's M. NW6 1F 55
St Mary's Path *E1* *5K 69*
(off Adler St.)
N1 2K 59
St Mary's Pl. W8 7F 71
St Mary's Sq. W2 3K 63
St Mary's Ter. W2 3J 63
St Mary's Twr. EC1 2C 68
St Mary's Wlk. SE11 1J 83
St Matthews Ct. SE1 7B 76
St Matthews Ho. SE17 5D 84
St Matthew's Lodge
NW1 4A 58
St Matthew's Row E2 7K 61
St Matthew St. SW1 7B 74
St Michael's All. EC3 6E 68
St Michael's Ct. SE1 5C 76
St Michael's Flats NW1 5B 58
St Michael's Gdns. W10 4A 62
St Michaels M. SW1 2F 81
St Michael's St. W2 5A 64
St Mildred's Ct. EC2 6D 68
St Nicholas' Flats NW1 5B 58
St Olaf Ho. SE1 2E 76
St Olaf's Rd. SW6 7A 78
St Olaf Stairs SE1 2E 76
St Olave's Ct. EC2 6D 68
St Olave's Est. SE1 4G 77
St Olave's Gdns. SE11 1H 83
St Olave's Mans. SE11 1H 83
St Olave's Ter. SE1 4G 77
St Oswald's Pl. SE11 3F 83
St Oswalds Studios SW6 5D 78
St Oswulf St. SW1 2C 82
St Owen Ho. SE1 6G 77
ST PANCRAS 1F 67
St Pancras Commercial Cen.
NW1 2A 58
St Pancras Way NW1 1K 57
St Paul's All. *EC4* *6A 68*
(off St Paul's Chyd.)
St Paul's Bldgs. *EC1* *1A 68*
(off Dallington St.)
St Paul's Cathedral 6B 68
St Paul's Chyd. EC4 6A 68
(not continuous)
St Paul's Cres. NW1 1C 58
(not continuous)
St Paul's M. NW1 1C 58
St Paul's Studios W14 3A 78
St Pauls Ter. SE17 5A 84
St Paul St. N1 3B 60
(not continuous)
St Pauls Vw. Apartments
EC1 7H 59
St Peter's All. EC3 6E 68
St Peter's Av. E2 5K 61
St Petersburgh M. W2 7F 63
St Petersburgh Pl. W2 7F 63
St Peter's Chu. Ct. N1 4A 60
St Peter's Cl. E2 5K 61
St Peters Ho. SE17 5D 84
WC1 7E 58
St Peters Pl. W9 2F 63
St Peter's Sq. E2 5K 61
St Peter's St. N1 3A 60
St Peter's St. M. N1 4A 60
St Peter's Way N1 1G 61
St Philip Ho. WC1 7H 59
St Philip's Way N1 2C 60
St Richard's Ho. NW1 6B 58
St Saviour's Est. SE1 6H 77
St Saviour's Wharf *SE1* *4J 77*
(off Shad Thames)
SE1 4J 77
(Mill St.)
St Stephen's Cl. NW8 3C 56
St Stephen's Cres. W2 5E 62
St Stephen's Gdns. W2 5D 62
(not continuous)
St Stephens Ho. SE17 5D 84
St Stephens M. W2 4E 62
St Stephen's Row EC4 6D 68
St Stephen's Ter. SW8 7F 83
St Stephen's Wlk. SW7 1H 79
St Swithins La. EC4 7D 68
St Thomas Ct. NW1 1A 58
St Thomas St. SE1 3D 76
St Thomas's Way SW6 7B 78
St Vincent Ho. SE1 6H 77
St Vincent St. W1 4G 65
Salamanca Pl. SE1 2F 83
Salamanca Sq. SE1 2F 83
Salamanca St. SE1 2E 82
SE11 2F 83
Salem Rd. W2 7G 63
Sale Pl. W2 4B 64
Sale St. E2 1K 69
Salisbury Cl. SE17 2D 84
Salisbury Ct. EC4 6K 67
Salisbury Ho. EC2 4E 68
N1 2K 59
SW1 3C 82
SW9 7J 83
Salisbury M. SW6 7B 78
Salisbury Pas. SW6 7B 78
Salisbury Pavement
SW6 7B 78
Salisbury Pl. W1 3E 64
Salisbury Sq. EC4 6J 67
Salisbury St. NW8 2A 64
Salters Ct. EC4 6C 68
Salter's Hall Ct. EC4 7D 68
Saltram Cres. W9 6C 54
Saltwood Gro. SE17 4D 84
Salusbury Rd. NW6 2A 54
Sambrook Ho. SE11 2H 83
Samford Ho. N1 3H 59
Samford St. NW8 2B 64
Sampson Ho. SE1 2K 75
Samuel Cl. E8 2J 61
Samuel Ho. E8 3H 61
Samuel Jones Ind. Est.
SE15 7G 85
Samuel Lewis Trust Dwellings
SW3 2B 80
SW6 7E 78
W14 1B 78
Samuel Richardson Ho.
W14 2B 78
Samuel St. SE15 7H 85
Sancroft Ho. SE11 3G 83
Sancroft St. SE11 3G 83
Sanctuary, The SW1 6C 74
Sanctuary St. SE1 5C 76
Sandalwood Mans. W8 7F 71
Sandbourne NW8 3F 55
W11 5D 62
Sandby Ho. NW6 3D 54
Sandell St. SE1 4H 75
Sanderling Lodge E1 1J 77
Sanders Ho. WC1 6H 59
Sandfield WC1 7E 58
Sandford Row SE17 3D 84
Sandford St. SW6 7G 79
Sandhills, The SW10 5J 79
Sandland St. WC1 4G 67
Sandpiper Ct. *E1* *1K 77*
(off Thomas More St.)
Sandringham Ct. W1 6A 66
W9 7J 55
Sandringham Flats WC2 7C 66
Sandwich Ho. WC1 7D 58
Sandwich St. WC1 7D 58
Sandys Row E1 4G 69
Sans Wlk. EC1 1J 67
Santley Ho. SE1 5J 75
Saperton Wlk. SE11 1G 83
Sapperton Ct. EC1 1B 68
Sapphire Ct. E1 7K 69
Saracens Head Yd. EC3 6H 69
Sarah St. N1 6G 61
Sarah Swift Ho. SE1 4E 76
Sara La. Ct. N1 4G 61
Sardinia St. WC2 6F 67
Satchwell Rd. E2 7K 61
Satchwell St. E2 7K 61
Saul Ct. SE15 6H 85
Saunders St. SE11 1H 83
Savage Gdns. EC3 7G 69
(not continuous)
Savannah Cl. SE15 7H 85
Savile Row W1 7K 65
Savona Ho. SW8 7K 81
Savona St. SW8 7K 81
Savoy Bldgs. WC2 1F 75
Savoy Ct. WC2 1F 75
Savoy Hill WC2 1F 75
Savoy Pl. WC2 1E 74
Savoy Row WC2 7F 67
Savoy Steps WC2 1F 75
Savoy St. WC2 7F 67
Savoy Theatre 1E 74
Savoy Way WC2 1F 75
Sawyer St. SE1 4B 76
Saxon Ho. E1 4J 69
Scafell NW1 6K 57
Scala St. W1 3A 66
Scarborough St. E1 6J 69
Scarsdale Pl. W8 6F 71
Scarsdale Studios W8 7E 70
Scarsdale Vs. W8 7E 70
Scawfell St. E2 5J 61
Sceptre Ct. EC3 1J 77
Schafer Ho. NW1 1K 65
Schiller International University
3H 75
Schomberg Ho. SW1 1C 82
School App. E2 6G 61
School Ho. SE1 1F 85
Science Mus. 7K 71
Sclater St. E1 1H 69
Scoresby St. SE1 3K 75
Scorton Ho. N1 4G 61
SCOTCH HOUSE 5D 72
Scotland Pl. SW1 3D 74
Scotson Ho. SE11 2H 83
Scotswood St. EC1 1J 67
Scott Ellis Gdns. NW8 7K 55
Scott Ho. N1 2D 60
NW8 2B 64
Scott Lidgett Cres. SE16 5K 77
Scott's Sufferance Wharf
SE1 5J 77
Scott's Yd. EC4 7D 68
Scovell Cres. SE1 5B 76
Scovell Rd. SE1 5B 76
Screen on Baker Street (Cinema)
3E 64
Screen on the Green Cinema
3K 59
(off Upper St.)
Scriven Ct. E8 2J 61
Scriven St. E8 2J 61
Scrope Ho. EC1 3H 67
Scrutton St. EC2 2F 69
Seaford St. WC1 7E 58
Seaforth Pl. SW1 6A 74
Seagrave Lodge SW6 5E 78
Seagrave Rd. SW6 5E 78
Seal Ho. SE1 6E 76
Searles Rd. SE1 1E 84
Searson Ho. SE17 2A 84
Sears St. SE5 7D 84
Seaton Cl. SE11 3J 83
Sebastian Ho. N1 5F 61
Sebastian St. EC1 7A 60
Sebbon St. N1 1A 60
Sebright Ho. E2 4K 61

Talbot Sq.—Walbrook Ct.

Talbot Sq. W2 6A 64
Talbot Wlk. W11 6A 62
Talbot Yd. SE1 3D 76
Talgarth Mans. W14 3A 78
Talgarth Rd. W14 3A 78
Tallis St. EC4 7J 67
Tamar Ho. SE11 3J 83
Tamarind Ct. W8 7F 71
Tamarind Yd. E1 2K 77
Tamplin Ho. W10 6B 54
Tamworth St. SW6 5D 78
Tangmere WC1 7F 59
Tankerton Ho's. WC1 7E 58
(off Tankerton St.)
Tankerton St. WC1 7E 58
Tanner Ho. SE1 5G 77
Tanner St. SE1 5G 77
(not continuous)
Tanswell St. SE1 5H 75
Tapley Ho. SE1 5K 77
Taplow NW1 6J 57
Taplow SE17 3E 84
Taplow Ho. E2 7H 61
Taplow St. N1 5C 60
Tarns, The NW1 6K 57
Tarn St. SE1 7B 76
Tarranbrae NW6 1A 54
Tarrant Pl. W1 4D 64
Tarver Rd. SE17 4A 84
Tasso Rd. W6 5A 78
Tasso Yd. W6 6A 78
Tate Britain 2D 82
Tate Modern 2A 76
Tatham Pl. NW8 4A 56
Tatsfield Ho. SE1 6E 76
Tatum St. SE17 2E 84
Taunton Ho. W2 6H 63
Taunton M. NW1 2D 64
Taunton Pl. NW1 1D 64
Tavern Ct. SE1 7C 76
Taverners Cl. W11 3A 70
Tavistock Ct. WC1 1C 66
WC2 7E 66
(off Tavistock St.)
Tavistock Cres. W11 4B 62
(not continuous)
Tavistock Ho. WC1 1C 66
Tavistock M. W11 5B 62
Tavistock Pl. WC1 1D 66
Tavistock Rd. W11 5B 62
(not continuous)
Tavistock Sq. WC1 1C 66
Tavistock St. WC2 7E 66
(not continuous)
Taviton St. WC1 1B 66
Tavy Cl. SE11 3J 83
(not continuous)
Tay Bldgs. SE1 6F 77
Tayler Ct. NW8 2K 55
Tayport Cl. N1 1E 58
Teal Ct. E1 1K 77
Teale St. E2 4K 61
Tea Trade Wharf SE1 4J 77
Tedworth Gdns. SW3 4D 80
Tedworth Sq. SW3 4D 80
Telegraph St. EC2 5D 68
Telephone Pl. SW6 5C 78
Telfer Ho. EC1 7B 60
Telford Ho. SE1 6B 76
Telford Rd. W10 3A 62
Telfords Yd. E1 1K 77
Telford Ter. SW1 5K 81
Templar Ct. NW8 7K 55
Temple Av. EC4 7J 67
Temple Bar 6H 67
Temple Bar Gate 6A 68
Temple Chambers EC4 7J 67
Temple Ct. SW8 7D 82
Temple Gdns. EC4 7H 67
Temple La. EC4 6J 67
Temple of Mithras (remains)
6D 68
Temple Pl. WC2 7G 67
Templeton Pl. SW5 2E 78
Temple W. M. SE11 7K 75
Tempus Wharf SE16 4K 77
Tenby Ho. W2 6H 63
Tenby Mans. W1 3G 65
Tenison Ct. W1 7K 65
Tenison Way SE1 3G 75
Tenniel Cl. W2 7G 63
Tennis St. SE1 4D 76
Tennyson Ho. SE17 3C 84
Tennyson Mans. W14 5A 78
Tennyson Rd. NW6 2B 54
(not continuous)
Tenterden Ho. SE17 4F 85
Tenterden St. W1 6J 65
Tenter Ground E1 4H 69
Tenter Pas. E1 6J 69
Terling Wlk. N1 2B 60
Terminus Pl. SW1 7J 73
Terrace, The EC4 7H 67
NW6 2D 54
Terraces, The NW8 4K 55
Terrace Wlk. SW11 7D 80
Terretts Pl. N1 1K 59
Territorial Ho. SE11 2J 83
Tetbury Pl. N1 3K 59
Tetcott Rd. SW10 7H 79
(not continuous)
Thackeray Ct. SW3 3D 80
Thackeray Ho. WC1 1D 66
Thackeray St. W8 6G 71
Thamesbrook SW3 4B 80
Thames Ct. SE15 7H 85
Thames Exchange Bldg.
EC4 7C 68
Thames Ho. EC4 7C 68
SW1 1D 82
Thames Wlk. SW11 7B 80
Thanet Ho. WC1 7D 58
Thanet St. WC1 7D 58
Thavie's Inn EC1 5J 67
Thaxted Ct. N1 5D 60
Thaxton Rd. W14 5C 78
Thayer St. W1 4G 65
Theatre Mus. 7E 66
Theatro Technis 3A 58
Theberton St. N1 2J 59
Theed St. SE1 3H 75
Theobald's Rd. WC1 4F 67
Theobald St. SE1 7D 76
Theseus Wlk. N1 5A 60
Thessaly Ho. SW8 7K 81
Thessaly Rd. SW8 7K 81
(not continuous)
Thetford Ho. SE1 6H 77
Third Av. W10 6A 54
Thirleby Rd. SW1 7A 74
Thirlmere NW1 6J 57
Thistle Gro. SW10 3J 79
Thomas Darby Ct. W11 6A 62
Thomas Doyle St. SE1 6A 76
Thomas More Highwalk
EC2 4B 68
Thomas More Ho. EC2 4B 68
Thomas More Sq. E1 1K 77
Thomas More St. E1 1K 77
Thomas Neal's Shop. Mall
WC2 6D 66
Thomas Pl. W8 7F 71
Thompson's Av. SE5 7B 84
Thomson Ho. SE17 2F 85
SW1 4C 82
Thorburn Sq. SE1 2K 85
Thoresby St. N1 6C 60
Thornbury Ct. W11 7D 62
Thorncroft St. SW8 7D 82
Thorndike Cl. SW10 7H 79
Thorndike Ho. SW1 3B 82
Thorndike St. SW1 2B 82
Thorney Ct. W8 5H 71
Thorney Cres. SW11 7A 80
Thorney St. SW1 1D 82
Thorngate Rd. W9 1E 62
Thornhaugh M. WC1 2C 66
Thornhaugh St. WC1 2C 66
Thornhill Bri. Wharf N1 3F 59
Thornhill Cres. N1 1G 59
Thornhill Gro. N1 1G 59
Thornhill Ho's. N1 1H 59
Thornhill Rd. N1 1H 59
Thornhill Sq. N1 1G 59
Thornton Ho. SE17 2F 85
Thornton Pl. W1 3E 64
Thorold Ho. SE1 4B 76
Thorparch Rd. SW8 7C 82
Thorpe Cl. W10 5A 62
Thorpe Ho. N1 3G 59
Thrale St. SE1 3C 76
Thrasher Cl. E8 2H 61
Thrawl St. E1 4J 69
Threadneedle St. EC2 6D 68
Three Barrels Wlk.
EC4 1C 76
Three Colt Cnr. E2 2K 69
Three Cranes Wlk.
EC4 1C 76
Three Cups Yd. WC1 4G 67
Three Kings Yd. W1 7H 65
Three Oak La. SE1 4H 77
Three Quays EC3 1G 77
Three Quays Wlk. EC3 1G 77
Threshers Pl. W11 7A 62
Throgmorton Av. EC2 5E 68
(not continuous)
Throgmorton St. EC2 5E 68
Thrush St. SE17 3A 84
Thurland Rd. SE16 6K 77
Thurloe Cl. SW7 1B 80
Thurloe Ct. SW3 2B 80
Thurloe Pl. SW7 1A 80
Thurloe Pl. M. SW7 1A 80
Thurloe Sq. SW7 1A 80
Thurloe St. SW7 1A 80
Thurlow St. SE17 3E 84
(not continuous)
Thurlow Wlk. SE17 3F 85
(not continuous)
Thurnscoe NW1 3K 57
Thurso Ho. NW6 5F 55
Thurstan Dwellings
WC2 5E 66
Thurtle Rd. E2 3J 61
Tibberton Sq. N1 1B 60
Tiber Gdns. N1 3E 58
Tickford Ho. NW8 7B 56
Tideway Ind. Est.
SW8 6A 82
Tideway Wlk. SW8 6A 82
Tilbury Cl. SE15 7J 85
Tileyard Rd. N7 1D 58
Tilleard Ho. W10 6A 54
Tillet Way E2 6K 61
Tilloch St. N1 1F 59
Tilney Ct. EC1 1C 68
Tilney St. W1 2G 73
Tilson Cl. SE5 7F 85
Tilton St. SW6 6A 78
Timberland Cl. SE15 7K 85
Timber St. EC1 1B 68
Tintern Ho. NW1 5J 57
SW1 2H 81
Tinworth St. SE11 3E 82
Tisbury Ct. W1 7B 66
Tisdall Pl. SE17 2E 84
Titchborne Row W2 6B 64
Titchfield Rd. NW8 3D 56
Tite St. SW3 4D 80
Tiverton St. SE1 7B 76
Tobin Cl. NW3 1C 56
Tokenhouse Yd. EC2 5D 68
Tolchurch W11 5C 62
Tollbridge Cl. W10 1A 62
Tollgate Gdns. NW6 4F 55
Tollgate Ho. NW6 4F 55
Tolmers Sq. NW1 1A 66
(not continuous)
Tolpaide Ho. SE11 2H 83
Tolpuddle St. N1 4H 59
Tom Blau Gallery *4H 77*
(off Queen Elizabeth St.)
Tomkyns Ho. SE11 2H 83
Tomlinson Cl. E2 7J 61
Tompion Ho. EC1 1A 68
Tompion St. EC1 7A 60
(not continuous)
Tomson Ho. SE1 6H 77
Tom Williams Ho.
SW6 6B 78
Tonbridge Ho's. WC1 7D 58
Tonbridge St. WC1 6D 58
Tonbridge Wlk. WC1 6D 58
Toneborough NW8 3G 55
Took's Ct. EC4 5H 67
Tooley St. SE1 2E 76
Topham St. EC1 1H 67
Torbay Ct. NW1 1J 57
Torbay Mans. NW6 1B 54
Torbay Rd. NW6 1B 54
Torbay St. NW1 1J 57
Tor Ct. W8 4E 70
Tor Gdns. W8 4D 70
Tornay Ho. N1 4F 59
Torquay St. W2 4F 63
Torrens St. EC1 5K 59
Torridon Ho. NW6 5F 55
Torrington Pl. WC1 3B 66
Torrington Sq. WC1 2C 66
Tothill Ho. SW1 1C 82
Tothill St. SW1 5B 74
Tottenhall NW1 1G 57
Tottenham Ct. Rd. W1 2A 66
Tottenham M. W1 3A 66
Tottenham St. W1 4A 66
Toulmin St. SE1 5B 76
Toulon St. SE5 7B 84
Tourist Info. Cen.
City of London 6B 68
King's Cross 6E 58
Leicester Sq. 1C 74
Southwark 2C 76
Waterloo International
Terminal 4G 75
Tournay Rd. SW6 7C 78
Tovy Ho. SE1 4K 85
Tower 42 5F 69
Tower Bri. SE1 3H 77
Tower Bri. App. E1 2H 77
Tower Bridge Experience
3H 77
Tower Bri. Plaza SE1 3H 77
Tower Bri. Rd. SE1 7F 77
Tower Bri. Sq. SE1 4H 77
Tower Bri. Wharf E1 3K 77
Tower Ct. N1 1B 60
NW8 4C 56
WC2 6D 66
TOWER HILL 1H 77
Tower Hill EC3 1G 77
Tower Hill Ter. EC3 1G 77
Tower Ho. E1 4K 69
Tower Mill Rd. SE15 7F 85
(not continuous)
Tower of London, The 1H 77
Tower of London Vis.
Cen., The 1G 77
Tower Pl. EC3 1G 77
Tower Pl. E. *EC3 1G 77*
(off Lwr. Thames St.)
Tower Pl. W. *EC3 1G 77*
(off Lwr. Thames St.)
Tower Royal EC4 7D 68
Tower St. WC2 6C 66
Townley St. SE17 3D 84
(not continuous)
Townsend St. SE17 2E 84
Townshend Ct. NW8 4C 56
Townshend Est. NW8 4B 56
Townshend Rd. NW8 3B 56
(not continuous)
Toynbee St. E1 4H 69
Tradescant Rd. SW8 7E 82
Tradewinds Ct. E1 2K 77
Trafalgar Av. SE15 4J 85
Trafalgar Chambers
SW3 3A 80
Trafalgar Gdns. W8 6G 71
Trafalgar Ho. SE17 3C 84
Trafalgar Point N1 1E 60
Trafalgar Square 2C 74
Trafalgar Sq. WC2 2C 74
Trafalgar St. SE17 3D 84
Trafalgar Studios 2D 74
Trafford Ho. N1 5E 60
Traitors' Gate 2H 77
Transept St. NW1 4C 64
Tranton Rd. SE16 6K 77
Treasury Pas. SW1 4D 74
Treaty St. N1 3F 59
Trebeck St. W1 2H 73
Trebovir Rd. SW5 3E 78
Trederwen Rd. E8 2K 61
Tregunter Rd. SW10 5G 79
Trelawney Ho. SE1 4B 76
Trellick Twr. W10 2B 62
Trematon Ho. SE11 3J 83
Trenchold St. SW8 6D 82
Tresco Ho. SE11 3H 83
Tresham Cres. NW8 1B 64
Tressell Cl. N1 1A 60
Tress Pl. SE1 2K 75
Trevanion Rd. W14 3A 78
Trevelyan Ho. SE17 7A 84
Treveris St. SE1 3A 76
Trevor Pl. SW7 5C 72
Trevor Sq. SW7 6C 72
Trevor St. SW7 5C 72
Trevor Wlk. SW7 5C 72
(not continuous)
Trevose Ho. SE11 3G 83
Triangle, The EC1 1A 68
Tricycle Cinema *1C 54*
(in Tricycle Theatre)
Tricycle Theatre *1C 54*
(off Kilburn High Rd.)
Trident Pl. SW3 5A 80
Trig La. EC4 7B 68
Trigon Rd. SW8 7G 83
Trimdon NW1 3K 57
Trinity Chu. Sq. SE1 5C 76
Trinity Ct. N1 2F 61
SE1 6C 76
W2 5H 63
WC1 1G 67
Trinity Ho. SE1 6C 76
Trinity Pl. EC3 1H 77
Trinity Sq. EC3 1G 77
Trinity St. SE1 5C 76
(not continuous)
Trinity Twr. E1 1K 77
Trio Pl. SE1 5C 76
Triton Sq. NW1 1K 65
Trocadero Cen. 1B 74
Trocette Mans. SE1 6F 77
Trojan Ct. NW6 1A 54
Trothy Rd. SE1 1K 85
Troutbeck NW1 7J 57
Troy Ct. W8 6D 70
Trump St. EC2 6C 68
Trundle St. SE1 4B 76
Tryon St. SW3 3D 80
Tudor St. EC4 7J 67
Tufton Ct. SW1 7D 74
Tufton St. SW1 6C 74
Tunbridge Ho. EC1 6K 59
Tupman Ho. SE16 5K 77
Turin St. E2 7K 61
Turk's Head Yd. EC1 3K 67
Turk's Row SW3 3E 80
Turnagain La. EC4 5K 67
Turnbull Ho. N1 2A 60
Turner Ho. NW8 4B 56
SW1 2C 82
Turner's All. EC3 7F 69
Turneville Rd. W14 5B 78
Turnmill St. EC1 2K 67
Turnpike Ho. EC1 7A 60
Turnstone Ho. E1 1K 77
Turpentine La. SW1 3J 81
Turquand St. SE17 2C 84
Turville Ho. NW8 1B 64
Turville St. E2 1H 69
Tuttle Ho. SW1 4B 82
Tweezer's All. WC2 7H 67
Twyford Pl. WC2 5F 67
Twyford St. N1 2F 59
Tyburn Tree (site of) 7D 64
Tyburn Way W1 7E 64
Tyers Est. SE1 4F 77
Tyers Ga. SE1 5F 77
Tyers St. SE11 4F 83
Tyers Ter. SE11 4F 83
Tyler Cl. E2 4H 61
Tyler's Ct. W1 6B 66
Tyndale La. N1 1K 59
Tyndale Mans. N1 1K 59
Tyndale Ter. N1 1K 59
Tyne St. E1 5J 69
Tyrrell Ho. SW1 5A 82
Tysoe St. EC1 7H 59
Tyssen St. N1 4G 61

UCI Cinema
Whiteleys Cen. 6G 63
Udall St. SW1 2A 82
Ufford St. SE1 4J 75
Ufton Gro. N1 1E 60
Ufton Rd. N1 1E 60
(not continuous)
UGC Cinema
Chelsea 5A 80
St James's 1B 74
South Kensington 4J 79
Trocadero 1B 74
Ulster Pl. NW1 2H 65
Ulster Ter. NW1 2H 65
Underhill Pas. NW1 2J 57
Underhill St. NW1 3J 57
Undershaft EC3 6F 69
Underwood Rd. E1 2K 69
Underwood Row N1 6C 60
Underwood St. N1 6C 60
Union Ct. EC2 5F 69
W9 3D 62
Union Sq. N1 3C 60
Union St. SE1 4K 75
Union Theatre 3A 76
Union Wlk. E2 6G 61
Union Wharf N1 5B 60
(Wenlock Rd.)
N1 3C 60
(Arlington Av.)
Union Yd. W1 6J 65
Unit Workshops E1 5K 69
Unity M. NW1 4B 58
Unity Wharf SE1 4J 77
University College London
Gower St. 2B 66
University of London
Institute of Education
1B 66
Institute of Latin American
Studies 1C 66
Senate Ho. 3C 66
University of Westminster
Marylebone Campus
3F 65
University of Westminster
(Cavendish Campus)
Bolsover St. 3J 65
Hanson St. 3K 65
University of Westminster
(Regent Campus)
Lit. Titchfield St. 4K 65
Regent St. 5J 65
Wells St. 4K 65
University St. WC1 2A 66
Unwin Cl. SE15 6K 85
Unwin Mans. W14 5B 78
Unwin Rd. SW7 6K 71
Upbrook M. W2 6J 63
Upcerne Rd. SW10 7H 79
Upnor Way SE17 3G 85
Up. Addison Gdns
W14 4A 70
Up. Belgrave St. SW1 6J 73
Up. Berenger Wlk.
SW10 7K 79
(off Berenger Wlk.)
Up. Berkeley St. W1 6D 64
Up. Blantyre Wlk. *SW10 7K 79*
(off Blantyre Wlk.)
Up. Brook St. W1 1F 73
Up. Camelford Wlk. W11 6A 62
Up. Cheyne Row SW3 6B 80
Up. Dartrey Wlk. *SW10 7J 79*
(off Whistler Wlk.)
Up. Dengie Wlk. *N1 2B 60*
(off Baddow Wlk.)
Upper Feilde W1 7F 65
Up. Grosvenor St. W1 1F 73
Upper Ground SE1 2H 75
Up. Hawkwell Wlk. *N1 2C 60*
(off Maldon Cl.)
Up. James St. W1 7A 66
Up. John St. W1 7A 66
Upper Lodge W8 3G 71
Upper Marsh SE1 6G 75
Up. Montagu St. W1 3D 64
Up. Phillimore Gdns.
W8 5D 70
Up. Rawreth Wlk. *N1 2C 60*
(off Basire St.)
Up. St Martin's La. WC2 7D 66
Upper St. N1 1K 59
Up. Tachbrook St. SW1 1K 81
Up. Talbot Wlk. W11 6A 62
Up. Thames St. EC4 7A 68
Up. Whistler Wlk. *SW10 7J 79*
(off Worlds End Est.)
Up. Wimpole St. W1 3G 65
Up. Woburn Pl. WC1 7C 58
Upwey Ho. N1 3F 61
Urlwin St. SE5 6B 84
Usborne M. SW8 7G 83
Utopia Village NW1 2F 57
Uverdale Rd. SW10 7J 79
Uxbridge St. W8 2D 70

Vale, The SW3 5K 79
Vale Cl. W9 7H 55
Vale Ct. W9 7J 55
Valentine Pl. SE1 5K 75
Valentine Row SE1 5K 75
Vale Royal N7 1D 58
Vale Royal Ho. WC2 7C 66
Vallance Rd. E2 7K 61
Valois Ho. SE1 6H 77
Vanbrugh Ct. SE11 2J 83
Vanbrugh Ho. E1 3H 69
Vandon Ct. SW1 6A 74
Vandon Pas. SW1 6A 74
Vandon St. SW1 6A 74
Vandy St. EC2 2F 69
Vane St. SW1 1A 82
Vanston Pl. SW6 7D 78
Vantage Pl. W8 7E 70
Vantrey Ho. SE11 2H 83
Varley Ho. NW6 3D 54
Varna Rd. SW6 7A 78
Varndell St. NW1 6K 57
Varnishers Yd. N1 5E 58
Vassall Rd. SW9 7K 83
Vat Ho. SW8 7E 82
Vauban Est. SE16 7J 77
Vauban St. SE16 7J 77
Vaudeville Theatre 1E 74
Vaughan Est. E2 6H 61
Vaughan Ho. SE1 4K 75
Vaughan Way E1 1K 77
VAUXHALL 4E 82
Vauxhall Bri. SW1 3C 82
Vauxhall Bri. Rd. SW1 7K 73
VAUXHALL CROSS 4E 82
Vauxhall Distribution Pk.
SW8 6B 82
Vauxhall Gro. SW8 5E 82
Vauxhall St. SE11 3G 83
Vauxhall Wlk. SE11 4F 83
Venables St. NW8 2A 64
Venice Ct. NW8 1A 64
SE5 7C 84
Venn Ho. N1 3G 59
Verdi Ho. W10 5A 54
Vereker Rd. W14 4A 78
Vere St. W1 6H 65
Verney Ho. NW8 1B 64
Vernon Ho. SE11 4G 83
WC1 4E 66
Vernon M. W14 2A 78
Vernon Pl. WC1 4E 66
Vernon Ri. WC1 6G 59
Vernon Sq. WC1 6G 59
Vernon St. W14 2A 78
Vernon Yd. W11 7B 62
Verulam Bldgs. WC1 3G 67
Verulam St. WC1 3H 67
Verwood Ho. SW8 7G 83
Vesage Ct. EC1 4J 67
Vesta Ct. SE1 5F 77
Vestry Ct. SW1 7C 74
Vestry St. N1 6D 60
Viaduct Bldgs. EC1 4J 67
Vibart Wlk. N1 2E 58
Vicarage Ct. W8 4F 71
Vicarage Gdns. W8 3E 70
Vicarage Ga. W8 3F 71
Viceroy Ct. NW8 4C 56
Vickery Ct. EC1 1C 68
Victor Cazalet Ho. *N1 2K 59*
(off Gaskin St.)
Victoria & Albert Mus. 7A 72
Victoria Arc. SW1 7J 73
Victoria Av. EC2 4G 69
Victoria Colonnade
WC1 4E 66
Victoria Cotts. E1 3K 69
Victoria Emb. EC4 5E 74
SW1 5E 74
WC2 2E 74
Victoria Gdns. W11 2D 70
Victoria Gro. W8 6H 71
Victoria Gro. M. W2 1E 70
Victoria Ho. SW1 3H 81
(Ebury Bri. Rd.)
SW1 1A 82
(Francis St.)
SW8 7E 82
Victoria Mans. SW8 7E 82
Victoria M. NW6 2D 54
Victoria Palace Theatre 7K 73
Victoria Pas. NW8 1K 63
Victoria Pl. Shop. Cen.
SW1 1J 81
Victoria Ri. NW6 1J 55
Victoria Rd. NW6 4B 54
W8 5H 71
Victoria Sq. SW1 6J 73
Victoria St. SW1 7J 73
Victoria Yd. E1 6K 69
Victor Wharf *SE1 2D 76*
(off Clink St.)
Victory Ct. W9 2D 62
Victory Pl. SE17 1C 84
Vigo St. W1 1K 73
Viking Ct. SW6 6E 78
Villa St. SE17 4E 84
Villa Wlk. SE17 4E 84
Villiers St. WC2 1D 74
Vincent Ct. W1 5D 64
Vincent Ho. SW1 2B 82
Vincent Sq. SW1 1B 82
Vincent Sq. Mans. *SW1 1A 82*
(off Walcott St.)
Vincent St. SW1 1B 82
Vincent Ter. N1 4K 59
Vince St. EC1 7E 60
Vinegar Yd. SE1 4F 77
Vine Hill EC1 2H 67
Vine La. SE1 3G 77
Vine Sq. W14 4C 78
Vine St. EC3 6H 69
W1 1A 74
Vine St. Bri. EC1 2J 67
Vine Yd. SE1 4C 76
Vineyard M. EC1 1H 67
Vineyard Wlk. EC1 1H 67
Vinopolis 2C 76
Vinson Ho. N1 5E 60
Vintners Ct. EC4 7C 68
Vintner's Pl. EC4 7C 68
Violet Hill NW8 5H 55
Violet Hill Ho. NW8 5H 55
(not continuous)
Virgil Pl. W1 4D 64
Virgil St. SE1 6G 75
Virginia Ct. WC1 1C 66
Virginia Rd. E2 7H 61
Virginia St. E1 1K 77
Visage NW3 1A 56
Viscount Ct. W2 6E 62
Viscount St. EC1 2B 68
Vittoria Ho. N1 3G 59
Vixen M. E8 1H 61
Vogans Mill SE1 4J 77
Vollasky Ho. E1 3K 69
Voss St. E2 7K 61
Voyager Bus. Est. SE16 6K 77
Vue Cinema
Fulham Broadway 7E 78
Islington 4J 59
Leicester Sq. 7C 66

Wadding St. SE17 2D 84
Wade Ho. SE1 5K 77
Wadham Gdns. NW3 2B 56
Waite St. SE15 5H 85
Waithman St. EC4 6K 67
Wakefield M. WC1 7E 58
Wakefield St. WC1 7E 58
Wakelin Ho. N1 1K 59
Wakley St. EC1 6K 59
Walberswick St. SW8 7E 82
Walbrook EC4 7D 68
(not continuous)
Walbrook Ct. N1 4F 61

Walbrook Wharf—Zoar St.

Walbrook Wharf EC4 1C 76
Walcorde Av. SE17 2C 84
Walcot Gdns. SE11 1H 83
Walcot Sq. SE11 1J 83
Walcott St. SW1 1A 82
Walden Ho. SW1 2G 81
Waldron M. SW3 5A 80
Waleran Flats SE1 1F 85
Walham Grn. Ct. SW6 7F 79
Walham Gro. SW6 7D 78
Walham Yd. SW6 7D 78
Walker Ho. NW1 5B 58
Walker's Ct. W1 7B 66
Walkinshaw Ct. N1 1C 60
Wallace Collection 5F 65
Wallace Ct. NW1 4C 64
Wallgrave Rd. SW5 1F 79
Wallis All. SE1 4C 76
Wallside EC2 4C 68
Walmer Pl. W1 3D 64
Walmer Rd. W11 7A 62
Walmer St. W1 3D 64
Walnut Ct. *W8* *7F 71*
(off St Mary's Ga.)
Walnut Tree Ho. SW10 5G 79
Walnut Tree Wlk. SE11 1H 83
Walpole Ho. SE1 5H 75
Walpole M. NW8 3K 55
Walpole St. SW3 3D 80
Walsham Ho. SE17 3D 84
Walsingham NW8 2A 56
Walsingham Mans. SW6 7G 79
Walston Ho. SW1 3B 82
Walters Cl. SE17 2C 84
Walters Ho. SE17 6K 83
Walterton Rd. W9 2C 62
Waltham Ho. NW8 2H 55
Walton Cl. SW8 7E 82
Walton Ho. E2 1H 69
Walton Pl. SW3 6D 72
Walton St. SW3 1C 80
Walton Vs. N1 1G 61
WALWORTH 3C 84
Walworth Pl. SE17 4C 84
Walworth Rd. SE1 1B 84
SE17 1B 84
Wandle Ho. NW8 3B 64
Wandon Rd. SW6 7G 79
(not continuous)
Wandsdown Pl. SW6 7F 79
Wandsworth Rd. SW8 7D 82
Wansey St. SE17 2B 84
Wapping High St. E1 3K 77
Wardens Gro. SE1 3B 76
Wardour M. W1 6A 66
Wardour St. W1 5A 66
Ward Point SE11 2H 83
Wardrobe Pl. EC4 6A 68
Wardrobe Ter. EC4 7A 68
Wareham Ct. N1 1G 61
Wareham Ho. SW8 7F 83
Wargrave Ho. E2 7H 61
Warham St. SE5 7A 84
Warlock Rd. W9 1C 62
Warmsworth NW1 2K 57
Warner Ho. NW8 6H 55
Warner Pl. E2 5K 61
Warner St. EC1 2H 67
Warner Yd. EC1 2H 67
Warnham WC1 7F 59
Warren Ct. NW1 1K 65
Warren Ho. W14 1C 78
Warren M. W1 2K 65
Warren St. W1 2K 65
Warrington Cres. W9 2H 63
Warrington Gdns. W9 2H 63
Warwick W14 2C 78
Warwick Av. W2 2H 63
W9 2G 63
Warwick Bldg. SW8 6H 81
Warwick Chambers W8 6D 70
Warwick Ct. EC4 6A 68
WC1 4G 67
Warwick Cres. W2 3H 63
Warwick Est. W2 4G 63
Warwick Gdns. W14 7C 70
Warwick Ho. St. SW1 2C 74
Warwick La. EC4 5A 68
Warwick Pas. EC4 6A 68
Warwick Pl. W9 3H 63
Warwick Pl. Nth. SW1 2K 81
Warwick Rd. W14 7B 70
Warwick Row SW1 7J 73
Warwick Sq. EC4 5A 68
SW1 3K 81
(not continuous)
Warwick Sq. M. SW1 2K 81
Warwick St. W1 7A 66
Warwick Way SW1 3H 81
Warwick Yd. EC1 2C 68
Watercress Pl. N1 1G 61
Waterford Ho. W11 7B 62
Waterford Rd. SW6 7F 79
(not continuous)
Water Gdns., The W2 5C 64
Watergate EC4 7K 67
Watergate Wlk. WC2 2E 74
Waterhead NW1 6K 57
Waterhouse Sq. EC1 4H 67
Water La. EC3 1G 77
NW1 1J 57
Waterloo Bri. WC2 1F 75
Waterloo Pas. NW6 1C 54
Waterloo Pl. SW1 2B 74
Waterloo Rd. SE1 2G 75
Waterloo Ter. N1 1K 59
Waterman's Wlk. EC4 1D 76
Waterside W2 4K 63
Waterside Cl. SE16 5K 77
Waterside Pl. NW1 2G 57
Waterside Point SW11 7C 80
Waterson St. E2 6G 61
Water St. WC2 7H 67
Water Twr. Pl. N1 3K 59
Watling Ct. EC4 6C 68
Watling St. EC4 6B 68
SE15 6G 85
Watson's M. W1 4C 64
Wavel M. NW6 1F 55
Waveney Cl. E1 2K 77
Waverley Ct. NW6 1A 54
Waverley Pl. NW8 4K 55
Waverton St. W1 2G 73
Waylett Ho. SE11 4H 83
Weatherbury W2 5D 62
Weavers La. SE1 3G 77
Weavers Ter. SW6 6E 78
Weaver St. E1 2K 69
Weavers Way NW1 2B 58
Webber Row SE1 6J 75
Webber St. SE1 4J 75
Webb St. SE1 7F 77
Webster Rd. SE16 7K 77
Wedgewood Ho. SW1 4J 81
Wedgewood M. W1 6C 66
Wedgwood Ho. SE11 7H 75
Wedlake St. W10 1A 62
Weighhouse St. W1 7G 65
Weir's Pas. NW1 6C 58
Welbeck Ct. W14 1B 78
Welbeck Ho. W1 5H 65
Welbeck St. W1 4G 65
Welbeck Way W1 5H 65
Welford Ct. NW1 1J 57
W9 3D 62
Wellclose Sq. E1 7K 69
Wellclose St. E1 1K 77
Wellcome Cen. for Medical Science 1B 66
Wellcome Mus., The *5G 67*
(in Royal College of Surgeons, The)
Well Ct. EC4 6C 68
(not continuous)
Weller Ho. SE16 5K 77
Weller St. SE1 4B 76
Wellesley Ct. W9 6H 55
Wellesley Ho. NW1 7B 58
SW1 3H 81
Wellesley Mans. W14 3B 78
Wellesley Pl. NW1 7B 58
Wellesley Ter. N1 6C 60
Wellington Arch 4G 73
Wellington Bldgs. SW1 4G 81
Wellington Cl. W11 6D 62
Wellington Ct. NW8 4K 55
SW1 5D 72
Wellington Monument 4G 73
Wellington Mus. 4G 73
Wellington Pl. NW8 6A 56
Wellington Rd. NW8 4A 56
Wellington Row E2 6J 61
Wellington Sq. SW3 3D 80
Wellington St. WC2 7E 66
Wellington Ter. W2 1F 71
Wells Ct. NW6 4E 54
Wells Ho. EC1 6J 59
Wells M. W1 4A 66
Wells Ri. NW8 3D 56
Wells Sq. WC1 7F 59
Wells St. W1 4K 65
Wells Way SE5 5E 84
SW7 6K 71
Welsford St. SE1 3K 85
(not continuous)
Wendle Ct. SW8 6D 82
Wendover SE17 3F 85
(not continuous)
Wendover Ct. W1 4F 65
Wendover Ho. W1 4F 65
Wenham Ho. SW8 7K 81
Wenlake Ho. EC1 1B 68
Wenlock Barn Est. N1 5D 60
Wenlock Ct. N1 5E 60
Wenlock Rd. N1 4B 60
Wenlock St. N1 5C 60
Wentworth Ct. W6 6A 78
Wentworth Dwellings E1 5H 69
Wentworth St. E1 5H 69
Werrington St. NW1 5A 58
Wesley Cl. SE17 2A 84
Wesley's House, Chapel & Mus. of Methodism 2E 68
Wesley St. W1 4G 65
Wessex Ho. SE1 3J 85
Wesson Mead SE5 7C 84
West Block SE1 5F 75
Westbourne Bri. W2 4H 63
Westbourne Cres. W2 7K 63
Westbourne Cres. M. W2 7K 63
Westbourne Gdns. W2 5F 63
WESTBOURNE GREEN 5C 62
Westbourne Green Sports Complex 4E 62
Westbourne Gro. W11 7B 62
Westbourne Gro. M. W11 6D 62
Westbourne Gro. Ter. W2 5F 63
Westbourne Ho. SW1 3H 81
Westbourne Pk. Pas. W2 3E 62
(not continuous)
Westbourne Pk. Rd. W2 4E 62
W11 6A 62
Westbourne Pk. Vs. W2 4E 62
Westbourne St. W2 7K 63
Westbourne Ter. W2 5H 63
Westbourne Ter. M. W2 5H 63
Westbourne Ter. Rd. W2 4H 63
Westbourne Ter. Rd. Bri. W2 3H 63
WEST BROMPTON 4F 79
W. Carriage Dr. W2 1B 72
(not continuous)
W. Central St. WC1 5D 66
Westcliffe Apartments W2 4A 64
Westcott Rd. SE17 5K 83
W. Cromwell Rd. W14 3B 78
W. Eaton Pl. SW1 1F 81
W. Eaton Pl. M. SW1 1F 81
West End Ct. NW6 1F 55
West End La. NW6 1E 54
(not continuous)
W. End Quay W2 4A 64
Westerham NW1 3K 57
Westerham Ho. SE1 6E 76
Western Ct. NW6 5C 54
Western M. W9 2C 62
Westfield Cl. SW10 7H 79
West Gdn. Pl. W2 6C 64
Westgate Ter. SW10 4G 79
W. Halkin St. SW1 6F 73
W. Harding St. EC4 5J 67
Westhope Ho. E2 1K 69
WEST KENSINGTON 5B 70
W. Kensington Ct. W14 3B 78
W. Kensington Mans. W14 4B 78
WEST KILBURN 7B 54
Westland Pl. N1 6D 60
Westmacott Ho. NW8 2A 64
West Mall W8 2E 70
West M. SW1 2K 81
WESTMINSTER 5D 74
Westminster Abbey 6D 74
Westminster Abbey Chapter House 6C 74
Westminster Abbey Mus. 6D 74
Westminster Abbey Pyx Chamber 6C 74
Westminster Bri. SW1 5E 74
Westminster Bri. Rd. SE1 5F 75
Westminster Bus. Sq. SE11 4F 83
Westminster Children's Sports Cen., The 3K 63
Westminster Gdns. SW1 1D 82
Westminster Hall 5D 74
Westminster Mans. SW1 7C 74
Westminster Pal. Gdns. SW1 7B 74
Westminster RC Cathedral 7K 73
Westminster Theatre 6K 73
Westmoreland Pl. SW1 4J 81
Westmoreland Rd. SE17 5C 84
(not continuous)
Westmoreland St. W1 4G 65
Westmoreland Ter. SW1 3J 81
Westmoreland Wlk. SE17 5D 84
(not continuous)
Westonbirt Ct. SE15 6H 85
W. One Ho. W1 4K 65
W. One Shop. Cen. W1 6G 65
Weston Ho. NW6 1A 54
Weston Ri. WC1 5G 59
Weston St. SE1 4E 76
(not continuous)
West Point SE1 3K 85
W. Poultry Av. EC1 4K 67
West Ri. W2 7C 64
West Rd. SE1 4G 75
SW3 4E 80
Westside Ct. W9 1E 62
West Smithfield EC1 4K 67
West Sq. SE11 7K 75
West St. WC2 6C 66
W. Tenter St. E1 6J 69
W. Warwick Pl. SW1 2K 81
Westway W2 3D 62
W10 5A 62
W11 3D 62
Wetherby Gdns. SW5 2H 79
Wetherby Mans. SW5 3F 79
Wetherby M. SW5 3F 79
Wetherby Pl. SW7 2H 79
Weyhill Rd. E1 5K 69
Weymouth Ct. E2 4J 61
Weymouth Ho. SW8 7F 83
Weymouth M. W1 3H 65
Weymouth St. W1 4G 65
Weymouth Ter. E2 4J 61
Whalebone Ct. EC2 5D 68
Wharf, The EC3 2G 77
Wharfdale Rd. N1 4E 58
Wharfedale Ho. NW6 2F 55
Wharfedale St. SW10 4F 79
Wharfedale Yard N1 4E 58
Wharf Rd. N1 5B 60
(Baldwin Ter.)
N1 3C 58
(Camley St.)
Wharton Cotts. WC1 7H 59
Wharton Ho. SE1 6H 77
Wharton St. WC1 7G 59
Wheatley St. W1 4G 65
Wheatsheaf La. SW8 7D 82
(not continuous)
Wheatstone Rd. W10 3A 62
Wheeler Gdns. N1 2E 58
Wheler Ho. E1 2H 69
Wheler St. E1 2H 69
Whetstone Pk. WC2 5F 67
Whidborne Bldgs. WC1 7E 58
Whidborne St. WC1 7E 58
(not continuous)
Whiskin St. EC1 7K 59
Whistler Twr. SW10 7K 79
Whistler Wlk. SW10 7J 79
Whiston Ho. N1 1A 60
Whiston Rd. E2 4H 61
Whitacre M. SE11 4J 83
Whitby Ho. NW8 3H 55
Whitby St. E1 1H 69
(not continuous)
Whitcomb Ct. WC2 1C 74
Whitcomb St. WC2 1C 74
Whitebeam Cl. SW9 7G 83
White Bear Yd. EC1 2H 67
WHITECHAPEL 4K 69
Whitechapel Art Gallery 5J 69
Whitechapel High St. E1 5J 69
Whitechapel Rd. E1 5K 69
White Chu. La. E1 5K 69
White Chu. Pas. E1 5K 69
White Conduit St. N1 4J 59
Whitecross Pl. EC2 3E 68
Whitecross St. EC1 1C 68
Whitefriars St. EC4 6J 67
Whitehall SW1 2D 74
Whitehall Ct. SW1 3D 74
(not continuous)
Whitehall Gdns. SW1 3D 74
Whitehall Pl. SW1 3D 74
White Hart Ct. EC2 4F 69
White Hart St. EC4 5A 68
SE11 3J 83
White Hart Yd. SE1 3D 76
Whitehaven St. NW8 2B 64
Whiteheads Gro. SW3 3C 80
White Heather Ho. *WC1* *7E 58*
(off Cromer St.)
White Horse All. EC1 3K 67
Whitehorse M. SE1 6J 75
White Horse St. W1 3J 73
White Horse Yd. EC2 5D 68
White Ho., The NW1 1J 65
White Kennett St. E1 5G 69
Whitelands Ho. SW3 3D 80
Whiteleys Cen. W2 6G 63
Whiteley's Cotts. W14 2C 78
White Lion Ct. EC3 6F 69
White Lion Hill EC4 7A 68
White Lion St. N1 5H 59
White Lyon Ct. EC2 3B 68
White's Grounds SE1 5G 77
White's Grounds Est. SE1 4G 77
White's Row E1 4H 69
White Tower *1H 77*
(in Tower of London, The)
Whitfield Ho. NW8 2B 64
Whitfield Pl. W1 2K 65
Whitfield St. W1 2K 65
Whitgift Ho. SE11 1F 83
Whitgift St. SE11 1F 83
Whitley Ho. SW1 5A 82
Whitmore Est. N1 3G 61
Whitmore Ho. N1 3G 61
Whitmore Rd. N1 3F 61
Whittaker St. SW1 2F 81
Whittaker Way SE1 2K 85
Whittington Av. EC3 6F 69
Whittlesey St. SE1 3J 75
Whitworth Ho. SE1 7C 76
Wickham St. SE11 3F 83
Wicklow St. WC1 6F 59
Wicksteed Ho. SE1 7C 76
Wickway Ct. SE15 6H 85
Widegate St. E1 4G 69
Widford Ho. N1 5K 59
Widley Rd. W9 7E 54
Wigmore Hall 5H 65
Wigmore Pl. W1 5H 65
Wigmore St. W1 6F 65
Wigton Pl. SE11 4J 83
Wilbraham Ho. SW8 7D 82
Wilbraham Pl. SW1 1E 80
Wilby M. W11 2C 70
Wilcox Cl. SW8 7E 82
(not continuous)
Wilcox Pl. SW1 7A 74
Wilcox Rd. SW8 7D 82
Wild Ct. WC2 6F 67
(not continuous)
Wilde Cl. E8 2K 61
Wilde Ho. W2 5G 63
Wild's Rents SE1 6F 77
Wild St. WC2 6E 66
Wilfred St. SW1 6K 73
Wilkes St. E1 3J 69
Wilkie Ho. SW1 3C 82
Wilkins Ho. SW1 5J 81
Wilkinson Ho. N1 5E 60
Wilkinson St. SW8 7F 83
Wilks Pl. N1 5G 61
Willesden La. NW6 1A 54
William IV St. WC2 1D 74
William Cobbett Ho. W8 6F 71
William Dromey Ct. NW6 1B 54
William Dunbar Ho. NW6 5C 54
William Ellis Way SE16 7K 77
William Fenn Ho. E2 6K 61
William Gibbs Ct. SW1 7B 74
William Henry Wlk. SW8 6B 82
William M. SW1 5E 72
William Rd. NW1 7K 57
William Rushbrooke Ho. SE16 1K 85
William Saville Ho. NW6 5C 54
Williams Cl. SW6 7A 78
Williamson Ct. SE17 4B 84
William St. SW1 5E 72
Willoughby Highwalk EC2 4D 68
Willoughby Ho. EC2 4D 68
Willoughby St. WC1 4D 66
Willowbrook Est. SE15 7K 85
Willow Brook Rd. SE15 6J 85
Willow Ct. EC2 1F 69
NW6 1A 54
W9 3E 62
Willow Pl. SW1 1A 82
Willow St. EC2 1F 69
Willow Wlk. SE1 1G 85
Willsbridge Ct. SE15 6H 85
Wilman Gro. E8 1K 61
Wilmcote Ho. W2 3F 63
Wilmer Gdns. N1 3F 61
(not continuous)
Wilmington Sq. WC1 7H 59
(not continuous)
Wilmington St. WC1 7H 59
Wilmot Pl. NW1 1K 57
Wilsham St. W11 2A 70
Wilson St. EC2 3E 68
Wilton Cres. SW1 5F 73
Wilton M. SW1 6G 73
Wilton Pl. SW1 5F 73
Wilton Rd. SW1 7J 73
Wilton Row SW1 5F 73
Wilton Sq. N1 2D 60
Wilton St. SW1 6H 73
Wilton Ter. SW1 6F 73
Wilton Vs. N1 3D 60
Wiltshire Cl. SW3 2D 80
Wiltshire Row N1 3D 60
Wimbolt St. E2 6K 61
Wimborne Ho. NW1 2C 64
SW8 7G 83
Wimbourne Ct. N1 4D 60
Wimbourne St. N1 4D 60
Wimpole M. W1 3H 65
Wimpole St. W1 3H 65
Winchester Av. NW6 2A 54
Winchester Cl. SE17 2A 84
Winchester Ct. W8 4E 70
Winchester Ho. SW3 6A 80
SW9 7J 83
W2 6H 63
Winchester Rd. NW3 1A 56
Winchester Sq. SE1 2D 76
Winchester St. SW1 3J 81
Winchester Wlk. SE1 2D 76
Winchester Wharf SE1 2D 76
Winch Ho. SW10 7J 79
Winchilsea Ho. NW8 7A 56
Wincott St. SE11 1J 83
Windermere NW1 7J 57
Windermere Av. NW6 3A 54
Winding, The W2 4A 64
Windmill WC1 3F 67
Windmill Row SE11 4H 83
Windmill St. W1 4B 66
(not continuous)
Windmill Wlk. SE1 3J 75
Windsor Cen., The N1 2A 60
Windsor Ct. SW3 3C 80
W2 7F 63
Windsor Gdns. W9 2D 62
Windsor Ho. N1 4C 60
NW1 6J 57
Windsor Pl. SW1 1A 82
Windsor St. N1 2A 60
Windsor Ter. N1 6C 60
Wine Office Ct. EC4 5J 67
Wingfield Ho. E2 7H 61
NW6 4F 55
Wingrave SE17 1D 84
(not continuous)
Wingreen NW8 2G 55
Winicotte Ho. W2 3A 64
Winnett St. W1 7B 66
Winnington Ho. SE5 7B 84
Winsham Ho. NW1 6C 58
Winsland M. W2 5K 63
Winsland St. W2 5K 63
Winsley St. W1 5K 65
Winslow SE17 4F 85
Winston Ho. WC1 1C 66
Winterbourne Ho. W11 1A 70
Winterleys NW6 5C 54
Winterton Pl. SW10 5J 79
Wisden Ho. SW8 6G 83
Wisley Ho. SW1 3B 82
Withers Pl. EC1 1C 68
Witley Ct. WC1 2D 66
Woburn M. WC1 1C 66
Woburn Pl. WC1 1C 66
Woburn Sq. WC1 2C 66
Woburn Wlk. WC1 7C 58
Wolcot Ho. NW1 5A 58
Wollaston Cl. SE1 1B 84
Wollett Ct. NW1 1A 58
Wolseley St. SE1 5J 77
Wolsey Ct. NW6 1J 55
Wolverton SE17 3E 84
Wontner Cl. N1 1B 60
Woodbridge St. EC1 1K 67
(not continuous)
Woodchester Sq. W2 3F 63
Woodchurch Rd. NW6 1E 54
Wood Cl. E2 1K 69
Woodfall St. SW3 4D 80
Woodfield Pl. W9 2C 62
Woodfield Rd. W9 3C 62
Woodhall NW1 7K 57
Woodlands Ho. NW6 1A 54
Woodseer St. E1 3J 69
Woodsford SE17 3D 84
Woodsford Sq. W14 4A 70
Woods M. W1 7E 64
Woods Pl. SE1 7G 77
Woodstock Ct. SE11 3G 83
Woodstock M. W1 4G 65
Woodstock St. W1 6H 65
Wood St. EC2 6C 68
Woodville Ho. SE1 6H 77
Woodville Rd. NW6 4C 54
Wooler St. SE17 4D 84
Woolf M. WC1 1C 66
Woolstaplers Way SE16 7K 77
Wooster Pl. SE1 1E 84
Wootton St. SE1 4J 75
Worcester Ct. W9 3D 62
Worcester Ho. SE11 7H 75
SW9 7J 83
W2 6H 63
Wordsworth Ho. NW6 6D 54
Wordsworth Rd. SE1 2J 85
Worfield St. SW11 7C 80
Worgan St. SE11 3F 83
Worlds End Est. SW10 7K 79
World's End Pas. SW10 7K 79
World's End Pl. SW10 7J 79
Wormwood St. EC2 5F 69
Wornum Ho. W10 5A 54
Woronzow Rd. NW8 3A 56
Worship St. EC2 2E 68
Worth Gro. SE17 4D 84
Worthington Ho. EC1 6J 59
Wrayburn Ho. SE16 5K 77
Wren Ho. SW1 4B 82
Wren St. WC1 1G 67
Wrestlers Ct. EC3 5F 69
Wright's La. W8 5E 70
Wrotham Ho. SE1 6E 76
Wrotham Rd. NW1 1A 58
Wyatt Ho. NW8 2K 63
Wybert St. NW1 1K 65
Wyclif Ct. EC1 7K 59
Wyclif St. EC1 7K 59
Wycombe Ho. NW8 1B 64
Wycombe Sq. W8 3D 70
Wymering Mans. W9 7E 54
(not continuous)
Wymering Rd. W9 7E 54
Wyndham Deedes Ho. E2 5K 61
Wyndham Est. SE5 7C 84
Wyndham M. W1 4D 64
Wyndham Pl. W1 4D 64
Wyndham Rd. SE5 7A 84
Wyndhams Ct. E8 1H 61
Wyndham's Theatre 7D 66
Wyndham St. W1 3D 64
Wyndham Yd. W1 4D 64
Wynford Ho. N1 4G 59
Wynford Rd. N1 4F 59
Wynnstay Gdns. W8 6E 70
Wynyard Ho. SE11 3G 83
Wynyard Ter. SE11 3G 83
Wynyatt St. EC1 7K 59
Wythburn Ct. W1 5D 64
Wythburn Pl. W1 6D 64
Wyvil Rd. SW8 7D 82

Yalding Rd. SE16 7K 77
Yard, The *N1* *5E 58*
(off Caledonian Rd.)
Yardley St. WC1 7H 59
(not continuous)
Yarmouth Pl. W1 3H 73
Yates Ho. E2 6K 61
Yeate St. N1 1D 60
Yeoman Ct. SE1 4J 85
Yeoman's Row SW3 7C 72
Yeoman's Yd. E1 7J 69
York Av. SE17 3C 84
York Bri. NW1 1F 65
York Bldgs. WC2 1E 74
York Ga. NW1 2F 65
York Ho. SE1 7G 75
W1 3D 64
York Ho. Pl. W8 4F 71
York Mans. SW5 3F 79
W1 3F 65
York Pas. W8 4F 71
York Pl. WC2 1E 74
York Pl. Mans. W1 3E 64
York Rd. SE1 4G 75
Yorkshire Grey Yd. WC1 4F 67
York St. W1 4D 64
York St. Chambers W1 3D 64
York Ter. E. NW1 2G 65
York Ter. W. NW1 2F 65
Yorkton St. E2 4K 61
York Way N1 5E 58
N7 1D 58
York Way Ct. N1 3E 58
Young Ct. NW6 1A 54
Youngs Bldgs. EC1 1C 68
Young St. W8 5F 71
Young Vic Theatre, The 4J 75

Zander Ct. E2 6K 61
Zetland Ho. W8 6F 71
Zoar St. SE1 2B 76

HOSPITALS and HOSPICES
covered by this atlas
with their map square reference

N.B. Where Hospitals and Hospices are not named on the map, the reference
given is for the road in which they are situated.

ABBEY CHURCHILL LONDON, THE 6J **75**
22 Barkham Terrace
LONDON
SE1 7PW
Tel: 020 7928 5633

CHELSEA & WESTMINSTER HOSPITAL 6J **79**
369 Fulham Road
LONDON
SW10 9NH
Tel: 020 8746 8000

CROMWELL HOSPITAL, THE 1F **79**
162-174 Cromwell Road
LONDON
SW5 0TU
Tel: 020 7460 2000

EASTMAN DENTAL HOSPITAL & DENTAL INSTITUTE, THE 1F **67**
256 Gray's Inn Road
LONDON
WC1X 8LD
Tel: 020 7915 1000

ELIZABETH GARRETT ANDERSON & OBSTETRIC HOSPITAL, THE
....2A **66**
Huntley Street
LONDON
WC1E 6DH
Tel: 020 7387 9300

EVELINA CHILDREN'S HOSPITAL 6F **75**
St Thomas' Hospital
Lambeth Palace Road
LONDON
SE1 7EH
Tel: 020 7188 7188

FLORENCE NIGHTINGALE DAY HOSPITAL 3C **64**
1B Harewood Row
LONDON
NW1 6SE
Tel: 020 7725 9940

FLORENCE NIGHTINGALE HOSPITAL 3C **64**
11-19 Lisson Grove
LONDON
NW1 6SH
Tel: 020 7535 7700

GORDON HOSPITAL 2B **82**
Bloomburg Street
LONDON
SW1V 2RH
Tel: 020 8746 8733

GREAT ORMOND STREET HOSPITAL FOR CHILDREN 2E **66**
Great Ormond Street
LONDON
WC1N 3JH
Tel: 020 7405 9200

GUY'S HOSPITAL 3E **76**
St Thomas Street
LONDON
SE1 9RT
Tel: 020 7188 7188

GUY'S NUFFIELD HOUSE 4D **76**
Newcomen Street
LONDON
SE1 1YR
Tel: 020 7955 4257

HARLEY STREET CLINIC, THE 3H **65**
35 Weymouth Street
LONDON
W1G 8BJ
Tel: 020 7935 7700

HEART HOSPITAL, THE 4G **65**
16-18 Westmoreland Street
LONDON
W1G 8PH
Tel: 020 7573 8888

HOSPITAL FOR TROPICAL DISEASES 2A **66**
Mortimer Market,
Capper Street
LONDON
WC1E 6AU
Tel: 020 7387 9300

HOSPITAL OF ST JOHN & ST ELIZABETH 5K **55**
60 Grove End Road
LONDON
NW8 9NH
Tel: 020 7806 4000

KING EDWARD VII'S HOSPITAL SISTER AGNES 3G **65**
5-10 Beaumont Street
LONDON
W1G 6AA
Tel: 020 7486 4411

LATIMER DAY HOSPITAL 3K **65**
40 Hanson Street
LONDON
W1W 6UL
Tel: 020 7380 9187

LISTER HOSPITAL, THE 4H **81**
Chelsea Bridge Road
LONDON
SW1W 8RH
Tel: 020 7730 3417

LONDON BRIDGE HOSPITAL 2E **76**
27 Tooley Street
LONDON
SE1 2PR
Tel: 020 7407 3100

LONDON CLINIC, THE 2G **65**
20 Devonshire Place
LONDON
W1G 6BW
Tel: 020 7935 4444

LONDON FOOT HOSPITAL 2K **65**
33 & 40 Fitzroy Square
LONDON
W1T 6AY
Tel: 020 7530 4500

LONDON LIGHTHOUSE 6A **62**
111-117 Lancaster Road
LONDON
W11 1QT
Tel: 020 7792 1200

LONDON WELBECK HOSPITAL 4H **65**
27 Welbeck Street
LONDON
W1G 8EN
Tel: 020 7224 2242

MIDDLESEX HOSPITAL, THE 4A **66**
Mortimer Street
LONDON
W1T 3AA
Tel: 020 7636 8333

MILDMAY MISSION HOSPITAL 7H **61**
Hackney Road
LONDON
E2 7NA
Tel: 020 7613 6300

MOORFIELDS EYE HOSPITAL 7D **60**
162 City Road
LONDON
EC1V 2PD
Tel: 020 7253 3411

NATIONAL HOSPITAL FOR NEUROLOGY & NEUROSURGERY, THE
....2E **66**
Queen Square
LONDON
WC1N 3BG
Tel: 020 7837 3611

NHS WALK-IN CENTRE (SOHO) 6B **66**
1 Frith Street
LONDON
W1D 3HZ
Tel: 020 7534 6500

PORTLAND HOSPITAL FOR WOMEN & CHILDREN, THE 2J **65**
209 Great Portland Street
LONDON
W1W 5AH
Tel: 020 7580 4400

PRINCESS GRACE HOSPITAL 2F **65**
42-52 Nottingham Place
LONDON
W1U 5NY
Tel: 020 7486 1234

PRINCESS GRACE HOSPITAL ANNEXE 3G **65**
29-31 Devonshire Street
LONDON
W1G 6PU
Tel: 020 7486 1234

ROYAL BROMPTON HOSPITAL 3B **80**
Sydney Street
LONDON
SW3 6NP
Tel: 020 7352 8121

ROYAL BROMPTON HOSPITAL (ANNEXE) 3A **80**
Fulham Road
LONDON
SW3 6HP
Tel: 020 7352 8121

ROYAL LONDON HOMOEOPATHIC HOSPITAL, THE 3E **66**
Great Ormond Street
LONDON
WC1N 3HR
Tel: 020 7391 8864

ROYAL MARSDEN HOSPITAL (FULHAM), THE 3A **80**
Fulham Road
LONDON
SW3 6JJ
Tel: 020 7352 8171

ROYAL NATIONAL ORTHOPAEDIC HOSPITAL (OUTPATIENTS) 2J **65**
45-51 Bolsover Street
LONDON
W1W 5AQ
Tel: 020 7387 5070

ROYAL NATIONAL THROAT, NOSE & EAR HOSPITAL 6F **59**
330 Gray's Inn Road
LONDON
WC1X 8DA
Tel: 020 7915 1300

ST BARTHOLOMEW'S HOSPITAL 4A **68**
West Smithfield
LONDON
EC1A 7BE
Tel: 020 7377 7000

ST JOHN'S HOSPICE 5K **55**
Hospital of St John & St Elizabeth
60 Grove End Road
LONDON
NW8 9NH
Tel: 020 7806 4040

ST LUKE'S HOSPITAL FOR THE CLERGY 2K **65**
14 Fitzroy Square
LONDON
W1T 6AH
Tel: 020 7388 4954

ST MARY'S HOSPITAL 5A **64**
Praed Street
LONDON
W2 1NY
Tel: 020 7725 6666

ST PANCRAS HOSPITAL 3B **58**
4 St Pancras Way
LONDON
NW1 0PE
Tel: 020 7530 3500

ST THOMAS' HOSPITAL 6F **75**
Lambeth Palace Road
LONDON
SE1 7EH
Tel: 020 7188 7188

UNIVERSITY COLLEGE HOSPITAL 1A **66**
Gower Street
LONDON
WC1E 6AU
Tel: 020 7387 9300

WELLINGTON HOSPITAL, THE 6A **56**
8a Wellington Place
LONDON
NW8 9LE
Tel: 020 7586 5959

WESTERN EYE HOSPITAL 3D **64**
171 Marylebone Road
LONDON
NW1 5QH
Tel: 020 7886 6666

RAIL, RIVERBUS AND LONDON UNDERGROUND STATIONS

with their map square reference

Aldgate East (Tube) 5J 69
Aldgate (Tube) 6H 69
Angel (Tube) 4J 59

Baker Street (Tube) 2E 64
Bankside Pier (Riverbus) 1B 76
Bank (Tube & DLR) 6D 68
Barbican (Rail & Tube) 3B 68
Barons Court (Tube) 3A 78
Bayswater (Tube) 7G 63
Blackfriars Millennium Pier (Riverbus) 7J 67
Blackfriars (Rail & Tube) 7K 67
Bond Street (Tube) 6H 65
Borough (Tube) 5C 76
Brondesbury Park (Rail) 2A 54

Cadogan Pier (Riverbus) 6C 80
Camden Road (Rail) 1K 57
Camden Town (Tube) 2J 57
Cannon Street (Rail & Tube) .7D 68
Chancery Lane (Tube) 4H 67
Charing Cross (Rail & Tube) .2D 74
City Thameslink (Rail) 5K 67
Covent Garden (Tube) 6E 66

Earl's Court (Tube) 3E 78
Edgware Road (Tube) 4B 64
Elephant & Castle (Rail & Tube) 1B 84
Embankment Pier (Riverbus) 2E 74
Embankment (Tube) 2E 74
Essex Road (Rail) 1B 60
Euston Square (Tube) 1A 66
Euston (Rail & Tube) 7B 58

Farringdon (Rail & Tube) 3K 67
Fenchurch Street (Rail) 7G 69
Festival Pier (Riverbus) 2F 75
Fulham Broadway (Tube) 7E 78

Gloucester Road (Tube) 1H 79
Goodge Street (Tube) 3A 66
Great Portland Street (Tube) 2J 65
Green Park (Tube) 2J 73

High Street Kensington (Tube) 5F 71
Holborn (Tube) 4F 67
Holland Park (Tube) 3B 70
Hyde Park Corner (Tube) 4G 73

Kennington (Tube) 3K 83
Kensington Olympia (Rail & Tube) 7A 70
Kilburn High Road (Rail) 3E 54
Kilburn Park (Tube) 4E 54
King's Cross St Pancras (Tube) 6D 58
King's Cross (Rail) 5D 58
King's Cross Thameslink (Rail) 6F 59
Knightsbridge (Tube) 5E 72

Ladbroke Grove (Tube) 5A 62
Lambeth North (Tube) 6H 75
Lancaster Gate (Tube) 7K 63
Leicester Square (Tube) 7C 66
Liverpool Street (Rail & Tube) 4F 69
London Bridge City Pier (Riverbus) 2F 77
London Bridge (Rail & Tube) 3E 76

Maida Vale (Tube) 6G 55
Mansion House (Tube) 7C 68
Marble Arch (Tube) 6E 64
Marylebone (Rail & Tube) 2D 64
Millbank Millennium Pier (Riverbus) 2E 82
Monument (Tube) 7E 68
Moorgate (Rail & Tube) 4D 68
Mornington Crescent (Tube) 4K 57

Notting Hill Gate (Tube) 2D 70

Old Street (Rail & Tube) 1E 68
Oval (Tube) 6H 83
Oxford Circus (Tube) 5K 65

Paddington (Rail & Tube) 5K 63
Piccadilly Circus (Tube) 1B 74
Pimlico (Tube) 3B 82

Queen's Park (Rail & Tube) 5B 54
Queensway (Tube) 1G 71

Regent's Park (Tube) 2H 65
Royal Oak (Tube) 4G 63
Russell Square (Tube) 2D 66

St James's Park (Tube) 6B 74
St John's Wood (Tube) 4K 55
St Katharine's Pier (Riverbus) 2H 77
St Pancras (Rail) 6D 58
St Paul's (Tube) 5B 68
Savoy Pier (Riverbus) 1F 75
Shoreditch (Tube) 2J 69
Sloane Square (Tube) 2F 81
South Hampstead (Rail) 1J 55
South Kensington (Tube) 1A 80
Southwark (Tube) 3K 75
Swiss Cottage (Tube) 1K 55

Temple (Tube) 7G 67
Tottenham Court Road (Tube) 5C 66
Tower Gateway (DLR) 7H 69
Tower Hill (Tube) 7H 69
Tower Millennium Pier (Riverbus) 2G 77

Vauxhall (Rail & Tube) 4E 82
Victoria Coach (Bus) 2H 81
Victoria (Rail & Tube) 1J 81

Warren Street (Tube) 1K 65
Warwick Avenue (Tube) 2H 63
Waterloo East (Rail) 3J 75
Waterloo International (Rail) .4G 75
Waterloo Millennium Pier (Riverbus) 4F 75
Waterloo (Rail & Tube) 4H 75
Westbourne Park (Tube) 3C 62
West Brompton (Rail & Tube) 4E 78
West Kensington (Tube) 3B 78
Westminster Millennium Pier (Riverbus) 4E 74
Westminster (Tube) 5E 74

QUEEN

THE NEW VISUAL DOCUMENTARY BY KEN DEAN

OMNIBUS PRESS
LONDON · NEW YORK · SYDNEY

QUEEN
A VISUAL DOCUMENTARY

First published © Copyright 1986 Omnibus Press
This edition copyright © 1991 Omnibus Press
(A Division of Book Sales Limited)

Edited by Chris Charlesworth
Art Direction by Mike Bell
Book Designed by Stylorouge & Michael Bell Design
Picture Research by Valerie Boyd & Dave Brolan

ISBN 0.7119.2828.2
Order No. OP46721

Exclusive distributors:
Book Sales Limited,
8/9 Frith Street, London W1V 5TZ, UK.

Music Sales Corporation,
225 Park Avenue South, New York,
NY 10003, USA.

Music Sales Pty Ltd,
120 Rothschild Avenue, Rosebery,
NSW 2018, Australia.

To the Music Trade only:
Music Sales Limited,
8/9 Frith Street, London W1V 5TZ, UK.

Picture Credits:
Back Cover: London Features International, Ilpo Musto, Pictorial Press and Duncan Raban.

Camera Press: 12TC.
Fin Costello: 39T, 46L, 47TL, 51TR.
Steve Double: 92T & C.
Devon: 82T.
Al Johnson: 17TR & BR.
Keystone Press: 15TR, 50TR, 78TR.
London Features International: 4L, 5R, 8, 11R, 20TR, 21, 23, 30TL & BL, 32TL & B, 36L,
38L & R, 43T, 44TL & BR, 47BL, 49, 51BR, 52, 53T, 54BL & BR, 64B, 69TL, 72L, 73C, 74-75,
83L, 90, 91R, 92B, 93, 95BR, 101T, 102B, 103C, 104BL & BR, 105, 106TL, 107BL, 108, 109,
110, 111, 112, 121, 125, 126.
Ilpo Musto: 70L, 72R, 73BL, 86BL.
Andy Philips: 79TL.
Pictorial Press: 6B, 7C, 11B, 12L, 13R, 13-13C, 14R, 15TL, BR & C, 17TL, 18, 19BL,
22T, 26, 27TL, 30TR, 31BR, 33L, 34R, 37, 40T, 68B, 86TL, 91L, 94B, 95T & C, 101C & B,
103TL & B, 104CR, 128(5,6,7).
Barry Plummer: 8-9, 14TL, 17BL, 20TL, 20BL, 25R, 27TR, 28T&B, 29T, 30CL, 36R, 39BL,
41, 42R, 46R, 48T & BR, 51BL, 55, 63, 65TL & B, 66, 67L, 70R, 78BL, 84BR, 87R.
Retna: 94T, 98, 99B, 102T, 103TR, 104TL, 113, 114, 115, 116, 117, 118, 119, 120, 128(1,3,4).
Duncan Raban: 77T, C & BC, 79B, 80B, 81TL & CR, 85TR, BL & BR, 89BR.
David Redfern: 10, 11TL, 19T & BL, 31T & BL, 35R, 76, 77BL & BR.
Relay Photos: 4R, 5L, 6T, 7R, 12B, 13TL, 15BL, 16, 17C, 19BR, 24, 17B, 29B, 30BR, 32TR,
33TR, 34L, 38TR, 39BR, 42L, 43B, 44TR & BL, 47TR, 48CL, 51TL, 53BR, 54T, 56, 57, 58, 60,
61L, 65TR, 67BR, 69TR & B, 73T, 78BR, 81BL & BR, 83R, 85TC, 87TL, 88TL & TR, 89T.
Rex Features: 96, 97, 99T, 100, 104TR, 128(2).
Shinko Music (Koh Hasebe): 88BL, 89BR.
Syndication International: 67TR, 79TR, 84.
Justin Thomas: 61B, 62, 64TL, 73R, 80TL, TR & C, 82B.
Press Association/Adam Butler: 106TR&B, 107T.

Special thanks to Jason Chinnery, Jon James, Simon Kitts and
Dave Thomas for all their help.

Typeset by The Type Bureau.
Printed and bound in Great Britain by
Ebenezer Baylis Ltd, Worcester.
A catalogue record for this book is available from
the British Library.

CONTENTS

BRIAN HAROLD MAY was born on July 19, 1947, in Hampton, Middlesex, just outside London, and was educated at Hampton Grammar School, also in Middlesex. Inspired by Lonnie Donegan, The Shadows, The Ventures and Buddy Holly, May began playing guitar in various local bands at the age of fifteen, though most of the groups he was involved with never made it past the stage of rehearsing in a garage. (Brian: "None of these groups really got anywhere because we never played any real gigs or took it that seriously.") Among his contemporaries at Hampton Grammar School was a group called The Others, who released a version of 'Oh Yeah' in 1964. May's penchant for jamming with anyone who would play may have led to rumours of his having been a member of the group, but this was not actually the case. Whilst The Others had their moment of glory – and one more single as The Sands – and disappeared, May was engaged in a long-term project: building an electric guitar of his own design.

4

Unable to afford the Fender Stratocaster he coveted, May set about designing and building his own personal guitar with the aid of his father. Both father and son were experienced in wood and metal work, and Brian was a star physics student, so the task was not as difficult as it might sound…though the choice of materials may sound a little odd. (The body of the guitar is solid mahogany, carved from the surround of a 200-year-old fireplace, and the springs of the tremolo unit were salvaged from an old motobike!) Despite its home-made nature, it is this 'Fireplace' guitar which May has played on all Queen's hit records, and which he favours both on stage and in the studio to this day. Its initial price in materials was just £8.

1967 and the summer of love found May enrolled on a degree course in Physics at Imperial College in London. Having decided that he could combine his studies with a part-time musical involvement, May placed a handwritten note on the college noticeboard, inviting other student/musicians to join him in forming a college band. One of the first to do so was bassist/ vocalist Tim Staffell, followed by drummer Roger Taylor.

"We thought he was the best drummer we'd ever seen. I watched him tuning a snare – something I'd never seen done before – and I remember thinking how professional he looked,'' Brian said later.

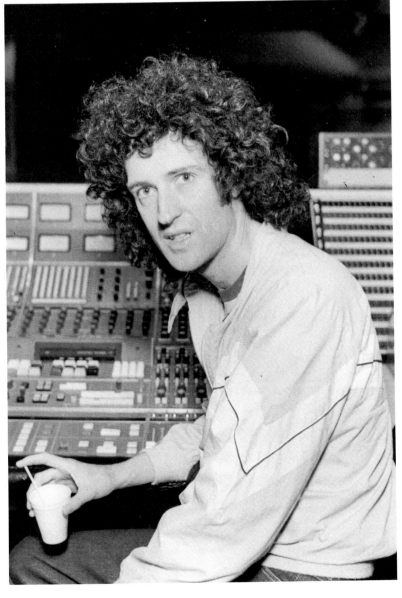

ROGER TAYLOR was born Roger Meddowes-Taylor on July 26, 1949, in Kings Lynn in Norfolk. His family moved to Truro in Cornwall when Roger was eight, and he was educated at Truro School. Taylor's own musical ambitions were frustrated by parental disapproval during his teenage years, though he too managed to play in various local groups – first as a guitarist, before settling down on a drummer's stool (*with* vocals).

Bowing to his family's wish that he pursue a serious career, Taylor came to London as a dentistry student, and studied at the London Hospital Medical School and the Hospital Medical School in Whitechapel. A year later he decided he'd seen enough teeth for one lifetime, and

switched to a straightforward Biology degree at Imperial.

Smile was the name adopted by May, Staffell and Taylor, and they soon built up a steady following – the hardcore of which were undoubtedly fellow students at Imperial – on the London pub and college circuits. May had by this time (1968) acquired an honours degree in Physics, and commenced postgraduate research in Infra-Red Astronomy, still at Imperial.

Despite studies, the three members of Smile were serious about a long-term career, but their inexperience with the music biz led them to sign a contract that was far from ideal. Mercury, at that time an American label with no real base in the U.K. other than a distribution arrangement,

signed Smile to a one-off deal, and sent them into the studio with John Anthony as producer. The result was one single, 'Earth', a Tim Staffell song, backed with 'Step On Me', a May-Staffell collaboration. The single did absolutely nothing, largely because it was released in the U.S. (with no group or record company support). Due to lack of action there, the single was never released in the U.K., and the group was quietly dropped from the label.

Perhaps it was this that caused Tim Staffell to drift away from the others and pursue solo plans that never reached fruition. Reports indicate that although Smile's material was well suited to the time (some of it was to surface on the first two Queen albums, after all), Staffell's voice may not have adapted to changing styles over the years in the way that his replacement's was able to do... so perhaps this departure was for the best.

Summer 1969 found May and Taylor somewhat depressed, to say the least. May took a job that autumn, teaching mathematics at a comprehensive school in London, uncertain whether to pursue his research studies. Tim Staffell was determined to pursue a solo career, and formed a new band called Humpy Bong for which he sang lead vocals. In the meantime, Staffell's flatmate – also a singer – joined Roger Taylor in running a secondhand clothes stall in Kensington Market. He was an ex-Art student with very definite ideas about how to run a pop group, and his first name was Freddie.

FREDDIE MERCURY was born Frederick Bulsara on September 5, 1946, in Zanzibar, an island that is now part of Tanzania. Despite his surname and birthplace, Freddie's parents are both British, his father being a British diplomat. As a result, Freddie attended boarding school in Bombay, India, until he was thirteen, at which time he returned to England. On leaving school, Freddie entered Ealing College of Art, where his contemporaries included Pete Townshend of The Who, Ron Wood of The Faces and The Rolling Stones, and Roger Ruskin Spear of The Bonzo Dog Doo Dah Band. Freddie graduated from Ealing with a Diploma in Art and Design, equivalent to a degree. Along with his artistic sensibilities, and in common with most art school students of the period, Freddie became intrigued by the possibilities of pop music, and in early bands like Sour Milk Sea and Wreckage he began to develop his songwriting, and his stage persona. He re-christened himself Mercury after the Gods' mythological messenger. He probably felt he had a message for somebody somewhere.

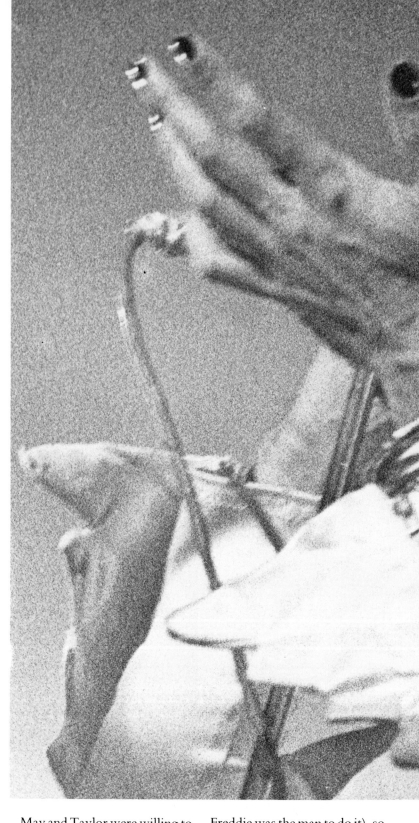

"My teeth... I don't like the way they protrude. I'm going to have them done but I just haven't had the time. Apart from that I'm perfect."

May and Taylor were willing to listen to Freddie's ideas, though May was intent on carrying on with his studies. Mercury's plan was simple enough: combine the 'heaviness' of Led Zeppelin with a new kind of visual flair. Outrageousness plus pop sensibility equals success. Why not? At this time, David Bowie was still a folk singer with one fluke pop hit. Glam and glitter hadn't been invented (though Freddie was the man to do it), so the obvious role model was Jagger, who'd been camping it all the way to the bank for years. Let's call the group Queen, said Freddie. Why not?

"Art School teaches you to be more fashion conscious, to be always one step ahead," Freddie told his new colleagues.

It was Smile's bassist Tim Staffel who introduced Freddie to Brian and Roger. After witnessing

several Smile gigs, Brian remembered Freddie was never slow to offer suggestions: "Why are you wasting your time doing this?", Freddie would exclaim. "You should do more original material. You should be more demonstrative in the way that you put the music across. If I was your singer that's what I'd be doing!"

May and Taylor had been soured by their experiences with Smile. May had painstakingly built a guitar that was as good if not better than anything commercially available. Freddie had *very* definite ideas about presentation. All of them were intelligent and qualified individuals who could easily have found well-paid careers in the 'real world' and if they were to form a rock group, they intended to take it seriously, and make a success of it. Consequently, they take things slowly. Throughout 1970 they

rehearse, write (all three were songwriters) and hone their material, playing in the main only at a friends' parties.

They have no intention of rushing into anything. After (according to legend) wearing out six bass players in rapid succession, they find the lucky seventh in John Deacon.

JOHN DEACON was born in Leicester on August 19, 1951. He attended grammar school in Leicester and did the usual round of teenage local groups before coming to London, where he was studying Electronics (he obtained a first class honours degree six months after joing Queen). Despite being a few years younger, Deacon meshed with the others. "We just knew he was the right one, even though he was so quiet. He hardly spoke to us at all," Brian was to say later.

Freddie designed a logo for the group, using their birth signs as inspiration (it *was* 1971; be fair!), and they were ready to be seen. In June 1971, they play the College of Estate Management in Hornsey for the first time as Queen.

It is with the addition of bassist John Deacon that Queen become the quartet which the rock world now recognise as one of the industry's most durable bands. John: "I was possibly the one person in the group who could look at it from the outside, because I came in as the fourth person in the band. I knew there was something there but I wasn't convinced of it…until possibly the *Sheer Heart Attack* album."

For most of 1971, life goes on as normal. The embryonic Queen play around the West Country, using Taylor's contacts, during the summer, and play some college gigs at Imperial that autumn. May and Deacon study; Mercury and Taylor run their stall, selling artwork as well as clothes. Much of their discussion centres around turning professional.

NOVEMBER
14th Ballspark College, Hertford.
DECEMBER
5th Shoreditch College, Egham.

1971

FEBRUARY
19th Hornsey Town Hall, London.
20th Kingston Polytechnic, London.
JUNE
College of Estate Management, London.
JULY
18th Imperial College, London
JULY – SEPTEMBER
A short tour of South West England. For some reason the only gig anybody remembers was in Truro! Tour organised by Roger Taylor.
OCTOBER – DECEMBER
Two concerts (for friends) at Imperial College, London.
DECEMBER
31st New Year's Ball at 'a rugby club' in London.

Freddie: "We said okay, we're going to take the plunge into rock and we're really going to do a job at it, no half measures. We all had potentially good careers and we weren't prepared to settle for second best if we were going to abandon all the qualifications we had got in other fields."

Roger: "For the first two years nothing really happened. We were all studying, but progress in the band was nil. We had great ideas, though, and somehow I think we all felt we'd get through."

Brian May, looking back on the beginning of Queen's career, recalls their early days thus: "If we were going to drop the careers we'd trained hard for we wanted to make a really good job of music. We all had quite a bit to lose, really, and it didn't come easy. To be honest, I don't think any of us realized it would take a full three years to get anywhere. It was certainly no fairy tale."
The gig played at College of Estate Management, London, was the group's first appearance using the name *Queen*.

Freddie: "Years ago I thought up the name Queen…It's just a name, but it's very regal obviously, and it sounds splendid…It's a strong name, very universal and immediate. It had a lot of visual potential and was open to all sorts of interpretations. I was certainly aware of the gay connotations, but that was just one facet of it."

"The reason we're successful, darling? My overall charisma, of course."

At the beginning of 1972, the group get a real break. De Lane Lea recording studios, anxious to (a) test our their equipment, and (b) have some kind of showcase material with which to interest new clients who would be exponents of the burgeoning 'heavy rock', are looking for a group who would be ready to give studio demonstrations for potential clients. Through friends, Queen get the gig. In return, they are given unlimited free studio time. They spend most of early 1972 using that studio time to make demos, using all the technology at their disposal to the full, and forging many new contacts. Still, none of the record companies they approach are impressed enough to sign them (including EMI, despite the fact that 'The Night Comes Down' on their first album is actually one of the De Lane Lea demos).

Among the many studio technicians who come to view the De Lane Lea/Queen set-up are Roy Thomas Baker and John Anthony, staff engineers at Trident Studios in Wardour Street. Anthony knows May and Taylor through producing their Smile single, and Baker has just set up his own production company. After hearing the group, both Baker and Anthony are convinced that this is the product they need, and they approach their employers at Trident, Barry and Norman Sheffield, who at the time are considering diversifying their studio and film interests by starting a record label.

1972

JANUARY – OCTOBER
Various club and pub gigs, including one at The Pheasantry, Kings Road, Chelsea, and one at Imperial College. Many pub gigs in the Shepperton area. The group spend this period making demos at De Lane Lea Studios.

15

1972

NOVEMBER
1st Forest Hill Hospital, London.
6th The Pheasantry, Kings Road,
London. This gig is arranged by
Roy Thomas Baker and Robin
Cable as an audition for Trident
Audio Productions.
DECEMBER
20th The Marquee, London.

Despite being impressed with the demo tapes, Trident want to see the group perform live, to see if they can cut it in person, so a 'showcase' gig is arranged by Baker on November 6, at The Pheasantry, a club in the Kings Road. Trident like what they see, and sign Queen to a production deal; in short, Trident will place a finished Queen album with a record company, having financed and produced the same.

Queen record their debut album with Baker and Anthony at the controls, but Trident can't have had that much confidence in them, because they are only allowed to record in 'dead time', i.e. when the studios aren't being used by anybody else. Despite the limitations this imposes, the group are seemingly pleased with the finished album; all that

remains is to find a record company. This task falls to Jack Nelson, an American A&R man who'd been brought in to try and find a deal for another Trident signing, a singer called Eugene Wallace, whose career was going nowhere fast. In a sense, Nelson will be selling Queen "off the back" of Wallace.

Nelson places the Queen album with EMI, who intend to use it as a launchpad for a new 'heavy rock' label. So far, so good. Then EMI just sit on it. Queen's relationship with Trident does not have the most auspicious of beginnings.

Recording sessions that result in 'Queen' commence at Trident Studios during December. These continue until the following May.

Brian: "Our stage act was a show, more rock'n'roll oriented than the album, actually, at that

stage of the game. You can only get so far in playing to audiences who don't understand what you're doing, so we did more heavy rock'n'roll with the Queen delivery to give people something they could get hold of – get on, sock it to 'em, get off! If you go on stage and people don't know your material, you can get boring if you do your own stuff all the time. So we did Bo Diddley's 'I'm A Man', Elvis Presley's 'Jailhouse Rock' and Little Richard's 'Shout Bama Lama'. Give 'em a show, but don't make anything but the music your foundation."

Freddie: "When I saw Baryshnikov
on stage I was so in awe I felt like a
groupie."

APRIL
9th The Marquee, London, a 'showcase' gig arranged by Trident.
JULY
6th 'Keep Yourself Alive'/'Son And Daughter' released. Rejected five times by the Radio One playlist, the single received virtually no airplay (licensed commercial radio stations did not appear until later this year), and never reached the charts.
13th 'Queen' released. (Spends 17 weeks on chart; reaches No.24. Status = Gold.)

AUGUST
'Queen II' recorded at Trident Studios, produced by Roy Thomas Baker and Queen.
SEPTEMBER
13th Golders Green Hippodrome, London. Recorded by Radio Luxembourg and broadcast just before Queen's visit there the following month.
OCTOBER
13th Frankfurt, Germany.
14th Le Blow Up, Luxembourg. (T.V. appearance. Between October 11 and 14 the group also appear on French and Dutch television.)
20th Paris Theatre, London. (Concert recorded by BBC Radio One for later 'In Concert' broadcast.)
NOVEMBER
2nd Imperial College, London.
12th Town Hall, Leeds. (First date of U.K. tour supporting Mott The Hoople.)
13th St Georges Hall, Blackburn.
15th Gaumont, Worcester.
16th Lancaster University.
17th Liverpool Stadium.
18th Victoria Hall, Hanley.
19th Civic Hall, Wolverhampton.
20th New Theatre, Oxford.
21st Guildhall, Preston.
22nd City Hall, Newcastle.
23rd Apollo, Glasgow.
25th Caley Cinema, Edinburgh.
26th Opera House, Manchester.
27th Town Hall, Birmingham.
28th Bragwyn Hall, Swansea.
29th Colston Hall, Bristol.
30th Winter Gardens, Bournemouth.

The April Marquee gig is the second time they've played there, so they aren't likely to be impressed by playing an 'auspicious' gig. Moreover, the concert is supposed to be a promotional gig for the new album. Well, they could promote the songs alright, but the album would take another three months to reach the shops; EMI still haven't finalized plans for their new label. Although the Marquee gig gets plenty of music press attention, the impetus of a press campaign for the album is lost.

Furthermore, when EMI do release the album, they do so with a promotional blitz that causes accusations of 'hype' to rear their heads. In the days before Malcolm McLaren and Sigue Sigue Sputnik, this was still an ugly word, and perhaps as a consequence the first single, 'Keep Yourself Alive', is rejected no less than five times by the faceless panel who control the Radio One playlist.

Neverthless the group have reason to feel optimistic. Summer 1973 sees them recording their second album, and (thanks to the Marquee gig) about to embark on their first U.K. tour as support act to Mott The Hoople, at the time a very hot group indeed (courtesy of David Bowie, who by this time had made the transition from Beckenham hippie to something else altogether). This tour establishes the beginning of a Queen 'following', the audience reaction being so good that Mott asked them to play support in the States the following year, and the booking agency MAM immediately signs them for a headline tour of the U.K. in the early spring. The rock press continue to ignore them; of such things is antipathy born.

In June, using the name 'Larry Lurex' (a send–up of the then popular Gary Glitter), Queen plus friends release a single, a cover version of the Beach Boys' hit 'I Can Hear Music', backed with the Goffin/King song 'Goin' Back'. Recorded at Trident Studios after the sessions for the first Queen album, with Roy Thomas Baker producing.

19

1974 is the year it begins to happen for Queen. 'Seven Seas Of Rhye', a Freddie Mercury song they'd included on the first album, is re-recorded for the second time around; it is indisputably a hit, not only in Britain and Europe, but also in the U.S.A. and Japan.

Things are shaping up nicely in America. Elektra, their label there, still has enough kudos left over from the sixties to attract good media coverage for Queen, especially when their debut tour is as support to Mott The Hoople, as hot in the colonies as they are back home. Then, after five nights in New York, Brian May comes down with hepatitis. The rest of the tour is scratched, Kansas step in as support band, and Queen head home to lick their wounds.

They seek consolation in writing material for a third album, only to have the initial recording sessions scuppered by the discovery that May has an additional problem – a stomach ulcer. They are effectively out of action. As it is, they do the best they can, recording as and when May's fluctuating health permits. Against all odds, the album is finished to a standard acceptable to all. It also yields an enormous hit – 'Killer Queen' – which only teenie idol David Essex's 'I'm Gonna Make You A Star' keeps from hitting the number one slot. More importantly (in the long term) they are back on the road, and ready for another crack at America.

DECEMBER
1st The Kursaal, Southend.
2nd Central Hall, Chatham.
7th Leicester University (without Mott The Hoople).
8th Liverpool University (without Mott The Hoople).
10th Court Hall, Taunton (without Mott The Hoople).
12th Cheltenham College (without Mott The Hoople).
14th Hammersmith Odeon, London.
28th Top Rank, Liverpool (without Mott The Hoople).

1974

FEBRUARY
Sunbury Music Festival, Melbourne, Australia. (A three day open air festival.)
25th 'Seven Seas Of Rhye'/'See What A Fool I've Been' released. (Spends 10 weeks on chart; reaches No.10.)
MARCH
1st Winter Gardens, Blackpool. Opening night of Queen's first headlining U.K. tour; support group – Nutz.
2nd Friars, Aylesbury.
3rd Guildhall, Plymouth.
4th Festival Hall, Paignton.
8th Locarno, Sunderland. 'Queen II' released. (Spends 26 weeks on chart; reaches No.5. Status = Gold.)

9th Corn Exchange, Cambridge.
10th Greyhound, Croydon.
12th Roundhouse, Dagenham.
14th Town Hall, Cheltenham.
15th Glasgow University.
16th Stirling University. A riot breaks out in the audience after Queen fail to return for a fourth encore. Two members of the audience are stabbed, and two crew members injured. The next night's concert at Barbarellas in Birmingham is cancelled and re-scheduled for April 2.
19th Winter Gardens, Cleethorpes.
20th Manchester University.
23rd Links Pavilion, Cromer.
24th Woods Leisure Centre, Colchester.
26th Palace Lido, Douglas, Isle Of Man.
28th Aberystwyth University.
29th Winter Gardens, Penzance.
30th Century Ballroom, Taunton.
31st The Rainbow, London.

"When I look back on all that black nail varnish and stuff I think, 'God, what did I do?' I used to feel a need for all that on stage. It made me feel more secure. But now I don't – I've grown up a bit."

Brian: "'Killer Queen' in 1974 was the turning point. It was the song that best summed up our kind of music, and a big hit, and we desperately needed it as a mark of something successful happening for us. We were penniless, you know, just like any other struggling rock 'n' roll band. All sitting around London in bedsitters, just like the rest."

Freddie, on 'Killer Queen': "It's about a high-class call girl. I'm trying to say that classy people can be whores too."

1974

APRIL
2nd Barbarellas, Birmingham.
16th Regis College, Denver, Co.
Opening night of Queen's first U.S. tour, supporting Mott The Hoople.
17th Memorial Hall, Kansas City, Ks.
18th Keil Auditorium, St Louis, Mo.
19th Fairgrounds Appliance Building, Oklahoma City, Ok.
20th Mid South Coliseum, Memphis, Tenn.
21st St Bernard Civic, New Orleans, Lo.
26th Orpheum Theater, Boston, Mass.
27th Palace Theater, Providence, RI.
28th Exposition Hall, Portland, Or.

MAY
1st Farm Arena, Harrisburg, Pa.
2nd Agricultural Hall, Allentown, Pa.
3rd Kings College, Wilkes-Barre, Pa.
4th Palace Theater, Waterbury, Ct.
7th Uris Theater, New York City.
8th Uris Theater, New York City.
10th Uris Theater, New York City.
11th Uris Theater, New York City.
12th Uris Theater, New York City.

JULY — SEPTEMBER
Recording sessions for 'Sheer Heart Attack' take place at Trident, Wessex, Rockfield and Air studios in England. Production by Queen and Roy Thomas Baker.

OCTOBER
11th 'Killer Queen'/'Flick Of The Wrist' released.
(Spends 11 weeks on chart; reaches No.2. Status = Silver.)
30th Palace Theatre, Manchester.
Opening night of U.K. tour with Hustler as support.
31st Victoria Hall, Hanley.

NOVEMBER
1st Empire, Liverpool.
'Sheer Heart Attack' released.
(Spends 40 weeks on chart; reaches No.2. Status = Gold.)

2nd Leeds University.
3rd Coventry Theatre.
5th City Hall, Sheffield.
6th St Georges Hall, Bradford.
7th City Hall, Newcastle.
8th Apollo, Glasgow.
9th Lancaster University.
10th Guildhall, Preston.
12th Colston Hall, Bristol.
13th Winter Gardens, Bournemouth.

In 1975 Queen were finally back in the USA, and with massive backing from Elektra, Queen set off on a nationwide tour – this time as headliners. Unfortunately, the group are clobbered again, firstly by critics comparing them unfavourably to Led Zeppelin, and – more seriously – further medical problems. Freddie comes down with laryngitis half way through the tour, and is diagnosed as having suspected throat nodules – a common enough singers' complaint, but a fairly serious one nonetheless. Rest is ordered, and seven concerts are cancelled. The tour then takes off again, with only one concert having to be cancelled through a recurrence of the same problem.

With single and album both high in the U.S. charts, the tour seems a success, and the group grab a short holiday in Hawaii before their first trip to Japan. The entire group fall in love with the country, especially Freddie, who becomes (overnight) a fanatical collector of Japanese art and antiquities.

Autumn sees the recording of Queen's most ambitious project to date. Despite two months rehearsing the new material, recording sessions grow more and more complex, dragging on for over a month longer than originally planned. The album is 'A Night At The Opera', and Queen are determined that it should be a total state of the art

recording (without resorting to the use of synthesizers). At least six different recording studios are used, sometimes with one band member playing in a totally different studio to the rest of the group! The drum tracks are recorded at Rockfield studios in Newport, Wales, famous for its association with Dave Edmunds; multi-track vocals are recorded at Roundhouse studios; and Brian May's layers of guitar parts are recorded at Sarm. Slowly, Roy Thomas Baker helps piece the whole thing together.

In the middle of all this, business problems rear their head. Despite the departure from Trident that July of Jack Nelson, the group's liaison figure (almost a manager,

24

and one with whom they were less than satisfied: Mercury dedicated the song 'Death On Two Legs' to him), the group remain unhappy with Trident. The final rift comes in September, and the group sign their own record deals with EMI and Elektra, and take on Elton John's dapper but quick-tempered manager, John Reid, to handle their affairs.

Freddie: "As far as Queen are concerned our old management is deceased. They cease to exist in any capacity with us whatsoever. One leaves them behind like one leaves excretia. We feel so relieved!"

Their business house set in order, Queen are ready to unveil their masterpiece. The first fruit of the new album is a single, 'Bohemian Rhapsody'. Almost endless debate surrounds whether the single should be released or not, but in the end EMI decide to take a chance. Despite the song's six minute length, the record's very uniqueness ensures airplay and carries it to the number one position. There *was* nothing around that was comparable. Freddie's 'Opera' has found form under the guidance of May and Baker, with 180 vocal overdubs in one section, and enough guitar parts to drown out a *real* orchestra. To cap it off, Queen make a film to go with the song. True, it only takes four hours to make and costs a modest £4,500, but it is still fairly revolutionary; the age of the video as standard promotional tool is still far in the future.

The single creates enough demand for the album to place that too at the top of the charts over the Christmas period. Queen celebrate with a televised concert on Christmas Eve from Hammersmith Odeon, bringing a successful U.K. tour to a close. Things couldn't have been better.

Freddie is taken to a throat specialist after the February 24 concert at Washington D.C., virtually unable to speak. Nodules on his vocal chords are suspected, and he is ordered to rest. As a result, concerts in Pittsburg, Kutztown, Buffalo, Toronto, Kitchener, London and Davenport are cancelled. The tour recommences on March 5.

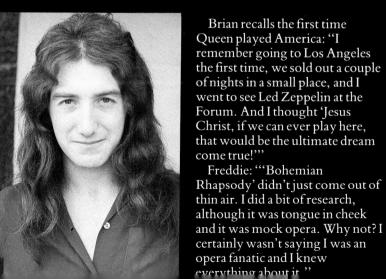

Brian recalls the first time Queen played America: "I remember going to Los Angeles the first time, we sold out a couple of nights in a small place, and I went to see Led Zeppelin at the Forum. And I thought 'Jesus Christ, if we can ever play here, that would be the ultimate dream come true!'"

Freddie: "'Bohemian Rhapsody' didn't just come out of thin air. I did a bit of research, although it was tongue in cheek and it was mock opera. Why not? I certainly wasn't saying I was an opera fanatic and I knew everything about it."

Producer Roy Thomas Baker recalls the problems recording the single: "It wasn't all recorded in one go. We did the whole of the first section and the rock section, and for the middle part, we just hit some drums now and then, after which it was basically edits – we just lengthened the middle section depending on what vocals were put in, because Freddie would come up with amazing ideas. He'd walk in and say, 'I've got some new ideas for the vocals – we'll stick some Galileos in here'…The basic backing track was done over a two day period.

29th Civic Auditorium, Santa Monica, Ca. (Two shows.)
30th Winterland, San Francisco, Ca.

APRIL
2nd Edmonton, Cananda.
3rd Calgary, Canada.
6th Seattle, Wash.
7th Final U.S. concert in Portland, Ore, is cancelled due to Freddie's throat problems. The band leave for a ten day holiday in Hawaii.
19th Budokan, Tokyo, Japan. Opening night of Queen's first Japanese tour.
22nd Aichi Taikukan, Nagoya, Japan.
23rd Nokusai Kaikan, Kobe, Japan.
25th Kyuden Taiikukam, Fukuoka, Japan.
28th Okayam Taiikukam, Okayama, Japan.
29th Yamaha Tsumagoi Hall, Shizuoka, Japan.
30th Bunka Taiikukam, Yokohama, Japan.

MAY
1st Budokan, Tokyo, Japan.

JUNE – JULY
Rehearsals of material for 'A Night At The Opera'.

AUGUST
Mercury, May and Taylor record a session with London soul group Trax at Trident Studios. No material is ever released from this session.

AUGUST – NOVEMBER
Recording sessions for 'A Night At The Opera' take place at Sarm, Roundhouse, Olympic, Rockfield, Scorpio and Landsdowne studios in England. Production by Roy Thomas Baker and Queen.

SEPTEMBER
Release of Eddie Howell's single 'Man From Manhattan', on which Brian May plays guitar, and Freddie Mercury sings and plays piano. Recorded at Sarm East Studios the month before.

OCTOBER
31st 'Bohemian Rhapsody'/'I'm In Love With My Car' released. (Spends 17 weeks on chart; reaches No.1. Status = Platinum.)

NOVEMBER
Filming of 'Bohemian Rhapsody' video, now widely regarded as the first ever pop promo video to be made by any performer or group.
14th Empire, Liverpool. Opening night of U.K. tour; support group – Mr. Big.
15th Empire, Liverpool.
16th Coventry Theatre, Coventry.
17th Colston Hall, Bristol.
18th Colston Hall, Bristol.
19th Capitol, Cardiff.
21st Odeon, Taunton.
23rd Winter Gardens, Bournemouth.
24th Gaumont, Southampton.
26th Free Trade Hall, Manchester. (Two shows.)
29th Hammersmith Odeon, London.
30th Hammersmith Odeon, London.

"The opera section was done over a seven day period of at least 10 to 12 hours a day continual singing, and also continual laughing, because it was so funny to do that we were all in hysterics while it was being recorded. Then there were all the guitar overdubs and getting on for two days to mix it. I'd say that that track, on its own, took getting on for three weeks, because it's three songs merged together to make up this one track... People were getting value for money – they were able to buy a single which was seven minutes long, and was three weeks work on the A-side alone!"

Freddie: "A lot of people slammed 'Bohemian Rhapsody', but who can you compare that to? Name one group that's done an operatic single. We were adamant that 'Bohemian Rhapsody' could be a hit in its entirety. We have been forced to make compromises, but cutting up a song will never be one of them!"

John, on the video: "People used to have clips before, but they were often shot on film. It was quite accidental...at the time we were touring England, and we knew we wouldn't be able to get to record 'Top Of The Pops' on the Wednesday. Our managers at the time had a mobile unit, so it was actually shot on video, in about four hours!"

Freddie: "At one point, two or three years after we began, we nearly disbanded. We felt it wasn't working, there were too many sharks in the business and it was all getting too much for us. But something inside us kept us going and we learned from our experiences, good and bad... We didn't make any money until the fourth album, 'Night At The Opera'. Most of our income was consumed by litigation and things like that."

7th Civic Hall, Wolverhampton.
8th Guildhall, Preston.
9th Odeon, Birmingham.
10th Odeon, Birmingham.
11th City Hall, Newcastle.
13th Caird Hall, Dundee.
14th Capitol, Aberdeen.
15th Apollo, Glasgow.
16th Apollo, Glasgow.
24th Hammersmith Odeon, London.
This show was televised live in a special edition of BBC 2 T.V.'s 'The Old Grey Whistle Test'.

1976

The group spend the first third of the year promoting 'A Night At The Opera' with a U.S. tour followed by dates in Japan and Australia. Although initial radio resistance means that neither album nor single are as instant a success as in Britain, both lodge in the top ten by the end of the tour.

That summer – releasing 'You're My Best Friend' off the album to keep the public aware of them – Queen enter the studio to record a follow-up to 'Opera'. This is the first time they have total control of their own production, Roy Thomas Baker having parted company with the group on amicable terms – seemingly, both parties want to try something new. Recording sessions are interrupted for a few gigs in September, all of which add to the band's growing popularity. Perhaps the most notable of these is a free concert in London's Hyde Park, the site of such events since 1968, the most famous of which was the Rolling Stones July 1969 gig. Over 150,000 fans turn up to see Queen.

JANUARY
27th Waterbury Palace Theater, Ct. Opening night of extensive U.S. tour.
29th Music Hall, Boston, Mass.
30th Music Hall, Boston, Mass.
31st Tower Theater, Philadelphia, Pa.
FEBRUARY
Mercury, May and Taylor all sing and play on the track 'You Nearly Done Me In' on Ian Hunter's LP 'All American Alien Boy', released the following month.
1st Tower Theater, Philadelphia, Pa.
2nd Tower Theater, Philadelphia, Pa.
5th Beacon Theater, New York City, N.Y.
6th Beacon Theater, New York City, N.Y.
7th Beacon Theater, New York City, N.Y.
8th Beacon Theater, New York City, N.Y.
11th Masonic Temple, Detroit, Mich.
12th Masonic Temple, Detroit, Mich.
13th Riverfront Coliseum, Cincinnati, Oh.
14th Public Hall, Cleveland, Oh.
15th Sports Hall, Toledo, Oh.
18th Civic Center, Saginaw, Mich.
19th Veterans Memorial Auditorium, Columbus, Oh.
20th Syrian Mosque, Pittsburg, Pa.

Brian has especially fond memories of Hyde Park: 'The Hyde Park gig was really high. The occasion rather than the gig, you know, the tradition of Hyde Park. I went to see the first one with the Floyd and Jethro Tull – a great atmosphere and the feeling that it was free. We felt that it would be nicer to revive that but it was fraught with heartache because there were so many problems. Trying to get the place was hard enough, let alone in the evening. We had to make compromises and in the end, because the schedule overran by half an hour, the loss meant we couldn't do an encore.''

The title of 'A Day At The Races' identifies it as a 'sequel' to 'Opera' by continuing the Marx Brothers movie theme (Groucho Marx actually sends the group a congratulatory telegram to the launch party at Kempton Park race course). If the single 'Somebody To Love' isn't another 'Bohemian Rhapsody', nobody really expects it to be (it still reaches number two). The album is launched with half a million advance orders in the U.K. alone, and reaches No. 1 over the Christmas period.

Opposite page, top: Hyde Park, from the stage.
Right: A day at the races...with trainer Fred Winter (left), new manager John Reid (centre) and jockey John Francome (right).

22nd Auditorium Theater, Chicago, Ill.
23rd Auditorium Theater, Chicago, Ill.
26th Keil Auditorium, St Louis, Mo.
27th Convention Center, Indianapolis, Ind.
28th Dane County Coliseum, Wis.
29th Fort Wayne Coliseum, Ind.

MARCH
1st Auditorium, Milwaukee, Wis.
3rd St Pauls Auditorium, Minneapolis, Mi.
7th Berkeley Community Center, Berkeley, Ca.
9th Civic Auditorium, Santa Monica, Ca.
10th Civic Auditorium, Santa Monica, Ca.
11th Civic Auditorium, Santa Monica, Ca.
12th Civic Auditorium, Santa Monica, Ca.
13th Sports Arena, San Diego, Ca.
22nd Budokan, Tokyo, Japan. Opening night of Queen's second Japanese tour.
23rd Aichi Ken Gymnasium, Nagoya, Japan.
24th Kosei Kaikan, Himeji City, Japan.
26th Kyuden Gymnasium, Fukuoka, Japan. (Two shows.)
29th Kosei Nenkin Kaiken, Osaka, Japan. (Two shows.)
31st Budokan, Tokyo, Japan.

APRIL
1st Budokan, Tokyo, Japan.
2nd Miyagi-Ken Sports Centre, Sendai, Japan.
4th Nichidai Kodo, Tokyo, Japan.
11th Entertainments Centre, Perth, Australia. Opening night of Queen's first Australian tour.
14th Apollo Stadium, Adelaide, Australia.
15th Apollo Stadium, Adelaide, Australia.
17th Horden Pavilion, Sydney, Australia.
18th Horden Pavilion, Sydney, Australia.
19th Festival Hall, Melbourne, Australia.
20th Festival Hall, Melbourne, Australia.
22nd Festival Hall, Brisbane, Australia.

JULY
'You're My Best Friend'/'39' released.
(Spends 8 weeks on chart; reaches No.7. Status = Silver.)
Recording sessions commence for 'A Day At The Races', and continue until November.
Recorded at The Manor, Wessex Studios and Sarm East Studios. Production by Queen, with Mike Stone as engineer.

SEPTEMBER
1st Playhouse Theatre, Edinburgh.
2nd Playhouse Theatre, Edinburgh.
10th Cardiff Castle.
18th Hyde Park, London. A free concert, with Queen as headliners. Support acts are Kiki Dee, Supercharge and Steve Hillage. The concert is broadcast live by Capital Radio.

Freddie: "People are apprehensive when they meet me. They think I'm going to eat them. But underneath it all I'm quite shy."

1977 begins with a two month tour of America, with Thin Lizzy as support band. Critics slam Queen, but rave about Lizzy. The result is that many new fans are acquired while checking out Lizzy on the critics' recommendations.

Ironically, the very next single to be released by EMI after Queen's 'Somebody To Love' is The Sex Pistols' 'Anarchy In The U.K.' While the Pistols' stay on EMI is a brief (but colourful) one, their debut makes its mark on the whole record industry. The year of the Queen's Jubilee is also to be the year of punk, and The Pistols celebrate the dichotomy with their next single, 'God Save The Queen'. The other Queen, meanwhile, choose the celebrate the Jubilee in somewhat different fashion – after touring the U.S.A. for three months, they finish their European/British tour with two nights at London's Earls Court as part of the *official* Jubilee celebrations. Queen put on a lavish show, losing £75,000 in the process, so costly is the lighting and other effects.

NOVEMBER
12th 'Somebody To Love'/'White Man' released.
(Spends 8 weeks on chart; reached No.2. Status = Silver.)
DECEMBER
10th 'A Day At The Races' released.
(Spends 21 weeks on chart; reaching No.1. Status = Gold.)

28th B.B.C. T.V. repeats the Old Grey Whistle Test Queen concert first screened live the previous Christmas.

1977

JANUARY
13th Auditorium, Milwaukee, Wis.
14th Dane County Coliseum, Madison, Wis.
15th Gardens, Columbus, Oh.
16th Convention Center, Ind.
18th Cobo Hall, Detroit, Mich.
20th Civic Center, Saginaw, Mich.
21st Elliot Hall Of Music, Ky.
22nd Wings Stadium, Kalamazoo, Mich.
23rd Richfield Coliseum, Cleveland, Oh.
25th Central Canadian Exhibition, Ottawa, Canada.
26th Forum, Montreal, Canada.
28th Stadium, Chicago, Ill.
29th Hara Arena, Daytona, Oh. (Cancelled.)
30th St. Johns Arena, Toledo, Oh.

FEBRUARY
1st Maple Leaf Garden, Toronto, Canada.
3rd Civic Center, Springfield, Mass.
4th College Park M.D., Md.
5th Madison Square Gardens, New York City, N.Y.
6th Nassau Coliseum, Long Island, N.Y.
8th War Memorial Auditorium, Syracuse, N.Y.
9th Gardens, Boston, Mass.
10th Civic Center, Providence, RI.
11th Civic Center, Philadelphia, Pa.
19th Sportarium, Miami, Fl.
20th Civic Center, Lakeland, Fl.
21st Fox Theater, Atlanta, Ga.
22nd Auditorium, Birmingham, Al.
24th Keil Auditorium, St Louis, Mo.
25th Lloyd Noble Center, Ok.
26th Moody Coliseum, Dallas, Tx.
27th Sam Houston Hall, Houston, Tx.

In the music press, this doesn't exactly go down well. Hawkish young journalists are championing younger bands, to whom a musician like Freddie Mercury – who toasts his audience with champagne – is the personification of all that is wrong with rock. The NME runs what is less an interview than a confrontation between Mercury and journalist Tony Stewart under the heading 'Is This Man A Prat?' Communication between the two is virtually impossible: to Freddie rock bespoke glamour and always has done – he sees no reason to pretend otherwise.

As a result, Queen are even less fashionable, and their relationship with the press is even worse. They return to the studio to record 'News Of The World', before returning to the States for a two month tour. In the course of the tour they crack America wide open, with the next single – 'We

Are The Champions' – going Platinum and becoming a standard crowd sing-along chorus at sporting events of all kinds.

Brian: "We were just totally ignored for so long, then completely slagged off and slated by everyone. In a way that was a good start for us. There's no kind of abuse that wasn't thrown at us. It was only around the time of 'Heart Attack' that it began to change.

"I'm always affected by criticism. I think most artists are even if they say they're not. It doesn't matter how far you get, if someone says you're a load of shit it hurts.

"But that was just a press response, because for the rest it was always building up very steadily. 'Queen 1' sold really well over a longish period and coincided with our breaking ground concertwise. So we really had matured as a group and had

our audience before the press caught on to us. I think that actually gave us a better start because we were better prepared.

"Most people make the decision to take music seriously a lot earlier. Whereas we were not let loose on the public till a lot later. But we were around, and were playing pretty interesting material. I could play you tapes of Smile which have the same general structures to what we're doing today.

"I'll say one thing for punk rock at the moment. It is creating a way for groups which I think is maybe very healthy. I think maybe people are just being pushed into the limelight too soon, and there is a tendency to get swept along by image to the exclusion of musical direction, but if it's left I'm sure something valid will come out of it all.

1977

MARCH
1st Coliseum, Phoenix, Az.
3rd Forum, Los Angeles, Ca.
(Brian's 'ultimate dream' comes true!)
4th Forum, Los Angeles, Ca.
'Tie Your Mother Down'/'You And I' released.
(Spends 4 weeks on chart; reaches No.28.)
5th Sports Arena, San Diego, Ca.
6th Winterland, San Francisco, Ca.
(Concerts on March 8 and 9 in Sacramento and Fresno cancelled.)
11th PNE Coliseum, Vancouver, Canada.
12th Paramount, Portland, Or.
13th Arena, Seattle, Wash.
16th Jubilee Auditorium, Calgary, Canada.
17th Jubilee Auditorium, Calgary, Canada.
18th Northlands Arena, Edmonton, Canada.

MAY
8th Ice Stadium, Stockholm, Sweden.
10th Scandinavium, Gothenburg, Sweden.
12th Broendby Hall, Copenhagen, Denmark.
13th Congresscentrum, Hamburg, Germany.
14th Fest Halle, Frankfurt, Germany.
16th Philipshalle, Dusseldorf, Germany.
17th Ahoy Hall, Rotterdam, Holland.
19th Sporthalle, Basle, Switzerland.
23rd Hippodrome, Bristol.
24th Hippodrome, Bristol.
26th Gaumont, Southampton.
27th Gaumont, Southampton.
29th Bingley Hall, Stafford.
30th Apollo, Glasgow.
31st Apollo, Glasgow.

JUNE
Queen's 1st EP released.
(Spends 10 weeks on chart; reaches No.17.)
2nd Empire Theatre, Liverpool.
3rd Empire Theatre, Liverpool.
6th Earls Court, London.
7th Earls Court, London.

JULY—SEPTEMBER
Recording sessions for 'News Of The World' at Basing Street and Wessex Studios. Production by Queen, assisted by Mike Stone.

OCTOBER
7th 'We Are The Champions'/'We Will Rock You' released.
(Spends 10 weeks on chart; reaches No.2. Status = Gold.)
In America this is Queen's most successful record to date, reaching No.4 and achieving Platinum status.

35

Thin Lizzy as a support band is a real challenge. They'll want to blow us off stage, and that can be a very healthy thing. You feed off the energy of others and I know that if they go down a real storm then we're gonna go on feeling that much higher. It makes for good concerts. We've had it the other way round. I think we gave Mott The Hoople a hard time on our first tours of Britain and America."

Freddie: "The Jubilee's quite fun isn't it? I love the Queen. I'm very patriotic. I love all this pomp, of course I do. I love it. She does outrageous things!"

Roger: "We were recording an album next door to The Sex Pistols. One day Sid Vicious stumbled in and yelled at Freddie,

'Oho I fed, so you've really bought ballet to the masses then?' Freddie just turned round and said 'Ah, Mr. Ferocious. Well, we're trying our best dear!'"

Brian May joins Ringo Starr, Elton John, Ron Wood, Leo Sayer and others to play on Lonnie Donegan's 'comeback' LP, 'Puttin' On The Style'. He plays guitar on the track 'Diggin' My Potatoes'.

Freddie Mercury co-produces (with Roy Thomas Baker) an album by Peter Straker, entitled 'This One's On Me'.

Freddie: "I just like to think that we've come through rock 'n' roll, call it what you like, and there are no barriers; it's open. Especially now when everybody's putting their feelers out and they want to

infiltrate new territories. This is what I've been trying to do for years. Nobody's incorporated ballet. I mean, it sounds *so* outrageous and so extreme, but I *know* there's going to come a time when it's commonplace.

"The term rock 'n' roll is just a label one starts off with. I should like to think of it as a vast open door. We just carry on doing as many things as we can in different fields. Labels are confusing, they bounce off me.

"People want art. They want showbiz. They want to see you rush off in your limousine. If everything you read in the press about me was true I would have burnt myself out by now. We will stick to our guns, and *if* we're worth anything we will live on."

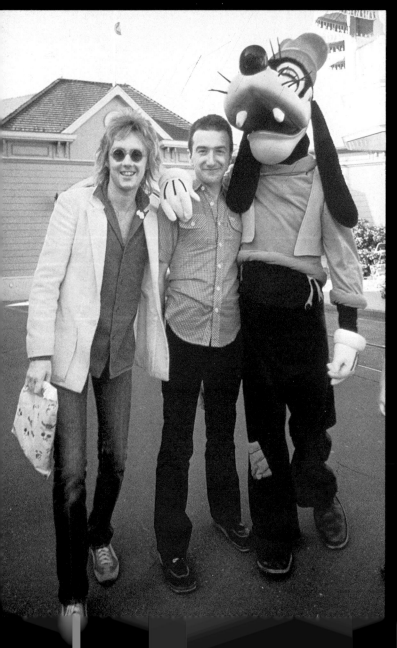

28th 'News Of The World' released.
(Spends 19 weeks on chart; reaches No.4. Status = Gold.)

NOVEMBER
11th Cumberland County Civic Center, Portland, Or.
12th Boston Gardens, Boston, Mass.
13th Civic Center, Springfield, Mass.
15th Civic Center, Providence, RI.
16th Memorial Coliseum, New Haven, Ct.
18th Cobo Hall, Detroit, Mi.
19th Cobo Hall, Detroit, Mi.
21st Maple Leaf Gardens, Toronto, Canada.
23rd The Spectrum, Philadelphia, Pa.
24th The Spectrum, Philadelphia, Pa.
25th Scope Arena, Norfolk, Va.
27th Richfield Coliseum, Cleveland, Oh.
29th Capitol Center, Washington D.C.

DECEMBER
1st Madison Square Gardens, New York City, N.Y.
2nd Madison Square Gardens, New York City, N.Y.
3rd University Of Dayton Arena, Dayton, Oh.
5th Stadium, Chicago, Ill.
8th The Omni, Atlanta, Ga.
10th Tarrant County Convention Center, Fort Worth, Tx.
11th The Summit, Houston, Tx.
15th Aladdin Center, Las Vegas, Ne.
16th Sports Arena, San Diego, Ca.
17th County Coliseum, Oakland, Ca.
20th Long Beach Arena, Long Beach, Ca.
21st Long Beach Arena, Long Beach, Ca.
22nd The Forum, Los Angeles, Ca.

"I like leather. I rather fancy myself as a black panther."

Above: Freddie meets his
macho...on the 1978 US tour.

FEBRUARY
10th 'Spread Your Wings'/'Sheer Heart Attack' released. (Spends 2 weeks on chart; reaches No.39.)

APRIL
12th Ice Stadium, Stockholm, Sweden.
13th Falkner Theatre, Copenhagen, Denmark.
14th Ernst Merck Halle, Hamburg, Germany.
16th Forest Nationalle, Brussels, Belgium.
17th Forest Nationalle, Brussels, Belgium.
19th Ahoy Hall, Rotterdam, Holland.
20th Ahoy Hall, Rotterdam, Holland.
21st Forest Nationalle, Brussels, Belgium.
23rd Pavillion, Paris, France.
24th Pavillion, Paris, France.
26th Westfallenhalle, Dortmund, Germany.
28th Deutchlandhalle, Berlin, Germany.
30th Hallenstadian, Zurich, Switzerland.

MAY
2nd Stadhalle, Vienna, Austria.
3rd Olympianhalle, Munich, Germany.
6th Bingley Hall, Stafford.
7th Bingley Hall, Stafford.
11th Empire Pool, Wembley, London.
12th Empire Pool, Wembley, London.

JULY – SEPTEMBER
Recording sessions for 'Jazz' take place at Mountain Studios in Montreux and Super Bear Studios in Nice. Production by Queen and Roy Thomas Baker.

OCTOBER
13th 'Fat Bottomed Girls'/ 'Bicycle Race' released. (Spends 11 weeks on chart; reaches No.11. Status = Silver.)
28th Convention Center, Dallas, Tx.
29th Mid South Coliseum, Memphis, Tenn.
31st New Orleans Auditorium, New Orleans, Lo.

NOVEMBER
3rd Sportorium, Miami, Fl.
4th Civic Center, Lakeland, Fl.
6th Capitol Center, Washington, D.C.
7th Coliseum, New Haven, Ct.
9th Cobo Arena, Detroit, Mi.
10th Cobo Arena, Detroit, Mi.
'Jazz' released. (Spends 26 weeks on chart; reaches No.2. Status = Gold.)

…And the touring continues in 1978, with a month in Europe. Queen finish with four U.K. dates – two at Bingley Hall in the North, and two at Wembley's Empire Pool. Then it's back to the studio for the recording of 'Jazz'. After producing two albums on their own, Queen once again recruit the aid of Roy Thomas Baker as producer. Whether or not this is move born of desperation is open to speculation.

39

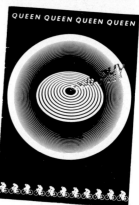

Two songs on the album are tied together as a single for (obvious) promotional reasons, an album insert is banned in the U.S.A. and a video is produced. May has a song called 'Fat Bottomed Girls', and Mercury has one called 'Bicycle Race'. Some genius therefore decides to gather together several dozen nude girls for a bicycle race, and the whole thing is filmed at Wimbledon Stadium by Steve Wood. A fairly innocuous rear view photo of one girl is used as the single sleeve and advertising poster. The whole thing reeks of cheap gimmickry, and – although doubtless meant simply as 'a bit of fun' – left the group wide open to charges of sexploitation (NME runs a suitable picture of Mercury with the caption 'Fat Bottomed Queen').

Not that the group have time to notice – they spend the rest of the year touring the States. Mind you, bringing naked girls on stage during the 'Jazz' section doesn't exactly quieten the controversy…

Brian on nude bicycle racing: "We lost some of our audience with that. 'How could you do it? It doesn't go with your spiritual side.' But my answer is that the physical side is just as much a part of a person as the spiritual or intellectual side. It's fun. I'll make no apologies. All music skirts around sex, sometimes very directly. Ours doesn't. In our music, sex is either implied or referred to semi-jokingly, but it's always there."

During the summer EMI International Records are awarded the Queen's Award To Industry. To celebrate the occasion they choose (appropriately enough) to press up 300 copies of 'Bohemian Rhapsody' in Royal Purple vinyl.

1978

11th Wings Stadium, Kalamazoo, Mi.
13th Boston Gardens, Boston, Mass.
14th Civic Center, Providence, RI.
16th Madison Square Gardens, New York City, N.Y.
17th Madison Square Gardens, New York City, N.Y.
19th Nassau Coliseum, Long Island, N.Y.
20th Spectrum, Philadelphia, Pa.
22nd Auditorium, Nashville, Tenn.
23rd Checkerdome, St. Louis, Mo.
25th Richfield Coliseum, Cleveland, Oh.
26th Riverfront Coliseum, Cincinnati, Oh.
28th War Memorial Auditorium, Buffalo, NY.
30th Central Canada Exhibition Centre, Ottawa, Canada.

DECEMBER
1st Forum, Montreal, Canada.
3rd Maple Leaf Gardens, Toronto, Canada.
4th Maple Leaf Gardens, Toronto, Canada.
6th Dane County Coliseum, Madison, Wis.
7th Stadium, Chicago, Ill.
8th Kemper Arena, Kansas City, Ka.
12th Coliseum, Seattle, Wa.
13th Coliseum, Portland, Ore.
14th PNE Coliseum, Vancouver, Canada.
16th Coliseum, Oakland, Ca.
18th Forum, Los Angeles, Ca.
19th Forum, Los Angeles, Ca.
20th Forum, Los Angeles, Ca.

Opposite page, below: "A Crazy Little Thing Called Love".

A two month European tour at the start of 1979 leads into a one month stay in Japan. The European dates are recorded, and a double album 'Live Killers' is released that summer. The sound isn't great, and the inclusion of 'Bohemian Rhapsody' (for a large section of which Queen were absent from the stage) seems to some to be extracting the Michael a little too far. Taylor hates the album and says so publicly.

Still, it frees them to take their time over the next studio album. Besides creating hits like 'Crazy Little Thing Called Love' and 'Save Me', Queen discover an unexpected asset in their engineer, (known only as) Mack. His ideas appeal to the group so much that he ends up with a co-producer credit, and has worked regularly with them ever since.

John Reid goes the same way as Trident (out of the picture), and the group opt to manage themselves, with the help of a fairly large retinue. John Deacon, the group's least conspicuous member, develops a flair for the business side of Queen's activities. And that summer Freddie finally gets a chance to do ballet, when Derek Dean and Wayne Eagling invite him to join them onstage at the Royal Ballet, in a dance interpretation of 'Bohemian Rhapsody' and 'Killer Queen'. Freddie rehearses for weeks. The rock press ignore the event.

The British tour that autumn features a number of small venue dates around London – Queen's 'Silly Tour'. Nobody had thought that Queen would even set foot in Purley or Tottenham, let alone play there!

They round off the year by playing one night of the benefit concerts for the people of Kampuchea (where, once again, The Beatles fail to reform), and by announcing that they are doing their first film soundtrack, for 'Flash Gordon'.

Film producer Dino de Laurentiis approached the group to write the soundtrack for this film, a remake of the 1930's science fiction serial. The group accept – their first movie soundtrack.

JANUARY
17th Ernsy Merckhall, Hamburg, Germany.
18th Ostee Halle, Kiel, Germany.
20th Stadhalle, Bremen, Germany.
21st Westfallenhalle, Dortmund, Germany.
23rd Messesportspalace, Hannover, Germany.
24th Deutchlandhalle, Berlin, Germany.
26th Forest Nationale, Brussels, Belgium.
'Don't Stop Me Now'/'In Only 7 Days' released.
Different B-side in U.S. — 'More Of That Jazz'.
(Spends **12 weeks** on chart; reaches No.9. Status = Silver.)
27th Forest Nationale, Brussels, Belgium.
29th Ahoy Hall, Rotterdam, Holland.
30th Ahoy Hall, Rotterdam, Holland.

FEBRUARY
1st Sportshalle, Cologne, Germany.
2nd Festhalle, Frankfurt, Germany.
4th Hallenstadium, Zurich, Switzerland.
6th Dom Sportova, Zagreb, Yugoslavia.
7th Tivoli Halle, Ljubljana, Yugoslavia.
10th Basketball Halle, Munich, Germany.
11th Basketball Halle, Munich, Germany.
13th Sporthalle Boeblingen, Stuttgart, Germany.
15th Saalandhalle, Saarbrucken, Germany.
17th Palais de Sport, Lyons, France.
19th Palacio de Deportef, Barcelona, Spain.
20th Palacio de Deportef, Barcelona, Spain.
21st Palacio de Deportef, Barcelona, Spain.
23rd Pabellon del Real Madrid, Madrid, Spain.
25th Les Arenas, Poitiers, France.
27th Pavillion de Paris, Paris, France.
28th Pavillion de Paris, Paris, France.

MARCH
1st Pavillion de Paris, Paris, France.

APRIL
13th Budokan, Tokyo, Japan.
14th Budokan, Tokyo, Japan.
19th Festival Hall, Osaka, Japan.
20th Festival Hall, Osaka, Japan.
21st Practica Ethics Commemoration Hall, Kanazawa, Japan.
23rd Budokan, Tokyo, Japan.
24th Budokan, Tokyo, Japan.
25th Budokan, Tokyo, Japan.
27th Central International Display, Kobe, Japan.
28th International Display, Nagoya, Japan.
30th Kyuden Athletic Association, Fukuoka, Japan.

'Live Killers' attracts criticism for inclusion of 'Bohemian Rhapsody', during which Queen left the stage while audience listened to pre-recorded tapes!

Brian: "'Rhapsody' is not a stage number. A lot of people don't like us leaving the stage. But to be honest, I'd rather leave than have us playing to a backing tape. If you're there and you've got backing tapes, it's a totally false situation. So we'd rather be upfront about it and say 'Look, this is not something you can play onstage. It was multi-layered in the studio. We'll play it because we think you want to hear it'."

Freddie: "I wrote 'Crazy Little Thing Called Love' in the bath. I actually dragged an upright piano to my bedside once. I've been known to scribble lyrics in the middle of the night without putting the lights on."

Brian, on 'Crazy Little Thing Called Love': "We're not a singles group. We don't stake our reputation on singles and we never have done, but I think it's brought in a lot of younger people to our concerts."

Roger: "Crazy Little Thing Called Love' – it's not rockabilly exactly, but it did have that early Elvis feel, and it was one of the first records to exploit that. In fact I read somewhere – in *Rolling Stone* I think it was – that John Lennon heard it and it gave him the impetus to start recording again. If it's true – and listening to that last album it certainly sounds as if he explored similar influences – that's wonderful."

Brian, on the British tour: "We thought it was important to actually visit people again. Unless people can see you in their hometown, it can almost seem like you don't exist. It's also a relief to us because, having done the big barns, it's nice to be somewhere where people can actually see and hear you.

"The advantage of what we're doing this time is that, because our sound and light systems are better than ever, we can really knock audiences in the stomach. The only real disadvantage is that not everybody can get to see us – but I think that those who do have a much better time. It's great fun, too, because the reward is much more immediate and rewarding.

"In the larger venues you tend to lose that intimacy, but on the other hand you gain something

MAY
1st Kyuden Athletic Association, Fukuoka, Japan.
2nd Prefectural Athletic Association, Yamaguchi, Japan.
5th Makomanai Ice Arena, Sapporo, Japan.
6th Makomanai Ice Arena, Sapporo, Japan.

JUNE
Recording commences on 'The Game' at Musicland Studios, Munich. Continues throughout July.
22nd 'Live Killers', a double album recorded on the European tour, January – March 1979, is released. Produced by Queen, engineered and recorded by John Etchells, using the Manor Mobile studio.
(Spends 28 weeks on chart; reaches No. 3.)
29th 'Love Of My Life' (Live) / 'Now I'm Here' (Live) released.
(Spends 2 weeks on charts; reaches No. 63.)

JULY
Recording continues on 'The Game'.

AUGUST
18TH Ludwigparkstadion, Saarbrucken, Germany, supported by Voyager.

OCTOBER
5th 'Crazy Little Thing Called Love' / 'Spread Your Wings' (Live) released.
(Spends 13 weeks on charts; reaches No. 2. Status = Gold.)
'Crazy Little Thing' shows a new Queen, a new sound, a new image (short hair) and a fun video. Even the critics like it.

NOVEMBER
22nd RDS Simmons Concert Hall, Dublin, Eire.
24th NEC, Birmingham.
26th Apollo Theatre, Manchester.
27th Apollo Theatre, Manchester.
30th Apollo Theatre, Glasgow.

DECEMBER
1st Apollo Theatre, Glasgow.
3rd City Hall, Newcastle.
4th City Hall, Newcastle.
6th Empire Theatre, Liverpool.
7th Empire Theatre, Liverpool.
9th Hippodrome, Bristol.
10th Brighton Centre.
11th Brighton Centre.
13th Lyceum Ballroom, London.
14th Rainbow Theatre, London.
17th Tiffanys, Purley.
19th Mayfair, Tottenham.
20th Odeon, Lewisham.
22nd Alexandra Palace, London.
26th Hammersmith Odeon, London.
(One of several nights on which England's premier rock acts play benefit gigs for the people of Kampuchea. Queen's whole set is recorded, but only one track — 'Now I'm Here' — is released.)

else. You get a feeling of an event, and the more people there are, the greater the tension becomes. As a result it makes you work harder, particularly to reach the people at the back.

"I doubt very much whether we'll be going back to large venues in England, because there aren't actually many good ones. Bingley was quite good, but it's dirty and nasty for the people who come to watch. The NEC in Birmingham was the same – and it was definitely far too big.

"It's nice to do those sort of places once and see what they're like, but there aren't many we'd want to go back to. I wouldn't want to do Earl's Court again, nor Wembley, and it's quite possible that after doing Alexandra Palace we won't want to do that. But it's

worth a try, because we're trying to do some special things with Ally Pally. We wanted to do one big gig in London to sweep up all the people we couldn't otherwise cover.

"We don't like to be artificially exclusive. I'd hate to get to the point where people who genuinely want to see us and who couldn't queue up for the tickets can't see us at all."

1980 was hectic – touring the U.S. and Europe, finishing off the sessions for 'The Game', and recording the 'Flash Gordon' soundtrack. Somehow, they get it all done. A 'Greatest Hits' album, scheduled for Christmas release, is shelved when the group decide to release the 'Flash' soundtrack as an official Queen album (to mixed reactions, it must be said).

It seems that 1981, not 1980, would be the band's official tenth anniversary.

'Another One Bites The Dust' becomes an Amercian number 1 on both the pop and soul charts. The song is written by John Deacon.

John: "I listened to a lot of soul music when I was in school and I've always been interested in that sort of music. I'd been wanting to do a track like 'Another One Bites The Dust' for a while, but originally all I had was the line and the bass riff. Gradually I filled it in and the band added ideas. I could hear it as a song for dancing but had no idea it would become as big as it did. The song got picked up off our album and some of the black radio stations in the U.S. started playing it, which we've never had before."

1980

JANUARY
25th 'Save Me'/'Let Me Entertain You' (Live) released.
(Spends 7 weeks on chart; reaches No.11.)

FEBRUARY – MAY
Sessions resume on 'The Game' at Musicland Studios in Munich. Production by Queen/Mack.

MAY
30th 'Play The Game'/'A Human Body' released.
(Spends 8 weeks on chart; reaches No.11.)

JUNE
Release of 'The Game'.
(Spends 18 weeks on chart; reaches No.1. Status = Gold.)

30th PNE Coliseum, Vancouver, Canada.

JULY
1st Coliseum, Seattle, Wa.
2nd Coliseum, Portland, Or.
5th Sports Arena, San Diego, Ca.
6th Compton Terrace, Phoenix, Az.
8th The Forum, Los Angeles, Ca.
9th The Forum, Los Angeles, Ca.
11th The Forum, Los Angeles, Ca.
14th Coliseum, Oakland, Ca.

AUGUST
5th Mid South Coliseum, Memphis, Tenn.
6th Centroplex, Baton Rouge, Lo.
8th City Myriad, Oklahoma, Ok.
9th Reunion, Dallas, Tx.
10th Summit, Houston, Tx.
12th Omni, Atlanta, Ga.
13th Coliseum, Charlotte NC.
14th Coliseum, Greensboro, SC.
16th Civic Center, Charleston, Va.
17th Market Square Arena, Indianapolis, Ind.
20th Civic Center, Hartford, Ct.
22nd Spectrum, Philadelphia, Pa.
'Another One Bites The Dust'/'Dragon Attack' released.
Different B-side in U.S. = 'Don't Try Suicide'.
(Spends 9 weeks on chart; reaches No.7.)
23rd Civic Center, Baltimore, Md.
24th Civic Center, Pittsburgh, Pa.
26th Civic Center, Providence, RI.
27th Spectrum, Portland, Ore.
29th Forum, Montreal, Canada.
30th PNE Coliseum, Toronto, Canada.
31st Convention Center, Rochester, N.Y.

Work commences on the 'Flash Gordon' soundtrack in May, and continues around the group's touring schedule until October. At least four different recording studios in the U.K. are used.

Brian: "We saw 20 minutes of the finished film and thought it very good and over the top... We wanted to do something that was a *real* soundtrack... It's a first in many ways, because a rock group hasn't done this type of thing before, or else it's been toned down and they've been asked to write pretty mushy background music, whereas we were given the licence to do what we liked, as long as it complemented the picture."

SEPTEMBER
10th Mecca, Milwaukee, Wis.
12th Kemper Arena, Kansas City, Ks.
13th Civic, Omaha, Ne.
14th St Paul Civic, Minn.
16th Hilton Arena, Ames, Iowa.
17th Checkerdome, St Louis, Mo.
19th Horizon, Chicago, Ill.
20th Joe Louis Arena, Detroit, Mich.
21st Richfield, Cleveland, Oh.
23rd Coliseum, New Haven, Ct.
24th War Memorial, Syracuse, N.Y.
26th Boston Gardens, Boston, Mass.
28th Madison Square Gardens, New York City, N.Y.
29th Madison Square Gardens, New York City, N.Y.
30th Madison Square Gardens, New York City, N.Y.

OCTOBER — NOVEMBER
Final recording sessions for 'Flash Gordon — The Original Soundtrack.' Recorded at Anvil Studios, England. Production by May/Mack. Executive producers — Queen.
Roger Taylor plays drums on Gary Numan's LP 'Dance'. Recorded at Roch City Studios, London.

NOVEMBER
23rd Hallenstadion, Zurich, Switzerland.
24th 'Flash'/'Football Fight' released.
(Spends **12** weeks on chart; reaches No.**10**. Status = Silver.)
25th Le Bourget La Retonde, Paris, France.
26th Sportshalle, Koln, Germany.
27th Groenoordhalle, Leiden, Germany.
29th Grugahalle, Essen, Germany.
30th Deutchlandhalle, Berlin, Germany.

DECEMBER
1st Stadhalle, Bremen, Germany.
5th NEC, Birmingham.
6th NEC, Birmingham.
8th 'Flash Gordon — The Original Soundtrack' released.
(Spends **14** weeks on chart; reaches No.**10**. Status = Gold.)

ORIGINAL SOUNDTRACK MUSIC BY QUEEN

Queen's relationship with the U.K. music press has always been ambivalent, and Brian reflects on that relationship after a decade: "There are lots of little mechanisms built into the relationships between a musician and the press, which means – almost inevitably – that you fall out. But it happened very early to us, so perhaps it doesn't apply. Generally, I could write the reviews of our albums, the good ones and the bad ones… It's a very limited view of what goes on, as soon as something becomes successful, it can't be worth anything… I did think in the beginning it was important to keep the lines of communication open, to talk to everybody. In the end though, after many experiences, you find that it really doesn't come out. If the guy has stated already that he hates you, and can't see anything in you that is worthwhile, then nine times out of ten, if you spend your time trying to convince him how good you are, he goes away and writes what he thought anyway!… We do have a reputation for not wanting to talk to people, which is really not that true most of the time, if we have time we'll always talk. But if somebody slags you off in a way you don't think is fair, you don't want to talk to them again."

Brian talks about Queen's audience and his attitude to performing: "We do have a lot of power. We just hope we can divert it in the right direction… I know it looks like a Nuremberg Rally, but our fans are sensible people, they're creating the situation as much as we are, it's not that we're leading them like sheep… You just play music which excites people, which interests them. It's rock 'n' roll, there's no philosophical reason why we should be there… Touring is certainly the most immediately fulfilling part of what we do, and it's not really a big strain – mentally or physically – because we're well organised, we know how to do it. All you have to worry about is playing well on the night. For me, it's by far the best part of being in the band. Suddenly life becomes simple again!"

Brian on Queen's growing stature: "You're progressing when you get to play Madison Square Garden for one night, then two, then three. You're reaching more people each time, and it's a recognition that the people who enjoyed themselves the first time have come back and brought their friends. It's a good feeling to build all the time. It doesn't mean that in some ways you're not conscious, it's not an artificial aim, getting bigger is not the be-all and end-all. Often if you sell more records, it doesn't mean that the quality of the record is any better."

8th Wembley Arena, London.
9th Wembley Arena, London.
10th Wembley Arena, London.
12th Forest Nationale, Brussels, Belgium.
13th Forest Nationale, Brussels, Belgium.
14th Festhalle, Frankfurt, Germany.
16th Hall Rhenus, Strasbourg, Germany.
18th Olympiahalle, Munich, Germany.

Roger on the New Romantics: "I just can't see how anybody can get excited over Spandau Ballet. It doesn't send shivers up my spine. I like listening to Bruce Springsteen."

This year the touring takes them to Japan again, but also – on two visits – to South America, almost virgin territory for rock music, other than via pirate tapes. It is a gargantuan task, and – despite thinking of themselves as apolitical musicians – forces Queen to confront political situations they visit, notably in Argentina. They are also – probably to their surprise – slagged off by the press for visiting areas deemed politically unsound. It won't be the last time.

They celebrate their tenth anniversary by releasing a 'Greatest Hits' album for the Christmas market, as well as a video and an official book.

Then they score a real surprise, by releasing a collaborative single with David Bowie, recorded during early sessions for 'Hot Space' that summer. Recording continues through the winter, and

the following spring.

The first of Queen's eight concerts in Brazil and Argentina attract a total audience of over half a million people. The first major rock act to tour these countries, Queen do so in style, flying in 20 tons of sound equipment from the Japanese tour, a further 40 ton load from Miami (including a full football field covering of artificial turf, to protect playing fields in the arenas they were due to play), plus 16 tons of stage scaffolding from Los Angeles. Not surprisingly, the tour has taken nine months to organise, and with estimated running costs of £25,000 per day, no one can accuse them of just doing it for the money – even with high ticket prices. It is a challenge, and it pays off – the audiences are amongst the most enthusiastic the group has ever seen.

Freddie: "We were really

nervous. We had no right to automatically expect the works from an alien territory. I don't think they'd ever seen such an ambitious show, with this lighting and effects."

Brian: "It's a long time since we've felt such warmth from a new audience, although we couldn't see much because of the size of the crowd. We feel really good about it now, as if our ambitions have been partly realised again."

Roger: "In a way I was surprised that we didn't get more criticism for playing South America. I didn't think we were being used as tools by political regimes, although obviously you have to co-operate with them. We were playing for the people. We didn't go there with the wool pulled over our eyes. We fully know what the situation is like in some of those countries, but for a time we made

FEBRUARY
12th Budokan, Tokyo, Japan.
13th Budokan, Tokyo, Japan.
16th Budokan, Tokyo, Japan.
17th Budokan, Tokyo, Japan.
18th Budokan, Tokyo, Japan.
28th Velez Sarfield, Buenos Aires, Argentina.
28th Velez Sarfield, Buenos Aires, Argentina.

MARCH
1st Velez Sarfield, Buenos Aires, Argentina.
4th Mar de Plata, Argentina.
6th Rosario, Argentina.
8th Velez Sarfield, Buenos Aires, Argentina.
20th Morumbi Stadium, Sao Paulo, Brazil.
21st Morumbi Stadium, Sao Paulo, Brazil.
'Future Management', a single from Roger Taylor's upcoming solo album — recorded in six weeks in Switzerland — is released.

APRIL
'Fun In Space', Roger Taylor's first solo album released.

SEPTEMBER
25th Poliedro De Caracas, Caracas, Venezuela.
26th Poliedro De Caracas, Caracas, Venezuela.
27th Poliedro De Caracas, Caracas, Venezuela.

OCTOBER
The 'Greatest Hits' LP spends 165 weeks on the charts.

9th Estadion Universitado, Monterrey, Mexico.
10th Estadion Universitado, Monterrey, Mexico.
16th Estadion Cuahtermoc, Puebla, Mexico.
17th Estadion Cuahtermoc, Puebla, Mexico.

thousands of people happy. Surely that must count for something?

"We weren't playing for the government, we were playing to lots of ordinary Argentinian people. In fact, we were asked to meet the President, President Viola, and I refused. Didn't want to meet him, because that would have been playing into their hands. We went there to do some rock music for the people.

"I wouldn't mind playing Russia at some time. But over there you have to be carefully vetted by the government. The Russian authorities like Cliff Richard and Elton John, but Queen are still considered a little bit wild."

Roger (on his solo LP): 'Afterwards I was so mentally exhausted that I couldn't even be trusted to select the single. There were certain things I wanted to do which weren't within the Queen format; in a way it's like flushing out your system, and until you've done it you just don't feel fulfilled. If I get more ideas for songs I might eventually do another solo thing, but Queen would always get priority."

"The title 'Fun In Space' doesn't mean that the album should be regarded as 'Son Of Flash Gordon', but in many ways it is nostalgic, capturing the old days when life was perhaps a little more uncertain. I've got some old Sci-Fi books and magazines which I browse through from time to time. Maybe there are things up there in space watching us. I wouldn't find that surprising at all."

A fourth Caracus concert, scheduled for September 30, is cancelled, and Queen take a two week break in the U.S.A. before returning to South America.

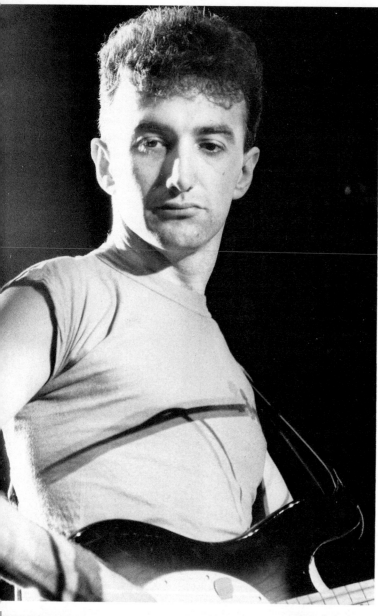

Recording sessions start for the 'Hot Space' album in July, at Queen's Mountain Studios in Montreux. One surprise development is 'Under Pressure', a collaboration with David Bowie which came about almost by accident.

Roger: "It's one of the very best things Queen have ever done, and it happened so casually, when David simply visited us at our studio in Montreux. As long as we can continue to do this, and surprise even ourselves, we'll carry on."

David Bowie: "They turned up in Montreux, so I went down to the studio and we just started one of those inevitable jams, which led to a skeleton of a song. I thought it was quite a nice tune, so we finished it off. It sort of half came off, but I think it could have been a lot better. It was a rush thing, one of those things that took place over twenty-four hours. I think it stands up better as a demo. It was done so quickly that some of it (the lyric) makes me cringe a bit, but the idea I like."

As part of their tenth anniversary celebrations Queen release not only their 'Greatest Hits' album, but also 'Greatest Flix', a video compilation, and 'Greatest Pix', a book which reprints articles by Paul Gambaccini, Ray Coleman and others, together with photos old and new (Quartet Books). A rival book published at the same time (by Judith Davis, and published by Proteus) is successfully injuncted by the group.

The 'Greatest Pix' book is compiled by Jacques Lowe, former house photographer at the White House in the Kennedy era. Lowe sorts over 3,000 photographs before making his final choice.

Track listing for the 'Greatest Flix' video is as follows: 'Killer Queen', 'Bohemian Rhapsody', Love Of My Life', You're My Best Friend', 'Somebody To Love', 'Tie Your Mother Down', 'We Will Rock You', 'We Are The Champions', 'Spread Your Wings', 'Bicycle Race', 'Fat Bottomed Girls', 'Don't Stop Me Now', 'Crazy Little Thing Called Love', 'Save me', 'Play The Game', 'Another One Bites The Dust', 'Flash'. All are promotional videos released at the same time as the songs, with the exception of 'Killer Queen', which is made especially for this compilation.

Freddie: "As long as we feel a sense of achievement and that we are breaking new ground, like doing the South American tours, and planning something like the Far East, we're happy, and we ought to continue."

Brian: "I'm into paradoxes. I wanted to make an album about them, but the group told me I was a pretentious fart. They were right."

54

NOVEMBER
2nd 'Under Pressure'/'Soul Brother' released.
Credited to Queen and David Bowie; produced by Queen/Bowie.
'Soul Brother' does not feature David Bowie and was recorded during sessions for 'The Game'. (Spends 10 weeks on chart; reaches No.1. Status = Silver.)
24th Montreal, Canada.
25th Montreal, Canada.

DECEMBER
Recording continues on the 'Hot Space' album. Completed in March 1982. Recorded at Mountain Studios, Montreux and Musicland, Munich. Produced by Queen/Mack, and engineered by Mack.
8th The Royal Philharmonic Orchestra, under the direction of Louis 'Stars On 45' Clerk, perform an evening of Queen compositions.
Proceeds from the concert go towards leukaemia research.

Roger, on Freddie's reluctance to deal with the press: "Freddie doesn't talk anymore because he's a little tired of Queen and himself being misrepresented. I think anybody who meets Freddie would be in for a bit of a surprise. He's not quite the prima donna you might imagine. Obviously, he's a positive character, but so are we all. When all is said and done he works damned hard and puts on a good show."

Freddie buys a 28 room mansion in Kensington for £500,000 – in cash! Despite carrying out extensive alterations to the property and furnishing it with Japanese antiques, he still hadn't moved in four years later.

Freddie: "Every person who makes a lot of money has a dream he wants to carry out, and I achieved that dream with this wonderful house. Whenever I watched Hollywood movies set in plush homes with lavish decor, I wanted that for myself, and now I've got it. But to me it was much more important to get the damn thing than to actually go and live in it. Maybe the challenge has worn off now. I'm very much like that – once I get something I'm not that keen on it anymore. I still love the house, but the real enjoyment is that I've achieved it.

"Sometimes, when I'm alone at night, I imagine that when I'm 50 I'll creep into that house as my refuge, and then I'll start making it a home. Anyways, as it is, I can only spend 60 days a year in England for tax reasons."

Freddie, on his audience: "I like people to go away from a Queen show feeling fully entertained, having had a good time. I think Queen songs are pure escapism, like going to see a good film – after that, they can go away and say that was great, and go back to their problems.

"I don't want to change the world with our music. There are no hidden messages in our songs, except for some of Brian's. I like to write songs for fun, for modern consumption. People can discard them like a used tissue afterwards. You listen to it, like it, discard it, then on to the next. Disposable pop, yes."

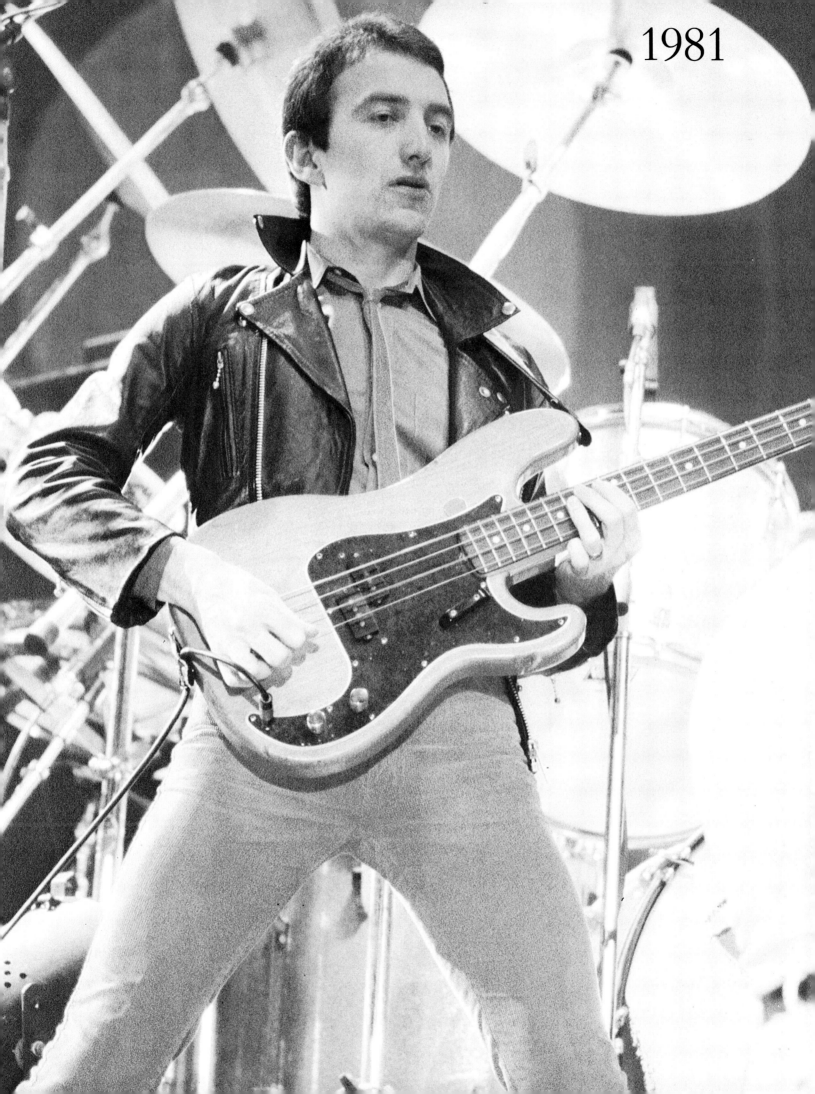

1981

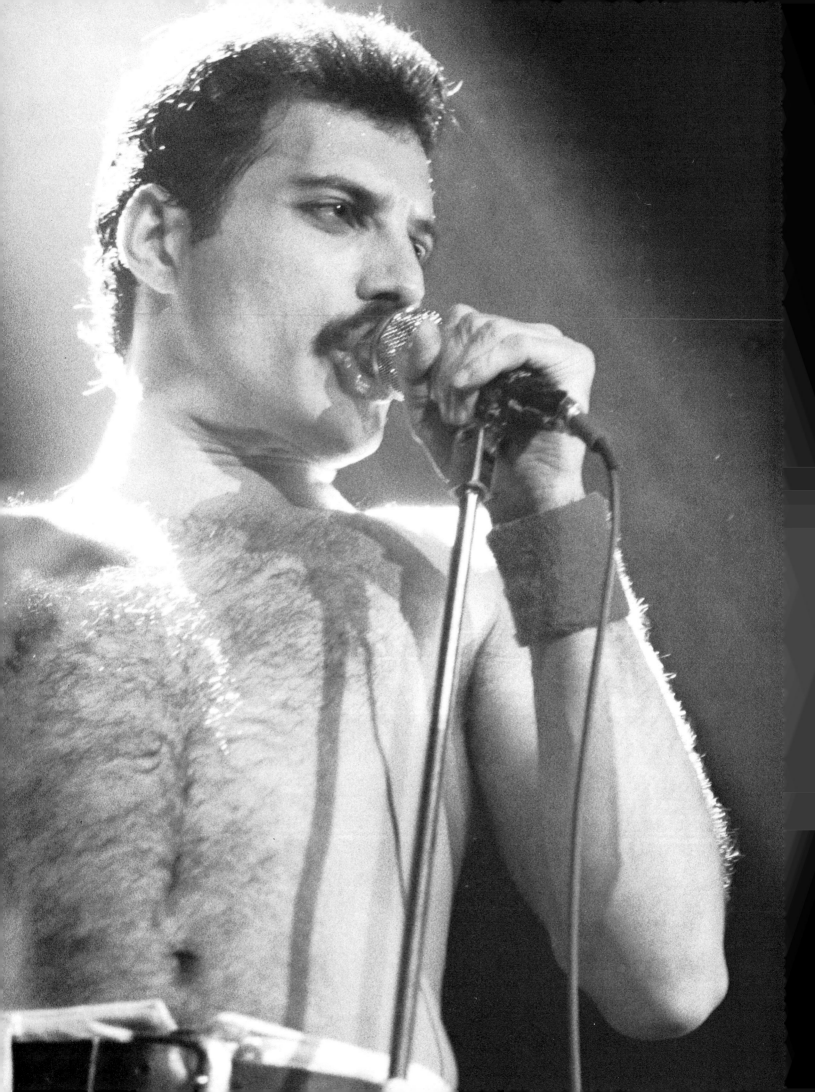

Freddie, on ballet: "I don't know how those ballet people do it – the same steps every night! I couldn't perform in that framework."

Freddie, on meeting Prince Andrew at a Royal Ballet party: "I was wearing a white scarf and holding a glass of wine when I was introduced to Prince Andrew. But I was so nervous I didn't realise my scarf was dangling in the drink.

"There I was trying to be really cool and suddenly the Prince said, Freddie, I don't think you really want this getting wet.' He squeezed out the scarf and that broke the ice between us.

"I said, 'Thank goodness you've put me at ease. Now I can use the odd bit of dirty language.' Then we both burst out laughing.

"He really got into the spirit of things and even had a dance. He's really quite hip in those sort of situations.

"I have a lot of respect for Royalty, I'm a tremendous patriot."

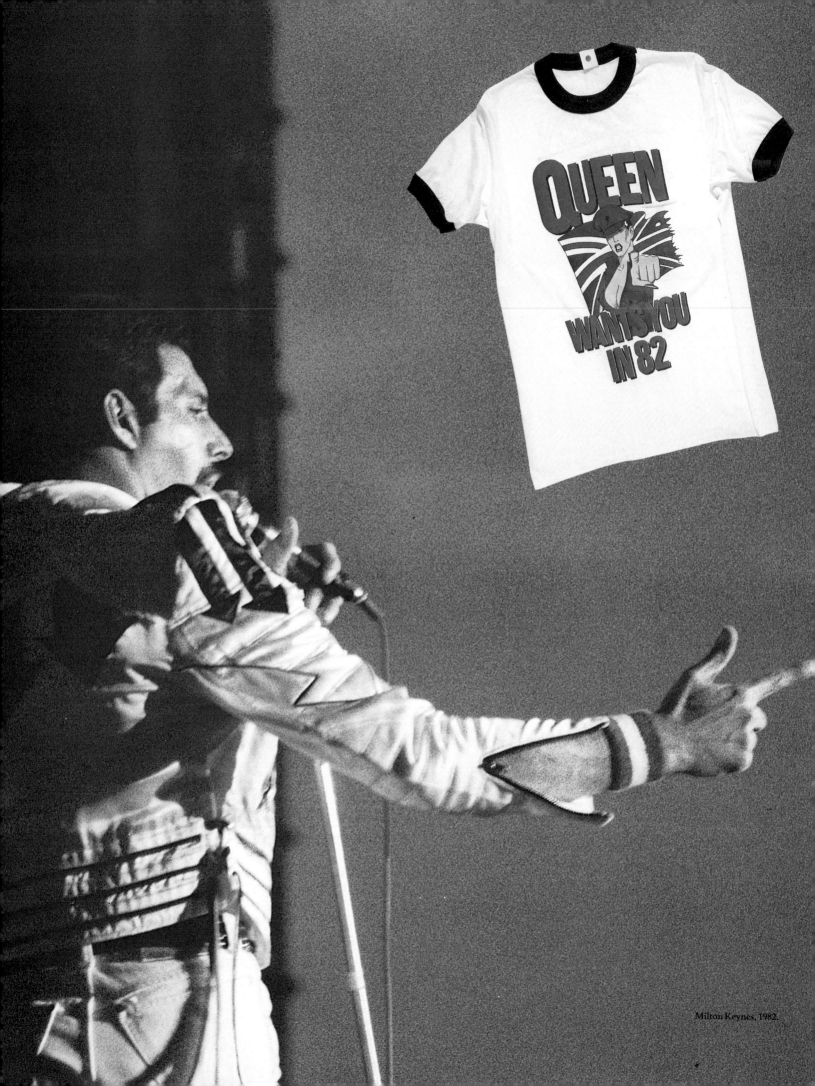

Milton Keynes, 1982.

Yet another year of heavy touring during 1982: little wonder that they decide to take the next year off.

Planned concerts at Manchester's Old Trafford football ground and London's Arsenal football ground, due to take place in May and June are cancelled. The reason given is lack of toilet facilities, as all portable chemical toilets in the country have been booked by cities being visited by Pope John Paul II.

The London date is replaced by a concert at the Milton Keynes Bowl on June 5, and the Manchester concert on May 29 is moved to Leeds United football ground, Elland Road.

Brian: "'Hot Space' is an attempt to do funk properly. It has a style of playing where you get in and get out quickly, hence the title 'Hot Space.'"

With 'Las Palabres De Amor' their current single, Freddie is asked to comment on the Falklands conflict between Britain and Argentina: "It's our young men killing their young men. There's no glory in being blown to bits."

Roger: "In Argentina we were Number One when that stupid war was going on and we had a fantastic time there, and that can only be for the good. Music is totally international."

APRIL
9th Scandinavium, Gothenburg, Sweden.
10th Isstadion, Stockholm, Sweden.
12th Drammenshallen, Oslo, Norway.
16th Hallenstadion, Zurich, Switzerland.
17th Hallenstadion, Zurich, Switzerland.
19th Palais De Sport, Paris, France.
'Body Language'/'Life Is Real' released.
20th Palais De Sport, Lyon, France.
22nd Forest National, Brussels, Belgium.
23rd Forest National, Brussels, Belgium.
'Hot Space' released.
(Spends **19 weeks** on chart; reaches No. 4. Status = Gold.)

24th Groenoordhal, Leiden, Holland.
25th Groenoordhal, Leiden, Holland.
28th Festhalle, Frankfurt, Germany.
29th Festhalle, Frankfurt, Germany.
MAY
1st Westfallenhalle, Dortmund, Germany.
3rd Palais De Sport, Paris, France.
5th Eilenriedenhalle, Hanover, Germany.
6th Sporthalle, Cologne, Germany.
7th Sporthalle, Cologne, Germany.
9th Carl-Diem Halle, Wuerzburg, Germany.
10th Sporthalle, Stuttgart, Germany.
12th Stadhalle, Vienna, Austria.
13th Stadhalle, Vienna, Austria.
15th Waldbuehne, Berlin, Germany.
16th Ernst-Merck Halle, Hamburg, Germany.
18th Eisspdorthalle, Kassel, Germany.
21st Olympiahalle, Munich, Germany.
23rd 'Hot Space' released.
29th Leeds United football ground, Elland Road, Leeds.
JUNE
1st Ingliston Showgrounds, Edinburgh.
'Las Palabras De Amour'/'Cool Cat' released.
2nd Ingliston Showgrounds, Edingburgh.
5th Milton Keynes Bowl. Recorded by Channel 4 T.V. and broadcast on January 7, 1983.

Freddie, on recording with Michael Jackson (several unreleased tracks were recorded in Michael's home studio): "I'd like to release something with Michael because he is a really marvellous person to work with. It's all a question of time because we never seem to be together at the same time. Just think, I could have been on 'Thriller'. Think of the royalties I've missed out on.

"Michael has been a friend of ours for a long time. He's been to our shows and enjoyed them. We make a great team."

Brian, on managing the group themselves: "We didn't particularly want the job, but we decided it was the best way of getting precisely what we wanted and controlling our own destiny."

Freddie: "It's not a question of money anymore. I spend money like it's nothing. You know, I could be penniless tomorrow, but I'd get back, somehow."

Roger: "We just don't want to be seen to fail. That's what keeps us going."

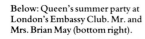

Below: Queen's summer party at London's Embassy Club. Mr. and Mrs. Brian May (bottom right).

JULY
'Calling All Girls'/'Put Out The Fire' released (U.S.A. only).
21st Forum, Montreal, Canada.
23rd Gardens, Boston, Mass.
24th Spectrum, Philadelphia, Pa.
25th Capitol Center, Washington, D.C.
27th Madison Square Gardens, New York City, N.Y.
28th Madison Square Gardens, New York City, N.Y.
31st Richfield Coliseum, Cleveland, Oh.

AUGUST
Roger Taylor sings backing vocals on three tracks — 'Play The Game Tonight', 'Right Away' and 'Diamonds & Pearls' — on the Kansas album 'Vinyl Confessions'.
2nd Maple Leaf Gardens, Toronto, Canada.
3rd Maple Leaf Gardens, Toronto, Canada.
5th Market Square Arena, Indianapolis, Ind.
6th Joe Louis Arena, Detroit, Mich.
7th Riverfront Coliseum, Cincinnati, Oh.
9th Brendon Burn Coliseum, Meadowlands, NJ.
'Back Chat'/'Staying Power' released (not released in U.S.A.).
10th Coliseum, New Haven, Ct.
11th Poplar Creek, Chicago, Ill.
13th Poplar Creek, Chicago, Ill.
15th Civic Center Arena, St Paul, Ill.
19th Civic Center, Biloxi, Tx.
20th Summit, Houston, Tx.
21st Reunion, Dallas, Tx.
24th Omni, Atlanta, Ga.
25th Mid-South Coliseum, Memphis, Tenn.
28th Kemper Arena, Kansas City, Ka.
30th Nichols Arena, Denver, Co.

SEPTEMBER
2nd Coliseum, Portland, Ore.
3rd Coliseum, Seattle, Wa.
4th PNE Coliseum, Vancouver, Canada.
7th Coliseum, Oakland, Ca.
10th Coliseum, Phoenix, Az.
11th Irvine Meadows, Irvine, NM.
12th Irvine Meadows, Irvine, NM.
14th Forum, Los Angeles, Ca.
15th Forum, Los Angeles, Ca.

OCTOBER
19th Kyuden Auditorium, Fukuoka, Japan.
20th Kyuden Auditorium, Fukuoka, Japan.
24th Hankyu Nishinomiyakyujo, Osaka, Japan.
26th Kokusai Tenjijo, Nagoya, Japan.
29th Hokkaiidoritso Sangyo Kyoshinkaijo, Sapporo, Japan.

NOVEMBER
3rd Seibu Lions Kyujo, Tokyo, Japan.

Freddie: "I can be very soft, very slushy and mushy."

During 1983 Queen take a year off from recording and touring, and concentrate their energies on solo projects.

Brian: "We were getting too close to each other…getting on each other's nerves which happens periodically. This time we said: 'Let's take a break and give ourselves some breathing space. Let's do individual things, then we can come back to Queen when we actually feel motivated.' We took about five months off work, up until August this year.

"During that time we met and talked a lot, but we didn't actually do anything. We wanted the next album we made to be in a new situation.

"We were trying to break from our old record company in America, which was important. We didn't want to deliver another album in that situation.

"There was that feeling that we might just be making another Queen album and putting it back into the machine. We didn't want that, and it's all worked out very well. We agreed on Capitol, and signed a deal with them. Suddenly, we have a company in America that's really *excited* to be getting their first Queen album.

"There's always been a lot of tension within Queen, because we don't like the same things as far as music is concerned and have to find common ground. We often disagree about how things should be presented. We're all very forthright and different. We are very stubborn, but there is a democracy. Nobody has a bigger share of the say than anybody else. But sometimes it's very tense and very hard.

"It's not the touring, though. That's the best and easiest part. You have to go out there and be as good as you damn well can be. But the thought of doing another album just didn't appeal to us after the last tour, so, we thought it was no use forcing it. Better to wait until we'd something to offer.

"We didn't want to split up because we felt that's a mistake so many people have made from The Beatles onwards. It would have been so good if they could have held together for longer. No matter how talented the individuals are, the group is always something more than its components. And we think Queen is an example of a proper group. With all its shortcomings, I think it's worth keeping together.

JANUARY
7th Film of June 5, 1982, concert at Milton Keynes broadcast by Channel 4.

Left: Roger on timpani during the "We Will Rock You" video.

65

After all the fights we still tend to come up with things that have been through the sieve and are worthwhile – *because* of all the fighting. We still care. I think our new album is damn good, much better than anything we've done for a while. It's going to be called 'The Works'. And it really is! There's all the Queen trademarks. Lots of production, arrangements and harmonies.

"We've experimented a lot in the past and some of the experiments didn't work. Our last album was one big experiment and a lot of people totally hated it. And it didn't sell very well – not compared to earlier stuff, anyway. We've had ups and downs. People don't realise that. They think Queen can't do anything wrong.

"People think we can just stick out an album and it's easy for us. But really it's not. There are varying degrees of success, and we are always conscious that our next album may also be our last. We don't like to repeat ourselves, so there is always the chance that people will hate what we do.

"It's funny; everyone thought Queen had this big master plan to conquer the world, but really we were so excited *just* to make an album – that was the amibition in itself. None of us knew what was ahead."

Roger: "After touring America, Europe and Japan we were totally knackered, so we thought we deserved a bit of a rest…It also had a lot to do with the last album not doing as well as previous LPs. We realised that it hadn't been what a lot of fans wanted or expected from us, so we thought a break would give us the opportunity to think things through a bit."

Freddie: "I used to think we'd go on for five years, but it's got to the point where we're all actually too *old* to break up. Can you imagine forming a new band at 40? Be a bit silly, wouldn't it?"

During the summer Brian co–produces (with Mack) the debut album by Heavy Pettin', 'Letting' Loose', recorded in London and Munich.

John Deacon plays bass on 'Picking Up Sounds', a single by Man Friday And Jive Junior.

Brian May plays guitar on two
tracks by Jeffrey Osborne, 'Two
Wrongs Don't Make A Right' and
'Stay With Me Tonight', which is
released as a single. Recorded at
Mad Hatter Studios in Los
Angeles.

Brian is interviewed by BBC
Radio One for their 'Guitar
Greats' series – hour-long
programmes which feature in-
depth interviews with the most
famous rock guitarists (Beck,
Townshend, Clapton etc). A
transcript of the interview is
published in the book of the series
in September 1983 (*Guitar Greats*
by John Tobler and Stuart
Grundy, BBC Publications).

Brian, on playing live with Def
Leppard at an L.A. Forum
concert: "I was bowled over by
them. Just amazing. Their show
was one of the highest energy
things I've *ever* seen. I was turned
on to them by Heavy Pettin'.
They destroyed the place. I went
back and told 'em so, and they
invited me to play with them the
next night. I was highly flattered,
so I went on and played a song
with them at the end, which was
great fun."

Top left: Freddie snapped by the
paparazzi.
"I hate pockets in my trousers. By
the way, I don't wear a hose. My
hose is my own...there's nothing
stuffed down there."

In October 1983 Brian becomes the second member of Queen to release a solo album, 'Star Fleet Project', a star–studded project which featured Van Halen's Eddie Van Halen and REO Speedwagon's Alan Gratzer. Also released in a single 'Star Fleet', an edited version of the title track.

Brian: "To be honest, I didn't even know if I could play with other musicians. I had been *so* long with Queen I thought, 'What kind of musician am I?' I had been working the machine, but maybe I had become too much a slave of it... Edward and I took a break from recording and started talking about how it was in the old days when Eric Clapton was doing his thing with John Mayall. We all found 'The Beano' album had been a big influence on us, remember, the one with Eric reading the comic on the cover? It was a classic collector's item for every guitarist. It sounded like they were having so much fun they couldn't stop...'Blues

Breaker', which takes up all of side two on the album, is my favourite part of the record. It seemed very indulgent putting out a long jam but, having listened to it, I think it's worthwhile...It's rock blues with all the mistakes left in."

Mercury and Taylor sing backing vocals on the title track of Billy Squier's album 'Emotions In Motion', recorded at Musicland in Munich.

Brian: "Recently, Guild guitars approached me and said they would like to make a Brian May model. So we got together and talked about it. They've been through the guitar, taken it to pieces and measured it up, and they reckon they can make something which is very close to the one I made myself all those years ago. Now, hopefully, there should be a Brain May guitar which sounds like my one."

Brian: "People have been rumouring that Queen are going to split up for the last eight years at least. I've got some great cuttings

at home from people saying, 'One thing is certain, Queen will no longer exist in a year's time'. And that was in 1973!"

1984 and back to serious business, though the first gig doesn't go well. At the San Remo song festival, Taylor and May are at each other's throats over material, the stage and a thousand other things. Freddie manages to crack them both up laughing, which saves the day, and possibly the group.

The new album does well, and the European tour is bigger, venuewise, than ever before. Then Queen play Sun City, the playboy paradise in South Africa. They knew before they go that it will be a controversial move, but feel it is worth it to take their music to a new audience. They are not to realise how long the controversy will rage.

Roger: "One day the radio came on in my house and my three year old son Felix came out with 'radio poo poo!' I thought that sounded

Below: Brian with 'Fireplace' guitar.

good, so I changed it around a bit and came up with 'Radio Ga Ga'. The song came after I'd locked myself in a studio for three days with a synthesiser and a drum machine…Giorgio Moroder had bought the film rights to *Metropolis* and he wanted us to write a song to go with it. We wrote him a song and we swapped it for the rights to use some footage from the film. It's a great movie, and I'd always been interested in using images from it…there's a sense of nostalgia in watching a silent film that links in with the nostalgic view of radio I got from remembering nights spent listening to Radio Luxembourg under the bedclothes."

One of the other acts at Italy's San Remo Song Festival is Culture Club.

Freddie: (on Boy George): "He's a great talent. That boy is so brave.

"When I started off, rock bands were all wearing jeans, and suddenly here's Freddie Mercury in a Zandra Rhodes frock with make-up and black nail varnish. It was totally outrageous. In a way, Boy George has just updated that thing, the whole glam-rock bit. George is more like a drag queen. It's the same outrage, just doubled.

"Rod Stewart, Elton John and I were going to form a band called Hair, Nose & Teeth after the three of us. But it hasn't happened because none of our egos can agree on the order of the words! Naturally, I wanted it to be called Teeth, Nose & Hair… Michael Jackson and I have grown apart a bit since his massive success with 'Thriller'. He's simply retreated into a world of his own. Two years ago we used to have great fun going to clubs together but now he won't come out of his fortress. It's very sad. He's so worried that someone will do him in that he's paranoid about absolutely everything."

Brian, on 'The Works': "I always got the most enjoyment out of the harder material. Actually, our new album is a lot harder…but I did fight to get it that way. We've done some fantastic over-the-top harmonies and a lot of heavy things that we haven't done for years.

"The pressure has always been against me, because not everyone in the band is into the same stuff as I am. I get the most pleasure out of things that I can hammer down and get some excitement out of. Basically, I'm like a little boy with the guitar, I just love the fat, loud sound of it. But that's not important to the others, and I agree with this, the songs come first. That's where the common ground ends and the arguments begin. The result is always a compromise."

JANUARY
23rd 'Radio Ga Ga'/'I Go Crazy' released.
(Spends 9 weeks on chart; reaches No.2. Status = Silver.)
The 'Radio Ga Ga' video includes footage from Fritz Lang's *Metropolis*.
FEBRUARY
San Remo Song Festival, Italy.
27th 'The Works' released.
(Spends 48 weeks on chart; reaches No.2. Status = Gold.)

APRIL
2nd 'I Want To Break Free'/ 'Machines (Or Back To Humans)' released.
(Spends 15 weeks on chart; reaches No.3. Status = Silver.)
MAY
12th Golden Rose Festival, Montreux, Switzerland.
JULY
16th 'It's A Hard Life'/'Is This The World We Created?' released.
(Spends 9 weeks on chart; reaches No.6.)
Rehearsals in Munich for the forthcoming tour, often lasting over twelve hours a day.
AUGUST
24th Forest National, Brussels, Belgium.
28th RDS Simmons Hall, Dublin, Eire.
29th RDS Simmons Hall, Dublin, Eire.
31st NEC, Birmingham, supported by General Public.

Left: Fritz Lang's *Metropolis*.

Brian, on their South African dates: "We've thought about the morals of it a lot, and it's something we've decided to do. This band is not political, we play to anybody who comes to listen. The show will be in Botswana in front of a mixed audience."

John: "Throughout our career we've been a very non-political group. We enjoy going to new places. We've toured America and Europe so many times that it's nice to go somewhere different. Everybody's been to South Africa, it's not as though we're setting a precedent. Elton John's been there, Rod Stewart, Cliff Richard. I know there can be a bit of a fuss, but apparently we're very popular down there…

Basically we want to play wherever the fans want to see us."

Roger on touring strange places: "The Russians still think we're very decadent. We want to play China as well, and Korea. John and I spent a holiday in Korea and it's a fascinating place."

Roger, responding to criticism of Queen's South African appearances: "'I Want To Break Free' is an unofficial anthem among the African Congress Movement, and 'Another One Bites The Dust' is one of the biggest selling songs in South African black history."

Nevertheless repercussions of the South African concerts continue to plague the band.

Roger: "In a way I do regret playing. In some ways I would

defend what we did. I mean, basically we play music to people – lots of them preferably – and I think a lot of crap is talked over here about things that people don't really know about."

Brian: "We're totally against apartheid and all it stands for, but I feel we did a lot of bridge building. We actually met musicians of both colours. They all welcomed us with open arms. The only criticism we got was from outside South Africa."

Roger: "It's not the money anymore, it's the thought of 'Christ, what would we do if we ended it?' Obviously we could all have our solo careers and put new bands together, but that would be like climbing Mount Everest again. Queen is what we do; it's

SEPTEMBER
'We Will Rock You', a video compilation, is released by Peppermint Video Music. Release of 'Love Kills'/'Rot Wang's Party', Freddie Mercury's first solo single, and a song written for inclusion in the soundtrack of the 'updated' version of *Metropolis*.

1st NEC, Birmingham.
2nd NEC, Birmingham.
4th Wembley Arena, London.
5th Wembley Arena, London.
7th Wembley Arena, London.
8th Wembley Arena, London.
10th 'Hammer To Fall'/'Tear It Up' released.
(Spends 13 weeks on chart; reaches No.8.)
12th Westfallenhalle, Dortmund, Germany.
14th Sportspalace, Milan, Italy.
15th Sportspalace, Milan, Italy.
16th Olympic Hall, Munich, Germany.
18th Omnisports, Paris, France.
20th Groenoordhalle, Leiden, Holland.
21st Forest Nationale, Brussels, Belgium.
22nd Europahalle, Hanover, Germany.
24th Deutchlandhalle, Berlin, Germany.
26th Schleyerhalle, Stuttgart, Germany.
29th Stadhalle, Vienna, Austria.
30th Stadhalle, Vienna, Austria.

OCTOBER
5th Sun City Super Bowl, Bophuthatswana.
6th Sun City Super Bowl, Bophuthatswana.
10th Sun City Super Bowl, Bophuthatswana.
13th Sun City Super Bowl, Bophuthatswana.
14th Sun City Super Bowl, Bophuthatswana.
18th Sun City Super Bowl, Bophuthatswana.
19th Sun City Super Bowl, Bophuthatswana.
20th Sun City Super Bowl, Bophuthatswana.
Release of the soundtrack album of *Metropolis* (CBS 70252), which featues Mercury's 'Love Kills' alongside songs by Pat Benatar, Jon Anderson, Cycle V, Bonnie Tyler, Loverboy, Billy Squier and producer Giorgio Moroder.

NOVEMBER
26th 'Thank God It's Christmas'/ 'Man On The Prowl'/'Keep Passing The Open Windows' released.
Produced by Queen/Mack.
(Spends 6 weeks on chart; reaches No.21.)

'The Works' EP, a four track video compilation, is released by Picture Music International.

what we're used to. But we'll only do it while the enthusiasm's there. The more interest that's shown in the band, the more enthusiasm is generated within the band; that's why it's been such a thrill that 'Radio Ga Ga' is such a big hit. Obviously, if people stopped buying our records and coming to our live shows, we'd knock it on the head pretty quickly.''

Freddie donates the song 'Love Kills' to Giorgio Moroder, for use in the soundtrack of the re-vamped version of Fritz Lang's classic silent film, *Metropolis*.

"People can think what they like about my bi-sexual stage image. That's what I want them to do. I want to keep the mystique."

Filming the video for "I Want To Break Free"

In February *The Sun* newspaper publishes an interview with Freddie Mercury, hooked around the admission, "Oh yes, I'm gay. I've done all that."

Freddie: "I was completely misquoted. But from the beginning, the press have always written whatever they wanted about Queen, and they can get away with it. The woman who wrote that story wanted a total scoop from me and didn't get anything. I said, 'What do you want to hear? That I deal cocaine?' But for God's sake, if I want to make big confessions about my sex life, would I go to *The Sun*, of all papers, to do it? There's no fucking way I'd do that. I'm too intelligent."

Roger (on the Golden Rose Festival at Montreux): "All things like that are farces, 'cause you're miming to playback, but Freddie made that pretty obvious. But 400 million viewers…who could say no?"

In June Roger's second solo album, 'Strange Frontier' is released. Cover versions of Bob Dylan's 'Masters Of War' and Bruce Springsteen's 'Racing In The Streets' are included, and the album includes a songwriting collaboration with Freddie Mercury ('Killing Time') and one with Rick Parfitt of Status Quo ('It's An Illusion') on which John Deacon plays bass.

Roger (on rehearsing after the long lay-off): "It's strange how rusty we are, and so we're trying to blow the cobwebs away. It's taking a lot of work. Usually we rehearse until about nine, and then we eat together and decide what we're going to do in the evening. The clubs here (Munich) are really fun. Something to cater for every taste or perversion."

"We still have the rock 'n' roll gypsy mentality. Even after 12 years without a line-up change we

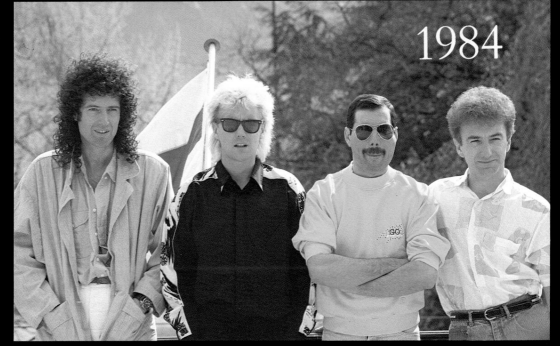

1984

still really enjoy the buzz from playing live and the fact that we have hit singles. Some bands in our position might take it all in their stride, but we're still like kids, we get very excited.''

'Keep Passing The Open Windows' is a quote from novelist John Irving's 'The Hotel New Hampshire'. The phrase basically means 'don't commit suicide', a message Queen have stressed before, on 'Don't Try Suicide', the American B-side to 'Another One Bites The Dust'.

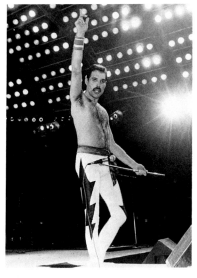

January's 'Rock In Rio' festival is an event of gargantuan proportions. The group must have thought at the time that they'd never face a larger audience. They were wrong.

'Live Aid' superseded even Woodstock in the public imagination (and almost certainly in the history books as well). Queen turned in a superb set, coming on just after David Bowie and running through almost all their hits. As a result, an awful lot of people realised they liked Queen after all, and record sales went soaring. Hopefully, the event saved a life or two as well.

JANUARY
11th Rock In Rio Festival, Rio de Janeiro, Brazil.
18th Rock In Rio Festival, Rio de Janeiro, Brazil.

APRIL
13th Mount Smart Stadium, Auckland, New Zealand.
16th Sports & Entertainments Centre, Melbourne, Australia.
17th Sports & Entertainments Centre, Melbourne, Australia.
19th Sports & Entertainments Centre, Melbourne, Australia.
20th Sports & Entertainments Centre, Melbourne, Australia.
25th Entertainments Centre, Sydney, Australia.
26th Entertainments Centre, Sydney, Australia.
28th Entertainments Centre, Sydney, Australia.
29th Entertainments Centre, Sydney, Australia.

MAY
8th Budokan, Tokyo, Japan.
9th Budokan, Tokyo, Japan.
11th Yoyogi Swimming Pool Auditorium, Tokyo, Japan.
13th Aichi Auditorium, Nagoya, Japan.
15th Jo Hall, Osaka, Japan.

JULY
13th Wembley Stadium, London. The 'Live Aid' concert.

AUGUST
'Made In Heaven', the second single from Mercury's 'Mr. Bad Guy' album is released.

NOVEMBER
5th 'One Vision'/'Blurred Vision' released.
Produced by Queen/Mack.

DECEMBER
5th 'The Complete Works' released. A limited edition boxed set of all Queen albums to date (excluding 'Greatest Hits'), with an additional album, 'Complete Vision', comprising singles and B-sides that have escaped inclusion elsewhere, up to and including 'One Vision'/'Blurred Vision'. All fourteen albums are digitally re-mastered and packaged in plain white sleeves (the original sleeve artwork is reproduced in one of the two booklets that came with the package). Lovingly put together, and good value for money: you even get a map of the world, showing Queen's conquests!

Left: Live Aid.
Above: Freddie on stage at Rio.

Top right: Status Quo's Rick Parfitt joins Queen.
Opposite page, top: Roger and Freddie arrive at Wembley for Live Aid; bottom left: the crowd in Rio; centre right: Roger with DJ Mike Read; bottom right: Brian at the BPI Awards, 1985.

In April actor Jimmy Nail releases a cover version of the Rose Royce hit, 'Love Don't Live Here Anymore', co–produced by Roger Taylor and David Richards. Taylor also arranges the song and plays on it.

The Taylor/Richards team are also reported to be producing Scottish band Sideway Look, with 'Bulletproof Heart' due for single release.

John Deacon reported to have begun work on a solo album.

In May Freddie Mercury releases a solo single, 'I Was Born To Love You'. His album 'Mr. Bad Guy' is released later this month.

Freddie: "I've put my heart and soul into this album. It's much more beat oriented than Queen's music, and it also has some very moving ballads.

"They're all love songs, things to do with sadness and pain. At the same time they're frivolous and tongue in cheek; that's my nature.

"I've wanted to do a solo album for a long time, and the rest of the band have encouraged me to do it. I wanted to cover such things as reggae rhythms and I've done a couple of tracks with a symphony orchestra. It will have a very rich sound."

'Live In Rio', a film of the group's January Brazilian concerts, is released on video by Picture Music International. It goes straight to No.1. on the video chart.

Freddie on life, love and the pressures of fame: "I seem to eat people up and destroy them. There must be a destructive element in me because I try very hard to build up relationships, but somehow I drive people away. They always blame the end of the love affair on me because I'm the successful one. Whoever I'm with seems to get into a battle of trying to match up to me, and over-compensating… Then they end up treading all over me!

"I can't win. Love is Russian roulette for me. No one loves the real me inside, they're all in love with my fame, my stardom. I fall in love far too quickly and end up getting hurt all the time. I've got scars all over. But I can't help myself because basically I'm a softie – I have this hard, macho shell which I project on stage but there's a much softer side too, which melts like butter.

"I try to hold back when I'm attracted to someone but I just can't control love. It runs riot. All my one-night stands are just me playing my part. What I really like is a lot of loving. And I spoil my lovers terribly, I like to make them happy and I get so much pleasure out of giving them really wonderful, expensive presents…

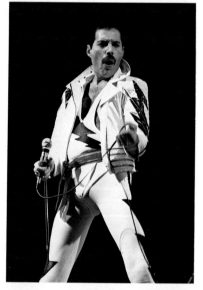

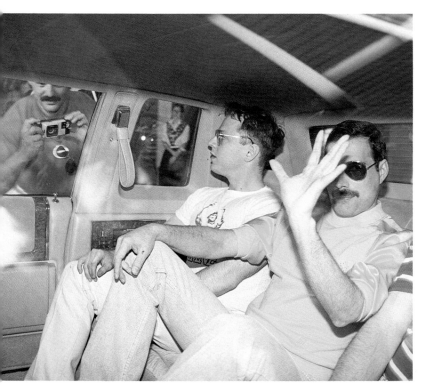

Below: Partying in Rio.

"You can have everything in the world and still be the loneliest man, and that is the most bitter type of loneliness!"

Freddie on money: "I love having so much money, but I don't believe in counting it. And because I have far more than I need, I give a lot of it away to people that I like. I try to enjoy life, and if there was no money, I wouldn't let it stop me having a good time. In the early days, when I had hardly anything, I'd save for two weeks and then blow it all in a day so that I could have a blast of fun."

And on bisexuality: "I couldn't fall in love with a man the way I could with a girl."

On ex-lover Mary Austin: "Our love affair ended in tears, but a deep bond grew out of it, and that's something nobody can take away from us. It's unreachable. All my lovers ask me why they can't replace her, but it's simply impossible.

"I don't feel jealous of her lovers because, of course, she has a

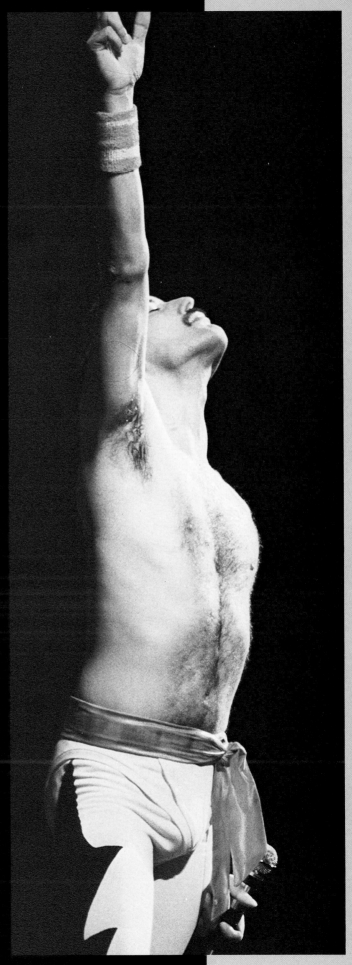

ife to lead, and so do I. Basically, I try to make sure she's happy with whoever she's with, and she tries to do the same for me. We look after each other, and that's a wonderful form of love. I might have all the problems in the world, but I have Mary and that gets me through. What better person to leave my fortune to when I go? Of course, my parents are in my will, and so are my cats, but the vast bulk of it will go to Mary.

"If I dropped dead tomorrow, Mary's the one person I know who could cope with my vast wealth. She works in my organisation and looks after my money side and all my possessions. She's in charge of the chauffeurs, maids, gardeners, accountants and lawyers. All I have to do is throw my carcass around on stage!"

Guild launch the BBM-1 guitar, modelled on the guitar Brian May made for himself all those years ago. Brian undertakes promotional appearances at trade fairs.

Live Aid began with Bob Geldof mustering many of British rock's leading acts to record 'Do They Know It's Christmas' in December 1984. No–one ever believed that a show on the scale of Live Aid could ever be realistically achieved, but a little over six months after Band Aid's single went on the become the U.K.'s best selling single ever, the rock world's leading acts took to the stages of Wembley and Philadelphia. Queen were originally approached by their keyboardist Spike Edney, who also doubled as trombonist for Geldof's band The Boomtown Rats.

John: "We didn't know Bob Geldof at all. When 'Do They Know It's Christmas' was out, that was a lot of the newer acts. For the gig, he wanted to get a lot of the established acts. Our first reaction was, we didn't know – 20 minutes, no soundcheck…!

"When it became apparent that it *was* going to happen we'd actually just finished touring Japan, and ended up having a meal in the hotel discussing whether we should do it, because obviously they wanted our answer, and we said yes. We didn't get involved in the running order thing, but strangely enough we did well coming on when we did…It was

the one day that I was proud to be involved in the music business – a lot of days you certainly don't feel that! But that day was fabulous, people there forgot that element of competitiveness…It was a good morale booster for us too, because it showed us the strength of support we had in England, and it showed us what we had to offer as a band."

Brian: "Actually, it's only by a narrow squeak that we got involved in it. Our first reaction was 'Oh, God! Not another one!' We'd been involved in quite a few and we were a bit disillusioned as to how the whole business works."

Below right: Freddie at Live Aid with bodyguard (right) and Queen manager Jim Beach (left); bottom right: Freddie and Brian at Live Aid.

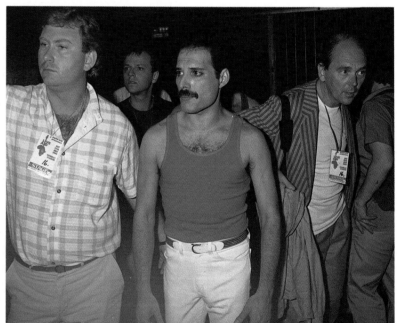

Roger: "Geldof's whole thing was magnificent. He did it out of the purest motives. I cannot believe *arseholes* like Johnathan King can denigrate something that's done real good when he's done no good to mankind except litter the planet with dreadful records! How *dare* he? How *worthless* parasitic *specks* like him can have a go at something that's so good, I don't know."

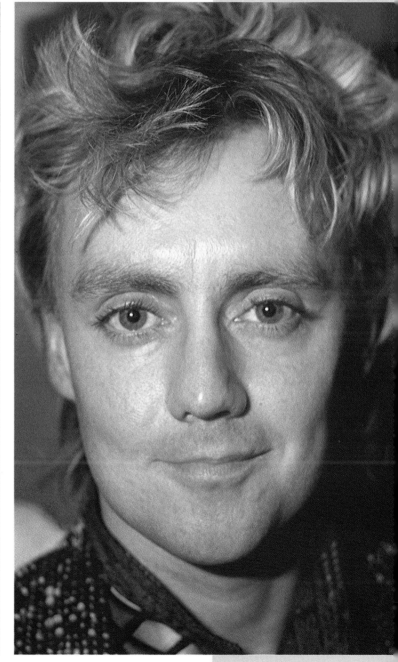

85

In August Freddie is seen in public with a new companion, 42–year–old German actress Barbara Valentin.

Freddie: "Barbara and I have formed a bond that is stronger than anything I've had with a lover for the last six years. I can really talk to her and be myself in a way that's very rare."

Roger Taylor is one of several 'guest' drummers who contribute to Roger Daltrey's tribute song to Keith Moon, 'Under A Raging Moon'. Recorded at RAK Studios in London.

Roger Taylor plays drums and synths on Feargal Sharkey's single 'Loving You', which he co-produced with David Richards. Recorded at Eden and Townhouse studios in London.

Freddie's third solo single from 'Mr. Bad Buy', 'Living On My Own' is released in September. Another track, 'Foolin' Around' is donated to the soundtrack of the Nick Nolte film *Teachers*.

Roger Taylor plays drums on Camy Todorow's single 'Bursting At The Seams', which

he again co-produced with David Richards. Recorded at Mountain Studios, Montreux.

'One Vision', released in November, is the first time in the band's career that all four members collaborate on a single. The video for the song is – for Queen – a subdued affair, simply showing the band hard at work in their Munich Studio, although they are initially in the head and shoulders set up in which they appeared in the seminal 'Bohemian Rhapsody' exactly 10 years earlier!

The accompanying press release for 'One Vision' states that the song was 'inspired' by Live Aid. As a result, accusations are rife that Queen are 'cashing in' on the event.

Roger: "I was absolutely devastated when I saw that in the press. It was a terrible mistake and I was really annoyed about it. Some public relations person got hold of the wrong end of the stick. I went absolutely bananas when I saw that."

Brian: "We do a lot of stuff for charities, but 'One Vision' was a way of getting back to what we're doing, and if we didn't run ourselves as a business, we wouldn't be around for the next Live Aid. We're not in the full-time business of charity at all. We're in the business of making music, which is a good enough end in itself."

On the 7th December Steve Van Zandt's Artists United Against Apartheid project is on the radio, in the charts, and the subject of a great deal of media discussion. Is *anyone* going to play Sun City now? Hazel Feldman, Sun City's entertainment director tells the *NME* that 'a return appearance by Queen should not be ruled out."

On the 14th December Queen issue the following statement:-
"Queen categorically state they they have no plans, at present, to return to Sun City and wish to make it plain that they have a total abhorrence of apartheid."

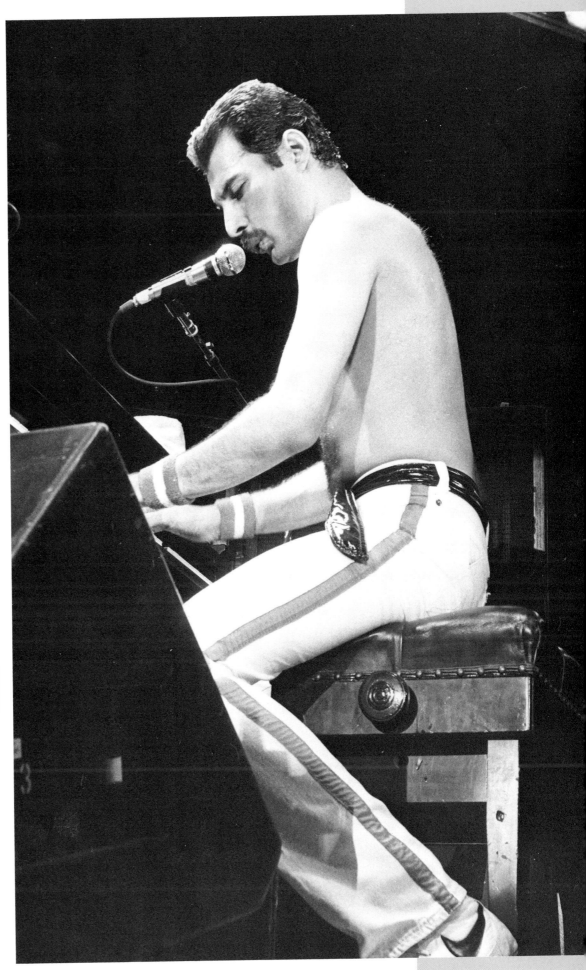

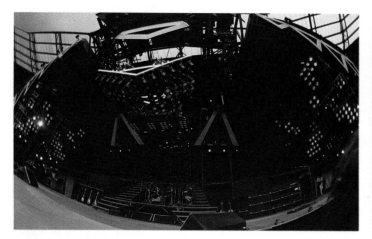

Above top, centre, left and opposite page: Wembley Stadium, 1986.

1986 saw Queen firmly back in the limelight. Their single and album 'A Kind Of Magic' both become best-sellers and in the summer the group undertook a series of massive open air U.K. concerts. Perhaps inspired by their appearance at Live Aid (or even Bruce Springsteen's Wembley concerts the previous year which various Queen members attended) the venue chosen was...Wembley Stadium.

'A Kind Of Magic' comes from the $20 million film *Highlander*, the second film for which Queen have supplied the soundtrack, (although Queen songs have also been heard on the soundtracks of films such as *Stripper*, *Revenge of the Nerds* and *IronEagle*).

Highlander marks the feature film debut of video director Russell Mulcahy, who has worked with such acts as Duran Duran, Elton John and Ultravox.

Mulcahy: "When I did this film, there was only one band in my mind to do the music, and that's Queen. Queen's music was just right for this film: they have a very keen sense of visuals. They write very powerful, anthem-type songs, and the film needed just that kind of energy. I've always been a fan of Queen's and for a long time have wanted to work with them."

The collaboration on the *Highlander* soundtrack is so successful that Mulcahy directs the video for Queen's 'A Kind Of Magic' single, which is filmed at the Playhouse in Northumberland Avenue, the former BBC studio from which such classic shows as The Goons and Hancock's Half Hour were broadcast.

Mulcahy: "It will please the six to 60-year-olds, with magic and fantasy like we used to see in the old musicals of Hollywood."

That 'magic and fantasy' also permeates *Highlander*, which stars

FEBRUARY
John Deacon records a song with Hot Chocolate singer Errol Brown.

MARCH
17th 'A Kind Of Magic'/'A Dozen Red Roses For My Darling' released.

MAY
21st 'A Kind Of Magic' is released; it spends 62 weeks on the chart and peaks at No. 1.

John's first solo single, 'No Turning Back', is released.
24th Freddie's rendition of the title theme of Dave Clark's stage musical *Time* enters the chart and reaches No. 24.
Brian's name is first romantically linked with actress Anita Dobson.

JUNE
'Friends Will Be Friends'/'Seven Seas Of Rhye' is released; it spends 8 weeks on the chart and reaches No. 14.
The 'Biggles' Soundtrack LP is released by MCA, credited to John Deacon and The Immortals.
7th Stockholm, Sweden.
11th Groenoordhal, Leiden, Holland.
14th Charletty Stadium, Paris, France.
14th 'A Kind Of Magic' peaks at No. 1 in the UK LP chart, residing in the chart for 62 weeks.
17th Forest Nationale, Brussels, Belgium.
21st Mannheim, Germany.
26th Waldbuehne, Berlin, Germany.
29th Munich, Germany.

the screen's best Tarzan (Christopher Lambert) and James Bond (Sean Connery) in an epic tale of love and revenge which spans four centuries. All four members of Queen contribute to the soundtrack, and those contributions form the bulk of their 1986 album 'A Kind of Magic'.

Roger on *Highlanders*: "There's some very heavy stuff in the film. It's a very heavy film.'

For the second single from the soundtrack, 'Princes Of The Universe', *Highlander* star Christopher Lambert flies in from Paris to London to appear in the video, and can be seen grappling with Freddie for supremacy!

On 25th April, the first International Queen Fan Club Convention is held at Great Yarmouth. Over 1,000 fans attend from as far afield as Australia and South America.

Queen aide Jim Beach: "We'd thought of a fan club convention like that a couple of years ago but never got round to organising it. If it works well I'm sure it will become an annual event."

Queen announce a series of open-air European concerts for summer '86. Over an eight-week period they will tour Scandinavia, Germany, France, Belgium, Switzerland, Spain and Eire.

Top U.K. promoter Harvey Goldsmith announces that Queen will headline an open air concert before 120,000 at Knebworth Park on Saturday August 9. Goldsmith tells a press conference at the St. James Club, Piccadilly, that ticket applications for Queen's two Wembley Stadium concerts number close to half a million, and that tickets for Queen's Newcastle concert sold out within one hour of going on sale. "The queue of ticket applicants at Newcastle was

longer than the queue for Cup Final tickets when Newcastle United were in the F.A. Cup Final," Goldsmith told assembled pressmen. "The Manchester show was the fastest selling show ever to be advertised in that city. I've never known anything like it. We were overwhelmed at the demand for Wembley Stadium tickets, but not surprised. However the rush for the Newcastle and Manchester show went beyond our wildest dreams."

The UK dates at Wembley on July 11 and 12 feature support acts Status Quo and The Alarm. As part of Capital Radio's Music Festival the concert is recorded for future broadcast and Harp Lager act as sponsors. The extra date was added after Wembley's 80,000 capacity sold out almost immediately by postal applications only. Harvey Goldsmith, the Live Aid promoter, was clearly delighted. "I'm really thrilled," he said. "It just shows that after 15 years Queen are bigger than they've ever been."

The new concerts début Queen's new stage show, based around a 160ft stage – requiring holes to be drilled in the Stadium's concrete foundations and big enough to fill one end of Wembley stadium – a new Clare Brothers sound system and the largest lighting rig ever assembled. The general effect, according to Roger, will be "bigger than bigness itself. It'll make Ben Hur look like The Muppets."

Queen's preparation included four weeks of rehearsals – "more than we have ever done in our career," admits Roger, adding "I think we are probably the best live band in the world at the moment and we are going to prove it . . . no-one who comes to see us will be disappointed."

'A Kind Of Magic' is released in June, and features the Queen material used in *Highlander*. It was to sell over a million units, and peak at No. 1 in Britain.

The same month sees the low-key release of John Deacon's first solo project – the soundtrack to the movie *Biggles* about W.E. Johns' fictional air ace. A single, 'No Turning Back', appears the previous month in 7 and 12-inch formats, credited to John Deacon and The Immortals: both are issued by MCA.

Freddie is also involved in a soundtrack project, lending his voice to the title theme of the stage musical *Time*. Released in May, it reaches No. 24, though like Stevie Wonder (another star name on the cast recording),

Freddie is not to take part in the West End production mounted by Sixties star Dave Clark.

Freddie follows up in July with his first (and so far only) video EP featuring four tracks: 'I Was Born To Love You', 'Made In Heaven', 'Time' and 'Living On My Own'. Having been banned from TV, the latter is an instant collector's item, depicting as it does the Bacchanalian scenes of 300 friends consuming caviar and champagne at the singer's 39th birthday party in Munich, October 1985.

A series of European dates follow Queen's epic Wembley appearances, notably in Germany where Level 42, Marillion and Gary Moore support, while the open air concert at Knebworth House, Hertfordshire, on August 9 (with special guests Big Country and Status Quo) is the band's biggest ever UK concert and is to be the last of the decade. An amazing show is marred by a small outbreak of violence in the mammoth 150,000 crowd and the death of a fan close to the stage.

A single, 'Friends Will Be Friends', is released in June to coincide with the live dates: a typically grandiose Queen anthem, it spends eight weeks on the chart and reaches the No. 14 position. Three months later, 'Who Wants To Live Forever' enters the chart and peaks at No. 24.

In May, Brian's name is romantically linked with actress Anita Dobson, best known for her appearances in the soap opera *EastEnders*.

November proves an expensive month for CD-equipped Queen fans as the entire back catalogue (barring the already digitally released 'The Works', 'Greatest Hits' and 'A Kind Of Magic') is issued on compact disc.

An eventful year in the Queen calendar ends with a bang in December, when 'Live Magic' finds itself in hundreds of thousands of Christmas stockings. A record of the eventful 'Magic Tour', it covers all aspects of their career, but omissions like 'Save Me', 'Somebody To Love', 'It's A Hard Life' and the whole first album raises eyebrows. Even without a single release, it sells 400,000 copies by Christmas and reaches No. 3.

JULY
Freddie Mercury's first video EP is released.
'A Kind Of Magic' released on compact disc.
1st Hallenstadion, Zurich, Switzerland.
5th Slane Castle, Dublin, Eire.
9th St. James Park, Newcastle.
Sponsored by Harp lager.
All profits from this concert are given to the Save The Children Fund.
"Queen were so bowled over at the amount of enthusiasm for their shows they wanted to say thank you. Princess Anne's dedication to Save The Children goes beyond the call of duty is an example to us all," comments Queen aide Jim Beech.
11th Wembley Stadium, London.
Sponsored by Harp lager.
12th Wembley Stadium, London.
Sponsored by Harp lager.
This show is filmed for worldwide television by Tune Tees T.V.
16th Manchester City Football Ground, Maine Road, Manchester.
Sponsored by Harp lager.
19th Cologne, Germany.
21st Stadthalle, Vienna, Austria.
22nd Stadthalle, Vienna, Austria.
25th Budapest, Hungary.
29th Cannes, France.
31st Bullring Monumental, Barcelona, Spain.

AUGUST
2nd Rayo Vollecano Stadium, Madrid, Spain.
4th Estadio Municipal, Marbella, Spain.
9th Knebworth Park.
Queen's biggest ever concert in the U.K.
As well as a six thousand square foot stage Queen use 180 Clare Brothers S4 speaker cabinets, 8.6 miles of cable, 5 power generators providing 5,000 amps, and immense sound system powered by half a million watts and special delay towers to take account of the size of the venue. Above the stage is a 20 by 30 foot Starvision screen, the extreme weight of which is counterbalanced by a huge water reservoir at the rear.

SEPTEMBER
'Who Wants To Live Forever'/ 'Killer Queen' released; it spends 5 weeks on the chart and peaks at No. 24.

NOVEMBER
Eleven Queen albums released on compact disc: 'Queen', 'Queen II', 'Sheer Heart Attack', 'A Night At The Opera', 'A Day At The Races', 'News Of The World', 'Jazz', 'Live Killers', 'The Game', 'Flash' and 'Hot Space'.

DECEMBER
'Live Magic' released; it spends 40 weeks on the chart and makes No. 3.

After the epic 'Magic' tour, 1987 was to be a year off for Queen as a record releasing and touring band. Roger has other ideas, though, telling the press "Queen is like a huge rolling machine and we're not working all the time. I am a musician by profession, that's my whole life. I don't want to waste it . . ."

Four days of auditions at Paramount City (the former Windmill Theatre) in London in July saw 250 musicians pass through the doors, all bar one recruited by an anonymous *Melody Maker* small ad. They play along to Roger's backing tracks of two songs, 'Cowboys And Indians' and 'Love Lies Bleeding'.

The final Cross line-up emerges as Roger (lead vocals, rhythm guitar), Spike Edney (keyboards, occasionally Queen's on-stage pianist), Josh Macrae (drums), Clayton Moss (lead guitar) and Peter Noone (bass, no relation to the Hermit). "I wanted to be in a working group," Roger explains. "I want to play music I sincerely believe in, that was heavy rock'n'roll, and I want to do it live.

"The solo LPs were my own expression of my own musical product at the time. This is a whole new group which is going to be taken seriously, I hope – this is a whole new career."

Top right and centre: The Cross. Opposite page, top: Brian with Ade Edmondson of Bad News; bottom: Freddie with Montserrat Caballe.

Someone else making giant strides with his own solo career is Freddie. Leaving CBS Records for Queen's EMI/Parlophone label, he releases 'The Great Pretender' in March which shoots up the chart to No. 4 – his biggest solo success yet, though a second solo LP is conspicuous by its absence. In contrast, the first Cross single, 'Cowboys And Indians', released on Virgin in October, just scrapes into the Top 75.

The Cross's first live performance is in the Thames TV studios for the *Meltdown* show, broadcast in December. Their hour-long set includes songs from the forthcoming 'Shove It' album, with Roger handling lead vocals and guitar with aplomb. Among the songs were his own Queen composition 'I'm In Love With My Car' – sung by its writer for the first time!

On the Queen front, the 'Live In Budapest' video is released in February. Recorded before 80,000 people (the largest concert crowd ever in Eastern Europe) at the capital's Nep Stadium, on June 25 1986, it includes many noteworthy performances – not least a Hungarian folk song, 'Tavaski Szel', which predictably brings the house down.

October sees the début album release from a new heavy metal group, Bad News. Produced by Brian May, it reaches No. 69 in the charts – a remarkable achievement for four actors, Rik Mayall, Ade Edmondson, Nigel Planer and Peter Richardson, the first three of whom are better known for their roles in *The Young Ones*.

JANUARY
'Live Magic' appears on compact disc, a month after its vinyl counterpart and the last 'non-simultaneous' Queen release. It is marginally longer than the LP.
Freddie can be heard at the start of Billy Squier's single release 'Love Is The Hero'.

FEBRUARY
Queen's 'Live In Budapest' video is released.

MARCH
'The Great Pretender'/'Exercises In Free Love' released by Freddie on EMI/Parlophone. It becomes his highest solo single to date, reaching No. 4 and spending 9 weeks in the chart. An accompanying video single also appears.

JULY
Roger auditions members for his new group, The Cross. He will play guitar and sing. Baktabak interview picture disc LP (BAK 2014) released.

SEPTEMBER
12th 'Bohemian Rhapsody'/'Life With Brian' by Young Ones spin-off group Bad News enters the singles chart and reaches No. 44 in a 5 week stay. It is produced by Brian.

OCTOBER
'Barcelona'/'Exercises In Free Love', a duet between Freddie and Spanish opera singer Montserrat Caballe, released. It stays in the charts for nine weeks, reaching No. 8.
The first Cross single, 'Cowboys And Indians', is released on Virgin Records label. It reaches No. 74 in the chart, where it remains for a single week.
24th 'Bad News' by Bad News, produced by Brian, enters the UK LP chart for a single week at No. 69.
The Cross' first live TV performance is broadcast by ITV.

Brian: "They didn't use their real names and we addressed each other in character. They weren't pretending they were rock stars, they *were* rock stars."

A single precedes the album by a month – the Bad News version of 'Bohemian Rhapsody', which staggers to No. 44. To further prove Brian can take a joke, the B-side is Pythonesquely entitled 'Life With Brian'.

Brian's verdict: "I think we made a great album but unfortunately it's not the kind of thing that can get commercial success as it's directed at a minority audience but I think it's a very astute comment on rock music and the way that it's moved over the last few years. It was recorded live and mainly unscripted."

Freddie is also making new friends, notably Spanish opera singer Montserrat Caballe. A single, 'Barcelona', is released and reaches the Top Ten. More fruits of the unlikely collaboration are promised by Freddie, who explains: "I just think she has this remarkable voice . . . I happened to mention it on Spanish TV and she called me up."

The Cross's first album, 'Shove It', is released in January. Recorded in Ibiza, Montserrat and London's Townhouse studio, it mixes Roger's backing tracks with the new musicians and some special guests.

There's no attempt whatsoever to play down the Queen connection: samples employed include Roger's own drum sounds from 'We Will Rock You'! 'Heaven For Everyone', a track Roger originally intended for close friend Joan Armatrading (who rejected it), features Freddie on vocals and another song, 'Love Lies Bleeding', incorporates guitar from Brian.

Brian's relationship with *EastEnders* actress/singer Anita Dobson (who reached No. 4 in 1986 with a vocal version of the soap opera's theme tune) extends into the musical arena when he produces and plays on her album 'Talking Of Love'. Released in June, he analyses it thus: "I think that we produced an album that strides across the two worlds in which we live. There's a certain amount of rock influence and a certain amount of show influence. Most of Anita's audience may have thought that it was getting too heavy and most of those in my world thought 'what the hell's he doing?' with

someone who's really only a show tune singer . . . I stand by the project as being very worthwhile."

Press gossip mistakenly suggests the romance is over in October, ironically the month Anita releases a single, 'To Know Him Is To Love Him'. "It's enough if you know I'm with him," she says. "I don't want to talk about it, about him or what he's doing. That's his business. Most of my fans are happy I'm with someone. We have to have something that is ours."

As compact disc players are reduced to affordable prices, Queen's fans rush to repurchase the entire catalogue – and record company EMI is happy to make the strain on their purse-strings a little lighter. June sees eight Queen albums released on mid-price CD with new catalogue numbers. These are 'Sheer Heart Attack' (CZ99), 'Flash' (CZ100), 'Hot Space' (CZ101), 'News Of The World' (CZ102), 'Jazz' (CZ103), 'The Game' (CZ104) 'Day At The Races' (CZ105), 'A Night At The Opera' (CZ106) and 'Live Killers' (CZ107).

Freddie's collaboration with Spanish opera diva Montserrat Caballe, previewed on single last year, reaches fruition in October with the release of 'Barcelona' and another single 'The Golden Boy'. Described by the record company press release as 'A glorious celebration of the

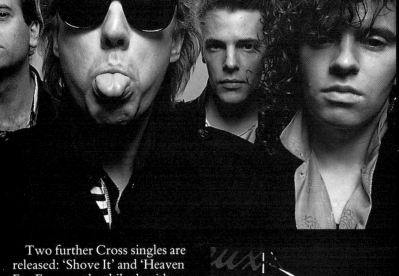

Two further Cross singles are released: 'Shove It' and 'Heaven For Everyone', while the title track reappears in April as lead track of a four-song CD EP. Roger on the state of pop music, especially Stock, Aitken and Waterman: "SAW are like second hand car salesmen or something. They're *awful*!"

The band plays live on television's *Number 73*. Roger on TV appearances: "I used to like doing *Top of the Pops* with Queen because you had to mime. It's the unions, you see." They then set off on a low-key, unpublicised tour of small British venues, later playing further club dates in Germany with a number of UK Queen fanatics making the journey with them.

Roger on The Cross: "We intend to build a powerbase with the intensity of our live performance. I think it'll be a force to be reckoned with in six months."

power of pop and the passion of opera', the work receives a mixed reaction from the press. The public elevate it to No. 25, 19 places below Freddie's solo long-player three years previously.

A gala concert, *La Nit* (The Night) is held at Barcelona's Avinguda De Maria Cristina, the city's equivalent of London's Mall, to celebrate the start of preparations for the city's hosting the 1992 Olympic Games. Support acts include Eddy Grant, Jerry Lee Lewis, Spandau Ballet and ballet dancer Rudolf Nureyev.

After this impressive build-up, a tuxedo-clad Freddie and befrocked Ms Caballe perform 'Barcelona' with a finale of fireworks, but the world's press are granted no interviews. The absence of microphones indicates that they are in fact miming: as Freddie notes later, "We'd need a lot of rehearsals (to sing live) . . . they're complex songs and we just didn't have enough time."

Two days later, the Crush Bar of the Royal Opera House, London sees Freddie break his silence: "I don't know how Queen fans will react to this," he admits nervously. "The worst thing they can call it is rock opera, which is so *boring* actually. You can't label it in any way because I'm doing songs that I've never done before, the sort of

songs to suit our voices. I found it very difficult writing them and singing them because all the registers had to be right and they're all duets."

November, traditionally a time for the release of greatest hits albums, sees all Queen's most memorable musical moments re-emerge in a format never before seen – three-inch compact disc! Playable on any CD machine with a special adaptor, they are housed in minute picture sleeves, making them even more collectable. A dozen are released simultaneously, making this the most expensive month for the dedicated Queen fan since the release of 'The Complete Works' back in 1985. All the CDs have

the original A and B-sides as they originally appeared on vinyl, together with a bonus track in each case.

The Cross resurface to play a short set at a Christmas party for Queen fan club members at London's Hammersmith Palais. They are joined for the encores by Brian and John who, together with Roger and keyboard player Mike Moran, play a set of blues standards and a raw but enjoyable 'I'm In Love With My Car'.

Also in action in December are Brian's comedians turned heavy metallists Bad News, who make their live début at London's Marquee Club. Their version of Queen's greatest hit predictably brings the house down . . .

JANUARY
The Cross release their first album, 'Shove It'. It spends 2 weeks in the chart, reaching No. 58.
The album's title track is released as a single, 'Shove It'/'Rough Justice'.

FEBRUARY
The Music & Media label release an interview picture disc.
The Cross tour the UK in low-key, unpublicised performances, also playing in Germany.

MARCH
'Heaven For Everyone'/'Love On A Tightrope (Like An Animal)', the third single from the album, released.

APRIL
'Shove It (Extended)'/'Rough Justice'/'Shove It (Metropolix)'/'Cowboys And Indians' released as a 4-track extended play CD.

MAY
EMI (Germany) release a 12-inch single, 'Crazy Little Thing Called Love'/'Spread Your Wings (Live)'
A US album 'Live In Concert' appears in import record shops.

JUNE
Eight previously released Queen albums appear on mid-price CD.
Actress Anita Dobson releases her début album, 'Talking Of Love', produced by boyfriend Brian.

OCTOBER
8th Freddie Mercury and Montserrat Caballe mime to 'Barcelona' in the city of that name.
10th The UK launch party for the album is held in the Crush Bar of the Royal Opera House, London.
22nd The duo's album 'Barcelona' enters the chart for the first of 4 weeks, in which it attains a highest placing of No. 25.
A single, 'The Golden Boy'/'The Fallen Priest' is released.
Anita Dobson releases a single, 'To Know Him Is To Love Him', produced by Brian. It fails to chart, amid press rumours of a split.

NOVEMBER
One dozen of Queen's singles are reissued in 3-inch CD form.

DECEMBER
16-17th Bad News perform their version of 'Bohemian Rhapsody' and other rock parodies at the Marquee Club in London.
Brian and John join The Cross on stage at London's Hammersmith Palais.

1989 dawns brightly for Queen fans, with a new album – their first studio recordings for three years – scheduled for spring release. It is previewed at the Queen Fan Convention in April and receives the expected unanimous acclaim – but a written communiqué from Freddie stating that he does not intend to tour takes the gloss off the occasion.

"I want to change the cycle of album, world tour, album, world tour," he says. "Maybe we *will* tour, but it will be for totally different reasons. I've personally had it with these bombastic lights and staging effects. I don't think a 42-year-old man should be running around in his leotard any more."

Despite this gloomy prediction, Freddie is far from idle, and visits co-producer/ engineer Dave Richards at Queen's Mountain Studios in Montreux to start work on his own track, 'Delilah', for the *next* album. A third single with Montserrat Caballe is released to end the collaboration.

The first single from the imminent LP, 'I Want It All', enters the charts at No. 3 early in May. Amazingly, it's Queen's highest ever débuting 45, beating 'Radio Ga-Ga' (No. 4 in 1984). Incidentally, 'Bohemian Rhapsody' entered at No. 47!

The promotional video, directed by David Mallet, is very different for Queen – a straightforward performance promo light years away from 'Rhapsody'. Queen aide Jim Beach describes it as "Simple and straightforward, showing Queen doing what they do best." Beach also adds revealingly: "A lot of videos which were received rapturously here weren't really appreciated in the States: they didn't see the humour of seeing Queen in drag."

'The Miracle', their first studio LP for three years, hits the shops in May. From the cover, a strange multi-headed photograph of the four members as one person, to the promotional gimmicks – a limited edition box with CD, 'teaser' tape, biography, press release and photo – it is a stunning album by any yardstick.

Curious fans can call an 0898 number to hear Brian May talking about the new album and playing selected tracks – but few have to be persuaded to put their hand into their pocket for the long-awaited sixteenth long-player. It enters the charts two weeks later at No. 1.

Brian May on the new democratic songwriting structure: "We wanted to record a really democratic album and each one of us would be involved in the songwriting. We created a real band feeling without any ego problems. That's one of the reasons that 'The Miracle' has turned into such a better album than 'A Kind Of Magic', for example."

Designer Richard Gray uses computer techniques to put the cover 'head' together, as well as a honeycomb of eyes and noses on the reverse side. Heads, noses and eyes all come together on in-store posters, which a fortnight before release promise 'Queen's Miracle arrives on May 22'. EMI's Tony Wadsworth the man behind the marketing campaign, comments: "Queen's 'Greatest Hits' was one of the best selling albums ever: the new album sounds like another Queen's 'Greatest Hits', except none of them are hits – yet!"

BBC Radio One broadcasts a Queen special, while ITV screen two programmes on the band. Disappointingly, both are already available on video: 'Queen: The Magic Years' (an edit of the currently already available three-volume anthology) and 'Live In Budapest'.

JANUARY
Freddie and Montserrat Caballe release a third collaborative single, 'How Can I Go On' which enters the chart at No. 95, spending one further week in the Top 100.

FEBRUARY
Channel 5 issue a three-track video EP of Mercury/Caballe performances. It is also released in the new CDV (CD video) format.

APRIL
Queen's forthcoming album 'The Miracle' is previewed at the Queen Fan Convention. Black Sabbath's 'Headless Cross', released this month, features Brian on the track 'When Death Calls'.

MAY
7th 'I Want It All'/'Hang On In There', the first single from the album, is released. It enters the charts at No. 3 on 13 May for a 7-week stay.
22nd 'The Miracle', Queen's first studio LP for three years, is released and enters the charts at No. 1 on June 3. It clocks up 27 chart weeks.
29th BBC Radio One broadcasts a special programme on the band.

JULY
1st 'Breakthru'/'Stealin'' enters the chart, and peaks the following week at No. 7 during its 7-week residence.

AUGUST
'The Invisible Man'/'Hijack My Heart' is released, remaining 6 weeks and reaching No. 12. The 'Rare Live' video is released. The press release describes it as 'A Queen concert from time and space designed for the collector starting with the first ever video (1973 in a rehearsal studio) through every stage of their career offering first performances and many little performed songs.'

OCTOBER
21st 'Scandal'/'My Life Has Been Saved' enters the chart at No. 26, but only goes one place higher in a 4-week stay.

NOVEMBER
9th 'The Miracle'/'Stone Cold Crazy' peaks at its entry position of No. 21, falling out of the chart after 3 weeks. The Baktabak label releases an unauthorised interview CD.

DECEMBER
Brian makes a rare stage appearance at a Jerry Lee Lewis concert at London's Hammersmith Odeon.
16th 'Queen At The Beeb', an eight-track radio compilation from 1973, spends 1 week in the album chart at No. 67. Picture Music International issues a four-track video EP, including 'The Miracle', 'Breakthru', 'The Invisible Man' and 'Scandal'.
The group work on ideas for their new album at Mountain Studios in Switzerland.

Roger makes an unscheduled personal appearance at the International Scrabble Convention, where he plays TV hostess Debbie Greenwood.

Roger on Queen and current musical trends: "It would be bloody ludicrous if Queen made a record using Acid House techniques. It would be jumping on bandwagons, and we've never been ones for that."

August sees the release of a true collector's item. The 'Rare Live' video includes 20 tracks from their first ever appearance on videotape (filmed in 1973 in a rehearsal studio) through every stage of their career with first performances and many little performed songs among them.

Brian May records a solo on the Black Sabbath track 'When Death Calls', though he protests "I enjoy doing that although I'm no session musician . . . Queen is and will stay the main thing in my life." He is also reported to be working on a solo project. "Hard pure heavy metal, weird acoustic songs and God knows what else. There isn't a direction to the album yet and I think that's one problem I have to sort out.

"The solo project is mainly about getting all the stuff I've had in my head onto tape, but I've found that some of the ideas I had in mind for solo work have ended up on the Queen album. I think that the best ideas should really be concentrated towards the

group because it's still the best vehicle I can find.

"It's a real strain doing solo projects because you are on your own. At the end of the day I am left sitting in a studio with an engineer saying 'Is this worth anything or not?' and it's very hard to make those judgements."

Brian, who has enlisted Manfred Mann's Earth Band singer Chris Thompson to help with his own album, is also involved in recording with ex-Genesis guitarist Steve Hackett. "Steve is a friend and he got halfway through his album and felt that he was short on ideas. He played me some of his material which inspired me to want to have a go at a couple of things."

Below far right: Brian and Tony Iommi.
Bottom centre: Brian and Dave Gilmour.

Late in the year, Brian is one of several special guests at a London concert by veteran rock'n'roller Jerry Lee Lewis, playing guitar on 'High School Confidential'.

Roger on rumours about Freddie's state of health or otherwise: "What? Stupid rumours! Freddie is as healthy as ever on the new album. We had a party at Brian's a few days ago and Freddie didn't exactly give the impression he was on his death bed. We've heard that rumour too, but it's ridiculous."

Four more singles are released from the album, each with less impact than the first. 'Breakthru' peaks at No. 7, 'The Invisible Man' No. 12, 'Scandal' No. 25 and the title track No. 21.

Biggest news for Queen's long-time fans is the December appearance of the long-awaited 'Queen At The Beeb' as the first release on Band Of Joy Records. It combines a session of four tracks recorded for BBC Radio One's *Sounds Of The Seventies* on February 5, 1973 (when they were still unsigned) and a similar session on December 3 of the same year, both produced by Bernie Andrews. All tracks except 'Ogre Battle' were versions of first album material, and provide a fascinating insight into the band's progress at that point.

In the words of sleevenote writer Malcolm Dome of *RAW* magazine, this is "an historic effort that still retains a contemporary resonance . . . vital, valuable and inexorable."

The album slips out relatively unpublicised in the frantic pre-Christmas sales period and spends just one week in the chart at No. 67.

Out of sight of their fans and critics, the group reconvene at their Swiss studio to record their next album. By Christmas, all four members are at Mountain Studios, kicking around ideas. "They were chomping at the bit," said Dave Richards. "They just got into the concert hall where I record them and started whipping each other on."

Brian on the early stages of recording: "We usually have two or three days just playing, finding sounds, just getting the feel of each other again. We keep the multi-track running and seem to find that there's little bits that really seem to gel."

If previous form was anything to go by, it seemed likely that 1990 would be another 'off year' for the band. Yet the four members are seen together as early as February when the British Phonographic Industry invites them to receive a special award recognising their Outstanding Contribution to British Music at the annual 'Brits' ceremony held on the 18th of the month. Their appearance in a televised show hosted by Jonathan King wins much applause, but Freddie's drawn appearance inspires further rumours about his health.

Roger's part-time band The Cross reappear, now on Queen's own label EMI/Parlophone after a flirtation with Virgin. Their second album, 'Mad, Bad And Dangerous To Know', appears in March with a single, 'Power To Love', appearing in April. Virgin reissue The Cross's first album, 'Shove It', at mid price to cash in on the publicity – which in most papers goes to another occasional outfit, Mark Knopfler's Notting Hillbillies, and 'Mad, Bad . . .' fails to chart.

Brian installs a new 16-track studio in his home over the summer. "I've been threatening to have it for a long time as I just had very simple equipment . . . it's all simple enough for me to work without too much of a problem. I hate too many buttons!"

In November, infamous tabloid newspaper The Sun clutches at straws and prints 'It's Official! Freddie is seriously ill', claiming he was a virtual recluse in his Kensington, London, home. Their justification was a compassionate quote from Brian: "He's OK and he definitely hasn't got Aids, but I think his wild rock'n'roll lifestyle has caught up with him.

"Freddie didn't want to do any videos for the next album. And he would prefer not to go out on tour either. I think he just needs a break."

Later that month the singer is pictured by *The Sun* leaving the Harley Street surgery of doctor F Gordon Atkinson 'looking haggard and gaunt'. A band spokesman said: "He has worked flat out for four months on the new album. He is just exhausted."

Not so Brian, who in September can be caught jamming (twice!) with Black Sabbath at London's Hammersmith Odeon on the encores 'Paranoid' and 'Heaven And Hell'.

In the same London suburb two months later, the Red and Gold Theatre Company's production of *Macbeth* opens at the Riverside Studios, with music specially composed by Brian as the first fruits of his home studio. "I'm very aware that the music could be irritating if not done well, and that a lot of people might feel that rock does not fit in with Shakespeare. But Will Shakespeare was into making direct contact with his audience – the way Queen has always done."

At the end of November, unknown US white rap artist Vanilla Ice (real name Robbie Van Winkle) hits the top of the UK chart with 'Ice Ice Baby', a rap track based on a none too subtle steal of the riff from 'Under Pressure'. It has already topped the American chart. Brian May: "I just thought, interesting, but nobody will ever buy it because it's crap. Turns out I was wrong . . . we don't want to get involved in litigation with other artists ourselves, that doesn't seem very cool . . . now I think it's quite a good bit of work in its way."

The Cross play a set at Queen's annual Fan Convention at London's Astoria Theatre in December, a month that also sees the release of a 'new' video – 'Queen At Wembley', a 75-minute record of their July 1986 shows at the Stadium.

Directed by Gavin Taylor, it uses time-lapse photography to show the erection of the massive 160ft stage – and, though no substitute for a live show (which shows as few signs as ever of happening), 'Queen At Wembley' is a creditable effort.

FEBRUARY
18th Queen receive an award for their Outstanding Contribution to British Music at the Brits.

MARCH
Roger Taylor's Cross release their second album, 'Mad, Bad And Dangerous To Know', on EMI/Parlophone. It does not chart.

APRIL
The Cross issue a single 'Power To Love'/'Passion For Trash', both tracks from the album, which reaches No. 83 in its one chart week.
Virgin reissue The Cross's first album, 'Shove It', at mid price.

JUNE
The Baktabak label issue a box set of 7-inch interview records entitled 'The Interview Collection'.

SEPTEMBER
8th & 9th Brian jams with Black Sabbath at London's Hammersmith Odeon.
'Message From The Palace', an unofficial picture disc interview LP, is issued.

NOVEMBER
13th *The Sun* prints 'It's Official! Freddie is seriously ill'.
19th The Red and Gold Theatre Company's production of 'Macbeth' opens at Hammersmith's Riverside Studios, with music by Brian.
25th Vanilla Ice's 'Ice Ice Baby', a rap track incorporating music from Queen's 'Under Pressure', reaches No. 1 in the UK singles chart.

DECEMBER
'Queen At Wembley' video is released.
The Cross play at Queen's Fan Convention at London's Astoria Theatre. Three tracks from the new album are previewed.

The New Year opens memorably for Queen watchers as the band's first single for 13 months, 'Innuendo', goes straight into the British chart at No. 1. It's their first ever to début in pole position and the 24th single in all to achieve the feat – and, at six and a half minutes in length, it's the longest UK Number 1 single since 'Bohemian Rhapsody'. The video, too, is a 'Bo Rhap'-style epic.

The track had received a standing ovation at the previous month's Convention. Fan club secretary Jacky Gunn: "You could have heard a pin drop when the song played . . . after it finished there was a second of awed silence, then they brought the house down."

Brian on the track 'Innuendo': "That was one of the first things that came. It's got this bolero-style rhythm, a very strange track. It's a bit of a risk (as a single), but it's different and you either win it all or you lose it all'. "

Freddie and Roger dine together over the New Year and decide the band should re-enter the studio to take advantage of a valuable spell of creativity. Talking of creation, Roger and model girlfriend Debbie Leng (well known for her appearance in a TV chocolate commercial) celebrate the birth of a son, Rufus Tiger, in February.

The album 'Innuendo' is also delivered in February and emulates its shorter namesake by entering its respective chart at the top (where it stays for 2 weeks before being toppled by Oleta Adams). Reviews, as ever, range from the sublime ("both enduring and endearing" – Q) to the ridiculous, a prime contender for the latter being a bitchy Tony Parsons who proclaims the result, in *The Daily Telegraph*, to be "A cross between Led Zeppelin and Kenneth Williams."

'Innuendo' is the first Queen album to appear (in America only) on Walt Disney offshoot Hollywood Records, whose price for signing the rights to their US releases is a reported $10 million.

Later in the month, Queen enter their Montreux studio to record material for their next album . . . at this rate, due for 1993 release!

Brian's liaisons with Black Sabbath produce an unusual by-product in March when 'The Stonk', 1991's Comic Relief charity anthem, is released. Sung by comedy duo Hale and Pace, it shoots to No. 1, with Brian credited with lead guitar, piano and production. Also in evidence as supporting musicians are Sabbath stalwarts Tony Iommi and Cozy Powell.

The video for Queen's March single 'I'm Going Slightly Mad' co-stars a flock of tame penguins and was shot at studios at Wembley at a cost of £200,000. As ever, *The Sun* had buttonholed the birdkeeper who said Freddie "didn't look very well at all." Despite (or because of) such positive coverage the single only reaches No. 22. A Queen spokesman on Freddie: "He's fine. He enjoyed making the video and he's delighted to be back."

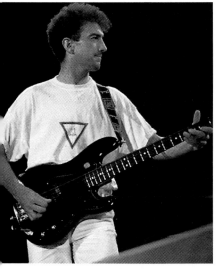

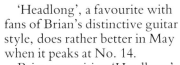

JANUARY
26th 'Innuendo'/'Bijou' enters
the UK singles listings at No. 1
and stays in the chart 6 weeks.

FEBRUARY
2nd 'Greatest Hits' re-enters
the album charts amid much
anticipation in the wake of the
single's success.
4th The album 'Innuendo' is
released, entering the album
chart at the top 12 days later
and staying in the chart 17
weeks (at time of writing).
Queen re-enter their Montreux
studio to record more new
material.
Roger becomes the father of
a son, Rufus Tiger.

MARCH
16th 'I'm Going Slightly Mad'/
'The Hitman' enters the charts.
It peaks at No. 22 and stays in
the chart 5 weeks.
23rd 'The Stonk', the Comic
Relief theme song sung by Hale
and Pace and produced by
Brian, reaches No. 1 in the
singles chart.

MAY
5th The *Sunday Mirror* prints
'revelations' about the theft of
a private video from Roger's
home.
25th 'Headlong'/'Mad The
Swine' enters the chart,
peaking at No. 14 the following
week and staying in the chart
3 weeks (at time of writing).

'Headlong', a favourite with
fans of Brian's distinctive guitar
style, does rather better in May
when it peaks at No. 14.

Brian on writing 'Headlong':
"I was in the studio for a couple
of days to get some things out
of my system . . . I came up
with 'Headlong' and 'I Can't
Live With You' . . . the guys
liked them."

Also in May, Roger's love life
makes tabloid headlines when
unknown musician Douglas Lean
tries unsuccessfully to sell a
private and allegedly salacious
home video of Roger and his
girlfriend, illicitly removed
from their second home in
Kensington, West London, to the
Sunday Mirror. The gates of their
Surrey estate also make news
when, after a row with the local
council about their permitted
size, they suddenly acquire a pair
of garden gnomes that light up in
the dark.

Brian on Queen, 1991-style: "The group tends to be the most stable family we've got, although it's hard to see how we've stayed together all this time. Roger is the most extreme in extravagance and the rock'n'roll lifestyle. Freddie is a mystery, nobody ever quite knows where he's coming from. John, too, the archetypal quiet bass player . . . but he's the leader on the business side, studies the stock market, understands the deals. And me, I think the others would tell you I'm the most pig-headed member of the band . . . !"

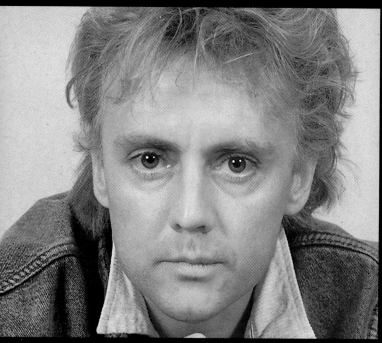

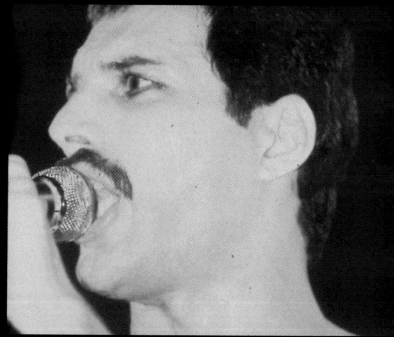

Months of speculation concerning Freddie Mercury's health came to a dramatic and tragic conclusion over the weekend of November 23/24, 1991. Within 24 hours of publicly admitting that he was suffering from Aids, Freddie died from bronchial pneumonia which his crippled immune system was unable to fight.

On Saturday, November 23, Freddie announced to the Press Association what tabloid newspapers had been suggesting for months. "Following the enormous conjecture in the Press over the last two weeks, I wish to confirm that I have been tested HIV positive and have Aids," he stated. "I felt it correct to keep this information private to date in order to protect the privacy of those around me. However, the time has now come for my friends and fans to know the truth and I hope that everyone will join with me, my doctors and all those worldwide in the fight against this terrible disease."

Freddie died shortly before midnight the following day at his palatial home in Logan Place, Kensington. Fans had gathered outside his house where there was a flurry of activity throughout the day. Among the last visitors were his parents, Bomi and Jer Bulsara, his former 'girlfriend' Mary Austin and Dave Clark, former drummer and leader of The Dave Clark Five, who was a close friend of Freddie.

Freddie was cremated four days later at the West London Cemetery in Kensal Green following a private service at which Zoroastrian Priests presided and sang ancient chants from the religion followed by Freddie's parents. The music of Spanish diva Montserrat Caballe was also played during the service.

Among those who attended the service were the three remaining members of Queen, Brian May, Roger Taylor and John Deacon, together with Freddie's friends Elton John and Dave Clark. Despite the secrecy with which arrangements were made, many fans made their way to Kensal Green but were held back by police lines.

Fans gathered at Freddie's home throughout the week and hundreds of floral tributes arrived. On Monday evening, 24 hours after Freddie's death, Queen aides staying at the Kensington house allowed fans to see inside the elegant garden where a carpet of floral tributes had been laid out before a large Christmas tree.

Freddie's death inspired a flurry of banner headlines in the British tabloid press, all of it sympathetic to the flamboyant star. BBC 1 televised a hastily assembled tribute on November 25 which was introduced by Elton John, evidently speaking off the cuff and clearly distressed at the events of the weekend. The 50 minute tribute featured scenes from Live Aid, from Queen concerts throughout the world over two decades and some rare footage of Freddie being interviewed on camera during the Seventies and early Eighties. The most recent footage was Queen's video for 'Innuendo' in which Freddie, dressed in a smart suit, looks gaunt but otherwise untroubled.

The tragedy was inevitably reflected in a welter of Queen back catalogue sales over the Christmas period. EMI re-released 'Bohemian Rhapsody' backed with 'These Are The Days Of Our Lives' which ended up as the second biggest selling record of 1991. Similarly, the recently released 'Queen's Greatest Hits Vol II' hogged the upper reaches of the UK LP charts during November and December.

After Freddie's death a billboard was mounted in his honour above the Hammersmith Odeon, the scene of some of Queen's earliest triumphs, and cab drivers driving close to Freddie's home along West Cromwell Road near Earls Court dipped their lights in tribute and declined to pick up passengers.

Freddie Mercury's grandiose performing style had attracted some derision from critics during his lifetime but all this was forgotten in the tributes that followed his death. As the antithesis of punk, Freddie – who occasionally toasted his audiences with champagne – was a sitting duck for the slings and arrows of hawkish critics offended by pomp and circumstance in rock and pop. Many of these same critics took a different tack in

their obituary notices: Freddie was now a natural showman who brought welcome good times to the concert scene, Queen's grandiose performances were no longer mocked as celebrations of rock's descent into moneyed decadence, his life was to be celebrated for its influence on the staging of rock concerts.

Many obituaries noted Queen's extraordinary success at Live Aid when everyone agreed they were the best band on the day. Bob Geldof was much quoted on this. "Queen had rehearsed their 20 minute set down to a tee," said the blunt Irishman. "Freddie was in his element – being able to ponce around with the whole world watching."

Other tributes noted Freddie's changing wardrobe and how he

had toned down his appearance
since Queen's breakthrough
in the mid Seventies. By the
Eighties he'd adopted the
traditional uniform of the macho
male gay stereotype – cropped
hair, bushy moustache,
bodybuilders' physique and tight
jeans and tee shirt, a mode of
dress which may have stunted
Queen's progress in America
where the heavy metal scene is
dominated by overt heterosexual
overtones.

Such sartorial factors made
no difference in the UK where
Queen's popularity seemed to
have reached an all time high.
They have become one of the
most collectable bands in the
world, with fans paying higher
and higher prices for Queen
memorabilia and artifacts.
Freddie's death can only have
enhanced this aspect of their
following.

It was a subdued Brian May
and Roger Taylor who appeared
on early morning television the
week after Freddie's death.
Adding little to the known facts,
they expressed their deep sorrow
and talked vaguely of holding
a concert in the near future
"to celebrate the life of Freddie
Mercury".

The same pair were slightly less subdued when they appeared together at the British Music Industry Rock and Pop Awards, broadcast from Hammersmith Odeon on February 12. Accepting their Brits Award for the best single of 1991 for 'These Are The Days Of Our Lives', Brian spoke warmly of Freddie's inspiration and talent while Roger concluded an emotional scene by announcing that there would be. . . "a concert that would be a tribute to Freddie's life at Wembley Stadium on April 20."

FEBRUARY
12th While collecting their Brit award for best single, Brian May and Roger Taylor announce that the Freddie Mercury Memorial Concert will be held at Wembley Stadium on April 20.

"I feel a great mixture of emotion," Brian told the gathering of musicians and industry figures. "If Freddie were here he would go and tell me to put this on the mantlepiece. He would say, 'Look mum, dad, that's what I did and I'm proud'. We're terribly proud of everything Freddie stood for. We feel his spirit is with us."

Roger then stepped forward to announce the date of the concert. "Aids affects us all," he said. "We see the Wembley concert as a tribute to his life and the fulfilment of his wish to get this message across. I hope you will join us at Wembley," he added before the Hammersmith crowd rose to give the duo a standing ovation.

Also included in the Brits show was a sequence from Queen's videos over the years which concentrated on Freddie's role in the band.

Much speculation then followed as to the line-up for the Wembley concert, tickets for which went on sale the day after the Brits awards. It was generally thought that Elton John would perform with Queen, probably taking over the role of vocalist with the band, and that many other guests would appear, performing either Queen material alongside Brian, Roger and John Deacon, or their own songs. Acts mentioned in the week following the announcement included U2, Guns N' Roses, George Michael, Eric Clapton and Rod Stewart. It was even reported that Madonna, already noted for her support of Aids related charities, had been approached to perform.

All the indications were that the memorial concert, which will benefit Aids charities worldwide, would rival Live Aid.

It was the wake to end all wakes, the biggest tribute concert in the history of rock and a fitting climax to Queen's glittering, often over-the-top, career. Madonna didn't turn up but Liza Minelli and Elizabeth Taylor did, and so did a host of rock's most illustrious figures, not to mention 72,000 rabid Queen fans from all over the world who snapped up their Wembley tickets within hours of them going on sale. Millions more watched the show on television and over £10 million was raised for various Aids related causes. Even the great weatherman in the sky looked down kindly on the Live Aid style event.

The tribute was divided into two halves. Various hard rock bands did their own thing during the first half, while Brian May, Roger Taylor and John Deacon of Queen, joined by an assortment of star guests, ran through Queen's catalogue of hits during the second section. The various performances were punctuated with Queen videos and past live footage, shown on the massive screens that flanked the stage and on television sets in living rooms across the globe.

Top thrashers Metallica opened the show, followed by Extreme who performed a well rehearsed medley of Queen songs sandwiched into 20 minutes in much the same way that Queen themselves did so successfully at Live Aid seven years earlier. After a considerable delay

Below right, Bob Geldof.
Bottom: Spinal Tap.

Def Leppard appeared, and they were joined by Brian May for their closing number. Bob Geldof, dressed like a species of pond life, followed with a Celtic romp which he'd apparently written with his 'unlikely' friend Freddie many years previously.

Spinal Tap made a big entrance on a red carpet dressed in ermine robes and crowns, but there was a long, perhaps deliberate, delay while the sound link to Nigel Tufnel's guitar was restored. They had thoughtfully cut down their normal set of 35 songs to just the one... "because Freddie would have wanted it that way." "Thank you, Wimbledon," they said as they left the stage, echoing the time honoured canard that rock stars never know where they are half the time.

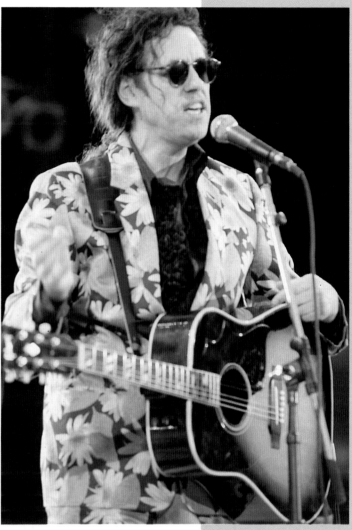

Top left: Axl Rose.
Top right: Elizabeth Taylor.
Right: Slash of Guns 'N Roses.

Following some moody new footage of U2 live from Sacramento during their current US tour, Guns N'Roses brought the first half to a climax with 'Paradise City' and an extended work-out on Bob Dylan's 'Knocking On Heaven's Door' which featured Slash on a twin necked guitar and Axl Rose on exaggerated histrionics. He was unquestionably the most powerful vocalist of the day, though his attire - skimpy white shorts beneath a slashed kilt and Union Jack top - seemed somewhat hastily considered for the occasion.

A sylph-like Liz Taylor, introduced by the gay actor Ian McKellen, made a regal entry to get the second half of the show under way. "Don't worry, I'm not going to sing," she joked before dealing deftly with one heckler. "I'll get off, but I've got something to say first. There are 72,000 people in this stadium, and in just two weeks there will be as many new (Aids) infections as there are people here tonight," she stated before urging the use of condoms on all, gay and straight alike.

The key element of the show, the part the 72,000 had been waiting for, followed: the three surviving

members of Queen performing their greatest hits with a variety of singers and guest guitarists. First up was Joe Elliott of Def Leppard singing 'Tie Your Mother Down', then Roger Daltrey, teasingly brought on to the riff from 'Pinball Wizard' and looking younger and fitter than many stars 10 years younger, offering 'I Want It All'. By this time Black Sabbath's Tony Iommi had joined the band on guitar.

Zucchero, Extreme's Gary Cherone, James Hetfield from Metallica and Robert Plant, an appropriate choice for the rockabilly styled 'Crazy Little Thing Called Love', all came, sang a Queen song with the band and went. Plant even crooned a few verses of Led Zeppelin's 'Thank You' which raised sufficient cheers to suggest that many in the crowd might have preferred to hear these mighty names performing songs associated with their own pasts rather than Queen's. Either way, none of the early guest vocalists managed to deliver Queen's material with the flamboyance - or pitch - of Freddie Mercury.

Left: Roger Daltrey and Brian May. Below: Robert Plant and Brian May.

115

Top left: Seal.
Top right: Lisa Stansfield.
Right: Annie Lennox and
David Bowie.

Paul Young sang 'Radio Ga Ga', traditionally a Queen song to inspire massed clapping and extended arms, while Seal calmed things down with a wistful but strangely off key rendering of 'Who Wants To Live For Ever'. Then came the first female performer, Lisa Stansfield, her hair in curlers and wielding a Hoover, to offer a gorgeous 'I Want To Break Free' of which Freddie, himself a housewife of some repute, would have been truly proud.

Lisa was succeeded by David Bowie in a smart green suit, and Annie Lennox, dramatically attired in a hooped black layered skirt which touched the floor, her eyes shaded as if for a masked ball. Together they performed 'Under Pressure', the song Bowie recorded with Queen in 1981. Next up was a genuine surprise: a partial Spiders From Mars/Mott The Hoople/ Queen joint reunion which featured Bowie on saxophone,

Ian Hunter on vocals, Mick Ronson on guitar, the three Queen men at the back and assorted Motts on back-up vocals. The song, inevitably, was 'All The Young Dudes', Bowie's 1972 gift to Mott which

temporarily rescued their career. In view of Queen's early relationship with Mott, this was an inspired bit of casting, an authentic reunion from the Glam Rock era, and it proved a crowd favourite too.

Left: John Deacon.
Below: Ian Hunter and David Bowie.

117

Right: David Bowie reciting the Lord's Prayer.
Below: Lisa Stansfield and George Michael.

It was difficult to follow but Bowie managed it with a spirited reading of his best ever song, 'Heroes', the same number that closed his inspired Live Aid performance, and a spontaneous Lord's Prayer, delivered on bended knee, to emphasise the reason why the concert was organised in the first place. It was easy to forget the Aids connection amidst the musical treats.

George Michael, too, had some special words to say about the Aids problem. He duetted with the irrepressible Lisa Stansfield – whom many considered the real star of the show – on 'Those Were The Days Of Our Lives' and sang 'Somebody To Love' by himself. Elton John followed and bravely tackled the opening lines of the complex 'Bohemian Rhapsody' but his range

was no match for the song's writer and despite Elton's new fringed hairstyle, which takes ten years off his age, his appearance as the penultimate performer somehow lacked the polish the audience might have expected from a star and elder statesman of rock who had been so closely identified with this concert from the start. Fittingly, Axl Rose joined Elton for 'Rhapsody's' tough HM style coda and 'The Show Must Go On'.

Left: Elton John and Axl Rose.
Below: Elton John.

Finally, Brian May introduced Liza Minelli, remarking as he did that Freddie would have been genuinely proud to have Liza stand in his footsteps on this occasion. Liza, who is more used to singing above a pit orchestra than a barrage of electric guitars and drums, performed Queen's traditional set closer, 'We Are The Champions'. She was joined by a chorus from the all star cast, none of whom seemed to have been offered microphones, so she was forced to belt out endless choruses of Queen's rabble rouser alone until, finally, Brian May and Roger Taylor brought this terrace favourite to a thumping close.

Appropriately 'God Save The Queen', with the ghost of Freddie Mercury leading a chorus of 72,000 from the video screens, ended a memorable day.

Right: Brian May.
Below: Liza Minelli leads the all-star cast in a climactic 'We Are The Champions'.

DISCOGRAPHY

PRE-QUEEN:

Singles

SMILE
(Brian May, Roger Taylor
and others):
'Earth' (Staffell).
'Step On Me' (May/Staffell).
U.S. release only (Mercury72977).

SMILE EP
'Doing Alright' (May/Staffell)
'Blag'/'April Lady'/'Polar Bear'/
'Earth' (Staffell)
'Step On Me' (May/Staffell).
Released in Japan only, and probably
a bootleg. Writing credits for 'Blag',
'April Lady' and 'Polar Bear' are
unknown. No label or serial number.

LARRY LUREX
(Brian May, Roger Taylor, Freddie
Mercury, John Deacon and others):
'I Can Hear Music'
(Spector/Greenwich)
'Goin' Back' (Goffin/King).
EMI 2030. Released June 1973.
Produced by Roy Thomas Baker.

It is rumoured that Brian May plays
guitar on a single by his school
contemporaries The Others, 'Oh
Yeah', released in 1964. In the light of
recent interviews, this seems unlikely.

QUEEN

Singles:

'Keep Yourself Alive'/'Son And
Daughter'
EMI 2036. Released 6 July 1973.

'Seven Seas Of Rhye'/'See What
A Fool I've Been'.
EMI 2121. Released 25 February 1974.

'Killer Queen'/'Flick Of The Wrist'.
EMI 2229. Released 11 October 1974.

'Now I'm Here'/'Lily Of The Valley'.
EMI 2256. Released 17 January 1975.

'Bohemian Rhapsody'/'I'm In Love
With My Car'.
EMI 2375. Released 31 October 1975.

'You're My Best Friend'/'39'.
EMI 2494. Released July 1976.

'Somebody To Love'/'White Man'.
EMI 2565. Released 12 November 1976.

'Tie Your Mother Down'/
'You And I'.
EMI 2593. Released 4 March 1977.

'We Are The Champions'/'We Will
Rock You'.
EMI 2708. Released 7 October 1977.

'Spread Your Wings'/'Sheer Heart
Attack'.
EMI 2757. Released 10 February 1978.

'Fat Bottomed Girls'/'Bicycle Race'.
EMI 2870. Released 13 October 1978.

'Don't Stop Me Now'/
'In Only Seven Days'.
EMI 2910. Released 26 January 1979.

'Love Of My Life' (Live)/'Now
I'm Here' (Live).
EMI 2959. Released 29 June 1979.

'Crazy Little Thing Called Love'/
'Spread Your Wings' (Live).
EMI 5001. Released 5 October 1979.

'Save Me'/'Let Me Entertain
You' (Live).
EMI 5022. Released 25 January 1980.

'Play The Game'/'A Human Body'.
EMI 5076. Released 30 May 1980.

'Another One Bites The Dust'/
'Dragon Attack'.
EMI 5102. Released 22 August 1980.

'Flash'/'Football Fight'.
EMI 5126. Released 24 November 1980.

'Under Pressure' (with David Bowie)/
'Soul Brother'.
EMI 5250. Released 2 November 1981.

'Body Language'/'Life Is Real'.
EMI 5293. Released 19 April 1982.

'Las Palabras De Amour'/'Cool Cat'.
EMI 5316. Released 1 June 1982.

'Back Chat'/'Staying Power'.
EMI 4325. Released 9 August 1982.

'Radio Ga Ga'/'I Go Crazy'.
QUEEN 1. Released 23 January 1984.

'I Want To Break Free'/'Machines
(Or Back To Humans)'.
QUEEN 2. Released 2 April 1984.

'It's A Hard Life'/'Is This The World
We Created?'.
QUEEN 3. Released 16 July 1984.

'Hammer To Fall'/'Tear It Up'.
QUEEN 4. Released 10 September 1984.

'Thank God It's Christmas'/'Man
On The Prowl'/'Keep Passing The
Open Windows'.
QUEEN 5. Released 26 November 1984.

'One Vision'/'Blurred Vision'.
QUEEN 6. Released 5 November 1985.

'A Kind Of Magic'/'A Dozen Red
Roses For My Darling'.
QUEEN 7. Released 10 March 1986.

'Friends Will Be Friends'/'Seven Seas
Of Rhye'.
QUEEN 8. Released 16 June 1986.

'Who Wants To Live Forever'/
'Killer Queen'.
QUEEN 9. Released September 1986.

'I Want It All'/'Hang On In There'.
QUEEN 10. Released May 1989.

'Breakthru'/'Stealin'.
QUEEN 11. Released June 1989.

'The Invisible Man'/
'Hijack My Heart'.
QUEEN 12. Released August 1989.

'Scandal'/'My Life Has Been
Saved'.
QUEEN 14. Released October 1989.

'The Miracle'/'Stone Cold Crazy'
(live).
QUEEN 15. Released November 1989.

'Innuendo'/'Bijou'.
QUEEN 16. Released January 1991.

'I'm Going Slightly Mad'/
'The Hitman'.
QUEEN 17. Released March 1991.

'Headlong'/'Mad The Swine'.
QUEEN 18. Released May 1991.

CD Singles

'Seven Seas Of Rhye'/'See What
A Fool I've Been'/'Funny How
Love Is'.
QUECD 1. Released November 1988.

'Killer Queen'/'Flick Of The Wrist'/
'Brighton Rock'.
QUECD 2. Released November 1988.

'Bohemian Rhapsody'/'I'm In Love
With My Car'/'You're My Best
Friend'.
QUECD 3. Released November 1988.

'Somebody To Love'/'White Man'/
'Tie Your Mother Down'.
QUECD 4. Released November 1988.

'Queen's First EP'
'Good Old Fashioned Lover Boy'/
'Death On Two Legs (Dedicated
To . . .)'/'Tenement Funster'/'White
Queen (As It Began)'.
QUECD 5. Released November 1988.

'We Are The Champions'/'We Will
Rock You'/'Fat Bottomed Girls'.
QUECD 6. Released November 1988.

'Crazy Little Thing Called Love'/
'Spread Your Wings'/'Flash'.
QUECD 7. Released November 1988.

'Another One Bites The Dust'/
'Dragon Attack'/'Las Palabras
De Amor (The Words Of Love)'.
QUECD 8. Released November 1988.

'Under Pressure'/'Soul Brother'/
'Body Language'.
QUECD 9. Released November 1988.

'Radio Ga Ga'/'I Go Crazy'/
'Hammer To Fall'.
QUECD 10. Released November 1988.

'I Want To Break Free'/'Machines
(Back To Humans)'/'It's A Hard
Life'.
QUECD 11. Released November 1988.

'A Kind Of Magic'/'Dozen
Red Roses For My Darling'/
'One Vision'.
QUECD 12. Released November 1988.

EPs:

Queen's 1st EP:
'Good Old Fashioned Loverboy'/
'Death On Two Legs'/'Tenement
Funster'/'White Queen'.
EMI 2623. Released June 1977.

Albums:

QUEEN
EMI EMC 3006
Released 13 July 1973.

Side One:
1. Keep Yourself Alive (May).
2. Doing All Right (May/Staffell).
3. Great King Rat (Mercury).
4. My Fairy King (Mercury).
Side Two
5. Liar (Mercury)
6. The Night Comes Down (May).
7. Modern Times Rock 'N' Roll
(Taylor).
8. Son And Daughter (May).
9. Jesus (Mercury).
10. Seven Seas Of Rhye (Mercury).

QUEEN II
EMI EMA 767
Released 8 March 1974.

Side One:
1. Procession (May).
2. Father To Son (May).
3. White Queen (As It Began) (May).
4. Some Day One Day (May).
5. The Loser (Taylor).
Side Two:
6. Ogre Battle (Mercury).
7. The Fairy Fellows Master Stroke
(Mercury).
8. Nevermore (Mercury).
9. March Of The Black Queen
(Mercury).
10. Funny How Love Is (Mercury).
11. Seven Seas Of Rhye (Mercury).

SHEER HEART ATTACK
EMI EMC 3061
Released 1 November 1974.

Side One:
1. Brighton Rock (May).
2. Killer Queen (Mercury).
3. Tenement Funster (Taylor).
4. Flick Of The Wrist (Mercury).
5. Lily Of The Valley (Mercury).
6. Now I'm Here (May).
Side Two:
7. In The Lap Of The Gods
(Mercury).
8. Stone Cold Crazy (May, Mercury,
Taylor, Deacon).
9. Dear Friends (May).
10. Misfire (Deacon).
11. Bring Back That Leroy Brown
(Mercury).
12. She Makes Me (Stormtrooper In
Stilettoes) (May).
13. In The Lap Of The Gods . . .
Revisited (Mercury).

THE OLD GREY WHISTLE TEST
BBC BELP 004
Released July 1975

(One track only: a version of 'Keep
Yourself Alive' recorded for 'The
Old Grey Whistle Test' BBC TV
programme in September 1973.)

A NIGHT AT THE OPERA
EMI EMTC 103
Released 3 December 1975

Side One:
1. Death On Two Legs
(Dedicated To) (Mercury).
2. Lazing On A Sunday Afternoon
(Mercury).
3. I'm In Love With My Car (Taylor).
4. You're My Best Friend (Deacon).
5. '39 (May).
6. Sweet Lady (May).
7. Seaside Rendezvous (Mercury).
Side Two
8. The Prophets Song (May).
9. Love Of My Life (Mercury).
10. Good Company (May).
11. Bohemian Rhapsody (Mercury).
12. God Save The Queen
(Trad. arr. Queen).

A DAY AT THE RACES
EMI EMTC 104
Released 10 December 1976

Side One
1. Tie Your Mother Down (May).
2. You Take My Breath Away
(Mercury).
3. Long Away (May).
4. The Millionaire Waltz (Mercury).
5. You And I (Deacon).

Side Two
6. Somebody To Love (Mercury).
7. White Man (May).
8. Good Old Fashioned Lover Boy
(Mercury).
9. Drowse (Taylor).
10. Teo Torriate (Let Us Cling
Together) (May).

NEWS OF THE WORLD
EMI EMA 784
Released 28 October 1977.

Side One:
1. We Will Rock You (May).
2. We Are The Champions
(Mercury).
3. Sheer Heart Attack (Taylor).
4. All Dead All Dead (May).
5. Spread Your Wings (Deacon).
6. Fight From The Inside (Taylor).
Side Two:
7. Get Down Make Love (Mercury).
8. Sleeping On The Sidewalk (May).
9. Who Needs You (Deacon).
10. It's Late (May).
11. My Melancholy Blues (Mercury).

JAZZ
EMI EMA 788
Released 10 November 1978

Side One:
1. Mustapha (Mercury).
2. Fat Bottomed Girls (May).
3. Jealousy (Mercury).
4. Bicycle Race (Mercury).
5. If You Can't Beat Them (Deacon).
6. Let Me Entertain You (Mercury).
Side Two:
7. Dead On Time (May).
8. In Only Seven Days (Deacon).
9. Dreamers Ball (May).
10. Fun It (Taylor).
11. Leaving Home Ain't Easy (May).
12. Don't Stop Me Now (Mercury).
13. More Of That Jazz (Taylor).

LIVE KILLERS
EMI EMSP 330
Released 22 June 1979

Side One:
1. We Will Rock You (May).
2. Let Me Entertain You (Mercury).
3. Death On Two Legs (Mercury).
4. Killer Queen (Mercury).
5. Bicycle Race (Mercury).
6. I'm In Love With My Car (Taylor).
7. Get Down Make Love (Mercury).
8. You're My Best Friend (Deacon).
Side Two:
9. Now I'm Here (May).
10. Dreamer's Ball (May).
11. Love Of My Life (Mercury).
12. '39 (May).
13. Keep Yourself Alive (May).

Side Three:
14. Don't Stop Me Now (Mercury).
15. Spread Your Wings (Deacon).
16. Brighton Rock (May).
Side Four:
17. Mustapha (Mercury).
18. Bohemian Rhapsody (Mercury).
19. Tie Your Mother Down (May).
20. Sheer Heart Attack (Taylor).
21. We Will Rock You (May).
22. We Are The Champions (Mercury).
23. God Save The Queen (Trad. arr. Queen).

THE GAME

EMI EMA 795
Released June 1980

Side One:
1. Play The Game (Mercury).
2. Dragon Attack (May).
3. Another One Bites The Dust (Deacon).
4. Need Your Loving Tonight (Deacon).
5. Crazy Little Thing Called Love (Mercury).
Side Two:
6. Rock It (Prime Jive) (Taylor).
7. Don't Try Suicide (Mercury).
8. Sail Away Sweet Sister (May).
9. Coming Soon (Taylor).
10. Save Me (May).

FLASH GORDON
(Original Soundtrack)

EMI EMC 3351
Released 8 December 1980.

Side One:
1. Flash's Theme (May).
2. In The Space Capsule (The Love Theme) (Taylor).
3. Ming's Theme (In The Court Of Ming The Merciless) (Mercury).
4. The Ring (Hypnotic Seduction of Dale) (Mercury).
5. Football Fight (Mercury).
6. In The Death Cell (Love Theme Reprise) (Taylor).
7. Execution Of Flash (Deacon).
8. The Kiss (Aura Resurrects Flash) (Mercury).

Side Two:
9. Arboria (Planet Of The Tree Men) (Deacon).
10. Escape From The Swamp (Taylor).
11. Flash To The Rescue (May).
12. Vultan's Theme (Attack Of The Hawk Men) (Mercury).
13. Battle Theme (May).
14. The Wedding March (May).
15. Marriage Of Dale And Ming (And Flash Approaching) (May/Taylor).
16. Crash Dive On Mingo City (May).
17. Flash's Theme Reprise (Victory Celebrations) (May).
18. The Hero (May).

CONCERT FOR THE PEOPLE OF KAMPUCHEA

Atlantic K 60153
Released April 1981.

(One track only: 'Now I'm Here', recorded live at the Hammersmith Odeon benefit concert, 26 December 1979.)

GREATEST HITS

EMI EMTV 30
Released 26 October 1981.

Side One:
1. Bohemian Rhapsody.
2. Another One Bites The Dust.
3. Killer Queen.
4. Fat Bottomed Girls.
5. Bicycle Race.
6. You're My Best Friend.
7. Don't Stop Me Now.
8. Save Me.
Side Two:
9. Crazy Little Thing Called Love.
10. Somebody To Love.
11. Now I'm Here.
12. Good Old Fashioned Lover Boy.
13. Play The Game.
14. Flash.
15. Seven Seas Of Rhye.
16. We Will Rock You.
17. We Are The Champions.

HOT SPACE

EMI EMA 797
Released 23 May 1982

Side One:
1. Staying Power (Mercury).
2. Dancer (May).
3. Back Chat (Deacon).
4. Body Language (Mercury).
5. Action This Day (Taylor).

Side Two:
6. Put Out The Fire (May).
7. Life Is Real (Song For Lennon) (Mercury).
8. Calling All Girls (Taylor).
9. Las Palabras De Amour (The Words Of Love) (May).
10. Cool Cat (Deacon/Mercury).
11. Under Pressure (Queen/Bowie).

THE WORKS

EMI EMC 2400141
Released 27 February 1984

Side One:
1. Radio Ga Ga (Taylor).
2. Tear It Up (May).
3. It's A Hard Life (Mercury).
4. Man On The Prowl (Mercury).
Side Two:
5. Machines (Or 'Back To Humans') (Taylor/May).
6. Want To Break Free (Deacon).
7. Keep Passing The Open Windows (Mercury).
8. Hammer To Fall (May).
9. Is This The World We Created? (Mercury/May).

THE COMPLETE WORKS

EMI QB1
Released December 1985

A boxed set of Queen's complete recorded output. In addition to the eleven studio albums and the 'Live Killers' double album, a new album was included which compiled the singles and 'B'-sides otherwise unaccounted for:

COMPLETE VISION

Side One:
1. See What A Fool I've Been (May).
2. A Human Body (Taylor).
3. Soul Brother (Queen).
4. I Go Crazy (May).

Side Two:
5. Thank God It's Christmas (Taylor/May).
6. One Vision (Queen).
7. Blurred Vision (Queen).

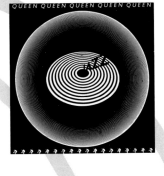

A KIND OF MAGIC
EMI EU 3509
Released May 1986

Side One:
1. One Vision (Queen).
2. A Kind Of Magic (Taylor).
3. One Year Of Love (Deacon).
4. Pain Is So Close To Pleasure (Mercury/Deacon).
Side Two:
6. Who Wants To Live Forever (May).
7. Gimme The Prize (Kurgan's Theme) (May).
8. Don't Lose Your Head (Taylor).
9. Princes of the Universe (Mercury).

LIVE MAGIC
EMI EMC 3519
Released December 1986

Side One
1. One Vision (Queen).
2. Tie Your Mother Down (May).
3. Seven Seas Of Rhye (Mercury).
4. A Kind Of Magic (Taylor).
5. Under Pressure (Queen/Bowie).
6. Another One Bites The Dust (Deacon).
Side Two
7. I Want To Break Free (Deacon).
8. Is This The World We Created? (Mercury/May).
9. Bohemian Rhapsody (Mercury).
10. Hammer To Fall (May).
11. Radio Ga Ga (Taylor).
12. We Will Rock You (May).
13. Friends Will Be Friends (Mercury/Deacon).
14. We Are The Champions (Mercury).
15. God Save The Queen (Trad. arr. Queen).

QUEEN AT THE BEEB
Band Of Joy BOJLP/MC/CD 001
Released December 1989

Side One
1. My Fairy King.
2. Keep Yourself Alive.
3. Doing Alright.
4. Liar
Side Two
5. Ogre Battle.
6. Great King Rat.
7. Modern Times Rock & Roll.
8. Son And Daughter.

THE MIRACLE
Parlophone PCSD 107
Released May 1989

Side One
1. Party (Queen).
2. Khashoggi's Ship (Queen).
3. The Miracle (Queen).
4. I Want It All (Queen).
5. The Invisible Man (Queen).
Side Two
6. Breakthru (Queen).
7. Rain Must Fall (Queen).
8. Scandal (Queen).
9. My Baby Does Me (Queen).
10. Was It All Worth It (Queen).
11. Hang On In There (Queen) (CD only).
12. Chinese Torture (Queen) (CD only).
13. The Invisible Man (12″ version) (Queen) (CD only).

INNUENDO
Parlophone PCSD 115
Released February 1991

Side One
1. Innuendo (Queen).
2. I'm Going Slightly Mad (Queen).
3. Headlong (Queen).
4. I Can't Live With You (Queen).
5. Ride The Wild Wind (Queen).
Side Two
6. All God's People (Queen/Moran).
7. These Are The Days Of Our Lives (Queen).
8. Delilah (Queen).
9. Don't Try Too Hard (Queen).
10. The Hitman (Queen).
11. Bijou (Queen).
12. The Show Must Go On (Queen).

Various

Interview Picture Disc LP
Baktabak BAK 2014.
Released July 1987.

Music & Media Interview
Picture Disc
Music & Media MM 1218.
Released February 1988.

'Crazy Little Thing Called Love'/
'Spread Your Wings (Live)'
EMI (Germany) 12″ 05263317.
Released May 1988.

Interview CD
Baktabak CD BAK 4022.
Released November 1989.

Interview Collection 7″ Set
Baktabak BAKPAK 1021.
Released June 1990.

Message From The Palace
Baktabak Pic LP BAK 6014.
Released September 1990.

Solo Recordings

FREDDIE MERCURY

Singles:

'Love Kills'/'Rot Wang's Party'.
CBS A 4735. Released September 1984.

'I Was Born To Love You'/'Stop All
The Fighting'.
CBS A 6019. Released May 1985.

'Made In Heaven'/'She Blows Hot
And Cold'.
CBS A 6413. Released July 1985.

'Living On My Own'/'My Love Is
Dangerous'.
CBS A 6555. Released September 1985.

'Love Me Like There's No
Tomorrow'/'Let's Turn It On'.
CBS A 6725. Released November 1985.

'Time'/'Time (Instrumental)'.
EMI 5559 (7″ only). Released May 1986.

'The Great Pretender'/'Exercises
In Free Love'.
Parlophone R 6151. Released March 1987.

With Montserrat Caballe
'Barcelona'/'Exercises In Free Love'.
Polydor POSP 887. Released October 1987.

'The Golden Boy'/'The Fallen Priest'.
Polydor PO 23. Released October 1988.

'How Can I Go On'/'Overture Piccante'.
Polydor PO 29. Released January 1989.

Albums:

MR. BAD GUY
CBS 28AP-3030. Released May 1985.

Side One:
1. Let's Turn It On.
2. Made In Heaven.
3. I Was Born To Love You.
4. Foolin' Around.
5. Your Kind Of Lover.
Side Two:
6. Mr. Bad Guy.
7. Man Made Paradise.
8. There Must Be More To Life Than This.
9. Living On My Own.
10. My Love Is Dangerous.
11. Love Me Like There's No Tomorrow.

BARCELONA (with Montserrat Caballe)
Polydor POLH 44.
Released October 1988.

Side One
1. Barcelona.
2. The Fallen Priest.
3. The Golden Boy.
4. Guide Me Home.
Side Two
5. Overture Piccante.
6. La Japonaise.
7. Ensueno.
8. Guide Me Alone.
9. How Can I Go On.

BRIAN MAY And Others.

Singles:

'Star Fleet'/'Son Of Star Fleet'.
EMI 5436. Released October 1983.

Albums:

STAR FLEET PROJECT
EMI SFLT 1078061/4. Released October 1983.
3-Track mini LP.

Side One
1. Star Fleet.
2. Let Me Out.

Side Two:
3. Blues Breaker.

ROGER TAYLOR

Singles:

'I Wanna' Testify'/'Turn On The TV'.
EMI 2679. Released July 1977.

'Future Management'/'Laugh Or Cry'.
EMI 5157. Released March 1981.

'My Country'/'Fun In Space'.
EMI 5200. Released June 1981.

'Man On Fire'/'Killing Time'.
EMI 5478. Released June 1984.

'Stranger Frontier'/'I Cry For You'.
EMI 5490. Released August 1984.
The 12″ version includes an extra track.
'Two Sharp Pencils'.

Albums:

FUN IN SPACE
EMI EMC 3369.
Released April 1981.

Side One:
1. No Violins.
2. Laugh Or Cry.
3. Future Management.
4. Let's Go Crazy.
5. My Country.
Side Two:
6. My Country 1 & 2.
7. Good Times Are Now.
8. Magic Is Loose.
9. Interlude In Constantinople.
10. Airheads.
11. Fun In Space.

STRANGE FRONTIER
EMI RTA 1.
Released June 1984.

Side One:
1. Strange Frontier.
2. Beautiful Dreams.
3. Man On Fire.
4. Racing In The Street.
5. Masters Of War.
Side Two:
6. Killing Time.
7. Abandon Fire.
8. Young Love.
9. It's An Illusion.
10. I Cry For You
(Love, Hope And Illusion).

THE CROSS

Singles:

'Cowboys And Indians'/'Love Lies Bleeding'.
Virgin VS1007. Released September 1987.

'Shove It' /'Rough Justice'.
Virgin VS1026. Released January 1988.

'Heaven For Everyone'/'Love On A Tightrope (Like An Animal)'.
Virgin VS1062. Released March 1988.

'Shove It (Extended version)'/ 'Rough Justice'/'Shove It (Metropolix)'/'Cowboys And Indians'.
Virgin CDEP 20. Released April 1988.

'Power To Love'/'Passion For Trash'.
Parlophone R6251. Released April 1990

Albums:

SHOVE IT
Virgin V2477. Released November 1987.
OVED302. Reissued April 1990.

Side One
1. Shove It.
2. Heaven For Everyone.
3. Love On A Tightrope (Like An Animal).
4. Cowboys And Indians.
Side Two
5. Stand Up For Love.
6. Love Lies Bleeding (She Was A Wicked, Wily Waitress).
7. Rough Justice.
8. The 2nd Shelf Mix (CD only).
9. Contact.

MAD, BAD AND DANGEROUS TO KNOW
Parlophone PCS7342.
Released March 1990.

Side One
1. Top Of The World Ma.
2. Liar.
3. Closer To You.
4. Break Down.
5. Penetration Guru.
6. Power To Love.
Side Two
7. Sister Blue.
8. Foxy Lady (CD only).
9. Better Things.
10. Passion For Trash.
11. Old Men (Lay Down).
12. Final Destination.

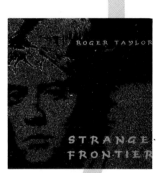

JOHN DEACON and The Immortals

Single:

'No Turning Back'/'No Turning Back (Chocs Away Mix)'
MCA 1057. Released May 1986

Album:

'Biggles' (Soundtrack LP)
MCA MCF 3328. Released June 1986

VIDEOS

1975 Bohemian Rhapsody
(Director: Bruce Gowers)
1976 You're My Best Friend
(Director: Bruce Gowers)
1976 Somebody To Love
(Director: Bruce Gowers)
1977 We Will Rock You
(Director: Rock Flicks)
1977 Tie Your Mother Down
(Director: Bruce Gowers)
1977 We Are The Champions
(Director: Derek Burbridge)
1978 Spread Your Wings
(Director: Rock Flicks)
1978 Bicycle Race
(Director: Dennis De Vallance)
1978 Fat Bottomed Girls
(Director: Dennis De Vallance)
1979 Don't Stop Me Now
(Director: Jorgan Kliebenst)
1979 Love Of My Life
(Director: Dennis De Vallance)
1979 Crazy Little Thing Called Love
(Director: Dennis De Vallance)
1980 Save Me
(Director: Keith McMillan)
1980 Play The Game
(Director: Brian Grant)
1980 Another One Bites The Dust
(Director: Daniella)
1980 Flash
(Director: Don Norman)
1981 Killer Queen
(Director: Brian Grant)
1981 Under Pressure
(Director: David Mallet)
1982 Body Language
(Director: Mike Hodges)
1982 Back Chat
(Director: Brian Grant)
1982 Calling All Girls
(Director: Brian Grant)
1984 Radio Ga Ga
(Director: David Mallet)
1984 I Want To Break Free
(Director: David Mallet)
1984 It's A Hard Life
(Director: Tim Pope)
1984 Hammer To Fall
(Director: David Mallet)
1984 Man On Fire
(Director: Tim Pope)
1984 Strange Frontier
(Director: George Bloom)

1985 I Was Born To Love You
(Director: David Mallet)
1985 Made In Heaven
(Director: David Mallet)
1985 Living On My Own
(Director: Hannes Rossacher/Rudolph Dolezal)
1985 One Vision
(Director: Hannes Rossacher/Rudolph Dolezal)
1986 Prince Of The Universe
(Director: Russell Mulcahy)
1986 A Kind Of Magic
(Director: Russell Mulcahy)
1986 Who Wants To Live Forever
1989 I Want It All
1989 Breakthru
1989 The Invisible Man
1989 Scandal
1989 The Miracle
1991 Innuendo
1991 I'm Going Slightly Mad
1991 Headlong

VIDEOGRAPHY

Queen's Greatest Flix
(Picture Music International:
MVP 99 1011 2/MXP 99 1011 4).
Released 12 October 1981.

We Will Rock You
(Peppermint Video Music 6122).
Released September 1984.

The Works EP
Picture Music International:
MVP 99 0010 2/MXP 99 0010 4).
Released 5 November 1984.

Live In Rio
Picture Music International:
MVP 99 1079 2/MXP 99 1079 4).
Released 13 May 1985.

A Kind Of Magic
(Picture Music International MVW 99 0059 2).
Released October 1986.

Live In Budapest
(Picture Music International
PMI MVN 99 1146 2).
Released February 1987.
(Also on CD Video, Polygram Music Video
080 510 1).
Released 1988.

Bohemian Rhapsody
(Gold Rushes PM 0022).
Released May 1987.

The Magic Years – Volume 1
(Picture Music International MVP 99 1154 2).
Released November 1987.

The Magic Years – Volume 2
(Picture Music International MVP 99 1155 2).
Released November 1987.

The Magic Years – Volume 3
(Picture Music International MVP 99 1156 2).
Released November 1987.

The Magic Years – The Complete
(Boxed) Set Vols 1–3
(Picture Music International MVB 99 1157 2).
Released December 1987.

Rare Live Video
(Picture Music International MVP 99 1189 3).
Released August 1989.

We Will Rock You (Reissue)
(Music Club MC2032).
Released September 1989.

The Miracle Video EP
(Picture Music International MVL 99 0084 3).
Released December 1989.

Freddie Mercury Video EP
(Picture Music International MVS 99 0055 2).
Released July 1986.

The Great Pretender
(Picture Music International MVP 99 0066 2).
Released March 1987.

(with Montserrat Caballe)
Barcelona
(Channel 5 CFV 00932).
Released February 1989.
(Also CD Video Polygram 0805482).

The Golden Boy
(Polygram Music Video 080580 2).
Released 1989.